**W9-BWD-288**

To Rosemarie Carbino—

Best wishes to a
dedicated advocate for
Positive change

Al Kadushin

Supervision in Social Work

Supervision in Social Work

Fourth Edition

Alfred Kadushin
Daniel Harkness

COLUMBIA UNIVERSITY PRESS
NEW YORK

Columbia University Press
Publishers Since 1893
New York & Chichester, West Sussex
Copyright © Columbia University Press, 2002
All rights reserved

Library of Congress Cataloging in Publication Data

Kadushin, Alfred.
   Supervision in social work.—4th ed. / Alfred Kadushin, Daniel Harkness.
      p. cm.
   Includes bibliographical references and index.
   ISBN 0-231-12094-X (cloth : alk. paper)
   1. Social workers—Supervision of. 2. Social workers—Supervision of—United
States. I. Harkness, Daniel. II. Title.
   HV40.54 .K33 2002
   361.3'2'0683—dc21

                                                              2002019588

∞

Columbia University Press books are printed on permanent and durable acid-free
paper.

Printed in the United States of America

c 10 9 8 7 6 5 4 3 2 1

Contents

» | Preface

The first edition of the book was published in 1976, the second edition in 1985, and a third edition in 1992. A fourth edition at this time seems necessary, given the continued concern with supervision and the sizable number of books and articles related to social work supervision published since 1992. Some older concerns have become archaic, and some new concerns have become increasingly visible.

The book provides an overview of the state of the art of social work supervision. It is addressed to supervisors and those preparing to do supervision, whatever their formal educational background may be. It is also useful to social work supervisees, students, and workers in enabling them to make more productive use of supervision.

The book is designed to help readers understand the place of supervision in the social agency, the functions it performs, the process of supervision, and the problems with which it is currently concerned. Although no book can directly further the development of skills, it provides the knowledge base that is a necessary prerequisite to learning how to supervise. The book frees the course instructor from the burden of presenting the general background of supervision so that more time can be devoted to consideration of clinical material and controversial points of view.

Changes in public social welfare policy over the past ten years have intensified concern about social work supervision, particularly its administrative responsibilities. Concerns for efficiency and productivity have been added to the continuing concern for accountability. Tax and spending limitations at all levels of government and growing budgetary stringency have resulted in reduction of financial support for social service programs. The current situation is characterized by reduction in staff, retrenchment in programming, and limitations in resources available to agencies.

Social agencies are labor-intensive operations. The current political context, which provides less financial support for social services, calls for doing more with less. One possible (if difficult) solution is to increase the productivity of each worker. Increasing productivity requires greater managerial efficiency and more imaginative agency management. With the constriction of resources, practice has become more time-limited and results-oriented. This has intensified requirements for accountability and the need to justify the legitimacy of the agency through the demonstration of efficiency and effectiveness.

Organizational survival may hinge on the ability of administrative supervision to fine-tune agency performance, increase efficiency, and deploy limited staff more effectively. Supervisory personnel are the crucial element in dealing with worker efficiency and productivity, as they were in meeting the demands for increased agency accountability.

More limited resources and the demands associated with taxpayer revolts have made issues of accountability a matter of much greater concern than ever before. Because agency accountability starts with the supervisor's review and evaluation of the work of the direct service staff, such issues intensify the visibility and importance of supervision.

The spread of managed care approaches to social agency management has intensified concerns with service efficiency and demands for accountability. The changing demographics of the client population and staff have increased the need for attention to the problems of diversity in supervision. The challenges of pressure toward privatization of social services and support for faith-based programs put traditional social work practice on notice.

The increasing dependence of agencies on governmental funding, third-party payments, and legislative mandates have resulted in the increasing external regulation of agencies. The need for documentation of agency activities through periodic reports further increases the need for administrative supervision to ensure that such information is available. Compliance with external regulatory requirements of funding sources, such as Medicaid, Medicare, and Title XX, puts a premium on the need for supervisory personnel. Community mental health centers are among the agencies that depend heavily on third-party payments for support and consequently face legislative mandates for rigorous accountability. A questionnaire study of community mental health center supervisors' perceptions of effective accountability mechanisms found that all 117 respondents saw a "well-coordinated and explicit system of supervision as the most preferred approach to facilitating a Community Mental Health Center-based quality assurance program" (Smith 1986:9).

Regulatory developments over the past ten years have once again increased the importance and significance of social work supervision. Licensing and registration legislation adopted by 2001 in the District of Columbia, the Virgin Islands, and all fifty states often requires that certified, licensed, or registered workers have formal access to supervision. This has particular relevance for the provision of health care, because third-party reimbursement by managed care organizations and insurers may be limited to those social workers practicing at the highest level of licensure, an achievement that typically requires an extensive period of supervision. Where exceptions exist, social workers are often required to receive formal supervision as a third-party condition for payment.

Reduction in services and resources available to social workers has resulted in a greater need to prioritize work and decisions regarding the allocation of scarce supplies. Now more than ever, social workers are faced with the necessity of making difficult decisions regarding what gets done, what is ignored, who is provided service, and who is denied service. Many triage decisions now require if not the help at least the shared responsibility of a representative of management. Such situations increase the need for supervisory personnel.

Supervision and in-service training and staff development share responsibility for helping the worker learn what he or she needs to know to do the job effectively. Cuts in agency budgets have frequently required cuts in staff development programs and in-service training. Agencies have increasing difficulty in funding worker attendance at workshops, institutes, and national meetings. As a consequence, supervision becomes increasingly more important as a source of training and often is the only resource available to help workers enhance their skills.

Recognition of the need for supervision has been formalized, in that candidates for the title of certified social worker (ACSW) are required to have been supervised for a minimum of two years after earning a master's in social work (MSW) degree. Similarly, other specialized professional organizations that enlist social workers require minimum hours of supervised practice for licensing or registration. This includes such organizations as the American Association of Marriage and Family Therapists and the National Commission for Credentialing of Alcoholism Counselors.

The ascendance of a political orientation that seeks to curtail the development of social programs and limit access to resources increases the importance of supervision for preserving the commitment of social work to a political orientation that is more humanistic. An orientation antagonistic to the objectives and values of social work has been made evident not only in legislative changes but also in attempts at imposing business management technologies on social agencies. The increasing tendency to appoint business managers to administer social agencies has been encouraged by the proliferation of business administration (MBA) graduates actively seeking such positions.

If social work, in defense of its own values, hopes to resist such impositions, it needs to be concerned with increasing the effectiveness of its own managerial practices. Concern by social agencies with improving the practice of supervision is one approach to contesting the imposition by outsiders of managerial practices that might conflict with the values, ethics, and philosophy of social work. "We" rather than "they" would formulate and implement the changes in managerial practice. In doing so, we would increase the certainty that social agency administration reflects social work ideology.

Changes in the relation between human service organizations and the courts over the past ten years have also increased the significance of supervisory personnel. The last decade has been characterized by increases in the frequency of legal challenges to human service programs as courts more actively inquire into areas previously left to the discretion of agencies. With increased attention to clients' rights and malpractice suits, many ethical and professional issues have been transformed into legal issues. The increased possibility of legal action against agencies by clients and community groups highlights the need for supervision to prevent damaging challenges from developing.

In a chapter devoted to negligent supervision as a basis for malpractice suits, Austin, Moline, and Williams (1990) advise supervisors to keep records that are complete and up to date, to document meetings with supervisees, and to take care in seeing that insurance forms for clients are completed properly. Risk management becomes a priority concern of supervision.

Since the publication of the first edition of this textbook, the problem of worker burnout was "discovered" and given considerable attention in the literature. The relevance to supervision of this new development lies in the fact that the research on burnout has concluded that supportive supervision is a key prophylactic and palliative for burnout.

Over the past ten years there has been a steady increase in research and exposition of studies of supervision in social work, supporting, supplementing, correcting, and edifying the content of previous editions. Studies of supervision in counseling psychology and psychiatry have provided additional updated material of relevance. The resulting accumulation of knowledge needs to be recognized in keeping the text current.

Some readers complain that the book presents an unrealistic, visionary picture of supervision—that it presents supervision as it should be rather than how it is. A letter from one reader said, "I just can't help but wonder where all those supervisors are that you describe so beautifully with all their right techniques and all their wisdom and all their understanding and time and patience. I can tell you I have never seen such a one and neither has anybody else here." Touché and mea culpa. In the real world of heavy caseloads, tight budgets, and increasingly difficult problems, these objections are admittedly well grounded. The text's image of supervision is an idealized image rather than a picture of supervision as it is actually practiced. Supervision as described in the text exists nowhere in practice. The reader need not feel quilt or anxiety that his or her experience with supervision falls short in some measure of the image presented in the text, as inevitably everyone's will. There is, however, some justification for presenting a systematic synthesis of the best in social work supervision. It suggests the ideal against which we can measure our practice and reveals the direction in which changes need to be made. It reflects Cicero's reminder that "no wind is favorable unless you know the port to which you are heading." The modern translation of this is: "If you don't know where you are going, you will probably end up somewhere else."

Because field instruction in graduate and undergraduate social work education have elements in common with agency supervision, we reviewed fieldwork manuals from fifty schools of social work and reviewed the rich literature on field instruction. In the end, the need to keep the length of the text within reasonable bounds dictated a decision not to include this material. Differences between agency supervision and field instruction in educational programs are sufficiently pervasive to justify this decision.

» | Acknowledgments

To the good people of Wisconsin who, for over half a century, have paid me for doing what I would choose to do even if I did not have to do it for a living—teaching, researching, and writing.

Over the fifty-five years that I have practiced, taught, and engaged in social work research I have learned a lot from clients, students, and academic and practitioner colleagues. I owe them all a deep debt of gratitude for what they taught me.

And above all, to Sylvia for a lifetime of help, support, comfort, laughter, friendship, and love. To Goldie and Raphael, perennial sources of interest, excitement, pride, warmth, and affection. And in loving memory of my parents, Phillip and Celia.

—A.K.

To the good people of Idaho as well—displaced farmers and ranchers, buckaroos and loggers, entrepreneurs and tycoons, migrant field hands, and single parents working three jobs—thank you for supporting social work education in our nation's most conservative state.

To my supervisors—Bob Dailey, Rea Stoll, and Sandra Shaw—thank you for modeling good social work supervision. To those who trained me—Arthur Katz, David Hardcastle, Ann Weick, Arno Knapper, Goody Garfield, Charlie Rapp, and John Poertner—thank you for your guidance and faith. To Cynthia Bisman, who supervised my first exploration of the supervision literature. To my colleagues—Doug and Francis in Kansas; Joe, Milt, Stan, and Marie in Idaho practice; and Rob, Dan, and Martha in the Idaho classroom—thank you for your inspiration, examples, and stalwart support. And to Jennifer Darling, Scott Curtis, and Shawna Manhire—my intrepid graduate research assistants—thank you for your important contributions to this book.

To Harriet, my wife, best friend, and the love of my life. To Julie, Geoff, Nick, and Sam, my treasured and talented children. And to Maxine and Orlo, dear friends and extraordinary parents. You are beacons of light.

D.H.

Supervision in Social Work

1 | History, Definition, and Significance

Historical Development

There are few and scattered references to social work supervision before 1920. Many of the references listed under supervision in the index of the *Proceedings of Conferences on Charities and Correction* or in older social work journals actually refer to quite a different process from the supervision of the past eighty years. Such references are usually concerned with administrative supervision of agencies by some licensing authority or governmental board to which the agencies were accountable for public funds spent and for their service to the client. *Supervision* referred to the control and coordinating function of a State Board of Supervisors, a State Board of Charities, or a State Board of Control. Originally, the term *supervision* applied to the inspection and review of programs and institutions rather than to supervision of individual workers within the program.

The first social work text that used the word *supervision* in the title—*Supervision and Education in Charity* by Jeffrey R. Brackett (1904)—was concerned with supervision of welfare agencies and institutions by public boards and commissions. Sidney Eisenberg, who has written a short history of supervision in social work, notes that Mary Richmond, "one of the most original contributors to the development of social work, made no mention of supervision in her published works" (1956a:1).

If the term *supervision* applied to the inspection and review of programs and institutions rather than to supervision of individual workers within the program, over time supervision became infused with additional duties. In addition to the efficient and effective *administration* of agency services, the *education* and *support* of social workers fashioned the three-legged stool of modern social work supervision. In the service of administering agency services and helping the case, social work supervision meant helping the social worker develop practice knowledge and skills, and providing emotional support to the person in the social work role.

With publication of *The Family* (subsequently *Social Casework*) by the Family Welfare Association of America, beginning in 1920, there are increasingly frequent references to supervision as we know it today—that is, supervision of the individual social worker.

Mary Burns (1958) comments that although components of the supervisory process were described in the literature as early as 1880 and 1890, the entity with which we are concerned in this book was not clearly recognized and explicitly identified until much later. It "was not included in the index of *Family* until 1925 and not until after 1930 in the *Proceedings of the National Conference on Social Work*" (1958:8).

Supervision as we know it today had its origins in the Charity Organization Society movement in the nineteenth century. A concern for the possible consequences of indiscriminate almsgiving led to organization of charity on a rational basis. Starting in Buffalo, New York, in 1878, Charity Organization societies soon were developed in most of the large Eastern cities. The agencies granted financial assistance after a rigorous investigation, but such help was regarded as only one aspect of the service offered. The more important component of help was offered by "friendly visitors," volunteers who were assigned to families to offer personal support and to influence behavior in a socially desirable direction. "Not alms, but a friend" was the catchphrase of the Charity Organization movement.

"Visitors" were the direct service workers, the foot soldiers, of the Charity Organization agencies. As volunteers they were generally assigned to a limited number of families (Gurteen 1882). Limited caseloads coupled with high turnover of volunteers meant that the agencies faced a continuous problem of recruiting, training, and directing new visitors. These tasks were primarily the responsibility of a limited number of "paid agents" employed by the Charity Organization societies. The paid agents were the early predecessors of the modern supervisor. Each agent-supervisor was responsible for a sizable number of visitors. The few statistics available testify to the fact that the principal burden of contact with the client was borne by visitors under the direction of a limited number of paid agents. Burns (1958:16) indicates that "by 1890 there were 78 charity organization societies with 174 paid workers and 2,017 volunteer friendly visitors."

Initially the paid agent shared responsibility for supervision of the visitor with the district committee. The district committee was in effect the local executive committee of the Charity Organization district office. The committee generally consisted of laypeople and representatives of local charitable agencies.

When a family requested help, the initial study was done by the agent, who then reported the findings at a weekly district committee conference. The committee discussed the case and decided its disposition. The fact that cases were brought directly to the district committee for determination of action meant that, initially, the paid agent-supervisor had relatively little managerial autonomy. He and the visitor were both "agents" of the district committee. Generally, however, district committees became more policy- and general administration–oriented. Gradually, responsibility for decision making on individual cases was given to the paid agent-supervisor. The visitors, and the paid workers who subsequently replaced them, discussed their cases with the agent-supervisor, who was responsible for the decision and its subsequent implementation by the visitor or worker. The agent-supervisor thus became the administrative-managerial representative of the organization and was most immediately responsible for the work of the direct service worker.

The agent provided a dependable administrative point of contact for the visitor, gave continuity to the work, and acted as a channel of communication. "The agent is always to be found at certain hours and, giving all this time, naturally becomes the center of district work, receiving both from visitors and [the District] Committee information and advice to be transmitted one to the other" (Smith 1884:70). As Fields says in one of the earliest social work texts, *How to Help the Poor*, "The agent becomes the connecting link for the volunteer visitors who come daily for advice and assistance" (1885:18). The agent-supervisor, the channel of communication, needed to be "careful to represent the Committee faithfully to the visitors and the visitors faithfully to the Committee" (Smith 1887:161).

All the significant components of current supervisory procedures can be discerned in descriptions of the activities of the paid agent-supervisors. From its inception in 1843, the New York Association for Improving the Conditions of the Poor "maintained a paid staff who were to supervise and train volunteers and thus provide continuity of service" (Becker 1961:395). The quote points to the historical antiquity of administrative and educational supervision.

Zilpha Smith, general secretary of the Boston Associated Charities and later director of the Smith College Training School of Psychiatric Social Work, was one of the first to write on supervision and training of visitors.

She exhorted the district agent to "look over the records of the visited families frequently to see if the work is satisfactory or if any suggestions can make it so" (Smith 1901b:46). Here the administrative requirement of ensuring that the "work is satisfactory" is coupled with the educational task of supervision.

According to a Boston Associated Charities report of 1881, the agent was charged with the responsibility of

> investigation and preparation of cases for the volunteer visitors and advising and aiding the visitors in their work. . . . The visitors . . . consult with the agent regarding the families they have befriended. Investigation by the agent precedes the appointment of a visitor in every case. This is necessary for the purpose of getting accurate and thorough knowledge; and when we know the family we can select the visitors whom we think most likely to persevere and be of greatest benefit. (Burns 1958:24)

Here the administrative task of differential case assignment is coupled with the educational task of "advising and aiding."

In an extended discussion of educational supervision of friendly visitors, Tenny (1895–1896:202) notes that "in the important work of starting a new friendly visitor," the conference worker (supervisor) tries "to show one or more things which may be done by a friendly visitor at the first visit; to show how to gain access to a family without seeming to have come to visit; to explain why a friendly visitor should not say 'I heard you were in trouble, what can I do for you'?"

Detailing the training of Boston friendly visitors, Thwing notes that they were first given educational literature, including rules and suggestions for visitors. Subsequently they attended the weekly conferences and had periodic talks with the agent, "who gave her general instructions as to the nature of the work" (1893:234). In reporting to the agent, "if mistakes are made they are more easily rectified" (1893:235). This is echoed by Gardiner (1895:4), who says that "ill results from mistakes" by friendly visitors "are easily guarded against by proper supervision."

Because visitors were always difficult to recruit, easy to lose, and often frustrated and disappointed, they needed supportive supervision from the agent-supervisor in addition to administrative direction and training. The paid agent or district secretary had to deal with the feeling responses of visitors to their work. On meeting the family to which she had been assigned, a "visitor returned immediately to say that those children must be taken away, the home was too dreadful. Then she was persuaded to try to make the home fit for them to stay in. As in this instance the new visitor often needs another's steady hand and head to guide her through the first shocks of finding conditions so strange to his experience that he cannot judge them rightly" (Smith 1892:53).

In the 1889 annual report, Boston Associated Charities stated that "a large part of the agent's day consists of consultation with visitors . . . and there is opportunity for much tact and personal power in helping new visitors to understand what aid will benefit and what aid would harm their families, and in inspiring those who become discouraged to keep on until things look brighter again." Here the supervisor's responsibility for consultation with visitors in furthering the visitor's understanding is supplemented by the need to offer support and inspiration for discouraged workers. One way of showing support in times of discouragement was to commend the worker for progress with families to whom they had been assigned:

> A lady who had shown herself a good visitor came to the office one day and said, "I think I may as well give up the Browns. I cannot see that I do any good there." But the agent said: "Think over last week. Do you remember what you said then?" "No." "You said those children's faces were never clean; they are clean now. That surely shows a little improvement. Do go once more." (Smith 1892:57)

The early literature points to many principles of supervision that are still accepted and desirable. For instance, the paid agents assigned work to visitors with a sensitive, contemporary-sounding regard for the visitor's needs.

> A visitor showed ingenuity and force of character but the first hint of responsibility frightened her. The Agent asked her to take a message to a serving woman, later to another, then when she was calling on a family near by, would she not slip in and see how she was getting on and after three or four times, the agent said, "Now I am going to put you down as a visitor to Mrs. B." She has been drawn in such a way into visiting seven families in all, more than we usually think wise for one visitor but she can give her whole time, is interested and enthusiastic. If anything like so much responsibility had been urged upon her at first, she would have been frightened away from the work entirely. (Smith 1892:54)

More than 100 years ago, Gardiner noted the need for individualizing workers in stating that "our workers have quite as varied natures as our applicants and require to be dealt with in quite as varied a manner" (1895:4).

The literature emphasized that the agent's administrative, educational, and supportive responsibilities were most effectively implemented in the context of a positive relationship. Smith said:

> In order to make friendly visiting succeed . . . the agents must care to really help the visitor—not merely to give what the visitor asks, but, with tact and patience what he needs and to go at it simply and informally. The agent . . . must learn patiently to know and understand the new visitor. . . . Thought must be given to his problems and both direct and indirect means used to help him help himself in working them out with the poor family. (1901a:159–60)

Earlier she had noted that "the agent should be one able to guide and inspire others, ready to step in and help when necessary in what is properly visitor's work but sufficiently patient with the imperfections and delays of volunteers not to usurp the visitor's place" (Smith 1884:69).

It was noted that education of visitors should emphasize the principles for worker action: "The meetings of visitors rightly managed are a great power of education. In these meetings, and in talking or writing to visitors, details should not be allowed to hide principles on which the work rests. The principles should be discussed and the reasons for them given again and again as new visitors come to the meetings or new knowledge invites a change of policy" (Smith 1887:160).

Although group meetings of visitors were frequently the context for such instructions, individual supervision, using the visitor's case record as the text for training, was employed more frequently.

Not only were the present functions and approaches of supervision foreshadowed in this earlier development of the process, but so was the present hierarchical position of the supervisor. While the "paid agent" acted as supervisor to the volunteer visitor, the paid agent "supervisor" was himself supervised by the district committee, which had ultimate authority for case decisions. Early charity organization records speak of members of the central executive committee coming to "consult and advise with Agent concerning the work" (Becker 1963:256). The paid agent-supervisor was then in a middle management position, as is true of supervisors today—supervising the direct service worker but being themselves under the authority of the agency administrators.

The amplifying effect of supervision in extending the influence of a limited number of trained and experienced workers was recognized early. "The agent's knowledge and experience was extended over a far wider field than he could have covered alone. The inexperienced worker was trained by actual service without the risk of injuring the beneficiaries in the process, and the family visited had the advantage of both the agent's professional knowledge and the visitor's more intimate and personal friendliness" (Conyngton 1909:22–23).

By the turn of the century, supervision was affected by a gradual change in the composition of agency staff. Difficulty in depending on a staff of volunteer visitors who needed to be constantly "obtained, trained and re-trained" became more evident as demands on agencies expanded. With the growth of industrialization and urbanization in late-nineteenth-century America and the large increases in immigration, the need for paid staff increased. As a consequence there was a gradual decrease in the ratio of volunteer friendly visitors to paid staff. Although such staff still initially required training by more experienced agent-supervisors, a cadre of trained workers who remained on the job for some time was being built up, and the demands for supervisory education and support became somewhat less onerous. At the same time the burden of educating workers in the supervisory context was partly relieved by other resources.

Development of Education for Social Work

From the very beginning of the Charity Organization movement, discussion groups of visitors and agents had been encouraged. Evening reading groups met to discuss current literature and to share experiences. The 1892 annual report of the Charity Organization Society of Baltimore notes that short papers, followed by discussion, were presented at meetings of visitors on the following topics: "How to Help Out-of-Work Cases," "The Treatment of Drunkards' Families," "Sanitation in the Homes of the Poor," "The Cost of Subsistence," "Deserted Wives," and "Cooking and Marketing." The Boston South End District visitors and agents heard lectures on "Housing the Poor," "The Sweating System of Boston," "Trade Unions," "The Social Situation at the South End," and one, by Professor John R. Commons of the University of Wisconsin, on "Training of the Friendly Visitor."

The better-established Charity Organization societies gradually began to conduct more formal training programs, which involved systematic education of those selected to be paid agents. For instance, the Boston Charities Organization initiated in-service training programs for new agents in 1891. The new agents were "apprenticed" to more experienced workers, participated in group teaching sessions conducted by the general secretary of the organization, and were assigned readings from the well-developed agency library. The supervising, experienced agents met periodically with the general secretary to discuss problems of educational supervision. By 1896 the Boston Organization stated in its annual report:

> We have a higher standard for our agents. When the society started, there were no experts at this work; the agents and committees had to work together to acquire their training as best they could; while now, we have a well-organized system for training agents by having them work under direction, both in the Conferences and in the Central Office, before they are placed in positions of responsibility; so that there is always an agent qualified for the place should a vacancy occur. . . . We have undertaken to prepare our [agents] for their work by a system of preliminary training which we hope will make them more positively efficient and guard them from errors unavoidable among the untrained. . . . We have had hopes of being able carefully to train new volunteer visitors. . . . We have thought, thus, to develop wisely the good intentions of those who join us with the generous, if sometimes indefinite, purpose to do good.

State and national conferences offered an opportunity for the exchange of information and ideas among people working in welfare organizations and institutions. They were, in effect, a source of training. The first National Conference of Charities and Correction was held in Chicago in 1879. In 1882 Wisconsin organized the first State Conference of Charities and Correction. The published proceedings of these kinds of conferences provided material for education and training. These were supplemented by a growing body of periodical literature that spoke to the concerns of people working in the field. Texts and tracts devoted to the work of charities' agency personnel were also published. In addition to the texts referred to previously, Mary Richmond, then general secretary of the Charity Organization Society of Baltimore, published *Friendly Visiting Among the Poor: A Handbook for Charity Workers* in 1899, and Edward Devine, general secretary of the Charity Organization Society of New York City, published *The Practice of Charity* in 1901.

The 1887 annual report of the Brooklyn Bureau of Charities states that "the nucleus of a library has been formed at the Central Office and now includes some twenty-five hundred books, pamphlets and papers relating to the principles and methods of charitable work and cognate subjects. The collection is already worth the attention of those interested."

Gradually a body of practice wisdom was being developed, codified, and made explicit for communication through published channels. A group of practitioners interested in a particular phenomenon that ultimately became known as social work was gradually being identified and developing a sense of conscious self-identification. The development of a knowledge base was accompanied by growing recognition that sympathy and interest alone were not sufficient to make a good worker. The twenty-second annual report of the Charity Organization of Baltimore (1903) comments that the "day is long passed when the only necessary qualifications for social service are good inclinations. To minister successfully to a family whose own resources have broken down requires intelligence and skill of a high order." The prerequisites associated with the emergence of a profession gradually began to become clear.

The development of a knowledge base made it possible to offer courses on social work content in colleges and universities—the beginnings of professional education—by departments of sociology and economics. These disciplines were closely allied with "social work" at that time and saw it as applied sociology. Frequently the academic courses used the Charity Organizations as social laboratories for student education. In 1894 it was reported that 21 of 146 colleges and universities contacted in a survey were teaching courses in charities and correction (Brackett 1904:158). For instance, the University of Wisconsin offered courses in practical philanthropy in the early 1890s. Professor Richard T. Ely, who was responsible for the development of that program, arranged for a course of lectures on charities by Dr. Amos G. Warner. "Expanded and published as 'American Charities' in the Library of Economics and Politics edited by Dr. Ely, these lectures became the first standard book on the subject" (Brackett 1904:162).

These various approaches to training personnel for the emerging profession culminated in the movement for development of a formal comprehensive program of specialized education. Anna L. Dawes is generally credited with making the initial suggestion for "training schools for a new profession." In a paper presented at the International Congress of Charities in Chicago in 1893, she argued that "it ought to be possible for those who take up this work to find some place for studying it as a profession." Students in such a training school could be taught "what is now the alphabet of charitable science—some knowledge of its underlying ideas, its tried and trusted methods and some acquaintance with the various devices employed for the up-building of the needy so that no philanthropic undertaking, from a model tenement house to a kindergarten or a sand heap, will be altogether strange." The motion was seconded by Mary Richmond, who argued for the need for a training school in applied philanthropy at the twenty-fourth National Conference of Charities in 1897. Richmond reported that although it was true that each Charity Organization Society took some responsibility for training its visitors and its workers through the district committee conferences and the activities of the paid agent-supervisors, such education was apt to be agency centered and parochial. "This training specializes too soon and our leaders have but the need for a more intimate and sympathetic acquaintance on the part of our agents with almshouse work, reformatory work, care of defectives and all the other branches of work represented at this [National] Conference. . . . The school that is to be most helpful to our charity organization agents, therefore, must be established on a broad basis" (Richmond 1897:184).

In June 1898 a six-week summer training program was offered to twenty-seven students by the New York Charity Organization Society. This program is regarded as the beginning of professional education in social work. The summer course was repeated for a number of years and then expanded to become the New York School of Philanthropy, the first full-time school of social work. It is now the Columbia University School of Social Work. A school for social workers was established by Simmons College and Harvard University in 1904; in 1907 the Chicago School of Civics and Philanthropy (now the University of Chicago School of Social Service Administration) was established.

By 1910 five schools of social work had been established in the United States. Primary responsibility for training a cadre of social work professionals was vested in such schools. Agency supervision was seen as a supplementary educational resource. But because the number of schools was so limited, the greatest bulk of paid agents (later called charity workers and ultimately social workers) still received their training through apprenticeship programs in social agencies under the tutorship of more experienced agent-supervisors.

Although charged with this responsibility for educational supervision, almost none of the supervisors had any formal training in supervision because none was available. A short course in supervision was offered for the first time in 1911 under the aegis of the Charity Organization Department of the Russell Sage Foundation. The department was headed by Mary Richmond at that time.

Thus, starting with the development of the Charity Organization movement in the 1880s, supervision gradually emerged as a necessary aspect of Charity Organization work. The agent-supervisor organized, directed, and coordinated the work of visitors and paid agents and held them accountable for their performance; he or she advised, educated, and trained visitors and paid agents in performance of their work and supported and inspired them in their discouragements and disappointments. The three major components of current supervision—administration, education, and support—were thus identifiable among the tasks assumed by the early agent-supervisor. The case record had been identified as the principal vehicle for supervision and the individual conference as the principal context.

By the turn of the century, the educational apparatus of a profession was being organized and was assuming the main responsibility for training. Supervision continued to perform an educational function but more as a supplement to such formal training institutions. Over time, supervision achieved more visibility in the agency administrative structure, and the process itself gradually became more formalized. Time, place, content, procedures, and expectations of supervisory conferences received clearer definition. As social work became more diversified, supervision took root not only in family service agencies, where it had its origins, but also in corrections, psychiatric social work agencies, medical school work agencies, and schools.

Primary responsibility for professional education was transferred gradually from the agency to the universities. However, agencies still retained primary responsibility for the administrative and supportive aspects of supervision and for residual, supplementary educational supervision.

Developing a Literature on Social Work Supervision

As supervision became a more identifiable process, it became the subject of social work scholarship. Between 1920 and 1945 *Family* and then *Social Casework* published some thirty-five articles devoted to supervision.

A number of books were devoted exclusively, or primarily, to social work supervision. Virginia Robinson published a pioneer work in 1936, *Supervision in Social Case Work,* followed by *The Dynamics of Supervision Under Functional Controls* (1949). In 1942, Bertha Reynolds wrote *Learning and Teaching in the Practice of Social Work,* which is devoted in large measure to educational supervision. Three years later, Charlotte Towle included an extended section on social work supervision in her widely distributed pamphlet *Common Human Needs,* published by the Federal Security Agency and later reprinted by the National Association of Social Workers (NASW). Towle enlarged on that work in *The Learner in Education for the Professions,* published in 1954.

A review of the published material indicates that the direction and concerns of social work supervision over time have mirrored some changes in the orientation of social work generally and of casework in particular. Early in the history of social work it was thought that the worker, or friendly visitor, knew what was best for the client. Knowing this, the worker offered the client clear advice as to what should be done, and he or she arranged, independently of the client, to make resources available on the client's behalf. This was sometimes called an executive treatment approach (Lee 1923). Analogously, the supervisor, knowing what was best, told the worker what needed to be done.

As social work developed a greater appreciation of the need to actively involve clients' participation in and planning of their own solutions to problems, there was a complementary change in the approach of supervision. Supervision moved from telling the supervisees what to do to a greater encouragement of supervisee participation in planning and an increased mutuality in the supervisor-supervisee relationship (Glendenning 1923).

Although the impact of psychoanalytic psychology on the actual service offered the client in the 1920s may have been exaggerated (Alexander 1972; Field 1980), many of its ideas do seem to have influenced the orientation of supervision during that period. Supervision was seen as a kind of relationship therapy analogous to casework for the client. To be effective with clients, workers needed to be aware of and have the help of the supervisor in resolving their own intrapsychic conflicts (Glendenning 1923). Marcus suggested that

> the supervisor consider herself a caseworker whose case work must embrace not only the student's cases but the student herself. This demands, of course, that the supervisor investigate and treat the personal problem of the student as the latter investigates and treats those of the client. . . . If casework is an art and a philosophy and not merely a trade practiced on the handicapped and helpless, it was to be just as thoroughly a part of the caseworker's attitude toward herself. (1927:386)

In the middle of the "psychiatric deluge," however, Paige (a supervisor) writes of supervision in terms that emphasize accountability. She talks about the supervisor's holding the worker "to the meticulous adherence to the enforcement of social legislation in which minimum social standards have been crystallized" (1927:307).

During the same period, Dawson explicitly stated the functions of supervision in traditional terms, as administrative (the promotion and maintenance of good standards of work, coordination of practice with policies of administration, the assurance of an efficient and smooth-working office); educational ("the educational development of each individual worker on the staff in a manner calculated to evoke her fully to realize her possibilities of usefulness"); and supportive (the maintenance of harmonious working relationships, the cultivation of esprit de corps) (1926:293).

At different points in time, the preferred model for the supervisor-supervisee relationship reflected the preferred model of the worker-client casework relationship rather than any of the models of group-worker or community-worker interaction. This is, of course, not surprising, because the supervisor-supervisee relationship, like the worker-client relationship, is dyadic. Whatever the profession at any one time thinks makes for an effective dyadic relationship will be reflected in the models applicable to both the worker-client and the supervisor-supervisee relationship.

The component of supervision that overall has received the greatest emphasis in the literature is educational supervision. Theoreticians of social work supervision have attempted to apply a more general theory of growth and change to the educational process in supervision. Robinson, in the first book written on casework supervision (1936) and in her subsequent work (1949), attempted to apply the Rankian-functional approach to behavioral change to the supervisor-supervisee relationship. Towle (1954), on the other hand, attempted to analyze the relationship between supervisor and supervisee in terms of Freudian ego psychology. Supervision was seen as a change-oriented process, the dynamics of which were made explicable by application of ego psychology theory.

Some explanation for the heavy emphasis in social work supervision on the educational component stems from the strong influence of psychiatry on social work. In the past, supervision in psychiatry was implemented almost exclusively in the context of the professional preparation obtained in the psychiatric residency program. The emphasis was on training and growth of a clinician and the supervision is clinically oriented. As Langs said in discussing psychiatric training, "The goal of supervision" is the "education of the therapist" (1979:83)—echoing another influential psychiatric supervision text by Ekstein and Wallerstein (1972).

The literature of psychoanalytic supervision talks of such educational objectives as "developing therapeutic competence" and the "acquisition of clinical expertise" accompanied by "personal growth." The context of psychoanalytic supervision is the "learning alliance" between supervisor and supervisee—through which the supervisee learns therapeutic skills while developing self-awareness. Primarily educational, psychoanalytic supervision has minimal administrative implications.

The balance between the administrative, educational, and supportive components of supervision has varied widely over the course of the twentieth century. Educational supervision, teetering toward therapy, was in ascendancy during the 1920s and 1930s, but the progressive development and diversification of large-scale public welfare programs nudged the administrative aspects of supervision toward center stage in the 1950s and 1960s.

During the period of intensified concern with social action on the part of social workers in the 1960s and early 1970s, there was a reaction against supervision generally. Sensitivity to the rights of all oppressed subordinate groups carried over to the supervisee as an oppressed group. Freedom from supervisory control, a greater emphasis on participatory democracy, and mutuality in the supervisory relationship were given greater attention (Mandell 1973).

Growing concern with accountability in the 1970s intensified a highlight on the administrative aspect of supervision, which was further accented by recurrent agency needs to accommodate to budgetary shortages and managed-care oversight. Subsequently, the "discovery" and growth of interest in burnout put greater significance on the supportive components of supervision.

Since roughly 1975 there has been a marked increase in the literature devoted to social work supervision. In addition to the three editions of this book, published in 1976, 1985, and 1992, there were books by Westheimer (1977), Abels (1977), Pettes (1979), Powell (1980), Austin (1981), Shulman (1982, 1991, 1993), Munson (1983), Middleman and Rhodes (1985), Bunker and Wijnberg (1988), Holloway and Brager (1989), Holloway (1995), Bernard and Goodyear (1998), Bradley and Ladany (2001), and Munson (2001). Collections of articles on supervision were edited by Kaslow and colleagues (1972, 1977) and by Munson (1979a). Books on field instruction in social work containing general material on supervision were published by Wilson (1981), Shaefor and Jenkins (1982), Ford and Jones (1987), Gardiner (1989), Bogo and Vayda (1988), Urbanowski and Dwyer (1988), and Schneck, Grossman, and Glassman (1990).

The Clinical Supervisor, an interdisciplinary journal of supervision in psychotherapy and mental health, began publication in 1983. The supervision literature has shown signs of interdisciplinary development and growing specialization since then. Now books exist on gerontological supervision (Burack-Weiss and Brennan 1991), supervision in residential settings (Brown and Bourne 1995), the supervision of child protection (Gadsby-Waters 1992), supervision in turbulent systems (Hughes and Pengelly 1997), the supervisory relationship (Kaiser 1992a, 1992b, 1997), and clinical supervision (Munson 1993a; Taibbi 1995). *The Handbook of Psychotherapy Supervision* (Watkins 1997) has chapters on the supervision of direct services to adolescents and older clients, group and family psychotherapy, cultural competence, and gender-sensitive practice. Articles are now published on the appropriate organizational response to post-traumatic stress disorder among AIDS social workers (Wade, Beckerman, and Stein 1996); the developmental supervision of therapists treating gay, lesbian, and bisexual clients (Bruss et al. 1997); and existential supervision (Mahrer 1998).

Not only is the supervision literature growing, but it has also become more empirical. The first review of supervision research found twenty-six empirical studies in journals, dissertations, and books (Harkness and Poertner 1989). Eight years later, Tsui (1997) examined thirty examples of supervision research, half of which had been published following Harkness and Poertner's review. Though primarily clinically oriented and almost exclusively educational in intent, our sibling disciplines, such as psychiatry, psychology, and counseling, have developed a rich literature on supervision. Borrowing from and citing this literature contributes to a greater understanding of social work supervision and of educational supervision in particular. In that light, a third review of the empirical literature is now most exhaustive of all. Ellis and Ladany (1997) have reviewed 104 studies of supervision in social work and psychology, one-fifth of which were found in journals identified with social work and 27 of which were published after 1990.

Supervision in Group Work and Community Organization

Almost all of the literature mentioned previously reflects a traditional casework orientation to direct social work practice in agency settings, rather than any of the models of group-worker or community-worker interaction.

As Kutzik notes, consultation rather than supervision "was the rule among settlement staff" (1977:37). The egalitarian nature of settlement-house movement ideology was less receptive to the hierarchical implications of supervision, and according to Kennedy and Ferra (1935), implementation of supervisory functions in settlement houses was limited through the 1920s.

With the development of group service agencies, supervision was enriched by contributions from this segment of social work. Williamson's book *Supervision* (1959; rev. 1961), though general in nature, was oriented toward the YMCA worker. Two additional texts on supervision were similarly directed toward group service agencies (Lindenberg 1939; Dimock and Trecker 1949).

Supervision nonetheless continued to be strongly influenced by its origins in casework. In one of the few articles written by a group worker on supervision, Miller (1960) deplores the tendency of group work to pattern its supervisory procedures in accordance with those developed by casework. Supervision is less clearly formalized in group work agencies. Spellman noted the "odd assortment of practices which had grown up" in response to the need to perform supervisory functions but without explicit consideration of the process:

> We've had the "trouble shooter method"; "let me know if anything goes wrong and you need me for any emergency—and I'll be right there." Then there is the "hit-and-run method"; "I'll see you in the hall a couple of minutes after the meeting is over and we'll check on what happened and what you want for next week." Others had worked out the "crutch philosophy"; "I'll help you get started until you can stand on your own two feet." (1946:125)

A 1972 study of Chicago group work agencies showed that "most executives confer with staff members individually when necessary without planned supervisory conferences" (Switzer 1973:587).

Supervision in community organization is even less explicitly formulated. Community organizers often work in agencies with limited staff or are members of a small specialized unit in large agencies. In either case there is no elaborate hierarchical structure that includes supervisory personnel. The nature of the work of the community organizer often tends to be diffuse and the goals amorphous. This requires a great measure of on-the-job autonomy in dealing with the demands of the nonstandardized situation.

Holloway and Brager (1989:94) note that the "supervisor who can observe the worker in action has a lesser need for formal monitoring mechanisms." Services performed in "the privacy of workers' offices are more apt to call for formal process reporting in regular supervisory conferences and similar structures than tasks that are more generally observable such as group and community services. Because the latter services are in themselves informal, there is a propensity for their oversight to be informal as well." Unlike casework performed in private, both group work and community organization are performed in a more public setting.

The functional requirements of supervision in community organization— assignment of work, review and assessment of work done—may be performed by the agency administrator. These functions have to be performed, however infrequently or casually, but often no one is clearly designated as supervisor, and there is no explicit recognition that supervisory tasks are being discharged. The failure to recognize supervision is intensified by the particularly negative connotations the term has for community organizers. Of all the specialized subgroups in social work, community organization feels most strongly the need for worker autonomy. Supervision suggests a subservience that runs counter to this strong value. "This generally activist philosophy of many community workers does not regard with enthusiasm such organizational concepts as bureaucracy, authority and accountability" (Pettes 1979:23).

A book devoted to the practice and training of community workers in England clearly reflects the community worker's uneasy attitude toward supervision while it indicates the value of supervision to the community worker (Briscoe and Thomas 1977). Community workers see their primary loyalty and commitment to the community in which they are working and to the people in that community. They are hesitant about being identified with an agency and its bureaucracy, which often represent what the community is struggling against. The community workers suspect that the purpose of supervision is to exact conformity with the goals and norms of the agency with which they are affiliated—an affiliation they would rather not acknowledge. They feel that supervision may also be perceived as a way of controlling community work activities that may be politically embarrassing to the department or local authority. Community workers generally see themselves as agents of social change, and they are suspicious of those in organizations, like supervisors, who seem to represent the status quo and who provide a method of control over field workers (Harris 1977:33).

Rejection of supervision is an effort to "avoid being contaminated" in the context of the community worker's conflicting loyalties and identification with the community and the agency. As part of their struggle to maintain their integrity in a situation of conflicting loyalties and commitments, "supervisors are kept at a safe distance" (Thomas and Warburton 1978:29).

Supervision is not only associated with the agency and its bureaucracy but also with professionalism. This, too, is resisted, because developing expertise and theorizing about community work increase the social distance between the worker and members of the community. Community workers "may feel morally or politically compromised in taking up skill development opportunities" (Thomas and Warburton 1978:28) within the agency. Consequently the educational as well as the administrative component of supervision is rejected. There is a tendency, then, to reject the idea that any supervision is appropriately associated with community organization, and there is an almost total lack of literature on this subject.

In some respects, however, the need for supervision is even more urgent in community organization than in other areas of social work. The community organizer inevitably represents the agency. Working in a highly politicized arena, the worker is subject to a variety of pressures and power plays. In dealing with community groups he may commit the agency to activity or to policies that the agency finds difficult to defend or support. Consequently there is a great need for the agency to know what might have been promised, what deals are being contemplated, what action the worker plans to take. This requirement for accountability to agency administration is a task of supervision.

Despite the desirability of supervision, the nature of the community organizer's work may sometimes make it difficult to apply supervisory procedures. "Community workers function frequently in less well defined situations than workers in other methods. In part this is due to the experimental nature of much of the practice" (Pettes 1979:24). Brager and Specht note that

> whereas casework interviews can be scheduled and group workers conduct meetings on some regular basis, the activities of community workers defy regulation and scheduling. Work time is absorbed with informal telephone conversation, attending meetings in which they may have no formal role, talking with other professionals, and other difficult to specify activities. (1973:242)

This argues for very loose supervision because the worker has to be provided with maximum discretion.

Wayne (1988) made one of the very few attempts to study the differences in supervisory practices and orientation between micro- (casework) and macro- (community organization) supervisors. Tape-recorded interviews were conducted with thirty-seven supervisors trained in and supervising micro-level practice and nineteen supervisors trained in and supervising macro-level practice. The supervisees in each instance were master's of social work (MSW) students. Micro-level supervisors showed a greater motivation to improve their supervisory skills and a greater interest in supervision. They were more likely to hold scheduled weekly conferences with supervisees and more likely to regularly require written material from supervisees for teaching purposes. Micro-level supervisors identified the ability to be "in touch with feeling" as the most important characteristic of a good social work student. Macro-level supervisors identified ability to "think critically" as the most important characteristic. Micro-supervisors were more affectively oriented; macro-level supervisors were more cognitively oriented. Although macro-level supervisors saw the relationship between themselves and supervisees as more desirably informal than micro-level supervisors, they were less egalitarian than micro-level supervisors. Though macro-level supervisors were more likely to see "no threat" in developing friendships between supervisor and supervisee, they were more ready than micro-level supervisors to exert their authority in the relationship.

Confirmation of the disproportionately greater concern with supervision in casework as contrasted with community organization and group work was indicated by the responses to the NASW 1982 Data Bank Survey of membership. Of the respondents who identified their primary job title as supervisor, 99.3 percent were from casework settings, 0.006 percent were from the community organization settings, and 0.002 percent were from group services settings. Information obtained from NASW in 1989 indicated that less than 1 percent of the supervisors were in group work services and less than 1 percent in community organization. The supervisory profile of the current NASW membership looks much the same, if only because few social workers report working as community organizers or group workers. Only 221 employed social workers of the 153,814 NASW membership identified themselves as primarily community organizers in 1995 (Gibelman and Schervish 1997a); NASW no longer collects discrete membership data for social workers employed in group services settings. Social work supervision is concerned primarily with casework.

Toward a Definition

The word *supervision* derives from the Latin *super* (over) and *videre* (to watch, to see). Hence, a supervisor is defined as an overseer, one who watches over the work of another with responsibility for its quality. Such a definition of supervision leads to the derisive phrase *snooper vision.* The orthodox definition stresses the administration aspect of supervision, the concern with seeing that a job is performed at a quantitatively and qualitatively acceptable level.

In developing a definition of supervision for our purposes, it is helpful to discuss in turn each of the different considerations, which, in aggregate, contribute to a comprehensive definition. These include (1) the functions of supervision; (2) the objectives of supervision; (3) the hierarchical position of supervision; (4) supervision as an indirect service; and (5) the interactional process of supervision.

The Functions of Supervision

A review of the social work literature shows that supervision has been defined primarily in terms of the administrative and educational function, the emphasis varying with the author. Robinson, in the first social work text on this subject, *Supervision in Social Casework,* defined supervision as "an educational process in which a person with a certain equipment of knowledge and skill takes responsibility for training a person with less equipment" (1936:53). The first edition of the *Encyclopedia of Social Work* defined supervision as an educational process. It is the "traditional method of transmitting knowledge of social work skills in practice from the trained to the untrained, from the experienced to the inexperienced student and worker" (1965:785). The sixteenth (1971) and seventeenth (1977) editions of the *Encyclopedia* emphasized the administrative function. They defined supervision as "an administrative function, a process for getting the work done and maintaining organizational control and accountability" (Miller 1977: 1544–1551).

Occasionally, both functions are included in the definition. Towle defines social work supervision as "an administrative process with an educational purpose" (1945:95; similarly Burns 1958:6). A standard group work text states that "the supervisor's responsibilities are both administrative and educative in nature. . . . The ultimate objective of supervision is that through more effective effort on the part of its workers, an agency's services are improved in quality and its central purposes come nearer to fulfillment" (Wilson and Ryland 1949:587).

Each of the definitions presented is only partially correct. It is true that supervision is both an administrative and an educational process. The social work supervisor has responsibility for implementing both functions in contact with supervisees. There is, however, an additional and distinctively different responsibility that needs to be included in the definition. This is the expressive-supportive leadership function of supervision. The supervisor has the responsibility of sustaining worker morale; helping with job-related discouragement and discontent; and giving supervisees a sense of worth as professionals, a sense of belonging in the agency, and a sense of security in their performance. In enacting this function, the supervisor provides workers with support.

The nineteenth edition of the *Encyclopedia* (Shulman 1995) provides a definition of social work supervision that addresses the complementary nature of administration, education, and support. All are necessary if the ultimate objective of supervision is to be achieved. Admittedly there is an overlap between the administrative, educational, and supportive functions of supervision. However, each function is different in terms of problems and goals. The primary problem in administrative supervision is concerned with the correct, effective, and appropriate implementation of agency policies and procedures; the primary goal is to ensure adherence to policy and procedure. The primary problem in educational supervision is worker ignorance and/or ineptitude regarding the knowledge, attitude, and skills required to do the job; the primary goal is to dispel ignorance and upgrade skill. The primary problem in supportive supervision is worker morale and job satisfaction; the primary goal is to improve morale and job satisfaction. The foregoing presents a functional definition of social work supervision.

The Objectives of Supervision

The objectives of social work supervision are both short range and long range. The short-range objective of educational supervision is to improve the worker's capacity to do his job more effectively. It is to help the worker grow and develop professionally, to maximize his or her clinical knowledge and skills to the point where he or she can perform autonomously and independently of supervision. The short-range objective of administrative supervision is to provide the worker with a work context that permits him or her to do the job effectively. The short-range objective of supportive supervision is to help the worker feel good about doing his or her job.

However, these short-range objectives are not ends in themselves but the means for achieving the long-range objective of supervision. This objective is to effectively and efficiently provide clients with the particular service the particular agency is mandated to offer. The ultimate objective is, then, efficient and effective social work services to clients. Toward this objective the supervisor administratively integrates and coordinates the supervisees' work with others in the agency, educates the workers to a more skillful performance in their tasks, and supports and sustains the workers in motivated performance of these tasks.

The Hierarchical Position of Supervisors

The position of the supervisor in the hierarchy of the agency further helps to define supervision. It is clearly a middle management position. The supervisor is responsible for the performance of the direct service workers and is accountable to administrative directors.

The supervisor is sometimes described as an "in-between" functionary. The position of the supervisor is aptly described by Austin, who notes that the supervisor has "one foot in the work force and one foot in the management module, not being clearly associated with either" (1981:32). They are "leaders of their subordinates" but are subordinate to agency administrators. The supervisor is sometimes referred to as the "highest level employee and the lowest level manager," a "sub-administrator and a supra-practitioner" (Towle 1962). A member of both management and the work group, he or she acts as a bridge between them.

Agency executive administrators are primarily responsible for program planning, policy formulation, agency funding, and community relations. Primary supervisory managerial responsibilities center on program management and program implementation. Unlike the supervisor, the administrator is externally oriented and is concerned with a broader perspective. His eyes are on the image of the agency as perceived by community and legislative boards, oversight bodies, and client groups. The administrator acts as a broker with other organizations, negotiating agreements for coordinated action and arranging the procedures for interagency accountability. The administrator is concerned with organizational stability and survival, external politics, and the donor constituency. Supervisors are, by contrast, internally oriented, focusing on the work environment and the job that needs to be done.

Supervision has a more pronounced internal operations focus as contrasted with the more external orientation of top agency administrators. It is said that administration controls the domain of agency policy and planning, supervisors control the domain of management, and workers control the domain of service.

Talcott Parsons (1951) identified the three different levels of organizational hierarchy as (1) the institutional level (relating the organization to the larger society), (2) the managerial level (mediating between the organization and the task environment), and (3) the technical level (direct service to organizational clients). Others have somewhat similarly identified the three levels as policy, management, and service.

Supervisors find their home at the second, managerial level. The supervisor is the only administrative person in immediate daily contact with the direct service worker. The supervisor's front-line position is at close contact with the coal face, the shop floor, the context where the work of the organization is actually done.

Supervision as an Indirect Service

The supervisor's position in the agency organizational structure further defines supervision as an indirect service. The supervisor is in indirect contact with the client through the worker. The supervisor helps the direct service worker help the client.

In exemplification of the indirect role, it is said that supervisors talk about clients, not to them.

Supervision as an Interactional Process

Supervision is defined as a process. In implementing the functions of supervision, the supervisor engages in sequential series of deliberately and consciously selected activities. There is an ordered beginning, middle, and end to the process of supervision, and the activities engaged in at each point in the process are somewhat different from activities engaged in at other points in the process.

The process of supervision is implemented in the context of a relationship. Being a supervisor requires having a supervisee, much as being a parent requires having a child. A supervisor without a supervisee makes as much sense as saying my brother was an only child. Because at least two people are involved, their interaction is a significant aspect of supervision. Supervisor and supervisee(s) establish a small, interlocking social system that at its best is cooperative, democratic, participatory, mutual, respectful, and open.

Supervision as the Means to an End

Socialized in the values and purpose of the social work profession, the supervisor socializes others in turn. Continuing a process that begins in the classroom, the supervisor helps the social worker internalize the service aspirations of social work practice. In concert, the delivery of efficient and effective agency services, the development of the front-line worker's knowledge and skills, and sustaining the worker-as-person in the face of difficult challenges—all target the end of improved client outcomes, in accordance with NASW (1999) standards for direct-practice supervision.

Definition of Supervision

A comprehensive definition of social work supervision attempts to combine all the elements noted in the five sections. As the term will be used in this book, then, a social work supervisor is an agency administrative-staff member to whom authority is delegated to direct, coordinate, enhance, and evaluate the on-the-job performance of the supervisees for whose work he or she is held accountable. In implementing this responsibility, the supervisor performs administrative, educational, and supportive functions in interaction with the supervisee in the context of a positive relationship. The supervisor's ultimate objective is to deliver to agency clients the best possible service, both quantitatively and qualitatively, in accordance with agency policies and procedures. Supervisors do not directly offer service to the client, but they do indirectly affect the level of service offered through their impact on the direct service supervisees.

Empirical Validation of Definition

Our definition is derived from a general analysis of social work supervision. To what extent do empirical studies of supervision support the validity of the definition—to what extent does it reflect the reality of social work supervision? We have only limited empirical data on this. In 1977, the Wisconsin Department of Health and Social Services sponsored a study of the tasks performed by those holding the position of Social Work Supervisor I. A task book of 574 possible supervisor tasks was developed, and the supervisors were asked to identify which of these tasks they actually performed. Usable responses were received from thirty-eight supervisors. The fact that only 20 percent of the 574 tasks were selected by 50 percent or more of the respondents indicates that there was considerable variation in the actual job tasks performed by those holding the similarly designated Supervisor I position.

The largest number of tasks performed by the largest number of supervisors were those that are essentially administrative in nature. This group of tasks constituted some 60 percent of all tasks performed. These included assigning, directing, reviewing, coordinating, and evaluating work; making personnel decisions regarding hiring, promoting, and termination; program planning and budget development; intra- and interagency communication of policy; and handling complaints.

Tasks related to educational supervision—staff development and training—constituted 10 percent of tasks performed. These included such activities as assessing training needs of workers; facilitating training; suggesting, teaching, and demonstrating; orienting and inducting new workers into their jobs; and providing needed information.

Tasks related to supportive supervision were rarely explicitly identified, although some of the task items selected indicated the supervisor's responsibility for maintaining productive levels of morale.

Patti (1977) asked ninety social welfare managers to delineate the activities they engaged in during a typical work week. The respondents included administrators and department heads as well as supervisors. Differences in activities were related to differences in levels of management. Executive management–level administrators were more concerned with "representing the agency in the community," "negotiating with groups and organizations," "setting agency goals and objectives," "designing program structures," and "budgeting," whereas respondents at the supervisory management level "spent a major portion of their work week in 'directing', 'advising,' and 'reviewing' the work of their subordinates" (Patti 1983:45). Supervisors were seen as having day-to-day contact with front-line staff, maintaining work flow, delegating and assigning work, seeing that services were provided in a manner consistent with policies and procedures, consulting with front-line workers on case-level decisions, providing advice and instruction on technical aspects of work, providing opportunities for upgrading areas of knowledge and skills, pointing out deficiencies, and evaluating individual performance (1983:44). Administrative and educational functions and activities of supervisors are clearly identified in the findings.

A detailed study between 1975 and 1977 of social work team practice in England, Scotland, and Northern Ireland involved repeated interviews with some 300 social workers and participant observation of their practice. Some 700 interviews were tape-recorded and transcribed. Asked about how they perceived the functions of supervision that they experienced, the practitioners identified administrative, educational, and supportive aspects, although support was given more explicit mention.

> In the social worker's eyes, the most important purpose was to provide them with the support which came from talking things over, sharing worries, and seeking practical and procedural advice. Reflection on interaction with clients was considered almost as important as immediate support. Social workers generally considered that another purpose of supervision and an appropriate one was checking on their work and, linked with this, ensuring that they were not making serious mistakes. Supervision, some mentioned, imposed a necessary discipline upon them. (Parsloe and Stevenson 1978:201)

Shulman reports on a study in which 109 supervisors were asked to "indicate the percentage of time they allocated to various tasks." Responses indicating that about 20 percent of the time was spent on "management,"

18 percent on "coordinating," and some 11 percent on "personnel" (all of which can be regarded as administrative considerations) led to the conclusion that about 49 percent of the supervisor's time was spent in administrative supervision. About 40 percent of the time was devoted to "supervision-consultation," which can be interpreted to mean educational supervision (Shulman 1982:22).

Poertner and Rapp (1983) did a task analysis of supervision in a large public child welfare agency. Having identified, through interviews with selected supervisors, the tasks that they performed, a refined listing of thirty-five explicit tasks of supervision was sent to 120 supervisors and 227 direct service workers. The supervisors were asked to state whether they performed the tasks listed, and the workers were asked to identify the tasks they perceived the supervisors performing. Responses indicated that supervisors performed administrative-management tasks primarily. Some 80 percent of the tasks performed were concerned with (1) caseload management ("evaluates case plans for compliance with department policy," "projects case placements and service needs," "examines case plans with case workers"); (2) worker control ("assigns new cases," "reviews forms for accuracy and completion," "monitors team goal attainment"); (3) organizational maintenance ("responds to instruction or requests from central office," "determines records-keeping procedures," "checks and approves forms"); and (4) interacting with community ("meets with community agencies to discuss service plans," "participates with community groups to identify and define new service priorities," "meets with community groups to elicit cooperation to meet department goals"). The remaining 20 percent of tasks performed were divided between supportive and educational supervision. In implementing supportive supervision, supervisors said they "encouraged, listened to, and responded to staff concerning cases." In implementing educational supervision, supervisors said they "educated caseworkers on the role of the juvenile court" and "taught caseworkers court procedures."

Here once again an empirical study of supervisors' tasks confirms the fact that administrative, educational, and supportive components are responsibilities of the position. In ranking the allocation of emphasis, administrative supervision once again has clear priority.

In 1989, Kadushin (1992a) distributed a questionnaire containing a series of questions about functions performed by supervisors to 1,500 randomly selected social work supervisors. Responses from 508 supervisors confirmed the fact that administrative, educational, and supportive functions were performed. In terms of ranking, 44 percent of the supervisors identified educational functions ("upgrading problem solving and practice skills, developing self awareness; instruct, advise, suggest regarding alternative case understandings and interventions") as most important. Some 32 percent of the supervisors cited administrative functions ("assigning, reviewing evaluating supervisee's work; planning unit work and unit budgets, coordinating work of unit") as most important, and 24 percent cited supportive functions ("maintain supervisee's motivation, morale, commitment, resolve dissatisfactions and grievances, mitigate job stress, prevent burnout") as most important.

Research by Erera and Lazar (1994a) operationalized and tested the tripartite definition of social work supervision in Israel. First, the investigators derived an exhaustive list of supervisory "action items" from the literature. Second, they asked independent judges to validate the list of action items to cull and refine it. Third, 233 supervisors employed in three types of agencies described how frequently they performed each of the remaining thirty-nine action items in the course of their daily work. Finally, the supervisors' reports were factor analyzed to determine the underlying structure of social work supervision. Seven distinct supervision factors emerged from social work practice in social service departments, social security and immigration agencies, mental health clinics, rehabilitation and addictions centers, probation offices, and hospitals. These were (1) policy modification, planning, and budgeting; (2) quality control; (3) contacts with community services; (4) professional skills and techniques; (5) professional boundaries; (6) knowledge and information; and (7) support. The first three factors were clearly administrative in nature, and the second three obviously served an educational function. The support factor stood on its own. In short, an operational form of Kadushin's (1976) definition of social work supervision has been found to be reliable and valid in practice.

Ecology of Social Work Supervision

Supervision, like any other process, is embedded in some ecological system, the components of which influence the process. Figure 1.1 describes a traditional view of the more consequential components of the supervisor-supervisee ecological system. Each component in the expanding set of components exerts some influence on the preceding component, the contiguous components of the system having the greatest influence on each other. The more distant component, as a rule, the less direct, immediate impact it is likely to exert. Wars, economic depressions, and other earth-shaking events are important and dramatic exceptions.

Community: General and Professional

The general community impacts on the supervisory system in terms of the sanction, support, and attitudes it communicates toward the social work

Figure 1.1

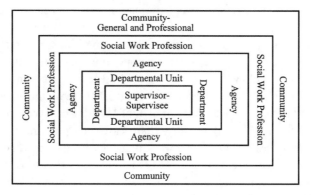

profession and the agency in which the supervisor operates. The general community provides the legitimation and funding that determines the organization's operations. Where legitimation is restrictive and funding inadequate, the supervisor works with considerable constraints and limited resources.

When the environment is stable, the impact of the community on social work supervision may go unnoticed. However, over the past twenty or thirty years, the landscape of social work supervision has undergone change of tectonic proportions. The so-called Reagan revolution and postmodern conservative government; welfare reform, managed care, and privatized human services; technological advances, a pulsing global market, the disappearance and creation of nations, human immigration, and the changing demographic profile of the nation shape the practice environment. As did the Great Depression and two world wars, inexorable forces from inside and outside our borders have an impact on social work supervision and social work practice.

In the 1980s the Reagan revolution set a sea change in motion. Government sought to downsize federal administration of human services with the Omnibus Budget Reconciliation Act of 1981. In large measure, block grants returned dollars and discretionary spending to the states. An explosion in national health-care expenditures alarmed the private sector and all levels of government. As public and private health care insurers adopted a variety of quality-assurance standards to slow the runaway growth in the health-care economy; for example, supervisors in the largest field of social work practice were compelled to review client charts by the thousands before auditors saw them. Random errors in recording or practice put agency revenues, social work jobs, and client services in jeopardy.

In the 1990s environmental demand for administrative supervision gathered force as welfare reform swept the nation. As foreseen by Stoesz and Karger (1990), *reform* meant (1) funding mandated services through the states, (2) privatizing human services, (3) inviting bids for human-service contracts to encourage private-sector competition, and (4) making clients pay for services. Following the signing of the Personal Responsibility and Work Opportunity Reconciliation Act on August 16, 1996, the organization, services, and administrative oversight of public welfare changed almost overnight (APHSA 1998), and public welfare caseloads plummeted (APHSA 1999). In the largest field of social work practice, rising costs of health produced a "managed care revolution" (Lohmann 1997) that took control of the health-care service-delivery system itself (Corcoran 1997). Now, argues Carlton Munson (1998a, 1998b), profiteering corporations are supervising social work practice. How social work supervision will manage managed care remains to be seen.

In the past, there was a more immediate community of allied professionals with which the agency cooperated and with which it coordinated some of its activities—the health service community; employment, housing, and educational services; and the law enforcement community. Agency supervision was effected by cooperative, coordinated, communicative relationships with these service providers. The immediate community in which the supervisor-supervisee dyad ultimately was embedded also included lay groups, such as foster and adoptive parents' associations and Families Anonymous, with which the agency had some working contacts. More than ever before, the community now includes federal, state, county, and local government (APHSA 1998) and private corporations (Munson 1998a, 1998b, 2001).

From an international perspective, Tsui and Ho (1997) argue that culture is the overarching environment of social work supervision. This requires thoughtful attention, as the United States absorbs an estimated 820,000 immigrants annually. Between 1991 and 1996, New York City and Los Angeles received 1.2 million immigrants, many from Central America and Asia. Another 400,000 immigrants became citizens of Chicago and Miami. In suburban Boise, Idaho, one can hear Chinese, Hmong, Korean, Nupe, Polish, Serbian, Spanish, and Russian being spoken on the streets. If current rates of immigration and population growth continue, in another fifty years the majority status of the white population will recede. Latinos will account for 22 percent, African Americans will become 14 percent, and the Asian population will rise from 3 to 10 percent of a U.S. population estimated to exceed 390 million (Spain 1999). Human diversity is reshaping the environment of supervised social work practice.

The Social Work Profession

The social work profession exerts an influence on supervision in terms of the values it dictates for supervisor and supervisee allegiance and the technology it makes available for solving human problems. The professionally educated supervisee and supervisor share norms, values, and objectives, derived from socialization to the profession and ethical standards, that determine their preferences and behavior in supervision. The profession as a source of identification for this ideology competes with the agency as a source of identification for determining behavior. The profession exerts a further influence on supervision through credentialing and licensing procedures, which set standards for practice.

The NASW Code of Ethics (NASW 1999) defines the values of the social work profession in behavioral terms that govern the transactions among the supervisor, the social worker, the client, and the practice environment. The abstract values underlying our ethical standards are immutable, but periodically the code of ethics is refreshed to clarify thorny issues of practice or rise to new practice challenges. In 1999, the NASW Code of Ethics was revised to address old ambiguities and new practice challenges in social work supervision.

Because the social work supervisor bears legal responsibility for the supervisee's actions and the outcomes of service and requires commensurate authority and resources to discharge his or her duties (Reamer 1998), supervisors have an ethical obligation to restrict the scope of their supervisory practices to their areas of competence, maintain up-to-date knowledge and skills, establish clear and appropriate interpersonal boundaries that avoid dual relationships, encourage their supervisees' professional development, evaluate their supervisees' performance, and promote and defend an ethical workplace (NASW 1999).

With more than half of NASW members now employed in private-sector settings (Gibelman and Schervish 1997b), social work supervisors are coming to grips with private sector values. Munson (1998a, 1998b) has described the NASW Code of Ethics as social work's moral compass, and points to sixteen ethical conflicts that supervisors are likely to face in the contemporary practice environment. Supervisors identified with social work's primary service obligation to clients may experience ethical tension with the goals and methods of welfare reform, for example, and supervisors committed to the ethical mandates of informed consent and client confidentiality may find it challenging to practice in managed care environments. Anecdotally, those conflicts find expression in the supervisory relationship. A new graduate, for example, socialized in client advocacy and empowerment practice, may view with suspicion ethical accommodations to welfare reform of an experienced supervisor, nearing retirement. By the same token, an experienced supervisor may question the ethical judgment of the young entrepreneur who, fresh out of school, forms a for-profit case-management agency. In the changing practice environment, supervisors will address ethical issues that are nuanced and textured, rarely clear-cut.

The Social Work Agency

The agency system determines the structure of agency supervision, the entitlements and obligations of the supervisory role within the agency, and the occupants of the role set. The culture of the agency, its mission and procedures, are determinants of supervisor-supervisee interaction. The discussion of supervision throughout this book is at a level of abstraction that ignores the specific agency context in which it is practiced. It needs to be recognized, however, that different agency settings require different adaptations of supervision. Supervising in a public hospital is different from supervising in a voluntary family service agency.

The Unit Within the Agency

The department within the agency in which the supervisor is located determines the specific tasks for which the supervisor is responsible and the situational specifics affecting supervision—the geography of the work unit, the support structure and resources available to the work unit, and so on. The unit peer group is, additionally, an influence on supervision at this point in the ecology of supervision.

Supervisor-Supervisee Dyad (Supervisee Group)

The worker-supervisor dyad (or group) provides the specific interactional system in which the supervisory process occurs. This interactional dyadic (sometimes group) context is the ultimate subsystem through which the wider influences of the broader ecological system outlined above are filtered. What happens here (and this is the continuing concern of this text) depends on the idiosyncratic nature of the supervisor, the idiosyncratic nature of the supervisee, and the special chemistry between particular supervisors and supervisees.

The Demography of Social Work Supervision

In 1995, information obtained from NASW indicated that 5,045 of its approximately 86,000 "working, non-student social workers" listed supervision as their primary function—about 5.5 percent of the membership (Gibelman and Schervish 1997b:7–8). An additional 18.3 percent listed supervision as a secondary function. Males were disproportionately represented among those for whom supervision was a primary function. The largest majority of supervisors (80 percent) were located in just three fields of practice—children, youth, and family services; medical social work services; and mental health services. Supervisors were relatively scarce in private for-profit agencies but overrepresented in private not-for-profit agencies.

The largest number, 23.7 percent, had eleven to fifteen years of experience in social work, followed closely by some 21.4 percent with six to ten years of experience and 18.7 percent with sixteen to twenty years of experience. Of the supervisors, 2.3 percent had a Ph.D./DSW, 92 percent had an MSW, and 5.7 percent had a bachelor's of social work (BSW). Of the supervisors for whom gender was reported, 72.5 percent were women and 27.5 percent were men. Supervisors had more experience, higher education, and a greater percentage of males than the NASW working membership as a whole.

The supervisors were more ethnically diverse than the NASW membership, which was 88.5 percent white, whereas only 83.3 percent of supervisors were white. Nine percent of the supervisors described themselves as African American, 2 percent as Asian, and 2 percent as having mixed ethnic heritage. Moreover, Native Americans, Chicanos, Puerto Ricans, and supervisors of other Hispanic ethnicity each represented approximately 1 percent of the NASW supervisors.

Although no overall information is available on the number or ethnicity of the social work supervisory cadre, the national social work labor force is more diverse than the NASW membership. In 2001, the U.S. Department of Labor reported that 22.7 percent of an estimated 828,000 employed social workers were African American, and 8.5 percent were of Hispanic origin. In a national study of child welfare supervisors, Vinokur-Kaplan and Hartman (1986) reported that 15 percent were African American, a percentage a little higher than the percentage of African Americans in the general population but substantially smaller than the percentage employed in social work labor force.

Gibelman and Schervish (1997b) reported that the median 1995 salary for social work supervisors was $37,499. The national salary range for supervisors in public state child welfare agencies in 1995 was $39,851 to $40,370, the midpoint of which is $38,823 (Curtis and Boyd 1997). These figures compare well with the 1999 median annual social work income of $31,252 (U.S. Bureau of Labor Statistics 2000c).

Span of control indicates the number of supervisees assigned to a supervisor. A detailed design of a social service system for children and families sponsored by the Child Welfare League of America advises that to fulfill the roles of supervisor "effectively it is recommended that a supervisor be assigned a maximum of five social workers, two case aides, and one or two clerk typists" (U.S. Dept. of Health, Education, and Welfare 1978:1989). In one instance, in which the courts mandated changes to agency practice in child welfare in response to a class action suit, the court decree specified a "maximum ratio of one supervisor to seven social workers" (Mushlin, Levitt, and Anderson 1986:48). Ten years ago, most of the supervisors (71 percent) participating in a national survey had responsibility for seven or fewer supervisees (Kadushin 1992a), but in all probability the span of control for social work supervision is now more diverse (Gibelman and Schervish 1997a). General trends suggest that although the span of control in social services agencies that receive public funding may be stable, the span of control in other settings has expanded. Thus, although the social work supervisor in a public child welfare agency may supervise seven or fewer supervisees, in a private case management agency his or her counterpart may supervise ten or twelve social workers. A growing number of private practitioners engaged in direct practice are supervising or receiving supervision from no one at all (Gibelman and Schervish 1997a).

The Significance of Supervision in Social Work

We have noted that historically, supervision has always been an important element in social work. Supervision is not, of course, unique to social work, but the function and process of supervision have achieved special importance in social work as contrasted with most other professions. This prominence might be explained by some distinctive aspects of the profession, the nature of its service delivery pattern, the problems with which it is concerned, the clientele to whom service is offered, and the characteristics of social workers.

1. Social work, as contrasted with other, more entrepreneurial professions, has traditionally offered service to the client group through an agency. An agency is a complex organization and therefore needs to develop some bureaucratic structure if it is to operate effectively. The work of different people, each performing some specialized task, has to be coordinated and integrated. The social agency thus requires a chain of command, a hierarchy of administrators. Because the greatest percentage of social workers perform their professional functions within an agency, they find themselves in a bureaucratic structure in contact with the supervision that a bureaucracy requires.

Until recently, a very small number of social workers operated autonomously as private practitioners outside an agency. This is no longer true. Although the majority of social workers continue to practice in bureaucratic organizational settings, Gibelman and Schervish (1997b:71) report that the private for-profit sector has become the primary auspice of social work practice for nearly 28 percent of the working membership of NASW. Solo or group private practice is the primary work setting for 20.3 percent of that membership (1997b:88), and 45.5 percent of working NASW members describe group or solo practice as their secondary work setting (1997b:95). To the extent that the profession moves toward implementation of its function outside an agency setting, traditional supervision may be de-emphasized. Supervisory practice is the primary function for less that 1 percent of the social workers engaged in solo or group private practice (1997b:92). However, the current situation—in which social work is practiced primarily in an agency setting—is likely to prevail for some time.

Other professions that find the bulk of their practitioners working in agency settings have been concerned with supervision for similar reasons. This is true particularly for teachers and nurses. As the more traditionally entrepreneurial professions become bureaucratized (as is happening currently with medicine and law), they find themselves building a bureaucratic apparatus that includes supervisory personnel and supervisory controls.

Social work, however, from its inception has been organizationally based. Having a longer history in an organizational context, it has had a more prolonged concern with supervision. Considerable educational and training effort is expended in helping social work recruits understand and identify with organizational models and values. Social workers are evaluated in terms of their identification with, acceptance of, and adherence to agency policies and procedures.

Social work education gives centrality to the agency. Other professions socialize recruits in terms of a professional image that is largely modeled after the independent entrepreneur, but social work has always heavily emphasized the organization-agency context as the locus of the worker's activity. Consequently, as Scott (1969:92) notes, "Social workers, unlike members of other professions, expect to enter an organization where their work will be subject to routine hierarchical supervision." As a result of tradition and training, the "social worker is a sophisticated and accomplished 'organization man' " (Vinter 1959:242; see also Epstein 1970; Rothman 1974:96).

2. A significant component of social agency activity is concerned with the distribution of services and supplies that the agency does not own. Very substantial amounts of agency resources, supplied from community appropriations, are allocated through decisions made by workers. Assigning a child foster care can involve the commitment of thousands of dollars over a five- to ten-year period. The decision to assign a homemaker to a family, provide day care at community expense, or institutionalize a brain-damaged child or

a senile aged person involves a substantial increase in community expenditures. The community feels entitled to know that such decisions are made with some oversight and procedural safeguards, not solely on the basis of the worker's autonomous discretion. As Levy notes, "Organization funds, materials, and all other resources placed at the disposal of staff members are not personal assets. They are assets held in trust for the community" (1982:51). Howe suggests that professions such as social work, which "involve economic externalities" that are provided by the community and whose use affects the community, cannot expect to be fully autonomous (1980:179). There is justification for community control of such organizations.

Accountability to the community is also required by the fact that the community provides the agency with its clientele. Policies established by the community regarding eligibility requirements for certain programs and definitions of needs channel people to the agencies. As a result, the social work situation brings great pressure from the community for explicit accountability procedures regarding agency activity. This again leads directly to a need for a supervisory apparatus.

One might argue that traditional accountability procedures in other professions require the professional to be self-disciplined and self-accountable, subject when necessary to peer review. However, even in the oldest and most solidly established professions there is a demand for more formal procedures of accountability once public funds are involved, procedures that are supervisory in nature.

In 1972 Congress passed legislation that provided for Professional Standards Review Organizations "to monitor the quality of every doctor's professional work whether it be performing open heart surgery or making a house call, if the services are being paid for by Federal [Medicaid and Medicare] programs" (*New York Times*, December 3, 1973). Neither Congress nor the American Medical Association (which ultimately approved the legislation) felt that the individual physician's self-accountability was sufficient. Given the large amount of public funds being expended for medical programs, supervision here, too, is regarded as necessary.

With the privatization of public human services under welfare reform and with the majority of health care managed, resource "ownership" and accountability have been realigned. Instead of relying on the supervisor to provide proxy oversight, the key to accountability has become the third-party contract. To obtain contracts to provide mental health services, for example, social workers have been required to obtain the highest level of clinical licensure first. In most states, that licensure follows an extended period of supervision, and in many states an examination must be passed. Ongoing supervision, if required, is a professional service that the social worker purchases independently. Instead of describing the process and outcomes of direct client services to the supervisor, a week or two later, under typical managed-care rules the social worker must obtain prior authorization to get paid for addressing a well-defined problem with a well-defined protocol for a predetermined number of sessions. Similar arrangements are being made between the public sector and human-service workers with less education, supervision, and training (U.S. Bureau of Labor Statistics 2000b). These trends may lead to growing demand for private social work supervision.

3. The finances and resources that the agency employs to help its clients, as well as the policies that the agency implements, often originate elsewhere. Policy for public social-welfare agencies often is created by political bodies, such as public welfare boards and commissions. The agencies are then answerable to these political entities for correct implementation of policy. This circumstance, too, creates an organizational pressure for some system of accountability for workers' activity within the agency.

Scott (1965) terms professional organizations that are controlled in some measure by external agencies "heteronomous organizations" and includes social agencies, schools, and libraries under this rubric. His study of their administration confirms their greater concern with supervision and supervisory procedures.

The outside dictation of agency policy is justified not only by the fact that public and private funds are being used to offer or purchase the service but also by the fact that social agencies are concerned with problem situations that present a great danger to the community, situations in which the community has a strong vested interest. Mental illness, crime, dependency, discrimination, and family breakdown are particularly costly financial and ideological threats to society. Response to these problems involves the embodiment of society's values, its ideological commitments in sensitive areas—family structure, legal conformity, sexual mores, the work ethic, racial conflict. The community and the corporation feel impelled to indicate how such situations should be handled through its articulation of social policy and the management of contracts. The fact that social work agencies are concerned with problems that pose not only a financial but also an ideological danger to the community again leads to external control of agency policy and internal agency control of work autonomy. The public is anxious about the kinds of decisions made by the agency that can affect public policy on controversial questions. The legislative consideration of various "patients' rights" bills suggests that the public is equally anxious about the kinds of policy decisions being made in the private sector as well.

4. The autonomy granted any member of a profession reflects the degree of autonomy granted the profession as a whole. If the community is hesitant

about granting full autonomy to a profession, there will be pressure toward supervision of the individual professional. The degree of autonomy granted is a function of the extent to which there is general consensus about the profession's objectives. Where powerful segments of the community disagree about the ultimate aims of a profession's activity, there will be greater reluctance to grant autonomy to the profession, as this will permit the profession to decide on its own objectives. Autonomy enables a few professionals to decide for the many in the community. There is less general consensus as to the objectives of social work than there is regarding, for instance, the fiscal objectives of welfare reform or managed health services. Hence, there is greater community reluctance to grant social work a full measure of autonomy. Research suggests that social workers have a tendency to base their practice decisions on values, not knowledge (Rosen 1994; Rosen et al. 1995), and whether deserved or not, social workers have acquired a reputation for spending other people's money.

Community confidence in the competence of a professional group to effectively implement society's mandate is a necessary prerequisite for the grant of full autonomy. Whether the opinion is justified or not, it seems clear that the community has doubts about social work competence. Because society's grant of autonomy to the profession is limited as a result of these considerations, there is less protection of the autonomy of any individual professional.

5. Research suggests that when a profession, such as social work, performs nonuniform tasks in an uncertain and unpredictable context toward the achievement of diffuse and ambiguous objectives with heterogeneous populations, there is more decentralization of decision making and a greater need for worker autonomy (Dornbusch and Scott 1975:76–87; Rothman 1974:152–57). These findings logically argue for less bureaucratic structure because they suggest difficulty in codification of procedures, formulation of standardized rules of action, and routinization of performance. They would also seemingly argue for a less elaborate supervisory apparatus. One can, however, deduce the opposite need from the same considerations. Where objectives are unclear, where there is great uncertainty as to how to proceed, where the effects of interventions are unpredictable and the risk of failure is high, workers may need and want the availability of an administrative representative with whom they can share responsibility for decision making, from whom they can receive direction, and to whom they can look for support. Consequently, the conditions under which the work of the profession is performed argue for the desirability of a supervisory cadre.

Because of the nonroutine, nonstandardized, unpredictable, highly individualized nature of social agency activities, it is difficult to design a comprehensive formal management information system. Even the best forms fail to collect a good deal of significant information about the worker's activity. Consequently the nature of the social worker's function and activities requires that the administration gather information through other channels. The conference between supervisor and supervisee is such a channel. The need for such personalized, intensive, and flexible channels for gathering this information further highlights the value of social work supervision.

On the other hand, some voices within the profession have advocated social work practice standardization. Howard and Jensen (1999), for example, believe that social workers should develop and follow practice guidelines, as physicians have begun to do. The motivation is both pragmatic and value laden. In the private sector, for example, insurers may deny payment for unproven methods of practice; in the public sector, perhaps foster care and family preservation will someday be judged by the same rule of thumb. In either case, providing clients with human services of the highest proven quality is a measure of client advocacy, because in principle adopting practice guidelines means determining what works best with whom for what problem and standardizing what we do. Munson (1998a, 1998b) advocates practice guidelines less stridently; he sees their value but doubts that social work has the scientific infrastructure to pursue them independently. As a remedy, Austin (1998) has called for increasing investment in research focused on the science of the helping professions. Guidelines already govern social work practice under managed care, but it is too early to determine whether social work will adopt guidelines of its own for the profession.

6. Social workers perform their functions under conditions that do not permit direct observation. The ethos of the profession encourages protection from such direct scrutiny, and practice principles further support it. We hold interviews in private and discourage observation as an intrusion on the privacy of the encounter. We contend that direct observation of our practice would create hazards for effective worker-client interaction. We thus create an unusual situation of role performance invisibility and interdicted observability. This being the nature of practice procedures, the client would be left without effective protection from practice that might be damaging if there were no system for supervisory review of what the worker is doing. Many other professionals perform their services publicly, and their work is thus open to more general evaluation. The lawyer can be observed in the courtroom; the musician, on the concert platform; the professor, in the lecture hall. These situations make less imperative the need for supervisory review of performance as a protection to clients. The fact that group workers to some extent, and community organizers to an even greater extent, perform "in public" mitigates some of the pressure for supervision in these areas of social work.

7. Certain other professionals, such as doctors and dentists, do perform their functions privately, but the outcome of professional activity is more objective and observable than in the case of social work. The doctor may perform his functions in private without benefit of supervisory review, but consistently inadequate professional performance means sick or dead patients. The cause-and-effect relationship between social work activity and changes in the client's situation is much more subtle and difficult to define. Because the damaging effects of poor practice are not so self-evident and observable, protection of the client requires a procedure for explicit periodic review of worker activity and practice outcomes.

8. Two additional aspects of the social work delivery system create a need for supervision: the agency provides the workers with their clientele, and clients are often "captives" of the agency.

A captive clientele reduces the need for self-discipline and critical self-evaluation. The professional entrepreneur, the lawyer or the doctor, pays a price for ineptitude, inefficiency, and outmoded professional skills by a reduction of income owing to loss of clients. The social worker, operating in an agency that provides the clients, does not face the same kind of penalties that alert him or her to the need for examining and correcting his practice. The setting again dictates a greater need for controls, as the practice does not automatically provide such controls.

Furthermore, the client's use of agency service is often involuntary, dictated by organs of social control, such as schools and courts. Even without such formal directives, situational imperatives may deny the client freedom of choice. The need for food, shelter, or medical care may determine the client's need for an agency service, a service for which the agency is granted a monopoly. The fact that the client's use of the agency is often compulsory means that greater provision needs to be made to protect the client than would be the case in situations in which the client could choose to withdraw if dissatisfied with the service.

Normally, professionals in independent practice or employed by a profit-making organization, such as a law or engineering firm, are subject to control by clients. Inadequate or incomplete service results in the loss of clients. In the past, human services agencies were immune, for the most part, from such punitive control by the client alerting them to deficiencies in performance. Human service agencies either had a monopoly on the particular service for all people in the community or had an effective monopoly on service for the poorest clients who cannot afford to purchase the service on the open market. The worker could afford to be somewhat more indifferent to client concerns in this context of limited client control. Given the chronic pressure of case overload, losing a client might even be perceived as rewarding. As compared with organizations that compete for clientele in the open market, social agencies were somewhat unaffected by client control through client defection. With third parties added to the contract between the social worker and the client, this may become less true.

9. Despite the fact that social workers use resources provided by the community, are required to implement policies formulated by groups outside the agency, perform their tasks in private on clients who often have no alternative options, and are concerned with outcomes that are difficult to discern and evaluate objectively, is there a real need for supervisory review and control in regard to accountability and client protection? One might counter that the supposition that such conditions argue for the necessity of supervision is demeaning and insulting to the worker. All of these conditions might accurately characterize the social work situation yet not require supervision if we granted the social worker his or her professional prerogative. One would expect that the direct service professional in contact with the client would be concerned about protecting the client and implementing agency policy in a clearly responsible manner. Operating autonomously, he or she would provide the controls of supervision. But here, once again, we encounter a situation characteristic of social work that creates a need for the development and elaboration of a supervisory apparatus.

Kaufman (1960) identifies the significant conditions that ensure that the autonomously operating worker will be self-supervised so that agency policy will be adhered to and the needs of the client protected. These conditions include extensive professional education, a strong interest in the tasks to be performed, a commitment to the ends to which these tasks are directed, and periodic agency indoctrination reinforcing the saliency and legitimacy of these goals. The result of these conditions is to socialize the worker so that he or she does, as a matter of personal preference and professional conscience, those things that are professionally required. The composition of social work agency staff, now and in the past, raises questions about the degree to which these conditions are met. In the absence of these conditions, there is greater pressure to develop a supervisory control system to ensure that work performance is in accordance with professionally desirable norms.

The process of professional recruitment, selection, and education has implications for the kind of supervisory system a professional establishes. If the process of occupational selection is deliberate, and the program of training is prolonged, the need for elaborate supervisory procedures is lessened.

A candidate who deliberately makes a choice of some profession after careful evaluation of alternatives is likely to feel a sense of commitment to the profession. The very process of applying for and being selected by a graduate professional school acts as a screen that ensures recruitment of those applicants who, in some way, share the values, assumptions, and predispositions characteristic of those performing the work. This is reinforced by the professional training experience.

The objective of professional training is not only to teach the knowledge, skills, and attitudes that would enable the recruit to do a competent job but also to socialize the student to the ways of the profession, to develop a professional conscience. It is the elaborate process of professional socialization, during a prolonged program of intensive training, that permits workers in all professions to operate autonomously, free of external direction and control but subject to internal direction and control on the basis of competence and values incorporated during training. The supervisor is, in effect, internalized during the transformation of the layperson into a professional, and supervision does not then need to be externally imposed. Discipline becomes self-discipline; accountability is accountability to one's professionalized self. Such constraints are further maintained and collectively sustained by strong professional organizations to which the professional feels an affiliation, even if he or she is not formally a member, and by periodic in-service training courses, conferences, meetings, and professional journals.

All this is quite different from the situation that characterizes job entrance for the largest percentage of social workers—currently and throughout the history of the profession. For most social workers, entrance to their jobs has not been the result of a serious commitment to social work as a lifetime career but rather a decision of limited commitment, frequently made because other, more attractive alternatives were not available. Workers often come to the job with no previous knowledge of social work and no firm identification with the profession, its objectives, standards, and values—an identification that might have been developed during a prolonged period of professional training—and with no resolute commitment to the profession.

The *2000–2001 Occupational Outlook Handbook* suggests that a bachelor's degree is the minimum requirement for many entry-level jobs, and that an MSW or a related field has become the norm for many positions. Although the BSW is the most desirable minimum requirement to qualify for a job as a social worker, applicants with bachelor degrees in history or literature may be hired. In the future, the *Handbook,* suggests that agencies will restructure services and hire more lower-paid human service workers and assistants instead of social workers. Although research by Shulman (1991) raises questions about the impact of social work education on client outcomes, the gap between trained and untrained social workers suggests the need for supervision.

How many of the people who carry the title *social worker* have been socialized and trained in schools of social work and how many have not is open to speculation. If you count all the graduates of MSW and Ph.D. programs between 1960 and 1997 and add to that the number of graduates of BSW programs since 1974 (when such programs who were first accredited) then deduct a reasonable number of graduates who left the profession, who died, who retired, and so on, a rough calculation give or take an error rate of 5 percent would suggest that there are some 325,000 Ph.D., MSW, and BSW social workers alive and well doing the work of social work (Kadushin 1999). The Bureau of Labor Statistics (2001) reported that 828,000 people were employed as social workers in the United States in 2000. This suggests that there are some 500,000 people providing social work services without prior training for the job—a group who require educational, administrative, and supportive supervision for effective job performance. The 325,000 professionally trained workers thus constitute a liberal estimate of some 40 percent of those holding the social work title, a minority of the social work labor force (see also Gibelman 2000).

The low ratio of professionally trained personnel to the total social-work workforce reflects a situation that has been typical throughout the history of the profession. In fact, the situation in 2000 is more favorable than in the past. A 1926 study showed that only 7 percent of the workers had full professional training (Walker 1928:108). Of the 69,000 social workers listed by the 1940 census, only 11,000 (16 percent) were members of the American Association of Social Workers, which enrolled most of the professionally trained social workers at that time (Hathway 1943). By 1960, some 25 percent of the 116,000 people holding social welfare positions had graduate social work degrees (National Social Welfare Assembly 1961:1).

Lacking control of job access and job entry, the profession can dictate to only a limited extent the educational and professional qualifications of social work personnel. Court decisions on discrimination suits filed under the Civil Rights Act of 1964 challenged the use of hiring requirements that could not validly be proven to be related to the job. As a consequence of the resulting declassification of civil service positions previously reserved for applicants who offered professional educational credentials, more people were hired who had no prior training in social work. Training by supervisors of such recruits was required to compensate for lack of pre-employment educational preparation. Nationwide declassification of social worker positions increased the importance of educational supervision.

There are, in effect, two different kinds of staff to which supervision is directed. One (often found in highly professionalized, generally voluntary agencies) is composed of people who have made a career choice of social work after considerable exploration and deliberation, who have invested effort and money in a prolonged program of professional education, and who have thereby developed both some beginning competence in performing social work tasks and some identification with and commitment to the social work profession.

At the same time, an even larger number of workers (more often concentrated in large public welfare agencies) hold the job title of social worker and perform social work tasks who often have come to the job fortuitously, because an opening was available. They often have had no prior exposure to social work, have not considered it seriously as a career, have had little (if any) education or training for the job, and have little (if any) identification with and commitment to social work. This second group is, of course, highly diversified.

Thus there always has been and continues to be a need for agencies to induct, train, and socialize new recruits. Because of tenuous commitment or lack of prior opportunity to socialize toward a firm commitment to the mission of social work on the part of many recruits, social work has had to assign supervisory personnel to perform the functions of educational and administrative supervision.

10. The need for organizational controls in supervision on the part of the agency is made more imperative by the absence of effective organizational controls on the part of the profession itself. The professional associations in medicine and law, controlling entry into and expulsion from the profession, can effectively be delegated the responsibility of policing their members to limit abuses of professional autonomy and guarantee professional responsible behavior. Twenty years ago the NASW did not even accept for membership the non-MSW social workers who filled the majority of social work positions. Though technically eligible, few such workers are affiliated with the professional organizations; only 3.6 percent of the NASW membership describe the BSW as their highest social work degree (Gibelman and Schervish 1997b). The ability of professional social work organizations to guarantee the conduct and competence of the social worker's performance is seriously limited. This absence of effective professional control groups in social work, as compared with more traditionally established professions, argues for an alternative control system, such as agency supervision.

11. Bureaucratization, of which supervision is a component, results not only from the limited training of a large number of people carrying the title of social worker but also from the limited knowledge base and technology available even to fully trained workers. In a profession in which the level of development of knowledge and techniques is such that the professional often finds himself encountering situations in which he cannot operate with full confidence that he knows what to do and how to do it, as is true in social work, there is a greater tendency to share the decisional responsibility with a supervisor and less readiness to resist supervisory "suggestions" and rules

that dictate action. A person needs to be very confident of his or her ability to make use of autonomy if he or she is going to claim it aggressively and defend it tenaciously. "Control over the work of semiprofessionals is possible because they lack the weapon—knowledge—with which professionals resist control. . . . The motives which drive professionals to seek autonomy are strong intrinsic commitment to specialize knowledge and skills together with confidence in their ability to exercise such skills" (Simpson and Simpson 1969:198–99).

12. The distinctive nature of the problems encountered and the tasks performed by social workers makes desirable, perhaps even necessary, the availability of supportive supervision. Social workers are in constant contact with highly charged affective situations that make heavy demands on emotional energy on behalf of the client. The problems encountered—parent-child conflict, marital conflict, illness, death, dependency, deviance—are those that a social worker struggles with in one way or another in his or her own life situation. The principal instrumentality for helping the client is the worker him- or herself so that failure to help may be sensed as a personal failure. The responsibilities are great, the solutions available are ambiguous, and the possibilities for happy solutions are limited. The risks of guilt, anxiety, discouragement, and frustration are numerous. There are few professions that come close to social work in developing in the worker the need for support, encouragement, reassurance, and restoration of morale—a need met by supportive supervision.

The nature of social work argues not only for the need for supervision for new recruits but also for the more experienced worker.

> The nature of social work . . . is work with people through relationships where the personality of the worker is one of the tools for the work. It can be argued that no one, however, skilled or experienced, can ever be entirely objective about the way they use themselves in relation to another person. A third person is essential to help the social worker stand back from the relationship and then return to it in ways which are helpful to the client. If one accepts such arguments then, in the words of one social worker, "supervision is essential for every social worker." (Parsloe and Stevenson 1978:205)

Summary

Following a brief historical review of supervision, we noted the variety of definitions of social work supervision. For the purposes of this book, the *supervisor* was defined as a member of the administrative staff offering an indirect service that includes administrative, educational, and supportive functions.

In explaining the prominence of supervision in social work, we noted that organizationally based workers offer resources provided by the community to implement community-formulated policies. Working with clients who often have few options, workers who are often untrained and need frequent support offer service under conditions of privacy, with ambiguous outcomes.

2 | Administrative Supervision

Introduction: Organizational Bureaucracy

Supervision is a special aspect of organizational administration. When a number of people are brought together and then provided with the necessary equipment and facilities to get a particular job done, there needs to be systematic coordination of effort if the objectives of the group are to be efficiently accomplished. The systematic cooperative, coordinated effort of a group of people in getting a desired job efficiently accomplished, if sustained for any period of time, leads inevitably to the development of some kind of formal organization of the work. Schein defines *organization* as "the rational coordination of the activities of a number of people for the achievement of some common explicit purpose or goal through division of labor and function and through a hierarchy of authority and responsibility" (1970:9). More tersely, Blau and Scott define an organization as "a social unit that has been established for the explicit purpose of achieving certain goals" (1962:1). Organizations are thus "consciously planned and deliberately structured" so as to increase the probability of achieving organizational goals and objectives.

A bureaucracy is a specialized kind of organization. The term *bureaucracy* is used here not pejoratively but descriptively and neutrally, to designate a particular organizational form. A bureaucracy is theoretically the most rational, efficient, and effective organizational format for coordinating the cooperative efforts of a sizable group of people, each of whom is engaged in a different task necessary for the achievement of common organizational objectives. A bureaucracy may be characterized as follows:

1. There is a specialization of function and task, a division of labor, among units of the organization and among different employees within each unit.
2. There is a hierarchical authority structure, different people being assigned positions of greater or lesser responsibility and power.
3. People in the hierarchy exercise authority on the basis of the position they hold.
4. People are recruited, selected, and assigned to positions in the organization on the basis of objective, impersonal technical qualifications rather than on the basis of who they are or whom they know.
5. There is a system of rules and procedures, universally and impersonally applied, that determine the rights and duties of people occupying each of the positions in the agency.
6. All organizational activities are deliberately and rationally planned to contribute to the attainment of organizational objectives. Bureaucracy is sometimes described as the "rational organization of collective activities."

These are the essential characteristics of the bureaucratic organizational structure in its ideal form; actual bureaucracies achieve the ideal in varying degrees. Consequently, any bureaucratic organization can be more or less bureaucratic.

Most social work organizations have employees who engage in specialized tasks and have an administrative hierarchy, a set of clearly formulated rules and procedures, and clearly defined roles and statuses, all designed to achieve specific objectives. In short, not only are social agencies organizational in nature, they conform to the definition of a particular kind of organization— a bureaucracy.

Any organization, and particularly a bureaucratic one, needs administration. *Administration* is a process that implements organizational objectives. Stein describes it as a "process of defining and attaining the objectives of an organization through a system of coordinated and cooperative effort" (1965:58).

In organizations with highly differentiated hierarchical structures, there are first-line supervisors, administrative personnel directly responsible for and in contact with the direct service workers. Our concern here is primarily with the front-line supervisors, those who supervise direct service workers.

The supervisor is a link in the chain of administration—the administrator who is in direct contact with the worker. Even in a turbulent environment, shaped by managed care (Kalous 1996), welfare reform (Drake and Washeck 1998; Pine, Warsh, and Malluccio 1998), adverse litigation (Wimpfheimer, Klein, and Kramer 1993), and postmodern management theory and practice (Boettcher 1998; Martin 1993; Pruger and Miller 1991; Smergut 1998), the supervisor has responsibility for agency management, and specific, clearly defined, administrative—managerial functions are assigned to him or her. These functions are the essence of administrative supervision.

Tasks

What specifically are the tasks the supervisor is called on to perform in discharging the responsibilities of administrative supervision? They include the following.

1. Staff recruitment and selection
2. Inducting and placing workers
3. Work planning
4. Work assignment
5. Work delegation
6. Monitoring, reviewing, and evaluating work
7. Coordinating work
8. The communication function
9. The supervisor as advocate
10. The supervisor as administrative buffer
11. The supervisor as change agent

Staff Recruitment and Selection

The effective achievement of organizational objectives requires making a collectivity out of a group of individuals. There has to be some consensus as to how individuals will work together, how they will perform their assigned tasks, and how they will coordinate their activities with others in the collective. Harnessing a group of people to work cooperatively and collaboratively toward a common objective necessitates limiting the effects of human variability.

One step in limiting variability lies in the process of selection for membership in the organization. Supervisors charged with hiring people as agency social workers seek to select candidates who are likely to "fit in." The task requires selecting applicants who have the personal characteristics, attitudes, and maturity that will allow them to feel comfortable and accepting in implementing agency objectives.

The process of prolonged education in other professions is a sorting mechanism that selects out those recruits who are not likely to be a good fit for the job. However, many people apply for social work jobs without having encountered the educational sorting process. Furthermore, the nature of the job is so ambiguously defined in the mind of the general public that many applicants cannot clearly determine whether they want to do it. As a consequence, the administrative gatekeeper has an important function in social work selection.

Because personnel recruitment and selection involve fitting people to a particular job, the nature of the job that needs to be done requires specification. The supervisor is often in the best position to know the details of the job and the attitudes, skills, and knowledge required to do it. Consequently, the supervisor should invite the work group to generate, test, and refine descriptions of essential job tasks before advising agency management about the position for which recruitment is being suggested. The work group not only has the most intimate and practical knowledge of the day-to-day job, their participation in this process tends to enhance human relations and build job satisfaction as well (Pecora 1996).

Because supervisors know the work that needs to be done, they participate in establishing criteria for hiring staff and in implementing these criteria in interviewing job applicants. Having interviewed applicants, they provide input into decisions about hiring. Even if they do not always make the final determination, supervisors' recommendations are invariably given careful consideration.

Supervisors, who are in immediate contact with the direct service workers, are in the best position to know if additional staff needs to be recruited. They are the first to know about anticipated resignations and staff turnover. Once again, their position in the agency calls attention to their administrative responsibilities in regard to recruitment and hiring.

It should be noted that although supervisors make a contribution to the hiring process, this is a secondary administrative function of supervision. Primary responsibility for recruitment and hiring is generally assigned to personnel units of social service organizations.

Inducting and Placing the Worker

Once an applicant has been recruited and hired, the supervisor to whom the new applicant is assigned has the function of placement and induction. Workers need to find their place in the organizational framework. Knowing clearly to whom they report (and who reports to them) enables workers to find their "particular location in the invisible geography" of the agency's human-relations network. Through the supervisor, their immediate administrative link, workers are tied into the total organizational apparatus.

In a study of the supervisory needs of beginning workers, Charles, Gabor, and Matheson found that supervisees wanted help "in fitting into the organization" and that supervisors "needed to consciously and consistently work at assisting the beginning worker to feel accepted as a valued member of the work environment" (1992:31).

The process of such placement and identification has its beginning in the worker's induction into the agency, a function for which the supervisor is administratively responsible. The supervisor prepares to induct the worker by prompting the office manager or personnel office to obtain required information and paperwork from the new worker, reviewing his or her personnel folder, informing other workers in the unit that a new worker has been hired, finding an office and a desk, selecting some reading material about the agency and its functions, and choosing a limited number of tasks to discuss with the worker for possible assignment.

Induction involves locating the new worker physically, socially, and organizationally in the agency. Because first experiences are very important in determining a person's feelings about the job, induction is a significant task. On meeting a newly hired worker, the supervisor discusses the function of the unit to which the worker has been assigned, how it fits into the total agency operation, the relationship of the supervisor to the worker and their respective roles and responsibilities (Freeman 1993), the worker's relationship with other workers in the unit, and the complex objectives of supervision (Harkness and Poertner 1989).

Hopefully, questions about job specifics have been discussed as part of the formal job offer, but they may need further clarification. Such specifics include details around salary, pay periods, work hours, health insurance, pension, vacations, holidays, absences, overtime, sick leave, reimbursement for travel, national meeting and workshop attendance support policy, receiving and making local and long-distance telephone calls. Induction includes sharing helpful information about parking, local eating facilities, and location of bathrooms. The supervisor makes arrangements for a door and/ or desk nameplate and a mailbox. A social worker in a family service agency says,

> If only my supervisor had provided me with a desk. When I started I had *no* surface for writing reports, notes, etc. My office became wherever a chair was to write on or my lap. Talk about not being one of the group. I also had the

feeling a lot of the time that either what I was doing wasn't worth even a card table or that my comfort level and sense of feeling that I belonged didn't really matter. Six months after starting I got a real desk. The desk gave me a space of my own and a sense of finally belonging.*

The supervisor tells the worker how to obtain business cards, forms, and office supplies and how and under what conditions to use the fax and copy machines. One supervisor says:

All this is nitty-gritty stuff but I have found that it is essential to outline these things for my supervisees so that they could provide themselves without having to ask me something or other every five minutes, but more important so that they could develop a sense of belonging to the agency. Knowledge of office operations allowed for a feeling of confidence, competence, and comfort and a sense of being one of the group.

If the worker is new to the city as well as the agency, there may also need to be at least an offer of help in finding such things as housing, day-care, a doctor, and a dentist.

The supervisor personally introduces the worker to peers, office personnel with whom he or she will be working, and administrative officers. A new person, in a new job, in a new organization, is likely to be lonely. The supervisor might ask one of the more experienced employees in the unit to act as sponsor for the new worker, answering routine questions and being available to help the new worker during the first week or so. It is also a great comfort to the new staff member if he or she is not isolated at lunch the first week, but is included in some group.

Unfortunately, employee recruitment and selection may engender or exacerbate organizational conflict in agency settings. The addition of new staff introduces change in the work place, threatening the group hierarchy of its members. Although some members of the work group may look forward to the new worker's arrival with eager anticipation, others may view personnel changes with anxiety or foreboding. As a result, some workers may embrace the new employee, as others ignore him or her, and a third group may circle its wagons.

*Throughout the text, the anecdotes and vignettes cited have been informally collected by the authors. They are derived from student assignments in supervision seminars, reports from supervisors and supervisees at supervision workshops, informal interviews with supervisors and supervisees regarding their experiences, and letters from practitioners in response to solicitations of critical incidents in supervision.

For the new hire, an overdetermined supervisor response to work-group behavior will make joining the work group more difficult, not easier. If the new worker has difficulty joining the work group, the best supervisory actions will be even-handed and restrained. Hurlbert (1992) contends that the supervisor who brings workers together for open communication may exacerbate the problem and impair organizational performance. A prudent supervisor will allow time to pass and carefully weigh whether further supervisory action, neither intrusive nor evasive, is called for.

New workers may have little if any idea of the purpose and nature of supervision, so there is a need for some kind of preparation for the role of supervisee. This will give the supervisee some idea of what to expect and will ensure the more active participation of the supervisee, who might otherwise see him- or herself as receiving supervision.

Some of the hazards of induction, and the supervisor's handling of them, are detailed in a social worker's recollection of her first day as a psychiatric social worker in a mental hospital:

> From the start, the supervisor seemed to be sensitively aware of possible anxiety on my part. The first day she arrived fifteen minutes early and met me at the door. We went to her office, she took my coat and offered me a cup of coffee. She then took me with her to get it so that I would know where the pot was for future use.
>
> We had to go through two locked doors and as we did so, Ms. B. explained that she would see that I got a set of keys for my own by the end of the day. (She did this, and I was to find that she was equally prompt with other matters as well. If I asked a question she would either answer it or be on the phone immediately to find out from someone who knew.) These two gestures served to make me feel like one of the staff and, as such, accepted and very comfortable.

Work Planning

Once the direct service worker has been recruited, hired, inducted, and placed, the supervisor has to plan what the agency needs him or her to do.

Administration sets general policies and objectives. These then need to be broken down into specific duties and, ultimately, into specific tasks—a certain unit of work to be completed within a given period of time. This is a process of progressively greater refinement of general policy objectives at each descending administrative level so that they can be parceled out in small, manageable units. It is at the first-line supervisory level that agency policies and objectives get their ultimate translation into tasks to be performed by direct service workers.

The supervisor is directly in charge of a group of employees responsible for maintaining a productive flow of work, which "flows from points of decision to points of action." In less elegant terms, this key administrative responsibility of supervision is called "getting the work out" or "putting the job description to work."

Providing service to the group of clients for which any unit has responsibility requires planning and the delegation of tasks. A unit may be allocated responsibility for 300 clients with a variety of social problems. Each supervisor, allocated five to seven workers, has the responsibility of delegating to each worker some component of the entire unit caseload so that in aggregate the 300 cases are covered. The supervisor is provided with human resources, staff resources, and service resources. The supervisor has to plan to organize the work force available, divide and assign the work, and allocate staff and service resources so as to accomplish the work assigned to the unit in a way that contributes to achieving the mission of the agency.

Planning the distribution of cases is not, however, an automatic mathematical process. Good planning requires familiarity with the supervisees and with the cases requiring action. It also requires familiarity with the tasks the unit is responsible for, so that all tasks will be concluded within a given time frame without unduly overloading the workers or requiring overtime work. The supervisor has to have the competence to plan for judicious deployment of his or her work force. Planning then involves deciding what needs to be done and how it is going to get done through selective assignment and delegation of tasks to staff. Planning involves decisions regarding scheduling and prioritizing work—not only who will do it, but when it has to get done. In deploying work force resources, the supervisor has to monitor absences, tardiness, vacation, and sick leave so as to know what personnel are actually available to cover the work at any time. Thus, of necessity, work planning precedes work assignment.

The unit supervisor has some responsibility for long-range planning as well as for immediate planning. Long-range planning involves preparation of a unit budget as a component of the total agency budget. This is based on some assessment of the future work load of the unit and the fiscal, technical, and human resources that might be required to complete it.

Work Assignment

Having planned the overall work of the unit, the supervisor selects tasks for individual workers in line with the total unit work plan. In making task assignments, the supervisor needs to take a variety of factors into consideration.

Criteria for Assignment

1. In social agencies, case or group assignment generally is made in terms of the specific strengths and weaknesses of individual workers. Consequently, in discharging this responsibility, the supervisor needs to know individual workers' capacities intimately. Implied here is not only a knowledge of the areas that are likely to be problematic for a certain worker but also the level of complexity of casework demands that the worker can handle with some likelihood of success.

2. Selection for assignment may depend on job pressures carried by the different workers for whom the supervisor has responsibility. Good administration requires an attempt to equalize the demands made on workers at the same title and salary level. The supervisor needs to consider the current total caseload carried by each worker in terms of number of cases, their difficulty, and the challenge of each new assignment. The supervisor then assigns new cases to ensure some equitable distribution of work load. Otherwise, for instance, a worker might be stigmatized by her peers as one who is not really carrying his or her full load in the group.

3. Another criterion in assignment of tasks should be variety. Too great a concentration on one particular kind of task, one kind of case, or a single kind of problem situation denies the worker the satisfactions and feeling of competence derived from variety in job assignments. This criterion needs to be balanced against assignment in terms of workers' strengths and weaknesses. Some workers do better and derive greater satisfaction from highly concentrated job assignments. Others find this stultifying and resent it.

4. The worker needs the stimulation of challenge as well as variety if motivation is to be sustained and professional growth increased. Assigning tasks clearly below the level of the worker's capacity is likely to be less desirable than the opposite. Whenever possible, workers should have an opportunity to express preference for certain kinds of case situations in which they may have a particular interest (Latting 1991).

5. Some consideration might need to be given to the question of matching worker and client in terms of age, gender, race, or ethnicity. In addition to McCroy et al. (1986), D'Andrea and Daniels (1997) and Stone (1997) provide rich discussions of these issues.

Work assignment and caseload management involve scheduling. Assignments need to be made and tasks allocated with some understanding of the time span in which the work needs to be completed, so that deadlines can be met. The pressure for timely completion of mandated tasks and the necessity for documenting every action makes much current agency practice "deadline driven" and "paper product" focused (Bannerjee 1995; Martin and Kettner 1997; Pruger and Miller 1991).

The supervisor is responsible for scheduling that ensures the workers' ability to perform their jobs without undue stress. The scheduling of meetings, supervisory conferences, dictation time, and deadlines must be made with some appreciation of the total load imposed on the workers and the time available to do the work.

Joint discussions of case assignment might further elicit the workers' subjective reactions to work loads. Though having the same number of cases as peers, a worker may nevertheless feel overloaded. Sharing his or her sense of resentment with the supervisor can be helpful. In addition, the supervisor has the opportunity to discuss techniques of caseload management with the worker. The total caseload might be reviewed and some decision made as to which ones can receive minimum effort because the situation is stable and not subject to much change. Other cases might be selected for more intensive consideration. The client may be more vulnerable, or the client and the social situation may be open to positive change in response to active intervention by the worker. At the same time the supervisor can make clear to the worker where the agency's preferred priorities lie, which cases should receive service if time and energy are limited, and which need not be done until time is available (Menefee and Thompson 1994).

Work Assignment Procedures

A study of case assignment procedures in voluntary and public welfare agencies shows that the most frequent system by far is for the supervisor or other administrator to assign cases "based on knowledge of case characteristics, worker ability and experience, etc." (Haring 1974:5). In only about 5 percent of the agencies did the procedure entail "division of labor by staff members among themselves either at periodic meetings or by rotating responsibility for intake" (Haring 1974:4). A high percentage of the workers reacted favorably to the assignment of work by the supervisor.

A supervisee writes about her reaction to case assignments by her supervisor:

> I, personally, felt that the supervisor's distribution of cases and task assignments provided me with a far greater array of experiences than would have been available had I selected cases and assignments more in accord with my own preference. Under these circumstances, I was often forced into situations that, had I been operating of my own volition, I might have tried to avoid. I

think that this produced an environment for substantial personal growth. Allowing an individual to select cases or work assignments which he feels are suited to his personal preferences may lead to stagnation, rather than the development of a flexible individual who can work with a diversity of problems and people. Too often personal preference can be used as an avoidance mechanism or a "cop-out." This does not mean that individual preferences should be categorically ignored or denied, but that the supervisor should evaluate the request for certain assignments or cases critically before giving his assent, to insure that such action would primarily be in the best interests of the client and/or the agency and not just the worker.

An innovative alternative to assignment of cases by the supervisor alone is assignment by unit members in a group meeting. The cases to be assigned are introduced and summarized, and supervisor and supervisees decide on assigning the cases together. Although this ostensibly is a more democratic procedure, a study of this procedure among social work teams showed that group pressure replaced supervisor authority. One worker said, "The allocation meetings allegedly allow a democratic choice. In reality it works out that the less strong-minded get lumbered. . . . However, in practice it was apparent that the social workers felt under an obligation to take a fair share of the referrals and not to leave all the work to their colleagues" (Parsloe and Stevenson 1978:73).

Group allocation did involve a considerable expenditure of worker time and worked best if the supervisor was willing enough and strong enough to exert authority to shield some workers from weakness or excessive self-demands. However, workers were stimulated by the discussion, got a better overview of the total referral caseload, and welcomed the status that came with involvement.

Problems in Work Assignment

In assigning cases the supervisor faces a number of contradictory pressures that are difficult to resolve. Though willing to accede to a worker's preference, the supervisor still must assign every case for service (Drake and Washeck 1998). Even if no supervisee has expressed preference for some particular kind of client, or worse, even if all supervisees have stated dislike for that kind of client, the supervisor must nonetheless assign the client for service.

Ms. P., a medical social worker, has been assigned cases on the pediatrics ward. The large number of handicapped and disabled children, especially children requiring institutional placement, has been disturbing to her. After three months at the hospital a case is assigned of a three-year-old disabled boy to discuss an institutional placement with his parents, who are felt to be receptive. Rather reluctantly, Ms. P. tells her supervisor that she would rather not be assigned this case, mentioning that the child of a friend was institutionalized a year ago. Ms. P. visited the child with her friend and found the setting depressing.

Rather than acceding to or rejecting the request or resorting to her positional authority to back up her assignment of the case, the supervisor engaged Ms. P. in examining her feelings about the assignment. The supervisor did this with the acceptance of the fact that every worker has limits to tolerance and there are some cases that should not be assigned because the worker has strong negative feelings about the assignment. At the same time, there was a recognition that workers have to be helped in extending their limits of tolerance. To permit Ms. P. to reject every assignment with which she might feel uncomfortable might limit her capacity for growth. In addition to discussing with Ms. P. her own feelings about the situation, the supervisor reviewed emerging knowledge about the advantages and disadvantages of institutionalizing children with similar disabilities. She helped Ms. P. apply this knowledge to the particular situation of the family of this particular child.

There are more conflicts—between the supervisor's desire to assign every case to the most competent and experienced workers and the need for equitable distribution of caseload, and between the desire to give each client the best worker and the need for new, inexperienced workers to learn the job.

A more global problem of case assignment for the supervisor is determining whether or not a case assigned by administration to the unit is appropriate. This is a gatekeeping function that guards against the unit being saddled with cases that are more appropriate to the functions and expertise of other units.

In assigning tasks the supervisor has the additional problem of deciding on the amount of direction given in assigning the task and the level of discretion permitted the worker. But this is a problem that relates more directly to another major function of supervision—work delegation.

Work Delegation

In assigning work the supervisor not only has to deal with the problem of task selection using the criteria discussed above but also has to decide the explicitness with which he or she instructs the worker about action that needs to be taken in implementing the assignment. Task assignment indicates what work needs to be accomplished. Task delegation indicates how it is to be accomplished. Where work is assigned under conditions of maximum worker autonomy and discretion, the objectives of task assignment are clearly stated, and the worker is permitted to initiate any action, at any time, that he or she feels will result in accomplishment of the objectives. Under conditions of more limited autonomy, the worker may be delegated authority to act only after obtaining prior approval, or he or she may be told in advance what to do.

There are a variety of procedures that can be used to delegate tasks in a way that can modulate the extent of autonomy granted. One can provide a series of explicit and detailed directives as to how the task should be carried out; one can provide a very general series of directives, giving the worker considerable flexibility on detail; one can plan cooperatively in discussions with the worker how the task should be carried out; one can even just leave the worker free to implement the task with no particular restrictions other than general objectives and a time limit. Supervisors tend to direct delegated tasks in terms of suggestions or advice. "It might be helpful if . . ."; "It might be advisable to. . . ." But advice, suggestion, or persuasion may not always be sufficient to direct or redirect the worker. In such cases, the supervisor has responsibility for being explicitly directive.

Frequently the more adequately trained and experienced workers are given the freedom of deciding the details in implementing an assignment. The supervisor assumes little responsibility for specifying how the assignment is to be implemented. In supervising less adequately trained and experienced workers, the supervisor may have to take more administrative responsibility for the specifics.

Intrinsic job satisfaction, heightened motivation, and increased productivity tend to be associated with greater autonomy in implementation of job assignments (Pine, Warsh, and Malluccio 1998). The more discretion he or she is given, the greater the likelihood that the supervisee will feel trusted and worthy of trust. Consequently on a continuum of directivity, the supervisor should permit the workers as much discretion as they can safely and productively handle (Hardcastle 1991; Veeder 1990). Whenever possible, the supervisor indicates what results need to be achieved without specifying the procedures to be employed. However, the supervisor should be ready, when necessary, to be more directive, not only assigning the task but clearly specifying how it should be done.

Often even the more experienced worker may want some directive assistance in task implementation. This function—analysis and planning of client contact with supervisees—is rated by supervisors as one that occupies a very high percentage of their time (Kadushin 1992a). In effect, such planning is like a briefing session. The assignment is explained, the objectives are clarified, and the method of implementation is discussed.

Even maximum worker autonomy, however, is exercised within constraints that derive from the objectives of the agency, the requirements of agency survival, and the tenets of the profession (Hardcastle 1992). Autonomy in task implementation is an exercise of discretion toward prescribed ends, within prescribed limits.

Delegation goes beyond the assignment of a task. It involves the supervisor sharing some measure of authority with the supervisee, who is then empowered to make decisions and to take action in the performance of the assigned task. But responsibility for the task and the authority to take action can be delegated but cannot be fully relinquished by the supervisor (Hurlbert 1992).

Delegating in social work, unlike some other supervisory situations, is risky, because there are more limited subsequent controls available permitting a check on the work. A work force whose activities are visible and subject to supervisory observation permits ongoing application of controls if the decision to delegate proves to be an error. In social work supervision, few controls are readily available to correct misdelegation (Boettcher 1998; Iberg 1991).

Task delegation is a complex function dependent on a number of interacting variables. These include supervisor attributes, supervisee attributes, the nature of the task delegated, and the organizational climate, all of which will be discussed in some detail in the following.

The amount of discretion that the worker is granted to operate autonomously is a function of the supervisor's ability and willingness to delegate responsibility, which in turn are affected by a variety of factors. Supervisors differ in the anxiety they feel about delegating tasks. Some are less willing than others to accept the risk of mistakes and failure in their supervisees, for which they might be held accountable. This unwillingness may stem from a supervisor's lack of confidence in him- or herself or from an anxious relationship with his or her own supervisor. Some are less ready to encourage the development of independence on the part of their supervisees and are gratified by the continuing dependency exemplified by controlling work decisions. Some obtain satisfaction by vicarious involvement in direct practice. More active direction of the work of their supervisees gives them a sense of being involved in the worker-client relationship. The more authoritarian, controlling supervisor will be less ready to delegate than will the democratic-egalitarian supervisor. The supervisor who is oriented toward upward mobility and anxious to please administration is less likely to delegate responsibility than is the supervisor who is free of such internal pressures. In summary, "the ability of a supervisor to delegate effectively depends on the way he relates to his job, his subordinates, his superior and himself" (Bishop 1969:112).

Other factors that determine delegation relate to the worker rather than the supervisor. A supervisor may be reluctant to delegate because he or she perceives the worker as incapable of operating independently at this point. The worker may be ambivalent about accepting responsibility because this implies accepting blame for failure as well as commendation for success.

The supervisor may be deterred from delegating because the worker communicates a reluctance and discomfort in accepting independent responsibility for the task. But worker readiness to accept responsibility reciprocally affects the supervisor's readiness to grant responsibility.

Supervisees who feel uncertain about their competence to do the job will press for greater direction and more precise delegation from supervisors than will their more confident peers. Supervisees who feel a strong need for independence, who are ready to risk mistakes, and who need less structure will encourage the supervisor to delegate tasks in a less specific way. Workers have different levels of readiness to tolerate ambiguity in a situation that is not clearly defined or structured for them.

Other factors that determine readiness to delegate relate to the task situation itself. If the nature of the situation is one that is likely to have high visibility, relates to a sensitive public policy question, or affects personnel and/or organizations that have considerable power, there will be increased hesitancy to delegate because embarrassing consequences of any error are more likely to be intensified.

Where clients are more vulnerable, as in the case of children who might be subject to abuse and/or neglect, where decisions might involve commitment of scarce resources such as large amounts of public money or large amounts of worker time, or where errors in worker judgment might have serious consequences for the client, the situation may dictate a reduction in delegated discretion (Hardcastle 1991; Wimpfheimer, Klein, and Kramer 1993).

The complexity of the task and the pressure of time available for completion also affect the nature of delegation. More complex tasks may require more precise specification in delegating. The pressure of time allows for fewer errors and less experimentation with possible false starts and consequently a greater measure of supervisor control.

Still other factors that determine the supervisor's willingness and readiness to delegate lie with administration. Supervisors are more apt to delegate responsibility if they have the assurance that administration will support rather than berate them if the worker commits an error.

Where there is pressure for precise accountability of agency activity from groups to which the agency is responsible, supervisors will feel a greater pressure to delegate tasks with clear boundaries that limit worker discretion.

Operating in a host setting alongside professionals of other disciplines increases the hesitancy to delegate. In schools, hospitals, and psychiatric clinics, supervisors are sensitive to the fact that their supervisees are being closely observed by others. Supervisors also have to negotiate with other professionals for the position and prerogatives of social work within the setting. This situation is more tenuous than one in a setting controlled by social workers.

In summary, the decision around task delegation and the degree of autonomy granted the worker in implementing a task are determined by such factors as the complexity of the task, level of worker skill and interest, worker caseload in terms of nature and number of cases, vulnerability of and risk to the client, sensitive nature of the problem, likely visibility of error, readiness of supervisor and supervisee to incur risk, and administrative penalties for supervisory failure.

Monitoring, Reviewing, and Evaluating Work

At this point the process leads to another distinctive function of administrative supervision. Having delegated the assigned task with the appropriate level of discretion, the supervisor has the further responsibility of monitoring the task assignment to see that it gets done in the allotted time and in a way that is in line with agency procedures.

An interview study of twenty supervisors in a state public welfare department found that 55 percent of the supervisors saw their primary role as monitoring worker performance (Weatherly 1980). Monitoring involves obtaining verbal reports from workers, reading records, and reviewing statistical reports. At a minimum, the objective of performance monitoring and review is to see that no harm is done. But in addition it may involve sharing favorable feedback and verbal approval. Work review is necessary to determine if the work is being accomplished as planned. Work review also involves the general responsibility of seeing that supervisees are available to cover the work load. This function, then, involves monitoring both the worker and the worker's work.

The principal resource the supervisor has available to ensure that the work of the agency gets done is the time and skill of the supervisees. In accepting the role of employee of an agency the supervisee implicitly agrees to place his or her time and skill at the disposal of the agency for some specific period during the day and week. Consequently, the supervisor has the responsibility of knowing when and if the supervisees are available for work during the agreed-on period. The supervisor needs to be concerned with tardiness, absences, requests for time off, sick leave, vacation schedules, and projected and emergency overtime personnel needs to ensure adequate coverage of work assignments. If the supervisor does not have final authority with regard to these questions, as he or she should, he or she often has the power of decisive recommendation. Paradoxically, supervisors have reported spending relatively little time monitoring worker performance; monitoring worker performance is an unsatisfying duty that supervisors tend to abjure (Kadushin 1992a).

Tardiness and absenteeism reduce the human resources available to the supervisor for getting the work done. Both are such routine occurrences that they need to be accepted by the supervisor as a fact of life. In time, supervisors get to know the tardiness and absentee patterns of their supervisees. They make decisions as to whether they are avoidable or unavoidable, controllable or accidental. Allowing for a certain amount of sanctioned tardiness and absenteeism, supervisors try to follow a policy that is reasonable, fair, equitable, and clearly and explicitly communicated to supervisees.

In implementing the work-assignment and work-delegating responsibilities of administrative supervision, the supervisor is concerned with assuring continuity of service. The worker represents the agency to the community. The supervisor represents the agency as well, though once removed. If a worker leaves the agency, the supervisor is there to step in and ensure that the agency is still responsible for offering service, so that there is no break in the continuity of contact but merely an interruption and possible delay. If the worker is absent or sick, the supervisor again ensures continuity of contact and work coverage.

The supervisor or administrator not only has to review the assignment to be assured that it is actually being accomplished and in accordance with agency policies and procedures, but also has to make some judgment as to whether it is being accomplished at a minimally acceptable level. The supervisor then has responsibility for evaluation. Formal evaluation of the workers' performances is an administrative act. If the agency is to operate efficiently, then someone has to share clearly with the workers an objective appraisal of the things they are doing right, the things they are doing wrong, and behaviors that require changing. Agency procedures regarding raises, promotions, and changes in job assignment require periodic formal evaluation if such decisions are to be implemented in a rational manner. Because evaluation is a very important function of administrative supervision and is the source of much confusion and difficulty, we have reserved a more detailed discussion for chapter 6.

Monitoring, review, and evaluation are the inspectional aspects of administrative supervision. Inspectional supervision deserves the onerous reputation it has achieved only if done autocratically and to excess. These are not inherently undesirable procedures; they are functions that are administratively necessary if the client is to receive satisfactory service. The administrative supervisory function of monitoring, reviewing, and evaluating work further implies the supervisor's responsibility to take disciplinary action if the work is clearly unsatisfactory.

Coordinating Work

The overall agency objectives have to be subdivided into manageable and differentiated tasks that are assigned to different units and then are once again subdivided and assigned to individual workers. If organizational objectives are to be effectively implemented all of this breaking down has to be coordinated and integrated. Coordination puts the pieces of the total work context together—relating one member of the unit to another, this unit to other units, this unit with support services, and a unit in this agency with a cooperating unit in another agency.

Through coordination the supervisor brings workers into relationship with other workers involved in activities that are reciprocal, supportive, or supplementary to their own work. Coordination unifies different workers' efforts toward achievement of agency objectives. Cooperation among workers and work units is maximized, conflict minimized, and greater complementarity ensured.

The supervisor also coordinates and integrates his or her own unit with other units of the agency and with other agencies in the community's social welfare network. Therefore, the supervisor not only occupies a position in the vertical hierarchy but relates horizontally to other administrative units on the same hierarchical level. The supervisor in the family service unit of a multiservice neighborhood center, for example, might help coordinate the activities of his or her supervisees with the homemaker unit, the employment unit, the day-care unit, and the protective services unit.

The supervisor activates support staff resources to facilitate the work of the direct service workers. Through coordination the supervisor makes available to the worker the human, fiscal, and physical resources required to do the job. He or she might help coordinate the supervisees' activity with that of the clerical unit, seeing that word processing is available and a tape recorder provided. He or she might help make available psychiatric consultation and psychological test resources to the supervisees. He or she functions to ensure the availability and smooth scheduling of a variety of different agency and community resources for the supervisees.

The supervisor organizes and orchestrates the activities of a number of different workers so that their joint efforts are cooperatively directed toward accomplishing some significant aspects of the mission of the agency. Coordination involves ensuring that the different workers understand the goals and objectives of the agency in the same way and accept them—or at least behave as though they accept them—so each worker can operate in the confident expectation that others in the group are working together rather than at cross purposes.

Coordination requires that the supervisor adjudicate conflicts between workers in his or her unit and between his or her unit and other units of the agency. Two workers may be competing for the same assignments or may disagree about who should be doing what with regard to a complex problem for which they have joint responsibility. For example, the unmarried mothers' unit may be dissatisfied about the availability of adoptive homes for which the adoptive unit is responsible; the family care worker may be getting little cooperation from the agency's employment unit or housing unit. The supervisor has the responsibility of seeing that such conflicts are satisfactorily resolved. Put positively, the supervisor maintains harmonious working relationships within the unit and between his or her units and other units in the agency. The failure to do so may hamper organizational performance (Hurlbert 1992).

Supervisors need the authority to require that facilities be made available. Strong chief unit clerks often contend with weak supervisors about the allocation of facilities and the work time of word-processing specialists and file clerks. Despite the fact that the agency table of organization gives the supervisor greater authority, inability to exercise this power effectively may put the supervisor's workers at a disadvantage regarding access to the resources they need to do their work effectively.

The Communication Function

The supervisor acts as an integral link in the chain of administrative communication. In the vertical line of authority, the supervisor faces two ways—toward the administrators above him or her in the hierarchy and toward the workers below. The supervisor's position is, then, one of the administrative control centers for gathering, processing, and disseminating information coming from above and below in the chain of command.

A small group cooperatively performing certain tasks can rely on face-to-face communication among all members of the group. A complex organization, in which administrators rarely have direct contact with workers, requires other approaches if messages are to reach their proper destinations and be understood and accepted. Formal channels of communication need to be provided, and the nature of the work to be done and the conditions under which it is to be completed need to be precisely stated and clearly defined.

Communication permits more effective coordination of the work of the agency through linkages provided by the flow of information and feedback. The volume of communication varies with the degree of diversity in a social agency. There is a greater necessity for communication in more complex organizations. Communication as a vehicle for coordination is particularly necessary in such organizations as social agencies, where tasks are ambiguously defined and when it is difficult to explicitly codify procedures for task implementation. Rather than being able to rely on written manuals and handbooks, administrators need to make frequent efforts to clarify and check to see if messages have been understood.

"In a sense the formal structure [of an organization] acts as a highway system guiding both the direction of information flow (up, down, sideways) and the distribution pattern and its terminal points" (Steiner 1977). The supervisor is one of the principal gatekeepers in the communications system, gathering, interpreting, distilling, and evaluating information received *from* others in the hierarchy and transmitting this information *to* others in the hierarchy.

Process in Organizational Communication

What administrators have to say to the workers in interpreting agency objectives, policies, procedures, and structure and what they have to share about proposed agency changes, they channel through the supervisor, who is administration's spokesperson to the workers. Downward organizational communication has been described as the top telling the middle what it wants the bottom to do.

Upward messages from workers to administration also have to be channeled through the supervisor. The administrator needs to depend on the supervisor to find out how agency policies and procedures are being implemented, the successes and problems in implementation, and the workers' feelings about agency objectives, policies, and procedures. This is the kind of information that only the direct service worker possesses and that the administrator needs to know about if the agency is to be run successfully. However, notwithstanding experiments in participatory human-service management (Pine, Warsh, and Malluccio 1998), the organizational chain of command in traditional settings sanctions only one primary upward channel of communication—from worker through supervisor to administrator.

The supervisor has the responsibility of encouraging relevant communication from supervisees and establishing a climate of receptivity and a readiness to listen. Conversely, the supervisor has to demonstrate a readiness to share relevant information with supervisees, keeping them informed, indicating a willingness to answer questions fully and to correct misconceptions. The supervisor should avoid assumptions. "Don't assume that the supervisees know; tell them. Don't assume that you know how they feel; find out. Don't assume that they understood; clarify" (U.S. Civil Service Commission 1955:22).

A large-scale study found adequate and effective communication within the agency to be a very important determinant of worker satisfaction. The study of 1,600 workers in thirty-one agencies found that "the biggest problem is that higher levels in an organization usually assume communication is adequate but lower level personnel do not agree. The great majority of personnel feel they do not have all the information they need to do their jobs effectively" (Olmstead and Christensen 1973:13).

Almost every aspect of the supervisor's work involves skill in communication. Clear, unambiguous communication is required in inducting the worker, assigning and delegating work, reviewing and evaluating work, giving feedback, and coordinating work. If communication between supervisor and supervisee is to be effective, it needs to be relevant, distortion-free, sufficiently detailed, and prompt.

In acting as a channel of communication from administration to the direct service staff, the supervisor has a responsibility beyond mechanical transmission of information. The additional responsibilities are to see that the message is understood and accepted and to motivate the worker to act in accordance with the information transmitted.

Concern with effective communication requires some decision as to how the message from administration to supervisees and supervisor to administer might best be transmitted. The supervisor has a variety of channels through which to communicate information: personal, face-to-face communication; phone communication; or writing e-mail messages, memorandums, or reports. The face-to-face choice provides instant feedback, which enables the supervisor to tailor the communication to fit the individual recipient. The message is apt to be more potent because it is transmitted personally. Phone messages are apt to be shorter or more abbreviated, and there is less feedback, both verbal and nonverbal.

However, both face-to-face and phone communication may get sidetracked and be dominated by other concerns, and because there is no record of the communication, it is not repeatedly visible as a reminder. Also, face-to-face and phone communication require additional time, because the message has to be repeated to every recipient. Furthermore, oral messages can be distorted in transmission.

In using the written channel of communication, the supervisor can be more precise. There is greater possibility for control of the content of the message. There is a record of the communication that can be reread by the recipient at his or her own convenience as a reminder. There is time saved in simultaneous distribution of the message to a number of recipients. However, written messages are less flexible, and there is no possibility of interpretation and elaboration to the individual recipient.

E-mail communication combines the advantages and disadvantages of face-to-face, telephone, and written communication. E-mail permits the rapid composition of messages lacking the contextual nuance and texture of nonverbal communication. Hasty e-mail, taken out of context, may invite misunderstanding. Moreover, e-mail is easy to distribute, allowing the recipients of e-mail messages to forward those messages to others. E-mail communications sent with private intentions may become public.

The supervisor may choose to employ multiple channels for repeated transmission of the same information. Redundancy in communication has the effect of reducing the possibilities of message distortion.

Because office geography affects communication, the supervisor should, if possible, arrange location of unit staff so that they are physically available for contact—on the same floor, with contiguous offices.

Problems in Organizational Communication

The foregoing discussion suggests one of the principal barriers to the free flow of communication up and down administrative channels: the supervisor may be reluctant to communicate negative information to people to whom he or she is administratively responsible or accountable, because he or she fears incurring hostility or displeasure. Similarly, the supervisee is reluctant to communicate negative information to the supervisor because he or she fears rejection, a negative evaluation, or a censuring reaction. Consequently, rather than sharing dissatisfactions and problems in offering service, communication is carefully restricted to telling others only what they want to hear or what will reflect favorably on one's own performance. The safest procedure may seem be to act the part of a not-too-obvious yes-man and "play it close to the vest." Freedom to speak is sometimes felt only as freedom to agree. This pattern operates more intensely for supervisees who are motivated to obtain the approval of supervisors and who are seeking a good evaluation.

Barriers to organizational communication result from conflicting group loyalties, as well as from a need for self-protection (Latting 1991). The supervisee may be reluctant to share information that may discredit peers or groups of clients with whom he or she might feel identified (Pine, Warsh, and Malluccio 1998). Supervisors may be reluctant to share with administration their critical but accurate assessment of some subsection of the agency with which they must continue to work (Boettcher 1998).

Information is power. The old saying "what people don't know won't hurt them" is not true. They can very well be harmed because they have not been informed about things they need to know to perform effectively. This suggests an additional barrier to the free flow of communication. The supervisor may withhold information from supervisees because this increases their dependency on him.

If these barriers to the free flow of communication do not result in withholding information that should be shared they more often result in "selective emphasis" and "selective omission" in transmission. Communication takes place but is tailored to the needs of the communicator.

One might realistically anticipate that every agency faces impediments to the free flow of communication. Even in the best of circumstances one might expect supervisees to be pragmatically self-protective in the information they choose to share. But if one cannot hope to achieve the best communication, one might perhaps attain better communication. Here the supervisor is a key figure. Olmstead claims that

> the climate created by an individual's immediate supervisor is probably the most important influence affecting his communication. Every encounter with the supervisor teaches him something. When the supervisor gives an order, reprimands, praises, evaluates performance, deals with a mistake, holds a staff meeting or contacts [supervisees] in any other way (or fails to contact them), the [supervisees] learn something. They learn about the kinds of information that will be rewarded or punished and the means of communication which the [supervisor] views favorably or unfavorably. (1973:47)

Credibility is important for effective communication. Supervisees need to have an attitude of confidence and trust in the motives and sincerity of the supervisor. This attitude develops when supervisors are truthful in their communications and when words and action go together. Supervisees are constantly engaged in "search behavior" in an effort to distinguish the reality from the rhetoric.

In general it might be said that communication in the agency flows down more easily than it flows up. Communication in the organizational hierarchy often has been described as a system in which information flows up through a series of filters and comes down through a series of loudspeakers. Good news is easy to communicate. Bad news—information about staff reduction, reduced agency funding, client complaints, and so on—intensify supervisor's communication hesitancy. However, the supervisor needs to clearly accept that he or she has the obligation to promptly and fully disseminate bad news. Bad news is included in "need-to-know" messages.

Even in a communications system free from inhibiting influences, the supervisor still has the problem of deciding what information needs to be shared and can be shared. Not all the information that comes from administration should be communicated automatically to supervisees; not everything shared by supervisees needs to be transmitted to administration. Applying some general principles of selectivity—such as that one should transmit only information that helps supervisees do their job more effectively—implies that the supervisor needs to have an intimate, detailed knowledge of the worker's job. Only on the basis of such knowledge and understanding can the supervisor assess the value of information for the supervisee.

Making human relationships work is supposedly the stock in trade of social work, and it applies as well to effective communications between supervisor and supervisee. A respectful, empathic, understanding orientation; a willingness to listen; and an accepting, nonpunitive attitude establish the context for good communications. Supervisees' willingness to talk is a function of their perception of the supervisor's willingness to listen understandingly, particularly to discomforting messages.

Because the orientation of the direct service workers to task-related information is different from that of the supervisor, the supervisor needs to be sensitive to the fact that the same communication may be perceived differently by them. A message from the administrator to the supervisor may consist of asking that the agency be more accountable to the community. This is translated by the supervisor to mean that he or she will need to assign tasks so that they are more objectively measurable, and this message is communicated to the workers. The workers translate the supervisor's message to mean that they will have to fill out more forms with greater care than previously. The responses to essentially the same message are apt to be different at the different levels of communication because the message has different implications for action.

Lateral Communication

We have noted that the supervisor is a channel of communication in the vertical hierarchy. The supervisor also communicates horizontally—within the agency and with other agencies, between his or her unit and other units through peers at the supervisory level. Lateral communication from supervisors in one unit to supervisors in related units is concerned with problems of conflict and overlap, changes that might make for more effective coordination of efforts, information about impending changes that may affect coordination of activities. Such communication may be for the purpose of reducing duplication of services, soliciting resources, increasing utilization of services, making referrals, reducing inappropriate referrals, or integrating services. Vertical channels of communication are hierarchically based on authority. Lateral channels of communication, based on a need to cooperate for purposes of coordination, are not hierarchical.

Informal Communication

The supervisor needs to be aware that in addition to the formal organizational communication network described here, there is a parallel communications network operating through the agency's informal structure. Colleagues and peers are a very rich source of information about the organization and about the work. Despite the aphorism "if they are talking, they aren't working," productivity increases with increases in interaction between staff members. Informal communication among peers is an important source of support as well as education.

Although this network transmits much in the way of gossip and rumors, it also acts to amend, interpret, and elaborate on the supervisor's communications up and down the hierarchical ladder. The informal channel is particularly active when the situation is ambiguous or unpredictable or when the formal channel has not provided sufficient information. Rumors and gossip, which may form a large component of such communication, needs to be the concern of supervisors only if such rumors are apt to be damaging to morale and one needs to correct disruptive distortions and half-truths.

An active rumor mill might suggest a failure of supervision. Gossip grapevines are most active in the absence of sufficiently detailed communications from supervisors about concerns that interest the staff. The more adequate the supervisory communication, the less need for the grapevine.

The Supervisor as Advocate

Advocacy is tied to communication. It is through vertical and horizontal communication that the supervisor advocates for staff with administration, other agency units, and with the community of agencies.

Downward communication requires being understood and accepted. There is no similar mandate in upward communication from supervisor to administrator. Such communication achieves acceptance through the supervisors' persuasive communication of messages and through active advocacy in behalf of messages with administration.

To be effective, the supervisor has to do more than act as a messenger. Lacking direct contact with administration, supervisees look to the supervisor to represent their interests and actively press for the implementation of necessary changes. Effective administrative supervision requires active representation of supervisees' interests and viewpoints as an intermediary with administration. Blau and Scott (1962:155) found that those supervisors in a public welfare agency who related to administrators in an independent manner and who regularly backed their subordinates commanded high loyalty from their supervisees. In the National Association of Social Workers (NASW) Code of Ethics (NASW 1999), advocacy is prescribed as a supervisory duty.

The act of communication is abortive unless it is accompanied by some confidence in the possibility that the message will have an effect. Supervisee satisfaction with supervision appears to be related to the level of influence the supervisor has with administration. There was dissatisfaction with the supervisor who promised much but was able to deliver little. There was high satisfaction with the supervisor who communicated worker requests and was able to get action. The lesson for administrators is that they should make a sincere effort to respond to communications from supervisees via supervisors. They must honestly share with the supervisees the limits of their power so as to forestall unrealistic expectations about the effects of upward communication.

Some studies have shown that workers are not confident that supervisors will take responsibility for decisions when these are questioned by higher-ups (Greenleigh Associates 1960:133). The most frequent complaint about supervisors listed by supervisees in a questionnaire study of NASW members is that the supervisor was "hesitant about confronting agency administration with the needs of his or her supervisees" (Kadushin 1992a).

Mr. E., a school worker, was indignant at the judgmental attitude of the Board of Education's policy regarding admission of unmarried mothers to special school programs. The supervisee informed his supervisor that it had been his experience that school officials were discouraging unmarried mothers from attending school by establishing unnecessary procedures for admission. Mr. E. had hoped that the supervisor would either join him in talking with Board of Education officials or support him in doing so. Instead the supervisor chose to focus on Mr. E.'s "indignation and hostility" toward the Board of Education and was insensitive to the need for change in school policy.

The supervisor has to assertively advocate for and protect his or her supervisees with clerical staff as well as with administrators. A worker in a large public welfare agency says:

> A member of the clerical staff (a very assertive person) has a number of social workers and their supervisors intimidated. Paperwork must be turned in according to the clerical person's format, or it is returned to sender (or, worse, it may be left floating in "the system"). It has been interesting to watch those "weak supervisors" and their workers doing their own clerical duties (time consuming and a poor use of social worker time) while the "strong supervisors" who are assertive with the clerical person get most of their documents printed.

In implementing advocacy, administrators appreciate and are more likely to be receptive to supervisor communications that outline the problem clearly and suggest alternative solutions for consideration.

Because the balance of power in this relationship rests with the administrator, the supervisor has to rely on rational arguments, ingratiation, or negotiating some kind of exchange in advocating for acceptance of suggestions. The sophisticated supervisor needs to be able to formulate the suggestion in the most acceptable or the least objectionable manner.

The Supervisor as Administrative Buffer

The supervisor serves as a buffer in relation to agency clients (Burke 1997). Administration looks to the first-line supervisory staff to handle problems relating to service. Consequently, the supervisor performs the function of dealing with clients who want to discuss a complaint with someone other than the worker. A child welfare worker writes:

> When an irate and emotionally disturbed parent wished to visit her child in foster placement and I had denied her request, she contacted my supervisor when I was out of the office. My supervisor listened supportively, gathered the facts, upheld me in my decision but suggested that the client come to the office to discuss the situation with both my supervisor and me.
>
> The parent came in a day or so later . . . and we had a very productive meeting. Client was able to express some of her hostility and anger at the child's removal from her home—which anger had been focused on me— however, my supervisor completely supported my position, which then freed me from becoming defensive and allowed me to support the client also. The result was a better relationship with the client and more cooperation from

her, which ultimately worked to her advantage in the later return of her children to her.

Having reviewed the case material, my supervisor had decided to support my decision. However, she also gave client respect and courtesy, which eased the tensions of the interview and allowed us all to gain by it. The client did not feel we were in league against her as she could have if my supervisor had not been skilled in encouraging her feelings and right to them; nor did the client manage to manipulate my supervisor and me into opposite corners.

The supervisor should be ready to accept appeals from clients who are dissatisfied with a worker's decision and want to speak to a higher authority. In doing so, they protect the worker from having to deal with clients' strong feelings about a negative decision and from a possible arbitrary or incorrect decision. They provide a channel for managing client complaints. Without such a channel, direct service workers may become overloaded with the extra time and effort required to deal with vigorous client dissent.

While serving as a buffer between client complaints and the agency, the supervisor also functions as a buffer between the worker and agency. The supervisor protects the worker from imposition by administrators of unreasonable work load standards, for example. The supervisors can modify the environment or act as a buffer in an agency that may be too bureaucratic, too authoritarian, or too undemocratic. Providing a "protective umbrella," the supervisor can soften the climate.

The supervisor also has the responsibility of protecting the supervisee from any kind of sexual harassment within the work unit for which the supervisor is accountable (Bonosky 1995; Dooley, Housley, and Guest 1993; Edelwich and Brodsky 1982; Hartman and Brieger 1992; Jacobs 1991; Larrabee and Miller 1993). The NASW definition of sexual harassment may be relevant here. "Sexual harassment includes sexual advances, sexual solicitation, requests for sexual favors, and other verbal or physical contact of a sexual nature" (NASW 1999:13). The NASW Code of Ethics (NASW 1999) explicitly prohibits the sexual harassment of students, supervisees, trainees, or colleagues, as well as sexual activities or contact between social work supervisors and those over whom they exercise professional authority (Reamer 1998).

The supervisor as a buffering person helping in negotiating organization complexities is described by a supervisee.

She was an intricate part of the system and really familiar with it; and I wasn't. And I think a knowledge of the hierarchy—of the system, the relationships that exist in it—is very important, and an ability to deal with those. If I had trouble with someone within the agency, she always dealt with it. She didn't do it for me but she helped me to deal with it. (Herrick 1977:128)

In addition, the supervisor is expected to protect the organization from potentially embarrassing deviance and heresy. *Deviance* involves behavioral contravention or subversion of agency regulations; *heresy* involves ideological opposition to the presuppositions on which the rules were formulated. For instance, a worker in a Catholic child welfare agency who helps an unmarried pregnant girl obtain an abortion is deviant in that context. If he or she instead champions the point of view that there is really nothing wrong with an out-of-wedlock pregnancy and questions the legitimacy of agency efforts to help women conform to society's traditional sexual mores, he or she would be considered heretical.

An agency operates in and is tied to an external environment whose components include clients, funding sources, regulatory agencies, and the general public as well as other agencies with which it competes for income and resources. The agency needs to maintain the goodwill and support of the external environment. Activities that undermine the legitimacy of the agency with its donor constituency threaten its very existence.

Agency self-preservation is a legitimate objective. More is involved than just a question of opportunistic defense of selfish vested interests. If agency workers have a sincere belief in the value of the agency's mission, their concern for agency preservation is ultimately a concern with providing a needed service. The failure to obtain continued funding results in denial of this service to a client group.

The supervisor acts as a guardian of the organization's belief system. For workers to reject significant aspects of agency policy and procedure is regarded as an act of hostility and a challenge to organizational authority. It threatens agency operation because "it suspends the rules that produce loyalty and cohesion" (Peters and Branch 1972:290), without which the agency finds it difficult to operate.

On the other hand, "although social work employees are generally expected to adhere to commitment made to their employers and employing organization, they should not allow an employing organization's policies, procedures, regulations, or administrative orders to interfere with their ethical practice of social work" (Reamer 1997a:120). The supervisor's duty becomes onerous in such cases.

The conflict between worker and organization is manifested first at the level of contact between worker and supervisor. Consequently, "in many organizations it seems systematically to become part of whomever is formally designated as first in command of each particular work unit to occupy the buffer zone which contains heretical confrontations between the individual and the social organizations" (Harshbarger 1973:264). The function is one of "crisis absorbency" and prevention of a threat to the agency's relationship with its supporting constituency.

This administrative function of supervision is implemented by offering workers the opportunity to discuss with the supervisor their questions and doubts about the agency's philosophy, rules, and procedures. Patient, open discussion of the workers' views in an accepting atmosphere is designed to help them understand the rationale of the agency's approach. If the workers remain unconvinced, the supervisory conference still offers a safe channel for the open expression of opposition. The cathartic effect of such an opportunity results, as Goffman (1952) says, in cooling the mark out—a reduction in the intensity of feeling of indignation, an increased readiness to conform to organizational demands. Another frequent procedure in the management of heresy is co-option, an attempt to retranslate the worker's opposition so that it can be channeled into kinds of behavior that the agency can accept.

The responsibility of acting in defense of agency policy can be a source of considerable dissatisfaction for supervisors. Frequently they find themselves in disagreement with some particular agency policy, rule, or procedure. Nevertheless, their role requires communication of the policy and attempts to obtain compliance with it. Forced by their position to perform such functions, supervisors often feel uncomfortably hypocritical. In a survey of "shortcomings" among social work supervisors, the need to "enforce policies and rules which give little meaning for work done with clients" was among the dissatisfactions most frequently checked by supervisors and supervisees (Kadushin 1992b:11).

The Supervisor as Change Agent and Community Liaison

Buffering client complaints and worker deviance and heresy suggests the exploitation of the supervisor in the service of preserving the agency status quo. Preserving organizational stability is, in fact, a function of administrative supervision. But the supervisor also has an equally significant, parallel administrative responsibility as an organizational change agent. Buffering contributes to the preservation of the agency, but rigidity and unresponsiveness to change threaten its preservation.

There is a danger that too rigid "management" of deviance and heresy, the "absorption of protest and domestication of dissent," may be counterproductive for the agency. An unperceptive supervisor would then be performing a disservice. The agency must balance contradictory needs—

accepting change while maintaining stability. It would be impossible to run an efficient organization and maintain effective working relationships with other agencies if the agency were not essentially stable and predictable. However, too much stability can foster rigidity. Ossification can disable the agency's ability to respond to a turbulent environment. Consequently, while defending the agency against deviance and heresy, the supervisor has to be open to suggestions for useful innovation. As Reich says, agency administration "is always neutral in favor of the Establishment" (1970:100). The bias needs to be explicitly recognized but lightly held.

The supervisor can be an active participant in the formulation or reformulation of agency policy. Having learned from the direct-service workers about client and community needs, having learned about the deficiencies and shortcomings of agency policy when workers have attempted to implement it, the supervisor should do more than act as a passive channel for upward communication of such information. The supervisor has the responsibility of using his or her knowledge of the situation to formulate suggested changes in agency policy and procedure. The supervisor is in a strategic position to act as a change agent. Standing between administration and the workers, he or she can actively influence administration to make changes and influence workers to accept them.

Supervisors may, however, hesitate to advocate change because of apathy, lack of conviction in the change being requested, competing pressures from routine work that demands all of their time and energy, or an unwillingness to take the risk of punitive reprisals if they challenge administration. In general, the administrator prefers a passive, conforming supervisor; the supervisees want an aggressive, advocacy-oriented supervisor.

In the service of agency preservation supervisors have to be sensitive and receptive to pressures from direct-service workers for changes in policies and procedures that they perceive as archaic, unworkable, ineffective, unproductive, inequitable, or oppressive.

If the supervisor sees a need for changes, then he or she should actually encourage and collaborate with supervisees in seeking them, rather than being a mere mediator. He or she must collect and organize supporting information, help staff clearly identify what it is they want changed, and help them articulate as clearly and as honestly as possible why they want change. Unless the desired change can benefit the agency and client group and receive the support of the staff, the chance for change is diminished. The supervisor has to mobilize allies in the agency that would support the change, maximize receptivity to the message, and minimize opposition and defensiveness on the part of the administration.

If unconvinced about the necessity for change, the supervisor may act as a mediator between direct service staff and administration around changes that supervisees see as necessary. The supervisor may arrange to have the administrator meet with the supervisee group to explain and, if necessary, defend policy in response to staff challenges.

It is at this juncture that conflict between the worker and the organization often become most clearly manifest. The philosophical debate regarding the obligation of civil disobedience to unjust laws is applicable to the problem faced by social workers in meeting agency requirements for conformity to policies and procedures that they are convinced are oppressive. Workers are encouraged to seek redress and change within the agency. There is a rich literature available on tactics that workers can employ in attempting to effect changes in agency policy and procedures in the face of resistant or inaccessible administrators (Resnick and Patti 1980; Holloway and Brager 1989; Gummer 1990). Going outside the agency, outside of channels that include the supervisor as the first point of contact, is enjoined—although there are frequent examples of such whistle blowing (Peters and Branch 1972; Nader, Petkas, and Blackwell 1974).

Although the problem that generates the most indignation is agency temporization (or outright rejection) of workers' suggestions for changes, there is often a problem in the other direction. Progressive, innovative administrators often have difficulty getting supervisees to accept changes in policies and procedures.

A whole host of factors understandably stand in the way of acceptance of change. Additional energy needs to be expended in overcoming habitual patterns of dealing with work problems, in unlearning old ways, and in learning new ways of working; there is anxiety about whether one can adequately meet the demands of new programs and new procedures; there is reluctance to accept an increased measure of dependency while learning new patterns; there is a struggle involved in developing a conviction in the value of the change; there is anxiety about rearranged interpersonal connections in the agency as work procedures change.

Change is best accomplished if supervisees participate from the start in planning the change; if they are informed early on of the nature of the planned change; if the change is introduced slowly, preferably with some initial trial effort; if expectations are made clear and understandable; if the change is in line with perceived agency norms and objectives; if there is some assurance that the change will have the predicted effect; if the administration, including supervisors, communicate strong belief in the desirability of the change; if there is some appreciation of and empathy with the difficulties that change generates for the staff; and if provision is made to reduce the costs of change to the staff. Putting him- or herself in the supervisees' place, the supervisor has to make an effort to understand the possible costs and benefits the change implies for them.

Not only is the supervisor responsible for changes within the organization, he or she must also be sensitive to needs for changes in the network of agencies whose operations affect the work of the supervisees. In reviewing, coordinating, and planning work, supervisors may become aware of a lack in the community social service system of some needed service. The supervisor contributes to facilitating the increased effectiveness of the work of his or her supervisees by advocating in the community for support of the needed service. By doing so, the supervisor enriches the resource network for both clients and supervisees.

Summary

The following principal administrative functions of supervision were identified and discussed: (1) staff recruitment and selection; (2) inducting and placing the worker; (3) unit work planning; (4) work assignment; (5) work delegating; (6) monitoring, reviewing, and evaluating work; (7) coordinating work; (8) acting as a channel of communication; (9) acting as an advocate; (10) administrative buffering; and (11) acting as a change agent and community liaison.

In implementing administrative responsibilities and functions, the supervisor organizes the work place, agency facilities, and human resources to achieve agency administration objectives in a way that, quantitatively and qualitatively, is in accordance with agency policies and procedures.

3 | Administrative Supervision: Problems in Implementation

Having outlined the functions, tasks, and responsibilities of administrative supervision in the preceding chapter, we are concerned here with some of the principal problems encountered by social work supervisors in implementing administrative supervision.

The Problem of Vicarious Liability

It was noted in the preceding chapter that the supervisor is ultimately responsible for the work that is assigned and delegated. Malpractice complaints and legal decisions have clearly confirmed the principle of the supervisor's responsibility for decisions and actions of supervisees (Reamer 1994, 1998). This is supported by doctrines variously known as vicarious liability, imputed negligence, and *respondeat superiore*. The doctrine states that the superior is responsible for the acts of his or her agents within the scope of their employment. The supervisee is legally regarded as an extension of the supervisor, and the two are considered a single persona.

When action is taken, the supervisor is perceived to have reviewed and sanctioned it. If the action was performed incompetently, the supervisor is responsible for having entrusted the implementation of the decision to a worker who he or she should have known was not competent to perform it. "It is assumed that the supervisor . . . knows or should know what is going on and that the supervisor has an impact on the quality of work done" (Slovenko 1980:60).

A worker's incompetence is an indictment of the supervisor. In a malpractice suit against the worker, the supervisor can be implicated as an accessory (Harrar, VandeCreek, and Knapp 1990). This is in response to the legal principle of *respondeat superiore*—let the master answer. Reviewing malpractice suits in social work practice, Reamer (1995) noted twelve malpractice suits filed against social work supervisors between 1969 and 1990 and in a more recent discussion (Reamer 1998) suggests that suits against supervisors are increasing.

The National Association of Social Workers' *NASW News* (June 1982:10) reported that "employees of the El Paso, Texas, Department of Human Resources, including the Director of the Child Welfare Division . . . were indicted by a county grand jury for criminal negligence in a child abuse case in which a fourteen-month-old girl under child welfare supervision died. . . . The supervisor of the social worker handling the case was also indicted." Following the death of an abused five-year-old boy under guardianship of the Illinois Department of Children and Family Services, a state legislator "demanded that the family services division caseworker and supervisor be suspended without pay pending an investigation (Madison [Wisc.], *Capital Times,* January 14, 1981).

In another case, a child who had been returned home by the agency after a short stay in foster care was fatally abused by the biological parents.

> An investigation by top state child welfare administrators into the events surrounding the decision to return the child to her home led to the highly publicized and controversial dismissal by DPW officials of social workers and two supervisors for professional negligence in the case. . . . the supervisors and administrators were found to be negligent because they failed adequately to review the clinical judgments of the workers under their supervision. (Aber 1983:217)

Slovenko reports the case of a client referred by the court to a mental health clinic for evaluation. "A social worker did the interviewing, found that he was without mental disorder, and the supervising psychiatrist signed the report without interviewing him. A few days later [the client] killed his wife and children. The supervisor was sued in a malpractice action" (Slovenko 1980:469)

A probation officer made a discretionary decision, in violation of department rules, not to take a probationer into custody on complaint by the probationer's girlfriend that he had physically and sexually assaulted her. Six weeks later the probationer sexually assaulted and killed a ten-year-old child. The probation officer "was suspended for three days without pay and his supervisor was suspended for five days without pay" (Madison [Wisc.], *Capital Times*, May 11, 1982).

Reamer describes the case of

> a social work supervisor in a family services agency, who was named as a defendant in a lawsuit filed by a former client. According to the client, who injured herself badly during an unsuccessful suicide attempt, her caseworker failed to properly assess her risk of committing suicide. Under the doctrine of vicarious liability, the client also alleged that the caseworker's supervisor was negligent because the supervisor did not meet regularly with the caseworker for supervision or talk to the caseworker specifically about suicide assessment procedures. (1998:152–53)

NASW (1997, 1999) has adopted guidelines and ethical standards for social work supervision. Ethical social work supervisors have the necessary knowledge and skills to supervise the services that clients receive, limiting the scope of their practice to those areas in which they have expertise. According to Reamer (1998), this obligates the supervisor to:

- Provide information for supervisees to obtain informed consent from their clients.
- Identify errors made by supervisees.
- Oversee workers' efforts to development and implement comprehensive planned interventions.
- Know when supervisees' clients must be reassigned, transferred, or have services terminated.
- Know when supervisees need consultation.
- Monitor workers' competence, addressing incompetence, impairment, and ethical lapses.
- Monitor the boundaries between workers and clients.
- Review and critique workers paperwork and case records.
- Provide supervisees with regularly scheduled supervision.
- Document supervision provided.
- Avoid dual relationships with workers.
- Provide workers with timely and informative feedback and evaluate their performance.

The doctrine of vicarious liability places the supervisor in a very vulnerable position. Schutz (1982:49) advises that "basically, any major decision that the [supervisee] makes ought to have been reviewed—and modified if necessary—by the supervisor." The NASW Professional Liability Insurance Agency warns that as a social work supervisor you are liable to be liable. To reduce liability risk, it suggests: "If you are responsible for the actions of other employees, be sure proper practices are fully understood and followed" (*NASW News*, February 1983:14).

Discussing the concept of *respondeat superiore* and vicarious liability, Cormier and Bernard note that it has far-reaching implications for supervisors. "The supervisor needs to ensure that supervision does occur. . . . In order to prevent negligent supervision, the supervisor has to be familiar with each case of every supervisee" (1982:488). The supervisor has to be clear about the level of competence of each supervisee to be able to guarantee that a case assigned can be competently handled.

Rowbottom, Hay, and Billis believe that because the worker is accountable: "Through the supervisor to the agency administrator and through the agency administrator to the legislature and ultimately to the public means that the supervisor not only has the managerial right but also the managerial duty to direct, instruct, review, appraise, and if necessary, discipline the worker" (Rowbottom, Hay, and Billis 1976:130). Although supervisors rarely make direct observations of supervisee behavior (Kadushin 1992a); despite evidence that what workers share with their supervisors may be highly selective (Ladany et al. 1996), empirical research suggests that social work supervision is the single most important factor affecting ethical decision making in social work practice (Landau and Baerwald 1999)—a finding with profound implications for preventing social work *mal*practice.

A recapitulation indicates that 634 malpractice suits were filed against social workers between 1969 and 1990 (Reamer 1995), the largest numbers being for incorrect treatment (18.6 percent) and sexual impropriety (18.4 percent). During this period, twelve social work supervisors were sued for failure to supervise properly (Reamer 1995).

The Problem of Authority and Power

Rationale for Authority and Power

If one agrees that the functions of administrative supervision reviewed in chapter 2 must be performed if the agency is to operate efficiently and effectively, and if it is further agreed that the supervisor is ultimately responsible for seeing that these functions are implemented, it follows that the supervisor needs to be granted the authority and power that would enable him or her to enact these tasks satisfactorily. As Studt says, authority is delegated and sanctioned when "to get the job done properly a person in one position in an organization is authorized to direct the role activities of a person in another position" (1959:18). Assigning supervisors the responsibility for implementing the essential functions of administrative supervision without simultaneously granting them the necessary authority is the organizational equivalent of asking them to make bricks without straw. The organizational axiom is that delegation of authority is a necessary concomitant of administrative responsibility.

The need for administrative authority in an agency derives from organizational complexity and task specialization. If groups of individuals are to work together to accomplish desired ends, their efforts must be integrated. Some administrative officer, in this case the supervisor, has to be given authority to direct and coordinate individual activities toward the achievement of a common purpose, to review and evaluate work, and to hold workers accountable. Formal channels of authority must be established because it must be clear who has the authority to assign, direct, and evaluate work and who is being directed and evaluated.

Because compliance with directives toward the achievement of joint efforts cannot be left to chance, individual desires, or whim, some kind of authority-control system is an organizational imperative. It is designed to "minimize discretion based on subjective considerations" (Stein 1961:15). Vinter says, "All organizations create means for ensuring that cooperative action is oriented toward desired objectives. To avoid a state of anarchy among participating personnel, an explicit structure of authority and responsibility is defined in every social agency. . . . This structure seeks to ensure predictable behavior of workers in conformity to policy" (1959:199–200).

In a study of the social work profession, Toren (1972:65) states: "Supervision is the institutionalized built-in mechanism through which the attitudes and performance of social workers are controlled." The rationale for any supervisory control review system is to ensure that the workers will act in ways that will lead to the achievement of organizational objectives. Weinbach (1990:232) notes that "controlling is an absolutely essential part of the job of the social worker as manager, and it is critical for the effective and efficient service to our prime beneficiary, the client."

The danger of indifference to procedures for controlling and/or influencing the behavior of workers is the possibility that the workers will make decisions and act in ways that reflect their own desires and preferences, whether or not they are congruent with organizational objectives. Furthermore, unless there is some predictability in the decisions and behavior of one worker—a predictability that reflects adherence to agency objectives and procedures—it is difficult to coordinate and integrate that worker's performance with that of other workers.

The authority delegated to the supervisor ultimately derives from the community. In public agencies the collective intent is embodied in the statutes that established the agency and in accordance with which the agency operates. In private agencies, the collective intent is manifested in the support the agency obtains for its existence and continuation through voluntary contributions. Agency objectives reflect what the community wants done; use of supervisory authority to ensure achievement of these objectives can be seen as an act in furtherance of the collective will.

Legal authority derives its legitimacy from the fact that it supposedly represents the common good. The objectives of the agency similarly are supposed to represent the common good. Authority employed to achieve the common good is regarded as legitimate.

The legitimacy of this ultimate authority may be questioned by workers, who thereby also question the legitimacy of the supervisor's authority. They may feel that neither the statutes that establish the public agency nor the community welfare council that sponsors the voluntary agency do, in fact, represent the will of the community.

The agency depends on the supervisee's acceptance of the legitimacy of organizational authority to achieve agency goals. When the agency and the supervisees are committed to the same objectives, the supervisee will more freely grant the right to be controlled if this contributes to the achievement of the accepted task. The common goal becomes the common good, which justifies acceptance of authority.

Supervisory Authority and Sources of Power

Authority needs to be distinguished from power. Authority is a right that legitimizes the use of power; it is the sanctioned use of power, the accepted and validated possession of power. Authority is the right to issue directives, exercise control, and require compliance. It is the right to determine the behavior of others and to make decisions that guide the action of others. In the most uncompromising sense, authority is the right to demand obedience; those subject to authority have the duty to obey.

This right of authority is distributed to the supervisor through the agency administrative structure. The supervisory relationship is established through authority delegated to the supervisor by the agency and through the supervisee's reciprocal acceptance of the supervisor's legitimate entitlement to authority.

A parallel source of supervisory authority derives from the social work profession. In most states, a period of social work supervision is required to earn licensure for advanced social work practice (Gray 1986); for the novice practitioner, supervision may be required to practice at all (DiNitto, McNeece, and Harkness 1997).

A third source of supervisory authority flows from the client. The ethical and legal principle of informed consent goes beyond the client's property right to control personal information; it affirms the client's right to decide whether to enter a contract for supervised social work services. Informing the client means providing the client with information about the supervisor's qualifications; the goals, methods, and responsibilities of the supervisor and supervisee; and any limits to client confidentiality (Bernard and Goodyear 1998; Ladany et al. 1999; McCarthy et al. 1995). The informed client who contracts for supervised social services delegates oversight authority to the supervisor (Harrar, VandeCreek, and Knapp 1990).

Authority is the right that legitimizes the use of power; power is the ability to implement authority. The word *power* derives from the Latin *potere*, to be able. If authority is the right to direct, command, and punish, then power is the ability to do so. The distinction is seen clearly in situations in which a person may have authority but no power to act, and vice versa. Extreme examples are a hijacker of a plane, who has power but no authority, and a prison warden held hostage by prisoners, who has authority but no power.

The distinction between authority and power is aptly illustrated by this discussion between a judge and a priest. The priest claimed that his position was more important because he could condemn sinners to hell; the judge countered by saying that his position was more important because when he condemned people to be hung, they actually were hung. The priest had the authority to condemn people to hell, but there was considerable question about his power to enforce the verdict. The same distinction is illustrated in Canute's law: "Even a king cannot control the tides." Authority is the right to supervise; power is the ability to effectively exercise that right. Authority can be delegated; power cannot.

The sources of the supervisor's authority are the agency administration, the profession, and the client, which in turn represent community will. What are the sources of power that energize authority and make possible the implementation of the right to command? Recognizing the legitimacy of the authority invested in the supervisor, what prompts the supervisee to actually comply with the supervisor's directives?

There are a variety of descriptive systems that categorize sources of power (Etzioni 1961; Presthus 1962; Weber 1946). Among the most frequently used is the classification developed by French and Raven (1960), who identified five distinctive bases of social power: reward power, coercive power, positional power, referent power, and expert power. We will attempt to apply these categories to the social work supervisory situation.

Reward Power

The supervisor has the ability to control tangible rewards for the supervisees, such as promotions, raises, more desirable work assignments, extra secretarial help, recommendations for training stipends, agency-supported attendance at conferences and workshops, a good reference on leaving the agency, and licensure recommendations. The supervisor further controls the work environment of the supervisee, for instance, office location and office appointments, and controls the level of work assignments and work procedures. Rewards can be psychic as well—approval, commendations, and supervisory expressions of appreciation.

Rewards such as pay increases and promotions are zero-sum. There is just so much to go around, and distributing these goodies to some means denying them to others. But there are many unlimited nonzero-sum rewards. Praise, recognition of achievement, and providing a feeling of satisfaction in work done can be freely given to one person without denying them to others.

If reward power is to be effective, it needs to be individualized and clearly related to differentials in performance. If rewards become routine, as in the case of across-the-board raises, they lose their power to stimulate improvements in worker performance. The supervisor, therefore, has to be knowledgeable about the quality of the performance of different workers if he or she is to make a fair determination of allocation of rewards. Furthermore, the supervisee needs some confidence that the supervisor does, in fact, control access to rewards, that administration has granted him or her the authority to make crucial decisions relating to dispensation of available rewards.

As contrasted with certain other employers, social agencies have limited reward power because they control only a limited range and variety of rewards. Production incentives, stock options, and so on are not available as possible rewards. Uniform pay scales dictated by civil service and/or union regulations make it difficult to reward meritorious performance.

A desirable reward system is one in which the supervisor has access to control of or, at the very least, decisive input into the allocation of rewards; the basis for rewards is explicit and clearly communicated; rewards are not politicized but based on competent contribution to agency objectives. Except for some formal occasions, rewards should be continuous in response to good work at the time good work is done.

The ethos of social work favors equality of rewards and decries the competition involved in striving for rewards. Consequently, this source of power tends to be employed sparingly and with uneasiness.

Coercive Power

The supervisor has the ability to control punishments for supervisees. These include demotion, dismissal, a poor "efficiency rating," less satisfying work assignments, and a negative reference. The client also has coercive power in the ability to seek a legal remedy for malpractice. This may include a financial payment to the client and the loss of a license to practice. There are psychic punishments as well—expressions of disapproval and criticism, snubs, and avoidance. Reward power and coercive power overlap because the withholding of rewards is in effect a kind of punishment.

In the case of reward power supervisees are induced to comply with supervisory directives and the contract with the client to achieve a reward, but in this case compliance results from the effort to avoid punishment. The strength of coercive power depends on the extent of belief in the likelihood of disciplinary action. If the supervisees have reason to believe that little serious effort will be made to apply punishments, this is not an effective source of supervisory power. However, "while most competent supervisors are reluctant to exercise coercive power, except in extremely serious conditions, the important point is that most subordinates behave in accordance with the belief that such power could be exerted at any time" (Austin 1981:21).

The general discomfort with punitive actions and the reluctance to hurt makes coercive power a relatively ineffective avenue for control in social work.

Legitimate or Positional Power

Holloway and Brager define *authority of position* as "the organizationally sanctioned right by virtue of occupying the role to initiate action, make decisions, allocate organizational resources and determine outcome for others" (1989:30). People have been socialized to accept and respond to positional power through experiences with parents, teachers, police, priests, swim guards, athletic coaches, and so on. We have learned the script and almost automatically follow it with people who occupy positions of authority. We respond to the authority associated with the position without reference to the particular person occupying the position. Positional incumbency activates a norm of compliance. The position evokes a sense of obligation to conform and the expectation that the obligation will be honored.

By virtue of being invested with the title, the supervisor can claim the authority that goes with the position. We accept the authority of the office and, in doing so, accept as legitimate the authority of the person occupying it. The supervisee, in taking a job with the agency, has implicitly contracted to accept direction from those invested with agency and professional authority. There is a sense of moral obligation and social duty related to the acceptance of positional authority. Consequently the supervisee feels that the supervisor has a legitimate right, considering his or her position, to expect that suggestions and directions will be followed.

Positional power derives its force not only from prior reinforcing experiences in which obedience to those in positions of authority was rewarded by acceptance and approval but also from its effect in making one's job easier. Barnard (1938) notes that the initial presumption of the acceptability of organizational authority enables workers to avoid making issues of supervisory directives without incurring a sense of personal subservience or a loss of status with their peers.

Referent Power

The supervisor has power that derives from the supervisee's identification with him or her, a desire to be liked by the supervisor and to be like the supervisor. Referent power has its source in the positive relationship between supervisor and supervisee, in the attraction the supervisee feels toward the supervisor. It is relationship power (Ellis 1991; Itzhaky and Ribner 1998; Keller et al. 1996). In effect, the supervisee says, "I want to be like the supervisor and be liked by him or her. Consequently, I want to believe and behave as he or she does," or "I am like the supervisor, so I will behave and believe like him or her." The supervisor is perceived as a model of the kind of social worker the supervisee would like to be.

A worker graphically describes the potency of referent power and some associated problems:

> My identification with my supervisor has allowed me to be influenced by him. Somewhere along the way, through his modeling in casework sessions, his respect for clients and his compassion for their struggles, I decided that I wanted what he had. I decided that I wanted to know how to do therapy as well as him. My desire and respect for his abilities has encouraged me to trust his advice and accept his direction.

The relationship, once established, provides the supervisor with a power base for influence. The stronger the relationship, the stronger the power of the supervisor to influence the behavior and attitudes of the supervisee.

As a consequence of a strong interpersonal relationship, the supervisee is receptive to influencing efforts on the part of the supervisor. As a result of identification, the supervisor's expectations become internalized. Supervisees then act as their own "supervisor," behaving as they expect the supervisor would want them to.

Expert Power

Expert power derives from the special knowledge and skills that the supervisor has and that supervisees need. This is the power of professional competence. The supervisee who attributes expertise to the supervisor must have trust in his or her decisions and judgments. The supervisor has the power to influence the kinds of behavior that supervisees will manifest because he or she has the knowledge that indicates the way in which it is desirable or necessary for them to behave if they are to deal satisfactorily with work problems.

Referent power has a potentially broader influence than expert power. The influence of expert power is confined to the content areas defined by the expertise. Expert power is difficult to achieve because the evidence of expertise needs to be validated continually. It can dissolve as the supervisee comes progressively closer to the supervisor in level of expertise. A supervisor's continued absence of contact with direct services can result in technical obsolescence and a consequent reduction in expert power.

Interrelations Between Types of Supervisory Power

The sources of power frequently have been subdivided into two groups, functional and formal power. Functional power, which includes expertise and referent power, depends on what the supervisor knows, is, and can do. Functional power resides in the person of the supervisor. Formal power is related more directly to the title the supervisor holds and the authority with which the title is invested. Formal power includes positional power and the power of rewards and punishments. The two groups of power are complementary. The most desirable situation for effective exercise of power is one in which the formal power and functional power are congruent. This is the situation when the person accorded positional authority and the power of the office to reward and punish is, by virtue of human-relations skill and knowledge of the job, also capable of demonstrating the power of expertise and of developing referent power. Functional authority tends to legitimize and make acceptable formal authority. Difficulty arises when the person with formal authority knows less or has less work experience than the supervisee or does not gain the supervisee's respect. The supervisee is therefore less willing to grant the person's entitlement to the power of his or her position and this tends to attenuate and undermine formal authority.

Because formal power is related to the office of the supervisor and functional power is related to the person of the supervisor, the latter is apt to be more variable. There is little difference between one supervisor and another in the same agency in their positional, reward, and punishment power. There may be considerable difference, however, in their total ability to implement their authority because of differences in their expertise and relationship skills.

The supervisees' readiness to accept the supervisor as an expert and as an object of identification and emulation is subject to change. Expert power tends to be eroded if supervisees find, as they grow in knowledge and experience, that they are less dependent on the supervisor for help in solving their work problems, if in testing the supervisor's advice and suggestions in practice they conclude that he or she is not the expert he or she claims to be or the expert they previously perceived him or her to be.

Formal authority is received automatically by ascription when a person is assigned to the position of supervisor. Functional authority has to be achieved by the supervisor and continuously validated. If the supervisees do not perceive the supervisor as an expert, the supervisor has no expert power; if supervisees feel no attraction to the supervisor and do not care whether or not the supervisor likes them, the supervisor has no referent power.

The different sources of power available to the supervisor to induce behavioral change in supervisees and to control their actions have different kinds of applicability and costs associated with their use. Both reward power and coercive power relate to specific kinds of supervisee behavior that are either encouraged or discouraged. The effect of using such power is apt to be rather limited in scope. Both require the opportunity and constancy of surveillance. Only if the supervisor knows what the supervisee is doing or not doing can these sources of power be applied (Holloway 1995). Supervisees feel a pressure to engage in the required behavior only if there is some chance that the supervisor will know about it. The use of reward and coercion as sources of power only achieves compliance.

Expert power and referent power, by contrast, are more diffuse in their effects. Once these sources of power have been established, then whatever the supervisor says or requests is likely to be considered seriously by supervisees. The effect of such power is internalization of the supervisor's authority, which then exerts pressure toward conformity whether or not the supervisor can witness the behavior. While reward and punishment power can achieve compliance and a change in behavior, the exertion of expert and referent power in achieving internalization of influence can achieve changes in feelings and attitudes as well.

Referent and expert power give the supervisory relationship a leadership orientation. As a consequence of the supervisee's liking the supervisor and admiring and respecting his or her expertise, the authority of the supervisor is freely accepted rather than felt to be imposed. The supervisee is voluntarily motivated to conform to the requests, suggestions, and tasks assigned by the supervisor. The supervisor obtains supervisee compliance with a minimum of resistance. The supervisee is open to and accepting of the efforts of the supervisor to guide and influence, and the supervisee feels led rather than bossed around.

Warren (1968) has analyzed the various sources of power as related to conformity to agency norms under conditions of the low-visibility performance characteristic of social work. Under these conditions, expert power and referent power are most effective in ensuring both attitudinal conformity (implying internalization of norms) and overt behavioral conformity.

Because the force of positional power as felt by supervisees is the result of earlier socialization, this source of power is vulnerable to problems concerning a supervisee's relationship to authority figures. The supervisee who has had developmental experiences that result in opposition to and hostility toward parents and parent surrogates is more likely to resist the power of position (Itzhaky and Ribner 1998).

Studies of worker satisfaction in a variety of contexts as related to supervisory sources of power show expert power and referent power to be positively related to supervisee satisfaction and coercive power to be least frequently related to satisfaction (Burke and Wilcox 1971).

Studying the relationship between supervisees' satisfaction with supervision and the perceived source of the supervisor's authority, Munson (1981) found that satisfaction with supervision was clearly related to competence and experience as the source of power. By contrast, supervisors whose power was perceived as deriving from hierarchical sanction of their positions were seen as less friendly, less open, and less understanding.

Coercive and positional power may be sufficient to induce supervisees to work at a level that meets the minimal requirements of the job. This is what they have technically contracted for in accepting the job. Referent and expert power, however, can induce supervisees to exert themselves beyond this level. They want to do better to please the supervisor, whose referent power makes him or her a person of significance for the supervisee. They get satisfaction doing a better job as they are helped with solving job problems through the supervisor's use of expert power. Reward power also can have this effect if the range of rewards available is sufficiently attractive to the supervisees and if they feel assurance that better work will, in fact, be rewarded.

The various sources of power are interrelated. Reward power increases the likelihood of developing a positive relationship. A positive relationship, once established, increases the potency of psychic rewards (praise, approval) offered by the supervisor. The use of coercive power tends to increase the difficulties of establishing a positive relationship and hence impedes development of referent power as a possible source of influence.

The exercise of power, when accepted by the supervisee, results in some change in his or her behavior. He or she acts and refrains from acting so that his or her behavior conforms to the needs of the organization in achieving its objectives. Power is used to attain some deliberate, intended effects. Where power is successfully applied, we can talk of control.

What sources of supervisory power are perceived by social workers as influencing their behavior? In a study of non–master's of social work (MSW) supervisees supervised by non-MSW supervisors in a public welfare agency, positional power was most frequently mentioned, followed by expert power (Peabody 1964). Referent power was seen as a less significant source of influence. In a second study involving MSW supervisors and supervisees, both groups saw expert power and professional competence as the main source of the supervisor's influence (Kadushin 1974). The supervisors saw this as almost the exclusive source of their power. A sizable percentage of supervisees, however, perceived positional power as a significant source of supervisory influence. Apparently, supervisees were more ready to grant supervisors the power of their position in the administrative hierarchy than supervisors were ready to accept this as a source of power. If social work values and hierarchical relationships are incompatible, as Munson (1997) contends, then recognizing that the supervisor's power derives not from competence but from the supervisory position may induce "cognitive dissonance" in the supervisor. It is interesting that neither study found referent power or relationship power as a significant source of supervisory influence. As was expected, neither reward power nor coercive power was seen as a preferred source of power, and Munson (1997) argues that power derived from position is incompatible with social work values.

A 1989 follow-up questionnaire study of 508 social work supervisors and 377 supervisees indicated once again that only expertise and positional power were perceived by both groups as salient (Kadushin 1992a). Supervisors overwhelmingly saw expertise as the source of effective power. Though supervisees generally agree, a high percentage saw positional power as the reason for agreeing to do what supervisors wanted them to do. A negligible percentage of respondents saw referent power, reward, or punishment as significant.

A study of some 16,000 employees in thirty-one social welfare and rehabilitation agencies shows the same relative ranking of the sources of supervisory power. "Expert power" was listed as the principal reason that induced supervisees to "do things my immediate supervisor suggests or wants me to do," followed by positional power as the second source of supervisory influence. Referent power was given middle-range ranking. Reward power and coercive power were perceived as the least potent sources of influence (Olmstead and Christensen 1973).

Although it is clear that expert power is the kind of power most readily acknowledged and most comfortably employed between social work supervisor and supervisee, the question might be raised whether this is a viable and potent power base for the social work supervisor.

The base of reward, coercive, and positional power is the community through the agency. The base of referent power is the person of the supervisor. The base of expert power, however, is the profession. The profession provides the knowledge that makes the supervisor an expert. Consequently, the potency of expert power depends on the "state of the art" of the profession. If a profession has well-developed, highly sophisticated techniques and the supervisor is well educated in what the profession has available, the gap in expertise between the supervisor and the supervisee recruit is very wide. If, however, there is little specialized knowledge available, if the techniques the supervisor possesses are limited, the gap is narrow and can be eliminated within a short period. Rapid changes in the field with reference to what is accepted theory, techniques, and interventions tend to erode the supervisor's authority of expertise. Socialized in terms of an earlier view of social work, skilled in approaches generally used in the immediate past but somewhat outmoded in the present, the supervisory may know less than the supervisee about what is au courant.

Difficult as it is for the supervisor to maintain authority on the basis of expert power when there is objectively little real expertise, the task becomes even more difficult in an ideological climate in which possible differences in expertise are explicitly rejected. Where the ideological emphasis is toward a declaration of equality between client and worker, teacher and student, supervisor and supervisee, where differences in roles are denied and all become peers and colleagues, authority based on expert power is further eroded.

It must be noted, however, that the preceding discussion refers to the extent of the gap in expertise relating general professional knowledge and skills. Expert power may be validated on the basis of other kinds of information. If the supervisor has more experience in the agency than the supervisee, as is usually the case, his or her greater expertise may only derive from specialized knowledge of the policy, procedures, and operations in that particular agency.

This base of expert power is supplemented by the supervisor's strategic position in the agency communications network. Not only does the supervisor know more about agency operations because he or she has had more intra- and interagency experience, but he or she also possesses much-needed knowledge about agency policies and procedures because of initial access to such information from administration.

Furthermore, every agency deals with a special social problem and a special clientele. The supervisor's specialized, more definitive knowledge of the particular agency's clientele and the particular social problem that is the focus of its concern may be a measure of the gap between the supervisor's expertise and the supervisee's need to know.

Legitimation of Authority

Despite our distaste for the words and our resistance to the activities implied, authority and power are built into the supervisory relationship. Miller suggests that

> it would help a great deal to give up the sentimental shame that the worker-supervisor relationship exists between equals or between professional colleagues who happen to have different functions and responsibilities. This kind of well-meaning distortion obscures the power and authority inherent in the supervisory function. (1960:76)

In an analysis of social welfare administration Patti (1983:26) says, "We acknowledge that authority is inherent to the administrative and management process. The manager does indeed direct and control and there is nothing to be gained by clouding the reality."

> Authority is intrinsic to the [supervisor's] role. Its constructive use is indispensable to the manager's performance and that of the organizational unit for which he or she is responsible. . . . The manager who consistently shrinks from using the authority of the office when there is disagreement with subordinates ultimately loses the ability to coordinate activities toward the achievement of organizational objectives. (Patti 1983:218–17)

The supervisor must accept, without defensiveness or apology, the authority and related power inherent in his or her position. Use of authority may sometimes be unavoidable. The supervisor can increase its effectiveness if he or she feels and can communicate a conviction in his or her behavior. If the supervisor acts with confidence and with an expectation that his or her authority will be respected, the directives are more likely to be accepted.

A supervisee in a school setting says:

> My supervisor told me directly and without any equivocation that my frequent coming late upset the schedule of the unit. She was straightforward and serious. She did not apologize, minimize, or press the comment. She just made the point, gave me a chance to respond (which I didn't, because she was right), and then she just moved on to the next time. Although uncomfortable, I had to admire her frankness and honesty.

Nonauthoritarian Authority

If, to perform functions that are necessary for achievement of organizational objectives, the supervisor must be granted and must exercise some measure of authority and power, how can this authority be most effectively manifested? The likelihood of the supervisees' accepting the supervisor's authority is increased if certain caveats are observed. They are designed to help the supervisor exercise authority without being officious or authoritarian.

In general, the most desirable use of supervisory power is "exerting power with minimal side effects and conflicts" and seeking approaches "for the limiting of the exercise of power to the least amount which will satisfy the functional requirements of the organization and for maximizing role performance without the exercise of power" (Kahn 1964:7).

Voluntary compliance with supervisory authority is apt to be greater if its sources are perceived as legitimate, the methods employed in its exercise are acceptable, the objectives of its use are understandable and approved, and it is exercised within the limits of legitimate jurisdiction.

The attitude, the spirit with which authority is employed, is significant. If it is used only when the situation demands it, when it is required to achieve objectives to which both supervisor and supervisee are jointly committed, it is more likely to be accepted. If it is exercised in a spirit of vindictiveness, in response to a desire for self-aggrandizement, a pleasure in dominance, a delight in self-gratification, it is less likely to be accepted. The best use of authority comes out of an expression of care and concern for the worker and clients.

Supervisees can more easily understand and accept the exercise of authority if it is clear that it is being used for the achievement of organizational goals rather than because it is intrinsically pleasurable to the supervisor. If supervisees are committed to the achievement of the organizational goal, acceptance of authority is then congruent with their own needs and wishes.

If authority is employed in a manner that indicates that the supervisor is flexible and open to suggestions for changes in "commands," on the basis of relevant feedback from supervisees, it is less likely to be viewed as capricious and arbitrary. If, in exercising authority, the supervisor shares with his or her supervisees the reasons that prompt the directive, if he or she gives an opportunity for questions and discussion of the directive, the supervisees' feeling that this is a rational procedure over which they have some control is further enhanced. Through such participation the supervisees share control.

If authority is exercised in a predictable manner, the supervisees again feel they have some control over the situation. They can clearly foresee the consequences of certain actions on their part. Arbitrary exercise of authority is unpredictable and inexplicable.

Authority needs to be used with a recognition that supervisees, as adults, tend to resent the dependence, submissiveness, and contravention of individual autonomy implied in accepting authority. And authority is best exercised if it is depersonalized. Even in the best of circumstances, we are predisposed to resent and resist authority. It is, in its essence, antiegalitarian. It suggests that one person is better than another. Depersonalizing the use of authority is designed to mitigate such feeling. The attitude suggests that the supervisor is acting as an agent of the organization rather than out of any sense of personal superiority. The supervisee is not asked to acknowledge the superiority of the supervisor as a person, merely his or her assignment to a particular function in the agency hierarchy.

If it is not to be resented, authority has to be exercised impartially. *Impartial* does not necessarily mean *equal*. It means that in similar situations people are treated similarly. If there is an acceptable reason for unequal, preferential treatment, this is not resented. One worker can be assigned a much smaller caseload than another. If, however, the smaller caseload includes difficult, complex cases, the assignment will not be regarded as an unfair exercise of supervisory authority.

The supervisor needs a sensitive awareness that his or her authority is limited and job-related. The administrative grant of authority relates to a specific set of duties and tasks. The legitimacy of the supervisor's authority is open to question if he or she seeks to extend it beyond recognized boundaries. For example, attempting to prescribe a dress code for supervisees or to prescribe off-the-job behavior causes difficulty because the supervisor is exceeding the limits of his or her legitimate authority.

The supervisor has to be careful to refrain from using authority unless some essential conditions can be met. Barnard (1938) points out that supervisory directives will tend to be resisted unless the supervisee can and does understand what needs to be done, believes that the directive is consistent with his or her perception of the purpose of the organization, believes it is compatible with his or her personal interests and beliefs, and is able to comply with it. Similarly, Kaufman (1973:2) notes that supervisee noncompliance results from the fact that the supervisee does not know clearly what needs to be done, cannot do it, or does not want to do it.

The most effective use of authority is minimal use. Persistent use of authority increases the social distance between participants in supervisory relationships and results in a greater formality in such relationships. It intensifies a sense of status difference between supervisor and supervisee and tends to inhibit free communication. The supervisor therefore should make authority explicit as infrequently as possible and only when necessary.

Using other means of influence as alternatives to the use of power is desirable. The desirable procedure is for the supervisor to use the least amount of authority and power to achieve the aims of supervision. If by providing certain information, or by modeling, or by expressions of empathic understanding and acceptance, one can induce the supervisee to behave in the desirable manner, this should be the most preferred intervention. As Sennett (1981:174) notes, "Naked power draws attention to itself. Influence does not." The veiling of power humanizes it.

Supervisory authority can be more effectively implemented if agency administration observes some essential considerations. Most basically, only those who are qualified as supervisors should be appointed to the office, and appointment should be a result of fair and acceptable procedures. Only then will supervisees be likely to grant the supervisor's legitimate right to the title and to the authority associated with it.

Administration needs to delegate enough authority to enable the supervisor to perform the functions required and to delegate it in a way that conforms to the principle of unity of command. This principle suggests that a supervisee be supervised by and answerable to one supervisor. The exercise of authority is difficult if more than one administrative person directs the supervisee with regard to the same set of activities. There is also difficulty if no one has responsibility for some significant set of duties that the supervisee has to perform. Both gaps and overlaps in administrative responsibility create problems.

When agency administration, as the immediate source of the supervisor's authority, consistently supports the authority of the supervisor, this tends to stabilize his power. Inconsistent, unpredictable support from the administration of a supervisor's authority tends to erode his or her power.

The administration needs to make clear to both supervisors and supervisees the nature of the authority delegated to the supervisors, the limits of that authority, and the conditions under which the authority can be legitimately exercised.

Problems in the Implementation of Supervisory Authority

Although theoretically social work supervisors have an impressive array of potential sources of authority and power, the available descriptive and empirical data tends to indicate that (1) social work supervisors are reluctant to use the authority and power they have available; (2) they are particularly reluctant to use their power and authority for implementing the administrative-instrumental productivity objectives of supervision (i.e., "getting the work out"); and (3) even if social work supervisors were more motivated to use their authority and power toward the administrative objectives of supervision, the likelihood of their success in achieving this objective can often be effectively blunted by the countervailing power possessed by supervisees.

Avoidance and Abrogation of Authority and Power by Supervisors

As Holloway and Brager (1989) note, the use of power and authority is based on the assumption that one person has the right to tell another person what to do and to expect compliance. The implication of superiority in the assumption embarrasses social workers and robs them of the ability to employ power without discomfort. Social workers resort to power and authority self-consciously, hesitantly, and apologetically. It evokes a sense of shame and guilt.

Administrative exercise of authority and power is perceived as being ideologically antithetical to some of the fundamental values of social work—values that emphasize egalitarian, democratic, noncoercive, and nonhierarchical relationships (Munson 1997). These practice precepts reinforce supervisors' ideological uneasiness about the exercise of administrative authority and power.

Vinter (1959), speaking to this problem, says that a "strain arises from juxtaposition of the nonauthoritarian ideology of social work and the exercise of authority and control within the administrative context. Valuation of autonomy and self-determination for the client has pervaded the administrative structure of social welfare" (Vinter 1959:262–63). Indeed, as Levinson and Klerman (1972:66) say, "The predominant view of power . . . in mental health professions is much like the Victorian view of sex. It is seen as vulgar, as a sign of character defect, as something an upstanding professional would not be interested in, stoop to engage in."

Unfortunately, but inevitably, it is difficult to respond to the need to exercise authority, power, and control in functional terms alone. Though authority, power, and control are functionally necessary for achieving organizational objectives, they get mixed up with feelings of prestige, self-esteem, superiority, inferiority, dominance, and submission. Strong currents of feeling are evoked by power relationships in any context because they reactivate memories of our first encounter with authority and control in the parent-child relationship.

Organizational studies of social agencies show that very few human service organizations have "management control systems that are in any way comparable in quality to those in the private sector" (Herzlinger 1981:207). Although some observers report that human services organizations are adopting private-sector management methods (e.g., Boettcher 1998; Martin and Kettner 1997), complex measures of quality control and customer satisfaction are rarely found in social work settings (Iberg 1991; Savaya and Spiro 1997). "Even if such data were present it is unclear that they would be used for control" because they are managed by professionals "whose norms are antithetical to the hierarchical corporate version of the control process" (Herzlinger 1981:209). Paradoxically, the private sector has begun to adopt management practices resembling in some respects those used in social work (Boettcher 1998).

The question of power and authority in the supervisory relationship is just a special instance of the problem of authority in social work generally, a difficulty that has received special attention in the professional literature (Yelaja 1971).

The reluctance of supervisors to express their authority is noted by Satyamurti (1981) in a participant-observation study of a British agency. In this excerpt supervisors are designated as "seniors."

In terms of the formal hierarchy, seniors had a supervisory role which implied the exercise of authority. It was apparent that this was distasteful to many seniors, particularly those with a traditionally professional orientation. Their model of the relationship between them and their team was far more along the lines of consultant to co-professionals, despite their awareness of wide differences among fieldworkers in respect of experience and skills. Even the more managerially oriented seniors were reluctant to insist on a social worker accepting their judgment if they were unable to persuade them to do so voluntarily. Thus one said that if he disagreed with a social worker over a financial payment, and was unable to convince him/her that it should not be made, then he would allow the payment to go ahead, and provide the required signature. Seniors' reluctance to exercise authority, and to emphasize the difference in organizational status between them and fieldworkers, made them open to pressure. (Satyamurti 1981:57)

In an interview study, more than 300 British direct service social workers identified "checking on their work" as an appropriate purpose of supervision. On the other hand, supervisors were more reluctant to acknowledge the "checking process." They "seemed to fight shy of what they regarded as authoritarian aspects of their role and concentrated on the supportive rather than the controlling aspects of supervision" (Parsloe and Stevenson 1978:202). A study of supervisors' activities found that they frequently fail to implement actions related to "performance evaluation and monitoring of supervisory activities" (Ladany et al. 1999:457)

Using standardized research instruments inventorying managerial styles and managerial philosophy, a number of different research reports concerning the approaches of social work supervisors lead to similar conclusions. They show social work supervisors having limited concern for monitoring task performance and worker productivity and greater concern for the human relations aspects of supervision.

Using a standardized leadership opinion questionnaire, Olyan (1972) obtained responses from 228 supervisors in three different settings. One scale included in the questionnaire concerned structure and is designed to reflect

the extent to which an individual is likely to define and structure his own role and those of his subordinates toward goal attainment. A high score on this dimension characterizes individuals who play a very active role in directing group activities through planning, communicating information, scheduling, criticizing, trying out new ideas and so forth. A low score characterizes individuals who are likely to be relatively inactive in group direction in these ways. (Olyan 1972:172)

Low scores on the structure scale suggest a reluctance to exercise control and authority.

A second scale included in the questionnaire was the consideration scale, designed to measure

the extent to which an individual is likely to have job relationships with his subordinates characterized by mutual trust, respect for their ideas, consideration for their feelings, and a certain warmth between himself and them. A high score is indicative of a climate of good rapport and two-way communication. A low score indicates the individual is likely to be more impersonal in his relations with group members. (Olyan 1972:172)

Though the social work supervisors scored relatively high on the consideration scale as compared with thirty-five other occupational groups for which scores are available, they ranked lowest of all thirty-six occupations on the structural scale. Olyan concludes that the data "suggests that supervisors in this study group are not oriented toward goal attainment techniques such as planning, communicating information, scheduling, criticizing" (1972:178). These are the activities central to implementation of the responsibilities of administrative supervision and related to the exercise of authority.

Granvold (1978) found along with Olyan (1972) that the 108 social work supervisors he tested using a leadership opinion questionnaire were high on consideration but low on the structure dimension that was "considered" to measure the supervisor attitudes that reflect a commitment to satisfying organizational objectives. Results indicated that "the study group ranked rather high on the consideration subscale and extremely low on the structure subscale" (Granvold 1978:42).

A major implication of this study is that social work supervisors "had the appropriate attitude set to effect worker objective satisfaction." However, with regard to organizational objectives, the findings suggested that respondents not only failed to manifest supervisor behavior in support of these objectives but that their attitudes toward such responsibilities were weak (Olyan 1972:44; see also Cohen and Rhodes 1977). Patti (1987) quotes a Ph.D. dissertation by Friesen, who studied first-line supervisors in community mental health centers and found that they tended to score much higher on consideration and support than on task-oriented behavior. Patti noted that the research literature indicates that social agency supervisors "tend to score low on task oriented behavior and high on consideration behaviors" (Patti 1987:379). Task-oriented behaviors include "specifying rules, procedures and methods and assigning specific tasks to subordinates" (Patti 1987:379). Patti concludes by saying that "apparently task related supervisory behavior needs to be emphasized more in outcome oriented agencies" (Patti 1987:379). A questionnaire study of supervisors and supervisees (Kadushin 1990) asked each supervisor to indicate briefly "their two greatest strengths displayed in performing the role of supervisors" and "their two greatest shortcomings." Four hundred eighty-three supervisors generated a total of 809 comments about their "shortcomings."

The largest cluster of comments by supervisors identifying shortcomings concerned the exercise of managerial authority. Two hundred twenty-four comments (28 percent) from supervisors identifying shortcomings cited problems around the use of administrative authority in reviewing, evaluating, and delegating work and a general antipathy to the bureaucratic requirements of a middle management position. This was the single largest coherent grouping of shortcomings cited. In detailing their shortcomings in supervision, supervisors said:

- I have a very hard time telling people what to do.
- I do not like to confront my staff with problems or inadequacies in their work.
- I hate having to reprimand or discipline a supervisee.
- I have difficulty confronting transgressions.
- I have difficulty terminating an employee even though it might be clearly indicated.
- I have weak confrontation skills.
- I avoid performance evaluations by prolonged procrastination.
- It's hard for me to set limits, to say "no."
- My problem lies in confronting poor, negative performance.
- I do not like to deal with monitoring, etc., paperwork requirements.
- I find it extremely difficult to enforce policies and rules that give little meaning for work done with clients.
- I lack optimal assertiveness in proposing unpleasant but necessary tasks to supervisees.
- I am too tolerant of incompetence and not enough of a disciplinarian.
- My disdain for bookkeeping, quality assurance, and red tape is one of my principal shortcomings.
- I am reluctant to give negative feedback.
- I hate the evaluation process, and I hate to reprimand and discipline.
- I hesitate to delegate work, out of concern for my supervisees, so that I end up doing a lot of the work myself.
- I find it difficult to confront supervisees on their failure to perform (repeatedly) necessary tasks. I tend to put it off.

In response to the problems that power and authority pose for social work supervisors, we might note that power and authority are intrinsically neutral. They can be used to coerce and dominate and to achieve socially undesirable objectives. However, power and authority can also be used to achieve highly desirable objectives. Civil rights leaders and unions used power to achieve greater freedom and benefits for their constituents. The most benign, productive use of power in social work is not for the purpose of control or self-aggrandizement, but for organizing human resources to achieve agency objectives; to get things done that help clients.

Organizational Factors Attenuating Supervisory Power and Authority

Reluctance and avoidance in the exercise of administrative authority by supervisors may be only partially the consequence of the fact that vigorous exercise of power and authority is antithetical to social work values and practice precepts. It may also derive from and be reinforced by a recognition that the supervisor's actual power and authority is more apparent than real.

Though the supervisor uses his or her authority to control, he or she is at the same time controlled by that authority. The nature of the delegated authority sets clear limits to a supervisor's jurisdiction and clearly prescribes boundaries to her authority. He or she is not authorized to employ certain sanctions, offer certain kinds of rewards, or intrude on certain aspects of the workers' behavior. Authority is the domestication of unregulated power; it explicates the prerogatives and limitations in the exercise of power (Dornbusch and Scott 1975).

Some of the attenuation of supervisory power results from factors that are inherent in a human service agency's organization and structure and in the nature of the social worker's tasks. Effective exercise of supervisory authority and power requires that certain prerequisite conditions be operative. Administrative control requires clarity in goals and objectives so that both the worker and the supervisor know the activities the workers should undertake. It also requires the supervisor to know clearly what the worker is doing and to judge whether or not it is being done correctly. None of these conditions, however, have been generally characteristic of the social work supervisory situation. Human services very often have had multiple, sometimes even conflicting goals expressing the ambivalence of the community regarding the problem the agency addresses and the clients they serve.

Handler (1979) points to the fact that the enabling legislation establishing most social service programs are replete with vague, ill-defined, and ambiguously stated objectives and criteria. "Vague language in the statues—creates a 'downward flow' of discretion—until the lowest level field officer interprets rules and guidelines for specific cases" (Handler 1979:9). The direct service worker was thus invested with a considerable amount of discretion in selecting objectives in individual cases.

In many fields of practice, managed care and welfare reform have effectively reduced supervisory and worker discretion by prioritizing policy goals and monitoring compliance (Corcoran 1997; Kalous 1996; Wexler and Engel 1999). But even if agency objectives have in the short run become less open to multiple interpretations, in time managed care and welfare reform will be compelled to respond to the need to individualize the application of agency service. Lipsky (1980:15) notes that the characteristics of the direct service social workers' jobs "make it difficult if not impossible to severely reduce discretion. They involve complex tasks for which elaboration of rules, guidelines, or instructions cannot circumscribe the alternatives." The situations encountered are too complicated, too unpredictable, too individualized, and too idiosyncratic to "reduce to programmatic formats." Workers need discretion "because the accepted definition of their tasks calls for sensitive observation and judgments that are not reducible" (Lipsky 1980:15) to specific rules, regulations, and procedures. To the extent that every client is like all other clients, the agency can standardize practice and direct the workers' behavior. But because each client is in many respects unique, discretion must be given the worker in responding to the unique aspects of the situation (Savaya and Spiro 1997). Invariably, both the external policy environment and the need to individualize social work practice compromise supervisory authority.

Direct service workers "enjoy considerable discretion in part because society does not want computerized public service and rigid application of standards at the expense of the individual situation" (Lipsky 1980:23), and only the worker can know the details of the individual situation.

The nature of the social worker's job makes it difficult to control, as each situation encountered is nonstandardized, diffuse, uncertain, unpredictable, and highly individualized. These are the characteristics of a work situation that demands allocation of a large measure of discretion to the person in actual contact with the client—the supervisee. The relevant research shows that the less specific the task and the less standardized the job, the less likely it can be controlled (Litwak 1964).

Complex, ambiguous, and uncertain situations can best be responded to incrementally, with each step determining the next step. Only the worker in direct contact with the client and aware of the details regarding each step is in a position to implement such a strategy.

Not only are the situations the worker needs to address nonstandardized, but so are the intervention techniques that the worker needs to apply. The services provided by most social agencies

> rely heavily on the application of technologies that are nonroutine, complex, and indeterminate. The variability of client needs and requests and the difficulties involved in understanding the problems they present when combined with the relatively unspecific nature of the techniques employed and the still considerable uncertainty about their effects, make it unfeasible for the organization to prescribe uniform technical processes. (Patti 1983:137)

Social work activity is characterized by what has been variously termed "role performance invisibility" and "low compliance observability." This factor, inherent in the work situation, further attenuates the supervisor's administrative power. The possibilities of direct control and observation of workers' behavior are very limited. Consequently, although the supervisor can "order" that certain things be done and that they be done in a prescribed manner, there often is no way he or she can be certain that the directives will be carried out. Ultimately, the supervisor is dependent on the worker's report that work has been done in the way it should be done. As Gummer notes,

> In social agencies supervision is based on the workers' reports of what they are doing rather than a supervisor's direct observation of the work. Organizations with this structure have significant control and accountability problems since the line workers are able to operate with a high degree of autonomy and can screen their behavior from the direct surveillance of administrators. These structural conditions promote discretionary behavior of workers, who in the privacy of the interviewing room are free to interpret and apply agency policy and procedure as they see fit. While confidentiality is designed to protect the client, it protects the worker as well. (1979:220)

Arguing that workers have too much autonomy, Handler notes that

> it is extremely difficult to monitor social service activity (i.e., to obtain reliable information on decision making so that performance can be evaluated); and if activity is not readily susceptible to monitoring then supervisory offices lack the necessary information to assert control. A system that limits the amount of information available to supervisors and controller increases the discretionary power of field-level personnel. (1979:18)

The less information the supervisor has about the worker's activity, the less amenable is the "worker to supervisory control and discipline" (Handler 1979:108).

Itse (1974), in their study of California foster care, found that workers had considerable decisional discretion. But the supervisor's failure to adequately monitor the worker activity, they note, is inherent in a situation in which a typical unit caseload for which the supervisor is responsible consists of 245 children. "Even if the supervisor was extremely conscientious there would have to be a well-developed monitoring system to enable him/her to keep up with what is happening to 245 different children. . . . The problem of too great a discretionary component is heightened by the impossibility of adequate supervision under the current system" (Gambrill and Wiltse 1974:18). Hasenfeld (1983:157) concludes that "these characteristics . . . accord line staff [the direct service worker] considerable discretion."

To sum up briefly, authority and power are difficult to exercise effectively in the face of ambiguous objectives, uncertain procedures, and indeterminate interventions about which the supervisor has only speculative knowledge.

The problem of control is intensified in the context of increasing caseload pressure. In an empirical study of the effects of higher caseloads on worker autonomy and discretion, Brintnall (1981:296) found that "caseload pressures tend to make effective supervision of staff by upper level officials unusually difficult increasing the latitude afforded lower level staff to act independently."

Supervisee Countervailing Power

The supervisor's authority and power are limited not only by ideology, reluctance, and organizational considerations but also by the countervailing power of the supervisees (Savaya and Spiro 1997). The traditional social work literature has underestimated the power of the worker and overestimated the power that the supervisor is actually able to exert in implementing the functions of administrative supervision. Although control in the relationship is asymmetrical, it is not unidirectional. The supervisor, clearly and admittedly, has more authority and power than the supervisees, but the supervisees also have some power in the relationship even though they may lack formal authority (Mechanic 1964; Janeway 1980). Supervisors have their measures of control; supervisees have their countermeasures. Both authority and power are transactional in nature. The reciprocal, in this case the supervisee, has to grant the authority of the supervisor and respond to the power the supervisor has the ability to exercise. Authority can be rejected, and power can be resisted.

The concept that power is ultimately based on dependency might be usefully applied in analyzing the countervailing power of the supervisees. The supervisees depend on the supervisor for rewards, for solutions to work problems, for necessary information, for approval and support. However, the supervisor is also dependent on the supervisees. The supervisor may have the formal power to assign, direct, and review work, but he or she is still dependent on the supervisees' willingness and readiness to actually do the work. If supervisees fail to do the required work because of opposition or resistance, the supervisor is in trouble with the administration, which holds him or her responsible for getting the work done. Supervisees thus have the power of making life difficult for the supervisor. In discussing her present assignment, one supervisee said she could

> drive her supervisor frantic if she wanted to—and she sometimes did. She was responsible for processing foster home applications. If she wanted to gum up the works she just took longer to do them—always for legitimate reasons— it was difficult to schedule an interview with the father or the last time she scheduled an interview with the family they had to cancel it when she got out there because of some emergency, or there were special problems which required more detailed exploration, etc.

> A supervisee writes that a supervisor newly appointed to the unit had the tendency to "command" his supervisees to carry out specific tasks and responsibilities, refusing to discuss the reasons behind them and replying coldly, "Because I said so," when asked. Our group of supervisees resented this approach to the extent that they "boycotted" the supervisor, flatly refusing to do anything more than minimum work required and giving him the "silent treatment." Once this reaction became apparent to the supervisor, he began to be more communicative and understanding and less strictly authoritative than he had been previously.

The willingness to obey is sometimes given key consideration in defining authority. In this view, authority is not delegated from above in the hierarchy but granted from below; it is based on the consent of the governed. If this is the case, then the legitimacy of the supervisor's authority is, in fact, controlled by the supervisees and can be withdrawn by them (Barnard 1938:161– 65). Although agency administration legitimates the authority of the supervisor, such authority must be endorsed by supervisees before it can be fully implemented. Both official legitimation and worker endorsement of authority are necessary (Dornbusch and Scott 1975:37–42). The power of the supervisees lies in their ability to withhold their work (as in the case of a strike) or to withhold their best effort in a slowdown or indifferent approach to their work.

The power of supervisees is of course constrained by ideological considerations. Professional ethics dictating an obligation to be available for client service inhibits the power available in withdrawal of effort, tardiness, and absenteeism. But in the final analysis the supervisees have the ultimate veto power—they can refuse consent to be governed by resigning from the organization: "You can't fire me, I quit." Power and authority are actualized as influence only as the reciprocal is responsive to these sources of power. The power associated with the authority to fire a person has no significance for someone who does not care if he or she keeps the job. The hijacker has no power over the passenger who is indifferent as to whether he or she lives or dies. The fact that power is given potency only in the response of the recipient to the manifestation of power gives substance to the contention that power and authority cannot be imposed; they need to be granted.

Workers not only have the power of not cooperating, they have the power of overcompliance or rigid compliance. Supervisees can effectively sabotage the work of an agency by the literal application of all policies, rules, and procedures. This is sometimes termed "malicious obedience."

The worker is the only one who has the knowledge of the intimate details of the client's situation. The worker comes into possession of this knowledge on the basis of a contact that the supervisor cannot observe. The worker then is in possession of considerable knowledge about the case situations for which the supervisor has ultimate responsibility. Such information, which only the worker possesses, can be shared freely, shared partially and selectively, distorted, or withheld in communications with the supervisor. This means that although the worker has no formal grant of authority in relation to the supervisor, he or she has considerable actual power in this relationship.

As a consequence, the supervisor is dependent on the worker for the information that is basic to the exercise of authority. Such information is provided by the workers in verbal reports and/or written records, the substance of which is determined by the workers. Outright falsification in records or verbal reports is infrequent and atypical. But there are no independent sources of information by which to check the reports made by the worker whose work is being supervised. The written and spoken records either support the worker's decisions or do not include information that might arouse doubts about the decision. Because the record is written by the worker, "it is not unreasonable to suppose that information would not be included that contradicts [the direct service worker's] judgments or that reports his unsanctioned behaviour" (Prottas 1979:153). The worker controls the nature of the information obtained from the client and controls the processing of selected information obtained (Yourman and Farber 1996). A study of information shared by supervisees with their supervisor noted in conclusion that "supervisors should be aware that there is significant information that supervisees do not disclose about themselves, their work with clients, and the supervision relationship" (Ladany et al. 1996:22).

Pithouse, in a detailed study of organizational interaction in a social agency, describes workers' "adroit management of supervisory encounters" (1985:78). In reporting on contacts with supervisors, one worker says:

Louise [the supervisor] is great. You know you could tell her anything—you can trust her. But when it comes to supervision I know my cases, so really I tell them from my point of view, do you see? I tell her what I want her to hear. I decide what to talk about and where I want advice, so in a sense it's not really supervision. If you like, I'm supervising her by what I say. I sort of control it—but it's alright, she knows how I work and I know how she ticks. (Pithouse 1985:86)

"Knowing" the supervisor, the worker skillfully assembles the information to be shared. "She is able to select, filter or avoid those aspects of the case that might elicit unwanted interest or interference from the supervisor" (Pithouse 1985:86).

The power of the individual supervisee in controlling the work flow (how much work or what kind is done within a given period of time) and his or her control of information fed to the supervisor may be augmented in coalition with other supervisees. Supervisees acting as a group can develop considerable power in controlling their supervisor. The supervisee peer group not only provides support but is also a base of organizational allies, a solidarity group that provides a source of power.

The supervisor is also dependent on the supervisees for some kinds of psychic rewards. Approbation from supervisees, expressions of commendation and appreciation from supervisees, is a source of intrinsic job satisfaction for the supervisor. It hurts the supervisor never to be told by a supervisee that he or she has been helpful or is a good supervisor. Supervisees can manipulate supervisors' dependence on such gratification by studied deference and apple-polishing. Blau and Scott (1962:162) found that one significant source of emotional support for the supervisor was the loyalty of his or her supervisees. The threat of withdrawal of loyalty acts as a constraint on the supervisor's exercise of his authority and power.

The power of the supervisee also derives from the supervisors need to be considered a "good" supervisor as described in the literature—a self-image the supervisor seeks to establish and maintain. Manifesting attitudes of unconditional acceptance and respect, adhering to the principles of participatory democracy and mutuality, communicating approachability and openness, the supervisor is vulnerable to pressure from a strongly motivated and assertive supervisee. The fact that the direct service worker has considerable power despite the fact that there is no formal grant of authority is aptly illustrated in the following vignette written by a supervisor in a day-care agency whose supervisee, Joan, was a child-care worker.

There were times that I thought Joan was taking advantage of my understanding nature. For example, I felt it was important for her to be on time so she could greet all the children when they arrived. This would establish for the children a mood for the day, a feeling of continuity, a trust that all is going to be well again. Often Joan would be late or would arrive early only to leave in order to buy coffee across the street. She had a million excuses—buses not being on time, dying of hunger, and alarms not going off. I had a feeling that Joan's most creative part of the day was in the morning thinking up excuses to give me for not being in the room when the children arrived. There was a point where I should have said something like, "All right, Joan, either you're here in the classroom at 8:40 or I will start taking money out of your paycheck." Why didn't I take action? There were several reasons, the most unattractive being that I didn't want Joan to see me as unfriendly, insensitive, and unempathetic. This was a mistake on my part. (Miller, Mailick, and Miller 1973:88)

The supervisee can control the use of power by the supervisor by appealing to the norms of fairness, collegiality, and professional behavior. This is not the way one should treat another human, another colleague, or another professional. To the extent that such norms are accepted by the supervisor, they act as constraints on his behavior. Holloway and Brager (1989) point out that the culture of human service organizations constrains the supervisor's options. "The centrality of themes in social work such as self-determination and empowerment, respect for the needs and interest of others, openness and mutuality . . . prescribes how human beings should interact with one another" (Halloway and Brager 1989:194). These values then prescribe the parameters that dictate some of the supervisor's behavior in supervision.

The countervailing power of supervisees relative to their supervisors has increased by subordinating both parties to the authority of the social work profession, embodied by NASW (Strom-Gottfried 1999), state licensing boards (Gray 1986), and the courts (Guest and Dooley 1999). In a review of 894 ethics complaints filed with NASW between 1986 and 1997, Strom-Gottfried (1999) found that 174 were filed against supervisors by their supervisees, typically for "poor supervision"—the failure to share or maintain performance standards with workers, flawed performance reviews, irregular supervision, or holding sessions that were ineffective or unclear. In an empirical investigation of the effects of social work licensure on social work supervision, Gray (1986:194) has reported that "with licensure comes a pattern whereby prominent supervisor qualities are those that represent efficient and effective supervision while those supervisor qualities associated with no licensure emphasize the affective components of the [supervisory] relationship." Examining malpractice claims filed against NASW members, Reamer (1995) found that 2 percent of the 634 claims filed between 1969 and 1990 were for improper supervision. Improper supervision, Guest and Dooley (1999) argue, makes the supervisor liable to the supervisee for malpractice.

Being in a one-down position relative to the greater power of the supervisor, the supervisees can claim the status of victims of oppression. Having generally become sensitive to the plight of victims, supervisors tend to respond with guilt to anyone implicitly or explicitly claiming the status of victim. The supervisees can use the power conferred by victim status to control the behavior of the supervisor. Appeals to professional values, the immorality associated with "blaming the victim," and appeals to fair play empower the supervisee.

A knowledge of agency rules can be used effectively by the supervisee in exerting influence on the supervisor. The supervisor is as much constrained by agency rules as is the supervisee. Quoting a relevant rule to the supervisor is among the more effective techniques used by supervisees in studies of upward influence procedures (Schilit and Locke 1982:310). Comprehensive knowledge of agency rules and procedures helps the supervisee equalize power with supervisors.

The countervailing power of the supervisee vis-à-vis the supervisor is central to the question of worker autonomy and the demands of the organization mediated by the supervisor. The strain between these often conflicting pressures is a persistent theme in organizational literature. This will be discussed again in chapter 9 in dealing with the question of worker independence from supervision and the problem of the professional in a bureaucracy.

The Problem of Rules, Noncompliance, and Disciplinary Action

Although the considerations cited above indicate the problems involved in implementing authority and power in monitoring and controlling supervisees' decisions and actions, it does not absolve the supervisor of the responsibility for performing those functions. The supervisor still has to implement administrative supervision in accordance with agency procedures and rules.

The Functional Value of Rules

In monitoring conformance to agency rules, standards, and procedures, the supervisor permits the agency to get its work done effectively. In prescribing and proscribing, in monitoring what should be done and what cannot be done, the supervisor is ensuring predictability and reliability of performance. Workers doing different things, whose work needs to be coordinated, can be assured that the work their partners are doing will be in accordance with some uniform expectations. The worker in the unit of the agency offering service to the unmarried mother interested in placing her child up for adoption can discuss the characteristics of an approved adoptive home without having herself seen one. The worker can do this because he or she knows the requirements and procedures that regulate the work of colleagues in the adoptive home–finding unit. Workers have to have confidence in the reliability with which these fellow workers will follow prescribed procedures as a prerequisite for performing their own tasks.

As protector of agency rules, standards, and procedures, the supervisor has the responsibility of seeing that policy is uniformly interpreted. If each worker were permitted to establish his or her own policies or to idiosyncratically interpret centrally established policies, this would ultimately set client against client and worker against worker. A liberal interpretation of policy by one client's worker is an act of discrimination against the client of a second worker. It would encourage competition among workers in an effort to tap agency resources to meet the needs of their own clients, with whom they are (understandably enough) primarily concerned.

The general emphasis in social work on autonomy, self-determination, and individualization tends to encourage a negative attitude toward rules. Rules suggest that people are interchangeable rather than unique and different. The negative attitude toward formalization of prescribed behavior in rules and procedures of course has support in the real negative consequences that can result from their application. They do limit the autonomy of the worker; they discourage initiative; they tend to make the agency muscle-bound, less flexible and adaptable, "set in its ways." They predispose the group toward a routinization of worker activity. Rules can become ends in themselves rather than means for achieving organizational objectives. They restrict the freedom to individualize agency response in meeting particular needs of particular clients and encourage deception and duplicity as workers feel a need to "get around" the rules.

Social workers are generally well aware of and sensitive to the negative consequences of rules. It might be helpful to the supervisor who inevitably faces the responsibility of communicating and enforcing rules and uniform procedures if some conviction could be developed regarding the positive aspects of rules.

Each rule, standard, and prescribed procedure, if taken seriously, limits worker autonomy by deciding in advance what action should be taken in a particular situation, but the rules may also permit more efficient agency operation. When the recurrent situation to which a rule is applied is encountered, it need not be subject to an exhaustive process of review and decision making. The supervisee does not need to discuss the situation with the supervisor and can act with the assurance that the decision, congruent with the procedure, has agency sanction. This relieves anxiety and frees the supervisee's energies to deal with those unique aspects of the client's situation that cannot be codified in some formal policy statement. If everything in every case had to be decided afresh, the worker could easily be overwhelmed and immobilized. Here, as elsewhere, there is no real freedom without clearly defined laws. They provide a structure within which workers can operate with comfort, assurance, and support. Rules provide a clear codification of expectations. They communicate to the worker how he or she is expected to respond in a variety of recurrently encountered situations. This understanding is particularly important in social work, where the various groups the social worker faces communicate contradictory and often conflicting expectations. The community may expect a worker to respond in one way to client problems, the client a second way, the profession in still another way. The rules offer a worker the serenity of unambiguous guidelines as to how the agency expects him or her to respond in defining clearly the "minimum set of behaviors which are prescribed and proscribed." The rules mitigate conflicts to which workers might otherwise be exposed.

Though rules and regulations have the negative effect of decreasing worker discretion and autonomy, they have the positive effect of decreasing role ambiguity and increasing role clarity. As a result of a set of formalized rules and procedures and a detailed job description, the worker knows more clearly and with greater certainty what he or she should be doing and how he or she should be doing it.

If the agency wisely formulates its rules, standards, and procedures with active worker participation, and if it further provides for a periodic critical review of them, the agency, of necessity, must make a systematic analysis of professional practice. The best rules are, after all, merely a clear codification of practice wisdom—what most workers have found is the best thing to do in certain situations. The call for rules and procedures is, consequently, a call for a hard analysis of practice.

Ultimately, rules protect clients, because the procedures to which all workers adhere in a uniform manner assure them of equitable service. The client is assured that another client will not be given preferential treatment because the worker likes him better or that the client will not be treated worse because he or she has antagonized the worker in some way. If a client meets the qualification as codified in agency procedures, the worker is under some constraint to approve the application for adoption, to authorize the request for a special assistance grant, or whatever. Rules and regulations are definite; the worker may be capricious. Disregard for agency rules and procedures enable the worker to meet client needs more effectively in some instances. However, it may also free the worker to act in arbitrary, inequitable, and opportunistic ways toward a client in other instances.

Rules reduce the possibility of friction between supervisors and supervisees. They set impersonal limits to exceptions that the supervisee might press for. They are also a source of support and sanction to the supervisor in making decisions that threaten the relationship. Rules depersonalize decisions that might be resented as a personal affront by the supervisee: "I wish I could go along with your request, but agency regulations prevent this." More positively, the procedural norms substantiate the desirability of the decision the supervisor is making: "In these kinds of problems we have found such an approach is not particularly helpful. In fact, based on our experience, we have developed a procedure that requires that the worker not take such action."

Rules protect the worker from arbitrary, personalized decisions by the supervisor, from favoritism, and from discriminating acts based on irrelevant criteria. Although rules constrain those to whom they are applied, they constrain the behavior of the rule applier as well. Rules provide protection to the supervisee. If rules are followed, even a bad outcome is excusable. "Rules and regulations [are used] for the purpose of legitimizing errors" (Benveniste 1987:16). If rules and professional standards are followed and mistakes are made, the agency has the obligation to defend a worker in attempts at innovative practice.

Rules reduce the possibility of supervisor-supervisee friction because they operate as remote-control devices. Supervision can occur through adherence to a universally applied rule rather than through the direct, personal intercession of the supervisor suggesting that this or that be done in this or that way. Control takes place at a distance in the absence of the supervisor. A rule is a definition of expectation. The explicitness of a rule makes clear when a required action was not taken or when a prohibited action did take place. A rule therefore provides the supervisor with a guideline to nonperformance and objectively legitimates the application of sanctions.

Gouldner (1954) has pointed out that rules can be used as devices to create social obligations. By deliberately refraining on occasion from enforcing rules, the supervisor can create a sense of obligation on the part of supervisees. If the supervisor has been lenient about enforcing certain requirements, he or she can more freely ask the supervisee to extend him- or herself to do some things that need to be done. Blau and Scott (1962) found that supervisors in a county welfare department actually did enforce rules differentially to attain the effect of developing loyalty and social obligation. The supervisor employing such an approach, however, needs to have a sophisticated knowledge of the work situation so that he or she can "judge which operating rules can be ignored without impairing efficiency" (Blau and Scott 1962:143). "The wise supervisor knows which rules should and can be ignored to facilitate worker morale or to promote unit goals and she will either modify them or look the other way as they are violated. Rules are the chips with which organizations stake supervisors to play the organizational game" (Holloway and Brager 1989:82).

The supervisor gives priority to behaviors that are "required" and those that are "prohibited." The rationale for designating the behaviors as either required or prohibited is, as we assume, that they have greatest potency for helping or hurting the client. Consequently, they have to be most carefully monitored. But between required and prohibited there are many behaviors that are less crucial and critical for the effective implementation of tasks the worker performs in offering service to clients. Consequently, the supervisor can view such modifications of prescribed role behavior with greater permissiveness and equanimity, formulating a zone of indifference.

A relaxed supervisor can adopt a flexible attitude toward agency rules. He or she accepts the fact that some degree of noncompliance is, in all likelihood, inevitable. The supervisor recognizes that not all procedures are of equal importance and that some can be ignored or subverted without much risk to agency or client.

Helping the staff understand clearly the nature and purpose of the agency's rules lessens the dangers of ritualism and overconformity. Rules, standards, regulations, and procedures often become ends in themselves rather than a means of more effectively serving the client. If workers are encouraged to participate in the formulation of rules and procedures, if they are helped to understand and critically evaluate the situations that required formulation of the rules, they will have less of a tendency to apply them in an overly rigid, routine way. Supervisees will be able to apply the rules more flexibly, more appropriately, and with greater conviction. Furthermore, understanding clearly the rationale for a particular rule, the worker will be in a better position to suggest modification in those situations in which the procedure seems inappropriate or self-defeating. To encourage and reward such initiative the supervisor needs to be receptive to such suggestions for change communicated by the supervisees.

Steggert speaks to this issue when he asks, "How then does the [supervisor] in a bureaucratic structure resolve the conflict between the organization's legitimate need for predictability (and thus for a variety of formal controls and coordination procedures) and the human unpredictability resulting from allowing subordinates to function more autonomously?" (1970:47).

Understanding Noncompliance

The supervisor should make an effort to understand and, if possible, help the supervisee understand failure to adhere to and implement agency rules, regulations, and standards. Here, as always, the assumption is that behavior is purposeful. It may be that the supervisee does not know clearly what is expected of him or her and does not clearly understand what he or she is supposed to be doing. Noncompliance might then yield to a clarification of what is called for by agency policy. The worker may understand what is required, may be in agreement with what is required, but be unable to meet the demands of the rule or procedure. He or she does not know enough or is not capable enough to comply. Education and training are required, rather than criticism, to obtain compliance.

> Although it had been agreed that Mr. F. would arrange for group meetings of the patients on his ward, he had consistently and adroitly avoided scheduling such meetings. Despite repeated discussion of the need for this and tentative plans, no meetings were held. Finally, in response to the supervisor's growing insistence and impatience, Mr. F. shared the fact that he knew very little about how to conduct a group meeting, despite all his early verbalized knowledge, and was very anxious about getting started with a group.

The rules, standards, and regulations of large, complex social agencies are often voluminous and sometimes contradictory, and are frequently undergoing revision and modification. Noncompliance may result from failure to know which rule to apply or how to apply it. Such actions might more properly be classified as practice errors rather than noncompliance. They are mistakes that are not due to any willful deviance or negligence.

Ability to fulfill task responsibilities may also relate to the client and the client's situation rather than to any inadequacies on the part of the worker. The client may be so resistive to help or the resources available to change the situation so limited that the worker avoids contact with the family.

> Children in foster care had been ordered by the court to be returned to the physical custody of the mother against agency recommendations. The worker, prior to this order, had been working with one of the teenage children, Sally, around school adjustment, adolescent conflicts, etc. Following the return of Sally to the mother, the worker failed to keep a scheduled appointment with Sally and did not schedule another appointment. When this was discussed in a supervisory conference, the worker indicated that with Sally's return to her own mother she felt no confidence that she could be of any help. The situation

in the house was such that she did not feel that anything she could do would enable Sally to change.

Noncompliance may result from a disagreement with policy or procedure. The worker may regard compliance as contrary to his definition of the agency's objective. This might require some discussion of the purpose of the policy in an effort to reconcile it with the worker's view of agency objectives. The worker may in fact be correct in claiming that agency objectives would best be served by ignoring the rules in this instance and amending or revising them. For instance, during the 1960s, social workers in West Coast public welfare departments were fired after they refused to conduct "midnight raids" to check on the continued eligibility of Aid to Families with Dependent Children (AFDC) clients. They strongly felt that such procedures were a violation of clients' rights and their own professional standards.

Noncompliance may result from some incompatibility between agency policy and procedures and the worker's personal values or the values of his reference group.

Mrs. R.'s caseload included a black family with four children. Part of the difficulty resulted from inadequate housing and Mrs. R, was helping them to find a larger apartment. However, she avoided exploring the possibilities which might be available in a large neighborhood housing project. In discussions with the supervisor, she indicated that she felt it inadvisable for black and white families to be living together and was reluctant to help her clients move into the housing project. This was in contradiction to the nondiscriminatory policies of the agency.

A point of persistent difficulty in Mrs. L's handling of her caseload is her consistent failure to inform clients of the different kinds of services and financial help to which they might be entitled, despite the fact that the procedure calls for sharing this information. She has a strong feeling that many of the clients are getting as much, or more, than they need and sharing this information is just inviting a raid on the county treasury.

Noncompliance may result from a conflict between bureaucratic demands and casework goals as perceived by the supervisee.

Ms. B had accepted a gift from a client. Her supervisor called attention to the fact that acceptance of gifts from clients was not in accordance with agency policy. Ms. B. said, in response, that she was aware of this but felt that if she had not accepted the gift the client would feel that she was rejecting her. She had accepted because this helped strengthen the relationship.

In general terms, this is the classic conflict between the bureaucratic orientation and the service orientation.

Workers may decide that some actions need to be taken in behalf of service to the client, even though the actions conflict with agency policy. In this sense, noncompliance comes close to innovation, permitting individualization of agency policy and enabling the agency to serve the client more effectively. It illustrates the fact that noncompliance may be functional.

Such noncompliance was noted by a participant observation researcher in a British social agency:

> Sometimes social workers found themselves in a situation of conflicting loyalties, particularly when a client was in conflict, or potential conflict, with authority—usually doing something that was illegal or which involved deception of some kind. Examples of this were dealing in stolen goods, taking drugs, "fiddling" with the gas meter, or withholding information about earnings from DHSS. Social workers, as part of "the authorities" themselves, felt that they were, at least in principle, expected to be on the side of respectability and observance of the law. But they also felt that their relationship to the client necessitated loyalty to him or her. In this situation there was a range of strategies that social workers could adopt. They could, first of all, avoid knowing about the client's deviant behaviour. Sometimes social workers confided in their colleagues that they suspected that Mrs. X was on drugs, or Mrs. Y had a cohabitee, but would not discuss this with the client concerned. Often clients played along with this, and withheld information from the social worker about some of their activities. Thus. Mrs. J only told her social worker that she was on drugs when the police had raided her flat and she was about to appear in court.
>
> Second, the social worker might know what was going on, but maintain a neutral attitude in relation to the client, neither encouraging the deviant behaviour nor informing the relevant authorities.
>
> Social workers might, on the other hand, side with the client secretly, so long as the conflict did not come out into the open. They might, for instance, encourage the client to earn extra money and not notify the DHSS. For some social workers, being "in on" the deviant act was to them a token of being trusted, which they valued for its own sake. (Satyamurti 1981:160)

A clear majority of the sixty-five social workers Pearson (1975) interviewed in a study of industrial deviance in a social agency admitted complicity in such acts of client violation of rules and procedures of the agency.

Pawlak (1976) reports a similar kind of tinkering with the system on the part of the worker.

A survey study of 1,300 workers in a state department of public welfare found that "more than two-thirds of the workers reported they bent, ignored, conveniently forgot or otherwise subverted departmental rules" (O'Connor and Spence 1976:178; see also Weatherly 1980).

Such noncompliance may be a necessary and useful expedient in dealing with conflicting and irreconcilable demands. The worker, subjected to the pressure of client needs in the context of bureaucratic rules and procedures that make difficult the satisfaction of such needs, bends or breaks the rules. In such instances supervisors often tolerate or ignore nonconformity (Jacobs 1969).

Green (1966) points out that the pull toward overidentification of social workers with the client is likely to be greatest in large, highly bureaucratic organizations. The client is often a victim of the same bureaucracy. "Thus the social work victim unconsciously identifies with the client victim" (Green 1966:75). This leads to the temptation to make an alliance with the client against agency regulations and procedures, resulting in noncompliance with agency policy.

Noncompliance may result from the fact that the supervisee is subject to a variety of pressures from the client and is dependent on the client for psychic gratification. In this sense the client has power over the supervisee that may force him or her to act in contravention to agency policy. Supervisees are subject to rewards from clients, such as expressions of gratification, praise, affection, and friendship. They are also subject to punishments from clients, such as expressions of aggression, hostility, and deprecation. Supervisees would like to be told that they have been helpful to the family, that they are loved for it, and that they are wonderful people; supervisees tend to avoid taking action that might result in the client's telling them, for instance, that they are "stupid bastards who never did know what it was all about and have never been of much help to anybody." Noncompliance may then follow from supervisees being pressured by the client to do what the client wants them to do, not what the agency or their professional conscience dictates as necessary and desirable. A supervisee in protective service writes:

> The agency is reasonably clear as to the circumstances which require initiating a petition for removal of the child. Of course, only the worker knows the specifics of a particular case so a lot depends on the worker's discretion. But in this instance of a black four-year-old boy in the home of a single-parent TANF [Temporary Assistance for Needy Families] family, I really knew the

kid was being abused. Yet whenever I even hinted at starting procedures to remove the child, which is what I should have done according to agency policy, the mother began to get hostile and abusive, accusing me of being a "meddling white racist." She knew how to manipulate me, making me feel anxious, guilty, and uncertain. I could, of course, have discussed this with my supervisor but I was afraid that it would end in a firm decision to remove the child and, given the control this mother had, I did not want to have to fight with her in implementing such a decision.

Supervisee noncompliance may be prompted by a desire to make the job easier, less boring, or more satisfying. Noncompliance is, in such instances, a response to the worker's effort to "increase his own power and status and freedom and security while shedding uncongenial work and unwelcome responsibilities" (Jay 1967:89). These are the pragmatic rewards of noncompliance. As Levy notes in discussing the activities of some workers in a county welfare department,

> employees begin to identify with and work within the logic of the "system." This entails the playing of a highly elaborate game in which the general idea is to make one's job as easy as possible through meeting enough statistical requirements to keep administrators and supervisors off one's back, doing just enough for clients so [one] won't be bothered by them and keeping [one's] caseload as low as possible by "transferring out" as many cases as possible and accepting as few as [one] can. (1970:172)

Noncompliance may result from the effort to cope with the requirements and stress of the work. It may be an expedient adaptation in managing the work to get it done with the least possible harm to the client and reduced discomfort and increased satisfaction to the worker. The nature of the work and the stringent constraints that limit the ability to be of help pressures direct service workers to adopt such expedients in implementing their jobs. Noncompliance or modified compliance may then be seen to be the direct service worker's response to the problems the job poses. A supervisee writes:

> After a time you get to be self-protective. You learn how to "manage" the clients so that they impose less of a burden. I remember one case of a middle-aged woman in marital counseling. She was very dependent, talked incessantly, and called me continually. Even though I recognized it was part of the service, I always "arranged" to be going out if she caught me in. She gradually got the message, "Don't call us, we'll call you."

A supervisee in corrections writes:

> There are a number of different circumstances which require revocation of parole. But that's a lot of extra work and a lot of harder work because it means a big hassle with the parolee. Okay, if something is very serious you play it according to the regulations. But if it is something ambiguous and you figure that even if something happens you can justify not having revoked parole, you figure, "To hell with the regulations, why bust your ass?"

Noncompliance may be due to psychological considerations, as in the case of the worker who fails to turn in a sufficiently detailed record because of anxiety regarding self-exposure. Similarly, noncompliance may relate to developmental experiences. A supervisor writes:

> I had a twenty-five-year-old worker who seemed unable to follow rules. When she first came to the unit, she seemed bright, eager, and intelligent. I was aware her father was a judge in a small town in another state. I did not realize how this was affecting her until several months passed. She never let me know, through "out" slips, where she might be in case of emergency. One day she was needed for an emergency, had not left an "out" slip or any word of where she might be located. I kept going to her office and asking other workers if they had seen her. Finally, she came bursting into my office where my secretary and another worker were and started blasting me. I stated, "Just a minute, young lady." The two people in my office quickly left. I pointed out to her that certain rules and regulations are necessary for running our unit efficiently and why I had been requesting "out" slips from her. What I had failed to realize was that her actions were those of an adolescent, that she still was rebellious and was projecting some of her own rebellion toward her father (an authoritarian figure in two ways—father and judge) on me and the department (the "System").

The supervisor, of course, is making a speculative inference that needs confirmation in discussions with the supervisee. If confirmed, the incident illustrated noncompliance based on personal developmental problems.

Noncompliance may also be an act of hostility toward the supervisor or the agency he or she represents, as when the worker deliberately fails to implement agency policies or procedures as an act of defiance. There is personal satisfaction in such covert manifestations of hostility.

Noncompliance may be a deliberate act of defiance in a conscious effort to call attention to policies that need to be changed. In such cases the worker is pointing to the need for change by challenging the system (Merton 1957:360).

Noncompliance may be a response to real dangers encountered on the job. The worker, often a young, white woman, in many instances is obliged to go into apartment buildings in areas characterized by high rates of crime. Social workers have, in fact, been mugged, assaulted, and molested during the course of their work. As a result there is considerable anxiety, and visits to clients may be resisted and not scheduled (Mayer and Rosenblatt 1975a).

Monitoring Noncompliance: Supervisor Responsibility

Understanding the worker's behavior is not the same as excusing it. Even though there may be understandable reasons for noncompliant behavior, clients are still harmed as a result, and the agency's objectives are not implemented. Being "therapeutic" to workers in permitting them to continue to operate contrary to agency policy may be antitherapeutic to the clients.

From an ethical perspective, supervisors are in a defensible position in requiring workers to do what the agency asks of them and in enforcing agency policy, rules, and procedures. The Milford Conference Report early emphasized the professional obligation of the worker to adhere "to the policies and regulations of the organization. . . . Policies once adopted by an agency are binding upon its entire personnel" (1929:53–54). The NASW Code of Ethics (1999) states that the social worker should adhere to commitments made to the employing agency. Levy (1982:48, 50) notes that "the very acceptance of employment in a social organization constitutes, in itself, a promise of loyalty to the organization and devotion to its purpose and function . . . whatever procedures have been defined for accomplishing the work of the social organization nonadministrative staff are obliged to follow."

Compton and Galaway (1975) strongly support this obligation. They clearly state that they do not believe that a "worker who accepts a position as a member of an agency—and who utilizes agency resources—can act as though he were a private practitioner. As a staff member, the worker is bound by the policies of the agency" (Compton and Galaway 1975:481). Of course, "loyalty and devotion to the employing organization is neither absolute nor infinite" (Levy 1982:48). Opposition to and deviance from agency policy may be ethically required where clients are harmed by policy and the policy itself is unethical. Deviation is then justified on the grounds of superseding values.

The profession of social work and the community has looked to the supervisor as the first line of defense in behalf of the client, the agency, and the community in responding to worker behavior that might represent a danger to the client, agency, or community. This charge is embodied in the monitoring, review, and evaluative functions of administrative supervision. When the supervisor has failed—either because of ideological hesitancy, incompetence, or indifference in implementing the functions of administrative supervision—the community has imposed external review-control procedures on the agency.

The child welfare services system reflects the consequences of such failure. Widespread criticism was directed against foster care throughout the 1960s and 1970s. It was said that children were unjustifiably placed and replaced, that children were lost in a system insufficiently and carelessly monitored, and that damage was done to children who lived for long periods of time in limbo because of failure to review their situation. In the drive to achieve "permanence for children" as early as possible, procedures were developed outside the agency—in court review of placements and in citizen review boards.

In many states, Juvenile and Domestic Relations Courts are authorized to review child welfare cases to determine whether the worker's decision is in the child's best interest; this in effect is judiciary supervision of the agency's work. Citizen review boards are authorized to monitor and review the worker's activities to determine, among other things, what efforts have been made to carry out permanent placement plans for a child and make recommendations about actions that might be taken (Conte et al. 1981).

By 1980 there was, in most states, monitoring and review by some external agency of the decisions and the work of the direct service child-welfare social worker. The ultimate explanation of and justification for such procedures was the perceived failure of the internal agency monitoring and review system—a failure of agency supervision.

The fact that citizen review boards, generally consisting of volunteers, have been legally authorized and established in a number of states to assess the performance of direct service workers and recommend changes in service intervention is a testimonial to the perceived failure of supervisors, who initially had this review responsibility (Conte et al. 1981). It is clear that if first-line supervisors inadequately review and monitor the work of their supervisees, others outside the profession will take over a measure of this responsibility.

A more committed adherence to the implementation of the essential functions of administrative supervision may help to modify the stereotypical perceptions of "policy makers, governmental executives, and top level agency managers" as well as the public "that somehow social work is antithetical to good management." The training and personal predispositions of social workers, in this view, "make them ill-suited for managerial positions that require, among other things, rational analysis, a willingness to ferret out inefficient practices and force compliance with policies and procedures" (Patti 1984:25).

Taking Disciplinary Action

It needs to be noted that most workers on most occasions do conscientiously comply with agency policies, rules, and procedures. Noncompliance is the exception. However, the limited number of exceptions give the supervisor a maximum amount of difficulty. A disproportionate amount of time and psychic energy needs to be devoted to the few workers who frequently are noncompliant.

The supervisor in the role as protector of agency policies, rules, standards, and procedures may have to get supervisees to do some things or stop doing some things in some particular way. The supervisor may find him- or herself in a position in which sanctions must be employed to obtain compliance with agency policy, rules, and procedures, in which the supervisor has to take corrective action. Supervisors face situations in which workers consistently fail to get work done on time; are consistently late or absent; fail to turn in reports; complete forms carelessly; conspicuously loaf on the job; disrupt the work of others by excessive gossiping; are careless with agency cars or equipment; are inconsiderate, insulting, or disrespectful to clients; or fail to keep appointments with personnel of cooperating agencies and services.

Such situations should not be permitted to develop unchecked. If a worker, aware of agency requirements, chooses to violate them, the supervisor has little choice but to engage in some form of discipline. There generally are prior indications of resistance or opposition to compliance. If earlier manifestations have been ignored, if the supervisor "looks the other way," it becomes progressively more difficult to take action when it can no longer be avoided. The supervisee can rightly claim that the supervisor has been remiss in never having earlier discussed the behavior he or she now wants stopped. The supervisor's effectiveness in dealing with the situation is reduced by feelings of guilt and defensiveness. A supervisor writes:

> In our last conference of the year, I hesitantly raised the question of B's persistent lateness to meetings and conferences. I had been aware of this failure on her part, but for a variety of reasons, had overlooked dealing with this directly. At this time, my opening this issue resulted in [B's] unburdening herself of a number of severe personal and family problems. I dealt with these as appropriately as possible, but referred back to the lateness, etc. B acknowledged her discomfort with her behavior, but felt she had not been sure about my expectations because I had not previously made an issue of this. I agreed

. . . and we ended with some appreciation for not having completely over-looked an important part of her development. The timing was unfortunate, in that this problem should have been dealt with much earlier in the year for it seemed to be symptomatically tied to important personal blockings that were interfering with [B's] development. Perhaps my "better late than never" behavior was similar to what she had been doing all year!

The supervisor should discuss in private any problem that calls for a reprimand. To criticize a worker in front of his or her colleagues and peers makes it more difficult to help him or her change the behavior. One supervisee writes that she was late in submitting a monthly statistical report:

The supervisor, meeting me in the hall, loudly reprimanded me in the presence of other workers and threatened to put my report-lateness in his evaluation. The supervisor returned to his office without giving me a chance to reply. The supervisor had a chance to release his anger but he was unsuccessful in getting my report in any sooner. I was sore. He publicly called attention to what I had done. It was nobody else's business. He never gave me a chance to explain—or even asked for an explanation.

A reprimand is also best delivered at a time when the supervisor is not upset about the incident. These last two suggestions, which require delay, contradict a third suggestion: that a discussion of the incident should take place as soon as possible after it occurs. However, they can be reconciled by noting that although a delay is desirable for cooling off and for provision of privacy, the delay should be as short as possible.

In what follows, a supervisor takes peremptory but necessary action in dealing with noncompliance. The context is a probation and parole office.

I happened to be passing by Helen's door as a client was leaving and overheard her say that he shouldn't worry about completing auto operation and permission forms (an agency requirement) because "they weren't that important." I felt upset that she was cooperating with a client to decrease compliance with important agency regulations. I asked that she meet with me and asked if her client had secured a car, if she had seen proof of a driver's license, insurance, and really thought about giving him permission to drive? I was being accusatory and Helen stated that it was stupid that a grown man should have to have our permission to own and operate his own car. I suggested that perhaps she wasn't aware that without completing the procedures with the required proof, if he committed another offense in which the vehicle was used, the agency would be accountable—that if he were stopped without a permission form he would be taken to jail. It became more of a rebuking lecture than I meant it to be. She said that she wasn't aware of all of this (another failure on my part) and thought that it was just a repressive measure to keep the clients under control. I left her office with the comment that the forms must be completed (an order), that they protected the agency, the client, the community, her, and myself.

The best approach is one which communicates concern for the supervisee, a willingness to listen to his explanation of what happened, a desire to understand how he sees the situation, and a readiness to help him change. The emphasis is on a change of behavior so as to increase the agency's effectiveness of service rather than on the apprehension and punishment of noncompliance. If the supervisor perceives noncompliance as a threat or an act of hostility, any discussion of the incident is apt to be emotionally charged. Regarding it as a learning opportunity for the worker or as an opportunity for improving the supervisor-supervisee relationship generates a different, more positive attitude.

The objective of such supervisory intervention is preventative and corrective rather than punitive. In reprimanding, the supervisor must be impersonal, specific as to the facts, and consistent in approach. The supervisor needs to be aware that in disciplining one he or she is disciplining all. Supervisor behavior manifested in dealing with one supervisee in a disciplinary action will affect the reactions of all supervisees.

Discipline effectively requires some confidence on the part of the supervisor in the correctness of what he or she is doing, a lack of defensiveness, and an ability to control the interaction calmly. The supervisor should make some record of the incident so that if there is a recurrence and more severe sanctions need to be employed, they can be justified by the record. There is a series of actions the supervisor might take, graded in terms of increasing severity. The first is a joint review of the situation by supervisor and supervisee. The supervisor can offer the worker a warning, followed with a verbal reprimand if the behavior continues. This might be followed by a written reprimand placed in the record, a lower-than-average evaluation rating, suspension for a limited period, demotion, and, ultimately, dismissal.

Serious disciplinary action, such as suspension without pay for a period of time, demotion, or firing, requires documentation. Such action will in all probability require a defense in response to a grievance procedure currently operative in most agencies, particularly those under civil service or union contracts.

If individual noncompliance is not effectively dealt with at the supervisory level, the administration may make it a matter for agency policy decision making. Such matters, when made agency policy, reduce flexibility at the direct service level. All the workers then suffer from some reduction in autonomy as a result of the dereliction in compliance by a few workers. Because of the possibility of such an eventuality, workers tend to support supervisors in their efforts to obtain compliance.

However infrequent termination might be, it is a necessary option in the case of a supervisee whose work is clearly inadequate, clearly unethical, or in consistent clear violation of agency procedures (Rivas 1984). The supervisor is generally the agency functionary who is allocated dismissal responsibilities.

Summary

This chapter reviewed some of the significant problems in implementing administrative supervision. The supervisor is responsible for the actions of her supervisees in accordance with the principles of vicarious liability and *respondeat superiore*. The supervisor is granted a measure of authority and power by agency administration in support of this ultimate responsibility. *Authority* was defined as the legitimation of the use of power. *Power* was defined as the ability to implement the right of authority. Five sources of power were discussed: reward, coercive, positional, referent, and expertise. A further distinction was made between functional power (relating to the personal attributes of the supervisor) and formal power (inherent in the position of supervisor).

The supervisor needs to come to terms with the delegation of authority and power. Power and authority should be used only when necessary to help achieve the objectives of the organization in a flexible, impartial manner and with a sensitive regard for worker response.

Despite the grant of authority, supervisors are reluctant to actively employ their power. Power and authority are further eroded by the nature of social work tasks and by the countervailing power of supervisees. As a consequence of the reluctant and difficult utilization of supervisory power, external sources of control have been developed, particularly in child welfare.

In implementing the functions of administrative supervision the supervisor needs some appreciation of the utility of rules and an understanding of the factors relating to noncompliance. The process of disciplining workers for noncompliant behavior was reviewed.

4 | Educational Supervision: Definition, Differentiation, Content, and Process

Educational supervision is the second principal responsibility of the supervisor. Educational supervision is concerned with teaching the worker what he or she needs to know to do the job and helping him or her learn it. Every job description of the supervisor's position includes a listing of this function: "instruct workers in effective social work techniques"; "develop staff competence through individual and group conferences"; or "train and instruct staff in job performance."

Studies of functions that supervisors identified as those they performed included such educational activities as teaching, facilitating learning, training, sharing experience and knowledge, informing, clarifying, guiding, helping workers find solutions, enhancing professional growth, advising, suggesting, and helping workers solve problems.

Educational supervision is concerned with teaching the knowledge, skills, and attitudes necessary for the performance of clinical social work tasks through the detailed analysis of the worker's interaction with the client. In the general literature on supervision, this function is more frequently identified as *clinical* supervision. The standard definition of clinical supervision is that of a situation in which a more experienced professional oversees the work of a less experienced professional with the objective of helping that person develop greater adequacy in professional performance. We have used the term *educational supervision* rather than clinical supervision here and throughout the text because we see it as the less ambiguous term.

Educational Supervision Distinguished from In-Service Training and Staff Development

We noted earlier that one of the singular aspects of social work is that a very sizable percentage of agency staff comes to the job without prior training. There is also considerable turnover and lateral movement from agency to agency. Consequently, there is a constant need to train people to do the job of the social worker and to do the job in a particular agency. The responsibility for such training is assigned to staff-development personnel, which includes first-line supervisors when they are engaged in educational supervision.

Some distinction needs to be made between staff development, in-service training, and educational supervision (Gleeson 1992). *Staff development* refers to all of the procedures an agency might employ to enhance the job-related knowledge, skills, and attitudes of its total staff, and includes in-service training and educational supervision. Training sessions, lectures, workshops, institutes, information pamphlets, and discussion groups for caseworkers, administrators, clerical staff, and supervisors are staff-development activities.

In-service training is a more specific form of staff development. The term refers to planned, formal training provided to a delimited group of agency personnel who have the same job classification or the same job responsibilities. In-service training programs are planned on an a priori basis in terms of the general educational needs of a group of workers. The generic teaching content is applicable to all members of the group but is specifically relevant to none.

Educational supervision supplements in-service training by individualizing general learning in application to the specific performance of the individual worker. Educational supervision is a more specific kind of staff development. Training is directed to the needs of a particular worker carrying a particular caseload, encountering particular problems, and needing some individualized program of education.

In discharging the responsibilities of educational supervision, the supervisor helps the worker implement and apply the more general learning provided through the in-service training program. He or she teaches "the worker what he needs to know to give specific service to specific clients" (Bell n.d.:15) and helps the worker make the transition from knowing to doing. In-service training and educational supervision complement each other. The supervisor will reinforce, individualize, and demonstrate the applicability of the more general content taught in planned, formal in-service training sessions (Meyer 1966).

In-service training is context-free and concerned with practice in general; educational supervision is context-bound and concerned with practice in specific situations. Educational supervision provides personalized learning concerned with the supervisee's assigned tasks.

Significance of Educational Supervision

The need for educational supervision in response to the lack of previous training of public agency social workers is noted in two different national studies of children's services made at two different periods. In the earlier study, Children's Bureau (1976:72) noted that "often the first line supervisor is practically the only source of in-service training." The second study indicated that the largest percentage of the caseworkers (75 percent) "were dependent on in-service training and supervision to acquire the knowledge and skill needed for the work" (Shyne 1980:31).

A study of the sources of knowledge social workers actually use in practice by Demartini and Whitbeck (1987) once again empirically confirms the crucial importance of supervision. Questionnaires returned from ninety master's of social work (MSW) direct service workers indicated that supervision was cited as the principal source of knowledge for practice, in terms of frequency of use as well as importance to practice of such knowledge. Education for social work provided the general framework of the knowledge needed for practice. But supervisors, along with on-the-job experience, on-the-job training, and colleagues provided the instrumental translation of the general knowledge to the specific requirements of the tasks workers performed. Supervision was noted as more important than graduate training in determining the actual use of knowledge. Interviews with supervisors and supervisees found that "good teaching/instruction" was associated with effective supervision; "It included processes involved in the teaching and learning connected with becoming a competent clinician" (Henderson, Cawyer, and Watkins 1999:67).

Educational supervision is a very significant dimension of the supervisor's activities and responsibilities. Two of the three strongest sources of satisfaction for supervisors are "satisfaction in helping the supervisee grow and develop as a professional" and "satisfaction in sharing social work knowledge and skills with supervisees." Two of the three main sources of supervisee satisfaction with supervision are related to educational supervision: "my supervisor helps me in dealing with problems in my work with clients" and "my supervisor helps me in my development as a professional social worker." In addition both supervisors and supervisees agreed that "ensuring the professional developments of the supervisee" was one of the two most important objectives of supervision (Kadushin 1974, 1990). Summarizing studies of ineffective supervision, Watkins (1997:166) found that "failure to teach or instruct" was consistently identified as among the negative aspects of poor supervision.

Conversely, when supervision fails, the failures are most keenly felt in the area of educational supervision. Two major sources of dissatisfaction expressed by supervisees relate to this function: "my supervisor is not sufficiently critical of my work so that I don't know what I am doing wrong or what needs changing" and "my supervisor does not provide much real help in dealing with problems I face with my clients" (Kadushin 1974, 1990).

Shulman (1982) studied the reports from both supervisees and supervisors regarding the actual functions the supervisors were perceived to perform and their preferred functions. Both groups indicated that a considerable amount of the supervisor's time was spent in teaching-consulting. Furthermore, the "largest increase of preferred to actual time spent" indicated by both supervisors and supervisees involved increased time in "teaching practice skills" (Shulman 1982:22–23). Although case consultation occupied only 40 percent of time on the job for a sample of sixty-eight social work supervisors examined by Shulman (1993), interacting with supervisees in case consultation was their most satisfying duty. Finally, an experiment that increased by one weekly hour the amount of time a supervisor and his or her supervisees dedicated to the discussion of cases produced substantive improvements in client satisfaction (Harkness and Hensley 1991).

Relation of Educational Supervision to Administrative Supervision

Administrative supervision and educational supervision share the same ultimate objective: to provide the best possible service to the clients. Administrative supervision provides the organizational structure and the resources directed toward this goal; educational supervision provides the training that enables workers to achieve it. Although complementary, administrative and educational supervision are independent. In their factor analysis of supervisory practice across a wide range of human service organizations in Israel, Erera and Lazar (1994a) found that the functions of administrative and educational supervision were empirically discrete.

Administrative supervision is concerned with structuring the work environment and providing the resources that enable workers to perform their jobs effectively. Educational supervision provides the knowledge and instrumental skills that are the workers' necessary equipment for effective practice. Administrative supervision serves the needs of the organizational bureaucracy; educational supervision serves the needs of the profession in developing competent, professionally orientated practitioners. If administrative supervision requires that the supervisor have managerial skills, educational supervision requires technical and pedagogical skills and, looking ahead, supportive supervision requires human relations skills.

Educational and administrative supervision also reinforce each other. Educational supervision is designed to increase the effectiveness of administrative supervision. As a consequence of educational supervision the tasks of administrative supervision are alternatively implemented. "Training and guided experience [take] the place of detailed and close supervision as a means of accomplishing the same control functions" (Olmstead 1973:90). With more education, workers can act more autonomously and independently, reducing the burden of administrative supervision.

Attitudes of commitment and loyalty to agency values, aims, and procedures are developed through educational supervision. If the agency can indoctrinate workers with a personal interest in doing what the agency wants done in the way the agency wants it done and toward objectives the agency wants to achieve, the agency will be less hesitant to delegate authority for autonomous performance. Educational supervision provides administrative controls through a process of helping the worker internalize such controls.

Educational supervision involves the communication of a belief system that has as one of its tenets the legitimation of the agency's authority structure. Such socialization has as one of its aims the "engineering of consent," so that ultimately the supervisee voluntarily endorses the legitimacy of the supervisor's positional authority.

Simon cogently summarizes the relationship between the functions of educational and administrative supervision:

> Training influences decisions "from the inside out." That is, training prepares the organization member to reach satisfactory decisions himself without the need for the constant exercise of authority or advice. In this sense training procedures are alternatives to the exercise of authority or advice as means of control over the subordinate's decision. . . . It may be possible to minimize or even dispense with certain review processes by giving the subordinates training that enables them to perform their work with less supervision. Training may supply the trainee with the facts necessary in dealing with these

decisions, it may provide him with a frame of reference for his thinking; it may teach him "approved" decisions: or it may indoctrinate him with the values in terms of which his decisions are to be made. (Simon 1957:15–16)

Social work recruits from a wide variety of backgrounds and with different sets of experiences, having learned the language and mind-set of different academic disciplines, need to be educated to a common frame of reference, a common view of agency objectives, and a uniform commitment to common goals. Unless differences can be reduced, there is little possibility of having a staff operating in some consistent manner. One of the educational tasks of supervision is to help the worker accept the frame of reference, point of view, and objectives to which other workers in the agency subscribe and that guides their actions and behavior.

Though the organization's control apparatus, manifested in administrative supervision, exerts an external pressure encouraging workers to conform to agency policies and procedures, educational supervision ultimately results in an internalization of such influence efforts. Both administrative and educational supervision are directed toward changing worker behavior in the direction necessary for effective performance as an agency worker. The achievement of this objective in moving from administrative supervision to educational supervision is the shift from direction by the supervisor to self-direction by the supervisee.

Professional socialization involves the reduction of idiosyncrasy. Lay attitudes and approaches to problems are diverse; professional approaches tend to be more homogeneous. Professional socialization involves taking on a professional identity and a special outlook regarding one's work, which is shared with colleagues. Educational supervision is the context for role transition from layperson to professional, providing the supervisee with this sense of occupational identity.

Because administrative supervision and educational supervision provide alternative procedures for control of workers' performance, more of one requires less of the other. Hall concluded from a study of the relationship of bureaucracy and professionalism in a number of different professions, including social work, that "an equilibrium may exist between the levels of professionalization and bureaucratization in the sense that a particular level of professionalization may require a certain level of bureaucratization to maintain social control" (Hall 1968:104). Higher levels of professionalization were associated with lower levels of bureaucratization. Similarly, Hage and Aiken, in a study of sixteen social welfare and health agencies, found that "close supervision is less likely when members of an organization . . . have been professionally trained" (1967:90).

Development of knowledge and skills, as a consequence of educational supervision, permits relaxation of administrative controls. Not only will the worker feel a personal obligation to do a good job, he or she will have the necessary competence and capability to do so.

Educational supervision permits smoother administrative coordination and more effective communication. Having learned how the agency operates, and what the functions of other people are in the agency, the worker can coordinate his own work with others. Having learned the specialized language of the agency and the profession, the worker can communicate with colleagues with fewer risks of misunderstanding. The shared "universe of discourse" aids communication. Making decisions on the basis of mutually shared values, presuppositions, and knowledge increases the predictability of the workers' actions. This is achieved as a consequence of the fact that educational supervision provides, in effect, a socialization experience acculturating the supervisee to the culture of the social work profession. "The supervisee is socialized in the language of therapeutic discourse, value orientation, and modes of thinking and problem solving that are characteristic of the profession" (O'Bryne and Rosenberg 1998:46). Thinking in a way that is similar to the thinking of their fellow professionals, they are likely to come to the same conclusions independently. Homogeneity of thinking among fellow agency workers makes it easier to coordinate the work of different groups in the agency.

Education of the supervisee to the consensus of values, uniformity of perspectives, and standardization of language shared by other workers in the agency reduces the likelihood of intra-agency conflict while increasing the level of intra-agency cooperation.

As a result of educational supervision, the worker is in a better position to evaluate his or her own performance. The worker learns the difference between good and poor practice and has some criteria by which he or she can be self-critical. Thus the administrative supervisory functions of control, coordination, communications, cooperation, and evaluation are all made easier as a consequence of educational supervision. Despite these elements of complementarity between educational and administrative supervision, there are aspects of incompatibility as well (Erera and Lazar 1994b).

Content in Educational Supervision

Any delineation of the content of supervisory teaching necessarily has to be general. An overview of supervision, such as this book, is directed toward workers in many different kinds of agencies who must learn different kinds of content to do their jobs well. However, because all social work agencies have elements in common, there are certain uniformities in what needs to be taught. The following discussion of the basic content of educational supervision is derived from material developed by Helen Harris Perlman. Perlman (1947) points out that what every social worker needs to know is concerned with people, problems, place, and process—the four *p*'s. To this might be added a fifth *p*—personnel, the person of the worker offering the service.

The nuclear situation for all of social work is that of a client (individual, family, group, or community—*people*) with a *problem* in social functioning coming, or referred, to a social agency (*place*) for help (*process*) by a social worker (*personnel*).

Supervisors in every social agency will be teaching something about each of these five content areas. However diverse the specifics of people, place, process, problems, and personnel, these will be matters for the agenda of educational supervision (Holloway 1995). Despite differences in specifics, in each instance there is a particular group of people, either an individual or collectivity, presenting a particular kind of social problem, seeking help from a social worker who is affiliated with a particular social agency and offers some particular approach to helping. The worker, to perform the job effectively, would need to know about the process by which he hopes to help, about the agency through which he is offering such help, about the people with whom he will be working, about the problems they present, and about himself as the principal instrumentality for helping.

For each of these content areas—people, problem, place, process, and personnel—there are objectives in terms of knowledge, attitudes, and skills.

However diverse the agency, the supervisor has to teach something about how this particular agency (place) is organized and administered, how it relates to other agencies and fits into the total network of community social services, what the agency's objectives are, what kind of services it offers and under what conditions, how agency policy is formulated and can be changed, and the nature of the agency's statutory authority. Knowledge of place (agency) also includes a knowledge of the community of social agencies in the area with which the agency is related, as well as the geographical community in which the agency is embedded. Systems knowledge is critical for social work practice with HIV-infected persons in medical settings (Itzhaky and Atzman 1999), for example.

However diverse the social problems with which different agencies are concerned, the supervisor will have to teach something about the causes of social problems, community response to particular social problems, the psychosocial nature of these problems, the impact of social problems on different groups in the community, the effect of a particular problem on social workers' and people's lives, and the relationship of agency services to the social problems that are of primary concern to the agency's mandate. This may be nowhere more evident than in the supervision of child protective work (Rushton and Nathan 1996).

However diverse the clientele served, the supervisor will have to teach something of human behavior in response to the stress of the social problems faced by these particular clients. Although the casework supervisor might be primarily concerned with teaching how individuals and families respond and adjust to social problems, the group work supervisor and community organization supervisor might be more concerned with teaching how people in collectivities (such as groups and communities) behave in responding to social problems. For the supervisee to understand problematic individual and collective responses to social stress, the supervisor needs to teach something of "normal" individual and collective development and behavior.

Whatever the processes employed in helping the client to a restoration of a more effective level of social functioning or ameliorating or preventing social dysfunction, the supervisor will have to teach something of the technology of helping. In medical settings, for example, the technology of social work practice far exceeds what students typically learn in graduate school (Berkman et al. 1996). This, in the end, is where everything gets put together. Knowledge about people, problem, and place is taught because ultimately it enables the worker to help more effectively. The supervisor has to teach what the worker is to do, how he or she is to act if he or she is to help individuals, groups, or communities deal effectively with their social problems. The supervisor has to teach something of the theory that explains why the particular helping technology the agency espouses (whatever it is) is likely to effect change.

In any agency, no matter what the methodology for helping, the supervisor teaches something of the sequential nature of the helping process. It is described in a variety of ways: social study, diagnosis, treatment, data gathering, data processing, intervention, obtaining information, processing information, and exerting social influence. All of these descriptions, however diverse, imply a process of remedial action based on understanding derived from the facts.

The supervisor further has to educate the worker (personnel) toward the development of professional identity. This includes helping the worker develop those attitudes, feelings, and behaviors that initiate, enhance, and maintain effective helping relationships with clients. This means revising prejudiced and stereotyped ageist, racist, sexist, and homophobic attitudes, education toward acceptance of social work values regarding self-determination, confidentiality, and nonjudgmental respect. In effect, this is socialization to the frame of reference and ethos of the profession.

People are, of course, not helped by a social agency in dealing with problems of social functioning but by social workers representing the agency. Furthermore, the principal instrumentality for helping is generally the social worker him- or herself. There are social utilities administered by social workers that are essential resources for helping, such as homemaker service, foster care, institutional care, day care, and grants of income. Most frequently, however, the principal resource the agency makes available in the process of helping people is the skill and competence of the worker. It is the social worker who leads the group, organizes the community, acts as advocate, supports, sustains, clarifies, offers him- or herself as a model for identification, rewards and shapes behavior, and so on. In social work, where the worker is the main instrumentality, the person of the worker determines what is done and how it is done.

Because the worker's personality and behavior are significant determinants of what happens in the worker-client interaction, the supervisee him- or herself and his or her attitudes, feelings, and behavior become a necessary and inevitable subject of educational supervision. The aim is to develop a greater measure of self-awareness in the worker so that he or she can act in a deliberate, disciplined, consciously directed manner in the worker-client interaction so as to be optimally helpful to the client. The capacity to perceive one's behavior as objectively as possible and to have free access to one's own feelings without undue guilt, embarrassment, or discomfort is a necessary prerequisite (if not sufficient in itself) for the controlled subjectivity the helping process demands. The freedom to use feelings imaginatively and creatively for helping also requires considerable self-awareness.

Nathanson defines *self-awareness* as "the capacity of an individual to perceive his responses to other persons and situations realistically and to understand how others view him" (1964:32). Grossbard (1954:381) notes that "broadly speaking, self-awareness is a person's ability to recognize with a reasonable degree of accuracy how he reacts to the outside world and how the outside world reacts to him." Self-awareness is central to the social worker's professional development (Stoltenberg and McNeill 1997).

Self-awareness involves the objectification of self. The self examines itself. Developing self-awareness is an exercise in self-reflection in which the self is the object of attention, study, and examination. Educational supervision needs to be concerned with the purposeful, consciously directed use of the professional self, which requires self-awareness as a necessary prerequisite.

Developing a high level of worker self-awareness is further necessary because the social problems that are the professional concerns of the worker also affect him or her personally. Here, unlike the situation in many other professions, there is considerable interplay between life and work. The worker may be involved, to some extent, in many of the kinds of problems encountered by the client—parent-child conflict, aging, marital conflict, deviance, illness, financial problems, death. "Living on a job that is so closely allied to life itself makes separation of work from other areas of life exceptionally difficult. Since, in social work, the work task and living are often simultaneously experienced, anxiety is greater than in many other fields of endeavor" (Babcock 1953:417).

Education toward a greater development of self-awareness permits the worker to think objectively about these matters. It provides a greater assurance that the worker's personal reactions to these professional problems will not adversely contaminate the helping relationship. One worker in a mental health clinic says:

> I have always been uneasy with clients about anything that has to do with money. In my family money was never discussed. It was a secretive thing, I see this affecting my work now. I was never comfortable asking my parents about their financial situation, and there is a twinge of uncomfortableness when I ask my clients. Because it was not normal to talk finances in my family, it is difficult for me to discuss it in a casual way with my clients. This is problematic, because the more anxious I am about it, the more anxious they will be. Ah, a new discovery in self-awareness.

In the following brief excerpt, the worker is talking to the supervisor about a twelve-year-old girl named Thelma. The youngster is described by the worker as provocative, snide, impudent, and upsetting. She teases adults, including the supervisee.

> As the [worker] talked about Thelma's behavior and described it in some detail in response to my questioning, she suddenly looked as though a thought had struck her and said, "You know, I was very much like her when I was her age." The [worker] went on to describe how she had taunted a Junior High School teacher with certain remarks, daring the teacher to punish her. I felt that the worker was really working on something and confined myself to listening and encouraging her to speak, with an occasional comment. (Gladstone 1967:11)

Awareness of similar life experiences permits the worker to understand the client's behavior.

A somewhat different group of problems relating to educational supervision also calls for developing self-awareness. Any systematic educational program is in essence a program of planned change, the teacher being the change agent, the learner being the target for change. Teaching involves a deliberate effort to change behavior in some selected direction. But the pressure to change, resulting from learning, generates ambivalence and resistance (Itzhaky and Aloni 1996; Itzhaky and Ribner 1998).

The particular content that needs to be learned, the attitudes that need to undergo change, sometimes result in blocks or problems in learning. We learn only what we can emotionally afford to learn. If the content to be learned threatens our self-esteem or challenges our core attitudes and beliefs, the lesson is avoided. The repertoire of maneuvers that permit us to shield ourselves from such threats includes all the mechanisms of defense. Educating toward self-awareness may help the supervisee resolve some of these resistances to learning. Persistent blocks to learning are the exception rather than the rule, however; such problems are encountered in a less intense and less pervasive form by all learners. For the reasonably mature learner the work of the ego in the service of adaptation is sufficient to counter the work of the ego in the service of defense. Learning takes place despite resistance because of the learner's need and desire to meet the demands of the job.

In a supervisory context that supports freedom and safety to do this, the healthy supervisee is open to introspective self-analysis. Introspectively examining his or her responses, the worker is in a double position—both the subject and the object of self-examination. Aware that he or she is reacting resentfully or punitively, or warmly or sympathetically to some clients; feeling intimidated or threatened or repulsed by other clients; and introspectively examining the basis for such responses helps the worker develop self-awareness. The supervisee, in applying knowledge of human behavior to him- or herself and his or her own interactions, understands this material in a more meaningful, affective way. Education in self-awareness has as one of its objectives this kind of heightened affective sensitivity.

This discussion of the justifications for concern with development of self-awareness reflects the fact that it is an important content area of educational supervision. The supervisor has the responsibility of advancing the worker's self-knowledge as well as teaching the worker about people, problems, place, and process. Apparently, social workers tend to perceive education toward self-awareness as one of the unique aspects of social work supervision. In a study that asked about factors that differentiated social work supervision, "the commonest theme expressed" by the 100 social work respondents was the following: "Because the skill to be developed is the disciplined use of self in professional relationships, supervision in casework affects personality more closely than supervision in other fields which are more dependent on objective skills" (Cruser 1958:23).

Self-awareness is a central feature in models of the development of the helping professional (Stoltenberg and McNeill 1997), and the requirement of a didactic psychoanalysis for certification as an analyst is an institutionalized testimonial to the importance of self-awareness in the people-helping professions (Baudry 1993; Brandt 1996; Pegeron 1996). The desirability of this objective of educational supervision receives support from several empirical studies of social workers, which suggests a relationship between level of self-awareness and practice competence (Bruck 1963; Charles, Gabor, and Matheson 1992; Crisp and Cooper 1998; Gray, Alperin, and Wik 1989; Greenspan et al. 1992; Knight 1996). But self-awareness by the worker of his or her contribution to the interaction does not necessarily automatically result in changes in behavior. The supervisor has to exploit self-awareness in helping the worker achieve behavior change.

An additional aspect of educational supervision that has been receiving more recognition is the need to help the supervisee develop a sensitivity to and awareness of ethnicity, gender, and sexual orientation (Beckett and Dungee-Anderson 1996; Crespi 1995; Niolon 1997; Russell and Greenhouse 1997).

The increased responsibility of supervisors to educate toward a greater knowledge and acceptance of cultural factors is related to the growing multicultural diversity of the client population as well as increased sensitivity toward discrimination related to gender and sexual orientation. Developing greater multicultural clinical competence involves education toward a recognition that culture may contribute some component to the clients' problem and that interventions to be maximally effective might need to take cultural factors into consideration. It involves helping the supervisee develop a greater consciousness of his or her own racial and gender identity and a clearer recognition of his or her own biases and prejudices (see Coleman 1999).

A male supervisee says:

I had recently become a member of a men's "consciousness-raising" group. We spent a lot of time trying to identify ways in which "macho" socialization had developed attitudes relating to oppression of women. Without realizing it, I became more solicitous, deferential, and protective in my interactions with women clients. In some dim way maybe I was trying to make up for what men had done to women or maybe to prove how enlightened I was. In any case, I had become less helpful to my women clients as a result. I became aware of this in supervision as my supervisor pointed out the differences in the way I related to women clients previously as contrasted with my more recent interactions.

A white female supervisee says:

> I was assigned to work with a black male with alcoholism. I found myself becoming uncharacteristically impatient and pushy in my interviews with him. My supervisor noted my change of tone. As we discussed this, I became more aware than I would have liked that there were some aspects of racism as well as sexism in my attitudes toward the client. I sensed that I didn't feel you could accomplish much with a black client and felt antagonistic in response to my perception of black males as being generally macho and irresponsible.

Bruss et al. report:

> One of the authors supervised a trainee who expressed openness about [gay/lesbian/bisexual] issues. However, in working with a lesbian client on relationship issues and on her partner's family's lack of comfort with their lesbian relationship, the trainee managed to avoid any discussion of sexuality or sleeping arrangements during visits with the partner's family, even when these seemed natural questions in some of the sessions. Rather than explore the client's feelings further, the trainee immediately launched into ways for the client to avoid the visit altogether. (1997:70)

Developing a heightened sense of self awareness and educating toward changes in attitudes, feelings, and behaviors has therapeutic connotations. This raises questions about possible conflicts and confusion regarding the dangers of a dual relationship—therapist and educator—involving the supervisor.

Of the considerable teaching syllabus outlined above, what content do supervisors themselves assign priority? Findings gathered from structured interviews with fifty public welfare supervisors concluded that they gave high ratings to content involving interpersonal skills—"know how to relate well, communicate, listen, interview and understand the client" (Brennan et al. 1976:20). Lowest priority was given to content "concerning the role of the social worker in relating to the community and in bringing about change in the agency" (Brennan et al. 1976:21).

Supervisees themselves see problem-solving content as important. York and Hastings (1985–1986) found that among supervisees at all levels of professional development the supervisors' work-facilitation help (shows how to improve performance; offers new ideas for solving job-related problems) was highly conducive to supervisees' satisfaction in supervision. York and Denton (1990) received questionnaire responses from ninety-three direct service workers evaluating the leadership behavior of their supervisors. The objective was to determine which supervisory behaviors were most clearly associated with a positive evaluation by the supervisee of the supervisor's job performance. The behavior that was by far most clearly associated with positive evaluations was "the supervisor communicates to his/her people what they need to know."

The educational content of supervision as actually practiced is less certain than what supervisors and supervisees prefer. In general, supervisees report that educational supervision is dominated by *practical* content that speaks to case management (Charles, Gabor, and Matheson 1992; Gray 1990; Gray, Alperin, and Wik 1989; Greenspan et al. 1992; Rogers and McDonald 1995). Some direct observations of the focus of educational supervision appear to confirm those reports (Keller et al. 1996), but others do not. In an experiment designed to increase the client focus of social work supervision in a mental health setting, for example, through direct observation Harkness and Hensley (1991) found that a supervisor and her supervisees spent 35 percent of their time discussing cases, but that otherwise little time was spent discussing cases in routine supervisory meetings. It seems safe to conclude that the content of educational supervision is variable.

The Individual Conference

The individual supervisory conference is a process with three phases. To begin the process, the supervisor structures and schedules the conference, and prepares for the meeting. In the middle phase, the supervisor adopts an orientation to the process of teaching and offers helpful feedback to the worker. The supervisor ends the conference, finally, by setting the stage for subsequent meetings.

Beginning the Conference

Structuring and Scheduling

The most frequent context for supervision is the individual conference (Gray 1990; Kadushin 1992a). It is often supplemented and sometimes replaced by such alternatives as the group conference (see chapter 9). Nevertheless the individual conference is still the principal locus of supervision; 82 percent of supervisors and supervisees indicated, in response to a questionnaire, that this was true in their experience (Kadushin 1990).

We believe that weekly individual supervision of new workers is required to balance the supervisor's duty to the organization, its staff, and its clients (Bullis 1995; Knapp and VandeCreek 1997; Rubin 1997; Saltzman and Proch 1990; Swenson 1997).

Our view is closely aligned with Scott and Farrow (1993), who argue that scheduling and keeping weekly one-hour individual conferences meets a minimum standard for the supervision of new workers. Although Barretta-Herman (1993) and Veeder (1990) discourage the individual supervision of professional social workers in the belief that close supervision erodes professional autonomy, supervisors who fail to provide adequate staff supervision may become liable for worker malpractice (Guest and Dooley 1999; Reamer 1989, 1994). Second, supervisors who fail to supervise staff adequately may be in violation of social work ethical standards (National Association of Social Workers 1999). Third, although staff may passively withhold their practice mistakes and ethical violations from the supervisor (Ladany et al. 1996), empirical evidence suggests that supervision is the prevalent mode that social workers use to resolve their ethical practice dilemmas (Landau and Baerwald 1999). Furthermore, 100 hours of supervision over a period of two years are typically required to advance social work licensure, and not more than 50 of those hours may take the form of group supervision (American Association of State Social Work Boards 1997). Empirical evidence suggests that social work supervision may affect client outcomes (Ellis and Ladany 1997; Harkness and Hensley 1991); even seasoned practitioners express a need for educational supervision (Schroffel 1998).

The individual conference is essentially a dyadic interview to fulfill the administrative, educational, and supportive functions of supervision. For educational purposes, it is an individual tutorial. Like all interviews, the individual conference requires certain formalities, structure, and differential role assignment. It should be a regularly scheduled meeting at some mutually convenient time. It should be conducted in a place that ensures privacy and protection from interruption, is physically comfortable, and is conducive to good, audible communication.

Availability relates to the regularity with which scheduled meetings are held, holding to the scheduled length of the meeting, and protection from frequent interruptions during the meeting. Time is a necessary prerequisite to accomplish any of the tasks of supervision.

A questionnaire study involving 885 supervisors and supervisees found that conference time was identified as a problem in supervision. In identifying their shortcomings in supervision, 18 percent of the supervisors noted that they did not readily make themselves available to supervisees, did not make sufficient time for supervision, and that they tended to allocate their time so that supervision was given low priority. Supervisors commented that supervision suffered from the multiple responsibilities and heavy workload that they carry. Supervisors said things like:

"I am not always there when they need me."

"I am not as available to supervisees as frequently as I would like."

"Not making enough time to meet with workers on a weekly basis."

"Too busy with other things to give much time to supervision."

"Overworked and tend to have too many things going at once to maintain consistency in supervision."

"I shortchange supervision time due to a busy schedule and emergencies."

If supervisors identify a lack of time to devote to supervision as a significant shortcoming in their supervisory practice, supervisees concur. Eighty-three comments (17 percent) by supervisees point to lack of time available for supervision due to missed, shortened, and interrupted conferences. Supervisees had such comments as:

"He needs to hold our time sacred."

"[She] tries to do too much in her job so that there is little time available for supervision, or less than desirable."

"He shows a chronic inability to structure conferences so as to avoid interruptions."

Interruptions occur because the majority of social work supervisors have competing administrative or direct-service assignments (Gibelman and Schervish 1997a). However, interruptions in supervision may have dire consequences for the working relationship between supervisor and supervisee (Shulman 1993). The effects of failure to guard against interruptions and of differences in supervisor-supervisee orientation to conferences are illustrated in the following comment by a supervisee:

We only have one hour, which is really poor because when I do see him there are constant interruptions. And I make a list before I go in there. First of all because I know I have to go boom, boom, boom. And John doesn't go boom, boom, boom. He's much slower than me in his pace of communicating, much more thorough. I would take a quick answer and go on to the next thing. . . . Today he couldn't see me at the regular time but could see me for half an hour after the staff conference. Well the conference was late and then there were interruptions. So it's gotten so that I reduce my discussions to the most specific, concrete kinds of things. (Amacher 1971:71)

Although formal scheduling is desirable, there may be occasions when informal, on-the-spot conferences are necessary. Social work is full of stressful emergencies that often cannot wait for the regular conference. At the point of crisis the worker's motivation for learning is apt to be most intense. Consequently, it is good to seize the teachable moment.

However, the unscheduled, off-the-cuff, "may-I-see-you-for-a-quick-minute" conference has its own disadvantages. Because it does come up suddenly, there is no time for preparation. Judgments are made without sufficient opportunity to carefully consider alternatives. A worker in a family service agency said:

> Only when we finally were able to establish a set time for individual confer-ences did the disadvantages of the "I'll-catch-you-when-I-can" type of con-ference become clear to me. In these kinds of conferences, I now recognize that I had always felt as though I were imposing, that I needed to be as quick, specific, succinct, and brief as possible, and I generally forgot to ask something I needed to know. I was never able to explore the wider implications of the questions I did raise.

Because such conferences snatch time from other scheduled activities, they are likely to be hurried and harried. The worker may feel guilty and apologetic about intruding on time the supervisor had scheduled for other activities. In contrast, the worker can comfortably use the scheduled confer-ence time with a guilt-free sense of entitlement. A separate time, a separate place, and a planned encounter symbolically affirm the importance of su-pervisory conferences. Persistent requests for conferences on the run tend to depreciate their significance.

An attempt to understand the individual worker's pattern of using su-pervision may be helpful. Some workers may deliberately (if not entirely consciously) force the supervisor into frequent informal conferences as a way of avoiding formal conferences. This pattern may express the worker's undue dependence on or hostility toward the supervisor. The supervisor must de-cide when an emergency is truly a crisis and when it is more an expression of a supervisee's rather than a client's need.

Meetings between supervisor and supervisee may not be regularly sched-uled because the supervisor has confidence in the worker's performance. But if meetings are not scheduled because of confidence rather than indifference, can the supervisor make explicit the basis for such confidence? Does the supervisee share a similar level of confidence in his or her work in the absence of regular supervision?

Preparing

A scheduled conference begins before it actually starts, and this is one of its prime advantages. It begins in the preparation for the conference by both supervisee and supervisor. The supervisee submits some record of his or her work—written records, tape recording, case files, work schedules, reports completed, a work plan. The supervisee's formal preparation of this material requires some explicit self-review of the work.

A good conference requires necessary preparation. A study of lousy supervision noted that such supervisors "would approach supervisory sessions without adequate preparation . . . with no particular goal in mind . . . and without reviewing notes before meeting with the supervisee" (Magnuson, Wilcoxon, and Norem 2000:198).

Supervisors differ with reference to deciding on cases for review. Some supervisors review selectively, spot checking some percentage of the worker's caseload. Some cover the entire caseload over a period of a limited number of conferences, so that all cases receive some review. Some review only the cases with which the worker is having some difficulty or is expected to have some difficulty. Some review with the worker only those cases the worker has selected for discussion. Giving the worker total discretion or covering the caseload selectively might do a disservice to clients who are receiving less than adequate service but whose cases are never reviewed.

Having made a selection of some aspect of the worker's performance for conference discussion, the supervisor reviews this material in preparation for the conference. Reviewing the material with the responsibilities of educational supervision in mind, the supervisor develops the teaching syllabus for the next conference or series of conferences. A conscious effort is made to select some cluster of information or concepts for teaching. The supervisor, in preparation for teaching, might review his or her own notes and the relevant literature on the material he or she plans to teach. Preparation for a tutorial deserves the same care as teaching a seminar in a school of social work.

The worker's activity, as evidenced in the material submitted, is the "textbook" for the "course." It provides the basic relevant material for teaching, and the teaching objectives selected should be tied in with the worker's on-the-job activity. Therefore the supervisor not only needs to know the content to be taught but also needs to be thoroughly familiar, through preparatory review, with the worker's activity.

In administrative supervision, case records, worker's reports, and other forms are reviewed for evidence of services rendered in compliance with agency procedure; in educational supervision the same records are reviewed for evidence of deficiencies in performance that require training.

In addition to the content and context of the material to be taught, the supervisor also has to review his or her knowledge of the learner. Given the special learning needs and unique learning patterns of a particular supervisee, how can the selected teaching objectives best be presented? What teaching techniques and approaches might work best with a particular supervisee? To answer these questions, the supervisor should review the educational diagnosis of the supervisee and where he or she is now in his or her learning. In preparation, the supervisor reviews both the material presented by the supervisee and the supervisee who is presenting it.

Preparation involves ensuring the availability of instructional materials that might be needed in conference teaching. If the use of certain agency forms is to be taught, copies should be at hand. If policies are to be discussed, the agency manual should be accessible. If references are to be cited to support teaching and to stimulate out-of-conference reading by the supervisee, the books and articles should be obtained in advance and made available.

The advance planning and preparation provide the supervisor with a focus and a structure that he or she holds lightly and flexibly, ready to discard or change in response to a supervisee's learning needs as they are actually manifested in the conference. Selectivity in choosing what to teach is a significant aspect of preparation. To attempt to teach everything all at once is to guarantee failure to teach anything. The supervisor has to sharpen the focus of supervision for teaching and learning.

Conferences concerned with the supervisee's clinical work generally have two interrelated objectives. One focus is on case management—enhancing an understanding of the client in his or her situation, planning strategies for intervention, and so on. The second focus is on developing the knowledge and skills of the worker, the worker's professional self and identity.

In summary, to paraphrase Kalous (1996), in planning the conference the supervisor should be prepared to: (1) evaluate and address the learning needs of the supervisees, (2) review legal and ethical issues, (3) monitor and document the progress of supervisees and their clients by observing actual work samples, and (4) evaluate the performance of supervisees and elicit their feedback. The evidence suggests that supervisory structure supports and advances social work practice.

The Middle Phase

Teaching and Learning

Once the conference is under way, how does the supervisor teach? We have noted that the starting point for educational supervision is the report of the worker's activity on the job, shared with the supervisor in advance or verbally during the conference. "Supervision is 'post-facto' teaching, a retrospective scrutiny of interactions and their reciprocal effects" (Fleming and Benedek 1966:238). The supervisor engages the worker in a systematic, explicit, critical analysis of the work he or she did and the work he or she is planning to do with an individual client, a family, a group, or a community. The endeavor is to provide the worker "with a structured learning situation which facilitates maximum growth through a process which frees potentialities" (Ekstein and Wallerstein 1972:10). The conference is an opportunity for guided self-observation, for systematic introspective-retrospective review of work that has been done, for thinking about the work as "recollected in tranquility." Experience is fragmented and seemingly chaotic. The supervisor helps the supervisee impose some order and meaning on experience and identify the principles that can guide him or her in understanding what needs to be done.

The supervisor does this by asking questions; requesting clarification; and freeing, supporting, stimulating, affirming, directing, challenging, and supplementing the worker's thinking. The supervisor calls attention to errors in the worker's performance, missed opportunities, apparent misunderstandings, gaps, and inconsistencies. The supervisor introduces new ideas, shares relevant knowledge and experience, and explains and illustrates similarities and differences between this and other situations, enlarging the worker's perspective. The supervisor poses relevant alternatives for consideration. A study of tape-recorded conferences indicated that the supervisor's questions very seldom came across with the meaning of the following.

> "I am testing you to see if you know this," but more often as "What do you think, because we have to decide this together?" or "What do you know about this, because I want to help fill in what you don't know so you can help the client more effectively?" That is, [supervisors] seemed interested in knowing what the [worker] thought, to put their ideas together or to help the [worker] become more knowledgeable, not to evaluate in the judgmental sense the worker's amount of knowledge. (Nelsen 1973:190)

The supervisor engages in a dialogue with the supervisee. It is a voyage of joint exploration in which the supervisor, through probing question and response, provides the supervisee with the opportunity to think more perceptively about the client's situation and what interventions might be helpful. The questions and responses encourage divergent rather than convergent thinking, postponing premature closure. What are the possible explanations for the client's situation? What observations can the supervisee offer in support of an explanation and alternative explanations? What inferences is he or she making from these observations, and what theory is he or she employing in making such inferences? What theoretical presuppositions are available that might lead to alternative inferences?

The dialogue is not over until explanation-understanding is tied to some plan for helping. The intent in educational supervision is to transform information into knowledge, knowledge into understanding, and understanding into action. Theory is reformulated as practice principles, which are then adapted to the situational requirements of the tasks the supervisee is asked to perform.

The supervisor has some idea, based on knowledge and experience, of how a competent professional would have responded to the client at the specific point in the case interaction being discussed. Using this image of competent professional behavior as a template, the supervisor makes some assessment of what the supervisee actually did in this situation.

The supervisor can offer a small lecture, engage the supervisee in a Socratic dialogue or a give-and-take discussion, offer a demonstration, role-play, listen to and analyze with the supervisee a tape-recorded playback, and offer material for reading.

Most supervisors apparently use a mix of expository, didactic teaching and dialectical-hypothetical indirect teaching procedures. *Didactic* teaching amounts to "telling"; *dialectical-hypothetical* teaching involves questions and comments that help the supervisees think things out for themselves and attempt to find their own answers. It comes close to the guided discussion method.

The supervisor acts as a catalyst to induce self-initiated learning. The workers can learn some things themselves from an analytical examination of their own experience with the client. For such kinds of learning the best approach by the supervisor is to be like a midwife, helping the worker give birth to his or her learning, assisting by active listening, guiding questioning, clarifying, paraphrasing, encouraging elaboration. "Tell me more of what you felt at that point"; "Could you explain that?"; "What prompted you to say that then?"; "What were you thinking when the client told you that?" This kind of learning depends on supervisee self-discovery, but the supervisor engages in actions that increase the probability that self-discovery will take place. This approach is in line with the recommendations of the classical educator Comenius, who noted that the principal objective of the educator is "to find a method of instruction by which teachers teach less but learners may learn more." Comenius is seconded in this by Rousseau, who noted that "our urge to instruct leads us to teach that which the student could better learn on his own."

Some things cannot be learned by even the most astute, insightful examination of the worker's interactional experience with the client. Some things have to be taught didactically—the agency's eligibility requirement for the variety of services it offers, the research findings regarding factors associated with success in adoption, community resources available to help with problems of single parenthood, and so on.

Most of the teaching for which the supervisor is responsible in implementing educational supervision results from a process of reciprocal interaction between the teacher and learner, both actively participating in and contributing to the process. It is a combination of didactic teaching and dialectical-hypothetical self-discovery learning.

Some significant content cannot be taught either didactically, through discussion, or experientially. Such content can only be taught through modeling. A good deal of what is most effective in social work is based on a special human attitude and approach to the client. As Grotjohn (1945:141) asks, "How can this be taught? How do you teach patience and devotion, tact and timing, decency and tolerance, empathy and intuition, modesty and honesty and frankness . . . the dangers of abusing a position of confidence and trust?" Such things are learned more effectively through an emotionally charged identification with a supervisor who models such attitudes rather than through didactic teaching or discussion.

Modeling involves deliberately selected displays of behavior by the supervisor for didactic purposes. Imaginative modeling involves more than watching the supervisor as implied in the term *role modeling*. Modeling involves observing desirable worker behavior available from a wide variety of sources—reading transcripts of interviews, listening to audiotapes, watching movies and videotapes, watching interviewing through a one-way screen, or sitting in on an interview. All these procedures provide the supervisee with a model of how a worker should behave in contact with a client.

It should be noted that incidental learning goes on side by side with intentional teaching. Much is caught that is not explicitly taught. Consequently the supervisor has to be careful that his or her interpersonal behavior is congruent with his or her teaching about such interpersonal behavior. The supervisor who behaves unacceptingly toward workers is not likely to teach the concept of acceptance successfully. In such a case, the supervisor does not exemplify in his or her own behavior the attitudinal approach he or she is professing to teach. The supervisor who says, "I am telling you that what you are supposed to do is to let the client make his own decision about what he wants to do," is not teaching what he or she intended to teach, namely self-determination. The supervisor models not only attitudinal behavior but, in analyzing the case along with the supervisee, the procedures employed in the problem solving approach as well.

Good supervision is good social work practice once removed. Much of what is desirable behavior in the worker-client interaction is analogous to desirable behavior in the supervisor-supervisee interaction. Good supervision is then a model for what the supervisee needs to learn and an instrumentality for facilitating such learning. Educational supervision is both a model and a method.

Given the fact that supervision is conducted in the context of an interpersonal dyadic relationship, with the objective of effecting change, it is not surprising that the approach that supervisors adopt in supervision reflects the approach they employ in casework therapy. Lacking training in teaching but possessing clinical skills, the temptation for the clinician-turned-supervisor is to utilize her preferred clinical approach in teaching.

The behavior modification caseworker is a behavior modification supervisor. The Rogerian caseworker is a Rogerian supervisor; the ego-psychology-oriented caseworker is an ego-psychology-oriented supervisor. Even the family therapist is likely to transform supervision into a replica of family therapy. For prescriptive examples, see Watkins (1997).

Detailed studies of the supervisory interactions of leading theoreticians supervising the same supervisee substantiated the hypothesis that "the work of the supervisor like that of the counselor will be affected by his or her theoretical orientation." (Goodyear, Abadie, and Efros 1984:236). McDaniel, Weber, and McKeerer (1983) found that a supervisor's choice of supervisory techniques is isomorphic to his or her theoretical orientation, a finding supported in a study by Wetchler, Piercy, and Sprenkle (1989).

But the choice of approach should depend not only on the nature of the content to be taught and the supervisor's preferred approach but also on the nature of the learning preferences of the learner. Even content that lends itself to learner self-discovery through Socratic questioning by the supervisor some learners may prefer to learn didactically. A supervisee says:

> I am aware, or at least I hope, that the supervisor knows some of the answers. Maybe it's better to do things for yourself. You may learn better by trying to reach for the answers by yourself. But I know myself and I learn what I need to learn pretty effectively if I am just told what answers others have formulated. I can use their experience and know-how.

Ideally, the approach of choice is based on the fit between the content to be taught and the learning preferences of the supervisee, with supervisor theoretical preference being given lower priority. In practice, however, the supervisory style of a particular supervisor may vary little over time or between one supervisee and another (Krause and Allen 1988; Shanfield et al. 1992; Worthington 1987).

If the supervisor selects an approach so that it is not only congenial with the learning patterns of the supervisee but also appropriate to the content to be taught, more efficient learning will occur. Agency forms and procedures can be taught didactically and by providing relevant reading material. Interviewing techniques cannot be effectively taught in that manner: role-playing is the more appropriate teaching approach for this kind of content.

A supervisor says, "The worker expressed his anxiety about medical terms and his limited understanding of them, and I recommended a book which contained useful information about them," illustrating an appropriate approach for the content to be taught. In a different situation, however, another supervisor says that her supervisee "faced a difficult decision whether to recommend foster care for these children or placing a homemaker in the home. I engaged [her] in a discussion [in which we thought] of the advantages and disadvantages of each of the alternatives." In each of these conferences the teaching methods were appropriate for the different content that needed to be taught.

The methods employed have to be appropriate to the ultimate objective of educational supervision, which is knowledge for use. Rapoport's (1954) definition of *supervision* as a "disciplined tutorial process wherein principles are transformed into practice skills" calls explicit attention to this focus. The classroom teacher can be satisfied with intellectual acquisition of content by the learner. Educational supervision has to aim at emotional assimilation of the content so that behavioral changes result from teaching. The progression is from information into knowledge, knowledge into understanding, and understanding into changed behavior. New behavior is then tested in interaction with the client to see whether the change is effective. Feedback from the client and the supervisor permits the worker to correct his or her learning, modify his or her behavior, test it again, and examine the second feedback.

To promote transfer of learning so that the same problems do not have to be rediscussed as they are encountered in different cases, the teacher directs learning toward a clarification of general principles that can be validly applied from case to case. He or she moves from the specific to the general, relating the case situation to the principle and vice versa.

Situational learning of the technical requirements for dealing with the particular case situation, which is the subject of the conference, is supplemented by an effort to conceptualize and generalize what is taught. Conceptual teaching generalizes the particular experience; practice teaching particularizes the generalization. The supervisor's approach in moving from the specific to the general, in helping the supervisee conceptualize practice, is illustrated in the following comment:

Oh, one other thing that I think has to do with his teaching style is that when we're talking about a specific client, he will often now—he didn't at first—

but now he will say, "Well, what do you think about this general issue of—?" and then he'll take what we're talking about—say it's a very verbal client or a very nonverbal client, or it's a client who has terminated early—he'll say, "What do you think about this style in general?" not just related to this client, but with others. Or a client who terminates: "If you had it to do over again with this client, what might you have done differently now that you have hindsight?" I guess it's typical of him to say, "Now that we're operating on the basis of hindsight, what might we do differently?" which does not mean to me, "Well, schmuck, what could you have done better with this case?" But "Now that we have all the data in, thinking back on it, do you have any thoughts?" So he pushes me to think in a more general way about the processes of therapy with particular kinds of people or particular kinds of techniques or whatever, and how I would do that again in the future—how I would use that. I guess sort of asking me to conceptualize things on a broader level, to think about things on a broader level than just one client. (Herrick 1977:143)

Teaching techniques have different effects depending on the attitude, skill, conviction, and appropriateness with which they are used. "What do you think?" and "How do you feel about it?" can sound like tired clichés. Alternatively, these can be asked in a spirit that suggests that the supervisor warmly welcomes more active participation of the supervisee in the learning process. The aim is to develop an interactional pattern of mutuality. Despite the elements of mutuality in the relationship there is (or should be) an imbalance in the knowledge and skills the participants bring to the encounter. The supervisor has to accept the responsibility for having more experience, being more knowledgeable and skillful and having available what the profession provides in practice wisdom and problem solutions. Supervisor and supervisee are not peers. As Robinson (1949:42) says, "to start with an assumption of equality is to deny the student her right to any learning process." The supervisor has the ultimate responsibility for what takes place in the teaching-learning situation.

In the following passage a supervisor describes how she found her own congenial approach to educational supervision in offering leadership in the context of mutuality.

Perhaps one of the most difficult aspects of the role of supervisor, for me, was making criticisms and suggestions. As nice as my supervisory theory sounded, when I attempted to put it into practice, I had trouble.

I found myself saying to Ruth, as she reported her meetings to me, "Did you find out about ? . . ." "Did you turn this in yet?" "Well, did you think of trying this . . .?" Ruth's reaction to all of these "did you's" was, naturally, very defensive. Her answer was, most often, something like "Well, I didn't have time" in a very cold, flat voice, or "It seemed more important to. . . ." I was sounding more like a policeman-mother than a helpful supervisor.

I began to experiment with different ways of saying the same things, or getting the same point across, without such an authoritarian ring. My first idea was to hedge a little, to not come on so strong. I began saying "Well, you know, you might be interested in trying something like this . . ." or "Maybe one thing you could do, too, is to attempt to. . . ." When I hedged and hawed in this manner, Ruth wasn't nearly as defensive, but I still wasn't getting the desired result. Now she wasn't taking me seriously. I seemed to have no authority at all now, rather than too much. Her answer very often was "Maybe I'll try it" or "I'll think about it," very lethargically. When I realized that this approach was failing also, I put my head to work, and came up with another idea. I was trying to learn from Ruth and she from me. I needed to respect her and encourage her: I needed to give her the chance to express herself in an open and nonjudgmental atmosphere.

What I was attempting to teach her was my own techniques, my way of doing things and of thinking, of handling groups, of being a social worker. Therefore, when I suggested something to Ruth, I was giving her my ideas, what I thought, what I needed to know, what I would do. Individual supervision is a very personal experience. Therefore, I felt I could say these things to Ruth in just that way. At our next meeting together I said to Ruth, "I think what I would like to know from this girl is, . . ." "I think the first thing I might try would be to, . . ." "For me to do this. . . ."

At first I was afraid of what Ruth's reaction would be to my great emphasis on "I," but my fears were quickly dispelled. It worked beautifully. Ruth's reactions were something like "Oh yeah? I didn't think of that" or "Wait a minute, why would you do that?" When I gave her my thoughts, as a person in a supervisory capacity, she was able to relate herself to me as a person in the student role.

I realize this type of approach wouldn't work well for everyone, although it did work for me in this one case. One snag, however, that came hand in hand with this new way of doing things, was that it evoked questions such as "Why would you do that?" I was pleased she wanted to know my thoughts and that she wanted to discuss it further. Nevertheless, I didn't feel comfortable just telling her my reasons, without her having to think about it. Yet I dislike it when someone tries to "play teacher" with me, and turns my questions back around on me. I didn't want to answer, "Because X, Y, and Z," nor did I want to reply, "Well, why do you think?"

My solution again stemmed from the philosophy I tried to adopt: that I was there to learn from her as well as she from me. The next time she asked me my reasons why, I told her of this dilemma: that I didn't want to give her all the answers, but I didn't want to be the quiz master either: and then we struck a compromise. If she would tell me some reasons she could find for doing it that way, I might learn some new things. Then I would tell her my reasons for taking that approach, and she might learn some new things from me.

As funny as it all sounds right now, and was at that time too, it really worked well. Whenever Ruth started to ask why, she would stop herself and say, "Is that because . . .?" To which I would always reply politely, "Yes, and not only that. . . ." It became a kind of a game I suppose, but the game, and the very ritualized aspect of it provided some very necessary elements to our interviews. It helped us both to realize our roles more fully, through spelling them out so clearly in this one aspect of the supervisory relationship. It added humor to our sessions. It helped us deal with our embarrassment, by laughing a little and thereby relieving the tension. And perhaps most importantly, it brought us closer to each other; we began to like each other and to work much better together.

Orientations to Teaching and Learning

Several distinctly different orientations to the supervisory process have been identified that tend to result in different approaches to teaching and learning social work practice. An experiential-existential, supervisee-centered orientation sees supervision as concerned with the development of supervisees' self-understanding, self-awareness, and emotional growth. The emphasis is on the worker's feelings. The supervisee has major responsibility for what he or she wants to learn, and the focus of supervision is on the *way* the worker does the work and the nature of his or her relationship to the client.

A didactic, task-centered orientation sees supervision as primarily concerned with the development of the supervisees' professional skills. The emphasis is on the workers' thinking. The supervisor has the primary responsibility for what is taught, and the focus of discussion is on the content of *what* the worker is doing, the activities with and on behalf of his or her clients.

An experiential-existential orientation to educational supervision involves establishing a relationship with the supervisee and engaging in interaction that is analogous to the worker-client relationship. The focus of interaction is the supervisee and the content for discussion is the supervisee's feelings about the case problem, his or her reaction to and feelings about the client, the client's response to the supervisee as the supervisee perceives it, the supervisee's feelings about the client's response, and so on.

The supervisor concentrates on this focus by reflecting, clarifying, probing, and interpreting the feelings of the supervisee. Suggestions, advice, and evaluative comments that might reinforce or discourage certain supervisee behaviors are held to a minimum. The goal of educational supervision here is to help the supervisee to find his or her own orientation through an exploration of his or her own experience. Attempting a balance between challenging and being supportive, the supervisor acts as a catalyst in helping the supervisee experience self-initiated discovery.

A scale listing these two orientations (didactic versus experimental) as opposite poles was offered to supervisors and supervisees (Kadushin 1990). They were asked to indicate the point on the scale that denoted the orientation that they thought worked most effectively for them. The tendency for both supervisors and supervisees was to check the midpoint, indicating that the most desirable orientation was a rather even mixture of the two approaches. Despite the general overall agreement, however, supervisors leaned toward the didactic, task-oriented, professional-growth approach somewhat more decidedly than did supervisees.

The supervisor's orientation affects how supervisees learn to practice. A recent review of ninety-seven studies of counselor supervision and training (Lambert and Ogles 1997) suggests two overarching conclusions. First, reading and viewing examples are the most efficient methods of mastering basic interviewing skills and goal-setting with clients, but didactic-experiential training is the most effective way to master the interpersonal helping skills of empathy, warmth, and respect. Thankfully, supervisees may acquire such skills without especially high levels of supervisory empathy, genuineness, and unconditional positive regard, as long as they perceive that their supervisors are trying to be helpful. Second, systematic training advances the development of interviewing and interpersonal skills, but helping skills learned in the classroom may not generalize well to actual practice settings. A period of retraining is often required and, if counselors are to retain and generalize those skills, supervision is helpful. Although the acquisition of advanced interpersonal skills takes time, those skills improve with modeling, rehearsal, and feedback. Unfortunately, empirical research has rarely examined the client outcomes of counselor supervision and training (Ellis and Ladany 1997).

The question that has been posed more and more insistently for social work outcome research generally seems equally applicable here: What kinds of approaches to educational supervision work best with what kinds of supervisees under what kinds of circumstances? There is no one best way to teach; similarly, there is no single best way to supervise, given the infinite variety of supervisors, supervisees, and supervisory interactions.

Providing Helpful Feedback

The supervisor teaches and the supervisee learns through feedback. It would be impossible to learn to play golf if we never saw where the ball went after we hit it. We need to know how we are doing, what we are doing right, what needs to be changed. Feedback reinforces learning that "works" and helps correct faulty learning. We learn from our mistakes only if we can find out what they are and have the opportunity of analyzing them. A flexible supervisor accepts the idea that supervisees will definitely make mistakes but rejects the idea that mistakes should be tolerated indefinitely.

As Middleman and Rhodes note, the old maxim "practice makes perfect" needs revision. It is "practice plus feedback (knowledge of results) that makes perfect" (Middleman and Rhodes 1985:36). Whereas supervisors tend to hesitate about being critical of a supervisee's work, supervisees welcome appropriate and constructive criticism. Two surveys have found that among the main sources of supervisee dissatisfaction was with "shortcomings in reviewing, monitoring, and evaluating supervisees' work so as to provide critical constructive feedback necessary to improve professional performance" (Kadushin 1974, 1992b:15). Workers seem to both anticipate and welcome instruction, direction, and structure from the supervisor. They do, apparently, look to a supervisor to learn what they need to know to do their jobs effectively. Supervisees deserve and appreciate explicit, definite feedback. Goldhammer, discussing supervision of schoolteachers, makes this point:

> Perhaps the most rapid and efficient way to alienate one's supervisees is by hedging and by pussyfooting. Teacher: So you think I was really sarcastic with them? Supervisor: Uh, no. I didn't really say that. You are generally sympathetic and friendly with the youngsters, but some of your remarks today, were, uh, less kindly than I've known them to be in the past. Teacher: Some of my behavior today was unkindly? Supervisor: Well, uh, no, not really, but, uh . . . (1969:344)

To engage in the following kind of dialogue is not very helpful either: "You're doing fine! Keep it up." "Keep what up?" "Just what you're doing" (Ekstein and Wallerstein 1972:145)

Heppner and Handley (1981) researched the behaviors of supervisors that correlated with counselor trainees' perceptions of their supervisor's trustworthiness. The results "seem to indicate the importance of providing honest evaluative information on teaching with a supportive relationship. Perhaps when supervisors only provide positive feedback and do not confront trainees with nonfacilitative behaviors, trainees question what is not being said and subsequently the trustworthiness of the supervisors" (Heppner and Handley 1981:244).

In a study that asked supervisees for their perceptions of their supervisor's shortcomings, a lack of critical feedback was cited in 27 percent of the comments. Supervisees said:

> There is a lack of periodic feedback about quantity and quality of work performance. I need to have more constructive criticism so I know what I need to change.
> I sometimes feel I am manipulated by praise. Where is the criticism?
> She is almost too complimentary. Sometimes I do not feel that her evaluation of my work has too much basis in fact. I can't fix it if I don't know it's broken. (Kadushin 1990:191)

We can expect the workers, as reasonably healthy people, to be able to take valid criticism without falling apart. Therefore it is not necessary to balance every criticism with a compliment. Not only does this often put the supervisor in a false position, it is also demeaning to the worker. One supervisee said, "I knew something bad was coming up because she started to give me all that sweet-talking praise." A supervisor expresses her own response to the dilemma:

> Should I always temper a criticism with a compliment? Should I make up compliments or pick out small good points if I can't find enough to go around? Should I just offer each compliment as it occurs to me? I'm sure it sounds silly now, but at the time, it was really a problem. The solution I arrived at was simply to play it by ear. I couldn't bring myself to make up phony compliments or pick out petty points to compliment her on or to temper each criticism with a compliment. My main focus here was to be open, honest, and realistic. If something could have been done better, I felt it was important to let Carol know. If something was done well, this was also important information.

Ratliff, Wampler, and Morris (2000) have researched the delicate dance involved in concern for the supervisee's feeling about his or her work and the supervisor's responsibility to ensure competent clinical practice. Discussing 120 episodes in which some corrective action was required, they found that supervisors made suggestions and evaluations in a very tentative manner and (supervisees) responded with deference and cooperation (Ratliff, Wampler, and Morris 2000:385).

The supervisor should not apologize for corrective feedback. This discounts its importance and attenuates its impact. The supervisee needs feedback to help overcome performance deficiencies so that he or she can do better work. Feedback helps make learning explicit and conscious. The supervisor has the perspective, the objectivity, and the knowledge of what good performance is supposed to look like—a *super vision*, so to speak.

Clients, of course, are sources of feedback in their reaction to workers, and workers are sources of feedback for themselves as they examine their performance. Aside from the client and the worker, the supervisor is the only other person who has detailed knowledge of a supervisee's performance. However, the supervisor is the only one sanctioned and obligated to give feedback and is explicitly charged with this responsibility. Given these considerations, the supervisor is most often the primary source of feedback for the supervisee, and supervisees are eager for this.

Receptivity to feedback is a function of the source of the message and the nature of the message. If the source of the feedback has credibility for the receiver, if the source has power over the receiver, if the source is regarded as an expert, the feedback is more likely to be regarded seriously. Supervisors frequently meet these conditions, increasing receptivity to their feedback.

Feedback is more effective if certain guidelines are observed by the supervisor in offering feedback (Abbott and Lyter 1998; Roberts 1992).

1. Feedback should be given as soon as possible after the performance. This increases motivation and interest in learning what might have been improved. Rewarding commendable performance by praise as soon as possible after the event increases the potency of reinforcement.

2. Feedback should be specific. One should be able to point to a specific intervention, act, or comment that needs praise or correction. A specific illustration of poor question formulation or a ragged, ambiguous transition is better than general feedback, which suggests a need to improve interviewing skills.

3. Feedback should be objectifiable. One should be able to point to the concrete behavior that illustrates a deficiency in performance. Vague, general, global statements have less credibility.

4. Feedback should be descriptive rather than judgmental. "I notice that your response to Mrs. P. resulted in her becoming silent and changing her focus," rather than, "Your response to Mrs. P. was not very good."

5. If possible, it is desirable to highlight the effects of good performance: "I was glad to see that you were more accepting of Mrs. H., and I notice she was less resistant to sharing her troubles with the nursing home."

6. Feedback should be focused on the behavior of the supervisee rather than on the supervisee as a person. "After he told you he was gay, your next

series of comments had a punitive phrasing," rather than, "From your comment, it seems that you don't like gays or are uncomfortable with them."

7. Feedback should be offered tentatively for consideration and discussion rather than authoritatively for agreement and acceptance.

8. Try to tie feedback as explicitly as possible to what you want the supervisee to learn, what you think he or she needs to learn.

9. Good feedback involves sharing ideas rather than giving advice, exploring alternatives rather than giving answers. It is focused on behavior that can be modified and is accompanied by specific suggestions for change.

10. Feedback needs to be selective in terms of the amount that a person can absorb. The principle is to keep the amount to what the supervisee can use, not all of the feedback you have available to give.

Feedback is important for the supervisor as well as the supervisee. Monitoring verbal and nonverbal responses, specifically requesting reaction where only limited or ambiguous reactions are communicated, the supervisor needs to be constantly alert to whether teaching is resulting in learning. What has been well taught is not necessarily well learned. The communication of feedback about performance does not in and of itself generate a change in performance. The information needs to be accepted by the workers as descriptive of their performance. There needs to be motivation to change, and the problem needs to be perceived as susceptible to change.

Although the supervisor is ultimately responsible for supervisee performance, typically the supervisor must rely on reports from the worker, through whose eyes the process is filtered, to get the job done. For another perspective, supervisors and workers should obtain feedback from clients to round out the picture. Empirical research suggests that supervision designed to obtain client feedback may improve supervision, worker performance, and client outcomes.

Harkness and Hensley (1991), for example, described an experiment in which the focus of social work supervision in a mental health setting was changed by asking experienced workers a series of ten questions designed to elicit client feedback:

> What does the client want help with? How will you and the client know you are helping? How does the client describe a successful outcome? Does the client say there has been a successful outcome? What are you doing to help the client? Is it working? Does the client say you are helping? What else can you do to help the client? How will that work? Does the client say that will help? (Harkness and Hensley 1991:507)

Across workers and caseloads, the findings suggested that a 10 percent improvement in client satisfaction with goal attainment, a 20 percent improvement in client satisfaction with worker helpfulness, and a 30 percent improvement in client satisfaction with worker-client partnership were the outcomes of using social work supervision to elicit client feedback.

Although client outcomes may improve if supervisors and workers obtain client feedback on an ongoing basis, supervisees may perceive the supervisor as having less empathy for workers if the focus of supervision is changed to obtain client feedback (Harkness 1997), and practitioners may passively resist the adoption of information systems designed to produce it (Savaya and Spiro 1997). It appears that overreaching for client feedback breaches a firewall between administrative and educational supervision; Erera and Lazar (1994b) fear that such breaches impede the supervisory process.

Ending the Conference

A supervisory conference, like an interview, is hard work. Consequently, after an hour, it is likely to be progressively less productive. The end of the conference should be planned at the beginning so that the agenda selected can be completed within the allotted period of time.

Toward the end of the scheduled time, the supervisor should be looking for a convenient point of termination. It should be at a point where closure has been obtained on a unit of work. The emotional level of the interaction should not be intense. The worker should have been given some prior opportunity to ask those questions and discuss those issues that were of most concern. It is very frustrating to say to the supervisee, "We have two minutes left for the conference. Was there something you wanted to bring up?"

Termination involves a summarization of the conference and a recapitulation of points covered and content taught. A supervisor says, "The sessions seemed more worthwhile when I reiterated at the end what we had talked about because it made it seem like we covered a lot. The ending seemed much more together and planned out when I summarized. We both saw these conclusions as a pronouncement of the end of the session. We consequently then proceeded to relax."

Because the conference terminates before it actually ends in the minds of the participants, it might be good to finish with some explicit questions for the worker to think about or some specific reading suggestions relevant to what has been discussed and in line with his or her interests. The questions might serve as a transition to the next conference. Thinking about the questions raised, both the supervisor and supervisee would be preparing for their next meeting.

In general, it might be said that a good conference in educational supervision has the following characteristics:

1. It involves planning and preparation by both supervisor and supervisee.
2. It has a shared, consensually agreed-on objective.
3. Its focus is the clinical work of the supervisee.
4. It gives priority to critical self-analysis by the worker of his or her performance, assisted by the guidance of the supervisor and supplemented by the supervisor's contributions as a resource person.
5. It provides the worker with clear, unambiguous, relevant feedback designed to help improve performance.
6. It takes place in the context of a facilitative learning atmosphere.
7. It follows desirable principles of learning and teaching.
8. It provides follow-through and a tie to the next conference.

It might be noted that although the supervisor has the primary responsibility and sanction for formal education of the supervisee, the supervisor needs to remember that considerable informal, unsanctioned education of the supervisee is going on at the same time. Workers turn to their peers in learning how to do the job. The client is actively engaged in teaching by responses to what the worker does. When interventions work, the client is helped and the worker is rewarded. The worker learns that this is a good way to go. As Langs (1979:205) notes, the "ultimate supervisor for the therapist is the patient." Supervisors need not feel competitive about these auxiliary teachers but welcome their assistance.

Process Studies

There are few social work studies available that attempt a systematic and detailed examination of what actually goes on in individual conferences. Nelsen (1973, 1974) studied tapes of sixty-eight supervisory conferences conducted in a variety of casework agencies. Although these conferences were between students in a school of social work and their field instructors (supervisors), the findings are applicable to supervisory conferences generally. In response to the question, "What do participants really talk about in supervisory conferences?" Nelsen found that

> by the fourth taped conference, the following discussion pattern was fairly common. First, field instructor and student would together go case by case through the student's submitted written material, with field instructor asking questions for clarification or student volunteering extra details, with interrelated discussion of dynamics and handling, with occasional brief exposition by the field instructor of relevant theoretical or skills information which the

student had apparently not known, and with eventual agreement on what was going on with the client and what to do next. Second, there might be brief discussions of cases on which there had been new developments but not dictation, e.g., a broken appointment requiring further action from the student. Third, there might be some, usually brief, discussions of learning content such as whether a student was recording properly, or agency-field content such as monthly statistics or the need to find a resource for a client. (1973:189)

Both field instructors and students usually participated actively [in the discussion]. The field instructors freely gave didactic material although not often lengthy exposition. (Nelsen 1974:149)

Supervisors also engaged in supportive activity (discussed in chapter 6) and gave directives "requiring particular behavior" by the supervisee, such as, "fill in social service cards in each case"; "to find a nursing home, call the homes; find out whether they have a bed; if not find out when they will; find out the cost." Directives tended to be associated with agency administrative procedures and concrete services. The context in which the directives were given indicated a sort of summing up of mutual discussion rather than the issuing of an order. The reciprocal interaction between supervisor and supervisee is suggested by the fact that supervisors gave more directives to supervisees who often requested direction than to those who did not.

Busso (1987) studied thirty audiotapes of educational supervision sessions between three social work graduate students and an experienced MSW supervisor. The basis for the supervisory conferences was the audiotapes of the first, third, and last interviews with three of each of the students' clients in a medical social work setting. The tapes of the educational supervision conferences were analyzed by independent raters in terms of the task-centered approach to social work practice. The analysis showed that by far the greatest amount of time in the educational supervision conference was devoted to "understanding problems," "examining what was a problem to a client and who supported the problem in the client's environment" (Busso 1987:70). Much less time was devoted to "selecting a strategy; designing specific steps of strategy" (Busso 1987:69). Supervisory behaviors in support of the worker were not included in the analysis.

Studies of supervisory conferences in closely related fields are instructive. Culatta and Seltzer (1976, 1977) developed an instrument for scoring categories of interactional events in supervisory conferences of communicative disorder clinicians. Six categories were related to the interventions of the supervisor and six to analogous contributions by the supervisee.

The supervisory conference event categories included positive or negative evaluation statements (supervisor evaluates observed behavior or verbal report of supervisee and gives verbal or nonverbal approval or disapproval); strategy interventions (statement by supervisor given to clinician for future therapeutic intervention); questions (any interrogative statement made by the supervisor relevant to the client being discussed); and observation or information statements by supervisor.

The two different studies yielded very similar findings. The principal activity in the supervisory interaction tended to be concerned with provision by the clinician-supervisee of "information about therapeutic sessions while supervisors essentially used this information to suggest strategy for future sessions—the picture that evolves is one of the clinicians feeding raw material to the supervisors who used it to plan overall therapy strategy for the clients." This was in marked contrast to the supervisors' perceptions of "themselves as sounding boards to be used by the supervisee as resource people" (Culatta and Seltzer 1976:12)—a perception similar to the one generally held by social work supervisors of their activity.

In analyzing differences in talk-time by supervisors and supervisees in the conference, supervisors almost invariably talked more than supervisees.

Questioned about their style of supervision, supervisors were sorted into three distinct groups: "Those who felt they were directive in style by providing specific suggestions and comments about methodology and client performance; those who believed they were nondirective, using a nonprescriptive method relying on the clinician to explain the methodology employed; and a group who said they favored a combination of approaches" (Culatta and Seltzer 1976:12). However, analysis of the content and sequence of the conference revealed that all supervisors seemed to function in similar patterns regardless of their own evaluation of their supervisory styles.

A surprising finding was the very limited number of evaluation statements made by supervisors. This generally left the supervisees with little explicit guidance as to what they were doing correctly and/or well and what was done incorrectly and/or poorly.

Schubert and Nelsen (1976) corroborated the Culatta and Seltzer findings using a somewhat different instrument for explicitly analyzing supervisors in the conferences. They found that supervisors were most frequently engaged in providing opinions or suggestions. The second most frequent behavior was providing information. In this study as well, supervisors talked more than supervisees.

Keller et al. (1996) have used direct observation to describe the communication content and patterned interactions of supervisors and supervisees. They found that imparting knowledge, achieving personal growth and self-understanding, and managing the hierarchical supervisory relationship dominated communication in a four-stage pattern that emerged across supervision meetings: (1) rapport-building, (2) getting down to work, (3) resolving questions and options, and (4) wrapping up.

Another direct-observation study provides a somewhat different view of interactional styles and patterns found in supervision. Heppner and colleagues (1994) observed six dimensions of supervisory intervention behavior: (1) directing-instructing versus deepening, (2) cognitive clarification versus emotional encouragement, (3) confronting versus encouraging the client, (4) didactic-distant versus emotional involvement, (5) joining versus challenging the trainee, and (6) providing direction versus resignation. What remains to be seen is how supervisees respond to supervisory interventions.

Case Illustration

The following vignette illustrates the supervisor implementing the responsibilities of educational supervision in an individual conference with a worker in a child welfare district office regarding a child in foster care.

> Jim began by saying that he wanted to talk about Frank. He brought out that it was important to preserve Frank's placement—he did not think the problem would be solved by replacing him and I agreed. He thought he had made some impression on the boy, and that Frank realized he wanted to help him. I said this was good, and suggested that worker was really on the spot with foster mother ready to put Frank out if his behavior did not change. He agreed to this and said he had made it clear to Frank that he must get a job and stay away from the old crowd, since they are undesirable. I said from his recording I could see he had tried very hard with Frank—did he think it had worked?

The worker here selects the content for the teaching agenda ("he wanted to talk about Frank"). This is in accordance with the principle that learning takes place when the supervisee actively participates in the learning process. It also ensures a higher level of motivation to learn, because the worker, given the opportunity, will select for discussion content that presents a problem for him or her.

The supervisor helps clarify and define the nature of the problem situation that confronts the supervisee. The problem is not Frank's replacement but how to preserve the current placement for him.

The supervisor rewards by explicitly commending ("I said this was good"), in accordance with the principle that we learn best when we receive rewards for learning.

The supervisor communicates empathic understanding and acceptance of the worker's situation (he was "really on the spot"). This probably will be regarded as emotionally supportive by the worker, and this helps establish a good atmosphere for learning. Recognition that the supervisor is empathic and accepting makes the supervisee more receptive to content. The supervisor, however, might be concerned with teaching in saying that the worker is on the spot. The supervisor is redefining this matter as a problem for Jim in his responsibility as the social worker assigned to the case. The supervisor is not concerned with Frank's behavior; that is Jim's responsibility. The supervisor is, however, concerned with Jim's behavior and case planning. The worker, rather than the client, is the immediate responsibility of the supervisor.

After Jim has shared with the supervisor what he has done on the case, the supervisor confronts him with a challenging question: Did he think it had worked? Because the question is challenging and apt to induce defensiveness, it is preceded by an introduction that makes it emotionally easier to accept: "I said . . . I could see he had tried very hard with Frank." The question of whether he thought it had worked solicits an objective, self-critical analysis. In inviting reflection, the supervisor is increasing the worker's involvement, intensifying his level of participation in learning.

Didactically stating that the approach was mistaken—or, more gently, that it left something to be desired—might have engendered a need for Jim to defend his behavior, as this might be perceived as an attack. People learn less effectively when psychic energy is devoted to self-defense. Encouraging self-examination may result in the worker's explicit recognition of some of the shortcomings of his approach. He may then be more ready to consider alternatives.

It might be noted, too, that the supervisor has actually read the record and is using his knowledge derived from it in this conference. This in itself is encouraging to the supervisee because it indicates that the supervisor is serious about these encounters, is interested in preparing for the supervisory sessions, and is keeping to their mutual agreement. Because the justification for recording lies partly in its utility in supervision, use of the recording in the supervisory session rewards the worker for having done the work. It further helps develop a positive supervisor-supervisee relationship. Emotional interaction between the two is more apt to be positive if the supervisor shows respect for the supervisee by respecting his product—the recording.

So far, the supervisor has not taught much, at least not explicitly, although he has taught something about good human relations. He has taught by implication that it is helpful to define a problem clearly and to partialize it if possible. He has encouraged an attitude toward work—a reflective, self-critical approach—that is a necessary prerequisite for the development of self-awareness. Principally, however, the supervisor is not so much concerned with teaching at this point as he is with developing an atmosphere that is conducive to learning.

> Jim shook his head, indicating he was very doubtful, then burst out with, "Frank makes me mad, he's just lazy like Mrs. D says. He doesn't ever try to get work." He went on to tell how at Frank's age he had been earning his own spending money for several years by doing odd jobs that he found himself. I agreed that it would be hard for him to understand why Frank could not do this too—could he see any difference in Frank's situation and his own. He thought for a moment and then pointed out that he had his family and Frank was in a foster home. I wondered what difference that would make? He could not see that it would make any. After all Frank was only two when he went to a foster home and does not even remember his own family—it was probably the best thing that could have happened because his mother did not take care of him.

Here the atmosphere of psychological safety established by the supervisor permits the supervisee to express negative feelings about the client. It frees the supervisee to express disagreement with some of the things for which social work supposedly stands. In effect he says the client is lazy and no good; if he's in trouble, it's his own fault; he makes me mad; each man is the architect of his own fate, and if Frank just tried harder, he would be able to resolve his problems.

The supervisor is understanding enough to accept this outburst, and, rather than express disappointment or chagrin that a social worker should react to his client in a manner that suggests rejection, he expresses empathy with the supervisee's difficulty in understanding Frank. Responding in this way, the supervisor is teaching by example the concept of acceptance—that judging the client and his behavior in moral terms may be satisfying, but it is not very helpful; in problem-solving it is more helpful to try to understand than to judge. He then asks a question that shifts the focus from an evaluation of Frank's behavior to an attempt to understand the behavior: What helps explain Frank's actions, what prompts him to act differently from the supervisee?

The supervisee, whose thinking has been channeled by the question, comes up with a descriptive statement of difference. The supervisor further questions him because this, as yet, does not explain why people should behave differently when confronted with similar situations. A less perceptive supervisor might be satisfied with the answer and develop a short lecture on the implications of differences in developmental history. This supervisor prefers to elicit the supervisee's perceptions of the implications that differences in developmental history have for behavior. Once again, this maximizes supervisee participation in learning. Implicit in the supervisor's questions are some behavioral concepts, for example, the past is structured in the present, behavior is purposive, all generalizations need to be individualized, feelings are facts and determine behavior. These ideas, however, are not taught explicitly.

The worker continues to voice doubts about the point the supervisor is making; he questions whether this difference in background explains the difference in behavior between himself and Frank.

> I suggested we think back to when all this happened. I asked how he thought Frank felt when he had to leave his parents and go to a strange place, or did it seem that he was too young for it to make any difference. Worker looked dubious and remarked that, after all, a kid of two could hardly talk. We discussed this for a while, and he was thoughtful at my suggestion that it might even be harder for a little child like Frank who could feel, but was too young to understand what was happening, than for an older child. I said here we were talking about what had happened to Frank and about his feelings when he was two years old, perhaps this did not seem to have much connection with the present. He said, thoughtfully, that he could see it might, adding that Frank never hears from his family and that must be "rough on the kid"; I said he was telling me that out of Frank's life experiences and his own they would bring something different in terms of feeling to the present. With an expression of surprise, Jim commented that he felt sorry, not angry at Frank anymore, how come? Did he think it was because we were trying to understand Frank? He decided this was it, and wondered why he had not thought about all that before.

The supervisor does not directly counter the worker's doubts about his implied "explanation." He invites the worker to examine his thinking further, but this time by attempting to empathize with Frank (how did he think Frank felt?). He goes on to suggest a line of thought which the supervisee grasps ("or did it seem that [Frank] was too young for it to make any difference?"). Such an approach can be helpful if the supervisor senses that this is the nature of the worker's thinking but that he is either not ready or not able to articulate it. The supervisor, in making it explicit, exposes it so that it can be discussed. Unless the message from a worker is clear, however, there is danger that this kind of interpretation will project onto the worker the supervisor's own conception of the situation, which the supervisee then employs for his own ends.

In any event, the supervisor is trying to make a teaching point: that a two-year-old can "know," and his knowing does affect later behavior—an idea with which the supervisee disagrees. At this juncture the supervisor, if he thinks the point important enough to warrant concern with its acceptance, should be prepared with didactic research material to reinforce it. What studies, if any, support the contention that a child of two can remember and that such memories affect later behavior? What clinical material supports the contention? The student has a right to know and the supervisor has an obligation to make this information available. Otherwise, the supervisor is exploiting the authority of his position to solicit acceptance of what may well be a presumption with little supporting evidence.

The past is of concern not for itself but only as it affects the present. The supervisor shifts the discussion back to this area of greater importance. He does so by a question that suggests another principle in learning—that we learn best when the material being presented is meaningfully related to problems that concern us. The supervisor is trying to relate the questions he raised about Frank's past to the problems Jim faces in dealing with Frank. The supervisee makes this connection and makes a deduction in line with what the supervisor is attempting to teach about the effects of the past.

The supervisor then summarizes and makes explicit the meaning of the interaction ("I said he was telling me," and so on). In summarizing, the supervisor uses another principle in learning—namely, we learn best and retain best if we are clear about what we have learned, if we can put it into words and examine it.

What needs to be taught is not only a change in thinking, not just the injection of new ideas for the worker's consideration (some of which may affect his thinking, some of which may not), but a change in feeling as well. The supervisor's approach, which focuses on understanding rather than judging, leads to a change in feeling. The worker begins to feel sorry for Frank, rather than angry at him. This is an advance toward greater helpfulness, but it is still not as helpful as an understanding of Frank, which the supervisor is aiming to teach. The approach toward developing understanding is only partly in the questions the supervisor raises ("could he see any difference between Frank's situation and his own?"; "I wondered what difference between Frank's situation and his own"; "I wondered what difference that would make"; "I asked how he thought Frank felt?"). It is also in the supervisor's approach to the worker. He is not judging the supervisee and his responses but rather attempting to understand why he answers in the way he does. She presents a pattern for identification, which the worker might emulate in thinking about Frank.

Jim then reminded me of the foster mother's complaints and of how he had tried to handle this with Frank by telling him he should find a job and give up his "bad" associates. I said he seemed to be questioning this himself, did he think people always did what they were told to do? In the Army they did. This was always true? What about the men who went AWOL? He pointed out that they took the consequences and I agreed that we all have to do that. He reminisced about the difference in officers, how some were not liked and had a lot of trouble because the men would not obey them. In other words, I said, it made a difference how the men felt about their superiors. Of course, if they trusted them it was OK. I said I was sure this was true, and suggested we get back to Frank. "You mean with Frank it's different, I'm not still in the Army." I thought it must be hard getting away from giving orders or carrying them out. "Yes, I see what you mean. I don't think mine are going to work with Frank."

Earlier in the conference the worker has allied himself with the foster mother against Frank ("He's just lazy like Mrs. D. says"). Here the supervisee is separating himself from the foster mother, and this change follows from his change of feeling about Frank.

The supervisor uses comparison and contrast to teach a sensitivity to the unique, individualized aspects of this situation. He helps Jim factor out the essential differences between this and an apparently comparable situation, his army experience. The supervisor employs a context that is meaningful for the supervisee and also follows the principle of moving from the familiar to the unfamiliar. The supervisor keeps to a relevant focus, however, by relating this situation to the problem that is of concern to them, how best to help Frank. To the good teacher, nothing introduced by the worker is irrelevant. It is the responsibility of the supervisor to take what has been presented and relate it to the tasks of the supervisory conference.

I asked Jim how, then, he thought he could help Frank, and he replied ruefully that he was not sure—it had seemed simple before, he would just tell him what he should do. Now he realizes Mrs. D. has been doing this right along and it hasn't worked. I asked if he thought he could help the foster mother understand Frank better. He thought he could try and added that he guessed she felt annoyed at Frank like he did. "How do you think Frank feels?" He said he had just been thinking about that and thought he might well be feeling all alone, like nobody cared, and that must be awful. I agreed and said, "I can see you do care what happens to Frank, and I think if you got that over to him, maybe in time Frank can learn to trust you."

Having helped Jim come to the conclusion that the approach he had been using with Frank was not likely to work and having helped him learn why it was not likely to work, the supervisor returns to the basic question that is the focus of the conference—how to help Frank. Now the question can be discussed with greater clarity and with greater motivation on the part of Jim to consider new approaches. The preceding discussion has made a teachable moment possible. The supervisor optimizes the supervisee's involvement by asking how Jim now thinks he can be helpful to Frank.

The supervisor recognizes and accepts the supervisee's dependence on him for suggesting possible new approaches at this point. In response to this need he suggests an approach ("I asked if he thought he could help the foster mother understand Frank better").

Jim is not only achieving a greater understanding of Frank but, in applying a general approach focused on understanding rather than judging, he is achieving greater empathy with the foster mother as well ("He guessed she felt annoyed at Frank like he did"). The supervisor teaches here, as she did somewhat earlier ("It made a difference how the men felt about their supervisors"), the importance of feelings in relationships—the fact that people behave toward one another in terms of how they feel about one another ("You do care what happens to Frank and . . . maybe in time Frank can learn to trust you"). The supervisor goes on to teach that the worker is part of this complex interaction; that his feelings toward the client are a determinant of the interaction in the relationship (feeling frustrated, he might feel angry toward Frank); that the worker's feelings that intrude on the relationship, once identified, can be controlled.

> Jim said he too could see how it would take time, whereas he had thought he could do it all in one interview. I said it was hard to realize that change comes slowly in people. I thought he had made a good beginning and realized that he had noticed Frank seemed more cheerful and spoke more easily at the end of the interview. He hoped so but felt he needed to do a lot more thinking before he saw Frank again.
>
> He guessed it wasn't the way he thought, that you can learn all about casework in ten easy lessons. I laughed and said it was good that he was realizing this, but I knew it was hard too when he wanted so much to know all the answers. When we didn't, we could feel frustrated, and perhaps that was some of the reason he had felt angry at Frank. Jim was very thoughtful and said this helped him to understand something that had happened in another interview and we went on to discuss that.

Utilizing the experience Jim has just gone through, the supervisor teaches about expectations for change. Inferentially the supervisor reassures and supports Jim by indicating that he does not expect him to change Frank overnight—nor should Jim expect this for himself. The supervisor supports and excuses his frustration at not being able to learn all about casework in a few lessons.

The supervisor's general approach is consistent with that communicated throughout the conference. His accepting, understanding, supportive attitude, readiness to praise the worker where commendation is warranted, and willingness to grant the worker autonomy and to move at his pace have created a nonthreatening climate favorable to learning.

The approach is not so permissive, however, as to be totally without anxiety. There is clear indication that although the supervisor accepts Jim's current professional deficiencies, he does expect him to learn to do better. This is the best kind of anxiety for learning—anxiety based not on fear but on the discrepancy between what the worker needs to know and perhaps wants to know and what he does, in fact, know.

This section of the conference concludes before the conference itself is ended. The next section is introduced by the supervisee once again, this time on the basis of association with related problems—a natural and desirable procedure for transition, indicating the supervisee's ability to generalize his learning.

Some readers might regard the supervisor's approach as too passive or too Socratic. He might have been more active in stimulating Jim to think about certain significant aspects of the case that were largely ignored. It might have been helpful to clarify the target of change efforts—Frank, the foster mother, or both. While suggesting that Jim help the foster mother to understand Frank better, he made no effort to develop how this might be accomplished. There was little exploration of how the foster mother felt and the basis for her reaction in the situation. Rather than agreeing readily with Jim that replacement was undesirable, the supervisor might have helped him clarify his thinking about the advantages and disadvantages of replacement in this particular situation. Though indicating the importance of developing Frank's sense of trust in Jim, the supervisor offers little in the way of specifics as to how this might be accomplished. The worker needs help in identifying more clearly the kinds of approaches and interventions on his part that will enhance trust. Little effort was made to explain the nature of the general social situation relating to Frank's employment and job-training opportunities. The fact that some things are not covered may reflect the principle of partialization. Only so much can be included on the teaching agenda of any one conference, and the supervisor always has to be somewhat selective.

We might further note that the supervisor was aided in her efforts by an apt, willing, and capable supervisee; the conference might have gone less smoothly if Jim had been less cooperative and more resistive. This observation illustrates that teaching and learning require the cooperative efforts of all the participants in the interaction. The best supervisor will fail with some highly sensitive supervisees with limited capacity for learning, and the worst supervisor will succeed with some highly cooperative and capable supervisees.

Summary

Educational supervision is concerned with helping workers learn what they need to know to do their jobs effectively. Educational and administrative supervision have the same objectives, and educational supervision supplements administrative supervision by furthering the internalization of administrative controls, developing a professional orientation and a sense of loyalty among colleagues.

The supervisor has the responsibility of teaching the worker content regarding people, problems, process, and place and developing the self-awareness of personnel with regard to aspects of functioning that are clearly job-related.

The regularly scheduled individual conference is the main locus of educational supervision. The teaching content is the supervisee's performance, and the teaching approach is based on an educational diagnosis of the supervisee. Preplanning and preparation are necessary, and during the conference the supervisor engages the supervisee in a systematic, critical analysis of the work he or she did and is planning to do.

5 | Principles and Problems in Implementing Educational Supervision

In implementing the responsibilities of administrative supervision, the supervisor acts as a manager. In implementing the responsibilities of educational supervision, the supervisor acts as a teacher. The previous chapter was concerned with what the supervisor teaches. The present chapter is concerned with how the supervisor teaches principles of teaching and learning. It is further concerned with some of the problems in implementing the process of educational supervision.

Conditions for Effective Teaching and Learning: Introduction

The supervisor's principal responsibility in educational supervision is to teach the worker how to do the job. Our task here is to delineate what promotes effective teaching and learning. The teacher can organize content, provide a suitable atmosphere for learning, and make learning available but cannot ensure its acceptance and certainly not its use. Only the learner can do this. Teaching is essentially the art of assisting another to learn. As Robinson says, "Teaching provides the subject matter, the stimulus, the materials, sets the tasks and defines the conditions. But learning is the process of utilizing opportunity and limits in one's way for one's own ends" (1936:128). Learning is a creative personal experience.

In implementing educational supervision, the supervisor has the responsibility of knowing the content that needs to be learned, knowing how to teach it effectively, and for creating, sustaining, and managing a social and emotional environment that facilitates learning.

A good teacher has expert knowledge of the content to be taught, is highly motivated to teach it, has a high level of teaching skills, is capable of designing an effective learning program, is enthusiastic about the subject, and has respect for and confidence in the learners. The necessary knowledge base required for good educational supervision is not confined to the subject matter to be taught. It also extends to necessary knowledge about teaching techniques, knowledge about the student who is the learner, and self-knowledge of the teacher.

Our interest here is in how learners learn. The supervisor needs to be aware of some of the factors that facilitate learning and know something about techniques that maximize it. In the following section we outline some general principles of learning and some techniques derived from these principles that are applicable to the supervisory conference.

Principle 1: We Learn Best if We Are Highly Motivated to Learn

In applying this educational principle the supervisor can use the following techniques:

1. Explain the usefulness of the content to be taught. We owe the worker some explanation as to why it might be important to know this material if he or she is to discharge his or her professional responsibilities effectively. Motivation increases as usefulness of the content becomes clear. A new worker may not appreciate the importance, for instance, of learning effective referral procedures. If we can show, by citing the relevant research, the sizable percentage of people who need referral service and the effects of different referral procedures on subsequent client experience, the worker may better understand the significance of this unit of learning. The adult learner (Memmott and Brennan 1998) is concerned with current problems that require learning for solution. In teaching-learning situations involving adults we can take advantage of this orientation by stressing the utility and applicability of what is learned.

2. Make learning meaningful in terms of the individual worker's motives and needs. However useful or significant the material is generally, the worker is not likely to be motivated unless one can show its usefulness and importance for a problem or situation that is meaningful to him or her. Showing how supervisees could have improved on their last interviews if they had had a surer grasp of the dynamics of behavior will do more to increase motivation than lectures on the general importance of such knowledge.

The closer the training is to the actual job of the worker, the more specific it is to the worker's problems, the more directly it is perceived by the worker as meeting his or her needs and satisfying any concerns. This has been found repeatedly in national (Vinokur 1983) and regional (Leung and Cheung 1998) studies of in-service training in child welfare.

3. Tie areas of low motivation to areas of high motivation. The worker may be very motivated to help the client but indifferent to the content the supervisor is attempting to teach—for instance, recording. If the supervisor can demonstrate that tape or video recording permits the worker to be more helpful to the client (Kivlighan, Angelone, and Swafford 1991), he or she may then be more motivated to learn it.

One needs to be aware of the variety of the possible motives for learning. Motivation is an internal process initiated by a need that leads to goal seeking. Intrinsic motives are tied to the content itself. People want to study the content because they are interested in the material, because there are intrinsic rewards in meeting and mastering the challenge of the content (Csikszentmihalyi and Csikszentmihalyi 1988), and because there is pleasure in acquiring knowledge that helps solve professional problems (Gleeson 1992).

Motives may be largely extrinsic, however. Learning the content is only a way of reaching subsequent goals. There may be psychic rewards from the approbation of peers, the supervisor, parents, or even one's own professional superego. Other psychic rewards are derived from competitively learning better than peers in the agency. Learning the content may be motivated by a desire for autonomy and independence, so that one does not have to turn to the supervisor for help. There may also be administrative rewards, such as pay raises and promotions.

Motives for learning may result from a developing commitment to the agency, its staff, and its objectives. Having a strong conviction in the agency's objectives, the worker wants to see them achieved as effectively as possible. Motivation is strengthened by identification with the agency and colleagues. Feeling identified with the agency, workers want the agency to be favorably perceived by the community; feeling loyal and close to their colleagues, they want their good opinion. As a consequence of these considerations, the worker is motivated to learn so as to be as competent as possible.

Research on the nature of job satisfaction helps clarify the incentives that are likely to motivate on-the-job learning. The main studies on job satisfaction have been done by Herzberg and his colleagues in a wide variety of contexts (Herzberg 1968; Herzberg, Mausner, and Snyderman 1959). Five factors were identified as the principal sources of job satisfaction for most people. Arranged in order of frequency, these are achievement (feeling pleased with something done in which one would take pride), recognition (good work was commented on and complimented), the work itself (the work was interesting, challenging, varied), responsibility (freedom to do the work independently and autonomously), and advancement (the possibility of moving up to more responsible positions). These factors can be used to motivate learning. For instance, there is greater possibility of meeting the need for achievement if the worker learns how to do the job more effectively; learning to do the job increases the probability that the worker will be granted more responsibility and more opportunity to work independently; and learning to do the job enhances the possibility of advancement.

We would do well to utilize any and all motives to optimize learning. If the worker wants a promotion or raise (or a student wants a high grade) we can tie these motives to the need to learn the content as a requirement for achieving their goals.

Motivation increases receptivity to learning and makes energy available for learning. It thus sets the stage for learning and provides the teachable moment. But it does not in itself make for learning. The supervisor has to take advantage of the teachable situation to teach something of significance. Motivation needs to be provided with a learning opportunity and direction. The supervisor provides guidance to the learning that motivation seeks.

4. Because motivation is of such crucial significance, the supervisor needs to safeguard and stimulate motivation where it exists and instill it where it does not. Motivation indicates a readiness for learning. Workers who lack motivation to learn certain content may have no perceived need for it. They are satisfied with what they are doing, in the way they are doing it. They have no problem that requires additional learning for its solution. The workers may be right, in which case the supervisor has nothing to teach them.

If the supervisor, however, is convinced that the workers' perception of their performance is wrong and that there is much they need to learn, he or she would first have to stimulate dissatisfaction with their performance. The supervisor may want to confront the workers with the gap between what they are doing and what they can do, what they are doing and what needs to be done, what they are doing and what they want to be able to do. Dissatisfaction with current performance is a necessary prerequisite before workers are ready to learn new and better ways of working with clients. Workers are more likely to be motivated when they are somewhat uneasy (Stoltenberg and McNeill 1997).

Consequently, the supervisor makes a deliberate but compassionate effort to create some desire for or curiosity about the learning he or she has to offer. Rather than being passive in the face of lack of motivation, the supervisor acts as a catalyst for change, creating tension that needs to be resolved.

The worker's equilibrium needs to be disturbed if receptivity to learning is to be stimulated.

At times the "supervisor must awaken anxiety by penetrating the rationalization and defenses that bind it. If the supervisor avoids conflict for purposes of keeping the supervisory relationship untroubled and outwardly smooth, he will have abdicated his responsibility to the supervisee and will have compromised his trustworthiness" (Mueller and Kell 1972:30–31).

Motivation for learning follows the general principle that all behavior is purposeful. We learn only when we want to learn, when we feel a need to learn. Although this justifies stimulation of a need, such a procedure may be unnecessary. The first assumption about an apparently unmotivated supervisee might well be that we are not sensitive enough to discern the motives that he or she does have. It would initially be better to attempt to understand and use those motives that the learner him- or herself brings to the situation. We might need to recognize that in some cases the problem is not that the worker is unmotivated but that he or she is *differently* motivated. The problem is not lack of motivation but difference in motivation. By discovering the nature of these different motivations, one might be able to exploit them in the service of motivating learning.

Principle 2: We Learn Best When We Can Devote Most of Our Energies to Learning

Energy needed to defend against rejection, anxiety, guilt, shame, fear of failure, attacks on autonomy, or uncertain expectations is energy deflected from learning. Using the following techniques, we can maximize the amount of energy available for learning.

1. Providing structure means clearly establishing the time, place, roles, limits, expectations, obligations, and objectives of supervision (Freeman 1993). Providing structure mitigates anxiety by focusing learning. If workers are anxious because they are uncertain of what is expected of them in the role of supervisee, they are not fully free to devote full attention to learning (Costa 1994). Therefore, the nature of the supervisory relationship should be clear. The frequency of supervisory meetings, the length of such conferences, the respective responsibilities, expectations, and obligations of supervisee and supervisor in preparation for and in the conduct of such conferences should be clearly established, mutually understood and mutually accepted. Such details provide the comfort of an unambiguous structure.

Clarity relates to learning objectives as well (Ching 1993; Talen and Schindler 1993). The supervisor needs to know, and to share with the supervisee, some idea of where he or she hopes the learner is going, what he or she will know and be able to do after learning what the supervisor hopes to teach. Objectives give meaning to each discrete learning unit and permit us to measure progress. As Seneca said, "No wind is favorable if you do not know your destination." We learn best if the learning objectives are clearly identified, if we know what to look for, and if we have a sense of priorities. However, Shulman (1991:166) reports: "When I ask participants in my supervision workshops to spell out their sense of their role . . . most tell me they never had a supervisor who was clear about purpose and role."

2. Respect the worker's rights, within limits, to determine his or her own solutions. The structure, though supportive in its clarity, should not be so rigid that it becomes restrictive. Supervisory rigidity contributes to poor supervisory experiences (Anderson, Schlossberg, and Rigazio-DiGilio 2000). Some flexibility needs to be permitted the supervisee to prevent psychic energy from being diverted from learning to deal with rising hostility and resentment at infantilization. This is particularly true in adult education, because learners operate with considerable freedom and autonomy in other significant areas of their lives. Here, however, they are partially dependent, as is every learner who needs to turn to others to teach what he or she does not yet know. As a generally independent adult, one is more apt to resent this necessary dependency. The supervisor should then permit the greatest amount of independence that the learner can profitably use without danger to the client. Respect for the worker's autonomy and initiative ensures that psychic energy necessary for learning will not be dissipated in defense of autonomy.

3. Establish an atmosphere of accepting, psychological safety, a framework of security. Learning implies a risk of mistakes and a risk of failure. It also implies a confession of ignorance. A worker who fears censure and rejection for admitting failure or ignorance will devote psychic energy to defense against such anticipated attacks. The supervisor should be the supervisee's mentor, not a tormentor. An atmosphere of acceptance permits a freer involvement in risk-taking and a greater psychic concentration on learning rather than on self-defense. Learning takes place best in an interaction that permits mistakes (if not condones them) and recognizes the ambiguity and indefiniteness of the available answers.

The effects of the supervisor's attitude of acceptance on the worker's performance is described by a worker.

I didn't feel that I was getting criticized for what I was doing. So a lot of my feelings of anxiety and discomfort began to dissipate as I was not getting criticism from him: therefore, I wasn't criticizing myself—as harshly anyway. And I was feeling more comfortable. As I began to feel more comfortable—

the more comfortable I felt, it's like the more ready I was to take that more critical look at what I had done. The more sure I felt that I wasn't a complete asshole, that I wasn't blowing it right and left, that I was OK in the room— I wasn't going to permanently damage anybody or any of that—and that the person I was presenting was really myself and not something that I was trying to do for my absent supervisor, the more ready I became to ask questions of myself and what I was doing in technique and all that. It wasn't laden with all the feelings and all the anxiety and all that. (Herrick 1977:136)

The impact on the supervisee of a supervisor who communicates non-acceptance is described by a supervisee.

I would just get angrier and angrier inside and I would get tighter and tighter and more closed, and whatever it was that we were supposed to be talking about around my client no longer became important because the dynamics that were going on between the two of us were so heavy that I couldn't even think about whatever it was that I was supposed to be thinking about. (Herrick 1977:95)

Learning does not merely result in adding knowledge and skills to those already available to the learner. It also involves the risk of change in attitudes, values, and behavior as the new learning modifies the learner's perception of the world and people. The risk of change is anxiety-provoking. We often fear what the consequences of change might be for us. If the supervisor is empathic in regard to the anxiety created by change resulting from learning and is supportive, there is less of a need to devote psychic energy to defend against change and to bind associated anxiety.

But acceptance involves expectations. Psychological safety does not mean a permissiveness that ignores the demand for adequate performance on the part of the worker. We must make firm demands on the worker for learning what he or she needs to learn. But demands should be made in a friendly way, out of a desire to help rather than to hurt. They do create tension, but such tension is necessary to motivate the supervisee to learn.

The supervisor has to be consistently helpful to the supervisee rather than consistently popular. This means challenging error, calling attention to ignorance, and pointing to mistakes and deficiencies in performance. The supervisor has to offer a judicious balance between stimulus and support. The supervisor is responsible for maintaining the balance between the level of tension that motivates and challenges and the level of tension that immobilizes a worker. We utilize the tension that derives not from the fear of failure but from the discrepancy between what the worker knows and what he or she wants to know. It involves making demands with the utmost possible respect, compassion, and understanding. It would be foolish to pretend that balancing these contradictory and vaguely defined variables is anything but the most difficult of tasks.

4. Acknowledge and use what the worker already knows and can do. This technique decreases anxiety because it indicates to the worker that he or she can draw on what he or she already knows to meet the demands of supervision. Affirmation and use of the already rich learning the worker brings to the teaching-learning situation is an advantageous aspect of adult education.

5. Move from the familiar to the unfamiliar. The unfamiliar provokes anxiety. If the supervisor can relate new material to familiar material, the new learning seems less strange and less difficult to learn.

6. Demonstrate confidence, if warranted, in the worker's ability to learn. He or she may have doubts about his or her own abilities, doubts against which he or she needs to defend at some expenditure of psychic energy robbed from learning. Communication of a feeling of confidence in the worker's ability, where warranted, helps allay feelings that detract from learning. Confidence in the learner's ability to learn is contagious. Communication of confidence increases motivation for and interest in learning.

At the same time the supervisor has to accept and make allowances for the fact that learning is a growth process and takes time. One must expect nonproductive plateaus where little progress is being made. There needs to be time for reflection, absorption, and consolidation of learning. There is likely to be some regression in learning, much zigging and zagging. Like all growth processes, it is uneven and variable; different kinds of content are learned at different rates of speed.

7. Know your content; be ready and willing to teach it. The supervisor needs not only the wish but also the ability to be helpful. The worker does not know what he or she needs to know, and this makes him or her anxious. This anxiety is tempered, however, by the fact that if the worker does not know, at least the supervisor knows the answer to some of his or her questions. The supervisor not only knows but is willing to share this knowledge with the worker, if necessary. If the supervisor does not know or seems unwilling to share knowledge, tension is increased because it suggests to the supervisee that he or she faces the prospect of dealing with situations with no adequate assistance available. Inevitably on some occasions, the supervisor might have to say, "I don't know." But then he or she needs to add, "We will try to find out." Lack of knowledge in a situation that requires responsible action is anxiety-provoking. Knowing that someone knows and is ready to provide helpful knowledge diminishes anxiety. It might be noted that

supervisor competence (rather than omniscience) is all that the supervisee does and can expect. But the greater professional competence of the supervisor can help meet the supervisees' legitimate dependence needs. The supervisor has to be capable and ready to meet these needs.

The negative effect on the supervisee when perceived legitimate dependency needs are thwarted is described by a supervisee.

> And sometimes her tone would get condescending: "Now, B., you're bright. You can think of that." For instance, if I was having difficulty with something and asked for some suggestions, that would be the sort of response she would give me. It was like, unless I did everything on my own, I wasn't putting forth enough effort. I could've used at times more help from her—very direct help— rather than, "What do you think?" There were a couple times when we went back and forth—it's amazing—where she'd say, "Well, what do you think?" after I asked for help; and I'd say, "I don't know, what do you think?" And she would—very straight-faced—come back with, "Well, what do you think?" And I'd say, "Look, H., I really thought about it very hard; and I can't come up with anything else. That's why I'm asking you." (Herrick 1977:154–55)

Principle 3: We Learn Best When Learning Is Successful and Rewarding

The following techniques help the worker repeat what is satisfying and avoid repeating what is painful.

1. Set conditions of learning to ensure high probability of success by optimizing the balance between the skills of the worker and the challenges of practice (Csikszentmihalyi and Csikszentmihalyi 1988). Intrinsically rewarding, each successful experience in one's practice reinforces the behavior associated with the successful experience.

It would be inadvisable to present the worker with a learning demand that is clearly beyond his or her capacity to meet. If there is little chance of success, there is little motivation to try. Learners need some assurance that they can succeed if they are going to risk themselves trying. On the other hand, the task needs to be sufficiently challenging to engage the workers' interest and prompt them to extend themselves. If a task is too easy, one is not likely to experience a feeling of success in achieving it. Selecting a learning task that is challenging but not overwhelming is a neat trick. Admittedly, it is much easier to describe than to do, particularly without any gauge by which to measure how much challenge a worker can hope to meet successfully.

2. We increase positive satisfactions in learning if we praise (where warranted) success in professional accomplishment. Praise is a psychic reward that reinforces the behavior prompting the commendation. Indiscriminate praise is counterproductive, however. The supervisee is an adult capable of independent critical assessment of his or her own performance. If we praise performance that he or she recognizes as substandard, we lose credibility and our subsequent assessments are discounted. The worker might feel he or she cannot trust our judgment. It is therefore important to commend only what can be defended as objectively praiseworthy. The supervisor should be specific about the behavior that has elicited approval. We should not use the general statement, "You really indicated your understanding of Mr. P.'s behavior," but the specific statement, "You really indicated your understanding of Mr. P.'s behavior when you said . . . in response to his comment about . . ." Such specificity not only ensures that such learning is attended by positive satisfactions because it is being rewarded but also makes conscious and explicit the behavior that the supervisor hopes to reinforce.

Pleasure and pain, reward and punishment overlap with the question of motivation in learning. We are motivated to learn so that we can avoid the pain that comes from inability to deal successfully with problems in job performance. We are motivated to learn to feel the pleasure of doing a job competently and effectively. We are motivated to learn so that we can avoid the punishment of being dependent and can obtain the reward of acting autonomously. We are motivated to learn so that we can avoid the pain of criticism and guilt and be rewarded with praise and approbation from ourselves and from significant others, including the supervisor. We are motivated to learn to avoid the dissatisfaction that comes from the uncertainty of not clearly knowing what we are supposed to be doing or how to do it. We are motivated to learn to feel the satisfaction in the security that comes from knowing, with assurance, what it's all about.

3. Praise through positive feedback also helps. Such reinforcement is most effective if offered while the learning situation to which it applies is still fresh and vivid. This fact emphasizes the importance of regularly scheduled conferences at reasonably frequent intervals (once a week perhaps) so that the supervisor can offer critical reaction to recently encountered experiences in which learning has been applied by the supervisees. Assessment of results is necessary if the learner is to experience a feeling of success, which is a reward.

4. Periodic stock-taking provided in a formal evaluation conference at less frequent intervals (every six months perhaps) further ensures learning attended by positive satisfaction because it permits a perspective on long-

range progress. The supervisee can get some sense of progress in learning over time, which is rewarding.

5. We ensure the greater probability of success if we partialize learning. As the adage goes, "A man can eat a whole steer—one steak at a time." We offer learning in digestible dosages. The agenda for a particular conference should cover a limited, defined unit of learning that is clear, acceptable, and attainable.

6. Success and positive satisfactions in learning are more likely if the material is presented in a graded sequence, from the simple to the complex, from the obvious to the obscure. It involves moving from more concrete consideration of case material to more theoretical conceptualizations of cases.

It is easier for a worker to understand concrete situational needs—such as a home for a totally dependent, abandoned infant—than it is to understand, say, the psychological dependency needs of a middle-aged neurotic. It is easier to understand that feelings are facts than to grasp the idea of ambivalence. Grading the complexity of content is more difficult in social work than it is in mathematics or chemistry. Seemingly simple situations have a tendency to present unanticipated complexities. However, to the extent that we can discern the measure of comparative difficulty of material to be taught, we should attempt to teach the simpler content first.

There are some general criteria for differentiating between simpler and more difficult social-work learning situations. The client who is motivated to use the service, has good ego strength, is not unduly defensive, and with whom the worker can identify in some way presents less difficulty. A situation in which cause-and-effect relationships are clear, for which remedial resources and services are available, and in which the problem is well focused, also presents less difficulty. These characteristics represent treatable clients in treatable situations, ensuring greater probability of the successful application of learning. Alternatively, the client who appears impulsive and predatory, unmotivated to use services, and threatening to the worker makes learning difficult.

7. We ensure the greater probability of positive satisfaction in learning if we prepare the worker for failure. It may be necessary to expose the worker to situations of a complexity and difficulty for which he or she is not yet fully prepared. The demands of case coverage may not always permit the assignment of cases that are within the worker's competence. In such instances it would be helpful to explicitly recognize with the worker the possibility of failure in the encounter. He or she is then less likely to be overwhelmed by personal guilt or shame and be more open to learning from the experience.

Principle 4: We Learn Best if We Are Actively Involved in the Learning Process

1. The supervisee should be encouraged to participate in planning the agenda for the supervisory sessions. This technique ensures the supervisee's active involvement in the learning situation. In addition, it increases the probability that content of primary interest and concern to the supervisee will be discussed.

Active participation in selecting the content for learning tends to heighten commitment to the task of learning. This is the content the learner suggested that he or she was motivated to learn. The objectives of the learning-teaching encounter are therefore probably acceptable to the worker. Although we might need to start where the worker is, we still have an obligation to educate toward where the agency wants him or her to be. There are objective performance standards that need to be met. In a gesture of mutual egalitarianism, we cannot give priority to the workers' educational choices. We are constrained to teach what they need to learn, not what they want to learn. But the two are often reconcilable; knowing what the individual learner is interested in learning may enable the supervisor to bring "wants" and "needs" closer to each other.

2. We ensure the greater active involvement of the supervisee in learning if we encourage and provide opportunity for the learner to question, discuss, object, express doubt. The supervisor should supplement (rather than substitute for) a supervisee's thinking. Thinking is trial acting. The worker will use what is being taught in active encounters with clients. He or she can, however, also be encouraged to engage with the content to be learned through discussion. This is a cognitive rather than behavioral engagement with the learning but one that nevertheless requires active participation in learning. Such involvement of the supervisees is only possible in an atmosphere of psychological safety in which the supervisees feel comfortable about questioning the supervisor and presenting their own, perhaps opposing, points of view.

3. Provide the explicit opportunity to utilize and apply the knowledge we seek to teach. If we are teaching the worker some of the principles of client advocacy, we would need to provide an assignment that involves the worker in client advocacy. The worker then, of necessity, is actively engaged in testing the learning through use. We learn by doing. Learning determines action, but successful action reinforces learning.

However, the worker may engage in incompetent practice. Consequently, providing practice experience has to be followed by a critical review of what was done. Such feedback enables the worker to know specifically what might need correction and change. This review should again be followed by the opportunity to practice the corrected learning.

Principle 5: We Learn Best if the Content Is Meaningfully Presented

1. As much as possible, select for teaching the content that is of interest and concern to the supervisee. Readiness for learning is often related to a specific situation of some sort. The worker needs to know what will help him or her deal with a problem with a particular client. This is the teachable moment for the presentation of the relevant content. At this point the content has meaning for the supervisee and can be taught most effectively.

2. Content is meaningfully presented if it fits into some general theoretical framework. Different supervisors adhere to different theoretical systems—psychoanalytic psychology, behaviorism, existential psychology, and so on. The choice of system is not as important as the fact that there is belief in some comprehensive, internally consistent configuration that satisfactorily explains the mysteries of human behavior (at least for its adherents). Our subject matter is people. We need some cognitive map, some cosmology, that makes sense of why people do what they do in the way they do it.

It is difficult to learn discrete, unrelated details of behavior. If, however, the supervisor is knowledgeable about some well-articulated scheme, he or she can relate details to principles that act as an organizing focus for details. Whatever one's opinion is regarding id-ego-superego or drive-stimulus-response, one needs to recognize that these ideas suggest large-scale, coherent, explanatory frameworks of human behavior that meaningfully organize details regarding the human condition. The supervisor needs to have available some reasonably comprehensive explanatory framework that meaningfully organizes the content he or she is attempting to teach. Such ideological scaffolding provides the "unity behind the plurality of experiences" and gives a sense of connectedness to discrete learnings.

Bruner notes that "perhaps the most basic thing that can be said about human memory after a century of intensive research is that unless detail is placed into a structured pattern it is rapidly forgotten" (Bruner 1963:24). "Organizing facts in terms of principle and idea from which they may be inferred is the only known way of reducing the quick rate of loss of human memory" (Bruner 1963:31). Bruner further comments that "the principal problem of human memory is not storage but retrieval" and that "the key to retrieval is organization" (Bruner 1963:32). We learn best if we can organize the discrete data in terms of some unifying concepts or some unifying theoretical framework. An ideological framework helps organize the chaos of unfamiliar and seemingly unrelated data.

3. Meaningful teaching is selective teaching. Some things are more important than others; some content requires more attention, emphasis, or repetition than other content. The supervisor needs to have priorities that guide the choice of content to be taught.

4. Imaginative repetition makes learning more meaningful. If we select a number of experiences that teach the same idea in different ways, it is easier for learners to grasp and accept. Through comparison and contrast and illustration of similarities and differences, the same content is more meaningfully presented.

Practice of skills is, after all, the opportunity to repeat in different situations the exercise of such skills. But repetition is not haphazard. It is carefully selected in terms of organizing principles. As Tyler (1971:83) states, "for educational experiences to produce a cumulative effect they must be organized so as to reinforce each other." The best repetition involves not sheer drill of old learning but some variation that includes new elements to capture the learner's interest. We learn best if the material is presented in a way that is novel, varied, and challenging. Such presentations tend to keep the learner stimulated and interested.

5. Teaching that is planned in terms of continuity (reiteration of important content—deepening learning), sequence (successively building toward greater complexity—broadening learning), and integration (relating different kinds of content to each other) is likely to be presented in a more meaningful context. Content has to be organized according to a plan and systematically presented if it is to be taught effectively.

6. Some of the techniques mentioned in relation to previously cited principles of learning are applicable here as well. The content is more meaningful if the supervisor can relate new learning to previously acquired learning, moving from the familiar to the unfamiliar, and if the content can be presented in logical progressions (moving from simple to complex).

7. Learning is more meaningful if it can be made conscious and explicit. We are not always aware of what we have learned. To the extent that we can consciously articulate and label what we have learned, the learning is apt to be more meaningful and transferable. This fact calls attention to the need for periodic recapitulation and summarization of units of completed learning.

Principle 6: We Learn Best if the Supervisor Takes Into Consideration the Supervisee's Uniqueness

1. Individualize the learner through educational diagnosis. Educational diagnosis involves a precise definition of the knowledge and skills a particular

worker needs to do the specific tasks required at a level of proficiency that meets agency standards and how he or she might best learn this. We study the learner so that we can understand how he or she learns. Although Lochner and Melchert (1997) have found that a supervisee's cognitive style predicts whether he or she prefers a task-focused versus relationship-focused supervisory learning environment, research by Itzhaky and Eliahu suggests that social work students and their supervisors tend to prefer a person-oriented supervisory style, characterized by "mutual communication, support, and emotional expression" (1999:77).

Educational diagnosis of supervisees includes a statement regarding what they already know well, what they need to learn, what they want to learn, and how they want to learn it. To individualize teaching we need to know not only where the worker is but where he or she wants to go. With such an educational diagnosis, we are in a better position to fit the learning situation to the learner rather than vice versa. The advantage of tutorial teaching in the supervisory context is precisely that the supervisor can tailor the choice of approach and content to the learning needs of the individual supervisee (Memmott and Brennan 1998).

In making an educational diagnosis of supervisees, one needs to consider the special attributes of the adult learner. Adult learners have a long attention span, can sustain learning activity and postpone gratification for long periods. A good deal of adult learning might more properly be termed relearning rather than primary learning, and the learning process therefore involves some necessary unlearning. There is more resistance to accepting the temporary dependency that learning often requires. Adult learners are, of course, often able to articulate what they want to learn and why they want to learn it. Maximum participation of the learner in the teacher-learner interaction is not only desirable but eminently feasible. The adult learner has a fund of learning and life experience that might be adapted to the current learning situation.

The educational diagnosis of the individual adult learner is developed in ongoing contact with him. The supervisor observes the supervisee's use of supervision, the level of motivation manifested, the balance of rigidity and flexibility in learning, the level of preparation for and participation in conferences, and the general attitude toward the content to be learned and toward the learning situation. The supervisor attempts to discern the procedures that elicit the supervisee's best response. Some people learn best in a highly structured situation; others learn best in a loosely structured situation; some learn through listening, others through reading; some learn only through action in a practice situation; others cannot begin to act until they have learned; some learn best in an individual tutorial situation; others learn best through group interaction; some learn best through ready acceptance of teaching; others learn best through active opposition to content presented; some are ready to learn but are less ready to be taught.

There are many questions to be considered when approaching this issue. Is resistance to learning (Itzhaky and Aloni 1996) manifested in submissiveness, detachment, arrogance, aggression, self-deprecation, dependence, and ingratiation? What failures in performance are due to ignorance or inexperience, amenable to change through education and experience, and what problems are the result of personality difficulties? What character defects impede learning and tie up psychic energy that might otherwise be available for learning? Is content learned for self-protection or for mastery of problem situations? Is learning collected as a possession or acquired for the aggrandizement of status? Does the supervisee think his or her way through a problem or feel his or her way through it? Is he or she responsive to a deductive pattern of instruction, moving from the general idea to the particular situation, or does the supervisee learn more readily inductively, requiring an experience with a series of similar situations before he or she can truly grasp the relevant generalization? Is he or she a fast learner, always ready and anxious for new material, or a learner who needs to take more time in integrating learning? Does the supervisee acknowledge his or her learning deficiencies and demonstrate a readiness to learn, or is his or her response characterized by denial and defensiveness? To what extent is the supervisee ready, willing, and able to take responsibility for his or her own learning needs? To what extent is the learner comfortable with uncertainty and ambiguity in the knowledge base available? To what extent does the supervisee need the certainty of unequivocal answers? The marginal learner needs to be distinguished from the resistant learner and the neurotically resistant learner from the situationally resistant learner.

How can the worker be described in terms of the variety of motives that energize people's interest and behavior? In McClelland and Burnham's (1976) terms, is the worker motivated by a need for interpersonal affiliation, for task achievement, or for power to influence others? In terms of Maslow's hierarchy of needs (Maslow 1968), is the worker motivated by a strong need for belonging, love, and social interaction, by a need for esteem and status, or by a need for self-actualization? In Herzberg's (1968) terms, is the worker motivated by maintenance needs, job security, salary, and working conditions or by needs for growth and development, increased responsibility, and recognition of accomplishment? What is the degree of cognitive complexity with which the worker approaches a situation—the extent to which he or she can perceive the multidimensional aspects of a problem?

A comprehensive educational diagnosis that individualizes the supervisee also includes some attention to learning problems associated with more personal aspects of the supervisee's functioning in interaction with the clients. These include learning problems relating to the reactivation of the worker's personal developmental problems in the interaction with the client and problems of selective identification with one aspect of the case situation. As a result of transference, the worker's perception of the client is distorted by seeing the client not as he or she actually is but as representing in some measure significant others from the worker's past. As a result of reactivation of developmental problems the worker may distort the client's situation by avoidance of significant content that would be important to recognize. As a result of selective identification, the worker may distort perception of the client's situation by "taking sides" with the child in a parent-child problem or with the wife in a marital problem. There are also difficulties that result from not only developmental problems but also problems with maturing—problems posed for the worker in moving from one state of life to another—from single to married, from nonparent to parent, from midlife crisis to retirement.

An educational diagnosis requires some attention to these sources of distortion, which can adversely affect the worker's ability to offer effective service. In the effort to identify such difficulty, the supervisor needs to be aware of some relevant symptomatic manifestations. The consistent failure on the part of the worker to discuss content that might logically be presumed to be important is a diagnostic clue. The total absence of any mention of the husband-father in the case of a child with a behavior problem or lack of any information regarding sexual adjustment in the case of a marital problem might also be suggestive.

An atypically sharp, disproportionate feeling reaction to some aspect of the client's situation might be another cue. The worker's response, if exaggerated, might suggest that the source of the reaction is only partially the client's situation and due more to the worker's own problems. Persistent stereotyping of the client based on limited evidence might suggest distortions in perception stemming from the worker.

Individualization implies some understanding of what the learner risks in learning this content; there are both internal risks and external risks. The internal risks relate to the meaning this learning has for the worker's self-image and current belief and attitudinal system. The external risks concern his or her relationship with his or her reference group. For instance, those who believe that the Bible is literal truth cannot afford to examine the proof in support of the theory of evolution; a right-wing conservative might feel out of place with his or her friends if he accepted liberal ideas about social welfare.

In an analysis of learning patterns of social workers as compared with other professional groups, Kolb (1981) identified the social worker's learning orientation as concrete-active. The pattern suggests a preference for learning through active involvement rather than detached, reflective, analytic observation of phenomena; learning through immersion in experience; or a tendency to solve problems in an intuitive trial-and-error manner. "The dominant philosophy is pragmatism and truth as defined by workability. Inquiry centers around the question of how actions shape events. The case study is the common method of inquiry and analysis" (Kolb 1981:244). (See also Anderson and Adams 1992; Kruzich et al. 1986; Van Soest and Kruzich 1994.)

2. The educational diagnosis should be used. The supervisor, in preparation for a conference, would need to review what the supervisee most needs to learn at this particular time, how best to approach teaching the content to this particular supervisee, how the supervisee is likely to react in response to the efforts to teach this content, and so on.

Individualization implies that each of us has a unique, best way of learning. However, though it is recognized that the supervisor may not always be capable of modulating the teaching approach to be neatly congruent with the needs of the learner, he or she should at least be understandingly aware of the nature of the learner's educational diagnosis.

3. It is desirable to engage the supervisee actively in an assessment of what he or she already knows and wants to learn. This once again individualizes the learning needs of the particular supervisee, spares him or her the boredom of redundant learning, and spares the supervisor the effort of teaching what does not need to be taught. In addition, the learner's employment record and record of experience at the agency give relevant information about his or her educational and experiential background.

Adult learners have at their command a variety of previously learned skills that may be retranslated for use in a social work context. In implementing educational supervision the supervisor might try to help the supervisee identify these skills and use them appropriately.

4. We individualize teaching according to differences in the pace of learning. It takes time to integrate newly learned material, to assimilate it with previous learning and make an accommodation to a new equilibrium in thinking and feeling, which the incorporation of learned material requires. Being asked to absorb too much too quickly threatens internal coherence and stability.

Although it is true that people learn more effectively when they learn at their own pace, there needs to be some recognition that both the agency and clients pay a heavy price for the slow pace of the slow learner. Neither can tolerate for long an excessively slow learner.

Establishing a Framework for Educational Supervision

Structure promotes conditions for effectively teaching and learning the social work job. This is achieved by establishing a framework for social work supervision. Freeman (1993) offers this advice for beginning supervision: (1) clarify the respective roles and responsibilities of the supervisor and supervisee, (2) describe how supervisory meetings will proceed, (3) explain the supervisor's theory of helping and its impact on performance expectations for the worker, (4) elaborate the process and standards for evaluating worker performance, and (5) describe the procedure for giving and receiving positive and negative feedback (see also Osborn and Davis 1996). At a minimum, the supervision contract should establish the format, day, time, place, and duration of supervisory meetings.

The Significance of the Supervisor-Supervisee Relationship for Educational Supervision

Throughout this chapter we have made allusions to the supervisor-supervisee relationship as having crucial significance for learning in supervision. The teacher-learner relationship is of prime importance because teaching is mainly a problem in human relationships. The term *relationship* as used here means the nature of emotional interaction. In general, learning can best take place when the nature of such interaction is positive, when teacher and learner accept each other and are comfortably relaxed with each other. The level of participation is higher and anxiety is lower in the context of a positive relationship, facilitating learning. There are a number of additional factors that suggest the importance of a good relationship for educational supervision.

Not only must the learner be motivated to accept the content of what needs to be learned, but he or she must be motivated and ready to accept it from the teacher. A worker resists accepting content offered by a supervisor he or she does not like and respect. The relationship, if positive, is the bridge over which the material passes from teacher to learner. If the relationship is negative, communication is blocked.

A positive relationship intensifies the impact of the supervisor's educational efforts. There is considerable empirical support for the contention that the nature of the supervisory relationship is a powerful variable in determining the supervisee's openness and receptivity to the supervisor's efforts to educate toward change (Goldstein, Heller, and Sechrest 1966:73–91). Relationship propels learning and makes content acceptable.

Identification with the supervisor heightens the worker's motivation to learn. As a consequence of identification, the worker wishes to be like the supervisor, to have his or her competence, and to learn to emulate him or her. Only if the relationship is positive will the worker identify with the supervisor.

The supervisor as model for identification is aptly described in the following, written by a supervisee:

> I guess his personal way of being was very strong in supervision. It was very warm, very relaxed, very comfortable—he smiled, laughed, sat back in his chair, and gazed off and smoked a cigar—and was just very interested but wasn't like sitting on the edge of his chair waiting for the next thing I would say so that he could respond to that. And I perceived that as indirectly giving me a model 'cause I figured that must be in some ways what he's like in therapy; and that's more what I would be like in therapy if I were myself. And it would also kinda make the client a lot more comfortable since it made me comfortable in supervision. "Aha!" I figured. "I should try to do that." It's very relaxing, and he uses strokes—makes supportive, reinforcing comments, but not overbearingly so—just does enough of that that I can believe it when he does it. And he never makes harsh, critical statements and his suggestions are usually specific, and he explains what he means by them and gives an example of it but somehow manages to do that without making me feel like a jerk for not having known to do that in the first place. (Herrick 1977: 139–40)

In learning through identification, the supervisor needs to give the supervisee the freedom to accept what he or she can use and reject or discard what does not seem appropriate. Such freedom leads to selective identification and selective learning rather than an indiscriminate mimicry of the supervisor.

Establishing and maintaining a positive relationship with the supervisee teaches essential social work skills, because in developing such a relationship, the supervisor is modeling the way in which the supervisee might effectively relate to the client (Bogo 1993). Having experienced a helping process in educational supervision, the worker is then in a better position to understand what is involved in seeking and using help. As Robinson (1949:30) states, "Since supervision in social casework teaches a helping process, it must itself be a helping process so that the [worker] experiences in his relationship with the supervisor a process similar to the one he must learn to use with his client." The educational alliance between supervisor and supervisee in significance and importance is analogous to the therapeutic alliance between worker and client.

The supervisory relationship itself, its nature and use, is an educational exemplification of what needs to be taught in developing clinical competence. An effective, positive supervisory relationship is analogous in many respects to a paradigm of the clinical helping relationship. The supervisory relationship is both the context for learning and a living learning experience in itself.

The influence effects in the supervisory relationship are like influence effects in the worker-client relationship, which is a two-stage process. The worker or supervisor, through communicating the facilitative conditions of empathic understanding, respect, and acceptance, establishes or increases his or her potential for influencing. Perceived as trustworthy, as having some expertise, and as a person the client or supervisee likes and wants to emulate, the worker or supervisor is in a position to influence toward change. The second stage in the process involves actually employing this influence potential to induce change.

Since Ekstein and Wallerstein (1972) emphasized the importance of the supervisory relationship, it has become the subject of considerable interest to researchers. Some empirical evidence suggests that the supervisory relationship affects the supervisee's development of counseling skills (Ellis and Ladany 1997:462–66), and that the supervisory relationship predicts the client outcomes of supervised social work practice (Harkness 1995, 1997; Shulman 1991, 1993). Such findings highlight the importance of research that seeks to identify additional factors and variables that influence the development and quality of the supervisory relationship. Thus, helping scientists have begun to examine how the supervisory relationship is affected by individual and developmental differences among supervisees and their supervisors on such dimensions as cognitive complexity and development, ego development, ethnicity and culture, experience, gender, learning and cognitive styles, personality, power, self-presentation (of anxiety, interpersonal attachment, and self-monitoring), sexual orientation, and theoretical orientation. Bernard and Goodyear (1998), Ellis and Ladany (1997), and Neufeldt, Beutler, and Banchero (1997) have conducted integrative reviews of this literature.

The Supervisor's Problems in Implementing Educational Supervision

To teach the content that is the curriculum of educational supervision, the supervisor needs to know the content. Keeping current with the relevant material in a fast-changing world with a rapid proliferation of new knowledge is a demanding task. Practice knowledge and competence are indispensable for effective first-line supervision generally and for educational supervision in particular. The power of expertise, a principal source of the supervisor's administrative authority, requires this. The responsibilities of educational supervision further require a solid grasp of the subject matter relevant to agency practice. The supervisor as a source of identification, as an admired practitioner, and as a model of effective practice, needs to project the image and the reality of competence. Consequently the supervisor faces the problem of assessing and, if necessary, upgrading theoretical knowledge and expertise.

Scott found that professionally oriented workers preferred a supervisor "to know the theoretical fundamentals of their discipline—be skilled in teaching casework methods and capable of offering professionally competent assistance" (1969:94–95). The supervisee looks to the supervisor to have available a knowledge base of previously developed solutions to practice problems. Studies of student evaluation of teaching show that a thorough knowledge of subject matter content is a necessary, if not sufficient requirement for good teaching.

In fact, in response to a question designed to identify their principal "strengths" in supervision, supervisors most frequently cited clinical knowledge, skill, and experience. Listing their greatest strengths, supervisors said:

> I have extensive knowledge and experience and am able to use that in developing skills in my supervisees.
> Experience and firsthand knowledge of the services I am supervising.
> Knowledge about what skills are needed to do the job and ability to impart that knowledge.
> My knowledge of public social service from budgeting to therapeutics. (Kadushin 1992b)

Many supervisees, responding to an analogous question about their perceptions of their supervisors' strengths, cited clinical expertise. Supervisees said:

> One of her principal strengths lies in her knowledge of theory and in her willingness to share this knowledge.
> Expert clinical knowledge which allows him to offer suggestions.
> Excellent knowledge he has of the theory, applied theory, agency dynamics and case work. (Kadushin 1992b)

In addition to the demand for practice expertise, there are additional problems in implementing educational supervision. Supervisors may exploit educational supervision to meet their own needs without being fully aware of it. The situation provides the opportunity for developing protégés, for making workers over into the supervisor's own professional image. In such instances, the supervisor becomes more an object of direct imitation than an object of identification. The worker's success is the supervisor's success; the worker's failures are perceived as the supervisor's failures. The supervisee is less an independent entity than an extension of the supervisor.

The supervisor who, in response to the triadic situation of client-worker-supervisor, is still more a worker than a supervisor, will focus too heavily on the client. Such a supervisor is still primarily interested in practice, albeit vicariously through the supervisee. He or she has not yet made the psychological transition from worker to supervisor. The consequence for educational supervision is that the supervisor denies the supervisee the freedom to learn. Giving exclusive priority to client needs, the supervisor is so fearful of mistakes by the supervisee that he or she tends to be overdirective and overcontrolling. The supervisor acts more like a guard than as a guide.

A supervisor may be hesitant in sharing knowledge and expertise with the supervisee out of anxiety about competition from a "sibling." If the supervisor derives gratification from the supervisee's dependency, he or she will perennially tend to perceive the worker as "not yet ready" for the next steps in education. In both these situations the supervisor tends to teach the content of educational supervision grudgingly, in small doses, and at an inappropriately slow rate. Evidence of workers' growing independence and competence is viewed with anxiety rather than pleasure. An imperious "need to be needed" on the part of the supervisor will further conflict with the responsibility to grant the supervisee as much autonomy as he or she can responsibly handle.

Overidentification with the worker may make the supervisor too protective, shielding the worker from possible mistakes, anxious that the worker may not be able to accept normal failures: "She was afraid to take the risks necessary for learning and I was afraid to let her."

A supervisor who is anxious about his or her own relationship with the administrator may overcontrol the worker to prevent embarrassment at worker errors for which the supervisor is held responsible. Conversely, supervisors may act out their own rebellious impulses toward the agency through their supervisees, from the safety of middle management positions.

The supervisor who has considerable therapeutic skills but limited pedagogic skills, or who feels more comfortable with the role of case-worker than with that of teacher, may convert educational supervision into psychotherapy. There is greater gratification in casting the supervisee in the role of client than in that of learner. Questions brought into the supervisory conference by the supervisee tend to become personalized and interpreted as problems of personal pathology with which the supervisee might need help.

A supervisor may be sufficiently uncertain about his or her own knowledge that he or she cannot permit the supervisee the freedom to experiment and to learn. A supervisor writes:

> Because of my discomfort with the supervisory relationship, I found it easier to simply introduce final decisions matter-of-factly, rather than risk challenge of my own choice of alternatives in a give-and-take process. I was perfectly happy with this "dictator" method but feared an open exercise of authority which might be called for in joint democratic decision-making if the worker didn't accept my reasons as valid and challenged my choices.

Such a supervisor may tend to be defensive and find it difficult to acknowledge ignorance.

Educational supervision provides the opportunity for a narcissistic display of knowledge and skills. Whether or not this is educationally helpful to the supervisee becomes a secondary consideration. The supervisor who made the following comment caught himself indulging in such behavior.

> In discussing the client with the worker during that session, I made another mistake: that of "lecturing" the worker on the psychological, social, cultural and economic factors affecting clients' behavioral patterns without any reference to the particular situation at hand. And when I did talk about the client, I started to discourse on the effects of emotional and cultural deprivation on the lives of children, and the psychoanalytical implications of Henry's father having run away from the home. . . . I finally caught myself in the middle of the oedipal complex bit. "B.S.!" I said to myself and changed the subject immediately, hoping that the worker had not realized the pompousness of it all, and if she did, that she would forgive me for it. I then realized how easy it is to get carried away when one has a captive audience. The "teaching" aspect of supervision is an art not easily mastered. I must remember to do more teaching and less preaching.

On the other hand, some more egalitarian supervisors may be afraid of showing what they know. Revealing that they are actually more knowledgeable than the supervisee destroys a pretense of equality in the relationship. Teaching freely requires the ready acceptance by the supervisor that he or she does, in fact, know more than the supervisee and is entitled to teach it.

Some supervisors are made uneasy by the inherently unequal nature of the supervisor-supervisee relationship in educational supervision. It needs to be noted that the superordinate-subordinate role relationship still holds, even in the educational component of supervision. The supervisor is sanctioned by the agency to engage in educational activity. Second, the supervisee, while participating in determining what should be taught and learned, faces constraints determined by what the agency requires that he or she learn to do. Educational supervision needs to maintain a balance between what the supervisees want to learn and what they need to learn. Consequently, the supervisor has considerable responsibility for what is included in the educational program. Third, the supervisor is responsible for evaluating whether or not the supervisee has in fact learned what it is that he or she has to know and what the supervisor has been mandated to teach. These considerations make it clear once again that supervisor and supervisee are not acting as equals in educational supervision.

Every supervisor has individual likes and dislikes regarding supervisee learning patterns. If they are not aware of such predilections, there is less probability that they can control differences in their responses to different supervisees. Some supervisors like rapid, avid learners who absorb teaching quickly and voraciously; some like the slow, plodding learners who are less challenging and for whom considerable repetition of content is required. Some supervisors prefer the supervisee who presses the supervisor-supervisee educational relationship in the direction of peer consultation and colleagueship; others find gratification in the supervisee who accepts a parent-child relationship. Some like the exuberant, extroverted learner; some like the shy, introverted learner. Some are more comfortable with learners who do best in the individual-tutorial situation; others are more comfortable with group-oriented learners.

Differentiating Educational Supervision from Therapy

One of the persistent problems encountered by educational supervisors is the task of differentiating supervision from therapy—differentiating teaching from treating (Neufeldt and Nelson 1999). The supervisory context is similar to the therapeutic context in many essential characteristics. Both situations involve a continuing, intimate, highly cathected, dyadic relationship in which an effort at exerting interpersonal influence to effect change is made by one member of the dyad toward the other. Both interactions are designed to develop a heightened sense of self-awareness (Stoltenberg and McNeill 1997; Sumerel and Borders 1996).

How then does the supervisor develop self-awareness in the supervisee without being accused of "caseworking the caseworker"? A distinction needs to be made between educational supervision and therapy to prevent problems in conflicting dual relationships and boundary violations.

Differences Between Supervision and Therapy

Differences between educational supervision, concerned with developing self-awareness, and therapy relate to (1) purpose and focus and (2) roles.

Purpose and Focus

The supervisor recognizes and respects the limits and restrictions of his or her purpose. His or her responsibility is to help the supervisee become a better worker—not necessarily a better person. The legitimate concern is with the professional activities of the supervisee, but the supervisor has no sanction to intrude into the worker's personal life. The concern is with changes in professional identity rather than changes in personal identity. The supervisor asks, "How can I help you do your work?" rather than "How can I help you?" Ekstein and Wallerstein (1972:92) note that "in supervision we aim at a change in skill, a change in the use of the professional self while in psychotherapy we aim at changes which embrace the total adaptive functioning of the individual."

The valid focus of attention is the supervisee's work, rather than the supervisee him- or herself. If the supervisee's behavior, feelings, and attitudes create some difficulty in the performance of professional tasks, then (and only then) do they become a legitimate matter for supervisory concern. The supervisor is not entitled to intervene with regard to behavior, feelings, and attitudes that, however problematic or deviant, are not clearly manifested in some job-related interaction.

In educational supervision we are not primarily dealing with the total person, as we would in a therapeutic milieu. We are dealing with only one of the many roles that make up the worker's total identity—the specific, particular role of agency employee. The supervisor, unlike the therapist, is not concerned with the causes of personal pathology, only with the consequences of such problems for the worker's performance on the job.

This is not to deny that professional growth does have consequences related to personal growth. The professional self is, after all, a significant aspect of the total personal-self configuration. But if the personal self undergoes growth and change, as is likely, it happens as an incidental, serendipitous, unplanned, unintended by-product of the focus on professional growth.

Although the following comments by Ekstein and Wallerstein (1972) relate to supervision of psychiatric residents, they are pertinent to this discussion. The authors comment that

> both supervision and psychotherapy are interpersonal helping processes working with the same affective components, with the essential difference between

them created by the difference in purpose. Though both are helping processes, the purpose of the helping experience is different. Whatever practical problems the patient may bring to his psychotherapist, they are always viewed in the light of the main task: the resolution of inner conflict. Whatever personal problems the student may bring to his supervisor, they are likewise always seen in terms of the main task: leading him toward greater skill in his work with his patients. . . . If the main purpose of a relationship is maintained throughout, the difference is clearly apparent between the type of relationship called psychotherapy and the one called supervision. . . . In psychotherapy the patient essentially sets his own goals. The therapist has no vested interest in any particular degree or direction of change. In supervision, on the other hand, the clinical setting, whose representative is the supervisor, sets both its requirements and its goals in terms of standards of professional performance and clinical service currently rendered and to be attained. (Ekstein and Wallerstein 1972:254–55, reprinted with permission of International Universities Press)

The therapist is free to work toward any goal the client selects. The supervisor is responsible for the behavior of the supervisee and is not free to work toward any goal the supervisee selects. The agency requirement is that the supervisor help the worker become an effective agency employee. The therapist helps the client achieve an individualized, personally satisfactory solution to his or her problem. The supervisor helps the worker achieve a resolution to a problem that is satisfactory to the organization. The objective of the supervision is improved technical performance in contrast with the therapist's objective of personality reconstruction or remediation. The objectives of educational supervision and therapy are different. Supervision is oriented to the needs of the client; therapy is oriented to the needs of the worker.

If the supervisee becomes a client of the supervisor in a shift from educational supervision to psychotherapy, the focus of supervisory attention must shift from the agency client to the worker. The needs of the supervisee as client then take precedence over the needs of the agency client. This is a subversion of the primary responsibility and obligation of the agency toward its client. Instead of the focus of attention being on service, the client is used to advance the therapy of the worker. This is an inequitable manipulation of the client, without his or her permission and in contravention to his or her objectives in coming to the agency. The client becomes an involuntary coparticipant in the worker's therapy.

To accept the supervisee for psychotherapy requires a modification of work standards. The criteria for a decision regarding enforcement of agency standards become the therapeutic needs of the supervisee-client rather than the needs of agency clients. This, too, is contrary to the primary obligations of the agency. Exercise of administrative sanctions required in maintaining adequate standards may be antitherapeutic for the supervisee-client. The supervisor cannot be a psychotherapist to the supervisee and at the same time a guardian of agency standards.

In implementing the focus on supervision as against therapy, the supervisor keeps the discussion centered on the client's situation and experience rather than on the worker's situation and experience. The discussion is work-centered, not worker-centered. Further, the focus is on *what* the worker did or failed to do, rather than *why* he or she did it. If there is any discussion of the reasons that may help explain the worker's behavior, it is centered on the current work situation rather than in any psychodynamic exploration of developmental antecedents.

Current reality as an explanation of workers' problems should always be examined first. Personal problems should be discussed only through their derivative manifestations in assigned work.

Unlike therapy, in supervision problems are alluded to but not explored for their developmental genesis. As Towle (1954:89) notes, "Our task is education not therapy. . . . We should deal with the student's emotional difficulties only insofar as they are interfering with his learning." Therapy explores the personal implications of problems; supervision explores the professional implications of problems.

Difference in Role Relationships

Shifting from educational supervision to psychotherapy involves an unwarranted and inappropriate shift in roles. As Stiles (1963:24) says, "A supervisory relationship contains an implicit contract: the worker is responsible for attempting to maximize his performance and continuing his professional development; the supervisor is responsible for helping him achieve these goals." The parameters of the contract, as noted, are the worker's performance and professional development. Concern with personal development is an unwarranted and unanticipated extension of the explicit contract. Having consented to an administrative-educational process, the worker cannot legitimately have a psychotherapy process imposed on him or her. Therapizing the relationship suggests that the supervisor is entering areas of the worker's life over which he or she has no organizational sanction or authority.

Unlike the client in psychotherapy, the supervisee did not voluntarily select the supervisor as his or her therapist, and unlike the client is not free to terminate the relationship with the supervisor. Thus, attempted transformation of educational supervision into psychotherapy is even more likely to be resented by the captive worker.

In educational supervision, the worker contracts for knowledge and guidance, not the alleviation of symptoms. There is no treatment contract that would sanction the supervisor to subject the supervisee to some of the psychic pain that may be necessary for effective therapy, no contract that would make the supervisee aware that he or she might have to accept some of the inevitable discomforts of therapy.

In accepting the role of patient to therapist, certain prerogatives of privacy are waived. In a supervisory relationship that is redirected to a therapeutic relationship, there is no clear agreement on the part of the supervisee that he or she has agreed to the suspension of such entitlements.

Subverting educational supervision so that it becomes psychotherapy in disguise not only contravenes the agreed-on nature of reciprocal supervisor-supervisee role relations, it also violates the conditions for effective therapy. Effective therapy is not likely to be possible unless a complete detailed history has been taken and a clear diagnosis of the problem formulated. Effective therapy would require considerably more detailed exploration of developmental data and current functioning than is possible, or acceptable, in the supervisory relationship.

Effective therapy requires a psychosocial diagnosis of the client and a therapeutic alliance between therapist and client. Effective educational supervision requires an educational diagnosis and a teacher-learner alliance between supervisor and supervisee.

In therapy, unconscious feelings are explored for their genesis and worked through for their resolution. In supervision, unconscious feelings may be identified, but they are neither explored nor resolved. Although listening with the understanding of a therapist, the supervisor responds not as a therapist but as an educator.

The supervisor seeks to promote identification but not transference (in which the worker's perception of the supervisor is distorted by seeing the supervisor not as he or she is but as representing in some measure significant others from the worker's past). If therapy depends for some of its effectiveness on transference elements, then converting the supervisory situation into a therapeutic relationship increases the probability that therapy will fail. In the usual therapy situation, the contact between patient and therapist is confined to their interaction during the therapy sessions. Supervisor and supervisee, on the contrary, have contact with each other in many different contexts in the agency. This tends to dilute the potency of transference for effective therapy.

The evaluative component inherent in supervision makes it difficult to engage effectively in therapy. In addition to the risk of loss of self-esteem and possible rejection and blame in sharing intra- and interpersonal problems, there is the added risk that this content might be used in evaluating the supervisee's potential for professional performance and advancement. There is increased tendency to share selectively rather than fully and openly. The responsibilities of supervision compromise the requirements for effective therapeutic interaction.

In therapizing the supervisor-supervisee relationship, the supervisor risks doing the supervisee an injustice. It reduces the supervisee's incentive to get outside help clearly designed to provide therapy and thus denies the supervisee the full benefit of a relationship exclusively devoted to his therapy.

Research studies indicate that supervisors tend to behave differently in supervision than in therapy. Lambert and Beier (1974) compared the interaction of five therapists with their own clients and with their supervisees. The focus of the tape-recorded comparison was the level of facilitative conditions (empathy, respect, genuineness, and specificity) offered in each of these interactional contexts. The levels of empathy and specificity were significantly lower in the supervisory context. A global rating showed that the interactional orientation in supervision was significantly less therapeutic than that offered in counseling. The results suggest that there is a recognition of the difference in objectives between therapy and supervision that requires the supervisor to behave differently in the two contexts.

To summarize, confusion results from the fact that educational supervision toward developing job-related self-awareness and psychotherapy are similar in some essential respects. Both encourage self-examination in the context of a meaningful relationship, both are directed toward personal growth and change, and both provoke anxiety. The psychodynamics of both processes and the techniques employed are the same. The distinction lies primarily in purpose and focus, and role parameters of the relationship.

Problems in Implementation of Therapy-Educational Supervision Distinction

These problems

> leave the supervisor in the dilemma of having to be more than a teacher, but less than a therapist. Inevitably this demands sensitive and difficult decisions on the part of the supervisor, who must always be aware of when his professional concern becomes personal intrusiveness and yet deal directly and realistically with counter-transference phenomena that interfere with the ongoing therapeutic work. (Gizynski 1978:203)

Furthermore, "It is a matter of extreme delicacy to maintain a warm and interested human relationship on the one hand and on the other not to respond to the therapeutic needs that the [supervisee] may reveal either directly by the development of symptoms or indirectly in the handling of case material" (Zetzel 1953:149).

Consequently, establishing guidelines for what is appropriate in a supervisory conference is easier than applying them (Sarnat 1992). The following excerpt is a supervisor's introspective review of the difficulty in making a decision in such a situation. The problem lies in deciding when a worker's difficulty is purely personal and when it is task-related.

Vera [the worker] brought up the fact that she was experiencing some confusion herself about the prospect of marrying her present boyfriend and that the two of them were involved in premarital counseling. She expressed doubt as to her ability to help someone else deal with a problem similar to the one she herself was experiencing.

I was caught a little off guard and likewise experienced a certain element of confusion—a few quick thoughts ran through my mind, and I responded by doing "nothing." My quick thoughts leading to this response went something like this: avoid taking on the role of therapist; personal problems of the supervisee are not relevant here unless they interfere with job or learning performance and there is not yet sufficient evidence to this effect. In starting the process of evaluating Vera's work, I have become aware of a tendency on her part to shy away from offering help to clients in the area of marital conflict, although not hesitating to offer and provide it in other problem areas (housing, child-parent relationships, etc.). Also, it now occurs to me that Vera may not have been asking for any help with her personal problems (she was already involved in outside counseling), but only for help in resolving her concern about being able to help someone else with a problem she saw was similar to her own. If this was the case, I would consider her concern to represent the kind of emotional aspect of learning which is the responsibility of the supervisor to deal with. In retrospect, viewing the pattern of Vera's work performance I think the problem was more job-related than I had originally thought.

The problem is noted by another supervisor in the following:

A recurrent problem was Dick's hesitancy about helping a family arrange for a nursing home placement for an aged client, even when this seemed clearly necessary. At some point, I felt that it was important to explore Dick's feelings toward nursing homes to be sure that he wasn't allowing a personal bias to interfere *against* nursing home placement. I attempted to deal exclusively with job-related awareness, but when Dick admitted that much of his feeling came from the experience of his own father being placed in a nursing home, the session began to focus more and more on the supervisee rather than on the work-related issue. We became caught up in dealing with the psychology of Dick's relationship with his father, but eventually I was able to redirect our attention and move back with some difficulty to the issue of nursing homes for his clients.

The problem is difficult because the worker is likely to react negatively to both indifference and excessive interest. If the supervisor ignores the supervisee's comment about what is apparently a purely personal problem, he or she is likely to feel rejected. If the supervisor shows excessive interest in the problem, it can be interpreted as an unwarranted intrusion. Recognition of the worker's statement without pursuing it might be the difficult response of choice. A frank, explicit statement by the supervisor of what he or she is doing might help: "I appreciate that this must be a difficult problem for you but I really don't think it is appropriate for us to discuss it at length here." However, it needs to be recognized that a "rigid boundary between the personal and professional lives of (supervisees) seems simplistic and artificial" (Gurka and Wicas 1979:404). What supervisees want and need from educational supervision tends to change over time (Glidden and Tracey 1992), and although advanced practitioners "have repeatedly expressed a willingness to examine personal issues that affect their relationships with clients" (Sumerel and Borders 1996:269), Schroffel (1998, 1999) reports that supervisors rarely offer the advanced educational content that experienced practitioners want, contributing significantly to worker dissatisfaction. In general, the evidence suggests that educational supervision is dominated by *practical* content, whether the supervisee is a student, a new social worker, or a senior practitioner (Charles, Gabor, and Matheson 1992; Gray, Alperin, and Wik 1989; Greenspan et al. 1992; Rogers and McDonald 1995). Apparently, experienced workers yearn for supervisory content that advances their personal growth, whereas supervisors emphasize content that gets the job done. However, the interest in supervised personal development shown by workers with experience may signal their desire for more challenging work, not psychotherapy (Goodyear and Bernard 1998).

Acceptance of Distinction Between Supervision and Therapy: Empirical Data

The available data suggest that most supervisors and supervisees understand and accept the limited definition of the supervisor's responsibility as outlined here. Most of the 853 respondents to one questionnaire made a clear distinction between professional development and personal development. The *professional* development of the supervisee was selected by both supervisors and supervisees as one major objective of supervision. Conversely, both groups selected "ensuring the more complete development of the supervisee as a mature person" as among the three least important objectives. Satisfaction "in helping the supervisee grow and develop in professional competence" was the main satisfaction in supervision for the largest percentage of supervisors (88 percent). Less than 1 percent of them, however, checked "helping supervisees with their personal problems" as a source of satisfaction (Kadushin 1974:291). Similarly, the statement of dissatisfaction in supervision least frequently checked by supervisees was "My supervisor tends to become too involved in my personal problems," indicating that transformation of supervision into psychotherapy was not then a problem for most of the respondents (Kadushin 1974:291).

Supervisors responding to admonitions that they have no right to casework the caseworker adhere to the dichotomy of professional versus personal development even more rigorously than do supervisees. If anything, supervisees indicate a greater willingness to accept the therapeutic intrusion of the supervisor than supervisors appear willing to offer it. In response to the incomplete sentence "If personal problems came up in my work with clients I would prefer that my supervisor, . . ." 48 percent of the supervisees said that they wanted the supervisor to "identify the problems and help me resolve them," whereas only 30 percent of the supervisors prefer this response. Conversely, 44 percent of the supervisors would "identify the problem and help supervisees get outside help," but only 11 percent of the supervisees preferred this response. Supervisors, more often than supervisees, saw the legitimate source of help for job-related personal problems as lying outside the supervisory relationship (Kadushin 1974:99). Kadushin (1992a) obtained similar responses in an updated survey of supervisors and supervisees. In a study of supervisor behavior as identified by ninety-three direct service workers, York and Denton (1990) found that the behavior least frequently engaged in by supervisors was to advise people on their personal problems. York goes on to comment that perhaps supervisors "are not engaging in therapy as supervision to the extent that some of us might have suspected" (York and Denton 1990:99).

The hesitancy of social work supervisors to therapize the relationship reflects a similar tendency in psychotherapeutic trainers of psychiatrists. Goin and Kline (1976) videotaped conferences between twenty-four supervisors of second-year psychiatric residents for the purpose of examining how the supervisors dealt with the residents' countertransference reactions to their patients. Countertransference was defined as the "therapist's conscious as well as unconscious reactions toward and feelings about their patients" (Goin and Kline 1976:41). Surprisingly "for a discipline that often stresses the need for open communication" (Goin and Kline 1976:42), only twelve of the twenty-four supervisors discussed countertransference at all, despite the fact that it was evident in each case. Of the twelve supervisors who did mention it, only four discussed it at any length. The supervisors tended to avoid such discussion because of hesitancy about converting the educational situation to therapy and because of hesitancy in creating anxiety in the supervisee.

When countertransference was discussed effectively, the supervisors, in a frank, no-nonsense way, called attention to the therapist's feelings about the patient that were affecting his or her work. There was no attempt to "explore personal motivations, conscious or unconscious, for residents acting or feeling as they did. It was merely an attempt to acknowledge the feelings that were there" (Goin and Kline 1976:43). The objective in raising these feelings for discussion was to make the resident aware of them so as to give him or her "a greater chance for rational control over his interactions with the patient" (Goin and Kline 1976:42). The objective was not to "probe deeper into the roots of these feelings" for the purpose of therapeutic resolution (see also Hunt 1981). As Haley (1977:187) notes, "A person's personal life is too important to be tampered with by teachers," including supervisors. (See also Mayer and Rosenblatt 1975b.)

An awareness of the parallel process phenomenon in supervision interaction is an additional consideration in appropriate application of the principles of teaching-learning and is related to the teaching-therapy dilemma just discussed.

The Parallel Process Component in Educational Supervision

The parallel process, sometimes called the reflection process, has been identified as a phenomenon in supervisory interaction that has considerable significance for educational supervision (Searles 1955; Marohn 1969; Mattinson 1975; Doehrman 1976; Sachs and Shapiro 1976; Kahn 1979; Calligor 1981; Bromberg 1982; Gasiorowicz 1982; Sigman 1989; Friedlander, Siegel, and Brenock 1989; Alpher 1991; Gray 1994; Harkness 1995; McCue and Lane 1995; Shulman 1995b; Patton and Kivlighan 1997; Raichelson et al. 1997; Williams 1997; Fox 1998; Mothersole 1999).

The parallel process is an exemplification of isomorphism—the tendency for patterns to repeat at different levels of the system. We can view the supervisor-supervisee-client interaction as one large system that includes two subsystems, the worker-client subsystem and the supervisor-supervisee subsystem. Isomorphism would suggest that the worker's dealings with the client in the worker-client subsystem would tend to get reflected in the supervisor-supervisee subsystem as a parallel process.

The parallel process suggests that the supervisee reenacts in the supervisory conference the behavior that the client manifested in the casework interview. The supervisor then has available in the immediacy of the supervisory conference this additional experiential dimension for understanding the worker's performance. Without being consciously aware of this, the supervisee, in attempting to understand the client's behavior, identifies with it and mimics it for presentation in the supervisory conference to obtain help in dealing with it.

The isomorphic nature of service and supervision is encapsulated in the statement that what the client does with the supervisee, the supervisee will, in turn, do with the supervisor. The client "comes" to supervision through this process. Parallel process events are replications across system boundaries. The problem is transferred from the worker-client setting to the supervisor-supervisee setting.

A client who evokes a sense of disorganization, confusion, and puzzlement in the worker is paralleled by the supervisee's evocation of confusion and puzzlement in the supervisor when the supervisee presents the case for discussion. After experiencing a client who is evasive and resistant, the worker, in discussing the case, may display an analogous kind of evasiveness and resistance in interaction with the supervisor. Just as the client generated a feeling of helplessness, frustration, and anger in the worker, the worker can evoke feelings of helplessness, frustration, and anger in the supervisor. If the supervisor is aware of the source of his or her feelings in the parallel process, he or she can more effectively help the supervisee in working with the client.

Manifestations of parallel process supposedly enable the supervisor to perceive what is occurring in the situation between worker and client as it is replicated in the supervisory interaction. Parallel process thus permits second-hand "observation" of the worker performance with the client through its reflection in supervision. A supervisor says,

> I became aware of the parallel process dynamics when I experienced an interaction that illustrated it. Penny, my supervisee, would shift away from troublesome significant problems by talking, apparently revealingly, about less important matters. Gratified at her open sharing, I rewarded her by going along with the shift and responding to her. In retrospect, I noticed that the client did the same thing with Penny. When Penny raised really difficult ques-

tions for discussion, the client would deftly digress to content, that while relevant, was less significant and less difficult to deal with. Penny rewarded the client's digression by responding and accepting the shift. Thinking about it, I planned to hold Penny to the difficult matters that needed discussion and in this way help Penny, in turn, to be less accepting of the client's evasions.

Parallel process events further the diagnostic and instructional objectives of supervision. Perception of a parallel process event enables the supervisor to understand the worker-client relationship as he or she sees it reenacted in the supervising interaction. It is a form of communication through which the worker, identified with the client, is trying to tell the supervisor about the problem. In responding therapeutically to the supervisee enacting the role of the client, the supervisor can then model the behavior that the supervisee can, in turn, manifest productively toward the client.

The parallel process may also work in reverse. If the supervisor does not actively extend him- or herself to help the supervisee, the supervisee may repeat this by being indifferent to the client. If the supervisor dominates the supervisee, the supervisee may dominate the client. One of the more frequently cited reverse parallel process examples is one where the supervisor refuses a request for an emergency meeting with the supervisee, followed by the supervisee's refusal of an emergency meeting with the client.

It is difficult to differentiate parallel processes in supervision from analogous processes that mirror interactional situations that may relate to each other. Much happens in the supervisor-supervisee relationship that is similar to what happens in the worker-client situation because of contextual, structural, and dynamic similarities. The worker-client interaction involves a process of growth and change. This is also true of the supervisor-supervisee interaction. In both interactions feelings of anxiety, dependency, anger, and resistance are activated. Both interactions involve differences in power and authority and evoke problems regarding openness and defensiveness. Both are highly affective, dyadic contexts in which emotionally charged material is discussed in private. Both contexts are conducive to transference and countertransference evocations. Given these similarities in the two situations and the fact that the dimensions of human relationships are limited and repetitive, similar things happening in the two situations should not be surprising.

The supervisee is the constant element in the two dyadic subsystems. Both involve interaction; both are concerned with the process of helping. Similar psychodynamics operate in both sets of relationships. It might be expected, then, that the feelings evoked in one context by and in the supervisee might be similar to the feelings evoked in the other context by and in the supervisor.

This provides the basis for a parallel process. From the vantage point of the parallel process the two dyadic systems, worker-client and supervisor-supervisee, become one triadic system.

The worker may act so as to obtain the approbation of the supervisor; this is parallel to the behavior of the client in attempting to solicit the approbation of the worker. In both situations, however, the "parallel" behavior is a very natural response to a person having positional power with reference to significant aspects of one's life. Structural and dynamic similarities between therapy and supervision foster parallelisms. Analogous situations evoke analogous behavior (Geidman and Wolkenfeld 1980). As Frawley-O'Dea and Sarnat note in reviewing the literature, "analytic and supervisory processes overlap and therefore invite regressive and progressive enactments of multidirectional parallelisms" (2001:173).

Correspondence between the elements in two contexts eventuates in analogous happenings in the two contexts. It might be more accurate to describe what is happening as analogous or isomorphic processes rather than parallel processes (Miller and Twomey 1999; White and Russell 1997).

Although many supervisors and supervisees observe parallel processes in their practice (Raichelson et al. 1997), very limited empirical research (Ellis and Ladany 1997; Mothersole 1999) is available beyond anecdotal and clinical accounts of the phenomenon (McNeill and Worthen 1989; Halberg, Berg, and Arlehamn 1994; McCue and Lane 1995; Etgar 1996; Lee 1997). Doehrman's (1976) frequently quoted study involved four psychology counselor trainees; a study by Friedlander, Siegel, and Brenock (1989) involved one counselor trainee. The anecdotal accounts of parallel process events depend on interpretation of the supervisee's behavior as reflective events and the occasional acceptance of the interpretation by the supervisee.

Findings from two larger studies of parallel process, lacking the nuance and texture of case studies, are also difficult to interpret. In a sixteen-week field study that examined the supervised practice of 1 supervisor and 4 workers serving 161 clients, worker ratings of the supervisory relationship were not associated with client ratings of the practice relationship (Harkness 1995). But in a study of twenty-five supervisors, seventy-five counseling students, and seventy-five clients, Patton and Kivlighan (1997) found that student ratings of their working alliances with their supervisors were associated with client ratings of their working alliances with their counselors.

Reviewing the literature on parallel process, Ellis and Ladany (1997:487) argue that there is too little evidence to support "inferences from the observed links between therapy and supervision to the parallel process," and Mothersole concludes that parallel process is a concept with a long history of wide use, "yet there is very little empirical evidence for its existence. What is required is further study" (1999:116).

Developmental Supervision

In discussing the different orientations to teaching in educational supervision, we concluded that it is difficult to select one best, most appropriate approach because much depended on the context of teaching and the content of teaching. Here we discuss an additional variable that contributes to the difficulty: developmental supervision. As foreshadowed, the teaching-learning principles discussed above need adaptation and revision at different points in the professional development of the supervisee. This reflects the findings regarding developmental supervision. The basic idea of developmental supervision is that the supervisee changes over the course of his or her development as a competent professional, and such changes in the supervisee require changes in the supervisor's approach. As learning needs change, educational supervision needs to change. Some early, classical expositions of stages in learning to become a social worker by Reynolds (1942) and Towle (1954) embody the ideas of developmental supervision.

A number of different attempts have been made to formulate the process of educational supervision in terms of stages of development (Hogan 1964; Littrell et al. 1979; Ralph 1980; Stoltenberg 1981; Hart 1982; Miars 1983; Friedlander 1983; Cross and Brown 1983; Friedman and Kaslow 1986; Holloway 1987; Stoltenberg and Delworth 1987; Worthington 1987; Bernard and Goodyear 1998). A detailed statement of the concepts and stages of developmental supervision is presented in a text by Bernard and Goodyear (1998). Ellis and Ladany (1997); Neufeldt, Beutler, and Banchero (1997); and Stoltenberg and McNeill (1997) have reviewed the related empirical research.

A developmental approach to supervision presupposes that there is growth in the supervisee and that each stage of such growth requires modification in the supervisor's approach to the supervisee. The modifications are required in response to changing needs of supervisees at different levels of the growth process.

The central idea in these formulations is that the supervisee moves through a series of identifiable, characteristic stages in learning to be a professional social worker, counselor, or clinical psychologist and in developing an identity as a professional.

According to the available research, at the beginning stages in the growth process supervisees need high levels of instruction, structure, and support.

They are method and technique oriented with a considerable concern for skill development. The focus in instruction is on the worker-client relationship and the instructional-expert role of the supervisor is given emphasis. The supervisee has a variable sense of professional identity. A coherent theoretical conception of practice is in the process of formulation. Expectations need modification toward a greater acceptance of realistic limitations. The supervisor is directive in a support-security context.

Dependent, anxious, and insecure supervisees at this point in their development are highly motivated to acquire technical skills. A considerable amount of learning is through imitation in a relationship that is hierarchical, the supervisor being an expert-teacher and proactive in terms of supervisee's performance.

Initially, the supervisee's theoretical base of practice is undifferentiated and unsophisticated. The image of professional identity is not yet clearly defined and not clearly owned. The supervisee's concern is primarily the worker's performance. The supervisee is very concerned about competence, needs answers to survive on the job, and is probably averse to risk taking. There is a naive optimism on the part of the supervisee that achieving a proficient level of competence would invariably permit the worker to be helpful to all clients.

With professional development changes are made. There is progressively less need for structure, directivity, and didactic instruction. Learning through identification and internalization takes the place of learning through imitation. There is a growing need for independence and autonomy as the ability to make use of such freedom increases. However, the movement in development is not uniformly linear. The supervisee who has achieved self-assured independence may temporarily become dependent again when encountering a difficult client.

The supervisor-supervisee relationship becomes less hierarchical and more collegial, and the supervisor is reactive to supervisees. Practice and theory become more integrated and theory more differentiated. There is a growing freedom to explore self-awareness issues and dynamics in the worker-client and supervisor-supervisee interactions, with a focus on the supervisee's contribution to transference and countertransference. There is a growing ability to see the situation from the client's perspective and to individualize the client. The image of self as a professional social worker becomes clearer and more stable, and there is growing consolidation and integration of professional identity. Confrontation and supervisor self-disclosure is more appropriate at this point in the supervisee's development than it was earlier. There is a growing acceptance of the limitations of what the profession can accomplish and acceptance of the reality that only some of the clients can be helped some of the time.

Professional development over time involves the growth of technical skills and the growth of a professional identity. The development is from a focus on and concern with self on the part of the supervisee to a gradual freedom to become aware of and appreciate the self-other transactions and their reciprocal effects. This implies a greater willingness to accept the collaboration of the client in problem solving. There is a gradual greater acceptance of the complexity, ambiguity, and multicausality of human behavior and the inevitability of failure in achieving definitive understanding.

Originally a figure of omniscience and transference, the supervisor came to be perceived as less infallible and more human. There is increased individuation and separateness from the supervisor (Watkins 1990). A Socratic approach, involving a series of challenging questions having an implied direction, stimulating inductive reasoning and self-discovery, is more appropriate with supervisees at more advanced developmental levels than with beginners (Overholser 1991). Stoltenberg et al. (1987) summarize these changes as being "a) from greater to lesser need for supervisor-imposed structure; b) from greater to lesser need for didactic instruction; c) from greater to lesser need for direct feedback of counseling behavior; d) from greater to lesser need for supervisory support and e) from greater to lesser training/supervision needs in general" (25).

Over the course of professional development, some needs—such as the need for continuing support and encouragement from the supervisor, the need to develop technical skills, and the need for a facilitative relationship—remain constant, if somewhat attenuated.

Although the concept of developmental supervision seems eminently sensible and intuitively logical, some scientists find the evidence lacking. Ellis and Ladany (1997), for example, describe the research on supervisee development as plagued with discouraging conceptual and methodological problems. At the heart of the matter is whether studies of the short-term training of practicum students in university settings are viable models of supervisee development across the professional life span in agency practice.

Attempts have been made to determine empirically whether supervisors actually modify behavior as supervisees change. The findings are contradictory. Some studies tend to show that supervisors do make changes in their approach to accommodate differences in needs of supervisees at different stages in development, more or less (Borders 1991a; Cross and Brown 1983; Miars 1983; Grater 1985; Rabinowitz, Heppner, and Roehlke 1986; Wiley and Ray 1986; Krause and Allen 1988; Tracey et al. 1989), but extensive reviews of the literature conducted by Worthington (1987) and Stoltenberg, McNeill, and Crethar (1994) found only weak support for the idea that they actually do so. In direct observation research, for example, Shanfield et al. (1992) were unable to determine that supervisory behavior with multiple supervisees varied at all. How supervision affects the development of novice therapists into seasoned professionals has not been explored (Neufeldt, Beutler, and Banchero 1997).

Applying the suggestions of developmental supervision requires some daunting prerequisites. It requires that the supervisor has a clear idea of the particular stage in development of the supervisee. It requires that the supervisor have a sufficiently varied repertoire of responses and flexibility in application so that he or she can select and implement the response most appropriate to the supervisee's changing needs. Given the varied competing pressures faced by supervisors, it requires the motivation and energy to make the changes. As Fisher says, developmental supervision suppositions may be valid and their validity acknowledged by supervisors, but given the fact that "practicing different supervisory approaches is a complex and challenging task" and given the "many demands on the supervisor—customizing supervision sessions may be unrealistic" (1989:71–72).

The literature on developmental supervision has considerable heuristic value, however. It provides the field of supervision with greater clarity regarding the subtle changes that supervisees experience over time and a more refined definition of the variables involved in such changes. These general considerations regarding modifications of supervisory behavior with increasing professional development and professional maturity of the supervisee need reviewing, however, when they are applied to an individual supervisee. Other, more idiosyncratic elements, aside from the level of professional development of the supervisee, need to be given consideration; among these is the supervisee's motivation to achieve and willingness to accept responsibility (York and Hastings 1985–1986).

The educational supervisor-supervisee situation is not only developmental it is persistently interactional. This further complicates the choice of teaching approach. Unlike classroom instruction, educational supervision is primarily tutorial. The one-on-one context demands the individualization of the teacher-learner interaction. Because the recipient of the supervisor's efforts is not inert but reacts in a highly idiosyncratic manner to the supervisor's actions and in turn affects the supervisor's response, this is a highly interactional situation. The same intervention by the supervisor may evoke different responses from two different supervisees whose learning needs, styles, and preferences are different. Hence, like the good social worker, the good supervisor has to be sensitive to how his or her interventions are being received and modify the approach to optimize the learning situation for the supervisee.

Summary

The following conditions make for an effective learning situation in the context of a positive relationship. We learn best if:

1. We are highly motivated to learn.
2. We can devote most of our energies to learning.
3. Learning is attended by positive satisfactions.
4. We are actively involved in the learning process.
5. The content to be learned is meaningfully presented.
6. The uniqueness of the learner is considered.

There are differences between educational supervision and therapy relating to purpose and focus, role relationships, and process. The distinction is difficult to apply with precision in supervision, although supervisors generally accept the distinction. Educational supervision requires a recognition of the different needs of supervisees at different points in their professional developments; these differences having been identified in studies of developmental supervision. Parallel process phenomena—reenactments in supervision of clinical problems—may be a component of the educational supervisory process.

6 | Supportive Supervision

Introduction and Overview

This chapter is concerned with the third major component of supervision—support. If the supervisor acts as a manager in implementing administrative supervision and acts as a teacher in implementing educational supervision, the supervisor acts as an adjustment counselor in implementing supportive supervision. Supervisees and supervisors face a variety of job-related stresses. Unless some resource is available to help them deal with these stresses, their work may be seriously impaired, to the detriment of agency effectiveness. The supervisor is responsible for helping supervisees adjust to job-related stress. The ultimate objective of this component of supervision is the same as the objective of administrative and educational supervision—to enable the workers, and the agency through the workers, to offer the client the most effective and efficient service.

The National Association of Social Workers (NASW 1981) *Standards for Social Work Practice in Child Protection* make this responsibility of the supervisor explicit. As one of the supervisor's tasks, the *Standards* lists "management of work-related stress and assistance to staff in coping with their work-related stress" (p. 15).

If one were to categorize the research findings on characteristics associated with effective supervision and leadership, two clusters of factors turn up repeatedly. One cluster relates to getting the job done—seeing that the people who do the job are provided with the facilities, services, information, and skills they need to do the job. These are the task-centered, instrumental considerations of supervision. The second cluster is associated with seeing that the people who do the job are comfortable, satisfied, and happy in their work and have a sense of psychological well-being. These are people-centered, expressive considerations of supervision. Expressive tasks meet the needs of system maintenance. They are the equivalents of oiling the parts and cooling the works of a mechanical system to reduce abrasion and the possibility of overheating. Such expressive system-maintenance functions permit the achievement of instrumental goals.

Blake and Mouton (1961) employ these two variables in the development of their managerial grid—concern for production (the instrumental consideration) and concern for people (the expressive consideration). The best managerial style, both psychologically satisfying and economically productive, is an optimum combination of the two concerns. The Ohio State Leadership Studies (Stodgill and Coons 1957) identified "initiating structure" and "consideration" as the two basic dimensions of leadership. A leader who rates high on initiating structure is task oriented, organizes the work to be done, and clearly defines work objectives, group member roles, and expectations. This is a concern with the instrumental aspects of the job. The leader who rates high on consideration communicates trust, warmth, friendliness, and support—a concern with expressive considerations. The Ohio studies found that the most effective leaders were those who rated high on both dimensions. The Michigan Studies on Management (Likert 1967) came to the same general conclusions. The supervisor who communicates both support and high performance-goal expectations is likely to have the most effective work group.

Fiedler's (1967) research on leadership suggested that the optimum mix of these two major dimensions was largely a function of the situation. Some jobs and some settings require a greater component of instrumental, task-oriented, production-centered concern; other situations require a greater emphasis on the expressive, worker-oriented, and human-relations aspects. The mix also depends on idiosyncratic needs and characteristics of the supervisees, some requiring more structure and direction, others requiring a more decidedly expressive orientation.

In studies of job satisfaction and dissatisfaction, these two aspects of supervision are again clearly distinguishable. Herzberg, Mausner, and Snyderman (1959) found that workers' dissatisfaction might be related to either "technical supervision" or "interpersonal supervision." Dissatisfaction with technical supervision resulted from the fact that the supervisors lacked competence in the technical skills they were assigned to supervise, the instrumental component of supervision. Dissatisfaction with interpersonal supervision resulted from failures in the human-relations responsibilities of the supervisor, the expressive component of supervision.

If these considerations operate even in the organizations that depend most on machines as the means of production, they are substantially more important for social work organizations in which the medium of service offered is the worker. Machines do not have to feel a conviction in the work they are doing to do it well; they never suffer from depression, guilt, or a sense of inadequacy. They are not jealous or envious of the achievements of other machines and do not feel competitive. They do not need to be inspired to work at an optimum level. But these kinds of feelings—and more—determine the effectiveness of the social agency worker. Consequently the social work supervisor must be concerned with the emotional reactions of supervisees to their jobs and their job situations. Where the technology is centered mainly in human resources, the protection and development of human capacities will be a dominant supervisory concern.

In terms of the categorization of the major components of supervision as used in this book, both administrative and educational supervision are primarily, although not exclusively, directed toward instrumental considerations. The supportive component of supervision primarily is concerned with expressive considerations.

Administrative supervision provides the organizational structure and access to agency resources that facilitate the worker's job; educational supervision provides the knowledge and skills required for doing the job; supportive supervision provides the psychological and interpersonal context that enables the worker to mobilize the emotional energy needed for effective job performance and obtain satisfaction in doing their job. Administrative supervision is concerned with organizational barriers to effective services; educational supervision is concerned with ignorance barriers to effective service; supportive supervision is concerned with emotional barriers to effective service. Administrative supervision is concerned with executive-managerial aspects, educational supervision with cognitive aspects, supportive supervision with affective aspects of supervision.

Administrative supervision is responsible for relating effective workers to effective organizations, increasing the effectiveness of the organizational structure and the resources available to the worker. Educational supervision is primarily concerned with increasing the effectiveness of the worker through upgrading knowledge and skills. Supportive supervision is primarily concerned with increasing effectiveness of the worker through decreasing stress that interferes with performance, and increasing motivation and intensifying commitment that enhances performance.

Performance is a function of ability, commitment, and motivation. Effective administrative and educational supervision may increase the supervisee's ability to do an effective job. The worker, however able, may still perform inadequately because he or she is not sufficiently committed or motivated. Motivation determines how vigorously, conscientiously, and persistently abilities will be mobilized to do an effective job. Motivation energizes behavior and sustains involvement in the work. Job commitment is associated with a feeling of loyalty to the agency, a conviction in the objectives of the organization, a positive identification with the group, and a desire to remain with the agency (Glisson and Durick 1988).

Social services are labor-intensive. To a considerable extent, productivity depends on the strength of motivation and commitment of the workers. Given limited access to powerful extrinsic rewards, such as high pay, the level of motivation and commitment is in response to intrinsic factors—how workers feel about their jobs, the rewards of the work itself, and how they are treated on the job (Wilkinson and Wagner 1993). Glisson studied the effects of leadership in a wide variety of social service organizations. He concluded that work groups headed by supervisors characterized as manifesting the attitudes and behavior associated with supportive leadership were more likely to be committed to organizational objectives. "Leadership affects organizational performance positively by creating a committed organizational climate within which workers can function" (Glisson 1989:113). Supportive supervision is concerned with increasing motivation, job commitment, and job satisfaction.

If administrative supervision provides supervisory authority with the power of position, reward, and coercion, and if educational supervision provides the power of expertise, supportive supervision provides supervisory authority with referent power. The worker complies with agency policies and procedures so that he or she can obtain the interpersonal support the supervisor can make available.

The different components of supervision provide the workers with distinct but complementary models of the social worker for emulation. Administrative supervision provides a model of an efficient worker; educational supervision provides a model of a competent worker; supportive supervision provides a model of a compassionate, understanding worker.

Once again it might be noted that administrative, educational, and supportive components of supervision are interrelated rather than categorically distinct. For instance, educational supervision, by helping the worker become more skilled, results not only in increased competence but also in greater job satisfaction and reduced anxiety about ability to meet job demands (Itzhaky and Aviad-Hiebloom 1998; Rauktis and Koeske 1994).

Supportive supervision includes those interventions that reinforce ego defenses and strengthen the capacity of the ego to deal with job stresses and tensions. Supportive supervision includes such procedures as reassurance, encouragement, and recognition of achievement, along with realistically based expressions of confidence, approval and commendation, catharsis-ventilation, desensitization and universalization, and attentive listening that communicates interest and concern (Erera and Lazar 1994a). In implementing the responsibilities of supportive supervision the supervisor attempts to help the workers feel more at ease with themselves in their work. As Bloom and Herman (1958:403) state, "One of the major functions of the supervisor is to provide certain emotional supports for the worker. She must encourage, strengthen, stimulate and even comfort and pacify him." The supervisor seeks to allay anxiety, reduce guilt, increase certainty and conviction, relieve dissatisfaction, fortify flagging faith, affirm and reinforce the worker's assets, replenish depleted self-esteem, nourish and enhance ego capacity for adaptation, alleviate psychological pain, restore emotional equilibrium, comfort and bolster, and refresh. Supportive supervision is concerned with tension management on the job (Itzhaky and Aviad-Hiebloom 1998).

If social workers are to do their jobs effectively, they need to feel good about themselves and about the jobs they are doing. However, the reality is that they often (for a variety of reasons to be discussed) feel discouraged, disaffected, powerless, frustrated, devalued, inadequate, confused, anxious, guilty, apathetic, alienated, and burdened with a sense of futility. A supervisor details a worker's disillusionment:

The supervisee is a male caseworker in a public welfare setting. He had had graduate training and this is his first job. He has been with the agency for nine months. While a number of clients have marital and parent-child problems, he feels that because of the size of his caseload he cannot furnish the psychosocial service he would like to offer and is trained to provide. Disillusioned, he says "The things I am doing, any intelligent clerk could do; they are hardly professional."

A supervisee expresses dismay:

I don't really know what the things are that are making me draw back. I think it's not really wanting to get involved in the world of Mrs. Garcia because it's such a horrible world. She has seven children and no husband and lives in a project and now she's very sick. You know that's not the nicest world and I'm not sure I want to be there. (Amacher 1971:164)

Another worker expresses discouragement:

First, the girl ran away from home, fine. She took an overdose, fine. Then her mother's boyfriend is living in the house; her father's an alcoholic; her boyfriend just gave her VD and then she found out she is pregnant. Bang, bang, bang, right down the line. (Amacher 1971:159)

Supportive supervision involves care for the carers, who feel disillusionment, disappointment, and disenchantment. If these feelings are frequent in an agency, the low level of morale results in high turnover, repeated absenteeism and tardiness, loafing and inattention to work, noncompliance, frequent grievance reports, and interpersonal friction—not a happy way to run an effective agency. Furthermore, only as the workers feel confident can they communicate confidence and hope to clients. A feeling of hope is an important variable in determining the success of worker-client interaction.

So far the general responsibilities of supportive supervision have been stated in a negative sense. A similarly restricted definition of physical health would be the absence of disease. We might broaden the definition of health to suggest well-being rather than just the absence of disease. In the same way, we might define psychological well-being, the goal of supportive supervision, as a state of complete emotional health, the maximum a person is capable of achieving.

In this sense the supervisor, in implementing the responsibilities of supportive supervision, not only relieves, restores, comforts, and replenishes but, more positively, inspires, animates, exhilarates, and increases job satisfaction. Such supervision makes the difference between joyless submission and eager participation—between playing notes and making music. A supervisee writes:

I am not sure what the supervisor did or how she did it, but the spirit she inspired in the group was unmistakable. Somehow we felt hopeful, light, cheerful, and optimistic. We felt confident that we could accomplish much that was good and worthwhile. It's a good feeling and it's hard to sustain but while it lasts it's a wonderful high, a really good trip.

The need for supportive supervision has long been recognized in social work supervision. One of the earliest studies of worker turnover, conducted in 1927–1928, noted "unhappiness in work," a question of worker morale, as the second largest category of reasons for leaving the job. It included such reasons as "dissatisfaction with social work," "depressing work," "clients hopeless," and "caseload too heavy" (Pretzer 1929:168). These problems would have been the concerns of supportive supervision at that time.

Supportive functions currently are seen as an important responsibility of supervision. A study of supervision in thirty-one social welfare and rehabilitation agencies, based on questionnaires to 1,600 employees and detailed interviews with a sample of direct service workers, showed "support" to be one of the key functions of supervision. It was defined as "provision of emotional support to subordinates and enhancement of subordinates' feelings of importance and self-worth." "Overall, personnel report that supervisors provide a great amount of support. . . . In fact, in comparison with scores on other scales, providing support is what supervisors do best" (Olmstead and Christensen 1973:189). An earlier study found that "support and encouragement" and "appreciation of efforts" ranked second and third, respectively, in a twelve-item listing of helpful aspects of supervision (Cruser 1958:20).

Nelsen (1973, 1974) studied tape recordings of a series of sixty-eight supervision conferences. She found that 69 percent of the taped units "contained three or more supportive comments" (Nelsen 1973:266), indicating the high frequency of such kinds of interventions. Relating the level of supervisor support to strain in the supervisor-supervisee relationship. Nelsen concluded that "the use of support was one of the most important skills for the [supervisor] to master if the relationship strain was to be avoided" (Nelsen 1973:340). She notes that the "technique of . . . offering support was used both more extensively and more flexibly than might have been expected" (Nelsen 1974:153).

In a study that asked supervisors to identify their strengths in supervision and asked supervisees to identify their perception of their supervisors' strengths, supportive behaviors were frequently mentioned (Kadushin 1992b). Three hundred and forty-seven supervisors offered 186 comments related to expressive aspects of the supervisor-supervisee relationship. Supervisees said:

My supervisor provides recognition and positive reinforcement about my work.
She is sensitive to work stresses and concerned for my well-being.
He is consistently available for support but makes it safe for me to be independent.
He frequently uses positive feedback, giving appreciation and recognition for good work. (Kadushin 1992b:9)

Supervisors listed their supportive behaviors as among their principal strengths. Four hundred and eighty-three supervisors provided 138 comments identifying supportive behavior as among their strengths in supervision. Supervisors said:

> My ability to relate positively, fairly, and supportively.
> Providing an empathic, supportive environment in which workers can comfortably discuss their clinical issues.
> I am empathic, respectful, caring, and provide a safe learning environment.
> My ability to relate to supervisees in an empathic, direct, understanding, and nonauthoritarian manner. (Kadushin 1992b:6)

A worker describes her supervisor as a "master of supportive supervision":

> She somehow had the ability to locate me when I was having a particularly bad day, would sit down and listen to me for awhile and would then find some way to make me laugh. She has a wonderful sense of humor. Then we would discuss the case or the situation that was troubling me and she would maybe offer a couple of suggestions. But I would leave these sessions feeling motivated and ready to go again. The connections we made seemed to change my whole outlook.

Burnout: Definition and Symptoms

Work stresses adversely affecting human services personnel have received explicit, almost explosive attention with the identification of the burnout syndrome. First named in the literature in 1974 by Freudenberger, burnout has been the subject of a small library of books and articles. (Brodsky and Edelwich 1980; Cherniss 1980; Freudenberger 1980; Pines, Aronson, and Kafry 1981; Maslach 1982; Paine 1982; Gillespie and Cohen 1984; Koeske and Koeske 1989; Wallace and Brinkeroff 1991; Koeske and Kirk 1995a, 1995b; Soderfeldt and Warg 1995; Drake and Yadoma 1996; Arches 1997; Itzhaky and Aviad-Hiebloom 1998; Um and Harrison 1998; Zunz 1998; Leon, Altholz, and Dziegielewski 1999; Anderson 2000). Clearly, burnout remains a hot topic. A major component of these studies is devoted to defining burnout and identifying the attitudes, feelings, and behavior associated with it. For the supervisor to help a worker with problems of burnout, the supervisor needs to be able to recognize its manifestation.

"Burnout can be defined as a syndrome of physical and emotional exhaustion" resulting from occupational stress "involving the development of negative self-concepts, negative job attitudes, and a loss of concern and feeling for clients" (Pines and Maslach 1978:233). Burnout has been defined as an "exhaustion reaction, the result of constant or repeated emotional pressure associated with the intense involvement with people over a long period of time" (Pines, Aronson, and Kafry 1981:15). Burnout is not the same as job dissatisfaction; it more closely resembles battle fatigue.

In characterizing a worker as burned out, we are not pointing to the transient, temporary feelings every worker experiences when a case has blown up. The term is validly applicable only to a persistent, chronic condition that results from a cumulative, prolonged, undissipated buildup of stress.

Mechanical devices have fuses that shut the machines down on overstress, computers display error messages when demand exceeds their capacity, and a pinball machine registers *tilt*. Humans have no built-in protective devices that indicate an overload.

An awareness of the symptom of burnout enables the supervisor to more easily recognize its onset. The symptoms are physical, emotional, and behavioral. Workers experiencing burnout manifest weariness and chronic fatigue. Feeling physically drained, they are often more susceptible to colds, tension headaches, digestive difficulties, and sleep disorders.

Emotionally burned-out workers feel a sense of disenchantment with the work and alienation from the work. Discouraged, hopeless, and pessimistic about the work they are doing, they feel depressed and emotionally depleted. Workers experiencing burnout tend to feel angry and resentful as a consequence of a sense of work failure and futility. There is a loss of enthusiasm, excitement, sense of mission, and a gradual erosion of commitment and interest in the job. Instead of being interesting and satisfying, the job becomes something to be tolerated and survived.

Behaviorally, workers suffering from burnout, or impending burnout, manifest a resistance to going to work, and increased tardiness and absenteeism. When at work they tend to watch the clock, postpone or cancel client appointments, and take more frequent and longer breaks. Where workers may have previously felt concern when a client failed to show up, they now feel relieved. They resist taking calls from clients and postpone calling back. They display a more cynical, detached, indifferent, or even apathetic approach to clients in an effort to distance themselves emotionally. There is an increased tendency to treat clients in a mechanical, rigid, petty, bureaucratic manner, making less of an effort to help. In discussing clients, they are more likely to stereotype and disparage them, show a loss of caring and concern, and talk about them as "cases" rather than as individuals (Kahill 1988).

When interacting with clients, burned-out workers are more likely to avoid eye contact, increase their physical distance from the client, subtly discourage the client from sharing emotional material, and keep the interview as short as possible. Feeling physically tired and emotionally depleted, burned-out workers tend to be more impatient with clients and more easily irritated by them.

Burned-out workers do only those things that enable them to get by. They are going through the motions, merely putting in their time.

A worker describes some of her behavior, which she identifies as associated with burnout.

> Sometimes I would be late for home appointments. I would make stops on my way to home visits and do my errands just to have time that had nothing to do with my work. I sometimes spaced out during interviews with clients and I started referring people to other agencies or counselors. I would have a negative attitude before I even went in; I would be very curt, with no warmth at all. In retrospect I think that I was fighting to create this distance so the clients wouldn't like me. I thought that if I wasn't helpful and I wasn't sympathetic, when I asked if they wanted another appointment, they would say no. (Pines, Aronson, and Kafry 1981:47)

Overall, the worker's behavior suggests emotional withdrawal from the job and emotional distancing and detachment from clients. Empathetic, accepting, and authentic responses are difficult to communicate when one is psychologically detached from the client.

Burnout results in a dehumanization of the client. Empathy, understanding, and individualization require a psychological effort that the worker can no longer emotionally afford. A worker in a community mental health agency expresses the sense of frustration and futility that characterizes burnout:

> The situations started looking so much alike to me. I could never see changes. It was always the same people, in the same situations. I would get angry when I'd go in. After a while, I stopped listening. I stopped being empathetic. I had to lose my compassion in order to survive emotionally. It wasn't a job where you got many thanks from the clients. It was a vicious circle: because the more angry I became, the less I felt like putting out in the counseling sessions, so of course less happened with the clients. (Pines, Aronson, and Kafry 1981:46)

Another worker details the changes she experienced in the development of burnout:

> When I started, I was deeply involved in every aspect of the sixty families I had. I really cared and was supportive of everything that went on. But if you continue at this level of involvement you get to be crazy very soon. So I started to withdraw a bit and see things as the client's problem. I went from total involvement to a kind of standing back. In the end I developed a callousness towards the people I was working with. I was so emotionally detached that I might as well

not have been there. I was earning money, but I didn't feel the work was part of my life. (Pines, Aronson, and Kafry 1981:58)

The feelings that contribute to the development of burnout are circular. Feeling disenchanted, hopeless, and cynical, sensing a growing hostility toward and resentment of clients and their unending problems, the conscientious human service worker responds with guilt, shame, and discomfort. The additional stressful emotional burden associated with such feelings further contributes to the development of burnout.

Burnout is a self-reinforcing process. The behavior associated with burnout reduces the likelihood of achieving a successful, satisfying case outcome. This reinforces feelings of helplessness and hopelessness, intensifying burnout.

The supervisor needs to be aware that there is an element of contagion in the loss of morale in the development of burnout. One worker's depressed, disenchanted feelings tend to contaminate other workers and reduce their levels of enthusiasm for the job.

Sources of Job-Related Stress for the Supervisee

Having learned to recognize burnout and the stresses and symptoms associated with its gradual development, the supervisor has to understand its etiology and the nature of the specific, recurrent sources of stress encountered by supervisees. The sources of stress include (1) various aspects of supervision itself (Bernard and Goodyear 1998; Erera and Lazar 1994b; Holloway 1995; Watkins 1996); (2) agency clients (Acker 1999; Iliffe and Steed 2000; Adelson 1995; Ryan 1999; Shulman 1993; Wade, Beckerman, and Stein 1996); (3) the nature and context of social work tasks (Itzhaky and Aviad-Hiebloom 1998); (4) the social work organization (Holloway 1995; Shulman, 1991); (5) community attitude toward social work (Brooks and Riley 1996; Donner 1996; Rubin 1997); and (6) the worker him- or herself (Fox and Cooper 1998; Horwitz 1998; Koeske and Kirk 1995a, 1995b). We will discuss each of these sources of tension in turn. The purpose of explicating this admittedly depressing litany of causes of stress is to help supervisors become more aware of the problems that might require their intervention.

Administrative Supervision as a Source of Stress

The previously discussed components of supervision are in themselves sources of tension for the worker. As covered in chapters 3 and 8, administrative pressures toward compliance with agency policies and procedures and the requirement for work assessment and evaluation are sources of tension for workers. Itzhaky and Aviad-Hiebloom (1998) have found that administrative supervision engenders role ambiguity and role conflict in workers; related to the conflict between bureaucratic and service orientations, these stresses appear to cause worker burnout. Although good administrative supervision is in and of itself supportive, supervisors who strive to offer their supervisees a well-defined structure in which to operate, a clear definition of realistic and appropriate objectives, and a chance to participate in agency decision making may find themselves swimming upstream in a turbulent practice environment (Brooks and Riley 1996; Jarman-Rhode and McFall 1997; Munson 1996a).

Educational Supervision as a Source of Stress

Similarly, educational supervision is a source of both tension and support. Education implies change, and the target of change efforts is the worker. Change involves, of necessity, a temporary disequilibrium, an unfreezing of the old equilibrium. Educational efforts, then, inevitably induce some anxiety (Birk and Mahalik 1996; Costa 1994; Frantz 1992; Hale and Stoltenberg 1988; Pepper 1996).

New situations are encountered for which the supervisee does not have a readily available solution. Ideas that were thought correct are explicitly examined and questioned; some are found to be incompatible with new ideas to which the supervisee is introduced. The transition period is characterized by anxiety and a temporary loss of confidence. The old procedures are being rejected, but the new procedures are not yet fully accepted. Besides, the supervisee is ambivalent about taking the next step. He is "not sure that he is willing to change what it took him so long to learn" (Rothman 1973:43).

All learning presents the learner with a need to adjust to these emotional concomitants, but their intensity varies, depending on the nature of the subject matter. The subject matter of social work is likely to develop the kinds of intrapersonal reverberations that make the changes resulting from learning more problematic. Social work content is emotionally charged and involves the ego. It is content that reflects the way a person views him- or herself and the surrounding world. In learning about human behavior, we are learning about ourselves—about our defenses, our motives, our unflattering impulses. Whereas the usual educational situation asks that the student critically examine and hence possibly change his or her ideas, social work supervision is often directed toward a change in behavior and perhaps personality.

The threat of change is greater for the adult student because learning requires dissolution of long-standing patterns of thinking and believing. It also requires disloyalty to previous identification models. The ideas and behavior that might need changing represent, in a measure, the introjection of previously encountered significant others—parents, teachers, highly valued peers—and the acceptance of other models implies some rejection of these people. The act of infidelity creates anxiety.

Much of social work education is concerned with secondary socialization. As a consequence of primary socialization, strong attitudes have developed toward minority groups, welfare recipients, divorce, discrimination, racism, sexual deviance, crime, juvenile delinquency, violent confrontation, the class struggle, and so on. The learner has become accustomed to particular patterns of behavior in relating to other people. Socialization in educational supervision requires changing those attitudes and behavioral patterns that impede competent job performance.

The supervisory tutorial is a threat to the student's independence. Readiness to learn involves giving up some measure of autonomy in accepting direction from others, in submitting to the authority of the supervisor-teacher. Supervisees also face a threat to their sense of adequacy. The learning situation demands an admission of ignorance, however limited. In admitting ignorance, supervisees expose their vulnerability. They risk the possibility of criticism, shame, and perhaps rejection because of an admitted inadequacy.

Supervisees have the choice of being anxious because they do not know how to do their work or being anxious about confessing ignorance and obtaining help. The recognition and acceptance of ignorance is a necessary prerequisite to learning.

Although educational supervision produces these kinds of anxieties, it also contributes to reducing tensions (Itzhaky and Aviad-Hiebloom 1998). The knowledge and skills, the problem solutions, that educational supervision makes available give the worker a feeling of confidence and a sense of assurance in job performance. In learning what he or she needs to know, the worker can adapt more successfully to the demands of the work situation. This is gratifying and supportively ego-enhancing.

The Supervisor-Supervisee Relationship as a Source of Stress

The relationship between supervisor and supervisee is another main source of both tension and support (Anderson, Schlossberg, and Rigazio-DiGilio 2000; Hagler and Casey 1990; Watkins 1997). Mayer and Rosenblatt, who obtained some 233 protocols of stress situations encountered by social work practitioners, state that "the worker's anxieties appeared to be basically a function of the two main relationships in which he was involved, his relations with his supervisor and those with his clients" (Mayer and Rosenblatt 1973b:3).

In her treatment of social workers, Babcock, a psychiatrist, maintained that they felt "less inadequate with clients than with the supervisor to whom they fear to reveal their inadequacies. . . . These patient-workers in discussing their work experience accept intellectually that they need the supervisor yet . . . they often admit to unreasonable anxiety" (Babcock 1953:418).

Why should the relationship be a source of tension? The supervisory relationship is an intense, intimate, personalized situation that has considerable emotional charge. As is true for any highly cathected, meaningful interpersonal relationship, it becomes infused with transference elements, with ambivalence and resistance, and with residuals of earlier developmental conflicts. It is a particularly fertile context for the development of transference.

The supervisor-supervisee relationship evokes the parent-child relationship and, as such, may reactivate anxiety associated with this earlier relationship. If the supervisor is a potential parent surrogate, fellow supervisees are potential siblings competing for the affectional responses of the parent. The situation therefore also threatens to reactivate residual difficulties in the sibling-sibling relationship.

The literature tends to support the contention that the supervisory relationship does, in fact, mobilize these kinds of tensions (Ekstein and Wallerstein 1972; Fleming and Benedek 1966; Schuster, Sandt, and Thaler 1972; Langs 1979).

There may be tension that results from the supervisor's legitimate need to discuss some of the emotional responses of the worker to the case situation. A supervisee says:

Feeling that "honesty" was the hallmark of the good caseworker, I included in my process recordings all of the doubts, fears and anxieties that I experienced in my interviews. At first the supervisor was delighted with my openness. However, in time she began to question what lay behind all my uncomfortable feelings. At one point, we were spending more time in discussing me than in discussing my patients. We explored my pathology in all its gory details. I would come out of the supervisory conference shaking with self-doubt and feeling vulnerable and picked apart. (Mayer and Rosenblatt 1975b:186)

In one case, a worker experienced stress as a consequence of unmet expectations from supervision:

Well, I don't get supervision, I don't get evaluation of cases and of me. When I get a problem case, I grab hold of Barry and force his attention—but that's not supervision. What all this means is that I'm not going to develop professionally unless I choose to read books. (Fineman 1985:57)

Another worker experienced stress related to supervision as a consequence of differences in style:

> Although technically I'm supervised by Joe, I soon found I couldn't stand his paternalistic style—and I told him this. He got very hurt. He's a very kind man, but he doesn't question things in a way that suits me. So I get my supervision and advice elsewhere. (Mayer and Rosenblatt 1975b:51)

For another worker, the conflict between the need to share and the possible consequences of this for evaluation was a source of stress:

> I have regular meetings with my supervisor, but always steer clear of my problems in coping with my report work. Can I trust her? I need her backing for my career progress, but will she use this sort of thing as evidence against me? There are some painful areas that are never discussed but *need* discussing so much. It's an awful dilemma for me. (Fineman 1985:52)

Responses by supervisees to a questionnaire recapitulate some of the additional sources of stress they associate with their supervisors (see Table 6.1).

Although the supervisory relationship may be inherently stressful, research suggests that supervisors vary on interpersonal dimensions that mitigate relationship stress. For example, several studies have found that the quality of the supervisory relationship hinges on supervisory empathy (Watkins 1997). Shanfield et al. (1992) and Shulman (1991) have reported that supervisees find empathetic supervisors more effective; Harkness (1995) found that supervisory empathy was not only associated with worker ratings of the supervisory relationship, but also with client ratings of the practice relationship. Thus, it appears that empathetic supervisory relationships both exacerbate and ameliorate stress for the worker.

The Client as a Source of Stress

Relationships with clients are an additional source of stress for the worker. Workers deal with people who are living under considerable stress, including children in need of protection and their families (Anderson 2000; Horwitz 1998), the elderly (Barber and Iwai 1996; Goodridge, Johnston, and Thomson 1996; Leon, Altholz, and Dziegielewski 1999), HIV-infected individuals (Garrett 1999; Itzhaky and Atzman 1999; Mueller 1995; Wade, Beckerman, and Stein 1996), persons with mental illness (Acker 1999; Koeske and Kirk 1995b), perpetrators and survivors of domestic violence (Iliffe and Steed 2000), and sexually abusive youth (Ryan 1999). Such clients are encountered at a time of crisis, when their emotional reactions are overt and strong. It is

Table 6.1 Sources of Supervisee Dissatisfaction in Supervision

Percentage of supervisees checking item as a strong source of dissatisfaction (N = 384)	
1. My supervisor is hesitant about confronting agency administration with the needs of his or her supervisees.	35
2. My supervisor is not sufficiently critical about my work, so that I don't know what I am doing wrong and what needs changing.	26
3. My supervisor does not provide much real help in dealing with problems I face with my clients.	25
4. My supervisor tends to be capricious and arbitrary in the use of his or her authority.	23
5. My supervisor does not provide enough regularly scheduled, uninterrupted conference time.	21
6. My supervisor is too controlling and dominant, so that he or she restricts my autonomy and initiative as a professional.	20
7. My supervisor shows little real appreciation of the work I am doing.	15
8. My supervisor tends to encourage unnecessary dependency.	14
9. My supervisor is hesitant about making decisions and/or taking responsibility for decisions, so that the total burden of case decisions rests with me.	12
10. Other (miscellaneous).	22

Source: Kadushin (1973).

very enervating to deal with a great deal of raw emotion—anxiety, anger, depression, grief—as well as deal with the constant exposure to highly charged emotional situations while controlling one's own emotional responses. "The worker, face to face with the client in the interview, is exposed continually to an onslaught of unrepressed primitive feelings. The avalanche of feeling with which the . . . social worker is confronted is an unusual stress situation peculiar to the task of extending psychological help. It is, in a sense, an occupational hazard" (Feldman, Sponitz, and Nagelberg 1953:153).

The effect of exposure to clients' feelings is intensified by the fact that social work training is designed to increase sensitivity and response to such feelings. The need to be empathetic implies the need to feel with the client. If the worker is truly empathetic, he or she must feel some of the pain, the anguish, the despair, the hurt that many of the clients feel. A supervisee says:

When you're working with people then you're under pressure straight away. You can't just treat a person like a piece of paper and file it away to be forgotten until another day. If that person came in to you with what to them is a very pressing problem, you have to do your damnedest to help them and therefore you put yourself under pressure, this is part and parcel of the work. (Parsloe and Stevenson 1978:300)

And during the course of the day's work, the emotional expenditures in each interview are cumulative, leaving the worker emotionally depleted and exhausted. A worker says:

A really bleak day. I had a series of four interviews, one right after another with several depressed women. The atmosphere in my office became progressively more funereal as the day went on. Gloom and doom, dejection and despair. And the very worst was the last interview of the day with Ruth, who, having been told by her lover that he was breaking off with her, wanted me to convince her that she has some reason for living. I had been contaminated by the mood of the other clients and feeling dejected, had a hard time screwing myself up to sound positive about life.

Workers may encounter clients who have neither asked for nor want agency service and who are hostile and resistant to their efforts to help. The caseload includes groups of clients whose behavior is offensive to many workers—child molesters, wife beaters, rapists, and child abusers.

Despite such hostility and the workers' own very human reaction of antipathy to some clients, professional practice principles require that they act acceptingly. In the following excerpt a worker describes her feelings before an interview with a hostile client. The worker was scheduled to visit a mother whose children had been removed and who wanted them back.

I was very frightened of the upcoming visit. I have a difficult time dealing with hostility and I expected Mrs. P. to be quite hostile. . . . My anxiety mounted steadily the morning of the visit. I lingered at the office as long as I could, wanting to remain in the presence of other workers. Finally I left to drive to Mrs. P's house. I arrived at her neighborhood only too soon. I trudged up the steep hill with dragging feet, wishing with all my strength that I was going in the other direction. . . . I remember hoping that Mrs. P. would have forgotten the appointment and wouldn't be at home. But there she was, opening the door for me. I felt somehow like a condemned man at his own execution. (Mayer and Rosenblatt 1973:8)

With limited capacity to effectively use the kind of help we can make available, often indifferent or resistant (if not openly hostile) clients can usually make only a limited tenuous adjustment, despite the best efforts of the social workers. The problems are often relatively intractable. The client's interpersonal environment is often unsupportive and deprived, if not actually noxious. Such clients make very heavy and stressful demands on the worker's time and emotional energy and offer limited professional satisfaction in return. Dependent and emotionally taxing clients drain the worker's store of emotional energy, leaving him or her feeling emotionally depleted and exhausted, powerless and impotent.

There is often no sense of closure—a feeling that the work is finished and the objectives accomplished. Experience has taught the worker that contact frequently is recurrent and episodic, rates of recidivism high. A community mental health clinic worker says:

> This woman had a boyfriend who moved in and out. While he was living with her, he gave her a lot of support with her children. Whenever they quarreled and he walked out, she'd call me in despair. At first I would go out and spend two hours saying whatever was needed to lift her out of her misery. This happened pretty regularly every few months, and after a year or so I became less responsive to her. Instead of going to see her, I'd talk to her on the phone. "So he left again," I'd tell her. "He's left before." If she remained upset, I'd tell her I'd be out to see her within a few days. Sometimes I never did go. I was beginning to put things off. (Brodsky and Edelwich 1980:186)

In a study of the satisfaction and stresses of psychiatrists, psychologists, and social workers, Farber and Heifetz (1981:626) found that "doubts regarding the efficacy of therapy was one of the principal sources of stress." They were stressed by "giving so much, receiving so little, and through it all remaining vulnerable to doubts that one's efforts are effective" (Farber and Heifetz 1981:674). "Most therapists cited lack of therapeutic success as the single most stressful aspect of therapeutic work" (Farber and Heifetz 1982:295).

A study that explored psychotherapists' perceptions of sources of stress pointed to clients. Clients who expressed anger, lacked motivation, made no observable progress, and terminated prematurely were cited most frequently by respondents as sources of stress (Deutsch 1984).

There is also stress associated with physical dangers encountered on the job. Reviewing a series of surveys and studies in England, Norris concluded that violence is an occupational hazard for social workers and that, proportionately, "social workers face a greater risk of violence than any other non-military profession apart from police" (1990:17). The book "highlights a major but as yet largely unrecognized form of stress for social workers" (Norris 1990:168).

"A survey commissioned by The (British) National Institute of Social Work found that almost a quarter of field social workers had been physically assaulted at work, nearly half threatened with violence, and over three quarters shouted out or insulted" (Wilmot 1998:24; Weinger 2000). Although actual physical abuse may be relatively infrequent, the worker is often subjected to verbal abuse. Clients under considerable stress are not always in full control, so that angry feelings are openly expressed in verbal attacks on workers. A foster care worker says:

> The interview left me shaken. When I told Mrs. N., that given her situation, we could not return Johnny home, she said "Could not? You mean *you* don't want to." Her voice rising and her face getting flushed, she lost her cool and she yelled. "You lousy bitch. You shit. I knew all along you didn't like me, but I didn't think you would go so far to hurt me, you little bastard." It's hard to get talked to like that without feeling upset.

Subject to abuse, the worker is not in a position to walk away or answer back, the usual measures of self-defense. The worker is obliged to continue client contact, making continued efforts to help. The worker's decisions often have considerable implications for the client's living situation. A child is placed for adoption, a parolee can be released from prison because a job has been found, or an abused child is separated from his or her parents. This is an awesome responsibility, and awareness of the possible consequences of such decisions is a source of occupational stress, anxiety, and guilt. The worker often has to make these crucial decisions in the face of unnerving uncertainty, ambiguity, and limited information and with a recognition that full understanding of the astounding complexities of unpredictable human situations is beyond the wisest person's full comprehension.

Many situations encountered by child welfare workers have all the essential elements of Greek tragedies. They involve conflicting but legitimate and justifiable interests and needs. There may be a conflict between the rights and privileges of a foster parent and the rights and privileges of a natural parent. The conflict may be between the right of grown children to live autonomously and the rights of aged parents for protection and support. Moreover, workers face the unnerving prospect of having their decisions reviewed. Social workers are accountable to the public generally and to their clients specifically. Clients now have the right to have access to their records and are entitled to activate complaint procedures and initiate lawsuits that name their social workers as defendants.

There are also problems of deciding between competing needs of different clients. Devoting a considerable amount of time to one client means neglecting another. As one worker put it,

> The conflict that I felt was not only between the regulations and the clients but between client and client. If you want to help clients get schooling or job training or discuss personal problems with people who may be very eager to talk to you about them, you do so with the knowledge that you are not using this time to help get basic material things to people who just as desperately need them. (Miller and Podell 1970:24)

The Nature and Context of the Task as a Source of Stress

Stress can result from the nature of social work tasks and the conditions under which the work is done. We noted earlier that the task in which the worker is engaged interpenetrates with his or her own life. Encountering separation experiences, the worker is made anxious as he or she remembers his or her own separation fears at the hospitalization or death of a parent, the threat of divorce, and so on.

Babcock (1953:417) says, "Living on a job that is so closely allied to life itself makes separation of work from other areas of life exceptionally difficult. Since the work task and living are often simultaneously experienced, anxiety is greater than in many other fields." One worker says,

> Sue was pregnant out of wedlock again. She went on and on about how easy it seemed for her to become pregnant—said it with pride as well as with some regret. And as she went on and on about this, my insides knotted with envy. Why so easy for her and so hard for me? We had been trying for a year and with increasing desperation, to have a child. I, who wanted a child so much, could not get pregnant; Sue, who did not want a child, got pregnant effortlessly. It was hard to keep listening to Sue discuss her problem, since listening increased the hurt I felt so deeply.

Other stresses result from the fact that the workers' responsibilities exceed their power and resources. Society supports social work agencies because they are part of the necessary apparatus for social control. They mitigate the effects of situations that might lead to social conflict and alleviate the most extreme effects of social dysfunction. The limited support given to agencies allows them to perform this secondary function. Society is not yet willing to grant the support necessary to carry out their primary functions—to provide adequate measures for prevention and rehabilitation. The workers therefore have to implement a policy that reflects society's ambivalence toward the groups whom they are asked to help. Very often what they are asked to do is in conflict with society's willingness to provide the resources to enable them to do it.

Furthermore, neither the worker nor the profession has the power to change those significant social pathologies—discrimination, unemployment, housing shortages, and so on—that directly limit what the worker can do. These crucial externalities, which are beyond the workers' power to remedy or change, affect their practice and determine the outcome of their efforts.

The results of the workers' best efforts to help the client in the face of overwhelming odds, under conditions beyond their control, lead to a sense of impotence, frustration, and failure. A clear sense of achievement is hard to come by.

A worker writes about her reaction to trying to help in the face of overwhelming odds:

I'm tired of hearing about rats and roaches, and politely ignoring the latter as they crawl over walls and floors. I'm tired of broken boilers, toilets, and refrigerators, plumbers who never come, junkies in the halls and junkies who break into apartments and steal clocks, irons, sheets, children's clothes, food—anything they can lay their trembling hands on. I'm tired of hearing about asthma, high blood pressure, anemia, arthritis, toothaches, headaches, and "nerves." . . . I don't want to hear the same things: "He just left . . . not enough for . . . I don't know where he . . . like to work but . . . think he's you know, slow . . . not sending up heat . . . some mornings it's so bad . . . went to the clinic but they . . . do you give money for . . . teacher sent him home because he . . . only got to the eighth. . . ." Poverty jams into a mold which permits few variations. (Walton 1967:5)

There is stress in working in the context of ambiguous objectives. Society often gives the agencies a poorly defined charge. The community sometimes does not make clear what response it expects from agencies in the face of social problems. Workers ultimately have the task of making decisions in the face of poorly defined or even conflicting objectives. Should the Temporary Assistance for Needy Family (TANF) mother be forced to work if her children need her at home? Should prisons serve the purpose of punishment or rehabilitation? Should the community share with the parents the burden of care for a severely retarded child? Should gay men and lesbian women be recruited as foster parents? In these situations and others, workers frequently face the stress of making decisions and taking action about moral and ethical questions on which both they and the community are still undecided.

Some of the occupational stress to which workers are subject stems from uncertainty about not only what they should be doing but also how they should be doing it. Techniques and approaches for helping the client are not so well established as to provide clear-cut guidelines for the workers' behavior. For many situations there is no validated professional consensus on the most effective approach. In addition to incomplete or imperfect mastery of available knowledge, workers have to accept the limitations of professional knowledge itself.

The worker is faced with the stress of balancing antithetical demands and expectations. He or she is required to be objective and maintain some emotional distance from the client. But at the same time, the worker is required to be empathetic, feeling what the client feels, and putting him- or herself figuratively in the client's situation. These are contradictory demands.

The worker is required to individualize the client, seeing him or her as unique. At the same time, the worker is often required to label the client for diagnostic reimbursement and administrative purposes. Labeling inevitably involves some deindividualizing and even stereotyping. There is a need to nonjudgmentally accept clients as they are. At the same time, the worker is expected to make assessments about the client's behavior, the client's treatability, the client's motivations, and the client's manipulations. The worker is asked to accept and respect the client as a person but reject dysfunctional behavior—to reject the sin but not the sinner. This is a difficult separation to make, as the behavior is a significant component of a person's identity. The worker is asked to accept the client as he or she is and is expected to help the client change what is not acceptable about him or her. The worker thus has to balance antithetical attitudes of acceptance and expectations of change.

We are asked to be authentic and genuine and at the same time consciously controlled in our interview behavior. The requirement for "spontaneously controlled" behavior once again involves contradictory demands. We are asked to respect client self-determination and simultaneously protect the client from self-harm.

There is stress associated with the antithetical pressures of being a professional in a worker-client relationship, on the one hand, and our humanistic tradition on the other. The professional relationship implies inequality in knowledge and power in our favor; the humanistic tradition strives for equality and collegiality in the relationship. As professionals we are "better" than the clients in the specific sense of expertise. The therapy relationship is inherently a relationship of unequals. We are the helpers; they are the ones needing help. But this inequality offends us, and we feel a sense of stress from the dissonance between the reality of difference and our egalitarian orientation.

The factor that tends to provide satisfaction and hence counter negative feelings in most jobs is the recognition by oneself (confirmed by others) that the work has been well done and that there is a desirable outcome. Social work does not confirm itself. There are no observable, objective, tangible indications of whether interventions have been successful. We do not see the car we helped build roll off the line, a defective heart corrected by a coronary bypass, or a jury verdict in favor of our client. Social workers are not often rewarded by unmistakable indications that interventions have made a difference.

Because the work is done in private, workers do not get the confirmation of their competence from other professionals who, having witnessed the performance, might commend the worker. The doctor in the operating room and the lawyer in the courtroom might be congratulated by peers who have observed the competent professional in action. The performance of actors, athletes, and musicians are applauded by their clients, the audience. Applause is an overt, instant expression of approval. In contrast, workers rarely get direct confirmation of their competence by applause from their clients. Most clients are too absorbed in their own troubles to concern themselves with efforts to express commendation or gratitude for the worker's efforts.

Working in private toward objectives the worker can only guess have been achieved and only rarely receiving spontaneous and voluntary gratitude by the client, the worker is under stress from doubts about his or her competence and about the significance of his or her work.

The worker is the principal instrumentality for helping the client. Failure in social work is more directly felt as a reflection on the adequacy and competence of the worker as a person, more so than in many other kinds of work. A facilitative relationship is the necessary if not the prime ingredient for success in much of our work. Developing such a relationship depends to a considerable extent on what we as people contribute to the interaction. Consequently, when things go wrong, in an exercise of self-awareness we tend to focus on ourselves to identify how our needs and feelings might have intruded in the interaction. More so than in most other jobs, the social worker *is* his or her work. Failure, then, is more easily personalized.

The occupational title social work professional arouses expectations in others that result in stress. Just as people who hold the title of minister, priest, or rabbi are expected to be more perfect morally than the population at large, the title social work professional leads to expectations that the person so identified would be better adjusted, be more successful in interpersonal relationships, be better at parenting, and have stronger marriages than others. Workers may feel a stressful pressure to live up to the expectations communicated by the title. When they encounter difficulties in relationships with their children and spouses—as is inevitable in any complex human relationship—social workers may feel more keenly than others a sense of disappointment and failure.

The Organization as a Source of Tension and Stress

Organizational turbulence, frequent reorganization, and rule changes are stressful. An organization oriented toward managed care with a high degree of centralization of decision making, a highly formalized hierarchical system, and elaborately structured rules and procedures is associated with a greater likelihood of a stressful work context.

Workers in many large public agencies face the stress of adapting to constantly changing directives.

> Frequent interruption of routine income maintenance and service activities further overburden caseworkers. An Atlanta caseworker says: "We get so many manual transmittals with so many changes that it's impossible to stay on top of everything." Changes are so frequent that agencies cannot keep manuals up to date. (Galm 1972:30)

Because the client's welfare is not necessarily equivalent to the agency's welfare, professional and bureaucratic orientations provide competing claims upon loyalty. Billingsley studied this conflict in child welfare agencies and found that

> in spite of the social worker's intellectual and emotional commitment to meeting the needs of his client it is apparent that these needs must be met within the framework of structured approaches imposed by the agency . . . even over the worker's own estimation of the needs of the client. This is consistent with findings in studies of other professions. (Billingsley 1964a:403)

The conflict between the two orientations leads to a strain between the agency demand that a given number of units of work be performed and the desire of the professional to do the best possible job. Billingsley identifies this as the conflict between quantitative output and qualitative performance.

There is stress associated with the salaries paid many workers, especially if coupled with high workloads (Rauktis and Koeske 1994). Admittedly, income may not have been a strong source of motivation in the choice of social work. Other kinds of satisfaction had greater priority. But if adequate income is not of first importance, it is, as someone said, "wonderfully soothing to the nerves," especially if faced with unrelenting demands for superhuman performance. We cannot ignore the fact that salary is often perceived as an objective measure of one's worth to society. Lower income levels signify that we are considered to be of lesser importance, and this makes it difficult to maintain a respectable level of self-esteem. Pay levels become particularly important as an objective measure of society's estimate of our worth in those instances where there is an absence of other objective measures of our work as noted previously.

The actual salary is not as important as equity, which requires remuneration consistent with one's workload, performance, and reference group peers. An equitable social work salary is one that provides reasonable compensation for performing a high volume of difficult work in comparison with persons of similar education, achievements, and background. The worker with a master's of social work degree (MSW) compares his or her salary and associated possible lifestyle with people in other professions who have also invested six years in professional preparation. The comparison often puts the social worker at a disadvantage.

Workers in some special settings face more particular stresses. All organizations interact, of course, with the environment in which they are embedded. However, not all professionals are required to interact on intimate terms with other professionals. The social worker in a host setting (for instance, the medical social worker in a hospital, the school social worker in a public school, the psychiatric social worker in a mental institution) is placed in this position. They have to justify and define their decisions to a critical audience of other professionals. They have to learn a pattern of deference in interacting with higher-status professionals. Research indicates that such "boundary positions" are apt to produce tension (Berkman et al. 1996; Brooks and Riley 1996; Itzhaky and Atzman 1999; Kahn 1964; Staudt 1997). For instance, even though doctors are supposedly colleagues and peers of the social worker in a hospital or mental health facility, the reality is that the doctor is *primus inter pares*—first among equals. A psychiatric social worker on an inpatient hospital psychiatric ward says,

> My feelings of anxiety and stress have been mainly a result of working in a host setting. Initially, I was extremely anxious about working with residents and psychology fellows. I felt inadequate even though I thought I had much better training and had better skills in working with people. I tended to be concerned with status, prestige, etc. They were psychiatrists—they had medical degrees or else they had Ph.D.s. I was really intimidated by their status.

When I began to work with residents, I tended to defer to them. I was sure that they knew what was best and that I shouldn't question them. Besides, if I did question them, I would have to be damned sure I could justify my position.

My one-down position became problematic and stressful for me. And the fact that I am a woman and almost all of the residents and psychology fellows are men didn't help either.

The hazards of sexism and the resentments associated with hierarchical elements in interprofessional relationships interact with each other. Hierarchy and gender segregation overlap. The higher-status psychiatrists and clinical psychologists are more apt to be men. Social workers are likely to be women.

There is stress that derives from the necessity of working cooperatively with other institutions in society that are based on values somewhat at variance with the values to which the social worker owes allegiance. The worker often has to work with the legal system, with the educational system, and the managed care system, which see the problems of his or her clients from different vantage points. The worker faces the stress of communicating in different milieus of discourse and accommodating to different points of view regarding the same problematic situation.

Community Attitudes Toward Social Work as a Source of Stress

The worker is affected by the general community attitude toward social work and the function it performs. The community has always been ambivalent about the profession, and more recently there has been an intensification of the negative components of the ambivalence.

Earlier in our history, the effectiveness of social work interventions was not critically questioned. It was presumed and generally accepted that our interventions had positive results. Not only was social work previously granted unquestioned presumptions about its expertise and effectiveness it was also granted a presumption about the benign nature of its intentions. There was a consensus that what the social worker did was done altruistically and unselfishly for the benefit of the client. The community attitude toward social work was generally respectful and approving and had given us high marks and prestige for our moral integrity, altruism, and disinterested benevolence.

However, during the recent past the thrust has been to challenge those assumptions. Some lawyers, historians, and radical therapists have argued that the apparent benevolence is a mask of social control for intrusion into client lives, a violation of client's rights, and coercive domination. They claim that in effect our work is an exercise of power and paternalism in disguise. Rather than acting in a benevolent manner for the client's own good, they argue, we actually represent an oppressive society, and the results of our interventions are often far from benign. Our focus on the intrapsychic and interpersonal problems of individual clients and their families suggested that we were "blaming the victims" of social pathology and social disorders and placing the burden for change on the clients. Clinicians were told that their work was futile and perhaps even destructive because they were ignoring the larger issues of racism, sexism, and failures in the economic system. This made clinicians defensive, ambivalent, and uneasy about their work.

Rather than being universally perceived as benevolent and benign, social workers now are more frequently perceived as intrusive and controlling. Although we intend to liberate human lives, some claim that we more often succeed in dominating our clients. Thus, over the years, public attitudes toward social work have moved from approval, trust, and confidence through questioning ambivalence to a greater measure of critical mistrust and cynicism. Certainly, past public attitudes were less stressful for workers than more current, more negative attitudes have become. With this growing public disenchantment, progressively greater encroachments were made on the autonomy of workers' decision-making power by community groups representing clients. Organizations of one kind or another representing various client groups, foster parents, adoptees, the mentally ill, physically disabled, battered women, substance abusers, and so on were empowered (or empowered themselves) to contest social workers' decisions. Workers face the stress of explaining and defending their decisions in response to critical questions from such groups.

In that climate, demands for accountability have become more insistent. Increasingly, the imputation of our competence and expertise now has to be demonstrated and validated. Managed care has put some social workers out of work, and empirical research has challenged the efficacy of our practice.

In summary, it is noted that the supervisor providing supportive supervision has to understand the stresses and tensions workers encounter on the job. Such understanding is a prerequisite to offering interventions that are likely to be helpful. The source of stresses and tensions include such factors as administrative and educational supervision, the client, the nature of the work itself, the social agency organizational structure, and the attitude of the general community toward social work and social workers. The worker encounters problems of role ambiguity, role conflict, role overload, and role strain.

Worker Personality as a Factor in Burnout

In effectively implementing supportive supervision, the supervisor not only has to be aware of the various worker stresses cited previously but also must understand the worker's reaction to stress. Just as the supervisor is guided by a diagnostic assessment of the learning needs and learning style of the supervisee in educational supervision, a diagnostic assessment of the needs for emotional support is useful in supportive supervision. For social workers providing services to AIDS patients, for example, Wade, Beckerman, and Stein (1996:85) describe such reactions as "a variety of emotional and physical symptoms of ill health, including stomach viruses, colds and flus, headaches, physical exhaustion, sleep disturbances, as well as loss of memory, lack of concentration, moodiness and flashbacks . . . [and] recurrent dreams involving death."

Subject to the same stressful stimuli, some workers burn out and others do not, and different workers manifest different degrees of burnout. The attitudes that people bring to the job are a factor (Koeske and Kirk 1995b). The worker who is relaxed and doesn't take the work too seriously, who has a high self-esteem that is not threatened by occasional failures on the job, and who is not too self-demanding and self-punitive is less frequently a candidate for burnout. Such attitudes help immunize the worker against burnout.

The worker who consistently tends to blame himself for failure rather than realistically assigning some component of failure to the client and the social situation is more likely to respond negatively to job stress.

The paradox is that the more conscientious, concerned workers may be more susceptible to burnout. It is said that "one has to be on fire to burn out." The commitment and dedication that characterize determined idealists may result in a greater discrepancy between effort expended, intensified expectations, and limited outcome. The sense of disappointment in their work is apt to be greater for such workers. The worker becomes a prisoner of his or her own sensitivity.

The self-image characteristic of many people who select social work as a career—the image of an accepting, tolerant, understanding, and helpful person—increases vulnerability to burnout. Encountering difficult problems, many workers find that they are, after all, not angelic but only human. When angry, unkind, or critical feelings about clients begin to surface, a considerable amount of psychic energy is expended in defending against such feelings in an attempt to preserve the more acceptable self-image. This reaction is often intensified when the client is of a different race or gender and the worker feels self-accused of sexism or racism.

There are differences among workers in the significance that the job has for them in regard to their total life configuration. For some workers, the job is the most important thing in their lives, having clear priority over other interests. For others, the job is a more peripheral aspect of their lives. The worker who builds his or her life around the job is more likely to risk burnout. Investing more of him- or herself in the job, he or she is more likely to be disappointed and depressed if things go wrong. Workers who have difficulty in separating work from the rest of life or are unable to balance idealism and realism are more likely candidates for burnout.

Stress is cumulative and incremental. Consequently, the worker whose off-job life is generally unstressful can withstand considerable stress on the job without risking burnout. However, if the worker's social, marital, or family situation is stressful, even limited additional stresses on the job may make him or her vulnerable. Stress from the home front spills over, adding to stress on the job.

Workers who have limited personal investment in their work, who are not strongly oriented toward seeking emotional fulfillment from their client contacts, who tend to make situational rather than personal attributions of failure in their work, or who are bureaucratically oriented toward acceptance of rules, regulations, and procedures are likely to have less need for supportive supervision. The nature of their orientation defends them from emotionally disturbing aspects of their work.

A worker who is concerned about but not emotionally involved in the job, who is satisfied with meeting minimal standards, and who is primarily concerned with extrinsic rewards—pay, job advancement, desirable office space—is likely to be in moderate need of supportive supervision when some situation is encountered that threatens job security.

Workers who are idealistic, independent, individualistic, and nonconforming are likely to need more supportive supervision. They are strongly affected by the conflict and the discrepancy between what they think service to the client should be like and what they actually experience it to be. They are sensitive to ethical conflicts in their work and are affected by the frustrated impulse to effect change. They chafe at requirements to conform to organizational needs. Such workers need supportive supervision in reconciling their conflicts, discontents, and disappointments. Where reconciliation is not possible, supportive supervision would at least provide the opportunity of openly discussing their disagreements with a receptive representative of the organizational hierarchy.

The more dedicated the worker, the greater the likelihood of the need for supervisory support. Workers who feel a strong sense of calling, who are imbued with a dedicatory ethic toward their work, and who have a strong professional superego are more strongly affected by inevitable failure. Such workers, who bring the best of what is needed to social work, are more likely to require the guilt-dissolving absolution of a supervisor, someone in a position of authority who gives permission to moderate the demanding rigidity of a strong, punitive superego. Supportive supervision provides the antidote to the tyranny of the ideal—the unrealistic expectations that such highly committed workers impose on themselves. Supportive supervision is designed to help such workers take themselves less seriously.

The worker who is upwardly mobile and achievement-oriented may need the frequent reassurance from supportive supervision that he or she is doing well. Any hint of work failure is threatening and anxiety-provoking to such workers and calls for supportive supervision.

In maintaining supervisor awareness of the negative effects of job stress and in raising supervisee consciousness of this, the periodic scheduled evaluation conferences might include a stress-check review. This would keep both supervisor and supervisee alert to the development of dangerously high levels of chronic tension.

Implementing Supportive Supervision

Having learned to identify burnout and understand the factors that help explain its development, the supervisor has the responsibility of responding to the problem in a way that might prevent the development of and/or mitigate the effects of stress and tension.

Supportive supervision is often implemented not as a separate, explicitly identifiable activity but as part of the work of educational and administrative supervision. Assigning work, reviewing work, or training for the work can be done in a supportive manner. The functions of educational and administrative supervision can be performed in a way that communicates respect for, interest in, and acceptance of the supervisee. As we discussed earlier, the consequences of good administrative supervision and good educational supervision can be supportive in the structure and the skills they offer the supervisees.

Administrative, educational, and supportive supervision have direct and indirect effects on social work burnout (Itzhaky and Aviad-Hiebloom 1998). If administrative supervision cannot alleviate burnout by reducing the ambiguity and conflict of the social work role, then supportive and educational supervision may help. Using supportive supervision to recognize personal accomplishments and increasing job performance and improving competence through educational supervision provides a sense of accomplishment, makes the job more meaningful, and leads to greater job satisfaction. In a study of how human service professionals cope with burnout and the suggestions they have for coping with burnout, "building competence" is the most frequently cited response (Shinn and Morch 1982:231). Helping the worker do his or her job and providing the information needed may be more effective in ameliorating stress than other kinds of supportive supervisory interventions, such as emotional support, that is, being warm and friendly (Himle, Jayaratne, and Thyness 1989; Itzhaky and Aviad-Hiebloom 1998). Contributing to worker competency and job mastery is perhaps the most important thing a supervisor can do to help ameliorate worker stress. Successful achievement of job objectives may ultimately be the most effective antidote to burnout.

Beiser notes that it is very difficult to separate the precisely educational from the purely supportive components of supervision. In discussing her own supervisory practice with child-psychiatry residents, she says that

> although I gave a great deal of didactic information both as to theory and specific skills, sometimes this was to alleviate anxiety, sometimes to encourage identification or to demonstrate a model of flexibility. When I tell of my own errors I use them not only to illustrate a particular point but to encourage a less experienced therapist or to interfere with hopes of omnipotence through identification with me. (Beiser 1966:138)

The supervisor's availability in and of itself is reassuring and supportive. A questionnaire study of worker reaction to supervision indicated that supervisors' availability and regularity of contact were positively correlated with satisfaction with supervision and the level of perceived helpfulness of the relationship (Shulman 1982:27–28). A replication of that research found that supervisors' availability was associated with worker ratings of supervisory skill, trust, rapport, helpfulness, morale, and stress in the social work job (Shulman 1991).

The negative effect of a harassed supervisor and his or her lack of availability in response to a worker's need for support is illustrated in the following:

> I had just completed my home visit with an extremely angry, hostile mother. She was angry with me because I had had to remove her child some time ago and still did not feel she was ready to assume her maternal responsibilities. I had endured her curses and hysterics; now, as I left her home I was trembling and angry. But, I was also filled with self-doubt. Was I doing the right thing? Maybe there was something I should have done differently or might do now

so that mother and child could be reunited? I returned to the office absorbed with the incessant dialogue taking place in my mind and proceeded to my supervisor's office. As she looked up, I blurted, "I am so angry with Mrs. S." Before I could finish my story we had several interruptions and then the phone rang. After the phone conversation, she said, "What is it you were saying?" "Nothing," and sulking I stalked out of her office. I was frustrated all afternoon.

The supervisor's response to the development of stress and tension on the part of the worker and the ultimate danger of burnout involves a series of specific interventions. The supervisor can act to (1) prevent stress and tension from developing; (2) remove the worker from the source of stress; (3) reduce the impact of stressors; and (4) help the worker adjust to stress.

Prevention of Stress

At the very beginning, the probability of burnout might be reduced by the supervisor's effective performance of the administrative supervisory function of hiring and inducting. This permits the selection of personnel so that there is a best fit between applicant and the work that needs to be performed.

Providing accurate information about the job permits the applicant to make a more objective decision as to whether it is the kind of job that fits his or her needs and expectations. As a consequence of clearly learning what the work realistically entails, some applicants who might have had difficulty on the job select themselves out.

But accurate objective information about the job is also helpful to those who decide to accept the position. As a result of having been clearly told what they might expect, new workers are less likely to be disillusioned and disappointed when they encounter the realities of the job. Such anticipatory guidance and realistic preview is a psychological inoculation associated with increased survival rate on the job.

Workers are hesitant to report incidents of violence or threatened violence because it might suggest a failure on their part in interacting with clients. They worry that they might have done something to annoy, irritate, or frustrate the clients (Norris 1990). Consequently, supervisors need to help supervisees communicate such experiences but, in addition, help the supervisee recognize danger signals that suggest impending violence so as to prevent such stress.

Reducing and Ameliorating Stress

The supervisor can supportively help reduce stress impinging on the worker or remove the worker temporarily from a stressful situation. These procedures are analogous to environmental modification procedures in working with the client. The supervisor can arrange for a temporary reduction in caseload or a temporary shift to less problematic clients. The supervisor might also arrange for a temporary increase in clerical help available to the worker.

Conferences, institutes, and workshops not only provide learning and stimulating personal contacts but also enable the worker to get away from the office and the caseload. They are, in effect, supportive rest and recreation devices, removing the worker from stress.

The supervisor might sanction time-outs as a tension-reducing measure. A day off in the middle of the week or an afternoon off after a difficult morning might be permitted, with the time to be made up when the worker feels more in control.

Imaginative, flexible work scheduling and arranging for job sharing of high-stress tasks are stress-reducing procedures. Helping the worker organize his or her work load, sanctioning the prioritization of tasks so that some responsibilities are temporarily put aside, and allowing for deadlines to be delayed with the supervisor's authorization help reduce the development of stress.

The supervisor can remove the worker from stress by job enrichment, job diversification, job rotation. As Davis and Barrett (1981:59) note, "Rotation of workers to alternate services within the agency can be used to provide a change of pace with relief from stressors."

Job enrichment attempts to help the worker find more meaning in tasks assigned, and job diversification involves increasing the variety of job-related tasks. Caseworkers might be assigned to work with a group, teach homemakers or foster parents, engage in work-related research, or write a work-related report for administration.

A temporary change of assignment from the field to the office with temporarily diminished responsibility for contact with clients helps the worker catch his or her psychic breath and recharge emotional batteries.

Careful assignment of a reasonable caseload balanced between cases with a high risk of failure and cases that might provide an experience of success prevents tensions arising from quantitative or qualitative role overload.

Overwhelming caseloads are stressful, and the supervisor can ameliorate this situation by helping the worker prioritize cases. Some may need less intensive contact than others. Giving permission to provide differential levels of service to clients may be helpful.

In an attempt more specifically related to helping the worker cope with developing tension, supervisors in some agencies have arranged for stress management workshops. This might include instruction on biofeedback, meditation, or relaxation techniques.

The supervisor can be supportive by sharing frankly some of his or her own difficulties with the supervisee. This confirms the fact that examined failure is acceptable and that the supervisee need not feel so guilty and inadequate. The supervisor reports her experience with Gretchen, her supervisee, who

> commented that it was so hard to know when she should say something to someone and when she should keep quiet. I asked her what she meant. She said, . . . "If the girls want to talk about sex, I let them talk about sex even if I know that maybe I am going further than they want to go." I agreed that this was a rough struggle, one that I was going through too. I elaborated by saying that many times I was torn when Gretchen asked me something as to whether or not to tell her or to let her do the work. This struggle, I said, I could feel with her since it was a struggle that I had too. Gretchen looked at me and said, "Do you really?" I said that I did. She looked very comfortable and at ease with this. (Gladstone 1967:9)

The worker may be upset about a problem he or she is facing with the client. Discussing it with a supervisor who is calm about the situation is supportive. Some of the supervisor's calmness is communicated to the worker. A supportive orientation encourages expression of feelings, which is supportive in itself. Nelsen found that supervisees "volunteered feelings after they had been encouraged *and* supported in expressing feelings on a conference by conference basis" (1973:209; emphasis in original).

It is presumed that anxiety is reduced by externalization, an open expression of anxious feelings. Perception by supervisees of the level of a supervisor's helpfulness was positively associated with the supervisor's encouraging such ventilation. Positive responses to the statement "When I am upset about something my supervisor says or does, he/she encourages me to talk about it" were highly correlated with supervisory helpfulness in Shulman's studies of social work supervision (1982:157, 1991:176).

The supervisor who suspects that the supervisee feels anxious about his or her next visit to a family, next group meeting, or next community-action planning conference, might supportively ask, "How do you feel about this meeting?" He or she might hazard an inference coupled with an invitation: "You seem somewhat upset about this upcoming meeting. Would you like to talk about it?"

Considerable stress is encountered in exercising control and communicating acceptance in response to a client's hostility and rejection. To react with anger, defensiveness, or withdrawal—eminently human and socially acceptable reactions—would be regarded as a violation of professional norms.

Such a response would then evoke guilt and a feeling of professional failure. Even the thought of such reactions creates discomfort. "The client aroused some negative feelings in me—like anger, impatience, and frustration. And I became angry at myself for having these feelings" (Mayer and Rosenblatt 1973a:8).

While still holding to the norms of professional conduct, the supervisor can supportively sanction such feelings. All thinking and feeling is acceptable as long as it is not manifested in unacceptable behavior. A worker says,

> I think that one of the important functions of supportive supervision is to help the worker deal with negative feelings about the client. Social work attitudes tend to reinforce general societal constraints about thinking negative thoughts about other people. So this is quite a job for supervision. In my case I was asked to physically describe a client. I proceeded along the line of height, weight, etc. When my supervisor asked me if the person was attractive, I was really caught off guard and felt hesitant about expressing my thoughts that, no, the person wasn't attractive at all. With the supervisor's support I have become more at ease with expressing negative thoughts and feelings and have come to accept these as part of any relationship.

The supervisor reduces stress by normalizing unprofessional feelings, noting that workers may often feel negative or critical about some clients. The supervisor supports workers in carrying out tasks that must be done but that cause anxiety. Workers are often initially reluctant to reverse the usual pattern of amenities and ask intimate details about the life of the client, who is a relative stranger. Such behavior is seen as an unwarranted intrusion of privacy, a manifestation of unacceptable "aggressive voyeurism." The supervisor supports the workers by reassuring them about their entitlement to such information if they are to do the job of helping the clients.

Reinforcement or confirmation of the workers' decisions is supportive because it assures them that the supervisor shares the responsibility for what they are doing or planning to do. It is reassuring for workers to know that their decisions are in line with more expert opinions.

The supervisor mitigates stress by supportively sharing the responsibility for difficult decisions with the worker. A social worker in a TANF program said,

> In talking with Mrs. H. about how she disciplined the children, she told me that yesterday she had caught her four-year-old playing with matches—lighting them and tossing them in the air. Frightened and anxious, she grabbed the kid, slapped his hand repeatedly, then lit a match and burned the kid's

hand slightly. Mrs. H. thought that feeling the pain would teach the kid to keep away from matches. She sure handed me a tough one. According to the law, I was really supposed to report Mrs. H. for child abuse. But if I reported her I would blow the chances of continuing a relationship with Mrs. H. and possibly being of help to the children. What to do? After discussing this with my supervisor, I held off reporting Mrs. H. for abuse. That shares the guilt for the decision.

Discussing this stressful aspect of the social worker's job, Brearley makes explicit the relation between work stress and sharing responsibility in supportive supervision:

Social workers are subject to many pressures which create stress. Working in a situation of uncertainty, having to deal with a lack of knowledge and often with uncontrollable factors in an environment which militates against change inevitably creates stress. Social work has therefore developed techniques to manage stress, particularly the supervision process. . . . Supervision is a way of sharing the burden of uncertainty, of gaining support in a practice context in which decisions are almost invariably made with incomplete information and knowledge. Through supervision, the worker is helped to manage his own response to being unsure and also helped to clarify decisions and share responsibility for decision making. (Brearley 1982:136, 139; see also Shapiro 1982)

Mayer and Rosenblatt (1973a, 1973b), in their study of stress among social workers, found that new workers had unrealistically high expectations of what social work could accomplish. When this overly optimistic picture met with inevitable failure, the workers tended to blame themselves. The supervisor can offer the exculpation of a practiced professional who reduces guilt by excusing failure. The supervisor helps workers move from an unrealistic sense of idealistic omnipotence to an acceptance of a realistic limitation of themselves, social work technology, and the clients. The shift is supportive and results in less anxiety and guilt. The supervisor legitimizes limits of expectations, depersonalizes responsibility for some failures, and relieves the worker of the burden of undeserved guilt.

One significant aspect of supportive supervision is concerned with what Stelling and Bucher have identified as vocabularies of realism. "Acquiring a language for coping with failure and human fallibility can be seen as part of the process of acquiring a professional orientation and frame of reference toward the work of the profession" (Stelling and Bucher 1973:673).

Vocabularies of realism help the worker cope with stress by a cognitive restructuring of his or her approach to the work. It helps reduce the pressure of work demands, providing sanction for detached concern and psychological distancing from the client. It revises expectations so that they are less idealistic and more realistic and depersonalizes failure when it occurs.

The need for vocabularies of realism is greater in those professions where risk of failure is high and the consequences of failure are significant. "A profession which rests on a body of knowledge characterized by uncertainties and gaps runs a relatively high risk of error and failure" (Stelling and Bucher 1973:673). These factors are operative in social work. Consequently, collective responses to recurrent probabilities of failure have tended to develop, and the supervisor passes these on in supportive supervision. Studying these procedures in medicine and psychiatry, Stelling and Bucher identify basic exculpatory themes that are similar to those employed in social work. One theme is "doing one's best"; a second is "recognition of limitations." In the following example we see the doing-one's-best theme communicated supportively by a supervisor to a psychiatric resident.

> Another very important time came when one of my supervisors said to me, in dealing with this very manipulative patient, "Look, you know, she may commit suicide, we may lose her—we could try, but there is a very good chance that she will kill herself sooner or later, no matter what you do," and I think once I had accepted that idea that patients do kill themselves and that . . . there are some things I can do to prevent this, but there are also some things that I can't, I think I had kind of an "aha" experience. (Stelling and Bucher 1973:667)

The second theme supportively communicated in supervision is a recognition of limitations, expressed by the following psychiatric resident:

> One thing one learns in this residency program is not to have therapeutic ambitions in anywhere near the quantities that you have when you first come here. Patients thwart that right, left, and center, and you learn that it is therapeutically unhelpful to have a large therapeutic ambition for patients. . . . I can now say that there are large numbers of people who suffer symptomatically, but who are untreatable. . . . I had many sorts of rescue fantasies about patients when I came into the residency, and it's taken me a long time to shift focus and learn that I didn't have to rescue everybody, that, one, it wasn't necessary, and two, it wasn't possible. (Stelling and Bucher 1973:669)

The supervisor helps the supervisee accept the reality of human fallibility and imperfection, the limits of technology, and the fact that all approaches are effective sometimes but never all the time. Supportive supervision is sometimes implemented by retranslating behavior deserving of criticism in a way that highlights the positive aspects of the worker's action. A supervisor talks about Jill (a worker), who was under

> constant pressure from a visit to a difficult family—she's spent months getting them back on their feet—very disorganized lot—and when she went back the other day they had slipped back into the same old mess, kids screaming, they hadn't learned anything—no movement at all. Just back in the same old mess and Jill lost her temper, got up and walked out! (laughs) She was overwrought but you see she had displayed temper to the client, she'd displayed emotion, she was showing she cared for them. Anyway she came back to the office and told me all about it. Well we had to laugh—she'd worked so hard with them, but I know she cares, she'll go back there and sort it out. (Pithouse 1987:70)

The worker demonstrates an awareness of failed performance. She shares this openly with the supervisor. The supervisor sees the behavior as true evidence of the worker's concern for the client and recognizes the "constant pressure" faced by the worker. The worker confesses and receives supportive absolution from the supervisor.

The supervisor can help the supervisee in modifying stress-producing self-statements through reframing and cognitive restructuring (Itzhaky and Aviad-Hiebloom 1998). Some of the kinds of disabling self-statements that the supervisor can help change follow:

- I must make the right decision, or something terrible will happen to the client.
- I should never feel bored or angry or disrespectful toward a client.
- I must always try to help if asked, even if it involves setting aside my own personal needs.
- When a client fails to make progress, I must have done something wrong.
- I should be a model of mental health.
- I must show my supervisor how perfect I am.

The supervisor communicates some ideas that help the supervisee become more realistic about the work, such as "Knowledge does not always lead to a solution," "Reality is contradictory and often characterized by mutually incompatible tendencies," and "Small changes, which is all that one can legitimately expect, are big victories, so that one can take satisfaction in doing some good some of the time."

When the elusiveness, ambiguity, and lack of clearly identifiable signs of success rob the worker of a significant source of work satisfaction, supportive supervision can be helpful. A protective service worker says:

> I find it extremely disheartening when so much of my work seems to have little or no effect. At times when I have been particularly discouraged and thinking about taking a construction job, a few words from a supportive supervisor have done wonders to boost my morale. I don't mean that he/she merely repeated empty clichés. Rather, they took the time to listen to what happened and had the insight and sensitivity to see and point out some positive effects in my interactions with clients.

The supervisor reduces tension by helping the worker resolve the problem of conflicting role obligations. If the worker is torn between finishing a report and helping a client facing an emergency, the supervisor can sanction delaying the report so that the worker can devote full attention to client needs. Where two performance objectives conflict—for instance detailed intensive interviews with clients at intake and the need to expeditiously complete intake interviews so as to process more applicants—the supervisor can reduce anxiety by officially assigning a higher priority to one of the objectives.

The supervisor provides the support of perspective. The view that both the client and the relationship are fragile often inhibits workers from doing what may be helpful. The supervisor can validly reassure the worker that both the client and the relationship can survive a mistaken intervention, a poor interview, or a temporary lapse in professional conduct. Unlike the experienced worker, the new worker "does not have a backlog of successful cases to which he can refer in reverie when things don't go well with the client who is sitting across from him. When things go awry in relationship to a particular client nothing can shore up a therapist's defenses faster than his recall of the many successful cases he has terminated" (Mueller and Kell 1972:104). Borrowing the perspective of the more experienced supervisor can be supportive.

A new worker might express doubts about his or her ability to be helpful to the client. The supervisor can supportively universalize by sharing the fact that most new workers feel this way, that he or she has been able to assist others to be helpful, that he or she has confidence in the worker's ability to learn, and that he or she would be available to discuss with the worker the problems that come up in trying to be helpful. This single intervention contains a number of different kinds of statements, all of which have a supportive intent.

Supervisors provide support for workers in helping them formulate a clearer conception of agency policies, their own work goals, and their role within the agency. Unless supervisees have a reasonably good idea of what they are supposed to be doing, why they are doing it, and toward what objectives, they are likely to be burdened with unnerving doubt and confusion. Uncertainty is generally related to increased tension. A worker whose supervisor clearly communicates performance objectives, performance standards, and performance expectations, feels a sense of support in such clarity.

If role ambiguity is a potential source of tension, clarity in definition of work objectives, expectations, and reciprocal responsibilities prevents the development of such tension. In the following, a supervisee writes of the nonsupportive effects of lack of clarity regarding objectives:

> I was given the task of being an indirect leader in a new setting. I continually reported back to the supervisor what I was doing and what problems existed. The supervisor briefly commented that what I am doing is good. When I asked direct questions such as what goal does the agency have as a priority now, or what are new developments from conferences, the supervisor answered that there are no new goals, no new developments, you do your own thing. I feel that a task like the above is extremely difficult and threatening, demanding support and a certain amount of direction from the supervisor, which serves the purpose of giving the supervisee a sense of direction and support in the work setting itself. The supervisor's lack of direction made my task more difficult.

The supervisor, in discharging the responsibilities of supportive supervision, attempts to provide workers with the opportunity to experience success and achievement in performance of professional tasks and provides increasing opportunities for independent functioning. Herzberg, Mausner, and Snyderman (1959) found that feelings of achievement and responsibility were two of the most potent sources of job satisfaction. Both help people feel good about the job they are doing.

The supervisor supports by praising and commending good performance and communicates agency appreciation for the workers' efforts. Short written communications can be helpful. One worker talked about "kudos memos," complimenting her on something she had done, that her supervisor occasionally dropped in her mailbox.

Compliments from the supervisor are particularly gratifying and ego-enhancing because they come from someone who is identified as capable of making valid evaluations. In sharing victories with an appreciative supervisor, workers know that they are talking to someone who understands the difficulty of the task they have successfully achieved. To perform this support function effectively, a supervisor

> must fulfill two important criteria: he or she must be an expert in our field and someone whose honesty and integrity we trust. In other words this person must understand the complexities of the job we do and must be courageous enough to provide honest feedback. If these requirements are met we can accept support as genuine. Mothers, spouses, or nonexpert friends can provide general encouragement but that is probably not as meaningful as support from someone who can appreciate the technical intricacies of our job. (Pines 1982:158)

Partial praise should be offered where warranted, perhaps saying something like "It was good you realized something was going on here, but I am not sure this was the best way to respond to it. Let's talk about how to handle clients' anxiety." The worker is commended for knowing that something needed to be done, even though what he or she did was not especially helpful. One supervisor, in detailing her supportive intervention, writes,

> On the days I didn't find a lot of glory to give her, I gave her encouragement and pointed out that at least she was aware of what she did wrong and how it could have been improved. When she had a miserable meeting with the girls and was angry with herself, I tried to interject some realistic reassurance. When she had a good meeting, I tried to help her feel justified in her high spirits. I'm sure that getting along together as people had a great deal to do with it as well.

Unwarranted praise, however, is antisupportive. It may reflect the supervisor's rather than the supervisee's anxieties, which then tend to decrease the supervisee's self-confidence: "He seems much too worried about me, like I am about to fall apart or something"; "I get the feeling he is afraid to criticize me, afraid that I can't take it"; "I don't think I am so fragile, but he is so supportive about not hurting my feelings that I begin to wonder if he thinks I am fragile"; or "I appreciate the gentleness of her approach to me, but it suggests a kind of condescension that I tend to resent."

As was true for educational supervision, the act and its intent may be at variance with the effect. Just as teaching is not learning, supportive activity on the part of the supervisor may not be perceived as supportive by the supervisee. The supervisor must be sensitive to any feedback that gives information as to the actual effect of his or her behavior. Reassurance may not reassure; catharsis may lead to an increase in anxiety.

The following are two examples of situations that were regarded by workers as good examples of supportive supervision:

> One conference dealt with the relationship of the supervisee in working with a group of severely mentally handicapped children. The worker mentioned the fact that such children "make me physically ill," "they are repulsive to me." I pointed out how I could understand her feelings and how I myself had at one time shared somewhat the same feelings. I went on to talk about my growth in this as a result of experiences I had had in working in a school for retarded children, the warmth of relationships that had developed.
>
> I do not know if she has changed her bias, but I know that she did a good deal of thinking about it, and told me how I had helped her manage her feelings so that she could work more effectively in that program. What helped the supervisee was some understanding and sympathy toward her feelings, coupled with warmth and empathy and a positive stand on what this type of work could entail, how it could be meaningful, etc.
>
> A worker in a surgical ward of an acute-care hospital expressed to her supervisor her resistance to visiting a patient, long known to her, who was in terminal stage of cancer. Supervisor helped worker to express her fear, and then to look at why she was afraid. Worker finally concluded that she was afraid patient might die while she [worker] was visiting her. Further exploration revealed that the worker had many warm, close, and positive feelings about the patient, and the worker was afraid she would break down and cry. The supervisor's response to this was, in effect, "So what!" Discussion followed regarding the reality of such fears and emotions, the need for the worker to remain an individual whose real feelings are not to be confused with concepts of "professionality," and that expression of honest feelings can only serve to strengthen relationships between people. Subsequently, the worker reported freedom to share feelings with the dying patient. The supervisor had effectively provided support to the worker, had accepted her fears and emotions, enabled her to express them, and freed her to overcome fears.

Recapitulation and Some Caveats

Generally, in implementing the responsibilities of supportive supervision, the supervisor engages in the same kinds of intervention that characterize supportive psychotherapy. The supervisor acts to prevent stress, reduce stress, or temporarily remove the worker from stress. The supervisor praises the workers' efforts where warranted, reassures and encourages, communicates confidence, depersonalizes and universalizes the workers' problems, affirms their strengths, shares responsibility for difficult decisions and/or lends sanctions to the workers' decisions, and listens attentively and sympathetically, providing an opportunity for cathartic release. All of this takes place in the context of a positive relationship characterized by respect, empathetic understanding, acceptance, and sympathetic interest in and concern for the worker as a person. The fact that such interventions are employed in the context of a meaningful positive relationship increases the saliency of the supervisor's communications. Praise, reassurance, encouragement—any supportive comment expressed by the supervisor—have greater significance for and effect on the supervisee because they come from somebody whose responses he or she values highly.

Last but far from least, the supervisor should not underestimate the importance of adequate salary levels and fringe benefits for increasing job satisfaction and reducing stress. As a consequence, the supervisor has to be an active advocate with management for salary increases for staff.

It needs to be recognized, however, that even the best supervisory relationship is not strong enough to resolve some dissatisfactions and job-related conflicts that derive from the nature of the work itself and the conditions under which it frequently has to be performed. Some potential dissatisfactions are inherent in agency structure, the social work task, the state of available professional technology, and the position of the social work profession in modern society.

It would be asking far more of supervision than it is capable of achieving if a good supervisory relationship is expected to eliminate completely work dissatisfaction, worker disenchantment, and worker turnover. This is part of the vocabulary of realism for supervisors.

Because of the selective emphasis on stresses and tensions associated with the social worker's job, there is a decidedly negative bias in the material presented above. Because of our conviction of the importance of the positive contribution that social work makes to people's lives, a parenthetical note seems necessary. The fact is that although the stresses and tensions noted above are real, most social workers do not burn out, and most find considerable satisfaction in their work.

A comparison of mean values for tedium and burnout for a variety of human service professions shows that social workers having a high mean value but on a lower level than in education or nursing (Pines, Aronson, and Kafry 1981:208, table A.3). A similar pattern has been described in a recent review of the literature; social workers suffer less burnout than comparable occupational groups (Soderfeldt and Warg 1995). A study of 108 family service agency direct service social workers found that "burn-out scores generally fell on the lower end of the scale, indicating that the majority of workers experienced little or no burn-out" (Streepy 1981:60). A national study of some 400 MSWs in a variety of agencies indicated a high level of satisfaction with their jobs. More than 80 percent of the workers stated that they were "very satisfied" or "somewhat satisfied" with their jobs (Jayaratne and Chess 1982:6).

More currently, Gibelman (1999) believes that external economic, social, and political forces now govern social work practice, which may explain why so many respondents to a random national survey of NASW supervisors have reported that job demands allowed little time for staff supervision (Kadushin 1992b). Findings of burnout among public service supervisors (Silver, Poulin, and Manning 1997) and veteran child protection workers (Anderson 2000) are consistent with a diminishing professional social work presence in public social services (Gibelman and Schervish 1996). Social workers who seek respite in the private sector may find little shelter from burnout; it appears that public sector refugees will encounter a new set of stressors in private social work settings, with limited supervision (Gibelman and Schervish 1997a).

This highlights the need for supervisors to be aware of stresses encountered by workers in doing their jobs. Worker and supervisor recognition of the significance of job stress is confirmed by the results of a 1980 national study (Vinokur 1983) of training needs of 1,500 child welfare supervisors and direct service workers. In selecting priorities for training from a list of forty-four content items, both workers and supervisors listed "identifying and lessening workers' stress" as among the very highest priorities (Vinokur 1983:78, 86; see also Pecora 1984).

The Value of Supportive Supervision: Research Findings

Studies are available that demonstrate the positive effects of supportive supervision. One study experimentally tested the effects of supportive and nonsupportive orientations to supervision (Blane 1968). Counseling students who experienced supportive supervision showed a significant difference in empathetic understanding after such supervision as compared with scores before supervision. Students who experienced nonsupportive supervision did not show this change.

Another study testing the differential consequences of the two approaches showed that nonsupportive supervision tends to shift the worker's focus of concern away from the client and toward him- or herself (Davidson and Emmer 1966). Blau (1960) found that reductions in the level of workers' anxiety as a result of supportive supervision were related to a less rigid use of agency procedures and encouraged better service to clients.

The available research also supports the supposition that good supervision reduces the development and negative effects of burnout. Berkeley Planning

Associates (1977), a research organization, studied worker performance in eleven protective service demonstration projects across the United States. Comparing differences in the level of burnout between workers in the different agencies, they concluded that the nature of supervision offered the workers was a crucial determinant of the level of burnout. "It was found that those demonstration projects in which workers report inadequate supervision had the highest incidence of burnout. Good supervision is crucial to workers' performance and satisfaction" (Berkeley Planning Associates 1977:57). Where workers experienced inadequate supervision, inadequate leadership, and inadequate communication, burnout was more frequent. Adequate supervisory structure and support and provision of timely, appropriate, and adequate information were associated with lower levels of burnout (Armstrong 1979).

In a study of stress encountered by 183 workers and supervisors in a public welfare agency, Munson (1983:217) found that "regular supportive supervision was the most effective aid in combating burnout." On the other hand, poor supervision is associated with increased risk of burnout. In a survey of 183 protective service workers, Gillespie and Cohen (1984) found that burnout was related to failure of supervisors to provide support and technical assistance to workers.

A research study of case management systems at four settings providing service to the chronically mentally handicapped found that "sites in which the content of supervision included supportive enabling and problem-solving activities were also sites in which case managers exhibited no antagonism toward management, low levels of absenteeism, no stereotyping of client groups, and less of the other symptoms associated with burn-out" (Caragonne 1979:24).

A detailed interview study of psychotherapists, including social workers in private practice, indicated that "most therapists found the role of support systems essential" in dealing with stress encountered in their work. "All who could, utilized supervisory relationships to help them through difficult moments" (Farber and Heifetz 1982:296).

A questionnaire study of forty direct care clinical staff at a psychiatric center found that emotional exhaustion and attitudes of dislike and cynicism toward clients were negatively correlated "with social support from one's supervisor—the supervisor's support of the worker was found to be a mediating factor in minimizing the negative effects of the work environment and was recommended as a strategy to prevent burnout" (Sullivan 1989:90–91). In another study, social workers identified "more support and appreciation" from supervisors as among the principal factors leading to the alleviation of job stress (Gibson, McGrath, and Reid 1989:15, table 7).

A participant observation and questionnaire study of ninety-eight social workers in a youth and community agency found that "the worker experiencing burnout perceived that there was little support from both their supervisor and their work environment" and they were "less satisfied with their supervisors' appreciation of their abilities and needs" (McCulloch and O'Brien 1986:85). A longitudinal study of changes in burnout over the course of a year found that the "variables related to social support (from supervisors and from peers) were most powerfully related to change in burnout levels" (Wade, Cooley, and Savicki 1986:170).

Supervisors were perceived as being one of the key figures in their social support network, along with co-workers and friends, as reported by human service workers in a number of related studies (Pines 1982:157). The availability of such support was significantly and negatively correlated with burnout; that is, the better the support network the less burnout occurred. The support network was defined as including people with whom one had "enduring interpersonal ties" and "who could be relied upon to provide emotional sustenance, assistance, and resources in time of need and who provide feedback and with whom we share values and standards" (Pines 1982:156).

Correlational data from 541 MSWs clearly support the existence of a negative relationship between emotional support from supervisors and co-workers and stress and strain. For example, "emotional exhaustion was negatively correlated with supervisor support" (Jayaratne, Tripodi, and Chess 1983:23).

A national sample of social workers provided questionnaire returns in a study of the relationship between emotional support and job stress and strain. The conclusions point to that fact that "both supervisor and co-worker support can help the practitioner cope with stress on the job and the strain that may result from this stress" (Jayaratne and Chess 1984a:448). A study involving about 2,000 American and Norwegian social workers found that "emotional support by both supervisors and co-workers is associated with lower levels of burnout, work stress and mental health problems" (Himle, Jayaratne, and Thynes 1989:35; see also Ross, Altmaier, and Russell 1989.)

In a study of organizational responses to burnout, White concludes that

the provision of effective *clinical case supervision* is the most consistent mechanism needed to provide staff with emotional rewards that may be only minimally provided by their clients with whom they work—the positive stroking of staff in the supervisory process may do more to enhance the treatment of clients than the actual supervision of details of the treatment process. (1978:15; emphasis in original)

Newsome and Pillari studied job satisfaction among 121 human service workers in a public agency. They found that "overall job satisfaction and the overall quality of the supervisory relationship were positively correlated" (1991:128).

Poulin studied job satisfaction of 873 social workers in a variety of settings. One of the significant research conclusions was that when "the level of supervisory support goes up then the level of satisfaction increases . . . This study's findings highlight the importance of supportive supervision" (1994:36).

A study of job satisfaction among 158 school social workers in Iowa found that "satisfaction with supervision has the most ability to predict job satisfaction" (Staudt 1997:49). "If the respondents were satisfied with supervision they were more likely to be satisfied with their jobs" (Staudt 1997:48).

A study by Schroffel of eighty-four professionally trained social workers serving mentally ill clients concluded that "workers who were satisfied with their quality of supervision are also satisfied with most aspects of their job" (1999:102).

A sophisticated investigation of supervision and role stress has found that these variables explain between 28 percent and 38 percent of the variance in social work burnout. Itzhaky and Aviad-Hiebloom tested 100 supervisees from 14 Israeli social welfare, mental health, rehabilitation, and family therapy agencies to examine the effects of two levels of supervisory orientation (psychodynamic and cognitive-behavioral), three supervisory functions (administration, education, and support), and two dimensions of role stress (role ambiguity and role conflict) on social work burnout. They found that "the higher the emotional-supportive function in supervision, the lower the role conflict and ambiguity, and consequently, the lower the level of burnout among social workers" (Itzhaky and Aviad-Hiebloom 1998:38).

A related study by Rauktis and Koeske (1994) examined the direct and moderating effects of supportive supervision on the relationship between social workers' work load and job satisfaction, a proxy measure for burnout. The investigators drew a systematic regional sample of 111 NASW members to survey their workloads, supportive supervision, and job satisfaction. In this study, all of the correlations between supportive supervision and job satisfaction were significant and positive, indicating that job satisfaction increased with supervisory support. The interaction between supervisory support and work load, however, made additional contributions to the prediction. In their final analysis, Rauktis and Koeske (1994:54) concluded, "There is an important limiting condition to supervision effectiveness; when work demands are high, emotionally supportive supervision loses its benefits. Apparently, even highly supportive supervision cannot overcome a work environment characterized by excessive work demands."

That cross-sectional finding was replicated in a panel study of supervised social work practice. Harkness (1997) examined variations in supervisory empathy and its effects on the supervisory relationship, worker skills and relationships with clients, and client outcomes over sixteen weeks of direct practice. Heightened expressions of supervisory empathy were associated with increased client ratings of worker skills and relationships, and with the client outcome of generalized contentment. As the experiment made client outcomes the focus of social work supervision, however, increased expressions of supervisory empathy diminished worker ratings of the supervisory relationship. Apparently, as supervisors coupled expressions of empathy with demands for more client-focused work, their supervisees found problem solving more helpful than empathy.

Additional Sources of Support for Supervisees

The Client

The supervisor is not the only source of support for supervisees in dealing with stresses encountered on the job. Clients can be a source of support as well as stress. In their responses to workers and to the service offered by workers, they confirm the workers' competence and sense of self-worth. Appreciative comments regarding the workers' efforts are supportive. Client movement and change for the better provide workers with a feeling of achievement.

The Peer Group

The supervisee peer group is an additional source of support for the supervisee that can supplement the supervisor's efforts. Workers turn to peers with whom they feel comfortable to talk about their dissatisfactions, discouragements, or doubt about the job and to express feelings of anxiety about inadequate performance and feelings of guilt about any mistakes. The peer group on the job, the work clique, is often the primary resource to which workers turn to talk about such concerns. These are people who most likely have experienced similar problems. They are knowledgeable about the job situation and can discuss these matters with some sophistication. The worker who feels the need to talk about these feelings and the peer group to whom he or she turns share experiences and a common frame of reference, increasing the likelihood of empathetic understanding. In addition, they have no administrative power to evaluate the worker. Consequently the worker may feel freer in sharing doubts and dissatisfactions with fellow workers than with the supervisor. The peer group has the additional advantage of being not only psychologically accessible, because social distance between peer and peer is minimal, but also physically available. You do not have to make an "appointment" with co-workers.

In providing supportive supervision, the supervisor can actively mobilize the assistance of the peer group resource. The supervisor can stimulate supportive peer-peer interaction and encourage cooperative, mutual relationships among staff in reinforcing the supportive activities of the supervisor.

Supervisors might facilitate the development of the peer-peer interactional system by arranging for group supervision and frequent unit meetings. The supervisor might also encourage supportive peer-peer interaction by helping organize peer supervision and consultation.

Though peer group support is an important resource, supportive supervision has some advantages that are simply not available from the peer group. Unlike peers, the supervisor has the power and authority to make stress-reducing changes in the worker's situation. Being responsible for evaluating the workers' performance, supervisors, in making supportive statements, have a more potent impact than peers who make similar statements.

Social Support Network

The supervisee's social support network also supplements supportive supervision. Although family and friends do offer a haven against stress, their lack of intimate knowledge of the nature of on-the-job stress limits the impact of their emotional support.

Because stress originates in the workplace, the workplace is the best context for dealing with work stress. The supervisor, who is intimately aware of the sources and nature of work stress, can offer the most relevant feedback to help the worker. Unlike family and friends, the supervisor is also more immediately available to deal with on-the-job stress.

To be effective, social support needs to be significantly related to the particular stress that is the source of strain. General undifferentiated social support may not provide effective buffering. The particularity of the supervisor's support directly related to specific work stress is likely to have more significant supportive effect.

In the final analysis, then, despite the availability of these additional sources of support, the supervisor is the best resource for dealing with supervisee work stress.

Supervisees' Adaptations

Supportive supervision is further supplemented by the workers' own capacities to adjust. Supervisees respond to the stress of supervision by actively "psyching out" the supervisor. Their purpose is to determine the kinds of behavior that will obtain acceptance and those that will elicit disapproval. Supervisees then manage a presentation of self that will net maximum approval and minimum disapproval. What Goldhammer says of teachers in supervision can be applied equally well to social workers. In adapting to stress in the supervisory relationship, they have learned "how to second guess the supervisor, how to anticipate what will please him, how to stage appropriate performances for him to observe and how to jolly him up for their own protection" (Goldhammer 1969:64).

Supervisees have developed a series of well-established, identifiable games that are, in effect, defensive adjustments to the threats and anxieties that the supervisory situation poses for them. In the description that follows, these games are grouped in terms of similar tactics. It may be important to note that some supervisees almost never play games. However, even the least anxious supervisees resort to such adjusting games occasionally. Supervisors also play games for similar reasons. These are discussed following the description of supervisees' games.

Supervisees' Games

Much of the material in this section originally appeared in the article "Games People Play in Supervision," *Social Work* 13 [1968]: 23–32. It is quoted with permission of the National Association of Social Workers.

Manipulating Demand Levels

One series of games is designed to manipulate the level of demands made on the supervisee. One such game might be known as Two Against the Agency or Seducing for Subversion. The game is generally played by intelligent, intuitively gifted supervisees who are impatient with routine agency procedures. Forms, reports, punctuality, and recording excite their contempt. The more sophisticated supervisee introduces the game by noting the conflict between the bureaucratic and professional orientation to the work of the agency. The bureaucratic orientation is centered on what is needed to ensure efficient operation of the agency; the professional orientation is focused on meeting the needs of the client. The supervisee points out that meeting client needs is more important, that time spent in recording, filling out forms, and writing reports is robbed from direct work with the client, and further, that when he or she comes to work and goes home is not important as long as no client suffers as a consequence. Would it not therefore be possible to permit the worker, a highly intuitive and gifted person, to schedule and allocate his or her time to maximum client advantage, and should not the supervisor be less concerned about the worker filling out forms, doing recording, completing reports, and so on?

It takes two to play games (Hagler and Casey 1990). The supervisor is induced to play this game because he or she identifies with the supervisee's concern for meeting client needs; the supervisor has frequently resented bureaucratic demands and so is initially sympathetic to the supervisees complaints; and he or she is hesitant to assert authority in demanding firmly that these requirements be met. If the supervisor chooses to play the game, he or she has enlisted in an alliance with the supervisee to subvert agency administrative procedures.

Another game designed to control the level of demands made on the supervisee might be called Be Nice to Me Because I Am Nice to You. The principal ploy is flattery, including such compliments as "You're the best supervisor I ever had," "You're so perceptive that after I've talked to you I almost know what the client will say next," "You're so consistently helpful," "I look forward in the future to being as good a social worker as you are," and so on. It is a game of emotional blackmail in which, having been paid in this kind of coin, the supervisor finds him- or herself unable to hold the worker firmly to legitimate demands.

The supervisor finds it difficult to resist engaging in this game because it is gratifying to be regarded as an omniscient source of wisdom: there is satisfaction in being perceived as helpful and in being selected as a pattern for identification and emulation. An invitation to play a game that tends to enhance a positive self-concept and feed one's narcissistic needs is likely to be accepted.

In general, the supervisor is vulnerable to an invitation to play this game. The supervisor needs the supervisee as much as the supervisee needs the supervisor. One of the principal sources of gratification for a worker is contact with the client. The supervisor is denied this source of gratification, at least directly. For the supervisor, the analogous satisfaction is helping the supervisee to grow and change. But this means that he or she has to look to the supervisee to validate his or her effectiveness. Objective criteria of such effectiveness are at best obscure and equivocal. To have the supervisee say openly and directly, "I have learned a lot from you" or "You have been helpful" is the kind of reassurance needed and often subtly solicited by the supervisor. The perceptive supervisee understands and exploits the supervisor's needs in initiating this game.

Redefining the Relationship

A second series of games is designed to lessen the demands made on the supervisee by redefining the supervisory relationship. These games depend on ambiguity in the definition of the supervisory relationship; it is open to a variety of interpretations and, in some crucial respects, resembles analogous relationships.

One kind of redefinition suggests a shift from the relationship of teacher and learner in an administrative hierarchy to worker and client in the context of therapy. The game might be called Protect the Sick and the Infirm or Treat Me, Don't Beat Me. The supervisee would rather expose him- or herself than his or her work, so he or she asks the supervisor for help in solving personal problems. The sophisticated player relates these problems to difficulties on the job. If the translation to worker and client is made, the nature of demands shifts as well. The kinds of demands one can legitimately impose on a client are clearly less onerous than those imposed on a worker. The supervisee has achieved a payoff in a softening of demands, and because so much time is spent discussing his or her personal problems, there is less time left for discussing his or her work.

The supervisor is induced to play because the game appeals to the social worker in him or her (since he was a social worker before he became a supervisor and is still interested in helping those who have personal problems); it appeals to the voyeur in him or her (many supervisors are fascinated by the opportunity to share in the intimate lives of others); it is flattering to be selected as a therapist; and he or she is not clearly certain that such a redefinition of the situation is impermissible. All the discussions about the equivocal boundaries between supervision and therapy feed into this uncertainty.

Another game of redefinition might be called Evaluation Is Not for Friends. Here the supervisory relationship is redefined as a social relationship. The supervisee makes an effort to take coffee breaks with the supervisor, invite him or her to lunch, walk to and from the bus or the parking lot with him or her, and discuss common interests during conferences. The social component tends to vitiate the professional component in the relationship. It requires increased determination and resolution on the part of any supervisor to hold the "friend" to the required level of performance.

A more contemporary redefinition of the supervisor-supervisee relationship is less obvious than the two kinds just discussed, which have long been standard. The game of Maximum Feasible Participation involves a shift in roles from supervisor and supervisee to peer and peer. The supervisee suggests that the relationship will be most effective if it is established on the basis of democratic participation. Because the worker knows best what he or she needs and wants to learn, he or she should be granted equal responsibility for determining the agendas of conferences. However, in the hands of a determined supervisee, joint control of agenda can easily become total supervisee control. Expectations may be lowered and threatening content areas avoided.

The supervisor finds him- or herself in a predicament in trying to decline this game. There is truth in the contention that people learn best in a context that encourages democratic participation in the learning process. Furthermore, the current trend in working with social agency clients is to encourage maximum feasible participation with ambiguously defined limits. To decline the game is to suggest that one is old-fashioned, undemocratic, and against the rights of those on lower levels in the administrative hierarchy—not an enviable picture to project of oneself. The supervisor is forced to play but needs to be constantly alert to maintain some semblance of administrative authority and prevent all the shots being called by the supervisee-peer.

Reducing Power Disparity

A third series of games is designed to reduce anxiety by reducing the power disparity between supervisor and worker. One source of the supervisor's power is, of course, his or her position in the administrative hierarchy vis-à-vis the supervisee. Another source of power lies in expertise and superior skill. This second source of power is vulnerable in this series of games. If the supervisee can establish the fact that the supervisor is not so smart after all, some of the power differential is lessened and with it some of the need to feel anxious.

One such game, frequently played, might be called If You Knew Dostoyevsky Like I Know Dostoyevsky. During the course of a conference, the supervisee alludes casually to the fact that the client's behavior reminds him or her of, say, Raskolnikov's in *Crime and Punishment,* which is, after all, somewhat different in etiology from the pathology that plagued Prince Myshkin in *The Idiot.* An effective ploy, used to score additional points, involves asking the supervisor rhetorically, "You remember, don't you?" It is equally clear to both supervisee and supervisor that the latter does not remember—if, indeed, he or she ever knew. At this point the supervisee proceeds to instruct the supervisor. The roles of teacher and learner are reversed; power disparity and supervisee anxiety are simultaneously reduced.

The supervisor acquiesces to the game because refusal requires a confession of ignorance on his or her part. The supervisee who plays the game well cooperates in a conspiracy with the supervisor not to expose this ignorance openly. The discussion proceeds under the protection of the mutually accepted fiction that both know what they are talking about.

The content for the essential gambit in this game changes with each generation of supervisees. Our impression is that currently the allusion is likely to be to the work of empowerment theoreticians—Goldstein, Saleeby, or

Weick—rather than to family therapists or literary figures. The effect on the supervisor, however, is the same: a feeling of depression and general malaise at having been found ignorant when his or her position requires that he or she know more than the supervisee. It has the same payoff in reducing supervisee anxiety.

Another game in this genre exploits situational advantages to reduce power disparity and permit the supervisee the feeling that he or she, rather than the supervisor, is in control. This game is So What Do *You* Know About It? The supervisee with a long record of experience in public welfare refers to "those of us on the front lines who have struggled with the multiproblem client," exciting humility in the supervisor who has to try hard to remember when he or she last saw a live client. A married supervisee with children will allude to marital experience and what it really is like to be a parent in discussing family therapy with an unmarried supervisor. The older supervisee will talk about "life" from the vantage point of a veteran to the supervisor fresh out of graduate school. The younger supervisee will hint at a greater understanding of the adolescent client because he or she has, after all, smoked some marijuana and has seriously considered cocaine. The supervisor, trying to tune in, finds his or her older psyche is not with it. The supervisor who is younger than the older supervisee, is older than the younger supervisee, or has never raised a child or met a payroll, finds him- or herself being instructed by those he or she is charged with instructing; roles are reversed, and the payoff to the supervisee lies in the fact that the supervisor becomes a less threatening figure.

Another, more recently developed procedure for putting the supervisor down is through the judicious use of strong four-letter words in the conference. This is Telling It Like It Is, and the supervisor who responds with discomfort and loss of composure has forfeited some amount of control to the supervisee, who has exposed a measure of the supervisor's bourgeois nature and residual Puritanism.

Putting the supervisor down may revolve around a question of social work rather than content. The social action–oriented supervisee is concerned with fundamental changes in social relationships. He or she knows that obtaining a slight increase in the budget for one client, finding a job for another client, or helping a neglectful mother relate more positively to her child are of little use because they leave the basic pathology of society unchanged. He or she is impatient with the case-oriented supervisor who is interested in helping a specific family live a little less troubled and a little less unhappily in a fundamentally disordered society. The game is All or Nothing at All. It is designed to make the supervisor feel that he or she has sold out, been co-opted by the establishment, lost or abandoned a broader vision of the "good" society, and become endlessly concerned with symptoms rather than with causes. It is effective because the supervisor recognizes that there is an element of truth in the accusation for all who occupy positions of responsibility in the establishment.

Controlling the Situation

The games mentioned have, as part of their effect, a shift of control of the situation from supervisor to supervisee. Another series of games is designed to place control of the supervisory situation more explicitly and directly in the hands of the supervisee. Control of the situation by the supervisor is potentially threatening because he or she can then take the initiative of introducing for discussion those weaknesses and inadequacies in the supervisee's work that need fullest review. If the supervisee can control the conference, much that is unflattering to discuss may be adroitly avoided.

One game designed to control the discussion's content is called I Have a Little List. The supervisee comes in with a series of questions about his or her work that he or she would very much like to discuss. The better player formulates the questions so they relate to problems in which the supervisor has greatest professional interest and about which he or she has done considerable reading. The supervisee is under no obligation to listen to the answers to these questions. When the first question has been asked, the supervisor is off on a short lecture, during which time the supervisee is free to plan mentally the next weekend, taking care merely to listen for signs that the supervisor is running down. When this happens, the supervisee introduces the second question with an appropriate transitional comment, and the cycle is repeated. As the supervisee increases the supervisor's level of participation, he or she is, by the same token, decreasing his or her own level of participation, as only one person can be talking at once. Thus, the supervisee controls both the content and the direction of conference interaction. The supervisor is induced to play this game because there is narcissistic gratification in displaying one's knowledge and in meeting the supervisee's dependency needs and because, in accordance with good social work practice, the supervisee's questions should be accepted, respected, and answered if possible.

Control of the initiative is also seized by the supervisee in the game of Heading Them Off at the Pass. Here the supervisee knows that his or her poor work is likely to be analyzed critically. He or she therefore opens the conference by freely admitting mistakes—he or she knows it was an inadequate interview and knows that by now, he or she should have learned to do better. There is no failing on the supervisor's agenda for discussion of those things that the worker does not freely confess in advance. The supervisor, faced with this overwhelming self-derogation on the part of the worker, has little option but to reassure the supervisee sympathetically. The tactic not only makes it difficult for a supervisor to conduct an extended discussion of mistakes in the work but also elicits praise for whatever limited strengths the supervisee has manifested. The supervisor once again acts out of concern for troubled people, out of a predisposition to comfort the discomfited, and out of pleasure in acting as a good, forgiving parent.

Another variation is Pleading Fragility. The supervisee communicates "that he is extremely brittle, is easily hurt, or may even go over the brink if pushed too hard. This communication effectively prevents the supervisor from exploring any painful or threatening issues with the supervisee" (Bauman 1972:253).

Woe Is Me trades on dependence and helplessness. This is a game most legitimately played by new workers. In playing the game they take advantage of legitimate deficiencies by exaggerating them so that it becomes a form of supplication. The social norms associated with responding to a supplicant reinforce the already existing professional obligation of the supervisor to help the supervisee.

Control can also be exerted through fluttering dependency, a case of strength through weakness. It is the game of Little Old Me or Casework à Trois. The supervisee, in his or her ignorance and incompetence, looks to the knowledgeable, competent supervisor for a detailed prescription of how to proceed, perhaps asking questions such as "What would *you* do next?" or "Then what would *you* say?" The supervisee unloads responsibility for the case onto the supervisor, and the supervisor shares the caseload with the worker. The supervisor plays the game because, in fact, he or she does share responsibility for case management with the supervisee and has responsibility for seeing that the client is not harmed. Furthermore, the supervisor often wants the gratification of carrying a caseload, however vicariously, so that he or she is somewhat predisposed to take the case out of the supervisee's hands. There are also the pleasures derived from acting the capable parent to the dependent child and from the domination of others.

A variant of this game in the hands of a more hostile supervisee is I Did as You Told Me. Here the supervisee maneuvers the supervisor into offering specific prescriptions on case management and then applies them in spiteful obedience and undisguised mimicry. The supervisee acts as though the supervisor were responsible for the case, the worker merely being the executor of supervisory directives. Invariably and inevitably, whatever has been suggested by the supervisor fails to accomplish what it was supposed to accomplish. I Did as You Told Me is designed to make even a strong supervisor defensive.

It's All so Confusing attempts to reduce the authority of the supervisor by appeals to other authorities—a former supervisor, another supervisor in the same agency, or a faculty member at a local school of social work with whom the supervisee just happened to discuss the case. The supervisee casually indicates that in similar situations his or her former supervisor tended to take a certain approach, which is at variance with the approach the current supervisor regards as desirable. It becomes so confusing when different authorities suggest such different approaches to the same situation. The supervisor is faced with defending his or her approach against some unnamed, unknown competitor. This is difficult, especially because few situations in social work permit an unequivocal answer in which the supervisor can have complete confidence. Because the supervisor was somewhat shaky in his or her approach in the first place, he or she feels vulnerable to alternative suggestions from other "authorities," and his or her sense of authority in relation to the supervisee is eroded.

A supervisee can control the degree of threat in the supervisory situation by distancing techniques. This game is What You Don't Know Won't Hurt Me. The supervisor knows the work of the supervisee only indirectly, through what is available in the recording and shared verbally in conferences. The supervisee can elect to share in a manner that is thin, inconsequential, and without depth of affect. He or she can share selectively and can distort (consciously or unconsciously) to present a more favorable picture of his or her work. The supervisee can be passive and reticent or overwhelm the supervisor with endless trivia. In whatever manner it is done, the supervisee increases distance between the work actually done and the supervisor who is responsible for critically analyzing it with him. This not only reduces the threat to him of possible criticism of his work but also, as Fleming and Benedek (1966) point out, prevents the supervisor from intruding into the privacy of his relationship with the client.

A supervisee can manipulate the level of the supervisor's response to worker performance deficiencies by games such as Who Me? Not Me and Mea Culpa, but Just This Once.

In playing Who Me? the supervisee tries to shift the burden of responsibility for his or her own shortcomings in task performance onto other things. Pointing to failures by others—the client, clerical staff, workers in other agencies, "the system"—acts to shift responsibility from the supervisee him- or herself. Pleading extenuating circumstances—traffic problems, the weather, temporary indisposition—mitigates responsibility.

Mea Culpa, but Just This Once is an apology coupled with a show of repentance that reduces the supervisor's inclination to reprimand the supervisee for task failures. The apology is an acknowledgment of error, a confirmation of the supervisor's right to point out the error. Repentance is both an act of self-punishment and a promise not to repeat the error. In the face of all of this, supervisors find themselves disarmed.

Yes-Butting is a game of seeming to accept what the supervisor says but in effect rejecting the communication. The *yes* signifies initial acceptance, which is then followed by a *but*, which introduces the rejections. *But* is often followed by some statement from the social work literature or from a social work guru who holds a position contrary to the one suggested by the supervisor. A sample statement in this game would be: "Yes, but isn't it also true, as noted by ——, that ——?"

Supervisors go along with these games because of their reluctance to reprimand workers. Along with the workers, they are looking for excuses that might make it possible to avoid confronting any performance deficiencies.

Countering Games

Although such defensive games help the supervisee cope with anxiety-provoking stress, they may be dysfunctional and subvert the purposes of the supervisory encounter. Consequently, the supervisor may be required to break up the games.

The simplest and most direct way of dealing with games introduced by the supervisee is to refuse to play. A key difficulty in this approach has been implied by discussion of the gains for the supervisor in playing along. The supervisee can successfully enlist the supervisor in a game only if the supervisor wants to play for his or her own reasons. Collusion is not forced but freely granted. Refusing to play requires that the supervisor be ready and able to forfeit advantages. For instance, in declining to go along with the supervisee's request to be permitted to ignore agency administrative requirements in playing Two Against the Agency, the supervisor has to be comfortable in exercising administrative authority, willing to risk and deal with supervisee hostility and rejection, and willing to accept the accusation that he or she is bureaucratically (rather than professionally) oriented. In declining other games, the supervisor denies him- or herself the sweet fruits of flattery, the joys of omniscience, the pleasures of acting as therapist, and the gratification of being well liked. He or she incurs the penalties of an open admission of ignorance and uncertainty and the loss of infallibility. Declining to play the games demands supervisors who are aware of and comfortable in what they are doing and who accept themselves in all their glorious strengths and human weaknesses. The less vulnerable the supervisor, the more impervious he or she is to game playing—not an easy prescription to fill.

A second response lies in open confrontation. Goffman points out that in the usual social encounter each person accepts the line put out by the other person. There is a process of mutual face-saving in which what is said is accepted at its face value and "each participant is allowed to carry the role he has chosen for himself" unchallenged (Goffman 1959:11). This is done out of self-protection, because in not challenging another, one is also ensuring that the other will not, in turn, challenge one's own fiction. Confrontation implies a refusal to accept the game being proposed; instead, the supervisor seeks to expose and make explicit what the supervisee is doing. The supervisory situation, like the therapeutic situation, deliberately rejects the usual roles of social interaction in attempting to help the supervisee.

Confrontation needs to be used, of course, with due regard for the supervisee's ability to handle the embarrassment and self-threat it involves. The supervisor needs to be aware of the defensive significance of the game to the supervisee. Naming the interactions that have been described as games does not imply that they are frivolous or without consequence. Unmasking games risks much that is of serious personal significance for the supervisee. Interpretation and confrontation in this situation, as always, require compassionate caution, a sense of timing, and an understanding of how they should be used.

Never openly confronting each other with what is happening protects the symbiotic nature of the relationship. A supervisee who was aware that she engaged in game playing, and who was aware that the supervisor was aware that she was playing games said, "In a sense, we collaborated to provide each other with what we wanted: I needed a good job reference; she needed to feel that she was a competent administrator and supervisor."

Another approach is to share honestly with the supervisee one's awareness of what he or she is attempting to do in adjusting to work-related stress but to focus the discussion neither on the dynamics of his or her behavior nor on one's reaction to it, but on the disadvantages for the worker in playing games. These games have decided drawbacks for the supervisee. They deny the possibility of effectively fulfilling one of the essential purposes of supervision—helping the worker grow professionally. The games frustrate the achievement of this outcome. In playing games, the supervisee loses by winning.

Kolevson attempted an investigation of the extent to which games are actually played in supervision by information solicited from social work student supervisees. The results indicated that "gamesmanship was relatively infrequent" but that "students who were more critical of their supervisory relationship" were more likely to engage in games (Kolevson 1979:243). The research goes on to note that the gamesmanship "in the supervisory relationship may be . . . difficult . . . to measure since exposing one's games may be a threatening venture" (Kolevson 1979:244).

Humor in Supervision

Humor, like games, helps control and mitigate job stress. In a study by Cross and Brown, supervisees reported frequent "use of humor in supervisory sessions" (1983:336; see also Consalvo 1989; Vinton 1989; and Decker and Rotondo 1999). Humor may be used by the supervisee to communicate gripes and dissatisfactions he or she may be hesitant to raise directly. Humor helps reduce worker tension by making the impermissible permissible. The friendly sarcastic remark permits an excusable expression of hostility toward clients and supervisors. It suggests that the worker does not really mean what he or she is saying and expects to be excused. If the supervisor reacts punitively, it is an indication that he or she cannot take a joke. "The supervisor said she was stumped, she really did not know what to suggest. A smile slowly spread over the worker's face as she said in a gentle voice, 'My, that really surprises me—I thought you were all-knowing, all-loving, and all-forgiving.'" A worker assigned an extra case says something like "Gee, you're really being generous today," communicating negative feelings about additional work in a positive way. Because opposition to the supervisor is risky, manifesting opposition in a joking manner reduces the threat. Stated in this way, the worker implies that he or she does not really mean it and it should not be taken seriously. Supervisees use humor to mask opposition and hostility to supervisors, whereas supervisors may use humor to mask the authoritarian nature of some of their communications. Messages are conveyed in a way that is less likely to create resentment or provoke repercussions.

Humor tends to reduce defensiveness and aids in tolerating conflicting points of view. It relieves tension and permits us to see problems in a different perspective through playful seriousness. It helps deal more effectively with some of the inevitable frustrations of work. It provides distance and detachment from stressful situations. Humorous interactions between supervisor and supervisee tend to reduce distance between them and increase a feeling of equality.

The supervisor has greater entitlement to make humorous, joking remarks than does the supervisee. Frequent use of humor by the supervisor in supervisory interactions communicates a message that humor is an acceptable kind of communication. This frees the supervisee to engage in humor. Generally, the supervisor is more frequently the initiator, and the supervisee is more frequently the butt of humorous remarks. However, a supervisor who accepts jokes directed at him or her reduces the social distance and increases the informality in the interaction (Duncan 1984). The supervisor is perceived as a good guy who can take it. Reciprocal humorous give-and-take increases a sense of bonding. Decker (1987) found that supervisee job satisfaction was higher in contact with supervisors who had a good sense of humor and used it in the interaction.

Humorous responses are most effective if communicated spontaneously, informally, and in interpersonally supportive ways. A lot depends on the ability to perceive the humor in a situation and the freedom to respond without defensiveness and inhibition. In short, it requires a sense of humor. The current increased concern about sexist and racist humor further requires that the humor expressed be sensitively and culturally appropriate.

There is a hesitancy to employ humor (1) because it is regarded as unprofessional and (2) in response to a recognition that the inappropriate use of humor can be demeaning and hurtful. Appropriate, productive use of humor requires some skill and a cast of mind that recognizes the humorous aspects of a situation. To achieve its purpose, humor needs to be a creative spontaneous response to a specific situation. Because humor depends on the reaction of the person with whom it is shared, supervisors might hold off employing humor until they get to know a supervisee better and a relationship established.

Summary

Supportive supervision is concerned with helping the supervisee deal with job-related stress and developing attitudes and feelings conducive to the best job performance. Whereas administrative and educational supervision are concerned with instrumental needs, supportive supervision is concerned with expressive needs.

The main sources of job-related stress for the supervisee are the performance and compliance demands of administrative supervision, the learning demands of educational supervision, the clients, the nature and organizational context of social work tasks, and the relationship with the supervisor.

In implementing the objectives of supportive supervision the supervisor seeks to prevent the development of potentially stressful situations, removes the worker from stress, reduces stress impinging on the worker, and helps him or her adjust to stress. The supervisor is available and approachable, communicates confidence in the worker, provides perspective, excuses failure when appropriate, sanctions and shares responsibility for different decisions, and provides opportunity for independent functioning and for probable success in task achievement.

The client, the peer group, and the worker's own capacities to adjust are additional sources of support for the supervisee.

Supervisees engage in a variety of procedures and games that can help deal with job-related tensions.

Judicious use of humor in the supervisory interaction is helpful in reducing stress and contributes to a more positive supervisor-supervisee relationship.

7 | Problems and Stresses in Becoming and Being a Supervisor

The previous chapter detailed some of the strains and stresses encountered by direct service workers that require a supportive response on the part of the supervisor. In this chapter we are concerned with the stresses and strains encountered by supervisors themselves. In chapter 8, however, there will be a fuller discussion of one of the more pervasive sources of stress and tension for supervisors, namely, the function of worker evaluation.

Selection of workers for the position of supervisor is most frequently made from direct service staff (Schwartz 1990). The rationale for this source of candidates is that supervision requires knowledge of direct service practice (Drake and Washeck 1998; Kalous 1996; Rich 1992). In addition to direct service practice experience, advanced educational credentials, such as a master's of social work degree (MSW), are sometimes required. The majority of social work supervisors with the National Association of Social Workers (NASW) membership, for example, report having six to twenty years of practice experience, and 95 percent report an earned MSW (Gibelman and Schervish 1997a). Apparently, years of practice experience can often be substituted for educational credentials (Barretta-Herman 1993).

At the upper echelon of administration, although it might be desirable to have social workers, it is not as compellingly necessary as it is at the supervisory level. A text on human services management (Weiner 1990) is based on the rationale that there is a "generic field of human services management" separate from a specific human service identification. This book, addressed to social service, nursing, hospital, educational, and mental health administrators, sees the tasks of all such administrators as having a similar focus.

However, at the supervisory level of management, expertise in core professional functions is clearly of dominant importance (NASW 1999). Though social workers can and have been widely replaced by business administration graduates at the executive level, such displacements have been rare at the supervisory level (Patti 1984). But in a recent analysis of social work supervision, Gibelman and Schervish (1997a) speculate that growing numbers of social workers are receiving supervision from non–social workers. This is consistent with Rich (1992:180), who reports that "supervisors of direct care staff are often untrained in clinical concepts," and with Munson (1996a:249–50), who contends, "supervision by a seasoned clinician has been replaced [in managed care environments] by telephone or written contacts with managed care case managers, many of whom have no clinical background." Paradoxically, in health care settings the supervisor's technical knowledge has become more important than ever (Berkman et al. 1996; Kalous 1996). This chapter presupposes that social work supervision is a distinct professional activity involving implementation of unique functions requiring differential knowledge, skills, attitudes, and behaviors.

Technical knowledge is the basic minimum requirement for any first-line supervisor, regardless of organizational affiliation. Social work ethics (Reamer 1998; NASW 1999) and many licensing statutes require that supervisors be technically competent in regard to functions performed by their supervisees, saying, "Social workers who provide supervision or consultation should have the necessary knowledge and skill to supervise appropriately and should do so only within their areas of knowledge and competence" (NASW 1999:19). Unfortunately, in our view, the Model State Social Work Practice Act, promulgated by the American Association of State Social Work Boards (1997), is silent on this issue.

In public agencies, promotion to supervisor is often associated with a written exam requirement. Only two states of forty-three reporting such information required an MSW for all supervisory positions (American Public Welfare Association 1990:chart C2).

Transition: Worker to Supervisor

Motives for Change

Different motives lead workers to become supervisors (Schwartz 1990). Some have had strong attraction to moving into a managerial position, and such a move is in line with their true intentions. Others move into supervision by reason of a lack of more preferable alternatives. Advancement up the career ladder in the direct service position is limited. Few agencies have super-advanced senior casework positions. For those who eschew private practice, career advancement in pay, status and prestige, and continuing professional growth and challenge, acceptance of the supervision option is virtually mandated.

A sizable percentage of social work administrators would have preferred to remain clinicians if salaries and status at the clinical level were the equiv-alent of those available with promotion to administration (Scurfield 1981). The current promotional situation risks the possibility that the agency may "lose a competent worker to gain an incompetent supervisor."

In their studies of workers' motives for transition to managerial positions, Schwartz (1990), Patti et al. (1979), and Scurfield (1981) found a variety of reasons, "interest in administration" being the principal motive of only a limited number of respondents. The decision to opt for an opening as a supervisor may result from a feeling of being burned out as a direct service worker. Movement into supervision comes almost automatically to "survi-vors," as a reward for the faithful who have considerable seniority on the job. There is often neither a great incentive nor a great opposition to the change.

In addition to extrinsic satisfaction associated with the move—such as better pay, better office, and more status and prestige—workers in transition mention intrinsic satisfaction. These most frequently include the opportunity to help supervisees develop professionally and the fact that as supervisors they will be in a stronger position to formulate and influence policy decisions (Pickvance 1997).

New supervisors, in explaining their motives for the change, say: "Being able to feel that I am able to do something to develop a better work force by stimulating the professional development of some supervisees and to assist some others in understanding that selling life insurance might be a better field for them" and "Opportunity to be involved in administrative or system change that would benefit practitioners and clients."

In general, as might be expected, work supervisors are older, better edu-cated, more experienced, and higher paid than supervisees (Poulin 1995; Gibelman and Schervish 1997a). Many have been employed in the agency in which they are supervising longer than their supervisees.

Preparation for Change

There is stress associated with the fact that many supervisors have limited preparation for assuming the position and little educational support available following assignment to the position (Blankman, Dobrof, and Wade 1993; Schwartz 1990; Erera and Lazar 1993; Rich 1992; Rodenhauser 1995; Watkins 1992b).

Some training in supervision is, of course, absorbed as a consequence of being a supervisee. In two studies, supervisors indicated that the most important source of learning their job was the role model of supervisors with whom they had had contact as supervisees (Olyan 1972; Rodenhauser 1995). Although all supervisors have experienced some anticipatory socialization to the position as a result of their experience as supervisees, there is an uneasy recognition that this is inadequate preparation. Being a supervisee does not make one a supervisor, just as being a student doesn't make one a teacher.

Many supervisors do not feel adequately prepared for the job (Rich 1992; Rodenhauser 1995). The average response of 109 supervisors who were asked by Shulman (1982) to respond to the statement, "I received adequate preparation for the tasks and problems I faced as a beginning supervisor" was between "uncertain" and "disagree." The largest group (42 percent) of sixty-two supervisors surveyed by Robiner et al. (1997:122–23) described the quality of their graduate training to become supervisors as "poor."

Some of the stress related to becoming a supervisor was detailed in a study of the reaction of forty supervisors to the experience of transition (Woodcock 1967). Becoming a supervisor was regarded as a career crisis, "the first and most striking finding being the degree of alarm that the prospect of supervision proved to arouse" (Woodcock 1967:68). Because few supervisors had formal training in supervision prior to the appointment, they felt considerable anxiety about whether they could do the job. This fear related particularly to the demand of educational supervision. Did they know enough to teach others to do the work? New supervisors reported "increased reading, thinking, consulting, attending lectures, seminars, meetings, anything which would illuminate the road ahead. . . . One supervisor said, 'I bought a pile of social work books, only one of which I read.' Another 'made notes on the principles of casework and determined to exemplify all these in all cases' " (Woodcock 1967:69).

Becoming a supervisor forces one to explicitly examine one's practice to conceptualize it for teaching. "Supervising forced me to put my ideas, knowledge and experience together. I was placed in the position of having to communicate or try to communicate what I knew." As Ewalt (1980:5) says, "Moving from doing to teaching requires what may be thought of as a conscious disintegrating process in which the supervisor purposefully recalls and conceptualizes elements in the decision-making process."

New supervisors, however, found that their prior casework training and experience was of considerable help in effectively dealing with the very significant interpersonal relationship aspects of supervision. In addition, their previous clinical experience was considered "to be a major source of credibility with their subordinates" (Patti et al. 1979:148). "The transition to management involved adapting knowledge and skills previously acquired, rather than comprehensive and fundamental retraining" (Patti et al. 1979:151).

Though most of the managers continued to feel that a clinical background was a necessary ingredient in preparation for human services administration, it is clear that there are some differences in the demands made of the direct service workers as contrasted with those made of the supervisor (Drake and Washeck 1998; Menefee and Thompson 1994; Watkins et al. 1995). The transition requires the mobilization of skills that are not so directly required in direct service practice. Direct services practice requires maximization of potentials for expressive behavior—caring, concern, empathy, compassion—but transition to supervisor requires maximization of potential for instrumental behavior—integrating, organizing, coordinating, manipulating. Bramford notes that

> the very qualities which make a good social worker are often the antithesis of those required in management. Talking things through patiently and determinedly is an admirable quality applied to work with clients. Applied indiscriminately to management decisions great and small, it is a recipe for administrative paralysis. (1978:11)

The skills of managing are different from the skills of doing.

Changes in Self-Perception and Identity

Promotion to supervisor involves a drastic change in self-perception for the worker (Blankman, Dobrof, and Wade 1993). The newly appointed supervisor "is essentially entering a new occupation, not simply a new position. This occupation will have its own set of job specifications . . . precedents . . . expectations. In the performance of his duties he finds himself in a new set of role relations with his former peers, with his new administrative colleagues and with his new superiors" (W. E. Moore 1970:213). A person disengages from an old role and takes on a new one.

The transition from worker to supervisor is in some measure analogous to developmental transitions "such as adolescence, marriage, or retirement. As with other transitions, it may involve a period of disruption, of depression or defensive hyperactivity, of personal and professional growth. . . . Changes in external aspects of the career are likely to be accompanied by inner changes in personality" (Levinson and Klerman 1967:13–14). Conceptions of personal identity change so as to be congruent with changes in professional identity (Yerushalmi 1993).

The transition involves a temporary disequilibrium in identity. The new supervisor had previously developed a firm sense of who he or she was and what could be done in his or her identity as a direct service worker. This identity had been repeatedly confirmed by responses from peers, supervisor, and clients, who accorded the worker the recognition that comes with this role identity. Moving into the position of supervisor required dissolving the old identity as direct service worker and slowly building a new sense of identity as supervisor. This new (and at the beginning alien) identity needs confirmation from supervisees, fellow supervisors, and administrators, whose behavior toward the new supervisor attests to the fact that they recognize and accept him or her as a supervisor. Initially the supervisor has to work to obtain this confirmation from others of the new position and title, which involves proving one's competence to others (Perlmutter 1990).

Becoming a supervisor often involves moving to a new agency (Gibelman and Schervish 1997a; Schwartz 1990) and all that this implies in the way of adjustment. But even if the worker stays in the same agency after becoming a supervisor, the shift requires some of the adjustments involved in accepting a new job. As one beginning supervisor said, "Rather than being at the top of the ladder as a caseworker, I was starting all over at the bottom again in my new trade—supervision" (H.C.D. 1949:161).

The shift from diagnosis of clients' social problems to diagnosis of supervisees' educational problems and from helping in the personal development of the client to helping in the professional development of the worker, involves a shift from therapeutic techniques previously acquired to pedagogic techniques that need to be learned (Kalous 1996). Accepting the title of supervisor involves a shift in self-perception from a treatment person to an administrator-teacher. The promotion involves learning to think like a supervisor (Borders 1992).

In moving into supervision, the worker assumes the stress of greater responsibilities. He or she has responsibility to the supervisees for administration, education, and support as well as ultimate responsibility for service to the client. The promoted worker assumes greater responsibility for policy formulation in the agency and community-agency relationships. Whereas previously the worker was responsible only for his or her own work, he or she now has the larger responsibility for the work of a number of others. Instead of being responsible for a single caseload, the supervisor is now responsible for a number of them. The shift has been compared with that of a person who has often ridden as a passenger in a car and now has the responsibility for driving the car, watching traffic, and getting the group safely to its destination.

Because of a frequently distorted perception of the supervisor's position, new supervisors often experience "reality shock" as they encounter the actualities of supervision. As one new supervisor said,

> When I was a caseworker, I thought the supervisors had it all worked out and knew what they were doing. It all looked so easy. Now I see how great the responsibilities are and that everything isn't so neat at the supervisory level. There are power struggles, games, and turf battles among the supervisors. When I first became supervisor, I felt very confused and depressed, and there was no one to help. (Abramczyk 1980:83)

The beginning supervisor also has to make other adjustments in perspective. He or she moves from a process orientation as worker to a more focused concern with product as a supervisor. He or she has to become more organizationally oriented.

Lieberman (1956) tested the hypothesis that a person's attitudes will be influenced by the role he or she occupies in a social system. "Johnny is a changed boy since he was made a monitor in school"; "She is a different woman since she got married"; "You would never recognize him since he became a foreman" (385). He studied the attitudes of men in industrial concerns before and after they became supervisors. He found that, because the supervisory role entails being a representative of management, workers who were made supervisors did tend to become more favorable to management.

The movement from worker to supervisor is accompanied by a stronger identification with the agency and increased support, loyalty, and commitment to the organization and its policies. Agency policy and actions now seem more justifiable, acceptable, morally correct, and fair. The new supervisor's attitudes become more like those supervisors whose ranks he or she is joining and different from the attitudes of direct-service workers from whom he or she is disengaging.

The change from worker to supervisor involves a change in reference group affiliation, which leads to changes in attitudes and therefore behavior. The change in functions performed also requires changes in behavior. Attitudes are revised so that they are consistent with changed behavior required by changed functions. One supervisor expressed her change in orientation as follows:

> My orientation definitely changed as I moved from the role of supervisee to the role of supervisor. In the first place, I took agency policy much more

seriously. I also felt a marked increase in responsibilities and in the importance of realizing the full responsibilities of this position. I also saw problems in a wider scope and found it easier to analyze them when the details and the client were not as close to me.

The closer one gets to administration, the more clearly one begins to respond to the pressures that administrators feel, that is, the pressure for meeting accountability demands of public, regulatory, and legislative agencies, the competition with other agencies for scarce resources, and agency survival needs.

The change in position and the responsibilities that go along with becoming a supervisor in and of itself force a change in the worker's perception of agency rules, policies, and procedures. But this change is reinforced by information about agency operation from a broader perspective than had been available earlier. Such change is also reinforced as a consequence of "experiencing" as supervisor the political effects of agency policy that the worker only "knows" about.

As a person moves from worker to supervisor, he or she becomes more sensitive to the effects—on policy, agency survival, and agency image—of actions taken with or in behalf of individual clients. He adopts an administrative perspective with regard to service decisions.

A change in perspective implies a change in perception of the effects of agency policy. As a former worker, the supervisor measured the effects of agency policy on the client with whom he or she had direct contact. As supervisor, that person is in a better position to see the effects of agency policy in a wider perspective. A policy that may have impacted negatively on his or her own former clients may be seen as meeting more effectively the needs of a wider group of clients as a collectivity.

The transition involves a change of orientation from individual justice in which the unique needs of the individual client are given priority to the idea of proportional justice that requires fairness and equity in prioritizing the competing claims of many clients.

The new supervisor has to reassess the balance in a conflict between an orientation that gave priority to resources and an orientation that gave priority to people. The conflict is often expressed by business managers who complain that "social workers don't care what they do with the money" and social workers who complain that managers "don't care what they do to people." In making the transition, the supervisor, as a member of the management team, has to give greater recognition to the fact that resources are scarce, painful choices have to be made, and priority of client needs is not absolute.

As a worker, the newly appointed supervisor may have thought of management as concerned primarily with survival, with little real commitment to the needs of the client. Now, as Matorin says, the practitioner as supervisor "has become a member of the 'establishment' and is propelled into what may have previously been the enemy camp. They are now responsible for all of the deficiencies of the system, yet expected to defend and identify with it" (1979:15).

From Clinician to Manager

Although relatively few social workers affiliated with NASW view supervision as their primary function (Gibelman and Schervish 1997a), in becoming a supervisor, a worker gives up some of the satisfaction of direct practice and contact with clients. He or she has to learn to offer service through others. From being an active participant in the process of implementing client change, the supervisor is a more passive facilitator of client outcomes.

One supervisor said, "As a caseworker I was very 'social work' oriented. I enjoyed working with clients and helping them if possible. As a supervisor I no longer feel the stimulation I did as a worker" (Miller and Podell 1970:36). Some supervisors ask for a small direct-practice caseload as a way of meeting the need for these satisfactions.

Some stress derives from the defensiveness that a supervisor might feel in comparing administrative work with direct service work. According higher status to direct service activity as the only work worth doing in an agency, the supervisor may be somewhat apologetic about a desk job without client contact.

As discussed earlier, some of the administrative requirements of the supervisor's job run counter to the ethos of social work. The need to exercise authority, the need to judge the worker, requires some adjustments in attitude. Patti et al., studying the problems of worker transition from the direct service position to the management position, found that "the use of authority, particularly as it implied directing, supervising, and changing subordinates, was the most difficult area of adjustment for respondents when they assumed their first administrative job" (1979:146–47).

A study of 285 social work administrators, most of whom had been clinicians, indicated once again that adaptation to authority was a problem in making the transition from direct service to administration. The move was from indirect leadership to more direct leadership, from permissiveness to assertive direction, from covert use of power to more overt use of power. In reporting the research, Scurfield (1981:497) says, "It is clear that the exercise of authority in relationships with subordinates in contrast with the exercise of authority in relationships with clients is a major area of change reported by some former clinicians in their transition to administration."

In direct service work, the workers may advise, suggest, and influence, but never direct the client to engage in certain actions. The ultimate decision and responsibility for action rests with the client and the consequences of the client's decision are borne only by the client. The authority of supervision extends beyond advice, suggestion, and influence to the imperative of directing the worker to act in some particular way. The consequences of the worker's decision to accept, reject, or modify the supervisor's directive is borne not only by the worker but by the supervisor and the agency as well. Because the supervisor is given the power to require certain actions by the supervisee, it is appropriate that supervisors accept responsibility for any worker's failure to act. The limits of authority and responsibility are broader and more pervasive in supervision as contrasted with direct service.

Worker adherence to the clients' right to self-determination permits the client, with worker acquiescence, to reject worker suggestions. The principal of self-determination is not applicable, however, to the supervisor-supervisee relationship.

> When a subordinate fails to accept the suggestion of the [supervisors] the latter must be prepared to press for compliance even in the face of appearing to be arbitrary. Certainly there are times when it is appropriate to defer to subordinates or engage in collaborative decision making, but inevitably there are occasions in which the manager must take courses of action that may not be agreed to or supported by staff. (Patti 1983:217)

The change in position may also at times require a change in language usage from expressions that connote egalitarian relationships to others that communicate a sense of hierarchy. Statements like "I might suggest that you—" or "I would encourage you to—"; suggest a relationship of mutuality. At some point the objectively hierarchical nature of the supervisor-supervisee relationship might need to be expressed in more direct language, such as "I expect you to—" or "I am telling you that—". To use the softer language when the supervisor has been directed to get certain procedures or objectives implemented leaves the supervisee with a sense of ambiguity as to what he or she is required to do (Furlong 1990).

The change from clinical to managerial frame of mind applies to changes in thinking about the supervisee as well as the client. Holloway and Brager point to the fact that beginning supervisors trained as clinicians and oriented toward psychological theories tend to focus on idiosyncratic behavior of supervisees as explanatory variables. Although supervisors still need to be sensitive to these factors, they need to give more explicit recognition to the organizational context, roles, and status of supervisees as sources of explanation for supervisees' behaviors (Holloway and Brager 1989:29).

Changes in Peer Relationships

Becoming a supervisor requires some changes in the worker's relationship with others in the agency (Blankman, Dobrof, and Wade 1993). The supervisor is no longer a member of the peer group of direct service workers. He or she has become one of "them." Not only is the new supervisor deprived of what may have been a satisfying source of pleasure and support, but he or she may be further penalized by feelings of rivalry and jealousy from former colleagues. There may be "a certain feeling of distance that I had arrived and they hadn't" or "that I was doing better than them" (Woodcock 1967:69). One new supervisor says,

> One's colleagues like to see a person get ahead all right—but not too far ahead, and not too fast. If fortune seems to be smiling too often and too broadly on one person, his friends begin to sharpen their knives to even up the score a bit. I was philosophical about this, as by this time I realized that an occasional knife in the ribs goes with supervision just as June bugs go with June and must be accepted as stoically; I marked my promotion by buying a bigger brief case, enrolling in an advanced seminar in supervision, and having a drink with a few sympathetic friends—also supervisors. (H.C.D. 1949:162)

Social distance is increased between the worker-turned-supervisor and his or her former peers. There is more formality, less spontaneity in their interaction and perhaps a greater guardedness and hesitancy in communication. The talk slows down and alters as the supervisor sits down to drink coffee with the workers. What was formerly identified as interesting in-group gossip is now perceived as squealing when shared with a former peer who is now a supervisor.

Charles Lamb noted this change in his essay "The Superannuated Man":

> To dissipate this awkward feeling, I have been fain to go among them once or twice since: to visit my old desk fellows—my co-brethren of the quill— that I had left below in the state militant. Not all the kindness with which they received me could quite restore to me that pleasant familiarity which I

had heretofore enjoyed among them. We cracked some of our old jokes, but methought they went off but faintly.

Describing this change from the supervisee's standpoint, a worker says: "I used to be close friends with Ruth but when she became a supervisor continuing as friends seemed 'funny.' As a result, I gained a great supervisor but I lost a good friend."

Having been a member of the supervisee peer group, the new supervisor has probably been party to all of the frequently unflattering characterizations made about supervisors. The new supervisor might be haunted by the memory of these remarks. "Are they saying about me what they said about so-and-so?" Former peers may wonder about the new supervisor. Will he or she act with favoritism toward best friends, pay off grudges against old enemies, grow into the job or just swell?

Some problems arise from the fact that the supervisor, in a position immediately adjacent to the caseworker, has the same professional background and experience as the supervisee. Identified and empathetic with the problems and orientation of the direct service worker, the supervisor nevertheless represents management. "This creates both a role conflict and a personal dilemma for the supervisor. Professional norms stressing autonomous integrity for practitioners still make a claim on him which he considers legitimate but so does the organization's need for control" (Abrahamson 1967:83).

The ghosts of one's predecessors can also be a source of tension. The new supervisor wonders if he or she can be as good as the former supervisor: if, in changing some of the patterns of work established by the former supervisor, he or she will challenge the established loyalties of the supervisees and incur their hostility.

Having lost the old peer group, the new supervisor has to obtain acceptance in a new peer group—that of the other supervisors. Maintenance of some marginality, some social distance from both groups to which the supervisor is hierarchically related, the supervisees who are his or her subordinates and the administrators who are his or her superiors, is functionally useful. Blau and Scott found that "detachment from subordinates was associated with high productivity and independence from superiors with greater solidarity in the work group and [that] both kinds of social distance, although the two were hardly related to one another, were associated with commanding the loyalty of subordinates" (1962:238).

Weinbach has offered a list of twenty-five questions that candidates for promotion to supervision might ask themselves on considering the change ("Am I comfortable with being directive and authoritarian with staff if the situation requires it; Can I handle being denied access to work place gossip and perhaps being the object of it; Would I like to assume the ultimate responsibility for others' actions?") (Weinbach 1992:206).

Summary: Stress Associated with Becoming a Supervisor

In accepting the transition, new supervisors face the complex processes of developing a clear conception of what the new position entails in terms of behavior and attitude; they have to divest themselves of old behaviors and attitudes appropriate to the direct service worker's position and learn and commit themselves to behavior and attitudes appropriate to the new position; they have to emotionally accept a changed image of themselves and a changed relationship with former peers and newly acquired colleagues.

Overall, however, clinicians moving to supervision see the transition as not being particularly problematic. Researching the actual experience of such a transition, Scurfield (1981). in reporting responses from administrators who made this transition, notes that he "expected that former clinicians would report that their transition to administration had been difficult. The findings show, however, that former clinicians tended to minimize differences between clinical and administrative practice. This suggests that little difficulty may be experienced in the transition period" (Scurfield 1981:498).

On the basis of their research of the actual transition experiences from clinician to administrator, Patti et al. second Scurfield's findings but are somewhat more sanguine. They note that "despite the obvious difficulties in making the transition to management, the data also suggests that in many respects the respondent's past clinical education and experience was perceived by them as an aid in the process. As a consequence the role discontinuity and identity problems encountered, although quite apparent, appear to have been much less intense than we had assumed" (Patti et al. 1979:151).

Ongoing Supervisor Stress: Problems in Being a Supervisor

In addition to the stresses encountered in becoming supervisors, there are ongoing job-related stresses involved in being a supervisor (Zunz 1998). Supervisors, like supervisees, face heavy work pressures.

The limits of the supervisor's responsibility are less definite than the worker's. Consequently, some beginning supervisors find themselves working harder than ever before. "I soon found that I was doing about twice as much work as I had done formerly. When I brought this to my executive's attention she was very nice about it. She patiently explained that this was one of the privileges of my new position" (H.C.D. 1949:161).

A study of supervisor's work load in a public welfare agency concluded that "casework supervisors did not have time to supervise" (Galm 1972:34). Apparently, this remains a problem throughout the social work profession (Hardcastle 1991; Kadushin 1992b) and in other fields as well (Johnson and Meline 1997). Faced with such pressures, supervisors feel anxious about the kind of job they can do. One supervisor writes:

> My greatest dissatisfaction came with the realization that supervision takes an incredibly large amount of time. I now understand why I have received so little of it in my former placements. To do the job correctly, one needs to devote great time and energy to supervising each [worker]. It resembles teaching anything. To maximize effectiveness, the teacher must prepare several hours for each hour spent actually instructing. I would have liked to have been able to analyze each recording of the worker, for instance, in depth, prior to our discussion of it, but instead I found myself listening to it for the first time in conference and responding spontaneously.

There is greater pressure to manifest exemplary behavior because the supervisor is perceived as a model. If the supervisor is frequently late, disorganized, or fails to keep work up to date, can he or she expect the workers to be punctual, organized, and efficient? A worker in a mental health agency said, "When the supervisor began to take days off at irregular intervals and without explanation, we began to follow his lead and took days off when we were feeling overwhelmed, calling them 'mental health' days."

Supervisors are aware of and feel concerned about the limits of the help they can give supervisees. A supervisor says: "A big part of my anxiousness is that I won't know the answers for them and that I won't satisfy them with the answers that I have to give. I think even our profession doesn't know that much and that's a hard thing. They walk out feeling they didn't get what they wanted" (Amacher 1971:262).

If supervisees see knowledge and practice competence as one of the principal "strengths" of their supervisor, they confirm that lack of clinical expertise is a significant "shortcoming" for them in their supervision (Greenspan et al. 1992; Hardcastle 1991). Of the supervisees responding to a questionnaire, 20 percent cited this as a problem for their supervisor. Supervisees said:

> He doesn't know enough to provide much help in difficult cases.
> When I don't know a particular form, process, procedure, policy, neither does my supervisor. I need to find this out for myself.
> She lacks knowledge about the particular clients and problems I work with.

Workers can stand the uncertainty and doubt better than the supervisor can because they feel that if they do not know the answers they need, the supervisor can make them available. The worker has the sanctioned luxury of acceptable dependence on the supervisor. The supervisor is granted the dubious prerogative of independence. He or she becomes the question-answerer rather than the question-asker. Furthermore, the supervisor has little opportunity to turn to others in the hierarchy who might be able to answer her own questions. The worker's status gives absolution from some mistakes; the supervisor's status reduces this grant of immunity. In meeting the needs of the worker, the supervisor requires a confidence in his or her convictions and in decision making that is hard to come by. The pressure to act with certainty, when inwardly one feels very uncertain, is stressful.

The supervisor has a more complex interpersonal configuration to monitor and understand than the direct service worker. She has to attempt an understanding of the client as described by the supervisee; she has to understand the nature of the relationship between the supervisee and client, and she has to understand the nature of the relationship between herself and the supervisee (Rubin 1997).

There is also stress that results from lack of clear definition of the supervisor's tasks, responsibilities, and authority. In one interview study of twenty supervisors, half said they were unclear about their role in the agency (Weatherly 1980), a phenomenon that Feldman (1999:281) describes as the Middle Management Muddle.

There is stress as a consequence of periodic challenges to the legitimacy of supervisory authority (e.g., Brashears 1995; Veeder 1990). The discussion in the literature (which suggests that supervision is an archaic, unnecessary drag on the profession) tends to erode the confidence of supervisors that they are engaged in an appropriate social work role.

Supervisors worry that they may be growing away from the job they have to supervise. In some measure the supervisor's image of practice is not as it is but as it once was; practice in the supervisee's experience is as it is today. Such anxiety is exacerbated by the rapid pace of change. "Given the rapid changes in knowledge and state of the arts, the administrative professional is in danger of losing 'professional authentication'" (S. Moore 1970:211). Changes involve new orientations and new techniques. Supervisors may often lack mastery of some of the new techniques and knowledge about some of the new programs. Hanlan cites an example of this:

> The merger of a number of small, independent, sectarian agencies in Philadelphia under one administrative organization is one illustration of how the change in functions has broad ramifications throughout all levels of the or-

ganization. In this particular case, the tension was particularly noticeable at the level of the first-line supervisor. The situation became critical when supervisors who formerly performed casework teaching functions were now required to train their staff and themselves in a wide range of community-organizing functions. (1972:43)

Formal supervisory conferences with supervisees are a source of stress for the supervisor. It is in this interaction that the supervisor has to prove his or her competence and value to the supervisee. The conference is the context in which the administrative, educational, and supportive abilities of the supervisor are subject to test. In providing materials for the conference agenda, the worker has exposed his or her work for critical analysis. The supervisor, in responding to the supervisee's work, questions, and problems, is subject to critical analysis by the supervisee. A supervisee notes:

> I had a systems-family perspective developed in family therapy training. My supervisor was psychoanalytically oriented. I had difficulty in relating what I was doing with my clients. Since we had adopted different perspectives, so too we had adopted different vocabularies to describe the dynamics of the problems and the proposed interventions. When I would indicate that a mystification process was operating or that an individual's matrix of identity was unbalanced or that a battle for bilaterality existed within the therapeutic relationship, my supervisor did not understand me. I found myself in an uncomfortable position of trying to explain these concepts and their applicability. My supervisor did not have any answers consistent with my perspective. It became difficult to rely on her for guidance questions concerning my analysis of a problem, my methods of intervention, or my goals for a client.

The supervisor has to deal with the stress of competitiveness between supervisees while diplomatically maintaining a cooperative spirit in the group. "Several workers with the same supervisor are like a big family, each demanding the . . . attention of a busy mother who has her own housework to do. The supervisor has to learn to give each what he needs without seeming to give anyone more than the others" (H.C.D. 1949:163). Here, too, the supervisor walks a tightrope.

We noted earlier that the supervisor is dependent on the worker to some extent. In terms of instrumental needs, the supervisor gets compliance, communication, and information from the worker; in response to expressive needs, the supervisor gets appreciation, respect, and loyalty from the worker. Failure or refusal of the worker to meet these needs creates stress for the supervisor. The worker can be uncooperative, be resistant, make the work of the supervisor more difficult, and threaten the supervisor's good conception of him- or herself and competence. The supervisor is identified with the supervisees in the agency and in the community and any complaints about their work reflects negatively on him or her.

A study of problems encountered by beginning supervisors in a counseling program found that supervisees' resistance to learning, a feeling of not knowing how to intervene in the supervisee's case, and a feeling of not understanding what was happening in the case were most frequently cited by supervisors (McColley and Baker 1982).

Satisfaction in helping the supervisee develop professionally can be achieved only with the cooperation of the supervisee. Workers who are not motivated to learn, resistant to learning, or incapable of learning deny the supervisor this source of satisfaction and create a problem for the supervisor.

Some groups of supervisees present problems for and tax the patience of supervisors more than others. Supervisors indicated that they tended to be impatient with and irritated by supervisees who were "uncooperative," "overly dependent," "hostile," "resistive," "failed to meet expectations." Supervisors said:

> I lack tolerance for people who work slowly, don't make an effort to learn on their own, the passive-dependent supervisee.
> I find it difficult to maintain an objective working relationship with complainers and narcissistic workers.
> I feel irritation at those unwilling to risk themselves and grow. (Kadushin 1992b:14)

Supervisors also talked about aspects of their own personalities that presented problems for effective supervision. Supervisors were concerned that they might be hyperverbal or too rigid, perfectionistic, demanding, and communicating unrealistic expectations (Kadushin 1992b).

Supervisors also face the problem of implementing seemingly antithetical demands: permitting the greatest degree of worker autonomy while adequately protecting the rights of the client; helping preserve agency stability while promoting agency change; being supportive to the worker while communicating challenging expectations; acting as an agent of the bureaucracy while being loyal to the profession; and balancing the individual needs of the worker and the needs of the organization. Workers want an aggressive supervisor; administrators generally prefer a more passive supervisor.

The supervisor is in the position of having to reconcile job demands with human demands, of managing with a focus both on productivity and quality and on worker satisfaction and morale. The supervisor has to balance these antithetical expectations. Thus the supervisor has to learn to live with the tensions generated by all sorts of conflicting demands and expectations. The more distasteful (but nevertheless necessary) aspects of the supervisor's managerial responsibilities include handling complaints, resolving grievances, and imposing discipline.

The supervisor is apt to be pulled between conflicting expectations from above and below. Placed at the boundary between the direct service worker and agency administration, the supervisor is simultaneously a member of both the working unit and the organizational unit. As is true for all who operate in boundary areas, the supervisor is in a difficult position. He or she has only marginal membership in each unit and is faced with pressure from both when attempting to act as a buffer and mediator between them. Sometimes the directives from administration and the demands from the workers are contradictory. In responding to one group, the supervisor risks incurring the hostility of the other group and compromising his or her power to influence.

The supervisor can effectively implement his or her responsibilities only if the agency provides enough resources to do the job. This means that the supervisor has to have enough workers assigned to the unit and enough workers with a particular level and variety of skills. Many supervisors face problems resulting from a short supply of workers available to cover the caseload or from assignment of workers with deficiencies in knowledge and skills that limit the productivity of the unit.

The supervisor, like the worker, faces the frustration of limits to autonomy and discretion. The sources of constraints may be different, but the experience of constriction is the same. The supervisor is constrained by administrative policy, union regulations, client advocacy organizations, the reporting requirement of legislative sources of agency funding, accrediting standards, licensing standards, and affirmative action and civil rights regulations.

The supervisor is authorized to make some decisions autonomously—such as assigning work. Some other decisions, however, may need to be reported to administration after they are made, and some decisions (such as hiring, dismissal, or purchase of assets) cannot be made without prior approval. Such internal and external constraints limit the supervisor's freedom to act vis-à-vis the supervisee in accordance with the supervisor's best judgment.

Ongoing Supervisor Stress:
The Challenge of Human Diversity

The growing human diversity of social work practice is an ongoing source of stress for supervisors. Supervisors, supervisees, and agency clients vary in race and ethnicity, gender, and affectional orientation (Beckett and Dungee-Anderson 1997; Bruss et al. 1997; Cashwell, Looby, and Housley 1997; Cook 1994; Daniels, D'Andrea, and Kim 1999; Fukuyama 1994; Granello 1996; Haj-Yahia 1997; Jayaratne et al. 1992; MacEacheron 1994; Porter 1994; Rasheed 1997; Russell and Greenhouse 1997; Stone 1997; Tsui and Ho 1997), challenging interactive assumptions about the process of helping. This has become the subject of a burgeoning theoretical (Arkin 1999; Bernard and Goodyear 1998; D'Andrea and Daniels 1997; Fong and Lease 1997; Holloway 1995; Munson 1997; Owens-Patterson 2000) and empirical supervision literature (Ellis and Ladany 1997; Ladany, Brittan-Powell, and Pannu 1997; Ladany et al. 1997; Leong and Wagner 1994; Lopez 1997; Neufeldt, Beutler, and Banchero 1997; Romans 1996).

Although there are numerous contexts for a discussion of cross-cultural supervision (class, age, race, ethnicity, religion, gender, affectional orientation), for purposes of simplicity we have elected to focus on two such contexts—race and gender. We hope this will provide analysis of some concerns that are ubiquitous and applicable in cross-cultural supervision generally.

Race and Ethnicity as Factors in Supervision

Conventional wisdom argues that race matters in social work supervision (Black, Mki, and Nunn 1997; Jayaratne et al. 1992; Rasheed 1997), because "patterned regularities" of identity and behavior, based on shared customs, language, traditions, values, and beliefs, have been traditionally organized around racial ethnicity in the United States.

White Supervisor–African American Supervisee

The most frequent cross-cultural pattern is of a white supervisor and an African American supervisee. A white supervisor supervising an African American worker should consciously make explicit to themselves their attitudes, feelings, prejudices, and biases relative to racial differences. They should clarify for themselves the nature of their own white identities.

They need to make an effort to learn some details about African American culture, lifestyles, communication patterns, discrimination experiences, attitudes toward authority, approaches to problem-solving, and so on.

In supplementation of such self-education, the supervisor should attempt to be openly nondefensive in learning about the culture of the supervisee (Ladany, Brittan-Powell, and Pannu 1997; Leong and Wagner 1994; McNeill, Hom, and Perez 1995; Williams and Halgin 1995). The supervisor should be sensitive to the fact that the supervisee, a member of a victimized group, will generally be vigilant in cautiously checking the speech and nonverbal reactions for any hint of prejudice or bias while assessing the level of sophistication of the supervisor's knowledge about African American culture. Supervisors suffer a disadvantage in discussing multicultural issues with younger supervisees in that few supervisors, unlike many supervisees, have ever had any training in multicultural counseling (Constantine 1997).

Any discussion of interracial concerns is likely to be uncomfortable and awkward. The supervisee, in a less powerful position, is likely to be more hesitant to initiate a discussion of such matters. Consequently, it is incumbent on the supervisor to be sensitively alert to the need for such dialogue and take the initiative in opening such discussions, assisting and encouraging the supervisee in the interaction.

The factor of race should not be ignored, nor should it be overemphasized. A sensible, relaxed sensitivity to race seems to be the most desirable approach.

A white supervisor in contact with an African American supervisee who ignores the factor of race may be perceived negatively. Saying, in effect, "You are like me; I don't think of you as black" may be seen by African Americans "as a negation of their black identity and a subliminal message that they would be acceptable if they were not black—that is if they would repudiate parts of themselves." If on the other hand, the African American supervisee "is asked to comment on every black patient or issue relevant to blacks he or she cannot help but wonder whether there is stereotypical thinking behind the question such as all blacks think alike" (Bradshaw 1982:205).

White supervisors of African American supervisees will have to work harder to elicit their trust and confidence and provide evidence of their ability to understand the African American experience (Jeanquart-Barone 1993). Studying workers in county welfare departments, McNeely found African American workers expressing dissatisfaction with their white supervisors because they were "unknowledgeable" (McNeely 1987:128).

A white supervisor says:

> The black worker felt that I was not meeting her needs, probably because of our racial differences. The worker was angry and I felt threatened (maybe I am a racist). We spent a great deal of time discussing these feelings. We got a lot of talk going but no real change in attitude. Finally I said, "Look, we've talked about it long enough. Let's get on to the business of the agency. If a specific example comes up that seems related to our differences in race we can then discuss it."

"A minority worker claiming the expertise of life experience can challenge the [white] supervisor's knowledge and ability to deal with racial/ethnic problems and issues" (Swanson and Brown 1982:65).

Providing a diverse caseload, the supervisor has the responsibility of reviewing and evaluating performance as objectively as possible. A white supervisor feeling guilty about discrimination might tend to be protective in compensating for victimization by lowering performance expectations. The supervisee, in turn, might exploit feelings of guilt by pressing for exceptions to standards.

Some supervisors out of sympathy, guilt, fear, or negative prejudice may evaluate minority group members differently and less confidently than would white workers. Fear of being labeled racist or the desire to claim openly that they are not racist may lead to a hesitance to criticize African American supervisees for deficiencies in their work.

The most powerful predictor of satisfaction with supervision for African American supervisees, reported in a study by Cook and Helms (1988), was whether they perceived that their supervisor liked them. The limited empirical evidence suggests that African American supervisees may expect their supervisors to be less empathetic and respectful than do white supervisees (VanderKolk 1974), but a study of African American workers by Jayaratne et al. (1992) found no significant differences in perceived levels of emotional support from white and African American supervisors. This is consistent with findings that psychological (Ladany, Brittan-Powell, and Pannu 1997) and ecological (Jayaratne et al. 1992) variables may ultimately be more relevant to supervisory relationship dynamics than racial matching.

African American Supervisor–White Supervisee

Although African American social workers constitute a mere 5.3 percent of the NASW membership, 9.2 percent of NASW supervisors identify themselves as African Americans (Gibelman and Schervish 1997a). An African American staff member newly promoted to the position of supervisor faces a number of possible problems. Some workers may perceive that promotion as a response to affirmative action mandates, not as a consequence of the new supervisor's professional competence (Jayaratne et al. 1992). This may generate some resentment and a derogation of the supervisor's ability to perform. The supervisor may need to establish his or her credibility rather than having the comfort of knowing it is taken for granted.

Administration may perceive the promotion as a having a "showcase" component, establishing the administration's credentials as nonracist. Administration may also hope the promotion may have a "fire-fighter" element, defusing any complaints about discrimination, or a "lightning rod" function, absorbing flak from the African American community.

An African American supervisor in an agency with a predominantly white staff tends to be perceived as the resident "expert" on the African American experience (Williams and Halgin 1995). He or she is expected to deal with racially related problems and answer racially related questions. The middle-class African American supervisor may feel apologetic and inadequate in answering questions about segments of the African American community about which, in reality, he or she knows very little.

Because promotion of an African American person to supervision might be an infrequent event in a particular agency, it suggests that there are few (if any) role models available for emulation (Rasheed 1997). As a member of a very limited, previously unrepresented member of his or her group in the supervisory cadre, the new supervisor may be more rigorously scrutinized in his or her performance. He or she carries the burden of representing a racial group and consequently is not given freedom to fail equal to that of a new white supervisor. Failure may be perceived as a group failure rather than an individual failure, which intensifies a feeling of being "on stage."

Although African Americans become social work supervisors somewhat frequently (Gibelman and Schervish 1997a), particularly in public agencies (Jayaratne et al. 1992), they may not have access to a great deal of significant information that is informally shared among the more numerous peer group of white supervisors.

When an African American supervisor supervises a white worker, positional authority is in contradiction to the usual social arrangement pattern. Few whites have experienced a situation of subordination to an African American person. For some white supervisees, the race variable may override the position variable. For a racist supervisee, "black" is associated with subordinate status and the etiquette of deference. This may override the superordinate status of the position of supervisor vis-à-vis supervisee. Because many white supervisees have not had experience with African Americans in the position of supervisor, there is a tendency to perceive them in terms of stereotypes (McCroy et al. 1986), which ends up with the supervisee withholding trust (Jeanquart-Barone 1993).

An African American woman supervising a white woman writes about the advantages of such an arrangement: "This was an opportunity for the worker to get information on black life-styles, feelings, etc., that she may otherwise not have had a chance to learn. It also gave me a chance to teach some therapeutic techniques to use in dealing with black clients that aren't usually printed in the literature." Royster, an African American social worker, notes that "the black supervisor must decide whether or not to assign white workers to black clients, given the prevailing belief in much of the community that black workers are more effective with black clients and given the knowledge of racism within each white person" (1972:81).

Feeling that they might be less acceptable to white supervisees, one might expect African American supervisors to have a tendency to be less directive and less assertive with such supervisees or hesitant to exercise close supervision even when necessary. However, the limited evidence suggests that a more nuanced supervisory pattern actually occurs. The African American male supervisors interviewed by Rasheed:

> described their cross-racial supervision as "laissez-faire," "laid back," "collaborative" or in other supervisee-centered terms, [but] modification of this style occurred in situations of conflict between the participants and their white supervisee. In these situations a more "autocratic" style was employed, with a clear exercise of managerial power and authority. In these situations, the participants expressed the need to be clearer and specific about job expectations and role relationships. In their experience, conflict that was racially based generally resulted from a particular white supervisee having difficulty in taking direction from a black male supervisor. In these situations the participants would tend to reinforce the supervisory role and responsibilities. In other words, the supervisor would clarify with the white supervisee, "who is in charge." The participants expressed reluctance about the use of managerial power and positional authority because of their prior experiences of being on the receiving end of the power spectrum in cross racial situations. Based on prior experiences as supervisees, the participants were sensitive to no mistreating their supervisees in ways similar to their experience as supervisees in cross racial supervision. (1997:100–101)

African American Supervisor– African American Supervisee

Royster feels that the African American supervisor may have more difficulty with African American workers. The African American supervisor, representing management in agencies that often have racist policies, may be in conflict with those African American workers who are more wholeheartedly oriented to the views of the African American community (Royster 1972:80).

A more positive view is that the African American supervisees may feel more comfortable with an African American supervisor and "they may see the black supervisor as a role model with whom they can unambivalently identify" (Bradshaw 1982:217). African American supervisees may resent African American supervisors, who may be perceived as identified with oppressive management and also as having betrayed their group in "acting white." It is felt that the process of acculturation to membership in the management team may tend to attenuate minority subcultural differences.

African American staff members may see the new supervisor as having a special responsibility to advocate for the special concerns of African American staff and clients. Failure to take an active stance in this regard leaves the new supervisor open to accusation of being an Uncle Tom or an Oreo—black outside, white inside.

African American staff members might look to the new supervisor as a "brother" or "sister" for greater empathy and more considerate evaluation. Supervisees may expect the supervisor to be more open, informal, or personal with them. Achieving effective distance in distinguishing personal from professional relationships creates a problem.

The African American supervisor may feel a special pressure to act as a representative of the agency's African American service workers with special advocacy responsibility and to help interpret the needs of African American staff members to agency administration (Vargus 1980). African Americans appointed to managerial positions are apt to feel that they are under constant scrutiny to prove they can do the job adequately. There may be some feeling of doubt not only on the part of their white colleagues but also on the part of their subordinate minority supervisees (Bush 1977:19).

On the other hand, African American supervisees in a study by Jayaratne et al. (1992) reported significantly more criticism from African American supervisors compared with white supervisors, an effect that grew more pronounced if the African American supervisor was female. African American supervisees perceived female African American supervisors as providing less emotional support, as more withholding of approval of and credit for good work, and as more undermining than white female supervisors. It was unclear whether this pattern reflected a tendency for female African American supervisors to use their authority to consolidate their competitive advantage in a turbulent environment, for African American supervisees to perceive their African American supervisors from the vantage point of "professional envy," or an ecological effect of social work practice in public agency settings.

Though the above discussion of racial differences has focused exclusively on African American and white supervisors and supervisees, it needs to be recognized explicitly that other kinds of interracial interactions also occur. However, as yet, the available literature presents very little information about interaction in Caucasian–Asian or Hispanic–non-Hispanic supervisory dyads.

Ryan and Hendricks (1989) have written one of the few articles on social work supervision of minority supervisees other than African Americans. They noted that Asian and Hispanic supervisees are comfortable in seeing the supervisor as an authority figure who gives direction and are uncomfortable with discussions focusing on self-revelation and self-awareness. Haj-Yahia

(1997) has made similar observations about supervisees of Arab heritage (see also Tsui 2001).

How significant is the racial factor in social work supervision? In a review of the limited empirical literature, Ellis and Ladany (1997:470) concluded: "The data indicated that race may play an important role in supervision process and outcome; however, the extent and nature of that role have yet to be adequately tested to make any tentative inferences."

Bernard and Goodyear (1998) have noted the limited empirical research on the effect of contextual variables—ethnicity, gender, sexual orientation—on the supervisory relationship. However, a study of 289 postdoctoral psychology interns indicated that discussion of cultural variables in the supervisory relationship "increased supervisees' satisfaction with supervision" (Gatmon et al. 2001:111). Both matched and unmatched dyads experienced increased satisfaction, indicating that it is not the cultural match between supervisor and supervisee itself that is important but the "presence and quality of the discussion of difference and similarity" (Gatmon et al. 2001:110).

Another study of sixty cross-cultural supervisory dyads found that despite differences in ethnicity, "supervisors and supervisees did not differ significantly in their overall high satisfaction with the supervisory relationship" (Duan and Roehlke 2000:138). Members of the dyad "who provided or received supervision from an individual with a different racial background than their own generally felt quite satisfied with their supervisory experience" (Duan and Roehlke 2000:141). Attitudes of respect and support and openness to discussing differences were associated with positive supervisory experiences.

Gender as a Factor in Transition to Supervision

Social work has been characterized as a "female" profession, with estimates that 83 percent of social workers are women (Munson 1997). Nearly three-quarters of NASW social work supervisors are female, and the percentage of female supervisors appears to be growing (Gibelman and Schervish 1997a). However, male supervisors earn more income than female supervisors (Gibelman and Schervish 1995), and men are disproportionately more likely than women to supervise (Gibelman and Schervish 1997a). Thus, social work supervision is gendered, with implications for leadership, influence, and power (Granello 1996).

Initiating structure—the instrumental component of supervision—has been associated with "masculine" characteristics (Crespi 1995). It is concerned with initiating activity, making decisions, organizing work, assigning work, and reviewing and evaluating work. It is concerned with task outcomes, accountability, standards, rules, competence, and effectiveness. This component of supervision requires the active use of authority and power deriving from position in the organizational hierarchy.

On the other hand, the expressive-consideration component of supervision reflects characteristics more commonly perceived as feminine (Crespi 1995). The focus here is on an empathetic understanding of people, and their satisfaction and dissatisfaction in their work, their self-esteem, and their need for appreciation and support, as well as awareness of workers' feelings. Power, authority, and hierarchical differences are downplayed in a press toward equality between supervisor and supervisee (Munson 1997).

At this point we refer back to a review of studies that suggest that the most desirable approach to supervision involves integrating instrumental and expressive behaviors, initiating structure and consideration behaviors. Content describing the "good supervisor" is relevant here as well. This material suggests that in terms of gender stereotypes, the most desirable approach to supervision is likely to be androgynous (Bernard and Goodyear 1998; Munson 1997; Powell 1993a, 1993b). Expressive, considerate behaviors in concern for people doing the job reflect the strengths of the female stereotype. Instrumental-initiating structure behaviors concerned with task accomplishment reflect the strength of the male stereotype. Because good supervision integrates concern for task accomplishment as well as concern for people, the good supervisor needs to possess characteristics that reflect maleness as well as femaleness. *Androgynous* here means the comfortable readiness and ability to manifest flexibly and adaptively either masculine or feminine traits as the situation requires. Males attracted to social work, a profession categorized as a female profession because a clear majority of workers are female, are likely to be more androgynously oriented than males in general.

Studying men in "female" professions, both Lemkau (1984) and Hayes (1986) found that, compared with men in more traditionally "male" occupations, such men held less sex-typed, more androgynous attitudes. They are consequently less likely to be uncomfortable about manifesting behaviors culturally defined or perceived as feminine. In addition to implementing instrumental behaviors in concordance with their maleness, they are likely to be capable of meeting the expressive needs of their supervisees. For male supervisors, such an approach to supervision may not present a problem.

The opposite may be the case for female supervisors. Although the expressive requirements of supervision are consonant with their gender identification, the executive demands of instrumental supervision require the manifestation of cross-gender, masculine-identified behavior. An androgynous orientation to supervision may consequently create discomfort and unease among female supervisors.

A male supervisor, in becoming a social worker, has already added some elements of feminine orientation to his behavioral repertoire. A female supervisor generally has not previously had to make this transition to androgyny by adopting male-identified behaviors. The need to act in an uncharacteristic gender manner in administrative supervision may stimulate feelings of discomfort (Watson 1988; Petty and Miles 1976).

In achieving comfort and competence in implementing the instrumental-structural component of supervision, female supervisors do not reject their socialization as women; rather, they transcend it. The gender-neutral requirements of good supervision may result in a positive or negative self-selection for the position. Women who see themselves as reflecting a more traditional feminine stereotype may show little interest in the position, seeing a supervisor as "unlike themselves." More androgynously oriented women might actively seek the position. As a consequence of self-selection and position retention, female supervisors, when studied, may demonstrate (as they empirically do) behaviors that are not significantly different from those of male social work supervisors (Ellis and Ladany 1997).

This is in accordance with the findings of a study by York. Studying social workers' orientation toward management, he found that "gender was not found to be a predictor of management orientation" (York 1988:37). He goes on to say that

> it is possible that females who achieve promotion into administrative positions are a select minority of females who happen to be more competitive or instrumental than other females. It is also possible that males in clinical positions are a select group of males who happen to be more inclined to embrace such clinically-oriented behaviors as expressiveness and mutuality than other males. This interpretation would suggest that a selection bias operates in the movement of males and females into various positions in social work organizations. (York 1988:38)

Male social work supervisors may be more "feminine" than men in general, and female supervisors may be more "masculine" than women in general.

Gender as a Factor in Ongoing Supervision

Differences in gender between supervisor and supervisee can present some problems. In an earlier study of the sociology of work, Caplow (1954) pointed to the fact that men find it contrary to the norm to be directly subordinate to women in the work situation and that they are resistant to accepting women supervisors. Subsequent research in a number of different occupations tended to confirm this as a prevalent attitude among males.

Although there might be a continuing discomfort felt by traditionally oriented male workers generally in being supervised by women, this does not seem to be true of male social workers. Male social workers tend to be more androgynous than men in general in their orientation toward sex role behavior and consequently are apt to be less disturbed or threatened by women in supervisory positions (Dailey 1983:22). The more accepting attitude toward supervision by women manifested by male social workers (as contrasted with men in general) is confirmed by their positive responses to their actual experiences as supervisees of female supervisors. In an interview study of the experience of sixty-five supervisees with their supervision, Munson (1979b) found that male social workers supervised by women reported high levels of satisfaction with their experience. The level of satisfaction of these male supervisees was even higher than the level expressed by males supervised by fellow males. A 1983 study of eighty-six supervisors and supervisees in social agencies in Michigan found that trusting relationships were just as likely between supervisees and supervisors of the opposite sex as between the same-gender pairs (Mathews 1983).

On the other hand Behling, Curtis, and Foster (1982) obtained responses from 276 graduate social work students about their experiences in supervision with field instructor supervisors; Focusing on the effects of sex matching between instructors, supervisors, and student supervisees, they found the female-student versus male-instructor combinations to be clearly the most stressful and problematic combination. "The stresses in the combination primarily were attributed to traditional sexist attitudes held by male instructors" (Behling, Curtis, and Foster 1982:96).

Though overall attitudes of male social work subordinates to female supervisors may be positive, this may be less true in relation to specific supervisory behaviors. Thus Petty and Odewahn (1983:19) found male social workers reacting negatively to assertive behavior from female supervisors.

Studying supervisee attitudes toward leadership in a social service organization, Petty and Miles (1976) found that both male and female supervisees held similar stereotypical views of supervisors. Both were significantly more satisfied with male supervisors exhibiting and initiating structure behaviors and with female supervisors exhibiting consideration behaviors.

For some men, working with a female supervisor is "the first time in their adult life, except in their relationship with parents, that they are presented with a woman in a position of authority. This experience exposes the beginning therapist to his own system of unrecognized values, attitudes, and thus potential countertransference problems" (Nadelson and Notman 1977:281).

The female supervisor can provide the male supervisee with a consciousness-raising learning situation regarding women's experiences. This can provide an antidote to the "countertransference deafness" of some males toward their women clients' needs and aspirations, increasing their capacity for empathetic understanding (Alonson and Rutan 1978; see also Scher 1981 and Granello 1996).

Theoretical presuppositions suggest that it might be desirable to assign supervisees to a supervisor of the other gender. Such arrangements should permit working out transference residuals to the opposite-sex parent. But empirical comparisons of gender matches and contrasts in supervision (e.g., Behling, Curtis, and Foster 1982; Ellis and Robbins 1993; Goodyear 1990; Hartman and Brieger 1992; McCarthy, Kulakowski, and Kenfeld 1994; Nelson and Holloway 1990; Petty and Odewahn 1983; Putney, Worthington, and McCullough 1992; Schiavone and Jessell 1988; Stenack and Dye 1982; Turner and Fine 1997; Vonk and Zucrow 1996; Worthington and Stern 1985) have produced an equivocal pattern of findings (Ellis and Ladany 1997), suggesting that the dynamics of gender in social work supervision are "subtle and highly complex" (Nelson and Holloway 1990). In general, empirical research currently available suggests a neutral approach to gender matching in supervision (Vonk and Zucrow 1996:418).

Much as it would be unwise and not expedient to ignore factors of racial difference between supervisor and supervisee, it would also be a mistake to regard gender differences between the two as a matter of no potential significance. For most supervisory dyads, gender differences may be of very little or no significance, with the supervisor and supervisee relating to each other as one professional to another. However, some female supervisees may exploit gender differences in seductive ploys, making their relationship with the male supervisor more advantageous. Some male supervisors may employ their positional power covertly to solicit sexual favors. In less extreme interactional encounters, gender difference may result in flirtatious displays of femininity and male narcissism that interferes with good supervision (Hartman and Brieger 1992). In response to stereotypic male roles, male supervisors may have difficulty with a manipulatively dependent female supervisee, and female supervisors may enact a nurturing role to male supervisees who need firm expectations.

Male supervisors may act in a traditionally courtly, protective manner toward female supervisees, being careful to avoid "hurting" them by being critical, even when criticism is appropriate. Or a female supervisor with a male supervisee may be reluctant to display the same level of assertive leadership behavior that she might comfortably manifest in contact with a female supervisee (Megargee 1969). Participants in cross-gender supervisory relationships may be hesitant to freely discuss the sexual problems of clients because of a fear of eroticizing the supervisory relationship (Brodsky 1980:516; Hartman and Brieger 1992).

Male and female supervisors may be perceived differently by supervisees in response to persistent stereotyping. One worker notes this when he says,

> In one work setting I had two supervisors—one male and one female. It almost felt like a family with two parents. If you needed support or validation you went to the female. If you had a question about policy or procedure, you went to the male supervisor. And, just like parents, the staff knew how to play them off. If you needed something, it depended on what you needed in order to make the decision about who to ask. If you wanted time off, you went to her even though he made the work schedule. If you wanted to order some supplies or equipment, you went to him.

Supervisors may assign cases in response to a perception of supposed gender differences in interest and aptitude. Child welfare cases might be more frequently assigned to female supervisees; cases involving delinquents more frequently to male supervisees. Gender might be a factor in assigning cases relating to incest and/or rape.

Something needs to be said in mitigation of some of the problems regarding race, ethnicity, and gender noted herein. In each instance, different stereotypes may tend to shape *initial* behavioral responses in the supervisory relationship. Unfortunately, much of the research examining the supervisory variables of race, ethnicity, and gender has sampled supervised students in training, the advent of professional practice, at one point in time. However, the actual experience of working with a supervisor or supervisee who is different in some way tends to vitiate the significance of these differences over time. Successfully working together results in people seeing one another as fellow professionals in a neutral race-ethnicity-gender context. Stereotypes tend to be modified or lose their potency to determine perception as people experience the actual person behind the label and as they get to know each other by working together.

The relationship between supervisor and supervisee established over time may be more significant than the factors of ethnicity, gender, and race. Prejudice, misunderstanding, and residuals of sexism and racism may decline or be resolved for the particular supervisee dyad as a consequence of continuing contact and development of a positive relationship. The supervisor's competence in performing administrative, educational, and supportive functions vis-à-vis the supervisee may take precedence over considerations of race or gender. Furthermore, cultural differences between supervisor and supervisee do not necessarily invariably make a critical difference. Though it encourages being sensitive and open to a recognition of difference, such an approach may not be a cogent variable in many supervisor-supervisee interactions (Fong and Lease 1997:403).

It needs to be noted that discussions of cultural differences require a very great simplification of reality. Talking about African Americans or females or gays and lesbians tends to ignore the very considerable heterogeneity and diversity within groups. Consequently, although approaching the supervisee with the recognition that he or she is in some way culturally different, the ultimate necessity of discovering and understanding the singular individuality of the particular supervisee needs to be constantly considered. The African American experience is not the same for every African American supervisee. In addition, culture is dynamic, and knowledge about culture is soon archaic. African American culture in 2001 is different from African American culture in 1950, and gender relationships in 2001 differ from those in the 1950s.

Sexual Harassment: A Problem for Supervision

Sexual harassment is a form of gender discrimination with grave human and institutional costs (Kaplan 1991; Singer 1994). In a recent review of the case law, Gould distinguished two forms of sexual harassment, *quid pro quo* cases, in which "harassment is said to occur when an employee's job is made dependent on performing sexual favors," and *hostile environment* cases, in which "unwelcome" and "offensive" sexual speech or conduct becomes "sufficiently severe or pervasive to alter the conditions of the victim's employment (Gould 2000:238). Social workers enjoy no immunity from sexual harassment (Maypole 1986; Risely-Curtiss and Hudson 1998). Although most victims of sexual harassment have been women (Cloud 1998), sometimes men also are victims of harassment (Maypole 1986; Stites, Brengarth, and Warefella 1983; Risely-Curtiss and Hudson 1998).

Supervisors are involved with questions of sexual harassment at two different levels. They might use their power position over the worker to make unwanted sexual comments and advances. They are also involved in protecting workers from sexual harassment from administrative superiors, peers, and clients.

Some of the general rulings that developed under the Civil Rights Act of 1964 have been applied to incidents of sexual harassment. In such cases, supervisors may be held liable for such acts perpetrated on supervisees for whom they have responsibility. Based on Title VII of the Civil Rights Act, courts have held agency administrators responsible for sexual harassment by subordinates, just as a taxi company would be held responsible for reckless driving on the part of its drivers.

Sexual harassment is a possible danger in cross-gender and same-gender supervision because the power differential is clearly in the supervisor's favor. As a consequence, the supervisee is vulnerable and the supervisor might use the position to obtain sexual advantages. Where there is a difference in power, there is no true voluntary informed consent. Because of differences in power, autonomy, and status, the supervisory relationship presents opportunities for unwanted, unsolicited, and unwelcome sexual behaviors.

The supervisor-supervisee relationship is one that provides the supervisor with the possibility of exerting "undue influence." "Undue influence" situations are defined as those situations in which there is inequality in the relationship, where one member of the pair is dependent for some reason on the other, where one member of the pair is induced to have confidence in the other. In the context of a relationship of undue influence, the potential impact of the supervisor's power is intensified.

The supervisee is vulnerable to advances from the supervisor because of the fact that the supervisor does possess real power with regard to the worker's career and that such power is exercised in response to evaluations that have considerable elements of subjectivity. Such vulnerability requires protection from sexual harassment. Differences in power might lead to quid pro quo forms of harassment, in which a supervisor implies the offer of some work-related benefit in return for sexual favors.

Furthermore, it needs to be recognized that the supervisor-supervisee relationship has many of the elements of an intimate relationship. People meet with some regularity in private to discuss matters that often are of an emotional or personal nature. The affective intensity of the relationship is deliberately fostered because it provides the necessary context for effective supervision.

Because the advantage of power lies with the supervisor, in this close relationship he or she must take greater responsibility for aborting any action that risks converting a professional relationship to an unethical dual relationship (NASW 1999). The supervisor has to be held to a higher standard of conduct than the supervisee. This does not absolve the supervisee from the responsibility of refraining from any action, suggestion, or innuendo that implies (directly or indirectly) interest in such a change in the relationship.

The possibility of sexual harassment seems most likely in the vertical hierarchical relationship (worker-supervisor; worker-administrator), where there is considerable power differential. However, the supervisor needs to be aware that co-worker relationships and worker-client relationships are also possible contexts for sexual harassment.

A questionnaire returned by 319 NASW members in a Midwest state in 1982 indicated that 36 percent of the female respondents and 14 percent of the male respondents had experienced sexual harassment on the job. The most frequent kind of harassment experienced was verbal—jokes, propositions, and demeaning flattery. Unwanted touching was less frequent. The person doing the harassing was equally often a client, co-worker, or supervisor/administrator (Maypole 1986). Such forms of harassment are experienced as a hostile work environment. The victim of sexual harassment is most often a younger female in a subordinate position. Among the most frequent perpetrators is an older male supervisor (Judd, Block, and Calkin 1985; Maypole 1986; Dhooper, Huff, and Schultz 1989).

In addition to achieving a measure of self-education regarding the subtleties of sexual harassment, supervisors have the obligation of interpreting to the staff the kinds of behaviors that are not acceptable. In light of recent Supreme Court rulings, Gould (2000) asserts that human service agencies should adopt and enforce antiharassment policies to achieve a nonsexist work climate.

The problem of sexual harassment in supervision requires educating workers as to what is involved. There is general awareness of harassing behaviors that are obvious, overt, and unambiguous. Education is necessitated by the need to bring to awareness the fact that looks, gestures, jokes, innuendoes, suggestive remarks, insulting comments, or ogling might also be perceived as sexual harassment. In fact, studies indicate that the most obvious forms of sexual harassment represent only a small percentage of the source of complaints. The more frequent source of complaints relate to the more subtle forms (Maypole and Skaine 1982; Maypole 1986; Risely-Curtiss and Hudson 1998).

The subtleties of sexist communications were listed by a worker in a probation and parole office. She said she was constantly subjected to seemingly innocent but nevertheless offensive "stone age" remarks, such as "women are better note takers than men, so you take the minutes" and "problems in decision making are just in the 'nature of the beast' for women." Being alert to the manifestations of sexual harassment is important to the supervisor as the administrative officer to whom formal complaints initially need to be addressed. Having educated workers and set guidelines, the supervisor has to communicate a receptivity to complaints regarding such behaviors and a serious response to such complaints.

It is disconcerting to note that workers who experienced sexual harassment from co-workers and/or clients rarely sought the protection of their supervisors or reported it to them (Maypole and Skaine 1982:690). It was felt that the report might be treated lightly if not ridiculed, and there was little conviction that any effective action would be taken. The typical response of the victim was either ignoring or avoiding the behavior, much less frequently confronting and/or reporting the behavior. Supervisors then have responsibility in encouraging and responding receptively to supervise reporting.

The current sensitivity to the possibilities of sexual harassment in supervision is justifiable and necessary. However, it may present a problem for both male and female supervisors. Maccoby (1976) notes that male supervisors, anxious about imputations of sexual harassment, often withhold needed encouragement from female supervisees; on the other hand, female supervisors may feel hesitant about assuming a warm, nurturing, supportive approach with male supervisees. Vigorous supportive supervision may be regarded as an invitation to intimacy.

A case that most graphically illustrates this complication involves, paradoxically, a charge by a male supervisee against a female supervisor. The worker alleged that his female supervisor made sexual advances, and when he failed to respond he was denied recommendation for promotion. A jury awarded the male supervisee $196,500 in compensatory and punitive damages. In commenting on the verdict, the Wisconsin assistant attorney general, who defended the supervisor, noted that "supervisors, especially those who are women, will have to step carefully through management techniques that call for being supportive to subordinate personnel. Otherwise it would be difficult to avoid the allegation of sexual harassment" (Madison (Wisc.), *Capital Times*, July 17, 1982). The accused supervisor said that as a result of the verdict, she was changing her approach to supervision, giving fewer compliments and being more direct in criticism (Madison (Wisc.), *Capital Times*, July 24, 1982).

Problems Related to Hierarchical Position

Special problems related to the unique position of the supervisor in the agency's hierarchical structure sometimes arise. The supervisor is a linchpin in the organization—he or she links two groups (direct service workers and administrators) and is a common member of the two dyads (supervisee-supervisor and supervisor-administrator), superordinate in one, subordinate in the other. Joining the two groups in which she is a member, the supervisor facilitates communications between them, advocates for one group with the other group, and attempts to mitigate distrust and friction between the two groups. The supervisor is sometimes involved in cross-role translation—communicating workers' concerns in a language that is comprehensible to administrators and, similarly, translating administrators' concerns to workers so that they are understandable.

In addition to translating communications, the supervisor is also concerned with reconciling differences in the problems and viewpoints between workers and administrators. The supervisor takes a multipositional orientation. The supervisor has to understand and accept the legitimacy of the different needs of the different members of the role set, to broker and negotiate between conflicting needs of the worker for autonomy and administrators' need for accountability. Allied with both, the supervisor must maintain some freedom from firm allegiance to either group. As a member of two different role sets, the supervisor has multiple and sometimes conflicting loyalties.

In a study of sixty-two public welfare supervisors, Erera (1991a, 1991b) found that implementing these responsibilities created stress because organizational policies were often ambiguous and incompatible.

Working with Administrators

It has been said that where you stand depends on where you sit. Administrators, supervisors, and direct service workers have different problems that need to be solved, different constituencies who are their primary concerns, different clusters of information to which they give attention, different sources of satisfaction, different prerogatives to be protected, and different personal anxieties. Administrators are concerned with policy reflecting the needs and preferences formulated in the politics of the general community. Service personnel are concerned with the needs and preferences of a particular segment of the community—the clients of the agency. The need to accommodate to simultaneous conflicting pressures from administrators and supervisees creates tension for the supervisor. Influence with supervisees in getting them to do a good job increases the supervisors' influence with administration, because administration admires a supervisor who achieves trouble-free, efficient, and effective production.

The supervisor who controls more resources has greater power. Making these resources available selectively, the supervisor has the possibility of dispersing a greater number of rewards. Control of resources results from the influence the supervisor has with administration. Influence with administration thus increases influence with supervisees.

Fluctuations in supervisory power are reflective of changes in reciprocal interaction with others in the supervisory role set. If the supervisor has effective influence with his or her work unit, able to motivate them to more effective performance, this increases the supervisor's power vis-à-vis the administrator. If the supervisor has more influence with the administrator, this increases the likelihood that his or her unit would have increased access to agency resources, which increases the supervisor's power with the work unit.

Understanding and Working with Administrators

Because the supervisor was more likely to have been a worker and less likely to have been an administrator, it is to be expected that supervisors would be more attuned, understanding, and empathetic with needs of the workers rather than the administrator. Bonding, alliance, and allegiance are stronger in the supervisor-worker relationship than they are likely to be in the supervisor-administrator relationship. However, supervisors, facing both ways, have the responsibility of working effectively with administrators as well as with supervisees. There has to be some understanding of where the administrator is coming from, what his or her needs and preferences are to implement the job successfully, and how the supervisor can help the worker achieve his or her objectives (Austin 1988).

The administrator is not the enemy, and acting to assist the administrator is not an act of disloyalty to the rank and file. But just as the supervisor has to empathize with supervisees, seeing the world from the perspective of client contacts, so the supervisor needs to empathize with administrators seeing the world from the perspective of the agency's relationship to the community. Administrators, like supervisees, need a trusting, supportive relationship with the people with whom they work. Administrators share with supervisors and supervisees a commitment to agency goals and objectives. They would like to see the agency operate as effectively as possible, not only because it makes them look good but because such an agency is best for the clients. Without feeling that it is demeaning and with some respect for the limited time most administrators have available, it might prevent problems if the supervisor were to discuss a difficult decision with the administrator beforehand. This signifies a generally positive attitude toward the administrator on the part of the supervisor. It suggests a cooperative stance in the mission in which both are jointly engaged. Most administrators appreciate a supervisor's approach to a problem if the discussion includes a clear statement of the problem, the possible alternatives to dealing with the problem, and the solution that the supervisor feels is the best alternative.

Acting effectively in a subordinate position to the administrator requires balancing a number of antithetical pressures on the part of the supervisor. The need to be open in discussing problems with the administrator conflicts with the need to be self-protective. The need to display initiative contradicts the need to appear noncompetitive with the administrator. There is a need to suggest explicitly what the workers want from the administration and still avoid being so specific as to deny the administrator some flexibility in response.

If supervisors have a problem with assertively employing power and authority in their relationship with supervisees, they have an analogous problem in being appropriately assertive in their relationship with administrators. Their position requires that they advocate assertively for staff and in behalf of necessary changes in policy, but many supervisors find this difficult to do.

In a questionnaire study of supervisors' shortcomings both supervisors and supervisees reported this as a problem. Supervisors said:

I tend to be hesitant to speak up for staff to higher administrators.
I have difficulty in negotiating between administrative demands and vested interests of supervisees.
I am reluctant to approach higher administrators with ideas for correcting inefficiency in service delivery.
Being weak in facing administrators with agency policy that is not in the best interests of the client. (Kadushin 1992b:12)

Supervisees said:

She does not have the backbone to stand up to the director.
Too eager to be a "good guy" to everybody and not willing to communicate workers' needs to administration.
His primary focus on covering his own tail keeps him from adequately supporting or advocating for his workers with administration.
She is ambivalent about her authority, which militates against her ability to advocate with administration in behalf of staff. (Kadushin 1992b:16)

Summary of Stresses Encountered by Supervisors

We have noted the stresses supervisors face in making a transition to the position and the stresses they encounter in implementing their responsibilities as supervisors. These relate to the demands of the position, the conflicting needs of administration, workers, and clients, and problems relating to gender and race.

Table 7.1 recapitulates some of the dissatisfactions with the supervisory role, as noted by supervisors, that reflect the different kinds of stress encountered on the job.

Table 7.1 Supervisor Dissatisfaction in Supervision

	Percentage of Supervisors Checking Item as a Strong Source of Dissatisfaction (N = 469)
1. Dissatisfaction with administrative "housekeeping"— red tape, details in caseload audits, time sheets, statistical reports, etc.	71
2. Dissatisfaction because other heavy responsibilities of the job not related to work with supervisees prevent me from giving as much time as I would like to supervisees.	53
3. Loss of the direct worker-client contact and relationship.	46
4. Dissatisfaction related to need to get workers' adherence to agency policy and procedure with which I disagree.	41
5. Dissatisfaction with having to work with supervisees who are resistive or hostile or dependent or slow learners, etc.	39
6. Dissatisfaction from being tied to the desk and to the office.	27
7. Anxiety at the responsibility of making decisions for which there is no clear-cut agency policy or procedure.	27
8. Dissatisfaction associated with the conflict between administrative, evaluative aspects of the relationship with supervisees and the educational aspects.	26
9. Anxiety from not feeling certain that I know enough to be an adequate supervisor.	22
10. The need to exercise administrative authority in relation to supervisee performance and to evaluate the work of the supervisee.	21
11. Dissatisfaction at the socially and professionally isolated position of the supervisor in my agency.	21
12. Dissatisfaction with the physical aspects of my job— office, equipment, parking, etc.	18
13. Dissatisfaction at finding myself becoming part of the Establishment.	15
14. Anxiety from being responsible for somebody else's work and being looked to for leadership.	12
15. Anxiety at having to supervise workers who are older and/or more experienced than myself.	2
16. Other (miscellaneous).	2

Source: Kadushin (1973)

Coping with Stress: Supervisors' Adaptations

In general, supervisors have fewer supportive resources available to help them cope with work-related stresses than do supervisees (Poulin 1995; Schwartz 1990; Silver, Poulin, and Manning 1997; Shulman 1993; Zunz 1998). Griping· or complaining as a form of cathartic release is not as readily available to the supervisor.

> Caseworkers could freely complain about agency policies and even, on occasion, defy them, but such options were hardly open to supervisors. Supervisors did critically discuss some aspects of agency functioning in supervisory staff meetings, and such discussions sometimes resulted in policy changes, but many regulations were outside their control, having been set by legislative bodies and the lay board. Regardless of their own feelings, supervisors were expected to enforce all current agency policies. These circumstances created problems for all supervisors, although professionally oriented supervisors were placed in a particularly difficult position. It was their task to help workers to accommodate to the agency's program—to reconcile bureaucratic requirements with professional principles. (Scott 1969:133)

Fewer provisions are made for the formal induction of supervisors into their new role, and fewer formal, regularized channels are provided to ensure support for new supervisors during the transitional period (Bernard and Goodyear 1998; Erera and Lazar 1993; Schwartz 1990; Watkins 1999).

Whereas the supervisee has a formal channel of feedback in the supervisor that provides opportunities for commendation, the supervisor has no such formally assigned sources of feedback. Many supervisors live with the stress of not knowing how well they are doing and what (if anything) they should be doing differently. Perhaps the assumption is that if the person is experienced enough to be selected for the position, he or she should be able to operate independently, without the need for such support. A supervisor wryly expresses some resentment about this:

> My first supervisee was a rather dependent person, who, as we expressed it professionally in her evaluation, "worked best with considerable reassurance and support." In practical terms, this meant that I propped her up while she propped the clients up, and in the end the whole weight fell on me. This left me in need of "considerable reassurance and support" too, but no one thought of that. I was the supervisor and I was paid to have shoulders that were broad. I soon became accustomed to this, however, and eventually I was able to prop

several workers up—something like the bottom man in a human acrobatic act—and hardly feel it at all. (H.C.D. 1949:162)

The supervisor rarely has interaction with some member of the hierarchy who has the responsibility of helping him or her become aware of countertransference toward supervisees. The supposition is that the supervisor is objective and self-aware.

The supervisory peer group is less often a resource for emotional support than is the direct-worker peer group. There are not as many supervisors, so there are fewer possibilities for choice of those with whom one might feel comfortable and congenial. Competition for promotion becomes keener as one moves up the administrative ladder because there are progressively fewer positions available. Consequently, there is less tendency for the supervisors to act as a group and a greater tendency to act as individuals in seeking administrative favor.

It is far more difficult for supervisors than for direct service workers to develop a colleague support group. There are few, if any, functions or activities that require that supervisors work together. There is no formal arrangement analogous to unit meetings that would enable supervisors to get to know each other and develop a relationship. The work of the supervisors, even more than that of the workers, tends to isolate them psychologically and geographically.

Studies of social interaction and peer consultation among direct service workers and supervisors showed a considerably greater amount of interchange among direct service workers as compared with supervisors (Blau and Scott 1962). Where opportunities for supportive collaboration exist, supervisors report more job satisfaction (Silver, Poulin, and Manning 1997).

Supervisees are a source of support for supervisors. Their positive response to the supervisor's efforts in helping them develop professionally, their efforts to do a good job, and the occasional compliments they offer the supervisor tend to provide the positive satisfactions that counter strain.

Supervisors are also subject to burnout (Shulman 1993; Silver, Poulin, and Manning 1997; Zunz 1998). High expectations that they can significantly influence supervisee professional growth while effecting consequential changes in the agency are often frustrated (Erera and Lazar 1994b). Supervisors experience burnout by balancing the needs of the organization against the needs of supervisees and/or clients, facing the necessity of obtaining compliance with policies and procedures with which they disagree, trying to carry out their responsibilities with increasingly limited resources of personnel and funds, emotionally depleted by the need to support and nurture and sustain a unit of supervisees while lacking a support group.

In adjusting, supervisors make deliberate efforts to buffer themselves from supervisees. Too much social contact and too little distance expose the supervisor to constant pressure from the demands and needs (explicit or implicit) of the supervisees. But because the supervisor needs the cooperation of the supervisee and a positive relationship with them, too great a social distance is undesirable. In a somewhat formalized, controlled contact the supervisor seeks an optimum balance between too great a familiarity, which risks constant pressure, and too little, which encourages supervisee resistance and alienation.

Supervisors adjust to their situation by developing their own vocabularies of realism. They learn to accept the limitations of their power and authority by discovering that, despite their restricted knowledge and control, most often the terrible things they fear just don't happen. They learn to turn a blind eye and a deaf ear to relatively inconsequential examples of deviance and noncompliance. They learn to recognize the limits of their influence: although they can teach the worker to be responsible for his or her learning and they can facilitate interest, motivation, and commitment in the work, but only the worker can *feel* that interest, motivation, and commitment.

A study of 101 human-services managers by Zunz (1998) identified a number of factors that predict supervisory resilience to burnout and stress. Supervisors may benefit from appropriate recognition and feedback, because burnout is associated with low feelings of self-worth. Supervisors need social interaction; low levels of interpersonal integration and attachment predict burnout. Opportunities for renewing the supervisor's sense of mission and skills may also be helpful, because the strongest predictors of resilience to burnout were commitment to mission and feeling able to get things done and done well.

In dealing with problems in supervision, supervisors can be helped by cognitive reframing. The supervisor who needs to do the very best with all supervisees, who attributes blame to self for every supervisee failure, who thinks he or she is indispensable, who thinks that all supervisees are lovable and that if you are nice to them they will be nice to you can profit from cognitive reframing. The middle-management position subjects the supervisor to pressure from those above and below, but it also presents opportunities for exculpation. The supervisors can explain failures to administration by pointing to the workers and explain failure to the workers by pointing to administration.

Some supervisors may adjust to the stresses of the position by becoming indifferent and doing the minimum to satisfy the requirements. Such a supervisor rewards supervisees who handle their assignments without bothering him or her, who do not bring up any problems, who do not generate any complaints from clients or other agencies, and who do not allow emergencies to develop and, when they do develop, handle them by themselves. The supervisor's actions are motivated not by a concern with helping the supervisees develop autonomy but rather by a desire to be trouble-free. He or she settles for the absence of negatives in the performance of his supervisees, rather than encouraging the presence of positives. He or she is not concerned with noncompliance as long as the supervisees take the risk and are not too blatant about it.

There are numerous compensating gratifications that offset and make acceptable the increased stresses occasioned by the appointment to supervisor (Poulin 1995; Schwartz 1990; Silver, Poulin, and Manning 1997). Table 7.2 ranks satisfaction in supervision as described by supervisors. The list points to the kinds of social and emotional returns from their jobs that sustain supervisors in dealing with job-related tensions.

Supervisors' Games

It would be doing both supervisor and supervisee an injustice to neglect a description of games initiated by supervisors (Hagler and Casey 1990). Supervisors play games for the same reasons that supervisees play. The games are methods of adjusting to stresses encountered in performing their role. Supervisors play games out of perceived threats to their position in the hierarchy, uncertainty about their authority, reluctance to use their authority, a desire to be liked, a need for the supervisees' approval, and out of some hostility to supervisees that is inevitable in such a complex, close relationship.

One of the classic supervisory games can be called I Wonder Why You Really Said That. This is the game of redefining honest disagreement so that it appears to be psychological resistance. Honest disagreement requires that the supervisor defend his or her point of view and be sufficiently acquainted with the literature to present the research evidence in support of the contention. If honest disagreement is redefined as resistance, the burden is shifted to the supervisee. He or she has to examine the needs and motives that prompt him or her to question what the supervisor said. The supervisor is thus relieved of the burden of validating what was said, and the burden for defense now rests with the supervisee.

Another classic supervisory game is One Good Question Deserves Another. A supervisor writes:

> I learned that another part of a supervisor's skills, as far as the workers are concerned, is to know all the answers. I was able to get out of this very easily.

Table 7.2 Supervisor Satisfaction in Supervision

	Percentage of Supervisors Checking Item as a Strong Source of Satisfaction (N = 469)
1. Satisfaction in helping the supervisee grow and develop, in professional competence.	88
2. Satisfaction in ensuring more efficient and effective service to more clients through my supervisory activity.	75
3. Satisfaction in sharing my social work knowledge and skills with supervisees.	63
4. Satisfaction in the greater opportunity and leverage to affect changes in agency policy and procedures.	45
5. Satisfaction in the stimulation provided by curious, idealistic, and enthusiastic supervisees.	44
6. Satisfaction in helping the supervisee grow and develop as a person.	37
7. Satisfaction in a more diversified job.	31
8. Satisfaction in having others look to me for leadership, advice, direction.	24
9. Satisfaction in being able to provide emotional support to supervisees when needed.	23
10. Satisfaction in increased salary that goes with job.	23
11. Satisfaction in contacts with professionally qualified and interesting fellow supervisors.	18
12. Satisfaction in the status and authority the position gives me.	9
13. Satisfaction in being free from contact with difficult clients and a heavy caseload.	5
14. Satisfaction in helping supervisees with their personal problems.	1
15. Satisfaction with the physical aspects of the supervisor's job— better office, parking privileges, etc.	1
16. Other (miscellaneous)	2

Source: Kadushin (1973)

I discovered that when a worker asks a question, the best thing to do is to immediately ask her what she thinks. While the worker is figuring out the answer to her own question (this is known as growth and development), the supervisor quickly tries to figure it out also. She may arrive at the answer the same time as the worker, but the worker somehow assumes that she knew it all along. This is very comfortable for the supervisor. In the event that neither the worker nor the supervisor succeeds in coming up with a useful thought on the question the worker has raised, the supervisor can look wise and suggest that they think about it and discuss it further next time. This gives the supervisor plenty of time to look up the subject and leaves the worker with the feeling that the supervisor is giving great weight to her question. In the event that the supervisor does not want to go to all the trouble, she can just tell the worker that she does not know the answer (this is known as helping the worker accept the limitations of the supervision) and tell her to look it up herself. (H.C.D. 1949:162)

Some games are designed to validate the supervisor's authority on the basis of ascription. Subtly appealing to experience or credentials, the supervisor solicits endorsement of authority and seeks to deflect any challenge to such authority. Playing Parents Know Best, the supervisor asserts his or her unquestioned authority on the basis of her education or years on the job (Hawthorne 1975). A milder form of the game is to openly recognize the supervisee's difference of opinion but not accept it: "I know you don't agree with me, but later when you get more experience you will find that I am right."

Some supervisor's games are concerned with protection from the burdens of supervision. The supervisor can avoid the inconvenience of individual conferences by finding justifiable reasons to postpone or cancel them or significantly shorten those that are unavoidable. The game might be called I Can Hardly Catch My Breath. The supervisor indicates that because he or she has suddenly received an administrative request for a special report or some special statistics, he or she is very sorry but the scheduled conference will have to be postponed (Hawthorne 1975).

A judicious arrangement of the supervisory conference agenda may provide protection from the need to confess inability to help. The more difficult questions are relegated to the last ten minutes of the conference. Then, regretfully noting that "I wish we had more time to discuss this," the supervisor gives these questions a cursory and hurried review, leaving no time for possibly embarrassing questions.

Protecting themselves from the necessity of exerting authority, supervisors play at being pseudodemocratic, trying to hide the fact that they are supervisors. The emphasis is on reducing any hierarchical differences and drawing the worker closer to the supervisor by drawing closer to the worker. The game is I Am Just Like You.

Appealing to the limits of the supervisory power protects the supervisors from some difficult decisions. In playing I Would If I Could, But I Can't, the supervisor indicates that he or she would be willing to go along with some request that the supervisee is making except for the fact that the administration will not permit it.

The worker has considerable administrative discretion in how liberally or rigidly he or she might interpret agency policy in contact with the client. The supervisor has similar maneuverability in applying administrative requirements in supervision. The supervisor creates an obligation by leniency in enforcing agency procedures. After All I Did for You is a supervisor's game that seeks to cash in on such obligations. It calls for explicit attention to the obligations the supervisee has incurred and asks that restitution be made. This game can be communicated almost as effectively nonverbally as verbally. The pained expression and a sigh of resignation at impending disappointment can bring a supervisee up short.

The supervisor might be selective in demands for adherence to agency rules and procedures or modulates the vigorousness with which he or she requires such adherence. The extent to which the supervisor feels free to do this depends on the security he or she feels in his or her own relationship with administrators and the number of reciprocity credits he or she has earned with them.

The obverse of reciprocity credits is, of course, obligation deficits. Supervisees seek to obligate the supervisor for extra work they have done in meeting the request for a report on short notice, in agreeing to cover an uncovered client, and so on. Being obligated to the workers, the supervisor has to reciprocate by softening (for a time at least) demands on the workers to maintain their loyalty.

Supervisors, in avoiding a response to a supervisee's request for a decision, information, or guidance, may engage in double-talk. From the supervisee's point of view this might be termed What Did She Say—sometimes called the old song and dance approach. The game involves using as many esoteric (preferably psychoanalytic) terms and lingo as possible, giving the appearance of knowing what one is talking about. It requires considerable self-assurance on the supervisor's part and the ability to phrase a response with considerable ambiguity. The effectiveness of this game derives from the fact that it is difficult for the supervisee to challenge the supervisor and request clarification and from the fact that the confusion generated by the statement makes it impossible to formulate a sensible question. Having made the statement, the supervisor prudently disappears in the smokescreen.

The "Good" Supervisor

At various points in the text, reference has been made in passing to factors that characterize "good" supervision. Our objective here is to pull together and highlight these factors in a systematic way. The recapitulation is based on reviews of the supervision research literature, empirical studies of effective and ineffective supervision, studies of supervision associated with supervisees' positive and negative responses to supervisors, and studies that define the kind of supervision that has the highest possibility of achieving the objectives of supervision (Hansen and Warner 1971; Nash 1975; Mayer and Rosenblatt 1975b; Hansen, Pound, and Petro 1976; Herrick 1977; Thing 1979; Ford 1979; Blumberg 1980; Lambert 1980; Hansen, Robins, and Grimes 1982; Shulman 1982; Kaplan 1983; Zucker and Worthington 1986; Allen, Szollos, and Williams 1986; Rabinowitz, Heppner, and Roehlke 1986; Carifio and Hess 1987; Kennard, Stewart, and Gluck 1987; Schacht, Howe, and Berman 1989; Wetchler, Piercy, and Sprenkle 1989; Baril 1989; Grube and Painton 1990; Wetchler and Vaughn 1991; Shanfield, Matthews, and Hetherly 1993; White and Russell 1995; Worthen and McNeill 1996; Lambert and Ogles 1997; Lazar and Eisikovits 1997; Vonk and Thyer 1997; Watkins 1997; Henderson, Cawyer, and Watkins 1999; Anderson, Schlossberg, and Rigazio-DiGilio 2000; Magnuson, Wilcoxon, and Norem 2000; O'Connor 2000; Wulf and Nelson 2000; Nelson and Friedlander 2001; Gray et al. 2001).

It needs to be noted that the picture of the good supervisor that emerges from the research is derived primarily from findings regarding supervisee satisfactions and preferences. The good supervisor is one the supervisees most prefer, find satisfactory, respond to positively, like, and trust.

Little empirical research has been done into outcomes related to the supervisee—and especially to the supervisee's clients (Lambert and Ogles 1997; Ellis and Ladany 1997). Outcome research would provide results showing that the good supervisor's supervisees are more efficient and effective, learn more and better than supervisees of other supervisors, or that clients of the good supervisor's supervisees made quicker and better progress in their treatment (Jaynes et al. 1979; Steinhelber et al. 1986; Ginsbery, Weisberg, and Cowan 1985; Kadushin 1981; Sosin 1986; Harkness and Poertner 1989; Harkness and Hensley 1991; Harkness 1997).

The following listing presents a composite picture of the good supervisor, organized in terms of the supervisory functions discussed in the text—administrative supervision, educational-clinical supervision, and supportive supervision.

As an *administrator* the good supervisor:

1. Accepts, is comfortable with, and appropriately implements the administrative authority and power inherent in the position in a nonauthoritarian manner; holds workers accountable for assigned work and sensitively but de-

terminedly evaluates supervisees practice; balances support and clear expectations of work in conformity with clearly defined performance standards;

2. Provides clearly structured procedures and constructive feedback for workers in their relation to the agency and their clinical practice: The "good" supervisor provides direction, confronts when appropriate, and provides constructive, honest, critical feedback in a way that respects supervisees' strength and confident growth toward independence;

3. Makes active efforts to integrate agency's need for production with the socioemotional needs of the workers, balances agency output objectives with workers' morale, makes task demands with concern for employees, balances instrumental tasks with expressive needs;

4. Is unobtrusive in supervision, so that supervisees know that they are being supervised but are not consciously and explicitly aware of this; availability without continuous presence is manifested;

5. Is generally physically available as well as psychologically accessible and approachable;

6. Develops and maintains good interpersonal relationships among the group of workers he or she supervises;

7. Communicates effectively up as well as down the hierarchical communication ladder, vigorously representing workers messages for administration's consideration, and representing administration's concerns fairly and understandingly to supervisees;

8. Balances the agency's need for stability with need to change and is ready to advocate for validated change.

As an *educator* the good supervisor:

9. Has a positive, forward-looking attitude toward social work and its mandate; displays a solidarity with and commitment to the profession; embodies the values of the profession in his or her behavior;

10. Displays a sincere interest in promoting supervisee learning and professional development, balancing control and direction with respect for supervisee's autonomy;

11. Has expert, updated knowledge of social work theory and practice and is ready to share such expertise in providing the supervisee with information and suggestions relevant to practice problems;

12. Has a problem-solving orientation toward the work of the supervisee based on consensus and cooperation derived from democratic participation rather than power-centered techniques and superordinate-subordinate relationships;

13. Provides a clear, flexible structure for the supervisor-supervisee relationship;

14. Actively prepares for conferences and group supervisory meetings; preparation involves review of knowledge of supervisees as well as knowledge of content;

15. Is culturally sensitive in helping the supervisee understand clients in their situation; is nonsexist and nonracist in orientation;

16. Establishes benign relationships with supervisees characterized by a sense of psychological safety—accepting, warm, empathetic, respectful, interested, supportive, flexible, and genuine;

17. Is ready, willing, and able to share expertise, effectively teaching practice in a way that optimally facilitates learning; sharing involves readiness to engage in appropriate self-disclosure;

18. Displays technical professional competence in helping supervisees with their work as well as competence in interpersonal human relations with supervisees;

19. Is ready to tolerate and accept mistakes and failures, recognizing these as a natural component of the learning experience.

In being *supportive* the good supervisor:

20. Projects an attitude of confidence and trust toward the supervisee, resulting in optimization of supervisee autonomy and discretion;

21. Is ready, willing, and comfortable in offering praise and approval for good performance; is equally ready to challenge and confront inadequate work;

22. Is sensitive to the manifestations of workers' stress and is flexible in adjusting work demands accordingly;

23. Establishes full and free reciprocal communication with the supervisee in an atmosphere that not only permits but encourages the expression of authentic feeling;

24. Is comfortable in nondefensively considering negative feedback and countertransference reaction and is tolerant of constructive criticism;

25. Though appropriately supportive, he or she is not emotionally intrusive on workers' private concerns.

In the end, it may all add up to the maxim "good supervisors are available, accessible, affable, and able." The general picture of the good supervisor shows him or her to be a person who is a technically competent professional with good human relations skills and good organizational-managerial skills.

But the contribution of the effective supervisor to the supervisor-supervisee interaction is only one factor in the equation. A detailed analysis of ninety-four supervisory experiences based on structured interviews found that supervisees also made a contribution to the kind of relationship that developed. Though supervisors were more or less inclined to be permissive or controlling, directive or nondirective, egalitarian or distant, accepting or disparaging, these tendencies were muted or intensified by the supervisees' own characteristic way of relating.

> In order for a supervisor to be collaborative, the supervisee must be some-one he can collaborate with; [supervisees] who have a collaborative approach to supervision themselves most probably elicit collaborative behavior from their supervisors. . . . In many cases a supervisor's coercive style may be the result of the [supervisee's] continually challenging or resisting his authority. . . . The exercise of coercive power is not necessarily attributable to the intrapsychic dynamics of the supervisor but may be the result of the supervisory interaction. (Nash 1975:26)

Some supervisors were described by some supervisees as their most preferred supervisor, whereas the same supervisor was described by others as their least preferred supervisor.

The configuration of effective and ineffective supervision that emerges is then in the nature of a generalization. This implies that an approach to supervision that mirrors the "good" supervisor configuration is more apt to lead to effective supervision. But like all generalizations, it suggests that this is not invariably the case. The complexity of bidirectional interaction between supervisee and supervisor precludes any such statement. A contingency model that takes into consideration the uniqueness of the relationship between these factors comes closer to the truth. It argues for a best-fit decision on the part of the individual supervisor in contact with a particular supervisee working in a particular agency offering service to a specific client in an idiosyncratic, problematic situation. But a generalization is useful. It suggests that among the myriad possibilities, the relevant literature shows the approaches listed above should be given priority for consideration because the research indicates they have been shown to be effective for many supervisors in many instances. Analogous to the frequent finding that there are few substantial differences in the effectiveness of various therapy models, there is no firm substantiation that the "good supervisor" can be identified as an adherent of this or that model of supervision.

Summary

Supervisors are subjected to a variety of job-related stresses. The transition to supervisor is a difficult change, involving a reorientation of relationships with colleagues and alterations in self-perception and in attitudes toward agency goals and procedures. The additional responsibility, along with the lack of preparation, ongoing support, and clarity in role differentiation combined with conflicting demands, all contribute to supervisors' feelings of tension. The problems of race, ethnicity, and gender in supervisory interaction are other sources of stress. Satisfactions, however, balance some of the dissatisfaction for supervisors. Games played by supervisors can help in their efforts to cope.

8 | Evaluation

Definition

Evaluation in supervision is defined as the objective appraisal of the worker's total functioning on the job over a specified period of time (Schmidt and Perry 1940). It is a process of applying systematic procedures to determine with reliability and validity the extent to which the worker is achieving the requirements of his or her position in the agency. An evaluation should be a judgment based on clearly specified, realistic, and achievable criteria reflecting agency standards. It is job related and time limited. It is concerned with both the quality of performance and the quantity of accomplishment.

Evaluation is an administrative procedure that can and should contribute to professional growth. It is therefore a component of both administrative and educational supervision. It is furthermore a component of supportive supervision. Explicit feedback helps the worker get a sense of meaningful achievement, reduces the tension associated with role ambiguity, and provides positive reinforcement for good work well done.

Written, signed evaluations have legal ramifications (Harrar, VandeCreek, and Knapp 1990; Millar 1990; Malos 1998; Reamer 1998; Strom-Gottfried 1999) as well as supportive, educational, clinical, and administrative implications. Due process requires that a worker be periodically informed of the acceptability of his or her performance to the agency. If a decision is made to dismiss the employee, failure to have provided the worker with such periodic assessments can legally be regarded as a violation of due process as well as being in contravention to many union contracts. Consistent with law, evaluation procedures should provide employees with a means of appeal.

Equal opportunity regulations require that any administrative personnel action requires validation by specific objective evaluation procedures. Much evidence suggests that the accuracy of performance appraisal varies with the gender and ethnicity of the supervisor and supervisee (Ilgen, Barnes-Farrell, and McKellin 1993; Arvey and Murphy 1998). Thus, without such substantiating documentation, decisions affecting women or minorities may be open to challenge.

Furthermore, evaluations are an ethical obligation of professional supervision. Principle 6.05 of the American Psychological Association's *Ethical Principles of Psychologists* (1992:23) lists the evaluation of "supervisees on the basis of their actual performance" and the establishment of "an appropriate process for providing feedback" as ethical mandates. By the same token, Standard 3.01(d) of the social work code of ethics (National Association of Social Workers [NASW] 1999:19; emphasis added) notes that "social workers who provide supervision should evaluate supervisee's performance in a manner that is *fair* and respectful."

Evaluations are as ubiquitous and necessary as they are inevitable. There is no way of not communicating an evaluative message. Refraining from evaluating is in itself an evaluation. An anxious worker to whom no evaluation is communicated may read the message as "I am so bad he can't even tell me about it"; the overly confident, conceited worker may read the same message as "my work is so exemplary that there is nothing to discuss."

Every time the supervisor nods in agreement, says "yes," "okay," or "you're right about that" in response to something the supervisee has said, an evaluation is being made. Every time a pained expression crosses the supervisor's face, every time he or she gestures impatiently, every time he or she says gently, "come now, I am not so sure about that,"—or more forthrightly, "I disagree with you about that,"—an evaluation has been made.

We cannot abstain from informal assessment, and workers are aware of this. Each supervisor has some idea of how he or she ranks a particular worker as compared with others in terms of a level of performance regarded as adequate. Evaluations require us to formalize such assessments, make them explicit, communicate them to the workers, and defend them if necessary.

The formal evaluation conference differs from the ongoing assessments that are or should be part of each supervisory conference. In the individual conferences the focus of concern is the current case situation. The formal evaluation conference is concerned with an overview of the entire caseload.

It is a period of stock-taking and review. Given the uncluttered opportunity to take a more general view of the worker's activity, the worker and supervisor make a conscious effort to discuss general patterns of performance.

At this point, greater precision in terminology might be helpful. One might reserve the use of the terms *evaluation* or *performance appraisal* for the formal, periodic event concerned with reviewing the worker's total performance. The term *assessment* might be an appropriate word for the ongoing, informal review of the limited segment of the worker's performance that is the concern of each particular conference. The formative *assessment* during each conference ultimately leads to the summative evaluation. Our concern in this chapter is with *evaluation* rather than *assessment*.

Values of Evaluation

Evaluation has value to the client, the agency, the supervisor, and, perhaps most important, to the supervisee. Thus, as codified in social work ethics (NASW 1999), evaluation is a supervisory duty (Bernard and Goodyear 1998; Borders et al. 1991; Bowers, Esmond, and Canales 1999; Bunker and Wijnberg 1988; Drake and Washeck 1998; Erera and Lazar 1994a, 1994b; Hardcastle 1991; Iberg 1991; Kadushin 1992a; Kalous 1996; Munson 1993; Rubin 1997; Savaya and Spiro 1997; Scott and Farrow 1992).

Value to the Worker

Evaluation relieves supervisees' anxiety, because it helps them know where they stand (Freeman 1993). The only thing more anxiety-provoking than evaluation is no evaluation. Supervisees are then in doubt about how adequately they are meeting agency expectations and how they compare with other workers of similar education and experience.

A period set aside for formal evaluation gives supervisees a perspective on change and achievement. Assuming that a worker has improved during the period of time covered by the evaluation, the process tends to encourage him or her and enhance a sense of accomplishment. For the worker, the evaluation is an opportunity to obtain explicit approval of his or her work from somebody who is thought to have the information, ability, and experience to make such a judgment. It provides the worker with a presumably objective, authoritative perspective on his or her abilities and deficiencies. Recapitulating the real progress in professional development made by the worker while acknowledging the existence of deficiencies, the supervisor helps the supervisee view his or her work more realistically and optimistically. This mitigates the counterproductive tendency (particularly on the part of young, conscientious workers) to deprecate their achievements.

Evaluations help motivate, direct, and integrate learning (Abbott and Lyter 1998; Latting 1991; Powell 1993a). The supervisee is stimulated to learn and change to achieve a good evaluation. A systematic review of what one has learned helps consolidate it. Having identified explicitly what he or she has learned to do, the supervisee can recognize learned behavior and more easily repeat it. Evaluation messages not only are designed to change behavior but also are important in maintaining or encouraging continuation of desirable behavior.

Evaluations help direct learning (Bernard and Goodyear 1998; Holloway 1995). The standards by which he or she is evaluated help clarify for the supervisee the specific kinds of activities on which he or she has to focus. Selection of a task for inclusion in an evaluation-assessment instrument increases the visibility and significance of that task. The workers are likely to expend more energy in learning such tasks and pay more attention to the performance of such tasks (Rapp and Poertner 1992).

Evaluation helps make learning conscious, because it requires an explicit assessment of performance. It points to how much the worker has learned, how far he or she has come. At the same time it helps clearly identify the nature of performance weakness and what needs to be learned more adequately. It makes possible further goal-directed teaching. An evaluation is concerned with an assessment in the present of work during the immediate past period for the purpose of determining future teaching and learning activity.

Evaluations help set the pattern for self-evaluation by the supervisee. Before standards of service can be internalized for self-regulation, they need to be clearly identified for the worker. Having become acquainted with performance standards and criteria as a result of evaluation conferences, the supervisee is in a better position to critique his or her own work. Evaluation increases self-awareness to further self-improvement.

Every worker has the responsibility for self-evaluation and self-regulation. The worker's continuous, critical assessment of his or her own performance is the best guarantee of effective and efficient service. But to do this analysis requires not only the will to engage in critical self-evaluation but a knowledge of the standards and criteria that distinguish good practice from poor practice, learned as a consequence of evaluation conferences.

Evaluations assist the worker in career planning. Many workers need reasoned feedback in helping them determine whether or not they have the necessary aptitude for success in social work. Marginal employees may be helped to consider alternatives as an outcome of evaluation. Others may find they have aptitudes for supervision and/or administration and can be helped by the evaluation conference to consider preparing themselves for these responsibilities.

Value to the Agency

Discharging the responsibility toward public accountability by evaluating the extent to which the agency is achieving its goals and objectives starts with an evaluation of the degree to which the individual worker's performance is meeting agency standards (Matheson, Van Dyk, and Millar 1995). Just as the agency is accountable to the community, the individual worker is accountable to the agency. Evaluation by the supervisor of the work of the supervisee is one link in the chain of accountability to the community for which the entire agency is responsible. Evaluation conferences provide the opportunity for structuring accountability.

Periodic systematic evaluation of worker performance may point to needed changes in agency administration. Careful review may show that the workers are not failing the agency but that, instead, the agency is failing them (Martin 1993; Murphy and Cleveland 1995). Evaluation leads to communication from supervisors to administrators regarding administrative procedures that are adversely affecting worker performance.

A review of a series of evaluations of a number of different workers can help in planning in-service training programs and staff development procedures. Such analysis may disclose consistent weak spots in staff performance to which agency administration needs to give attention. Evaluation helps define for the staff generally and for the individual worker in particular those aspects of professional performance that require further special attention and effort, and it points to the kinds of learning experiences that need to be provided. Evaluation further helps the agency identify special skills manifested by individual staff members who might then be assigned special tasks.

Evaluations are procedures for controlling and standardizing the behavior of the worker. The evaluation criteria make explicit and visible the kind of behavior expected, the kind of behavior that is approved, the kind of behavior that will be rewarded. As Dornbusch and Scott note, evaluation is an exercise "in the authorized use of power to control task performance by the distribution of organizational sanctions" (1975:157). Evaluations thus serve the agency purpose of administrative supervision.

If promotions, dismissals, reassignments, and merit pay increases are necessary and acceptable responsibilities of administrative supervision, then we must accept as legitimate and necessary the procedures that permit such decisions to be made on a reasonable and defensible basis. Evaluation also helps validate agency policy regarding worker selection. Through evaluation the agency can determine if its selection requirements do, in fact, tend to result in the recruitment of personnel capable of doing an effective job.

Evaluation of performance for administrative decisions becomes more important in the context of diminishing agency budgets and downsizing agency programs. If staff has to be cut, retaining the best workers depends on the accuracy and objectivity of performance evaluations.

Effective evaluation procedures can protect agencies against affirmative action challenges as well as ensure compliance with affirmative action procedures. Millar cites a series of court cases regarding personnel decisions in which the availability of valid evaluation instruments and procedures were involved in the decision (1990:68). See also Ladany et al. (1999), Guest and Dooley (1999), Murphy and Cleveland (1995), Reamer (1995), and Strom-Gottfried (1999).

Value to the Client

Social work, like other professions, claims the freedom to operate without control by outsiders. One justification frequently advanced to support the demand for autonomy is that professionals will regulate each other to prevent abuse and ensure efficient practice. The professional association code of ethics exemplifies such self-regulation by members of a profession. But the sanctions available in the professional codes of ethics are rarely applied and then only for the most egregious violations. The community, in granting a profession freedom from outside regulation, control, and interference has a right to expect some more immediate, more routinely applied measures of control. The principal benefit of evaluation for the client is that as a consequence he or she is more likely to be ensured of effective service and protected from continuation of inadequate service.

Value to the Supervisor

As a consequence of a systematic evaluation of the worker's performance, the supervisor knows what has been learned and what still needs to be taught. Evaluation provides the agenda for future educational supervision.

Explicitly evaluating the strengths and weaknesses of the individual workers in his or her unit, the supervisor is in a better position to efficiently deploy the human resources available. Assignments can be made more efficiently as a consequence of evaluation. The supervisor can make a better match between tasks that need to be completed and interests and abilities of individual workers.

Formal, explicit evaluation protects supervisors from their own biases in rewarding or sanctioning workers. The evaluation criteria and the need to justify judgments helps discipline the supervisor's thinking in assessing the worker's performance.

The evaluation report and associated documentation of the worker's performance provides protection for the supervisor in cases in which personnel decisions are contested. The requirements of the Equal Employment Commission, union contracts, and civil service regulations make supervisors vulnerable to such complaints.

The standards and criteria explicated in a good evaluation form are in effect a translation of the objectives of the agency at the administrator's level to specific tasks at the performance level. As such, it not only acts as an instrument of worker behavior control as noted above but also helps reduce role ambiguity and role conflict. Consequently, the evaluation form and process assist the supervisors in implementing the administrative functions of supervision.

Having noted the values of evaluation, we may now ask who might best be delegated the task of making evaluations. The logical response is that the person in the agency who is most directly and intimately acquainted with the details of worker's day-to-day activity would be in the best position to make a reasoned and defensible assessment of performance, that is, the worker's immediate supervisor. Consequently, it is not surprising that when any organization requires a formal, periodic evaluation of worker performance, the immediate supervisor is almost invariably given this responsibility.

Objectives of Evaluation

Having indicated the value of evaluations for the different constituencies that are directly or indirectly concerned with the process, the specific objectives of evaluation need to be noted. Evaluation has three principal objectives. One is an administratively focused objective. Evaluation provides a systematic product, a report, that management uses in making informed administrative decisions—retention, merit pay increases, promotion, suspension, reassignment, termination, and so on. A second primary objective is focused on the worker's professional growth and development. Evaluation is a teaching-learning process that identifies strengths and weaknesses in the worker's job performance to enable the worker to improve his or her performance. As a product for administrative purposes, evaluation focuses primarily on past performance. As a teaching-learning process, evaluation focuses on past performance for the purpose of improving future performance. As a product, the evaluation report is used by others to make decisions about the worker;

as a process, evaluation is used by the worker him- or herself for changing his or her way of working. Together, evaluation for administrative decision making and evaluation used by the worker to improve performance support a third, overarching objective—improving the outcomes of agency service (Daley 1992).

Both supervisor and supervisee perceive evaluations as used more frequently for administrative reasons (salary measures, retention or separation, promotion) rather than for staff development (for "making case load assignment," "differential work assignments") (Kadushin 1992a).

Dislike of Evaluations

Despite the value and necessity of evaluations, they trouble most supervisors and tend to be avoided, if not actively resisted. Performance appraisals have frequently been compared with motorcycle helmets and automobile seat belts. We agree that they are necessary, but we dislike using them.

The antipathy to performance evaluation is not peculiar to social work. The feeling is ubiquitous. An article in *Psychology Today* (September 1985) "Performance Review: The Job Nobody Likes," details the negative feeling about this task among supervisors in a wide variety of jobs.

A number of reasons explain supervisors' dislike of evaluations. Evaluation is among the supervisory procedures that most explicitly call attention to the difference in status between supervisor and supervisee. As such, it tends to increase the social distance between them. It is difficult to maintain the fiction that supervisor and supervisee are colleagues in a peer relationship when the supervisor has the responsibility and authority to evaluate the work of the supervisee. The possible reward-punishment consequences of evaluation clearly express the power of the supervisor, which may be muted and obscured on other occasions. Some supervisors feel uncomfortable with the authority inherent in their position. In many other kinds of supervisor-supervisee interactions their authority need not be explicitly employed and can be conveniently ignored; in evaluation, it is openly exercised.

Any evaluation of the worker is in effect an indirect evaluation of the supervisor. If the worker is performing inadequately, the evaluation might reveal that the supervisor has not taught the worker what he or she needs to know or has not given the worker the help he or she had the right to expect. A supervisor reports:

I felt a pressure to give her a good evaluation, and I wonder now if my desire to do this was because I felt it was therapeutic for her. It was also a kind of reward for myself for being a good therapist in helping Ms. G. become a better worker. Both of these reasons are inappropriate, but it was a kind of validation that I was a good supervisor.

Evaluation can evoke strong negative feelings. Supervisors may be anxious that evaluation will precipitate a hostile reaction from the supervisee; there is guilt at the possible consequences of a negative evaluation, consequences that have considerable significance for the job status and professional career of the worker. A supervisor says:

> If I told Mr. R. what I really think—that he's a lousy worker—he'd blow his top and I'd have psychic debris all over the office. Besides, he would challenge me on every word, and I am not so sure I could cross that *t* and dot the *I* on my judgments. So who needs all that grief? I kind of tone the evaluation down.

Whereas supervisors may feel uncomfortable and apologetic about making evaluations, supervisees are apt to be anxious and defensive. Comparative evaluation more often than not becomes a subject of agency gossip. Consequently, not only is self-esteem involved but standing and reputation in the peer group are affected by such assessments.

In addition, there are clear career-related penalties associated with a poor evaluation. The supervisor is keenly aware of the possible career consequences of evaluations for the supervisee. Many of the benefits that are possibly available as a result of very good evaluation are nondivisible—for instance, there are only so many promotion slots. Not knowing the rigor with which other supervisors are evaluating their supervisees, the supervisor is made hesitant by the realization that he or she might be placing the supervisee at a competitive disadvantage.

There is a reluctance to be appropriately critical because the criticism might be discouraging to the worker. The supervisor may hesitate to inflict pain and discomfort or may fear that the supervisee will like him or her less as a result. The supervisor's task is to be uniformly helpful stead of invariably popular, to be consistently useful and responsible rather than widely loved. Aware of this ambivalence, a supervisor notes:

> I was flattered by his evident liking and respect for me. It gave me pleasure. I was not so ready to risk this by arousing his hostility if I pressured him about some of the things he was doing poorly, which needed improvement. If I did what I thought I had to do I would be giving up, or at least risking, some of the satisfactions for me in the relationship.

To be comfortable with the threats posed by performance appraisal, the supervisor must accept the legitimacy of the evaluation process and feel entitled to make an evaluation. The supervisor has to feel confident that he or she is capable of making a valid judgment, that there is enough accurate information on which to base a valid judgment, and that the standards on which the judgment is based are clearly defined and defensible. However, many supervisors question the legitimacy of evaluation and lack a sense of entitlement. They do not think they can or should judge the work of another. Furthermore, they are oppressed by conflicting, ambiguous evidence of performance and by imprecise, vague standards available for judging performance. Consequently, they neither feel qualified to make such a judgment nor confident that they can make a valid evaluation. Such doubts may make supervisors hesitant about being critical; not being without sin, they are reluctant to cast the first stone. As one supervisor said,

> I know the agency wants us to recommend dismissal for workers who don't meet minimum requirements. But I am not so sure what these requirements are or how to measure them and how much emphasis to place on achievement versus individual progress. It's hard for me to be confident recommending dismissal for even my poorest supervisees, so I give them a passing evaluation.

A positive evaluation is an endorsement, a certification of proficiency. Hence, it involves a considerable responsibility to the general community, to the specific community of clients, to the agency, and to professional peers. Being invested with and having to carry out such a responsibility is apt to be somewhat unnerving.

The requirement for evaluation seems to contradict the ethos of social work. Our professional value orientation puts great emphasis on being nonjudgmental. Evaluations necessarily involve a judgment of performance. The admonition to be responsible, critical, frank, and direct in rigorous evaluation clashes with the professionally inculcated disposition to be accepting, compassionate, supportive, and reassuring. The conflict causes discomfort.

Most supervisors are aware of the possible loss of staff as a result of a negative evaluation. This realization suggests an additional motive for resisting evaluations. Every time a supervisee with some experience is fired or quits in response to a negative evaluation, a new, inexperienced worker has to be hired. During the period of transition, extra burdens are placed on the supervisor. The uncovered caseload has to be temporarily assigned. Prospective candidates for the position have to be interviewed and a selection made. Once a person has been hired, the supervisor again faces the tasks of introduction and orientation. The supervisor can avoid all this additional work by placating the supervisee with a laudatory (if not entirely accurate) evaluation.

On a cost-benefit analysis balance, supervisors have much to risk and little to gain by extending themselves to conscientiously undertake detailed formal evaluations. There is little overt reward. It is part of the job; there are no special compliments or fringe benefits that result. On the other hand, it is a difficult, time-consuming job requiring a lot of painful soul-searching. It involves a risk of evoking hostility, resentment, or rejection from the worker. It is understandable why evaluations are so often delayed and, when done, are done perfunctorily.

So evaluations generally tend to be avoided, but negative evaluations tend to be avoided most of all. Such evasion only compounds the supervisor's problem. Refraining from critical evaluation does the worker an injustice and promises future difficulty. Performance failures that are ignored do not disappear. The worker continues to practice mistakes and becomes more proficient in making them. With time the errors become more serious and, having been previously ignored, are more difficult to deal with. The easy avoidance of critical evaluation today comes back to haunt the supervisor tomorrow.

Hesitance to deal openly with deficiencies in performance becomes in itself an incentive to continued concealments. The supervisor is aware that if he or she raises the problem for discussion after some delay, the worker can justifiably accuse him or her of earlier dishonesty and deception.

Failure to be appropriately critical substitutes a problem of group morale for a problem of individual morale. The worker who is appraised too leniently may be happier, but his or her fellow workers will be less happy. Peers are perceptive in their evaluation of each other's competence. If a worker whom they know to be inefficient and ineffective is given a raise along with better workers because the supervisor has not been appropriately critical, they feel resentful and cynical. They become suspicious about the validity of the supervisor's evaluation of their own work. They are robbed of some of the motivation to improve their own performance because the system appears to reward good and bad work equally.

It might be reassuring for the supervisor to note that in employing sanctions in response to poor work he or she might have the support of other supervisees. Not only does the reputation of the unit suffer from the inadequate performance but other workers may have to pick up the slack that results from the sanctioned worker's failure to do his or her job.

It may further reassure supervisors to note that most social work supervisees recognize and accept the fact that the agency, as their employer, has a right to evaluate the work they are doing. They face this challenge along with millions of other employed workers. In fact, several studies have found that supervisees expressed strong dissatisfaction with the fact that supervisors were not sufficiently and specifically critical of their work. Anxious to do a better job, supervisees looked to their supervisor for help in identifying deficiencies in their work that needed correcting. They were disappointed when they failed to receive such critical analysis (Kadushin 1974, 1992a). When supervisees raise objections to evaluation, the reason is not the legitimacy of agency entitlement to evaluate their work but rather the fact that evaluations are often inequitable, arbitrary, and unhelpful.

Despite dislike of and resistance to evaluations, supervisors are likely to resist giving them up. They are the most definite expression of supervisory power and a potent instrument for control.

Desirable Evaluation Procedures

Despite the clearly identifiable reasons that feed supervisory antipathy toward evaluation, performance appraisals are both necessary and inevitable. What approaches are most likely to contribute to a productive evaluation?

1. Osborn and Davis (1996) contend that supervisors have a duty to evaluate their supervisees, and point to the failure to provide timely and relevant feedback as the root of most ethical complaints about the supervisory role: "Supervisees should be told the *amount*, *type* (formal or informal, written or verbal), *timing*, and *frequency* of evaluation procedures to be used. An explanation of how such information will be recorded by the supervisor (e.g., specific evaluation form, narrative, etc.), how it will be *used*, and with whom it will be *shared*, addressing the limits of *confidentiality* in supervision" (Osborn and Davis 1996:129; emphasis in original)—to prevent misunderstanding.

Supervisees may be less anxious if they know in advance when evaluations are to be scheduled, what information and standards are to be used as a basis for evaluation, what they might be expected to contribute to the evaluation, with whom the evaluation will be shared, and what use will be made of the evaluation. Of even greater importance, supervisees will be in a better position to prepare for the evaluation over a period of time and to participate more productively in the process.

2. Effective performance appraisal takes commitment and time. However, some evidence suggests that social work supervisors place a relatively low priority on evaluating supervisees (Menefee and Thompson 1994; Patti 1977), as do their managerial counterparts elsewhere (Napier and Latham 1986). Moreover, supervisors spend little time on the process—commonly

between three and seven hours per employee each year and often less than one hour per appraisal (Bretz, Milkovich, and Read 1992).

3. Evaluation should be a continuous process of systematic observation and assessment, rather than an occasional event, because the accuracy of ratings tends to increase with the amount of time supervisors spend observing supervisees (Favaro and Ilgen 1989). Research suggests that "careful attention needs to be paid to ensuring the systematic sampling of information," because supervisors "use cues from knowledge about the [supervisees] themselves, the jobs, the uses to which ratings will be placed, and other factors to form impressions of [supervisees], and these impressions influence the information to which [supervisors] attend" (Ilgen, Barnes-Farrell, and McKellin 1993:358).

4. In the service of accuracy, the supervisor might do well to maintain ongoing observational records or diaries of supervisee performance (DeNisi and Peters 1996; Bernardin and Walters 1997), The procedure might take the form of recording a brief summary note following each scheduled supervisory meeting. Otherwise, the supervisor may base annual performance appraisals on general impressions instead of specific past performance, reducing the accuracy of ratings with the passage of time (Ilgen, Barnes-Farrell, and McKellin 1993). The annual performance appraisal should be a summation of the small assessments that take place as part of each supervisory conference.

5. Regularly devoting some part of each conference to assessment, however brief, helps desensitize the worker's anxiety regarding it. This practice also helps prepare him or her for what is likely to be shared at the formal conference so that it does not come as an unexpected, disconcerting surprise. As one worker complained, "The supervisor never mentioned my overidentification with Jane [a girl on probation] until the evaluation conference. If I had been aware of it sooner I certainly could have made some effort to control overidentification in my contacts." The formal, periodic evaluation is a summary recapitulation of familiar, previously encountered assessments rather than an unexpected, unanticipated critique for which the worker is unprepared.

6. The evaluation should be conducted and communicated in the context of a positive relationship. The positive relationship acts as an anodyne to the pain of criticism (however warranted) and makes the worker more receptive to and accepting of the criticism as a basis for constructive change. If the supervisor and supervisee dislike each other, the supervisee is predisposed to reject the criticism as invalid and unfair. All criticism of performance should be offered out of a sincere desire to help, not out of pleasure and satisfaction in criticizing. The supervisor needs to be sensitive to the worker's reaction,

to manifestations of anxiety and resistance (Abbott and Lyter 1998). These feelings can then be discussed openly, and appropriate reassurance and support can be offered. The most important aspect of evaluation is the attitude with which the process is conducted. As one worker says about critical feedback from her supervisor, "Knowing that his feedback is not malicious but rather purposeful and beneficial helps me to accept feedback that I really would rather not hear."

A formal evaluation generates anxiety because it is a threat to narcissism and self-esteem. There is a fear of failure and rejection. It raises such questions as, "Will I be able to measure up to expectations?" "Will I be able to maintain the good opinion of me held by people I like and respect?" "How do I compare with my peers?" "What effect will this have on my professional future?" Evaluations become part of our official records. There is much at stake. A good supervisory relationship helps support the worker through this anxiety-inducing procedure. To the extent possible, the evaluations should be nonthreatening, protect the dignity and self-esteem of the supervisee, and suggest confidence in the supervisee's ability to do acceptable work.

Some social scientists believe that good supervisory relationships bias ratings of supervisory performance. Apparently, such fears have been based on the correlation between ratings of the supervisory relationship and ratings of supervisory performance in organizational research. When Lazar and Mosek (1993) found that supervisory relationships were better predictors of performance ratings than putative measures of supervisee ability, for example, this was construed as evidence that supervisory relationships interfered with supervisory evaluations.

The alternative explanation is that supervisors form more positive relationships with better performers. This conventional wisdom is consistent with findings from empirical research (Cardy and Dobbins 1986; Ferris et al. 1994; Robbins and DeNisi 1994; Varma, DeNisi, and Peters 1996) and the most recent reviews of the empirical literature (Bretz, Milkovich, and Read 1992; Ilgen, Barnes-Farrell, and McKellin 1993; Cardy and Dobbins 1994; Arvey and Murphy 1998).

7. The evaluation procedure should be a mutual, shared process. The supervisor should attempt to maximize the worker's participation in and contribution to the evaluation. Although self-appraisals tend to suffer from "positive leniency bias" (Ilgen, Barnes-Farrell, and McKellin 1993:354), the worker could be asked to write a self-evaluation or to write a critique of the supervisor's evaluation. The worker's reaction to the evaluation should be solicited. Mutuality implies not only encouraging the worker's participation but also active use of those contributions that are valid and applicable in the final evaluation write-up. Evaluation is done *with* the worker, not *to* the

worker. Mutual participation in the evaluation process increases the probability of a more valid evaluation and of its acceptance and use by the supervisee.

The good evaluation interview encourages open communication. The supervisee is encouraged to suggest changes in his or her performance, encouraged to formulate attainable change goals, and given the opportunity of explaining failings. The good evaluation acknowledges the possibility of different points of view regarding performance.

Participation lessens anxiety. Having been invited to participate, the worker retrieves a measure of control of the proceedings. Sharing in control and being able to determine content, direction, and emphasis (in some measure) in the evaluation conference, the supervisee tends to feel less anxiously helpless. Participation also tends to reduce the discomforting imbalance in power between supervisor and supervisee. Power is manifested in the ability to control. In encouraging the supervisee's active participation in the evaluation process, the supervisor is sharing control.

8. Evaluations should be made with some recognition and consideration of reality factors that might be determinants of the worker's performance. The supervisor needs to assess whether or not the worker's caseload was atypically heavy or included more than the usual number of especially difficult cases. Was this a period when the turnover in personnel was higher than normal, or when things at the agency were unusually hectic? Allowances need to be made for situational aspects of the job—lack of office space, lack of clerical help, unavailability of essential support services, or periods of low morale that adversely affect workers' performance. The worker who has a routine caseload of minimum complexity, imposing few unusual decision-making responsibilities, is in a different position from the worker with a caseload of clients who frequently present unique and complex problems.

9. The principal (if not exclusive) focus of evaluation should be the work performance of the supervisee rather than any evaluation of the worker as a person. The only social role of concern to evaluation is that of the supervisee as an employee of a social agency and, specifically, as the person assigned to do a particular job in that agency. None of the other aspects of the worker's life are legitimate areas for review. This concept was stressed by the Family Service Association of America in defining evaluation as "an accurate appraisal of the performance of the incumbent [of the position] in relation to specific duties assigned" (1957:53).

10. The evaluation should review both strengths and weaknesses, growth and stagnation, and should be fair and balanced. Isolated, atypical examples of the worker's performance should not be used to make a general case for failure. Rather, recurrent patterns of behavior in job performance are the

legitimate bases for evaluation statements. Nor should the supervisor's personal standards be substituted for agency standards as a basis for evaluation.

Fair evaluation focuses on behavior because "behavior provides structure and articulation for objectives and judgments that might otherwise be vague and excessively open to interpretation" (Goldhammer 1969:326). The total configuration of the worker's performance needs to be considered. Recent incidents may overinfluence the evaluation because of their very recency and dramatic incidents because of their vividness. Furthermore, if behavior patterns are cited as factors in the evaluation, there should be some reason to believe that the worker's behavior had some significant positive or adverse effect on the client.

11. A good evaluation should be specific and individualized. As one worker said in complaining of her evaluation conference, "The supervisor was satisfactory but what was satisfactory about it or why it was satisfactory she didn't say, so I don't know." General statements that apply to most supervisees—such as, "He is a conscientious worker who displays warmth in his interaction with people"—can be used interchangeably in evaluating most supervisees.

12. The evaluation should suggest tentativeness rather than finality and should focus on modifiable aspects of the worker's performance: this is the way the worker performs at this particular time; the expectation is that he or she will develop and improve. The good worker can become a better worker, and the poor worker a good worker. The spirit of the evaluation should communicate the idea that success is not final and failure is not fatal. After all, the evaluation is not an unchangeable verdict but an incentive for change.

In achieving comprehensiveness, an evaluation should look to the future as well as the past. The worker's performance speaks to what he or she has already done. Focusing on capacities and potentialities says something about what he or she might be able to do in the future.

13. Evaluations should be formulated with some consistency. Both intra- and intersupervisor consistency is desirable. The supervisor needs to apply the same standards in the same way to all of his or her supervisees who have approximately the same education and experience. Likewise, different supervisors responsible for different units of workers with similar backgrounds need to act similarly in evaluating their respective supervisees. It is difficult to think of any other factor so detrimental to morale as differences in evaluation procedures applied to a homogenous group of supervisees.

By the same token, evaluation should distinguish heterogeneous performance. Although many appraisal systems use five levels to evaluate employees, in general only three levels are used, with the top levels relatively "full" and the bottom levels relatively "empty" . . . "Labeling someone as satisfactory rather than above average or outstanding reduces commitment and satisfaction with the appraisal system" (Bretz, Milkovich, and Read 1992:329), but morale suffers when different levels of performance earn equal rewards.

14. It is desirable for the supervisor to indicate a willingness to accept evaluation of his or own performance from the supervisee. If the process of evaluation is helpful in the development of the supervisee, it can likewise contribute to the supervisor's professional development.

The supervisee will be more accepting of evaluation and less likely to see it as a manifestation of capricious authority if he or she has the opportunity, in turn, to evaluate the supervisor. Certainly, as a recipient of supervision, as the consumer of the product, the worker is in a position to assess the supervisor's performance. In academia, teaching faculty currently are more frequently open to student evaluation; it is difficult to defend supervisor immunity from supervisee evaluation. Two-way evaluations exemplify agency orientation toward evaluation. Evaluation of the worker's performance should be only one manifestation of the overall evaluation of personnel at all levels as part of a periodic review of the agency's total program.

15. Involvement of staff in establishing evaluation criteria is likely to ensure the selection of more relevant criteria, to intensify commitment to the evaluation process, and to clarify expectations with regard to evaluation (Millar 1990). Workers who have helped develop standards to which they will ultimately be held accountable will feel a greater obligation and responsibility to see that the evaluation process achieves its objectives. Research indicates that ability to have significant input in determining evaluation criteria and procedures is clearly related to satisfaction with evaluation (Dornbusch and Scott 1975:186–87). See Rapp and Poertner (1992) for systematic methods of describing desirable standards of practice behavior.

An acceptable evaluation process requires sound consensus between supervisor and supervisee about the objectives of the organization and the priorities among objectives. If the supervisor gives high priority to efficiency and the supervisee gives priority to client service, the two will evaluate the worker's behavior differently.

16. Because the worker does his or her work in an organizational context that might impede as well as facilitate satisfactory performance, some effort should be made to explicitly identify organizational difficulties over the evaluation period. One should ask whether there has been a change in administration, a reorganization of the agency, a temporary shortage of staff due to high turnover rates, new legislation directly affecting agency operations, and so on. Due allowance should be given these destabilizing considerations

in making the evaluation. In performance evaluation and feedback, context is important (Talen and Schindler 1993).

17. An effective evaluation procedure is integrated with other aspects of the organization. Administration should support performance appraisal, periodically review and revise the appraisal procedures, provide training for supervisors in the use of appraisal forms, and organize its reward and punishment system so that they support evaluation decisions.

Evaluation Conference: Process

Scheduling the Conference

The worker should be informed at least a week in advance about the specific date and time of the evaluation conference. In some agencies, evaluations are scheduled at regular intervals—every half-year or every year. In other agencies, evaluations are tied to transition points in the supervisee's professional career, for example, at the end of the probationary period, the hiring anniversary, when the worker's assignment is changed, when there is a change of supervisors, when the worker is leaving the agency, or when a merit increase is due.

Supervisor's Conference Preparation

The supervisor prepares by reading a sampling of the worker's recordings, reports, and special project write-ups; by reviewing the statistical material, time sheets, and supervisor's notes or logs covering the period of performance to be evaluated; and by reviewing previous examinations.

In a more general fashion the supervisor's preparation should be a continuous process. Utilizing all sources of information, the supervisor should make notes of ongoing activity that illustrates the worker's typical performance. He or she should be constantly alert for critical incidents that relate performance to agency standards. A thorough knowledge of the details of the worker's performance is one of the most effective antidotes to supervisory anxiety about making evaluations. Criticism can be shared with less anxiety if there is a feeling of certainty that it is warranted and if the criticism can be adequately documented.

Because the total caseload cannot be reviewed in equal detail, preparation involves selecting typical representative examples of the worker's performance for illustrative reference during the conference. This includes selection of good work showing specific skills, examples of poor performance illustrating the need for skills requiring additional work, and case examples indicating the worker's professional growth.

The supervisor further prepares by introspectively examining his or her attitudes toward and feelings about the supervisee that might contaminate an objective appraisal of performance. The supervisor needs to be aware of his or her own mood, which might make him or her expansive or narrowly focused; such feelings as hostility toward the supervisee, which might make the supervisor punitive in evaluation; a desire to control, which might make him or her manipulative; or a tendency to identify with and defend the supervisee, which might make him or her overprotective. The supervisor has an investment in the professional progress of the supervisees; eager for their success, which is the supervisor's success once removed, he or she may be reluctant to perceive a worker's failings.

The supervisor should also prepare for the conference by reviewing some of the classic and persistent pitfalls in evaluating to recognize and avoid them (Murphy and Cleveland 1995).

Worker's Conference Preparation

Workers should also prepare for the conference by reviewing the agency evaluation outline or evaluation rating form that has been shared with them. They might follow the outline in thinking about and making notes for self-evaluations. In addition, they might be asked to consider the way their performance six months or a year ago compares with their performance now, what they think they have accomplished over the period to be covered by the evaluation, where they think they need more help, and the kinds of professional experiences they missed and would like to have.

Despite the desirability of familiarizing the supervisee with the criteria of evaluation, a large percentage of supervisees responding to a national study reported that they were not given a formal statement that informed them of these criteria. Only about one in three supervisees was asked to formulate his or her own evaluation statement in preparation for the evaluation conference (Kadushin 1992a).

Evaluation Conference Interaction

At the beginning of the evaluation interview, it may be useful to deal explicitly with worker anxiety, review the procedure, and briefly recapitulate what will be covered. If made at all, these comments should be very brief; the worker is primarily concerned about the evaluation itself. Another tactic in opening the evaluation conference is suggested by a supervisor who said, "I asked the supervisee to check her caseload with me for the period to be sure nothing had been omitted. I find this is a good comfortable way for both supervisor and supervisee to get into the evaluation conference, and it sets the tone for the supervisee as an active participant."

It is suggested that the interview start with positives, move on to problems and deficiencies, and end with reviews of positive performance. This has been termed the sandwich approach—a slice of negatives between two positives.

Because the supervisee is probably anxious to hear what the supervisor has to say, this is one conference in which the supervisor should take the initiative. The supervisor should open the main body of the conference-interview by presenting clearly, simply, and unambiguously a general evaluation of the worker's performance as he or she sees it. Evaluation provides explicit formal feedback. Its effectiveness is intensified if it is specific, if it can be communicated so that it is appropriate to the needs of the worker, if it is clear and accurate.

The formal evaluation is the opportune time for plain, direct statements adequately supported by specific citations from job performance. Workers may feel puzzled by ambiguous evaluation statements, perhaps saying such things as "I guess I am doing all right because she didn't say I wasn't" or "She talked a lot about my mature approach to people, but I don't know exactly what she meant." Supervisees are interested in an honest evaluation of their performance. In expressing dissatisfaction with evaluations that failed to provide specific feedback in a supportive manner, a supervisee says:

> My evaluations were short, not in depth, and limited to general, positive feedback. Little criticism of my work was included. Overall my evaluations were positive but dissatisfying to me because they felt empty, as I really wanted to spend some time on areas on which I needed improvement.

Because a principal responsibility of the supervisor in this conference is to provide explicit, honest feedback in a supportive manner, the principles of effective feedback are applicable here.

The main body of the conference is a discussion of the worker's performance, using criteria such as those described in a later section of this chapter. If both supervisor and supervisee thoughtfully prepare for the evaluation, there may be much agreement to begin with. The following is an excerpt from a self-evaluation review by a supervisee and an excerpt, related to the same problem, from her supervisor's preliminary evaluation note.

Supervisee self-evaluation

With both Jane [an unmarried mother] and the Allens [a foster family] I continued to demonstrate what appears to me to be excess zeal. Jane was more capable of handling her problems than I gave her credit for and did not need as much help as I was ready and anxious to offer her. She was capable of applying for TANF [Temporary Assistance for Needy Families] without my intervention. The Allens too had enough skill and practice as parents to do an adequate job of making Paul [the foster child] comfortable with the transition to their home without all my hovering over them. In these, and in several other instances, I tend to be the all-loving, overprotective, anxious mother figure.

Supervisor's preliminary evaluation

Miss M [the supervisee] frequently manifests a need to be helpful, to encourage the dependency of clients, to solicit client approbation and appreciation by doing for them what they can, perhaps, do as well for themselves. The general attitude of concerned helpfulness which Miss M manifests is a desirable attitude for which the worker should be commended. However, Miss M's current indiscriminate helpful behavior needs to be exercised with more self-control and self-discipline. Miss M needs to learn to offer her help more discriminatingly in situations where it is appropriately required. In such situations and under such circumstances her help is likely to be more truly helpful. Perhaps we can, in future supervisory conferences, center on the criteria that will enable Miss M to distinguish when a client is truly objectively dependent on her for her intervention and when the client can do for himself.

The conference concludes, as does any good interview, with a summary of the main points covered. The implications of the conclusions for immediate future conferences are explicated and outlined. There is a clear statement of where to go from here. Attention is paid to the supervisee's emotional responses to the evaluation at the end of the conference, and an effort is made to resolve (or at least mitigate) the most disturbing feelings.

Having explicitly identified some aspect of the worker's performance needing improvement, the supervisor and supervisee might give some consideration in terminating the conference to a plan of action for change. Both participants should agree on a specific period of time during which the objective for change will be accomplished. Some evaluation forms even have an entry delineating a development plan, listing specific plans for improvements, objectives to be achieved, and schedules for development to be undertaken.

Even after the conference has ended, the evaluation process continues. Each evaluation is directed toward the ultimate achievement of a reduction of the frequency of evaluations, when the worker is truly self-directed and capable of valid self-evaluation. At that point in his or her professional development, an objective, critical outside review of his or her work can still be helpful, but the agency has sufficient confidence in the worker so that less frequent evaluations are administratively required.

Communication and Use of Evaluations

The supervisee is not in a position to accept or reject the evaluation, as would be true if the relationship were consultative. The agency cannot grant the supervisee this option if it is responsibly to meet its obligation to the community and the clients. Assuming the evaluation is valid, the supervisee is given the option of modifying his or her behavior so that it meets the standards of performance required by the agency.

The supervisor, in preparing an evaluation, needs to have confidence that recommendations for administrative action, which follow from the evaluation, will be supported by the administration. However, the ultimate responsibility for implementing the consequences of the evaluation rests with administration. This practice protects the supervisee from possible arbitrary evaluations and accompanying negative recommendations. Thus, if the supervisor needs the confidence that administration will generally accept his or her evaluative recommendations, he or she also needs to be aware that good administration will make a considered rather than an automatic decision to support such recommendations.

Once the evaluation has been formulated, it should be written out and the worker should have an opportunity to read it and keep a copy. NASW *Standards for Social Work Personnel Practices*, as revised in 1990, require a written statement by the agency "of standards of performance" as the basis for evaluation. Furthermore, "the evaluation shall be in writing . . . and the employee shall be given the opportunity to read it, to sign it (signifying he had read it) and to file a statement covering any points with which he disagrees. A copy of the evaluation shall be furnished the employee." The statement notes that "the authority of the evaluator must be recognized on both sides and final authority belongs to him" (NASW 1971:19).

In a written evaluation, the supervisor can be deliberate and precise. He or she can review it carefully and reconsider it at leisure for possible changes in content, emphasis, and balance. None of this is possible in the heat and stress of an oral evaluation, when a word uttered is beyond recall or change. Because they are a matter of record, written reports have the advantage of being available for use by those who might supervise the worker in the future.

Several arguments can be made in support of having the worker read the evaluation. Oral evaluation is open to misinterpretation and is the source of considerable fantasy or confusion about what the supervisor actually said. A written evaluation is definite and available for rereading and rechecking. Though still open to some misinterpretation, it is not as readily distorted as an oral evaluation. The worker may easily fail to hear what he or she does not want to hear or suppress what he or she has heard but is reluctant to remember. It is possible (but more difficult) to engage in such defensive maneuvers with a written document. The evaluation conference is often a stressful experience during which the supervisee finds it difficult to absorb what is being said. The opportunity to read the material improves the chances for distortion-free communication.

Being permitted to read the evaluation reduces any anxiety the worker may feel about whether the verbal evaluation is the same as the written evaluation actually filed with administration. The fact that the evaluation will be read acts as a constraint on the supervisor. It is likely to intensify the care with which the statement is prepared and increases the probability that the evaluation will be more objective and accurate.

The context provided for reading the evaluation is important. The worker should have the opportunity to read the evaluation in the presence of the supervisor. If the supervisee has questions or objections regarding content or desires clarification of ambiguously phrased material, it can be handled immediately. If the evaluation is negative, the presence of the supervisor is an immediately available source of reassurance and support.

If objections are raised that the supervisor accepts as valid, the evaluation statement is amended accordingly. If objections are raised that are not agreed to by the supervisor, the supervisee should have the right to ask that a statement of his or her reservations be included in the file in his or her own name. Evaluation forms often include provision for supervisor signature, supervisee signature, and signature of agency administrator. Alongside the supervisee's signature the forms might include a proviso, such as the following: "The contents of this evaluation have been shared with me. My signature does not necessarily mean agreement."

Some supervisors claim, with a certain amount of justification, that a careful safeguarding of the supervisee's right to read the evaluation will result in less useful and perhaps less valid evaluations. Torn between doing justice to agency administration and agency clients and protecting themselves from enervating argumentation, supervisors may choose to write bland, noncommittal, generally favorable evaluations, saying little to give offense but also saying little that is significant. Hunches, intuitions, sharp guesses that supervisors feel are true but that they cannot actually substantiate by citing the specific supporting evidence will tend to be excluded.

The agency should make available procedures for appealing an evaluation that the supervise thinks is unfair. The supervisor needs to support access to such procedures without any suggestion of retaliation. It is not the use of such procedures that is important to most workers but the knowledge that the option is freely available and accessible.

In summary, both supervisor and supervisee should prepare for the conference by reviewing their notes and tentatively formulating an evaluation. After they have discussed their respective perceptions of the worker's performance in the evaluation conference, the supervisor writes a formal evaluation statement. This is given to the worker for reaction and comment.

The discussed presentation indicates desirable social work evaluation procedures. We know little of how such evaluation conferences are actually conducted. Nichols and Cheers (1980) analyzed the recordings of twenty-three evaluation conferences. Although these were between supervisors and social work students, they may be instructive for what they can tell us about the conduct of practice evaluation conferences. In 30 percent of the cases no evaluative comments were made. With regard to about a third of the evaluative comments made, "little or no evidence was presented to support the evaluative comment. When evidence was produced, it was primarily a descriptive statement rather than a specific example" (Nichols and Cheers 1980:63–64). In 87 percent of the cases, the supervisor introduced the topics that were discussed.

A study of evaluation of workers in protective services concluded that

> where assessment skills of workers' performance has been rigorously examined, it appears that supervisors tend to make global assessments of workers' performance and fail to make discriminating ratings of different performance criteria. It was further noted that personal characteristics of the supervisors influenced their ratings. Supervisors, in general, were not prepared to carry out accurate and detailed performance assessment of supervisees' work. (Thomas and LaCavera 1979:4)

Errors in Evaluation

In making an appraisal of worker performance, supervisors are apt to make some human errors in information processing and judgment. Although there may be some question about the frequency and significance of such errors (Arvey and Murphy 1998:163; see also Ilgen, Barnes-Farrell, and McKellin 1993 for reviews of the literature), making them explicit gives them visibility that might help minimize bias and maximize fairness in performance appraisal.

1. The halo effect derives from the perception of one aspect of the worker's performance as outstanding. The very favorable impression result-

ing from this aspect then radiates to all other aspects of the worker's performance. Judgment in all aspects of performance is biased by the impression generated by a single aspect.

A dubious supposition of performance consistency supports the halo effect. The supposition is that the worker's performance is all of one piece. If he or she is good in this aspect, he or she is likely (if he or she is consistent) to be good in all aspects.

Halo effects operate in a negative as well as in a positive direction. Perception of a worker's total performance may be biased by deficiency in one aspect of his or her work.

The term *halo effect* is also used when the judgment of specific aspects of performance is biased by a global judgment of performance—the tendency is to make a global judgment and rate specific aspects of performance in a way that is consistent with the global judgment.

Green notes that research on supervisory evaluations tends to indicate that an evaluation "begins with a field instructor's assessment of a student's *overall* performance, which then determines whether he or she will not find any specific qualities that are being sought" (1972:53). This is the halo effect in operation.

Strong first impressions feed into the halo effect. Self-fulfilling prophecies involve the persistence of first impressions. In response to strong positive first impressions, the supervisor might tend to selectively perceive only the positive aspects of performance in confirmation of first impressions.

However, whether halo effects actually lead to inaccurate performance appraisals has been disputed. In general, the empirical evidence suggests that the correlation between discrete rating errors (due to halo effects) and the overall accuracy of performance appraisals is near zero (Murphy and Baltzer 1989). See Bretz, Milkovich, and Read (1992) for a review of the literature.

2. Leniency bias reflects a hesitancy to evaluate negative performance fairly and honestly. The evaluation is more positive than warranted by the actual performance. The result is that all ratings are skewed toward the positive end. There is little differentiation in the evaluation and the utility of the evaluation for administration is reduced.

Apparently common in practice, leniency bias may do the supervisee and his or her clients a disservice. It is falsely reassuring, encourages unrealistic confidence, and avoids coming to grips with performance deficiencies that require attention.

A leniency bias damages the morale of the best workers. If everybody gets a very good evaluation, questions are raised about the validity and fairness of the evaluation process. Objectively better workers wonder if extending themselves is really worth the effort, as superior performance is not differentially rewarded.

There is pressure toward leniency that derives from the perception that most supervisees have of their work. Most people believe they are above-average performers. Studies of evaluation talk of the "80/30 dilemma"—the fact that 80 percent of workers believe they are among the top 30 percent of performers.

Brandon and Davies note, in studying the process of evaluating marginal graduate social work students, that workers are evaluated as acceptable "if there is no evidence of incompetence." This is different from an orientation that requires "positive evidence of good practice" (1979:315). Leniency bias is reflected in the general conclusion of the study: that, in the program of professional education for social work, "people pass who do not fail."

Brandon and Davies's comments are supported by Brennan's findings that of a "combined total of 463 grades awarded first and second year graduate students in field instruction courses in a school of social work during the 1976–77 academic year, less than 1 percent of such grades were C or below" (Brennan 1982:77).

3. Central tendency error refers to the tendency when in doubt to rate all work as average. As a consequence, all evaluations are bunched together at the center of the distribution. An average rating may, in fact, reflect true performance. Central tendency error is only an error if it is made because an evaluation has to be given and the supervisor does not know enough about the worker's performance to make a defensible judgment. Average ratings are easy to justify, are rarely controversial, and meet the demands of the evaluation procedure. All in all, it is an easy way out and follows the line of least resistance.

4. Recency errors and errors of overweighting may also bias evaluations. Evaluations cover some definite time period, and the supervisor needs to make the evaluation in terms of performance over that time period. Otherwise, there is the tendency to be unduly influenced by recent performance. This is similar to the error of being unduly influenced by dramatic events, which tend to have disproportionate visibility. Both recency and drama distort perspective on total performance over the period to which the evaluation speaks. Evaluation should be based on patterned, typical performance.

5. Contrast errors are of two kinds. One is related to the field, the context in which the evaluation is embedded. If most of the supervisees in a unit are relatively poor performers, an average performer looks much better by virtue of the contrast. Rather than being evaluated in terms of performance based on some objective standard, the evaluation is based on the supervisee's performance as it compares with a poorly performing group.

The other contrast error is the result of comparing the supervisee's performance with that of the supervisor's assessment of how he or she might have performed in similar circumstances. Here the supervisor uses him- or herself as the standard against which the supervisee is contrasted. This is an idiosyncratic standard against which the worker is evaluated. Using our own performance as a standard against which we judge tends to make the worker who is similar to us look good.

6. Negativity effects may also cause problems. In evaluating, one has to be aware of the potency of what has been called the negativity effect. When presented with both positive and negative information about a supervisee, the negative information seems generally to be given greater weight in forming an overall impression. Because we expect supervisees to act in a positive manner, negative actions have greater visibility. When given equal amounts of positive and negative information about a supervisee, the evaluation will then tend to be negative.

Evaluation bias that is explicit, foreknowing, and deliberate refers to prejudicial evaluations in response to a personal bias against a worker or in response to a preferential relationship with a worker. However, much evaluation bias is unknowing and undeliberate. It is a consequence of skewed procedures in completing evaluation forms. These include halo effects, leniency errors, recency effects, central tendency effects, and contrast errors. In addition to these obstacles to a truly objective evaluation, one might note observational biases resulting from the ideological beliefs and personal values of the supervisor that color perception of the supervisee's performance. These, once again, are not deliberate biases, as the supervisor is often not explicitly aware of their influence on evaluation.

Evaluation Outlines and Rating Forms

Many of the suggestions to make the evaluation process more accurate, positive, and productive depend on the availability of an evaluation outline or guide for their effective implementation. An evaluation outline ensures more precise definition and specification of the criteria for evaluation. It also suggests the explicit kinds of information that need to be obtained for evaluation and ensures a greater likelihood that uniform standards will be followed by different supervisors and by the same supervisor with different supervisees. An outline tends to depersonalize the evaluation for the supervisee because the outline is an all-agency guide and reduces a supervisor's guilt and anxiety as he or she employs agency-sponsored standards and is protected from his or her own subjectivity. It also increases the certainty of covering the same points in successive evaluations. Finally, it simplifies sharing in advance with the supervisee the areas of performance to be covered by an evaluation.

It is generally agreed that a good performance evaluation instrument is (1) valid; (2) relevant—it actually evaluates what it is supposed to evaluate, and what it evaluates is relevant to the job; (3) reliable—it provides consistent evaluations across workers and time; (4) discriminating—it provides the possibility of clearly differentiating levels of performance; (5) free from bias—it maximizes objectivity and reduces opportunities for subjectivity; and (6) practical and relatively easy to use.

The availability of an evaluation outline related specifically to the job responsibilities of a specific group of workers in a particular agency ensures that the process of assessment will be directed to the worker's performance on the job, a job for which the duties have been clearly defined. The evaluation outline further serves as a convenient interview guide for evaluation conference discussion.

Evaluation outlines in any social work agency reflect basic social work skills, methods, and general objectives—the enhancement, support, or restoration of psychosocial functioning. Hence, it is to be expected that evaluation outlines have some general similarities. However, because each agency has a particular responsibility, a particular problem area, and operates in a particular community, with staff of some particular composition, each agency has to adapt and modify a generally applicable outline to make it optimally appropriate to its own situation. One agency may be concerned with use of community resources, another with the development of those resources. Workers in one agency may be involved in considerable collaborative effort with other professional workers; in another agency, they may have minimal working contact with other professionals. These factors alter the kinds of competencies that need to be evaluated.

Any evaluation necessarily starts with a statement of objectives and a description of the job the worker is being asked to perform. It is axiomatic that we cannot tell how well we are doing unless we know what we are trying to do. The process of evaluation involves the explication of worker tasks; the clear, concise, and meaningful definition of criteria by which we can measure the extent to which the tasks have been achieved; and the actual measurement of worker performance in terms of the criteria that reflect the task objectives. A criterion is a standard against which a comparison can be made.

Criteria are the specific aspects of the worker's performance that are given consideration in forming a judgment. Criteria should represent important, significant aspects of the worker's performance. In aggregate, criteria should cover the total job description. They need to be well defined and formulated so that they are measurable in objective terms.

A central problem for social work evaluations is the ambiguity relating to the definition of effective social performance, the competence required to achieve effective performance, and the outcomes desired from effective performance. Each of the key terms—*effective performance, competence required,* and *desirable outcomes*—is a controversial matter. Definitions for each of these terms are the sine qua non for a defensible evaluation.

Another difficult problem faced by the social work profession and shared with other human-service professions is establishing standards of productivity in the absence of a standard product. The target outcome of social work intervention is the more effective psychosocial functioning of the client—individual, family, group, or community. Perhaps the most readily accessible criterion for evaluating the productivity of the worker is how many—the number of clients who have been helped, as a consequence of the worker's activity, to achieve more effective psychosocial functioning over a given period of time. Alternatively, measures of how much clients or caseloads change are helping criterion that speak directly to agency goals and the social work mission. Any review of the literature concerned with evaluating the outcome of social work service will testify to the problems of definition, measurement, and data procurement that are encountered in applying such criteria in evaluating the worker's performance (Bannerjee 1995; Boettcher 1998; Harkness and Hensley 1991; Martin 1993; Savaya and Spiro 1997).

Unfortunately, attempts to evaluate worker performance on the basis of client outcomes by inducing workers to obtain such information has proved to be very difficult. Reviewing the relevant literature, Mutschler and Jayaratne found that "the research suggests that very few practitioners. . . . engage in the implementation of Single System Designs. . . ." (1993:124)—a much lauded procedure for obtaining outcome information. Savaya and Spiro (1997) made a determined but ultimately unsuccessful effort to obtain such information through the use of a validated clinical rating scale. Consequently, it is not surprising to note that "very little empirical research has been done on supervision from the perspective of outcomes" (Vonk and Thyer 1997:105).

In recognition of the difficulties of evaluating worker performance in terms of outcome, the content of evaluation in virtually all agencies has been generally concerned with second-order criteria, which are easier to apply. The use of such criteria is based on the supposition that if the worker possesses relevant knowledge, displays professionally approved behavior, manifests the proper attitudes, and follows professionally prescribed procedures, then clients will be helped. Consequently, the evaluation is focused on relevant knowledge, approved behavior, proper attitudes, and prescribed procedures rather than on the frequency, consistency, and quality of client change, as such, attributable to worker intervention.

Evaluation on the basis of process and procedure rather than outcome is defensible because so many factors that determine outcome are beyond the control of the worker. One might often legitimately claim that the operation was a success even if the patient died.

Despite the necessary emphasis on process, outcome data when available should be included as a consideration in evaluation. Such material helps increase the service-relevance of evaluative judgments (Bannerjee 1995; Rapp and Poertner 1992). For this reason, schools of social work have begun training students to evaluate the client outcomes of their practice and programs. On this basis, the worker's performance can be evaluated in terms of the degree to which specific, measurable objectives—in particular, client successes—have been achieved.

Evaluation Content Areas

Evaluations include cognitive criteria, such as values and ethics, understanding and knowledge, and self-awareness; affective criteria, such as interpersonal attitudes, feelings, and relationships; and performance criteria, such as skills in interviewing, assessment, and skills relative to the problem-solving social work process.

An overview of the principal content areas usually included in reasonably comprehensive evaluation outlines follows.

I. Ability to establish and maintain meaningful, effective, appropriately professional relationships with client system.
   A. Attitudes as manifested in appropriate worker behavior toward client: interest and desire to be helpful; respect; empathetic understanding; nonjudgmental acceptance; nonstereotyped individualization; assent to client self-determination; warmth and concern.
   B. Objective, disciplined use of self in relationship in behalf of client: empathy and sympathy without overidentification.
   C. Adherence to professionally accepted values and ethics in client contact: confidentiality.
II. Social work process—knowledge and skills.
   A. Data-gathering skills: discriminating ability to discern psychosocial-cultural factors of significance to service situation that needs to be explored; ability to gather relevant information from client, collaterals, records, tests; observation and exploration of relevant items of the client's psychosocial situation.

B. Diagnostic skills: demonstrates understanding of interrelationship of intrapsychic, interpersonal, and environmental factors; effectively applies knowledge of human behavior and social systems so as to derive meanings from social study data; shows appreciation and understanding of client's perceptual, cognitive, and emotional frame of reference; capable of formulating a descriptive, dynamic diagnostic or data-assessment statement.

C. Treatment (intervention) skills: capacity to plan and implement a program of remedial action based on understanding (diagnosis), derived from the facts (social study); ability to use, as appropriate to the client's situation, specific treatment interventions, for example, environmental modification, psychological support, clarification, insight, advocacy, brokerage, social action; interventions are appropriately timed and relevant.

D. Interviewing skills: ability to establish with client clear interview purpose; ability to maintain interview focus to achieve interview purpose; maintains a good balance between flexibly and responsibly following client lead and offering appropriate direction and control; ability to tactfully and nonthreateningly help client communicate feelings as well as facts.

E. Recording skills: recording demonstrates capacity for organization and communication of the worker's thinking and feelings: recording is discriminating, selective, accurate, succinct.

III. Orientation to agency administration—objectives, policies, procedures.

Knowledge of, commitment to, and identification with agency objectives, policies, and procedures; ability to work within limits of agency policies and procedures; imaginative use of agency policies and procedures in helping client; takes responsibility for working toward orderly change in policies and procedures that require improvement.

IV. Relationship to and use of supervision.

A. Administrative aspects: prepares adequately for conference, is prompt and regular in attending scheduled conferences, provides supervisor with necessary, appropriate material for conference.

B. Interpersonal aspects: freedom in seeking and using supervisor's help without undue dependency; acceptance of supervision and instruction without subservience; positive orientation to supervisory authority; active and appropriate participation in supervisory conferences; ability to recognize when consultation is needed and how it might be used appropriately.

V. Staff and community relationships.

Contributes to harmonious and effective relationship with agency staff at all levels; develops positive relationship with and makes appropriate use of colleagues from allied disciplines; constructively represents the agency to other professionals and to the general community; has good knowledge of relevant community resources.

VI. Management of work requirements and work load.

Covers work load with regularity and adequacy; shows ability to plan and organize work schedule within time allotted; shows capacity to set selective, valid priorities and to schedule work accordingly; is prompt in submitting recording, statistical reports, time sheets, service reports, and so on; absences and lateness infrequent and justified; productivity is at the expected level for workers of similar responsibility and experience.

VII. Professionally related attributes and attitudes.

Realistic critical assessment of own limitations without undue anxiety; adequate level of self-awareness and capacity for self-evaluation; flexible and cooperative on the job; enthusiasm for and conviction in the work he or she is doing. Generally behaves on the job in accordance with the values and ethics of the profession; shows identification with the profession; takes responsibility for continued professional development by reading, informal discussion, participation in relevant, available training programs.

VIII. Evaluating for cultural competence.

Recently, evaluating for cultural competence has been added to evaluation outlines. This includes assessing for the degree to which the supervisee is aware of his or her own culture-based values and biases; has some understanding and knowledge and acceptance of the values, attitudes, and behavior of different ethnic and racial groups; can implement techniques and strategies that are culturally appropriate to the needs of culturally diverse clients (Coleman 1999).

Evaluation outlines result in a narrative statement of performance. In the best of all worlds, a vivid narrative description lends rich nuance and texture to performance appraisal, but "thick" descriptions of social work practice require extensive observation and a lot of time to write and to read. Such a format then tends to fail the criteria for good evaluation procedures relating to practicality and ease in use. Several other formats available, such as Management by Objectives (MBO) and Behavior-Anchored Rating Scales (BARS), a job-oriented format for rank ordering of human performance, are infrequently utilized for similar reasons. See Pecora and Hunter (1988),

Millar (1990), Rapp and Poertner (1992), Matheson, Van Dyk, and Millar (1995), and Murphy and Cleveland (1995) for concise reviews of the literature and dimensional evaluations of each system. Unfortunately, research comparing different formats is rare (e.g., Kivlighan, Angelone, and Swafford 1991).

With staff involvement and effort, BARS methodology can produce reliable and valid measures of very abstract dimensions of professional performance, but their development and refinement may be labor-intensive. For this reason, Daley (1992) argues that BARS methodology is impractical in all but large public sector bureaucracies. However, see Taylor (1968), Taylor et al. (1970), Pecora and Hunter (1988), Conway and Ellison (1995), and Harkness et al. (2001) for BARS development procedures and practice applications.

Having worked to develop a behavioral rating scale, Conway and Ellison note that "the process is too consuming and difficult to be considered practical" (1995:117). Consequently, eschewing procedures that require large time investments, most human service organizations employ standardized check forms as guides to evaluation. The use of such a form imposes less of a burden on the supervisor; it strives for a more precise product for comparative evaluation of one worker with another or the same worker with him- or herself at different points in time, and it encourages greater standardization in evaluation. An expeditious way of summarizing evaluative statements, such methods, although vulnerable to error, may nevertheless classify supervisee performance with reasonable accuracy (Bretz, Milkovich, and Read 1992).

The following examples illustrate different kinds of formats used in social work evaluation forms. The material comes from evaluation forms obtained from a number of schools of social work and a wide variety of agencies. The items have been modified and edited to suit our present purposes. We have included only a limited number of items in each form but have varied the content so that, in aggregate, the items employed illustrate the kinds of content areas included in a comprehensive evaluation outline.

The following example illustrates the use of step scales. Each step in the scale identifies the level of performance that relates to a particular area of performance.

What are the worker's attitudes toward clients as shown in supervisory and/or group conferences?

1. Acceptance without sentimentality, without overidentification, without denial of unlikable qualities in client.
2. Acceptance tinged with overidentification, but not so much as to impede learning.

3. Acceptance varies in different cases; predominantly positive attitude toward clients.
4. Some negative attitudes toward clients, but these are not so excessive as to impede learning.
5. Strong overidentification impedes learning.
6. Hostile, withholding attitudes impede learning.
7. Neutral and guarded attitudes.

To what extent does the worker perceive his or her own part in the worker-client relationship?

1. Sees that his or her own feelings affect work with the client, and tries to handle his or her own feelings for the client's benefit.
2. Acknowledges feelings but does nothing about them.
3. Protests or denies feelings.
4. Guarded in acknowledging feelings; maintains a bland surface, so there is nothing to take hold of in teaching.

What is the quality of the worker's diagnostic perception as revealed in verbal and written evidence?

1. Very high quality both in recording and in verbal material. Expresses diagnostic thinking freely. See the total problem and implications. Sees the meaning of behavior both in the client's life situation and in the worker-client interaction. Explores supervisory suggestions rationally. Weighs evidence.
2. High quality, but less consistently or pervasively so than in 1.
3. Mixed quality: variations in different cases, or sees major problem but not its implications.
4. Mixed quality: does fairly well verbally but does not organize ideas on paper very well.
5. Limited quality: diagnostic thinking is in general rather thin or distorted, but enough is going on that there is something to take hold of in teaching.
6. Poor quality: distortions in thinking do not yield to discussion, or observation is so superficial that clues are not available for supervisory discussion.

What attitudes does the worker characteristically show in the conference with the supervisor?

1. Thoughtful, spontaneous, generally positive.
2. Somewhat scattered, spontaneous, positive.
3. Challenging and somewhat hostile, but hostility not so great as to impede learning.
4. Guarded: apparently, some fearfulness of the supervisor's intent; bland.
5. Passively hostile: negative attitude that impedes learning.
6. Actively hostile: negative attitude that impedes learning.
7. Other.

What is the level of the worker's attempts to engage client participation?

1. Very high: imaginative, individualized, relevant, with full recognition of obvious factors and some recognition of the less obvious. Flexibly related to case situation. Well-timed.
2. High: individualized and relevant, with recognition of obvious factors; fairly flexibly related to case situation; fairly well timed.
3. Moderate: incomplete or inadequate or superficial, but not predominantly irrelevant, inappropriate, inflexible, or poorly timed. May be somewhat inconsistent.
4. Low: predominantly somewhat irrelevant or inappropriate, and/or mildly distorted or rigid; not very well timed.
5. Very low: predominantly irrelevant or inappropriate, and/or grossly distorted or rigid; poorly timed.

Table 8.1 shows a five-step scale with a further gradation of two different points within each step.

Another and different evaluation instrument might be a check form with evaluation items stated, giving the supervisor four or five possible choices of responses. The performance response levels might be stated in several ways.

1 = clearly above expected level	1 = excellent	1 = outstanding
2 = above expected level	2 = above average	2 = very good
3 = at expected level	3 = average	3 = good
4 = below expected level	4 = below average	4 = poor
5 = clearly below expected level	5 = poor	5 = unsatisfactory

A zero is often provided to be circled when the supervisor does not have sufficient information or when the item is not relevant to the worker's job

Table 8.1 A Step Scale

For each factor to be rated, select the behavior description along the ten-point scale which *most nearly describes* the worker. Decide which of the two numbers above the behavior description represents the more accurate, most consistent description of the worker and circle this number. Rate each factor without reference to any other. If you have had no opportunity to observe the worker in the relevant activity, circle 0.

	0	1 2	3 4	5 6	7 8	9 10
1. Ability to develop and maintain working relationships with clients.	No opportunity to observe.	Difficulty in forming relationships, even in relatively uncomplicated situations.	Able to form productive relationships but this may be inconsistent and the range may be limited.	Generally forms productive relationships but has some difficulty in unfamiliar situations.	Consistently forms productive relationships in familiar situations and often in unfamiliar and challenging situations.	Unusual and consistent ability to form relationships with wide range of persons in complex situations.
2. Ability to take professional action on behalf of client.	No opportunity to observe.	Usually expresses little concern for the rights of clients.	Recognizes the rights of clients but generally does not stand up for the client.	Sensitive in general to the rights of clients and takes a stand for the client in usual situations.	Greater than usual sensitivity to the rights of clients and leadership in advocating for those rights.	Has indepth awareness of the rights of clients in complex situations and consistently takes a stand for clients.
3. Diligence and dependability in performing assigned work.	No opportunity to observe.	Frequently does not work hard or long enough and has "forgotten" to carry out assignments.	Some supervisory prodding necessary to get work done.	Works fairly steadily at assigned tasks.	Can be depended on to stick to a job until it is finished.	Puts every possible effort into his or her work.
4. Commitment to continuing professional development.	No opportunity to observe.	No apparent interest in professional development. Not self-critical, apathetic about increasing skill and knowledge, very limited view of professional responsibility. Does not respond to stimulus. Not committed to continuing professional development.	Inconsistently responds to outside stimulus to increase knowledge and skill, rarely takes initiative. Commitment somewhat questionable.	Usually responds to outside stimulus but does not initiate many efforts toward increasing knowledge and skill. Interest somewhat restricted, but there is some positive evidence of commitment.	Definite evidence of commitment to continuing professional develoment, although this may be spasmodic or limited to particular areas. Some initiative in self-evaluation. Demonstrates some sense of professional responsibility beyond immediate tasks.	Consistently seeks to extend knowledge and improve skill, evaluates own practice, formulates ideas and shares them, clear sense of professional responsibility beyond the immediate job. Systematically prepares self for new responsibilities.

Source: NASW (n.d.)

assignment. Any one of these three scales might be employed with the following evaluation-item listing.

Evaluation items	Performance level
a. Is aware of own feelings in relationship and controls them so as not to impede help to client.	1 2 3 4 5 0
b. Establishes a relationship characterized by rapport, ease, psychological safety.	1 2 3 4 5 0
c. Able to communicate acceptance of wide variety of different kinds of behavior while not condoning unacceptable behavior.	1 2 3 4 5 0
d. Able to obtain clear and accurate picture of problem situation with which client wants help.	1 2 3 4 5 0
e. Able to organize and synthesize social study data in understanding client in his or her situation.	1 2 3 4 5 0
f. Confirms, refines, modifies diagnostic formulation as appropriate.	1 2 3 4 5 0
g. Able to mobilize community resources on client's behalf.	1 2 3 4 5 0
h. Able to accept limited treatment goals without feeling immobilizing frustration.	1 2 3 4 5 0
i. Facilitates client communication in interview.	1 2 3 4 5 0
j. Understands and responds to nonverbal as well as verbal communication in interview.	1 2 3 4 5 0
k. Recording reflects nature of worker-client interaction and worker's diagnostic thinking.	1 2 3 4 5 0
l. Is constructively and appropriately critical of agency policies and procedures which impede service.	1 2 3 4 5 0
m. Able to contribute constructive disagreement in supervisory conference.	1 2 3 4 5 0
n. Takes responsibility for establishing own learning needs in supervision.	1 2 3 4 5 0

The following three items illustrate the use of a seven-point scale anchored by descriptive statements at the high and low ends, clearly defining the behavior being evaluated.

1. *Relationship* with client (individual or group); *level of rapport, warmth, acceptance*

   HIGH   Has regard, respect, and concern for person regardless of behavior that worker may reject; established warm, nonthreatening, nonpunishing, easy, relaxed, psychologically safe atmosphere; compassionate, gentle, sympathetic; client given freedom to be him- or herself, to express him- or herself freely, in all his or her unlovely as well as lovely aspects; client feels at ease and is encouraged to communicate because he or she trusts worker and has confidence in him or her.

___1. Extremely good

___2. Very much better than average

___3. Somewhat better than average

___4. Average

___5. Somewhat poorer than average

___6. Very much poorer than average

___7. Extremely poor

___8. Not enough information available to make confident judgment.

LOW   Moralistic and judgmental; cold, distant, aloof, derogatory, disapproving, critical; establishes an atmosphere that is psychologically threatening and potentially punitive; client not permitted freedom to be him- or herself; client feels uneasy, unrelaxed, hesitant to communicate, as he or she mistrusts worker and has little confidence in him or her.

2. *Diagnostic skills* (individual or group)

HIGH   Recognizes, identifies, demonstrates understanding of and appropriate use of psychosocial, individual, and group dynamics; tends to individualize diagnosis using pertinent social study material; capable of conceptualizing and verbalizing psychodynamics of client situation and psychodynamics of the worker-client (individual or group) interaction; uses theoretical constructs regarding individuals and groups to make relevant, valid inferences from appropriate case data; technical language precisely and/or appropriately used.

___1. Extremely good

___2. Very much better than average

___3. Somewhat better than average

___4. Average

___5. Somewhat poorer than average

___6. Very much poorer than average

___7. Extremely poor

___8. Not enough information available to make confident judgment

LOW Misses most significant psychosocial, dynamic cues; understanding of client's situation and dynamics of worker-client interaction superficial and/or distorted; tends to stereotype client and apply theoretical constructs inappropriately; technical language imprecise and/or inappropriately used.

3. *Management of work load*

HIGH Management of work load is smooth, efficient, inconspicuous, requiring little or no prodding or checking; worker output and efficiency high; meets deadlines, fulfills assignments.

___1. Extremely good

___2. Very much better than average

___3. Somewhat better than average

___4. Average

___5. Somewhat poorer than average

___6. Very much poorer than average

___7. Extremely poor

___8. Not enough information available to make confident judgment

LOW Management is poor, seems unable to manage work load without considerable reminding, prodding, checking; work output and efficiency low; frequently fails to meet deadlines or fulfill assignments.

More precise distinctions can be made on a graphic rating scale, as shown in Figure 8.1.

Figure 8.1

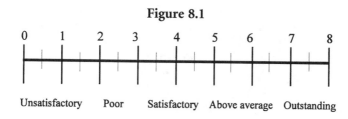

The supervisor is requested to circle the scale at the point that appropriately reflects level of performance. The scale is repeated for each of the items, such as the following:

a. Recognizes and disciplines own biases, prejudices, negative reactions to client.

b. Accepts limitations in clients' capacity and motivation and works with clients at their own tempo.

c. Uses good judgment in determining what information needs to be obtained in a particular situation.

d. Makes relevant inferences from social study data through appropriate application of social work theory.

e. Able to use the relationship as a medium for help.

f. Achieves good balance in treatment between stimulating the client to act on his or her own behalf and, when necessary, acting in behalf of the client.

g. Can identify and utilize appropriate strategies of intervention relevant to client system need.

h. Understands client's latent as well as manifest communication in interview.

i. Effectively handles pauses, silence, transitions in interview.

j. Recording is well organized and reflects essentials of case situation.

k. Understands his or her position in agency structure and the appropriate channels for intra-agency communication.

l. Shows little need to defend him- or herself against learning in supervision.

m. Shows evidence of use of supervisory learning in subsequent client contacts.

n. Able to function as a productive, contributing member of a team of colleagues.

Evaluation outlines might include a series of graded statements, the supervisor checking the one that most clearly approximates the worker's performance. The following are illustrations of this.

Supervisee's Relationship with Clients

__1. Shows an exceptional ability to relate.

__2. Demonstrates a high degree of relating.

__3. Relates adequately with most clients.

__4. Has difficulty relating to clients.

__5. Often relates in a manner that turns clients off.

Supervisee's Treatment Planning

__1. Has ability to formulate, develop, and implement sound treatment plans that prove effective for the client.

__2. Develops sound treatment plans but finds implementation difficult.

__3. Develops treatment plans that are sometimes questionable.

__4. Formulates treatment plans that prove ineffective for the client.

With recognition of the difficulty of making precise distinctions in levels of performance, some evaluation forms provide only for very broad categorizations, such as acceptable, needs improvement, unacceptable.

An evaluation form can include negative as well as positive and neutral statements. The following examples are taken from such a form.

Instructions: Below are listed some statements that relate to evaluation of worker task performance. Using your knowledge of the worker's activity, please mark each statement according to how strongly you agree or disagree that this is characteristic of the work. Mark the statement +3, +2, +1 or −1, −2, −3 to represent the following:

> +3 I strongly agree   −1 I disagree slightly
> +2 I agree   −2 I disagree
> +1 I agree slightly   −3 I strongly disagree

__a. Demonstrates an interest in client's problems.
__b. Tends to be cool and aloof in contact with client.
__c. Tends to respond punitively to the hostile, resistive client.
__d. Shows empathetic understanding of most client behavior.
__e. Participates actively and willingly in supervisory sessions.
__f. Accepts and acts on constructive criticism.
__g. Lacks sensitivity to dynamics of self in supervisory relationships.

The content of the evaluation outline and the content items included in the above example standardized forms are designed to be generic and applicable (with some adaptation) to all social work methodologies. In addition to the core generic items illustrated, it may be helpful to list some performance items that are more specific to group work and community organization.

Group work
1. Skill in the use of group process to effect individual change.
2. Skill in helping individuals establish positive, productive group relationships.
3. Skill in the use of program activities to effect group change.
4. Skill in participating effectively in group interaction.
5. Knowledge of and ability to use a variety of group roles in effecting group movements.
6. Skill in discriminating and appropriate use of program media.
7. Skill in effecting change in intragroup interaction.
8. Skill in relating to group members as individuals.
9. Knowledge of various types of groups and their differentiated structure and function.
10. Skill in group leadership.

Community organization

1. Skill in assisting community group to articulate needs and problems.
2. Skill in helping community residents develop organizational capacity necessary for effective social action.
3. Skill in establishing positive and productive relationships with leadership people at a variety of levels.
4. Skill in employing a range of educational and/or promotional techniques to enhance community understanding and support of social welfare programs.
5. Knowledge and understanding of community dynamics and power structure.
6. Skill in bringing together disparate citizen groups, professional groups, and social agencies in a working relationship addressed to the solution of community problems.
7. Skill in translating expressed community concerns into a feasible course of remedial action.
8. Skill in increasing motivation and participation of community residents in problem-solving activities in their own behalf.
9. Skill in negotiating with citizen's groups and community agencies.
10. Skill in effecting change in intergroup relationships.

In applying rating scales, supervisors make use of the knowledge that comes from experience in evaluating the performance of different workers. A lack of such experience makes it difficult to use some rating scales, as one supervisor notes:

> It was difficult to evaluate using ratings such as above average, average, below average. Having no substantial supervisory experience other than this year's, it was difficult to determine what average behavior would be. This must be a dilemma faced by other beginning supervisors, who have little other than their own behavior by which to compare.

Even the most detailed rating form may fail to include a performance item that is of particular significance in the case of an individual supervisee. Furthermore, a valid evaluation is a complex configuration of many discrete items. The standardized form tends to fractionate performance because it is generally a listing of separate items. It is clear that something more is required, something that involves putting the items together in some general, inclusive statement that relates the different items to each other. Using the same itemized information, one can get quite different evaluations, depending on how one interpretively puts the items together. Failure to understand the interrelationship of discrete performance items is illustrated by the satire of the efficiency expert who evaluated the work of members of a symphony orchestra. He noted that for

> considerable periods the oboe players had nothing to do. Their number should be reduced and their work spread out more evenly over the whole of the concert, thus eliminating peaks of activity. It is noted that all twelve first violins were playing identical notes; this seems unnecessary duplication. There is too much repetition of some musical passages. No useful purpose is served by repeating on horns and woodwinds a passage that has been already adequately handled by the strings.

In an evaluation, as in an orchestra, the whole is greater than the sum of individual parts.

In view of the need for a summary statement that integrates the itemized listing, most standardized forms leave space for this at the end. The instruction to the supervisor might be to consider and assess the staff member's total performance as a social worker during the period covered by the evaluation, taking into account those factors covered by the form and any others the supervisor might believe to be important. More succinctly, the form might end by asking for the supervisor's general overall impression of the worker. All items in the outline or on the standardized scale appear to have equal value, but some are more mechanical, are more peripheral, or require less skill than others. The overall summation is an opportunity to give differential weighting to the more significant aspects of the worker's performance that require more skill and competence.

The rating forms generally provide for fact-sheet information, which includes the name of the worker, classification of the worker, education, the name of the supervisor, the identifying department or unit, the date of the evaluation, the reason for it, the period it covers.

Once a standardized rating scale has been formulated, it might be helpful for the agency administrator to schedule meetings of supervisors alone, supervisees alone, and of the two groups together to discuss the use of the form. Such training in the use of the scale will ensure more uniform and efficient use of the instrument.

The evaluation outline or rating form is uniformly applicable to all the workers in the same job classification, that is, those positions having similar duties and responsibilities and requiring similar levels of knowledge and skill. Because the workers have the same classification, they have the same status in the agency and receive similar pay.

The standard for a job activity is defined as the quality of performance and the quantity of accomplishment that the agency feels is legitimate to ask from all the workers assigned this job activity who have similar levels of education and experience. Evaluations for the same job classification differ in terms of experience on the job. The evaluation outline for the Caseworker I employee with five years of service is necessarily somewhat different from that for the newly hired Caseworker I. The performance items are similar in many instances. The difference lies in the greater consistency, adequacy, appropriateness, and autonomy of performance by the experienced worker. It calls for a performance executed with greater self-assurance as applied to a caseload of greater complexity. For example, the evaluation outline in Table 8.2 makes distinctions in expectations varying with experience.

Sources of Information for Evaluation

In addition to knowing what to look for, which is spelled out in the criteria of the evaluation outlines, we have to know where to look in sampling worker performance. The supervisor needs to be able to obtain sufficient, valid, and reliable information representing the typical performance of the worker if he or she is to apply the criteria in making an assessment. The possible sources of information available to the supervisor regarding the worker's performance might include:

1. Supervisee's verbal reports of activity.
2. Supervisee's written records.
3. Audiotape recordings of supervisee-client (individual, group, or community) contacts.
4. Videotapes of supervisee-client contacts.
5. Observation of supervisee's performance via one-way screen.
6. Observation of supervisee in joint interviews.
7. Observation of supervisee's activity in group supervisory meetings.
8. Observation of supervisee's activity in staff meetings and/or joint professional conferences.
9. Client and peer evaluations of supervisee's performance.
10. Supervisees correspondence, reports, statistical forms, weekly schedule, daily action logs, monthly performance records, and so on.
11. Client and organizational outcomes.

Studies of the actual sources of information utilized by supervisors in formulating evaluations indicates high dependence on a very limited group of sources, principally the supervisee's verbal reports and written records of activity (McCarthy, Kulakowski, and Kenfeld 1994).

Written records include data regarding the worker's program efforts. Quantifiable productivity outputs such as the following are reviewed for eval-

Table 8.2 Distinctions in Expectations, Based on Experience

	Experience level		
Performance criteria	1st year	3rd year	5th year
Understanding of the relationship of this agency to other agencies	Beginning understanding	Good understanding	Full grasp
Commitment to agency program	Awareness and a feeling of responsibility	Growing facility	Full commitment
Anxiety level	Still a good deal of unfocused anxiety	No pervasive anxiety except in particular cases—expect some regression	Anxiety minimal worker should handle it him- or herself except in serious cases
Degree of enthusiasm for work	High degree	Still some unbridled enthusiasm	Seasoned with compromise
Capacity to take criticism and deal with it constructively	Accept with some objectivity; needs help in dealing with it	Take and use with a minimum of help	Take and use without defensiveness
Capacity for effective functioning as team member	Growing awareness of need to fit self in; still needs much help	Accomplished fact	Accomplished fact plus helping others to do it
Use of supervision	Willingness to expose but still quite dependent; produces material but not too clear on what needs to be learned	Takes initiative; use of time for specific needs; knows what he or she wants	Consultation

uation: number of interviews conducted, children placed, applications processed, discharge plans completed, home visits made, contracts written, institutions licensed, foster homes evaluated, group meetings held, number of collaterals contacted, and so on.

Less frequently utilized but of some importance are correspondence, reports, and statistical forms, as well as worker activity in staff meetings and group supervisory meetings. Audio- and videotape recordings, direct observation of the worker, and client evaluations are used rarely (Kadushin 1992a), although some recommend them (Braver, Graffin, and Holahan 1990; Bernard and Goodyear 1998). Of possible relevance, a study by Fortune and Abramson (1993) found that students who received performance feedback based on audio- or videotapes of their work reported more satisfaction with social work supervision.

The use of audio- and videotapes and one-way screen observation is discussed in detail in chapter 10, which is concerned with innovations in supervision. We might note here, however, that other human service professions use such devices in supervision much more frequently, and there is beginning to be an acceptance of their use in social work as well.

In all of the previously mentioned techniques, the worker, either alone or in interaction with the supervisor, generates the data that is utilized for evaluation. It must be conceded that supervisors see a worker's performance from just one vantage point. Others in different hierarchical relationships with the worker may see him or her differently because different aspects of the person's performance are manifested in the different relationships. Peers and clients may evoke different aspects of the worker's repertoire of behavioral responses. This argues for the fact that a more comprehensive appraisal of the worker's total performance would need to include the perceptions of not only the supervisors but also peers and clients. Obtaining so-called 360-degree feedback from multiple stakeholders has become a popular method of appraising performance in business and industry (Edwards and Ewan 1996; Carless, Mann, and Wearing 1998).

Some social workers argue that client satisfaction and other service outcomes should be used to evaluate social work practice (Rapp and Poertner 1987, 1992; Harkness and Poertner 1989; Harkness and Hensley 1991). However, although consumer satisfaction is an important source of feedback about the process and outcomes of supervised social work practice, clients are not in a good position to evaluate worker job performance. The client is not knowledgeable about agency job requirements, lacks a perspective on social work performance in general, and may find it difficult to be objective because of an intense personal relationship with the worker.

Client subjectivity is one explanation for the findings reported in a study by Bishop (1971), in which supervisor and supervisee evaluation ratings, significantly correlated with each other, were at considerable variance with much more favorable client ratings of the supervisee. Studies of the appraisal of managerial performance by superiors and subordinates have found similar patterns of disagreement but interpret them differently (Carless, Mann, and Wearing 1998). Good performance looks different from different perspectives (Edwards and Ewan 1996).

In principle, there is growing acceptance of clients' reactions as a source of information regarding worker's performance. Client reaction has frequently been a productive source of information in program evaluation research. Clients may provide equally valid information regarding their contacts with individual workers. Some evidence suggests that subjective client ratings of their relationships with workers are objectively determined by the outcomes of service (Harkness 1997). Moreover, some client outcomes are measurably improved when client feedback is used to focus supervision (Harkness and Hensley 1991). To the extent that using client feedback in supervision improves practice outcomes, the outcomes of performance appraisal may benefit from client feedback as well.

The research tends to indicate that peers make very accurate assessments of each other's performance, and organizations are said to make wide use of peer feedback when conducting management performance appraisals in business and industry (Edwards and Ewan 1996). However, efforts by the supervisor to solicit information from peers for purposes of evaluation presents problems. Peers are in a sort of competition with each other, and this may determine the nature of information selected for sharing. Peers telling on each other is apt to create morale problems within the peer group, and there is a question of violation of each other's confidentiality. Peer evaluation runs counter to the supposition generally held by the group that the unit is a company of equals. This inhibits the critical evaluation by one peer of another's work. But increased employee perceptions that appraisals are fair, positive changes in organizational behavior, increased productivity, and improved customer satisfaction are said to offset the untoward effects of appraisals by peers—albeit in business settings with organizational cultures and goals that may be quite different from those of social work services. See Edwards and Ewan (1996) for a selective review of the literature.

Evaluation of Supervisors

The supervisee is accountable to the supervisor, but in many agencies the supervisor is not formally evaluated by anyone else. There is frequently no evaluation of the supervisor's performance by agency administrators, leaving supervisors to evaluate themselves. A study of how sixty-two supervising psychologists evaluating their own competence found that most supervisors perceived their skills as adequate and were at least somewhat confident in their supervisory and evaluative skills, despite limited reading of the supervisory literature, poor supervisory training, and poor-to-fair preparation for the supervisory role (Robiner et al. 1997).

Although supervisors may be conscientious about self-evaluation and attempt to make efforts to modify performance accordingly, this may not be a sufficient incentive to effect change. Culatta and Seltzer instructed clinical speech therapist supervisors in the use of charting systems for their audio-taped supervisory conferences. Faced with a self-generated critique of their performance as a result of a charted analysis of their interaction, the supervisors became explicitly aware of some undesirable aspects of their supervision. Despite this, analysis of continuing supervisory sessions indicated that self-knowledge "*per se* of how a supervisory session is being conducted may not exert enough force to motivate change in supervisory behavior" (Culatta and Seltzer 1977:526; see also Dendinger and Kohn 1989). Apparently additional incentive through external feedback and evaluation may be necessary. However, Hegarty (1974) found that supervisors did change as a result of feedback from supervisees about their supervisory performance. This is not surprising, as organizational behavior appears to change at every level when human service providers obtain systematic feedback from their stakeholders (Boettcher 1998)—all the more so, perhaps, when supervisors seek feedback themselves.

To the extent that supervisee appraisal results in positive changes in the supervisor's performance, it makes a contribution to more effective supervision. It provides the feedback supervisors need to correct performance deficiencies. Supervisee appraisal of supervisors enhances worker morale, intensifies a conviction in the fairness of the organization, is in line with a more egalitarian ethos, and encourages the feeling that the supervisees have some power in the agency. The fact that such an appraisal is an accepted procedure in the organization may prompt supervisors to be more concerned about their performance and pay greater attention to supervisee needs.

Evaluation of supervisors presents more of a problem than evaluation of supervisees because supervisors produce fewer "products." In the absence of measured program outcomes, there are no case records and fewer reports of one kind or another. The supervisee has the most intimate, detailed knowledge of the supervisor's performance. Consequently, some efforts have been made to obtain evaluations of supervisors from their supervisees, despite the fact that the worker has information regarding a limited aspect of the supervisor's performance—namely, the supervisor's performance in supervising the supervisee. Despite the apparent value of supervisee evaluation of supervisors, only 18.5 percent of 377 supervisees answering a national survey said they participated in such a procedure (Kadushin 1992a).

A number of scales and coding systems have been developed to assess the supervisory process and its outcomes. Bernard and Goodyear (1998) have identified sixteen such scales, and Vonk and Thyer (1997) identified several more in a brief review of standardized self-report measures that rely on the perceptions of the supervisee, supervisor, or client. The recommended measures have been described as reliable and appear to tap key dimensions of effective supervision (Henderson, Cawyer, and Watkins 1999): (1) sound interpersonal skills for building relationships, (2) practice knowledge and experience, (3) goal-oriented structure and performance feedback, (4) a supportive attitude toward the supervisee, and (5) an effective balance between direction and autonomy.

Some of the items included in measures of supervisory performance concern the relationship with the supervisee (Shulman 1982; Munson 1983). The relationship measure might be in a semantic differential form.

Describe the response you think is characteristic of your supervisor's relationship to you.

Accepting	1__	2__	3__	4__	5__	Rejecting
Warm	1__	2__	3__	4__	5__	Cold
Cooperative	1__	2__	3__	4__	5__	Uncooperative

Sometimes it is in the nature of a scale soliciting different levels of agreement.

1. My supervisor recognizes and respects my autonomy.
   Strongly Agree __; Agree __; Undecided __; Disagree __; Strongly Disagree __.
2. My supervisor offers a supportive, open relationship that facilitates my learning needs.
   Strongly Agree __; Agree __; Undecided __; Disagree __; Strongly Disagree __.

Evaluations of supervisors by supervisees may be in the nature of a series of related statements. The supervisee is asked to choose the statement that best describes the supervisor's behavior.

__1. When conflict arises my supervisor tries to cut it off and win his or her position.

__2. When conflict arises, my supervisor tries to identify reasons for it and to resolve underlying causes.

__3. When conflict arises, my supervisor tries to be fair but firm and to get an equitable solution.

__4. When conflict arises my supervisor tries to remain neutral or stay out of it.

__5. My supervisor tries to avoid generating conflict, but when it does appear, he or she tries to soothe feelings and to keep people together.

It may be in the nature of a series of graded statements, the supervisee selecting the one most characteristic of the supervisor's performance.

My supervisor's attitude toward supervision is:

1. Enthusiastic—enjoys supervising
2. Very interested
3. Somewhat interested
4. Only routine interest displayed
5. Uninterested

My supervisor's apparent knowledge of social work is:

1. Very well informed
2. Well informed
3. Could be better informed
4. Not well informed
5. Misinformed

Sometimes evaluation items are in the nature of a scale indicating the level of consistency of behavior emitted by the supervisor. The scale uses terms like "almost always," "often," "sometimes," "rarely." Items may include such statements as:

1. My supervisor helps me gain a sense of achievement in my work.
2. My supervisor gives me an opportunity to do challenging work.
3. My supervisor is accessible when needed.
4. My supervisor provides opportunities for me to suggest changes in agency policy.
5. My supervisor treats me as though I could be easily replaced.
6. My supervisor helps me conceptualize my client's situation.
7. My supervisor confronts me with ineffective practice when this is appropriate.
8. My supervisor helps me assess my strengths and weaknesses.
9. My supervisor encourages me to find my own style in helping clients.

10. My supervisor provides direct suggestions and advice when appropriate.

The content areas of supervisor performance evaluations follow from the supervisor's functions. The supervisees are asked to evaluate the supervisor's adequacy with regard to:

1. The clarity of communication
2. Planning and assigning work
3. Delegating authority and responsibility
4. Guiding and reviewing work
5. Coordinating and integrating work
6. Resolving technical problems
7. Ability to motivate workers
8. Inducting and integrating worker into agency
9. Instructional skills
10. Supportive interventions
11. Objectivity and comprehensiveness of evaluation

Some content areas are concerned with the supervisor's attitudes and behavior regarding the responsibilities of supervision. Supervisees are asked to rate the supervisor's availability when needed, his or her level of commitment to supervision, his or her willingness to extend him- or herself to help supervisees, and the consistency with which he or she implements promises to the supervisee.

Supervisees might be asked to indicate (1) the extent to which they regard the supervisor as a desirable professional role model and (2) whether they would choose this supervisor for themselves if they had the option of making a selection.

It might be of assistance to supervisors in examining their own performance if supervisees were asked such questions as "What do you think are your supervisor's principal strengths?" Principal weaknesses?" or "What do you think your supervisor needs to work on?"

Questions have been raised about problems that might be associated with such an evaluation (Judge and Ferris 1993; Arvey and Murphy 1998). Will the supervisee assess the supervisor's performance primarily in terms of his or her own personal needs and preferences? Will such an appraisal encourage "gaming" on the part of both supervisor and supervisee—the supervisor acting to court a favorable evaluation, the supervisee evaluating to obtain the approval of the supervisor? Given the power of the supervisor, can the supervisee afford to be objective? Is the supervisee capable of making an objective evaluation of the supervisor's performance?

Dendinger and Kohn (1989) used questionnaires with 50 supervisors and 238 supervisees and found that supervisors' self-evaluations were very similar to supervisees' evaluation of supervisors. Reviewing the research regarding the effects of subordinates' appraisal of supervisors, Bernardin (1986) finds them largely positive, as do Edwards and Ewan (1996), who with Murphy and Cleveland (1995) caution that the anonymity of subordinate appraisals (and freedom from reprisal) may be crucial.

Vonk and Thyer (1997) and Bernard and Goodyear (1998) have identified a number of instruments that supervisors might adapt for appraisal by their supervisees. These include the Supervisor Feedback Rating System (Friedlander, Siegel, and Brenock 1989), the Supervisory Styles Inventory (Friedlander and Ward 1984), the Supervision Questionnaire (Ladany et al. 1996), and the Supervisory Working Alliance Inventory (Efstation, Patton, and Kardash 1990).

To counterbalance feedback from her supervisees, the supervisor might invite additional feedback from the agency administrator. An evaluation of supervisors by agency administrators might ask questions regarding such issues as (1) changes in the level of productivity of unit, (2) the unit's error rate, (3) number of complaints received from clients, (4) rate of staff turnover; (5) absentee and tardiness record of the unit, (6) relationships with other agencies, (7) interpretation of agency functions to the community, (8) ability to represent needs of his or her workers to administration, and (9) capacity to communicate service effects of agency policies and procedures to administration.

In accordance with the precept that he or she is ultimately responsible for the quality and quantity of agency services provided by the supervisees, the ambitious supervisor might seek systematic organizational feedback from external stakeholders and agency clients. In this regard, see Harkness and Hensley (1991), Iberg (1991), Rapp and Poertner (1992), and Bannerjee (1995), as well as a warning from Savaya and Spiro (1997).

Controversial Questions

Perhaps the key controversy in the evaluation of worker performance is whether individual performance should be evaluated at all. Overall, there is little evidence to support the contention that feedback from the evaluation of individual performance leads to meaningful performance improvements in organizational settings (Daley 1992), which leads many to believe that system factors (not individual factors) are the major performance determinant (Cardy 1998). Nevertheless, supervisors are unlikely to abandon the appraisal of individual performance in the foreseeable future.

There is some controversy about whether evaluation should be concerned with assessing the worker against objective, uniform standards or against the worker's own development. A profession accountable to the community and concerned with effective service to the client, it seems to us, cannot accept as legitimate an orientation toward evaluation that employs the worker's own development as the standard. Some minimal external requirements need to be met. Even if the worker is ten times more proficient today than yesterday, if he or she still does not meet minimum standards of acceptability, we do the clients an injustice in retaining the worker on the job. We are concerned about individual development but as measured against some general, established standards.

Earlier, we mentioned the controversy around separating administrative and educational-clinical supervision. Some proponents for separation suggest that the administrative responsibility of evaluation be given to the supervisee's peers. Studies have shown that when peers are provided with the necessary information about a worker's performance, their assessment of performance correlates very highly with evaluations of the same work made by the supervisor (Friesen and Dunning 1973). Under normal conditions, however, workers do not know enough about the work activity of their peers to make a reasoned judgment. Social work generally involves face-to-face activity between worker and client in privacy rather than any public performance open to observation by others. Studies of doctors in a clinic performing under analogous conditions indicated that they did not have enough knowledge of their peers' activities to judge their performance validly and reliably (Friedson and Rhea 1965).

Evaluation by peers would require sharing with each other all of the recordings, case reports, and statistical forms ordinarily used as a basis for evaluation. Even if such materials were shared openly and willingly, the peers would still be denied the rich information that supervisors obtain from the conference-to-conference discussion of work activity. The limited availability of basic information needed for valid evaluation and the time expenditure such a procedure would impose make peer evaluation for educational purposes open to criticism. Peer evaluation as a basis for administrative decision would be open to even more serious question. Where peers are in competition for scarce resources (a merit raise, a promotion, a more desirable caseload), the burden of trying to be fair, honest, and objective in evaluating one's competitors is very great. Some additional difficulties of the relationship of peers to the evaluation process have been discussed earlier.

The same problems regarding adequate knowledge of the worker's total performance would militate against assigning the responsibility for ongoing educational supervision to one person in the agency and responsibility for evaluation to another.

Another problem relates to the antithetical functions of education and evaluation (Erera and Lazar 1994b). We noted that the two principal objectives of a good evaluation are educational and administrative: evaluation is designed to further professional growth but also provides a basis for administrative decisions. Attempting to achieve both of these objectives in a single conference is likely to fail because the defensiveness generated by judgments operates against the openness required for learning. The suggestion is that these two objectives be separated. One evaluation conference would focus on professional development. Another conference, held at a different time, would focus on producing an evaluation report for administrative use.

In essence, evaluation for administrative purposes is uncoupled from evaluation for developmental purposes.

Uncoupling administrative and developmental evaluation conferences permits the supervisor to discuss salary and promotion decisions with regard to considerations other than the exclusive concern with performance competence. Salary, promotions, and layoff decisions may be communicated as the consequence of externalities having nothing to do with competence— such as agency financial changes, reductions in client applications, job seniority, and so on. In deciding to separate the administrative and developmental aspects of the evaluation into two separate conferences, there is the additional problem of determining which of these interviews will be scheduled first. If the developmental interview precedes the administrative review, the content of the first interview can be used to justify administrative decisions communicated in the second interview. However, supervisees may not be ready to fully engage with developmentally focused content until administrative issues have been discussed.

The priority supervisees give to administrative evaluation over developmental evaluation is exemplified by one supervisor who said, "Betty didn't want and wasn't ready to discuss anything about her work until she heard about her pay raise." Inevitably, there is some disjoint between performance standards formulated for an evaluation instrument and its relevance as perceived by any individual supervisee. Of necessity, performance standards have to be more general and less particular than any one supervisee's job. Consequently, the individual supervisee is likely to see any evaluation instrument as failing to do justice to and reflect accurately the specifics of his or her performance and the uniqueness of his or her tasks. It is not surprising, then, that in a study of differences between workers and supervisors regarding their reactions to performance evaluation, supervisors were significantly more likely than supervisees to see evaluation criteria as consistent with workers' duties and responsibilities and capable of accurately evaluating performance (Harkness and Mulinski 1988:342, table 2).

It may be that different evaluation procedures may need to be employed to meet the different objectives of evaluation.

Performance contract and MBO procedures are more clearly designed to serve the professional developmental purpose of evaluation (Daley 1992). In achieving this purpose, the criteria of evaluation are based on the individual performance and professional growth needs of the supervisee being evaluated. But because they are individualized or tailored to the needs of the particular supervisee, they are not useful in discriminating between the performance level of one supervisee as compared with another. This lack of discrimination makes this procedure ineffective for administrative purposes of evaluation.

A question arises about the reliability and validity of supervisors' judgments in evaluation. The supervisor is faced with a very difficult, albeit inescapable, task in evaluating. Unable to observe worker performance directly, denied access to a clearly defined finished product, employing imprecise criteria applied to activities that are difficult to measure, the supervisor is asked to formulate an evaluation that accurately reflects the reality of the worker's performance.

There is general agreement that standards for evaluation in social work have been vague, "pragmatic, observational and intuitive rather than precise, standardized and scientific" (Kagan 1963:18). But they have not been totally unsophisticated, casual, and without merit.

Some confirmation of the validity of a supervisor's assessments can be derived from the fact that such assessment shows significant correlation with scores achieved by workers on written tests developed from job analysis (Kleinman and Lounsbury 1978; Cope 1982).

In an experiment conducted in 1955 under the sponsorship of the Council on Social Work Education (Lutz 1956), records of four casework interviews were sent to casework faculty of schools of social work throughout the country for independent assessments. Records of four group-work meetings were sent to group-work faculty. Faculty members were asked to evaluate the performance of the caseworker or group worker as reflected in the record on a seven-point scale from "definitely inadequate" to "definitely superior." A total of 143 responses were received. In three of the four casework records the consistency in judgments made was at a level of statistical significance ($p = .01$). This indicates that there was a considerable consensus regarding judgments. However, there were some supervisors who rated the same record "definitely inadequate," whereas others rated it "definitely superior." Consistency in rating all of the group-work records was statistically significant, and there was less variability in the ratings. There is therefore reason to believe that supervisors can achieve close agreement about the level of performance of a particular worker based on some generally accepted criteria.

Kagle (1979) asked 435 registered clinical social workers to evaluate the social worker's performance in two case analogues sent to them. One was a case of child neglect, the second of marital conflict. The case evaluation form the respondents were asked to use included criteria generally employed in evaluating social work practice. Findings indicated that "there was much disagreement among evaluators on case one. Overall, less than 75 percent of the respondents agreed on thirty-nine of the fifty-four evaluation criteria. . . . Respondents failed to agree in twenty-nine of the fifty-four criteria" on case two (Kagle 1979:294). The researcher concluded that "a case record is clearly insufficient information on which to base a valid judgment" of the worker's performance (Kagle 1979:295).

Even if more adequate data were available to supervisors, some of the essential problems of evaluation would still persist. This is the conclusion of a study conducted by Liston, Yager, and Strauss (1981). They obtained videotapes of six psychiatric residents interacting with patients at midphase of psychodynamically oriented therapy. Using a previously validated schedule, the Psychotherapy Assessment Schedule, they asked thirteen board-certified psychiatrists, all experienced supervisors and clinicians, to evaluate the resident's performance based on the videotape. Interrater agreement was statistically better than chance. For practical purposes, however, it is noted that "the strength of interrater agreement was low on every case" (Liston, Yager, and Strauss 1981:1071). "Interrater agreement tends to be worse among ratings for those conditions or behaviors which are especially important to assess accurately. . . . The most difficult performance category for the raters to agree about was that of dealing with the specific skills of therapy" (Liston, Yager, and Strauss 1981:1072).

Chevron and Rounsaville (1983) arranged to have the work of nine psychotherapists evaluated by five different procedures:

1. Didactic examination.
2. A composite global rating by faculty in the training program attended by the subject therapists.
3. Therapists' self-ratings.
4. Independent evaluators' ratings of videotaped psychotherapy sessions.
5. Supervisor's traditional method of evaluation on the basis of the therapists' retrospective reports of therapy sessions.

Results showed little agreement among assessments of the therapists' skills based on the different data sources. The most disconcerting finding was the lack of agreement between ratings based on a review of videotaped sessions and those based on the supervisor's discussion of process material with the therapist. Optimistically, however, only the supervisor's ratings were correlated with client outcomes, indicating that the supervisor's ratings had validity in terms of positive client change.

In explaining these confounding findings, the researchers note that supervisees typically reported on client behavior, client themes, and client progress in discussions with supervisors. Thus the most salient information focus in supervisory sessions may be associated with client variables. In contrast, in evaluating videotaping of therapy sessions, the focus of attention tends to be on the therapist's behavior and interventions. What is discussed with supervisors in conferences is closer to client outcome than is the link between the videotape focus of evaluation and outcome.

Evaluations require some consensual agreement on the part of the profession about what constitutes good practice. Explicit criteria might have been formulated and standards established. Supervisors may be willing and able to evaluate, yet there may be problems in providing the worker with a fair evaluation. Because there are many schools of thought about what is good practice, the supervision might hold one theoretical position and the supervisee an equally acceptable but quite different position. Because the supervisor is charged with making the evaluation, his or her theoretical bias may determine the judgements made.

Until data firmly establishes the superiority of a well defined set of procedures or interpretation for a given clinical problem, the very same behavior of a clinician may be rated appropriate or inappropriate depending on the point of view of the observer . . . the behavior assessable only through the individual "filters" of a clinical supervisor. (Shriberg et al. 1975:159)

The fact that supervisors employ their own theoretical biases in evaluating the work of supervisees is neatly illustrated in the responses of three different supervisors to the same segment of work by a counselor.

This particular interview involved a beginning counselor and an exceedingly fluent and verbal high school senior who proceeded to monopolize the counseling hour so completely that the counselor actually said only two sentences, namely, "Would you tell me your reasons for coming to counseling," and "Our time is about up; would you like to make another appointment?" The three supervisors of varying theoretical positions proceeded to examine what should have been done in this particular interview, which perhaps in actuality was what *they* would have done under the circumstances. One of the supervisors, of a Freudian bent, asserted that he would have done exactly what the counselor in question had done; that is, permitted him to free associate as much as he pleased during this first interview without any direction or interruption. This supervisor felt the counselor had done a marvelous job. The second supervisor, of a more directive-clinical orientation, expressed the opinion that, as he saw it, the counselor had done an atrocious job and indeed posed the question, "Who was doing the counseling?" He felt that the counselor should definitely have curtailed the client's excessive flow of verbiage and probed, analyzed, hypothesized, and clarified to a greater degree. The third supervisor took a somewhat middle-of-the-road position and felt that there were several opportune times for the counselor to reflect, clarify, and recapitulate, but praised the counselor's permissiveness and patience. (Demos 1964:705)

The general difficulties in evaluation are compounded currently by rapid changes in social work responsibilities, procedures, and acceptable methodological approaches. For example, the psychoanalytically oriented supervisor has great difficulty in evaluating the work of the behaviorally oriented supervisee. Accepting that "different" does not necessarily imply "better" or "worse," the supervisor is not in a position to evaluate work based on a very different basic orientation to the clients.

Recognizing and accepting the necessity for evaluation and the difficulties that reduce the likelihood of achieving a wholly satisfactory, reliable and valid evaluation, what can one say to supervisors faced with this responsibility? The task and concomitant authority are inherent in the position. To accept the position of supervisor involves acceptance of the task. In accepting the task one must also necessarily accept the burden of guilt and anxiety associated with it. But this is a truth to which the supervisor is no stranger. The social worker offering service to the client accepts the burden of guilt and anxiety associated with implementing decisions that are frequently made on the basis of tenuous evidence and hazardous inference. Every decision of consequence to which one is a responsible party excites a keen and discomforting awareness of personal fallibility.

One might further say to supervisors that they should recognize and accept their humanity, that all evaluations inevitably have elements of subjectivity, that all are, in a measure, in error. But the supervisor, in immediate contact with the day-to-day work of the supervisee, is best informed about the work and best able to evaluate it. The measure of probable error in the supervisor's evaluation is less than the supervisee would be subjected to if evaluated by anyone else. The systematic, conscientious effort at assessments by the supervisor, despite subjectivity and error, is "far kinder (and more accurate) than the commonly employed gossip by which professional judgements are circulated in the absence of a structure" (Ekstein and Wallerstein 1972:291). If true, completely accurate, evaluations are not attainable, adequate and useful approximations are achievable.

It must be recognized and accepted that, however fallible it may be, the best instrument currently available to make complex judgments, such as performance evaluations, is the trained, perceptive, informed mind of the supervisor.

"Subjective judgements are imprecise and run to danger of being distorted by biases and preferences. But they are broader, richer, more complex and, in the end, perhaps truer to reality than highly specific, narrowly defined, objective criteria" (Haywood 1979). More precise instruments are desirable but not yet devised. Currently, "the making of such assessments is as much an art to be cultivated as it is a science to be applied" (Green 1972:54). Neither the community, the agency, the clients, nor the supervisee can legitimately ask for infallibility in evaluation. What they can ask for and expect-is a "reasonable approximation to an estimate" (Reynolds 1942:280). This most supervisors are capable of offering while striving for infallibility. Fortuitously, the empirical evidence supports measured optimism about the validity of subjective supervisory ratings. As Arvey and Murphy (1998:163) recently observed, "There is increased recognition that subjectivity does not automatically translate into rater error or bias and that ratings are most likely valid reflections of true performance and represent a low-cost mechanism for evaluating employees."

Summary

An objective appraisal of the worker's total functioning on the job over a given period of time, in terms of clearly defined criteria reflecting agency standards, has value for the supervisee, supervisor, agency, and client. It is a responsibility of administrative supervision.

Supervisors dislike evaluating because they are reluctant to accentuate status differences, feel dubious about their entitlement and ability to evaluate, perceive evaluation as an indirect assessment of supervision, regard it as contradictory to the ethos of social work, and fear the strong negative affect that might be evoked.

Evaluation should be a continuous process that encourages active supervisee participation and input. It is based on defensible related criteria that are openly shared with the supervisee. It takes situational factors into consideration and is tentative and concerned with both strengths and weaknesses. It is enacted in the context of a positive relationship, and the supervisor is ready to accept an evaluation of his own performance.

Both supervisor and supervisee prepare for the evaluation conference by reviewing the work done during the evaluation period. The conference is concerned with a mutual sharing of the outcomes of the review, using the evaluation outline as the basis for discussion. The final evaluation is written and given to the worker.

A variety of performance evaluation outlines were presented. The worker's written and verbal reports of his or her work are the principal data used in assessing performance. Evaluations are most frequently used in motivating professional growth and making personnel decisions.

9 | The Group Conference in Supervision

Although the individual conference is the most frequent context for supervision, it is not the only one available. In some agencies, the group conference is the principal form of supervision. In many more agencies, the group conference is used in addition to the individual conference.

A 1989 questionnaire study of some 900 supervisors and supervisees showed that the group conference was the principal context for supervision for about 18 percent of the respondents. For about 60 percent of the respondents the individual conference was the main context for supervision, supplemented by group conferences held once or twice a month. For about 22 percent of the respondents the individual conference was the sole context for supervision (Kadushin 1992a). Group supervision was much more frequently a supplement to individual supervision than was individual supervision a supplement to group supervision.

Group supervision may be the preferred modality for the supervision of social workers involved in group work. Interactions in group supervision can be used for illustration and discussion of problems and approaches that might be employed in working with groups of clients. What happens in group supervision can be used to foster understanding of the interactions in client groups.

For group workers, group supervision has the advantage that the context mirrors the modality in which they are primarily engaged. Participation in the group becomes the source of learning about group interaction, group process, group operations, and the supervisees' feelings about group membership. The principal focus in this chapter, however, is the use of group supervision in the supervision of caseworkers.

Definition

Group supervision is distinguishable from other procedures that employ a group setting to achieve agency administrative purposes. Staff meetings, in-service training sessions, agency institutes, seminars, and workshops all use the group setting as context for conducting agency business and for the purpose of educating staff. However, the term *group supervision* is defined here as the use of a group setting to implement the responsibilities of supervision. In group supervision, the supervisor—given educational, administrative, and supportive responsibility for the activities of a specific number of workers—meets with the group to discharge these responsibilities. In group supervision, the agency mandate to the supervisor is implemented in the group and through the group. Most simply, group supervision has been defined as supervision in a group format.

The supervisory conference group is a formed group. It is a structured group with a task and an agenda. Membership in the group is defined as a consequence of being a supervisee of a particular group leader-supervisor. These groups are organized under agency administrative auspices. They are formed with the expectation that certain objectives will be achieved; they have a designated place in the formal structure of the agency and have a designated leader in the unit supervisor.

This definition of group supervision solves some of the decisional problems regarding group formation. How large the group should be and whether it should be heterogeneous or homogeneous in composition are questions answered by the definition. The size of the group is determined by the number of supervisees for whom the supervisor has administrative responsibility (generally four or five). The supervisees assigned to any single supervisor probably have some similarity in education and training and likely are concerned with similar problems and similar service. As a result, the group is likely to be homogeneous with regard to significant factors that determine group interests and concerns.

The fact that members of the group share concern about the same social problems and the same group of services suggests that they have high interaction potential. Sharing significant concerns, they have much to talk about, and much of what they have to talk about is mutually understandable. Because they are all social workers in the same agency, they share a common frame of reference. These factors make for considerable mutual predictability, enhancing group members' trust and confidence in each other.

The primary ultimate objective of group supervision is the same as the ultimate objective of all supervision: more effective and efficient service to agency clients. Unlike group therapy or sensitivity training groups, group supervision is not directed toward the personal development of the supervisee, personal problem solving, or satisfaction derived from group activities and interaction.

Though the group explicitly meets to work on job-related concerns, the group meetings may have social and therapeutic pay-offs for supervisees. But these, like the therapeutic effects of educational supervision that relate to self-awareness, are not the intent, objective, or obligation of group supervision.

An agency introducing group supervision as a substitute for or a supplement to individual supervision needs to prepare its workers for the change. This modification of supervision should be introduced only with the concurrence of staff, with whom the reasons for the change have been discussed. The specifics of how group supervision will operate should be clearly interpreted following the acceptance of the desirability of the charge. There are distinct advantages and disadvantages to group supervision that can be made explicit.

Advantages of Group Supervision

1. One clear advantage of group supervision is economy of administrative time and effort (Hawkins and Shohet 1989; Bernard and Goodyear 1998; Hayes, Blackman, and Brennan 2001). Administrative communications regarding standardized policies and procedures can be communicated once to all the supervisees in a unit. Matters that are of common concern can be most economically communicated to individuals as members of a group. There are financial savings to an agency that moves from individual supervision to group supervision, as the latter involves less expenditure of supervisory personnel time. Group supervision is currently being recommended in redesigning supervision to lower costs in response to budget cuts. The recent growth of managed care service delivery has increased interest in group supervision as the more cost-effective approach to supervision.

2. Group conferences make possible the efficient utilization of a wider variety of teaching-learning experiences (Hawkins and Shohet 1989; Tebb, Manning, and Klaumann 1996). A presentation by a specialist can be scheduled, a film can be shown, a tape recording can be played, a role-playing

session can be organized, or a panel presentation can be arranged. Such learning experiences are designed primarily for use in a group context.

3. Group supervision provides the opportunity for supervisees to share their experiences with similar problems encountered on the job and possible solutions that each has formulated in response (Hawkins and Shohet 1989; Walter and Young 1999). All of us are smarter than any one of us; however similar the assignments, the aggregate of all the caseloads (which is the total pool for discussion in the group) provides a greater variety of experiences than is available in any single worker's caseload. Consequently, the sources for learning are richer and more varied than in the individual conference. Different members of the group can further provide a greater variety of points of view for learning.

The sharing of relevant experiences in the group supervisory conference is illustrated in the following excerpt. This conference of psychiatric social workers in a mental hospital setting is concerned with factors affecting casework movements with psychiatric patients. One supervisee, Mr. N, reported that his client

had regressed since his admission to the hospital. The patient's wife had noticed this further withdrawal and had discussed with Mr. N her concern about this observation. Mr. N pointed out that he felt he had been able to help the patient's wife understand that regressions during psychotic episodes occurred frequently.

Addressing the group, the supervisor pointed out that Mr. N had helped the relative to anticipate what so commonly happens during the course of mental illness and its treatment: that there were frequent vacillations in reality anchorage and in observable responses to treatment. The supervisor wondered if the others hadn't observed examples of these swings in their case assignments.

Miss Delmar said she had a patient who had recently been taken off of ECT [electroconvulsive therapy or shock therapy] and had regressed immediately afterward. Mr. Drake explained that he had a case like Miss D's and also one like Mr. N's. So far, most of Miss Gleeson's patients had been responding very well to treatment; however, when discharge plans had been mobilized with one of her cases, the patient had regressed, showing worse symptoms than had been shown on admission to hospital. The reversal had been sudden.

The group expressed its opinion that temporary regression at the time of discharge or termination is a common reaction among clients. (Abrahamson 1959:89–90)

4. Members of the group also act as a source of emotional support (Bernard and Goodyear 1998; Tebb, Manning, and Klaumann 1996; Walter and Young 1999). Group members console, sympathize with, and praise each other during the course of group meetings. The group not only provides the opportunity for lateral teaching—peer to peer—but also provides opportunities of mutual aid of various kinds. This opportunity for a supervisee to share his or her knowledge and to give emotional support to peers is a gratifying, morale-building experience that reinforces a feeling of belonging to the group.

In the following passage, Cohen (1972) notes the mutually reinforcing aspects of interaction in group supervision—for better and for worse. The setting is a geriatric center and the supervisor is reporting.

Vividly I can remember the day that the first client in the unit caseload had died. The [worker] rushed into my office, tears streaming down her face, sobbing "Mrs. H died and I wasn't there and I didn't know anything about it." Intuitively the three other [workers] in the unit came: out of their offices and the four of them sat with me for the next hour as we talked about their own feelings about dying and death. Real comfort was derived for each of them, and for me too, as in a very poignant manner we lent support to each other.

The reverse side of the coin of mutual support can be one [worker's] negativism or pessimism feeding into others. During a [group] meeting one [worker] began with "If this is what it's like to grow old who wants it. It's terrible." Whereupon each [worker] began to share the depressed, upset, gloomy feelings that had been accumulating. (Cohen 1972:175)

One supervisee spoke of group supervision as a forum for sharing common struggles. The group acts as a support system for its members.

5. The opportunity for sharing common problems encountered on the job is, in itself, a therapeutically reassuring contribution to individual morale. In the interchange made possible through group supervision, a worker often becomes aware that his or her problems are not unique, that failures and difficulties are not the result of ineptitude, that all the other workers seem to be equally disturbed by some clients and equally frustrated by some situations. The group context permits a living experience with the supportive techniques of universalization and normalization. The worker is given a keen appreciation of the fact that these are "our problems" rather than "my problems." It decreases the tendency to personalize problems and increases the likelihood of objectifying them.

6. Workers find it difficult to assess their comparative competence because they perform their tasks in private and discuss their performance in the privacy of the individual supervisory conference. Group supervision gives workers an opportunity to see the work of others and provides them with a basis for comparison (Hawkins and Shohet 1989; Getz and Agnew 1999; Hayes, Blackman, and Brennan 2001). A worker can develop a clear sense of how he or she is doing as compared with other workers of comparable education and experience. A worker in a court setting says,

> One of my major concerns is that I function pretty much on my own. I enjoy my autonomy but I have little opportunity to compare my work to my co-workers'. I have no standard to compare my efforts against but my own. My supervisor uses unit meetings for passing on new agency policies as well as troubleshooting unit concerns, but not for case staffing. When there has been an opportunity to team with another worker on a case, I found it interesting that much of what we did was similar, which reduced much of my anxiety. I was also surprised and excited about the different view they had of a situation and new methods of processing the same experience. Why couldn't we have done this in unit meetings of the group?

7. For some workers the group situation is the most comfortable learning environment. For some, the one-to-one tutorial conference is too intense a relationship. They need a more diffuse relationship with the supervisor to feel sufficiently comfortable to devote all their energies to learning; they need the give-and-take of the group interaction. It is easier for some workers to accept criticism, suggestions, and advice from peers than from parental surrogates, such as the supervisor. For some supervisees, then, the group context has the advantage of meeting idiosyncratic educational needs. Furthermore, because group members tend to implement different roles, people can gain recognition and approbation from having the opportunity to do what they do best.

8. The group context provides the safety in numbers that individual supervisees may need to challenge the supervisor. In the highly personalized, isolated context of the individual conference, the supervisee may be afraid to articulate his or her questions and objections to what the supervisor is saying. "In the individual conference . . . there are only two opinions available and in case of disagreement the supervisor's opinion will usually prevail" (Pointer and Fishman 1968:19). Given the support of potential allies, the supervisee may find the courage to present differing opinions in the protected setting of the group conference. The solidarity of a number of similarly iden-

tified professionals organized in a group permits more effective articulation of collective professional needs and orientation (rather than bureaucratic needs and orientation) (Getzel and Salmon 1985).

9. Group supervision is employed to encourage interaction among members of a work unit and to help develop peer group cohesion (Munson 1997; Hayes, Blackman, and Brennan 2001). Group supervision has the advantage of providing an opportunity for staff to meet each other. A supervisee in a mental health clinic says,

> A major plus of group supervision is the act of getting all these autonomous people together. Unless we pass each other in the hallway, meet at the bathroom, or use the appointment book at the same time, we are, for 90 percent of the day, behind our closed doors. After group supervision was started, there seemed to be a visible change in attitude and more people made an effort to stay in the hallway longer.

Through group conferences the individual supervisee develops a sense of belonging to a unit in the agency, a sense of group and professional identity, and of group cohesion. It is true that supervisees working in close proximity in a common enterprise develop some sense of solidarity through informal interaction. Group life is inevitable in any agency and is fostered by coffee breaks, lunching together, and working together on the job. The group supervisory conference supplements and reinforces what happens naturally and ensures that feelings of affiliation and commitment will in fact develop. Furthermore, formal group interaction in supervisory sessions feeds back to intensify and improve informal staff interaction outside these sessions (Joelson 1982).

10. The group conference provides the supervisor with the opportunity of observing the supervisee in a different kind of relationship (Bernard and Goodyear 1998; Hawkins and Shohet 1989). Individual conferences permit the supervisor to understand how a supervisee reacts in a dyadic relationship; the group conference shows the supervisee in action in a group. It provides the supervisor with an additional perspective of how the supervisee functions. As a consequence the supervisor may be in a better position to supervise the worker more effectively in the individual conference. This result is illustrated in the following vignette:

> Mrs. D is a kindly middle-aged worker who does a fine job with her clients but tends to overprotect the underdogs to the extent of denying them room for growth. Mr. L, her supervisor, has been unsuccessful in handling this with

Mrs. D in individual supervision. In group supervision Mrs. D assumes the same role, becomes protector of Miss T, the soft-spoken new worker. With direct observation of this interaction, Mr. L is able to assess with Mrs. D how needful Miss T is of this protection, how Miss T might be allowed to try coping with criticism on her own at future meetings, perhaps even considering how needful Mrs. D is of this role. (S. Moore 1970:19)

11. Group supervision permits an advantageous specialization of function. Any ongoing system, individual conference, or group supervisory conference requires the implementation of both expressive and instrumental roles. Some things need to be done to see that the system is kept operating harmoniously and successfully completes its assigned task. In the individual conference the supervisor has to perform both roles—to see that the work gets done while maintaining a harmonious relationship between supervisor and supervisee. The instrumental demands may at times be antithetical to expressive needs. To insist that expectations be met, to confront to get the work done, conflicts with the need to comfort and reassure. The supervisor has to be simultaneously both the good and the bad parent.

Group supervision permits the separation of these sometimes conflicting role responsibilities (Rosenthal 1999). While the supervisor is communicating support to some member of the group, the group may communicate expectations. While the supervisor is acting to confront, members of the group may act to reassure. Because the group situation allows delegation of different functions to different people, the task of the supervisor is in some ways simplified. He or she can let the group carry the instrumental tasks, confronting, demanding, raising uncomfortable questions, while he or she devotes attention to supportive interventions. At other times the supervisor can do the needling, counting on the group to be supportive.

12. It may be easier for the supervisor to achieve modification of a supervisee's behavior through the medium of the group conference than in an individual conference. If members of the peer group indicate, in the group discussions, an acceptance of the supervisor's point of view, the individual supervisee may be less resistive to change. Learning from peers with whom one feels identified can be easier than learning from a supervisor. Learning from peers is free of the feelings of dependency and authority that complicate learning from the supervisor. Taking advantage of these benefits of the group conference, the supervisor consciously uses them to influence workers toward desirable changes in behavior.

As Moore (1971:5) notes, "Norms formulated in the group through peer interaction are more readily internalized by workers than are the standards handed down from the supervisor as an authority figure. Workers are more apt to incorporate peer-formulated standards into improved work performance." This process is illustrated in the following extract:

> Shortly after the group supervisory meeting opened, Mr. L, a case-worker, complained that the meetings were dealing with material that was "too elementary," and they should move on to getting more "advanced" help with their cases. The supervisor, Mr. W, had anticipated this complaint and was prepared to answer; but he kept silent a moment and his patience was soon rewarded when Mr. M and Miss C came to his defense, itemizing instances where the so-called elementary material helped them with clients. Further, they suggested that some of the problems workers were having (the shoe seemed to fit Mr. L) were because they ignored elementary techniques and wanted to be self-styled psychiatrists. The force of the remarks at this point was greatly enhanced by having come from workers rather than the supervisor. (S. Moore 1971:5)

Clinically, the group modality has been employed in social work because of its potentially therapeutic effects. The supervisory group format offers analogous corrective possibilities (Bernard 1999; Geller 1994). In response to peer solidarity and identification, a supervisee may be induced to change professionally negative behaviors as a result of information and suggestions from the group. The incentive to change may be more powerful within the group than with the supervisor in the individual conference format.

13. Just as the group conference permits the supervisor to observe the supervisee in a somewhat different set of relationships, it permits the supervisee to observe the supervisor under different conditions.

Group supervision gives supervisees an opportunity to learn more about their supervisor. To what extent can he or she yield power gracefully, and to what extent does he or she need to feel in control? How does the supervisor react to different people in the group? Does he or she play favorites, have negative attitudes toward others, or treat group members similarly? How does the supervisor react to pressure when strong conflict around some consequential issue occurs?

14. The group setting provides the supervisee with the opportunity for using the supervisor as a model in learning group-interaction skills (Munson 1997). Through the individual conference, the worker learns something about dyadic interaction; through group supervision, the worker learns something about group interaction. With the growing acceptance of multimethod responsibilities for all workers and the increasing use of group approaches by caseworkers, there is clear advantage to learning about group interaction through group supervision.

15. Group supervision provides a gradual step toward independence from supervision. The movement is from dependence on the supervisor to a lesser measure of dependence on peers to autonomous self-dependence. Group supervision offers an effective medium for power sharing and power equalization between supervisors and supervisees. Consequently, it can serve as a halfway point in the movement toward independent functioning.

We have emphasized that the agency, and particularly the supervisory personnel, should move in the direction of actively encouraging the development of greater independence in functioning by all workers. For the worker who comes to the job with professional qualifications, such as a master's degree in social work (MSW), the move should be toward rapid and nearly total relinquishment of supervisory controls (Barretta-Herman 1993) to being governed by accountability and ethical constraints (Reamer 1998). For the worker who comes without any prior knowledge of social work, the tempo is less rapid and the relinquishment less total. The direction is the same for all workers—toward a decline in the amount and extent of supervision—although the rapidity with which the change is accomplished varies.

Group supervision requires active participation of the worker in lateral teaching of peers, by peers (Barretta-Herman 1993; Hawkins and Shohet 1989; Getz and Agnew 1999; Starling, Baker, and Campbell 1996). Such sharing among colleagues emphasizes a greater measure of practice independence than is true for individual supervision. Not only does the supervisor share with supervisees responsibility for teaching in the group conference, the power of the supervisor is also shared. The supervisees have a greater measure of control and a greater responsibility for the initiative in the group conference. Even responsibility for evaluation is shared. What is evaluation in the individual conference becomes feedback from peers in the group conference. Hence, if at the beginning there is much individual supervision and only a limited amount of group supervision, the movement toward independent, responsible practice should see a change in this balance. Gradually there should be less individual supervision and a greater measure of group supervision. In line with this idea, some agencies have used group supervision in explicit recognition of its potential as a vehicle for fostering independence and autonomy from supervision. Judd, Kohn, and Shulman have reported on their agency's use of group supervision "in helping the worker achieve greater independence and thereby accelerate his professional development" (1962:96).

16. Group supervision provides an opportunity for multicultural education. A racially heterogeneous group of supervisees in active interracial interaction permits exposure to challenges to stereotypes and biases. It may

help in the development of greater awareness and modification of negative ethnocentric attitudes.

Disadvantages of Group Supervision

1. The great advantage of the individual conference is that teaching and learning can be individualized to meet the needs of a particular supervisee. The group conference has to be directed toward the general, common needs of all the supervisees and the special, particular needs of none. As a consequence, the interest in group activity may be highly variable for the individual supervisee. At one moment the group may be concerned with something of vital interest to a particular worker; half an hour later the matter under discussion may be boring or repetitious and of no concern. The principal disadvantage of the group conference is that it cannot easily provide specific application of learning to the worker's own caseload. Given individual needs, it is very likely that any group supervisory session is likely to be perceived as less focused, less structured, and less relevant than individual supervisory sessions.

2. The supervisee may well learn more easily in a group conference through identification with peers, unencumbered by feelings of dependency and hostility toward the authority of the supervisor, but the group presents its own impediments to learning. The group situation stimulates a sort of sibling rivalry and peer competition (Bernard and Goodyear 1998). Each supervisee may be concerned that another will say the smart thing first or will get more of the attention, approval, and affection of the supervisor. Each may be anxious about how well he or she compares with others in the group.

This problem was noted by Apaka, Hirsch, and Kleidman in describing the introduction of group supervision in a hospital social work department: "There was hostility and competitiveness among workers that previously had been concealed effectively. It became clear that the group process was potent in underscoring and bringing out all the previously underscored or unacknowledged subtleties of staff interrelationships" (Apaka, Hirsch, and Kleidman 1967:58).

3. It is more difficult to incorporate a new appointee into a supervisory group than to provide the same appointee with individual supervision. A group with any continuity develops a group identity, a pattern of interpersonal relationships, an allocation of roles, development of cliques and subgroups, and a set of shared understandings. The newcomer, a stranger to all of this, threatens the established equilibrium and is apt to be resented. Group supervision thus imposes a particular problem for new appointees.

4. The individual conference forces the supervisee to come up with his or her own answers and decisions regarding the problem he or she faces. The group context permits the supervisee to abdicate such responsibility and accept group solutions and decisions. He or she is forced to participate and respond in the individual conference; he or she can hide in the safety of numbers provided by the group.

5. If a group offers a large pool of possible sources of insight and support, it also offers more sources of critical feedback. It is easier to expose your feelings to one supervisor in the privacy of an individual conference than to present somewhat inadequate work publicly to a group of four or five peers. If a worker is seeking and can accept critical feedback, the number of participants is an advantage of group supervision; if he or she is hesitant and anxious about critical feedback, it can be a disadvantage. There is a similar risk for the supervisor. The threat to self-esteem and narcissism from saying something stupid in front of a group is greater than the risk of a similar failure in the individual conference. Supervisory ineptitude is exposed simultaneously to many rather than to one.

6. Communication within a group risks a higher probability of failure than in the dyadic interaction. In the dyad the communicator can select ideas and choose words with regard for what may be specially required to ensure accurate reception by his or her one partner. In facing a group of people, each of whom requires a somewhat different approach to an idea and a somewhat different vocabulary for best understanding, the supervisor must compromise. He or she must select the message and words so that they can be received with reasonable accuracy by all, but they still may fail to meet the particular needs of any one.

An intervention that meets the needs of one person may at the same time create a problem for someone else. A complimentary comment to one member may seem like a rejecting comment to another member if the two are in rivalry for the supervisor's acceptance.

7. The safety of numbers that allows the supervisee to raise critical questions and comments also presents a danger that the peer group may organize against the supervisor in the group conference. The supervisor may feel more comfortable in the individual conference, where there is a greater likelihood that he or she can control the interaction. There is a greater threat to such control in the group situation. Consequently, some supervisors might be uneasy about employing group supervision.

In group supervision the supervisor risks loss of control of the meeting. Stimulating, encouraging, and supporting more active participation by the group and granting a larger measure of responsibility for interaction to the group are acts of control by the supervisor. He or she consciously decides to encourage such activity because he or she feels that it is desirable. But the group may decide to do some things the supervisor does not feel are desirable. Having encouraged maximum participation and fuller responsibility for action on the part of the group, the supervisor may find the group has taken the play out of his or her hands. In the individual conference, when something comparable to this occurs, the supervisor can reassert control. In the group situation, the supervisor is outnumbered. Faced with the solidarity of a group in opposition to him or her, the supervisor may find it difficult to regain control. Because of the risk in sharing control of the supervisory conference with the group, the need for personal security on the part of the supervisor is greater.

8. The more cohesive a group is, the more the individual member feels identified with the group, the greater are the pressures to conform to group thinking and attitudes. This cohesion is both a strength and a weakness of group supervision. On one hand, it operates as an advantage in influencing individual supervisees to accept agency procedures and professionally desirable approaches in interaction with clients. On the other hand, it tends to stifle individuality and creativity. Considerable strength and conviction are needed to express ideas and attitudes that run counter to those held by the group. Sometimes these atypical ideas may be valid and helpful to the group in more effectively implementing its tasks. The supervisor, as group leader, needs to act so as to preserve group cohesion but mitigate group tyranny and group think. In achieving this aim, the supervisor supports the expression of atypical attitudes and ideas, is sensitive to a supervisee's ambivalence about expressing them, and establishes as a norm for a group interaction the accepting encouragement of such contributions to group discussion.

9. Accepting the responsibility for group supervision imposes heavy, perhaps unfamiliar demands on supervisors and their knowledge and skills. As group leaders, supervisors have to learn about (or at least refresh their knowledge of) group interaction, group dynamics, and the psychology of individual behavior in the group context (Bernard and Goodyear 1998). Facilitators as well as supervisors, group leaders help develop and maintain group cohesion, monitoring group interaction so that it is productive rather than conflictual. They have to move from an accustomed focus on the individual as the center of interest to perceiving the group entity as the center of concern. If a supervisor cannot successfully reorient his or her focus, he or she may become engaged in an individual supervisory conference in the group context. The tendency might be to respond to a collection of individuals rather than to the group.

The situation for the supervisor is inevitably more difficult as a consequence of a need for a dual focus. The supervisor has to develop and maintain a relationship and a productive pattern of communication between him- or herself and each supervisee. In addition, the supervisor has to develop and maintain relationships and communication patterns between each group member and all the others.

Operating with confidence as a group leader requires more self-assurance than does successfully conducting an individual conference. The group context is more complex and demanding. The complexity of interaction increases geometrically as the number in the group increases arithmetically. Four times as many people makes a sixteenfold increase in possibilities for interaction. In any group there are simultaneous interactions among (1) individual group members, (2) individual group members and the supervisor, (3) the group as a whole and individual members, (4) the group as a whole and the supervisor, and (5) each subgroup, its members, and the supervisor. There is therefore a greater diversity of informational cues and pressures to which the supervisor has to adjust and accommodate as compared with the less complex and more manageable individual supervisory conference.

Individual and Group Supervision: Appropriate Use

Because both individual and group supervision provide special advantages and disadvantages and because both are more or less appropriate in response to different conditions and needs, it is desirable to employ them as planned, complementary procedures. Frequently, the agenda for group conferences derives from recurrent problems discussed in individual conferences; often, the group discussions are subsequently referred to in individual conferences on individual supervisee case situations. The flow is circular, from individual conferences to group conferences to individual conferences. Because the same supervisor is generally responsible for both the individual and group conferences, the different procedures can have unity and continuity. The supervisor has the responsibility of determining how each approach can best be used to further the learning needs of individual supervisees.

The decision as to what should be taught on an individual basis and what should be taught through the group must be based diagnostically on the educational needs of the learner. For example the staff member whose own personal deprivation in early childhood makes it difficult for him to accept placement of children away from their own homes will require considerable help and support in understanding how his own emotional experience influences the way he works with clients. For such a worker, learning would have to have an internal focus where, on a case-by-case basis, he could be helped to change his attitudes toward inadequate parents. The same staff member, however, could also profit from group consideration of this problem. He may discover, for example, that [other staff members] feel this way about such parents and that disapproving attitudes can stem from what is conceived to be a violation of our social values as well as from judgments growing out of individual developmental experiences. In a group the individual may get a different perspective which enables him to grapple more successfully with his own attitudes. This, in turn, may help him to feel less guilt as he works on the problem more introspectively in individual supervision. (Blackey 1957:62–63)

Research on Group Supervision

The question of the advantages and disadvantages of group supervision has been the subject of some empirical research. For reviews of the empirical literature, see Altfeld and Bernard (1997), Bernard and Goodyear (1998), Bradley and Ladany (2001), Holloway and Johnson (1985), and Prieto (1996).

Looking at the experience in supervision of 671 supervisees and 109 supervisors, Shulman found that group sessions were held on an average of twice a month and that "holding regularly scheduled group sessions correlated positively with a good working relationship" (1982:261) between supervisor and supervisee.

The University of Michigan School of Social Work conducted an experiment in which a sample of students assigned to group supervision in fieldwork was compared with a sample of students assigned to individual supervision (Sales and Navarre 1970). Comparisons were made in terms of student satisfaction with mode of supervision, content of supervisory conferences, time expended in supervision, the general level and quality of participation in conferences, and evaluation of practice skills as the outcome of training. In general the experiment indicated that "students performed equally well under each mode of supervision when supervisors' ratings of student practice skills were compared." However, "field instructors using individual supervision spent substantially more time per student in supervisory activities than those who employed group supervision." Because both "modes of supervision result in equivalent overall student performance" and because the difference in time expanded "unequivocally favors group supervision," "the time factor may become pivotal to a choice" (Sales and Navarre 1970: 39–41).

In addition to the greater efficiency in time expended in group supervision, the study further confirms some of the other hypothesized advantages of the approach: "students in group supervision felt greater freedom to communicate dissatisfaction with field instruction to their supervisors and greater freedom to differ with them about professional ideas"; "students in group supervision most liked the varying ideas, experiences, and cases made possible by this mode of supervision" (Sales and Navarre 1970:40). On the other hand, confirming the individualizing advantage of individual supervision, "students in individual supervision most liked the specific help, the help in specific problem areas provided by this method" (Sales and Navarre 1970:40).

An experiment that tested the two supervisory procedures in training counselors arrived at similar conclusions. The group of trainees were randomly assigned to individual supervision and group supervision. The data regarding training outcomes "suggest that the individual method is not significantly different from the group method in producing some desirable outcomes. It is reasonable, therefore, to use group supervision at least as an adjunct to individual supervision until further research suggests that a different method is obviously superior" (Lanning 1971:405).

Savickas, Marquart, and Supinski (1986) did attempt to determine empirically the variables of effective group supervision. Eighty-four medical students receiving group supervision in learning to interview were asked to provide critical incidents of effective and ineffective group supervision. Categorizing and factoring the responses, the researchers found that the effective group supervisor modeled good interviewing. The supervisor provided structured instruction; evaluated supervisee strengths and weaknesses through accurate, specific, and reinforcing feedback; and facilitated the development of independent functioning. In general, effective group supervisors provided structure and reassurance.

In studying the behaviors of peers in group supervision Hoese (1987) found that peers tended to provide mutual support to one another in developing a comfortable group environment. Supervisors were perceived as establishing goals, providing feedback in helping group members evaluate their work, and providing direct help or suggestions regarding client contacts. Kruger et al. (1988) observed and tape-recorded group supervision of four counseling teams in a children's treatment center in a forty-five-day period. Group meetings tended to be highly task-oriented, concerned with problems relating to resolving the emotional difficulties of residents. Participants rated the group experience as positive and satisfactory. Higher levels of satisfaction were related to higher levels of participation in group instruction.

Wilbur et al. (1991) describe an explicitly structured format for group supervision in which supervisees provide the group with a written request-for-assistance statement, and round-robin responses from the group are employed. A pilot research study of the format using a control group supported the desirability of a more structured approach to group supervision (Wilbur et al. 1994).

A qualitative study by Walter and Young (1999) compared student satisfaction with alternating weeks of individual and group supervision in a child welfare field practicum. In individual supervision, students appreciated the "individual attention, case-specific direction and support, being the initiator and director of their own learning process, developing their clinical skills, and acquiring the supervisor's increased understanding of the case material and the clinical process" (Walter and Young 1999:81). In group supervision, students were "able to validate one another, support one another, and to explore perhaps more deeply a particular point of intervention," as well as "see a larger view of the case" and its long-term goals (Walter and Young 1999:83–84). Despite complaints about the time required for writing process recordings, students preferred individual over group supervision. In the former, they learned to apply theoretical perspectives to a particular case, how to utilize short-term helping goals to focus their practice, and what to say and do in the next client interview. In group supervision, they learned to seek consultation from colleagues with different values, knowledge, and skills. Initially ambivalent about group supervision, the students came to value group encouragement and support for their work.

These limited citations suggest that there is relatively little empirical research regarding group supervision. Holloway and Johnson, in reviewing such research in 1985, noted that we were "at a very rudimentary level of explaining and understanding group supervision" (Holloway and Johnson 1985:333). A decade later, Prieto in updating the research available concluded that Holloway and Johnston's "recommendations to better research and understand the group supervision process . . . seems to have gone largely unheeded" (Prieto 1996:298)—a conclusion supported by Werstlein and Borders (1997).

Group Supervision: Process

Many considerations to which we might call attention regarding the process of group supervision are not particular or unique to the group supervisory situation. They are generally true for any circumstance in which a group is used as the vehicle for achieving the desired objective. Consequently, social workers familiar with the different uses of groups in providing agency service already know much that is applicable to the use of the group in supervision. This is true not only for group-service social workers but also for caseworkers who have employed group approaches in adoption, foster care, protective service, public assistance, corrections, health and mental health, and family therapy and for community organizers who operate in a group context. Awareness of the procedures that are most productive and the recurrent problems in group interaction that are likely to be encountered, is applicable (with some adaptation) to the group supervisory situation. The objective in this section is to review some of these considerations, translating the generally applicable material to the special context of group supervision.

Group Setting

Physical arrangement is a determinant of group interaction and needs to be given careful attention by the supervisor in preparing for a group supervisory conference. A circle of chairs in a room of moderate dimensions in terms of the size of the group is perhaps the most desirable arrangement. Too large a room makes the group feel insignificant and lost; too small a room may produce a cramped, uncomfortable feeling and may require too great a closeness and intimacy between members. A circular arrangement permits everybody to look at and talk to everybody else. Being able to look at as well as listen to everyone else permits easier perception of nonverbal communication messages. Furthermore, a circle has no identifiable status position, no front-of-the-group position. The supervisor can melt into the group by taking his or her place unobtrusively anywhere in the circle. Although the circle does not entirely neutralize the supervisor's dominant status in the group, it helps downplay it somewhat. Freedom from competing noises and interruptions are other components of desirable physical arrangement.

A schedule specifying the hour and day for meetings should be clearly established and adhered to with some regularity. It helps give the group continuity and becomes a necessary part of the group structure. It shows respect for the workers' time and permits them to schedule other appointments in advance with assurance that there will not be a conflict. In general, it might be good to avoid scheduling group supervisory meetings early in the afternoon. The lethargy that often follows lunch tends to hamper group interaction.

Though perhaps responsible for the initial series of meetings, the supervisor may subsequently delegate responsibility for calling and chairing the meeting to members of the group. Rotating responsibility for leadership among supervisees in the group optimizes participation and helps develop autonomy. Under the best of circumstances the group meeting agenda is preplanned by the group members, but where this has not been done the supervisor has responsibility for such preplanning.

Purpose

The group meeting, like the individual conference, needs to have a clearly defined purpose. Formed by the agency to achieve its purposes, the group is not entirely free to determine its own purposes. Group and individual supervision have the same ultimate objectives, and group conferences are required to have purposeful outcomes that further these objectives. A considerable amount of expensive agency and personnel time is invested in each group supervisory conference. A meeting of eight people for an hour and a half costs more than a day's pay for one worker. The supervisor consequently has some responsibility to attempt to direct the group interaction so that purposes congruent with the general objectives of supervision are selected and so that such purposes are more or less achieved.

Group members are also personally investing their own limited time and energy. If the group meeting serves no productive, useful purpose, they have every right to feel disappointed and resentful. In a study of social work students' reactions to group supervision, a major dissatisfaction was "time wasted in tedious, irrelevant discussions" (Sales and Navarre 1970:40).

Leadership and Planning

In group supervision, group interaction is employed as a "method used toward a specified end and group supervisory discussions are bounded discussions" (Perlman 1950:334) limited by the objectives of supervision. Consequently, the supervisor in the group conference is a leader in the explicit sense of having

> the authority and the obligation to guide and to direct and often to require. . . . He must take responsibility both for stimulating discussion and for controlling it; both for releasing the (supervisees') energies and for insistently directing them to the task for which they have been freed. He is responsible not only to promote movement but literally to 'steer the course' so that direction is not lost. He must not only keep the [group] going but help it to arrive. (Perlman 1950:335)

However egalitarian the approach, the supervisor cannot entirely shed the mantle of group leadership. His or her status in the agency hierarchy and his or her position inevitably denote a special status in the social system of the group. This status is reinforced by the supervisor's education and experience, which provide some special knowledge and skill that he or she is responsible for using (and is expected to use) in behalf of the group.

An egalitarian stance on the part of the supervisor ("I am just another member of the group"; "We are all the same here") is seen as false by some and as an abdication of responsibility by others. The very fact that the supervisor has the authority to define his or her position as not having authority is, in and of itself, proof of authority.

Because the supervisor, as designated leader, has authority not from the group but from agency administration and is responsible to agency administration for what the group does, the group is not democratic. In some instances, the supervisor may have to determine what decisions will be made and what procedures will need to be accepted by the group.

The group is not free to develop its own solutions but needs to recognize constraints imposed by agency budgets, legislative regulations, or agency policy. The supervisor has the responsibility of being knowledgeable about such constraints and sharing this knowledge with the group. Groups that formulate recommendations that cannot be implemented feel futile and discouraged.

Although leadership of the group is primarily the responsibility of the supervisor, it is not his or her responsibility alone. The group itself has considerable responsibility for the many decisions that relate to group purpose and functioning. As a matter of fact, a supervisor might react positively and with some relief to reduced hierarchical responsibility for the group sessions (Parihar 1983).

The supervisor here, as in the individual conference, is only the first among equals. Furthermore, it is clear that rigid, insistent adherence to an approach that emphasizes supervisory control is self-defeating and counterproductive. Supervisees can be required by the agency to attend group meetings, but there is no way to compel their participation. Though physically present, supervisees can defeat the purposes of group supervision. The purpose of the meeting and the nature of group interaction have to meet in some measure not only the needs of the agency but also the needs of the supervisees themselves.

The amount of leadership exercised by the supervisor should be the minimum necessary to assure that the group can do its job. As in the individual conference, the supervisor, as group leader, faces the dilemma of leading without imposing, directing without controlling, and suggesting without dictating. Over a period of time in the history of the group, the supervisor should be progressively less active, and an increasing proportion of the initiative, responsibility, control, direction, and activity should pass over to the group itself. The supervisor has to be flexible and comfortable enough to share this responsibility. Some roles are most effectively enacted by a member of the group rather than the supervisor. Leadership is then diffused rather than focused in the supervisor.

If the supervisor is invested with the responsibility for defining and implementing—however tentatively, however gently—the aim and objectives of the group, adequate preparation for group meetings is mandatory. The supervisor has to have a clear idea of what he or she will propose for group consideration, however experimentally. He or she must decide the points that need to be raised for discussion and the content that needs to be communicated and taught. The supervisor needs to think out the answers to some of the more difficult questions that can be anticipated. He or she needs to clarify which points will encounter greatest resistance and which may require repeated emphasis. In effect, he or she needs to imagine the general scenario of the meeting as it might unfold in reality.

Some plan—flexible, subject to change and, if necessary, to abandonment—is desirable. Having an outline of how the group meeting is likely to go is reassuring. However, a plan is advantageous only if it is used as a guide. If it becomes a crutch, the supervisor will resist deviating from it even when that appears necessary to follow the legitimate interests of the group, as he or she is psychologically dependent on it. The supervisor's preparation also involves bringing in supporting books, pamphlets, articles, forms, and directives that are pertinent to the content of the meeting.

The general purpose of group supervision may be clear, but because it is often stated in a very global way, the supervisor has to help translate it into specific, clearly identifiable objectives for each particular meeting. "Learning to offer more effective and efficient service" does not answer the question of what the group will actually do when it meets next Tuesday morning from 9 A.M. to 10:30 A.M. The supervisor, whose experience and perspective provide a clear idea of what supervisees need to know, to do, and to be, should be in a position to derive from the general purpose the topics for a series of meetings. However, though it would be helpful for the supervisor, as group leader, to propose specific topics for group meetings, it would be best if these were advanced tentatively as suggestions for consideration rather than as requirements for acceptance. The group itself may have suggestions for relevant and significant topics that have greater priority and interest for the members. However, achieving a shared purpose is not easy. Often the purpose that interests one subgroup is of little or no interest to others in the group. The objectives on which the supervisor is administratively required to focus may be accepted with reluctance or covert resistance.

A clearly stated purpose that has group understanding and acceptance is one of the best guarantees against overcontrol and overdirection of group activities by the supervisor. The group rather than the supervisor gives direction and meaning to group interaction, determines the relevance of contributions, and structures group activity. Knowing what to do and being motivated to do it permit the group to exercise self-direction.

Consideration needs to be given not only to the plan for a particular meeting but also to the way this meeting relates to the meeting that precedes and follows it. To what extent and in what ways does this specific meeting fit into some overall plan for group supervision?

Planning should include consideration of the most advantageous format for the kind of content with which the meeting is concerned. Sometimes a case presentation might be best; sometimes a movie, a role-playing session, or a panel presentation is appropriate. Different kinds of presentation procedures involve different levels of participation, involvement, and preparation from different members of the group.

Content and Method

The content of group supervisory meetings includes matters of general concern to social workers in any agency—recording, interviewing, referral procedures, psychological tests, caseload management, worker-client interaction, use of consultation, the ethics of practice, and so on. Often it is specific to the clientele served by a particular agency—understanding the delinquent, the adoptive child, the patient with a chronic or terminal illness, or the unmarried mother. Sometimes it is concerned with procedures, forms, and reports that are particular to a given agency, with communications to workers from administration, or with problems identified by workers that they are anxious to communicate to administration. It may also be concerned with the particular community in which the agency operates—community composition, community problems, agency resources in the community, and the nature of the relation between this agency and other agencies.

On occasion, general agency situations determine agenda items. If the agency is concerned with formulating a budget, this might be the opportune time to discuss budgeting matters as they relate to the unit's operations; if a state or other third-party case-audit is scheduled, it makes reviews of some related content relevant; if evaluations for unit members are scheduled for the immediate future, the evaluation form and associated questions might be discussed. Agenda items for group meetings are frequently and, most desirably, derived from interests and problems recurrently identified in individual supervisory conferences as common to a number of different workers.

By deliberate choice, group supervision may become individual supervision in a group setting. The group of supervisees might decide to conduct sessions in which the work of a particular member of the group is singled out for discussion. Rather than discussing matters that are of general concern, each meeting is devoted to the particular concerns of some individual member through case presentations.

Traditionally, clinical case material is the most frequently used stimulus for group supervisory discussions. Such material vicariously replicates actual situations with which group members are grappling, making those situations vivid and interesting, and motivating group involvement. For most productive use, case material needs to be carefully selected and prepared. Its very richness permits all sorts of digressions that have little real yield. Consequently, selection of case material should be in line with clearly defined objectives of the group meeting. In preparing the material for distribution, the supervisor may profitably condense and paraphrase so as to sharpen the teaching focus. Often, a section of dramatic interaction may be excerpted from a longer case record for group discussion purposes.

Although case material by definition is concerned with some individual instances, the focus of the discussion cannot remain tied to an individual case situation if learning is to be generalized and transferred. At some point the group (and if not the group, the supervisor) needs to determine what the particular case situation offers for learning about such situations in general.

When a group member presents his or her own material for discussion, there are additional problems. The supervisor may work with the supervisee toward selecting a case for presentation that is likely to have greatest value for both the supervisee and the group. The supervisee may need help in preparing the case for group presentation; he or she may also need the supervisor's support in coping with the anxiety that case presentation arouses and help in clarifying what group reactions are likely to be encountered. Because this is a case situation in which the agency has ongoing contact, the presentation may run the risk of group supervision of the worker that parallels the individual supervisory conference in deciding on specific planning for the case. The more appropriate use of the case situation in the group context would, again, be a general focus that permits group members to apply learning from this case to situations in their own caseloads.

Role-playing is a procedure often used in group conferences. It can be improvised readily and offers a dramatic episode for discussion. The outlines of the proposed role play have to be clearly presented to the group—what is the nature of the problem to be acted out, and who are the participants? Situations for role playing could include an application for temporary financial assistance at a department of public welfare, a rejection interview with an adoption applicant, an interview with an unmarried mother struggling to decide whether to surrender her child, a first interview with a parolee after his return to the community, an interview with a daughter concerned about institutionalization for her aged mother. Beyond the definition of the situation and identification of participants, the approach of the worker can also be defined. The worker can be asked to play the role in Rogerian, solution-focused, or behavioral terms—acceptingly, strategically, or directively.

Willingness to participate in role-playing requires a considerable sense of security in the group. Particularly in early meetings, obtaining volunteers may be difficult. It is easier if initially the supervisor volunteers to play the worker—the more difficult role. His or her playing the worker may inhibit spontaneous critical comment, but this depends partially on the freedom to criticize that the supervisor communicates to the group. Using the role-playing names of the participants helps depersonalize the discussion afterward. It is not "Mr. P" (the actual name of the supervisor whose work the group is discussing) but rather "Mr. Smith," the name the supervisor adopted for the role play.

The group can move into role playing through the use of brief playlets. In the midst of some discussion, the supervisor can suggest that, for the moment, he or she play the client they have been talking about. For example, the supervisor might suggest, "As the client, I have just said to the worker, 'I got so mad and discouraged that I sometimes feel like I just wanted to get away and never see the kids again.' How would you, as a worker, respond to that? Let's play it for a minute." Frequent use of such role-playing provides a good group introduction to role-playing.

Role-play participation enables the workers to understand more clearly, through vicarious identification, how an assistance applicant, an unmarried mother, an adoptive parent, or a parolee feels about his or her situation. However, like a thematic apperception test, role-playing permits and encourages self-revelation. Without realizing it, we tend to act ourselves and expose to the group some parts of ourselves that were previously hidden. Consequently, role-playing makes participants vulnerable. The supervisor has to be sensitive to the need to protect participants from destructive criticism. There is also a possibility that a role-playing session that generates strong feelings may become a group therapy session.

Audio- and videotapes are appropriately used as the basis for group discussions. Adequate preparation is invariably necessary. Audiotapes are often difficult to understand, and the strain of listening to unclear, disembodied voices can leave the group without energy for discussion. If possible, written transcripts of the tapes should be made available to the group. They not only permit people to follow what is said but also make subsequent discussion easier as people refer to the transcript in making a point. Playing a videotape without previewing it can often be disappointing and a waste of time. The catalog description of the tape may be only remotely related to its content. Familiarity with the equipment and with the room used for showing it is also necessary. Countless groups have been frustrated because an extension cord was not long enough to meet an outlet, because there were no blinds to darken the room, because no one could connect and operate the equipment, or because the audio or video portion of the film was garbled or defective.

Supervisor's Responsibility in the Group Conference

Just as the supervisor has inducted supervisees into the social system of the individual conference and has interpreted the respective, differentiated responsibilities of supervisor and supervisee in that system, he or she similarly inducts supervisees into their role as members of the group supervisory conference. The nature of reciprocal group-membership role expectations and obligations should be clearly outlined. Supervisees are given to understand that they have some responsibility for preparing for the meetings, for instance, reading any relevant material that is distributed in advance. They have responsibility for contributing to group interaction and keeping such contributions pertinent to the discussion; they have responsibility for listening to others with respect and attention and should refrain from making interventions that will create unproductive conflict and tension. They should also help in dealing with such conflicts and tensions as they arise. They need to indicate respect for other members of the group, to display a willingness to accept them as resources for learning, and demonstrate some commitment to help achieve group goals.

Early on in the group process the supervisor needs to make an explicit attempt to establish some group norms. The norms, if accepted and repeatedly implemented, help regulate the behavior of group members. Agreed-on norms of productive group supervision might include the following:

1. To allow everyone to have his or her say without undue interruption.
2. To listen carefully and attentively to what others are saying.
3. To respond to what others have said.
4. To keep one's contribution and response reasonably relevant to the focus of what is being discussed. Group membership requires a measure of deindividuation, some setting aside of one's own preferences to maintain the integrity of the group.
5. To share material and experiences that might contribute to more effective professional practice.

Most of the principles of learning that are applicable to the individual conference are equally applicable to the group conference. As in the individual conference, the supervisor is responsible for establishing a context that facilitates learning.

The supervisor, as group leader, engages in many of the same kinds of behavior he or she manifests in individual conferences—asking questions; soliciting and supporting the expression of ideas, attitudes, and feelings; requesting amplification of supervisees' points of view; restating and clarifying supervisees' ideas and feelings; summarizing, recapitulating, enabling, expediting, facilitating, focusing, and redirecting; resolving conflicts; making suggestions and offering information and advice; supporting and reassuring; and challenging and communicating agency expectations. The supervisor, as group leader, raises the provocative suggestion, acts as devil's advocate, calling attention to what has been missed, stimulating productive conflict to enhance instruction, and acting as a traffic cop to the interaction. He or she acts as catalyst, mentor, arbiter, and resource person.

The supervisor orchestrates the activities of the individuals who make up the group. He or she maximizes individual contributions, coordinates and synthesizes them, and weaves them together into a pattern. "The discussion leader must be able to focus discussion so that, for all its diversity, it maintains an essential wholeness, a basic unity. . . . Periodically the discussion leader 'pulls together' related points of the discussion. If discussion is visualized as the spokes of a wheel radiating from the hub, the leader may be said to 'rim the wheel'" (Perlman 1950:336).

Discussion in and of itself is not a particularly efficient procedure for learning, problem solving, or decision making. Discussion has been known to confuse and confound rather than to systematize and clarify thinking. As Towle said, discussion that is not focused through the direction of a leader and organized and reorganized through intermittent summarization can become a flight into purposeless activity—"activity which, in not attaining its aims, often breaks down into noisy fragments or sinks into silence. . . . For just as the client's unburdening will not necessarily reeducate or heal, just as the caseworker must direct him to talk to a purpose and help him focus and relate his production toward activity in the solution of his problem" (Towle 1954:359), so the supervisor as group leader must take some responsibility for purpose and focus of group discussion.

Groups, like individuals, resist the often difficult, unpleasant, or uncomfortable tasks that need to be worked on if productive purposes are to be achieved. Groups manifest ambivalence and resistance by irrelevant digressions, unproductive silences, fruitless argumentation, and side conversations among subgroups. The supervisor has the responsibility of holding the group to its purpose and stimulating and rewarding the kind of group interaction that will optimally help the group achieve its purpose.

At the same time the supervisor delays disclosure of his or her own views to prevent premature closure of discussion. Ultimately, of course, he or she is obligated to share them with the group, clearly and explicitly. But if, as in the individual conference, the supervisor indicated early in the discussion what he or she thought, this would act as a constraint on free exchange and would relieve supervisees of the stimulus and responsibility in finding their own answers. If challenged with "Well, what do *you* think?" the supervisor can legitimately respond, "I'll be glad to share that with you later, but at this point I think you all have some thoughts about this that we can profitably share with one another."

The pattern of informal group interaction that takes place in the agency outside the group meetings is brought into the group supervision meetings. Some people like each other, some dislike each other, some are indifferent to each other. Workers play out these feelings in the way they relate to each other. The supervisor needs to be aware of these patterns of relationship and how they might influence subgroup formation and reactions to what a particular individual says in the group. A knowledge of individual needs and the pattern of informal interaction outside the group helps the supervisor identify the nature of hidden agendas that help explain otherwise inexplicable in-group behavior. The supervisor knows a great deal about the individuals who make up the group and actively uses this knowledge in evaluating and understanding group interaction.

As Shulman (1982) points out, however, a deviant member of the group can be of considerable assistance to the supervisor as a catalyst in getting difficult work done. Shulman illustrates this by detailing a group supervisory meeting concerned with discussion of how to make do with less because of agency cutbacks and still maintain service. After the supervisor introduced the problem,

> a few people asked some questions, there was some silence, then Lou made a suggestion for a minor cutback in his area. I said I thought that was a helpful start. Frank jumped in and said he thought the discussion was a waste of time. I was angry at his cutting off what I thought was a beginning at a hard job. I said: "I'm sorry you feel that way, Frank. It's not a very constructive attitude. I don't think you are being helpful, and I am sure the others in the department feel the same way". . . . Frank was quiet for the remainder of the discussion. (Shulman 1982:239)

The supervisor's reaction made it difficult for other members of the group to express any strong feelings about the cutback. Recognizing this, at the next meeting the supervisor used Frank's remark to reopen the discussion.

> "I began by saying . . . that when Frank said the discussion was a waste of time, I felt on the spot, so I put him off. I didn't admit how uncomfortable the whole idea of talking to you about the cuts had made me. I suspect many of you probably agreed with Frank. Is that true?"
> Lorraine said she thought across-the-board cuts were unfair. The fact is, many other departments had fat in them, we all knew it, and yet each de-

partment was being treated equally in the cuts. I was surprised by how strongly she said this, obviously very upset. (Shulman 1982:240)

This was followed by similar expressions of dissatisfaction from other members of the group. Rather than planning on how to reformulate service delivery to accommodate the cuts, the group, as a result of this discussion of their feelings, planned on a meeting with the administrator to protest the cuts.

Each supervisee brings to the group meeting his or her own needs and anxieties, which eventually find expression in the way he or she behaves in the group. The supervisor has the problem of responding to individual behavior in a way that furthers the purposes of the group and at the same time meets the individual's needs. Often the best that can be achieved is some compromise between individual need and group need. Reconciliation of conflicting group and individual needs is sometimes impossible; the supervisor, giving priority to group needs, may have to ignore or actually deny the satisfaction of individual need. The persistent disrupter who seeks to use the group for satisfaction of insatiable attention-getting needs may have to be suppressed; the time allotted to monopolizers of group discussion may have to be firmly limited; the cynical demolisher of group morale may have to be resolutely moderated; the consistently passive supervisee may need to be prodded out of his or her lethargy. To keep all the group interested and motivated the supervisor must, without guilt, limit his or her concern for any one person in the group. Needs of the group, as a group, have priority.

The supervisor's responsibility denies him or her the flexibility of accepting any and every contribution, however subjectively correct for the person advancing it. If our claim to being a profession has substance, it means that we have established some procedures, practice principles, and approaches that are objectively more correct, more desirable, more efficacious than others. It is these responses that the supervisor is helping the group learn and accept. Consequently, some contributions from the group need to be challenged and rejected by the supervisor. Because the sting of rejection in the presence of a group is sharper than in the individual conference, the supervisor has to be even more sensitive and compassionate here.

The group supervision equivalent of rejecting the sin but not the sinner is to reject the comment but not the commentator. The supervisor does this subtly and understandingly, perhaps saying: "I see you have given this considerable thought but if we did it this way what negative consequences could result?" "It's easy to get confused about this. The point you are making is based on somewhat outmoded information. Actually the average assistance payments for a family of four is currently __" "I know that what you say is a point of view held by many people, but studies relating to this show that—"

Sometimes the supervisor can accept part of the comment and by reinterpretation or change of emphasis convert it into an acceptable contribution. "It may be, as you say, that the social system rather than the client needs changing, but how can we help Mrs. F, for whom something has to be done this afternoon?"

It would be best, of course, if the group itself takes the responsibility for correcting, rejecting, or amending erroneous information and approaches that might do a disservice to the client. But the group is not always aware of what needs correcting, and the supervisor cannot abdicate responsibility for this. Because members of the group are frequently on the same level in terms of education and experience, the nature of the error is not as readily evident to them. In addition, they identify as peers with other group members, and they are understandably reluctant to confront them. Reluctance to criticize also derives from hesitancy about creating friction in the group. Refraining from necessary criticism to maintain group harmony is one of the weaknesses of group supervision. Maintenance of a good group relationship may take precedence over the desirability of engaging in some difficult activities necessary for the optimum achievement of the group's objective. Expressive needs prevent fulfillment of instrumental tasks. Furthermore, because the supervisor has administrative responsibility for the work of every individual member of the group, there is hesitancy about intruding on his or her responsibility. Group members may feel limited responsibility to critique the work of a peer because this responsibility is formally invested in the individual supervisor-supervisee relationship.

For a number of different reasons, then, willingness to be openly critical develops slowly in most groups. In reporting on her own experience as a group supervisor, Smith notes that "for the first dozen sessions we were very supportive and encouraging towards the other participants, and few challenging or critical comments were made during the early reticent stage. Since then, workers have become more clear, direct and specific with their observations and thoughts" (Smith 1972:15).

When necessary expressive functions—group maintenance functions—are not performed by members of the group, the supervisor performs them. He or she mediates between conflicting subgroups; prevents, or tempers, scapegoating; offers help and support to group members who are fearful or reticent about participating; and tries to influence the monopolizer to accept a more quiescent role. Good discussion leadership does not necessarily imply that everyone participates equally, only that everyone has the opportunity for equal participation.

The supervisor attempts to protect individual members from the hostile reaction of the group and protects the group from its own self-destructive, divisive tendencies. While protecting the weak from the assaults of the strong, the supervisor has to act in a noncondemning manner, redirecting or redefining the hostile intervention so that only the comment is rejected.

In implementing the expressive-system maintenance responsibilities, the supervisor is friendly, warm, encouraging, and accepting in his or her interaction with the group, is sensitive to emerging feelings that may be disruptive to group interaction, moves to harmonize and resolve them, and exercises a gate-keeping function so that each member will have a safe opportunity to share thoughts and feelings. The supervisor has to be ready to find compromises for serious disagreements and in doing so be able to distinguish disabling disagreements from helpful differences of opinion.

The supervisor is responsible for keeping the tension at a level of optimum group productivity, heightening it by stimulation and/or confrontation when necessary and reducing it by reassurance, encouragement, and tension-releasing humor when it gets too high.

As in the individual conference, the supervisor must seek to establish and maintain an emotional atmosphere that will foster the achievement of goals. He or she seeks to establish a climate that will enable people to learn freely, to consider all alternatives to a decision, to risk change, and to communicate openly. The kinds of relationships between supervisor and supervisee that are helpful in the conference are similarly helpful in the group meeting. The supervisor's responses demonstrate to group members a model of tolerance, acceptance, and good patterns of communication. Research on the outcome of group experiences indicates that positive outcomes are associated with warm, caring group leaders who provide a cognitive framework for group interaction.

Task and group-maintenance problems are interrelated. The group that is effective in accomplishing its tasks is likely to have better morale and a greater sense of cohesion. A group that seems to accomplish little and never gets anywhere is more likely to encounter expressions of dissatisfaction and divisiveness. The supervisor who effectively aids the group in accomplishing acceptable objectives is also helping develop more positive patterns of interaction among group members.

In ending the group supervisory meeting, the supervisor summarizes the main points covered in the meeting, relates them (if possible) to conclusions of previous meetings, and ties them in with the topic of the next meeting. Material for the next meeting is distributed, and the group is reminded of specific responsibilities previously contracted for by individual members for the next meeting. If such continuity has not been previously established, the leader needs to reserve a block of time before the end of the meeting for a firm decision on what the group will be doing the next time it meets.

Whereas the frequency of participation on the part of the supervisor decreases (as it should) as the group continues to meet, the nature of his or her inventions remains rather constant. Most often the supervisor's interventions are concerned with direct teaching, for example, giving technical information about agency procedures; explaining agency policy; explaining social work theory; or questioning to stimulate further discussion, get clarification of thinking, elicit negative and positive feeling reactions, and get further information from the group. In addition, interventions offer support to the group or to some individual member, clarify the nature and direction of group discussion, provide active leadership to the group (i.e., initiating and terminating group activity), and summarize.

Humor in Group Supervision

Laughter provides a welcome break for the group. Serious consideration of clinical and administrative problems is stressful. The refreshing interposition of a moment of humor enables the group to return refreshed to its work. The group of medical social workers discussing terminally ill patients gets a respite when one of the group describes death as the ultimate discharge plan (Bennett and Blumenfield 1989). A supervisor chairing a group supervision meeting was asked to indicate where she stood in a heated debate about some clinical problem. Not ready to declare herself explicitly because this would cut off discussion, the supervisor said, "I feel like a politician who was asked where he stood on a certain bill. He said, 'Some of my constituents are for the bill, some of my constituents are against the bill, and I am for my constituents.'"

Humor acts as a safety valve for tension in the group. An acrimonious interchange between one member of the group and another or between one clique and another can be defused by an appropriately humorous remark. Group coherence is enhanced in the collective experience of laughter. Laughter together unites the group, performing an integrative function.

Kidding among peers is used to control deviance in the group and communicate group norms. People are kidded about behavior the unit regards as unacceptable. The judicious use of humor by the supervisor tends to help develop camaraderie and bonding, group cohesion and an atmosphere of playful informality.

A sense of humor is a positive attribute of the effective supervisor (Vinton 1989; Consalvo 1989). Laughing together means that supervisor and supervised share the same meaning of the situation. It tends to reduce status barriers.

There is a problem that stems from the fact that humor can have a covert aggressive component. Through humor the supervisee can risk derogating the person and skills of the supervisor. What we would never risk saying seriously, we can say humorously because humor contains the metacommunication that we don't really mean what we are saying. As La Rochefoucauld said, humor "permits us to act rudely with impunity."

The possibility of offending through the use of humor has increased with the growing concern about "politically correct" use of language, particularly in the group context. A supervisee in a mental hospital says,

> In staff meetings people seem uptight and careful about humor. We have very difficult cases, and at times I would feel better if I could just say, "you know, these people are crazy," but that's a no-no I would not care to risk in the group. In my individual conferences I am able to relax with my supervisor and can joke about some of my frustrations in an "unprofessional" way.

The comment also suggests the cathartic effect of humor. In group supervision, as in the individual conference, the supervisor should indicate a receptive reciprocal attitude toward nondisruptive, nonhurtful humor.

Illustration of Group Supervision

The following long quote is from the supervisor's report of a group supervisory meeting of a protective service unit in a county public welfare agency. It illustrates some aspects of the process of group supervision. The group consists of seven workers assigned to the unit. Five of them have an MSW. All have at least one year of experience in the unit. The group meetings, scheduled for one and a half hours every two weeks, supplement individual conferences, which are held once a week. The supervisor is responsible for scheduling and conducting the meetings. The meetings are held in the agency conference room around a large, boat-shaped table. The first thirty to forty minutes of this meeting are devoted to some general announcements and are followed by a discussion of techniques in helping abusive parents make changes in their behavior.

> George had been, as usual, a rather inactive participant. I observed that he had taken some notes, had nodded his head in apparent agreement with others at different times and had leaned forward at other times in apparent interest in what was being said. However, he himself had contributed little to the discussion. At this point, however, his nonverbal activity seemed to increase in intensity. He crossed and uncrossed his legs, leaned forward and back in his chair, and rubbed the back of his neck. I interpreted this to suggest that he might respond to a direct invitation to participate so I chanced it and, taking advantage of a slight pause in the discussion, I said, "George, I wonder if you would care to share your reactions to what has been said?" I tried to

make the invitation tentative and general so that he would not feel an obligation to respond to any particular point made in the discussion but could feel free to respond to anything that had been said. I attempted to make the tone of my invitation light rather than peremptory so as to suggest that it would be all right if he declined my invitation to participate. I tried to catch his eye as I said this, pausing a little after calling his name. He, however, kept looking at his notebook.

There was a moment of silence which increased the pressure on George to respond. Having initiated the invitation out of a conviction that George, like any other member of the group, had an obligation to contribute his fair share to the discussion, I wasn't going to rescue George too early by breaking the silence without waiting a while. He shifted in his chair but continued to look down. He said, "Well," and then paused. Then, looking at the wall, avoiding eye contact with any member of the group, he started up again, saying, "I guess the whole discussion kind of pisses me off. Here we are trying to figure out how to be nice and understanding and accepting of these lousy parents who crack skulls and belt a defenseless infant around. I say to hell with them. They had their chance to care for the kid adequately and they didn't. Out of protection to the kids we ought to petition the courts for termination [of parental rights] and place them. And then take legal action against the parents for abuse. That's the only way to discourage this sort of behavior and this is the way to protect other children from this sort of thing."

The more he talked, the more vehement he became. When he finished there was a kind of dead silence. I recognized that he had articulated a strongly felt, but often suppressed, attitude that was generally characterized as "unprofessional," a component of the protective social worker's ambivalence that was rarely openly expressed—at least in official sponsored meetings (it is frequently said by one worker to another in informal contacts in the washroom, coffee breaks, etc.). Consequently, after a short pause, but not giving anybody else a real chance to respond. I said, "Well, there is something to what you say. It's understandable that social workers concerned with child abuse might get to feel this way. What do others in the group feel about this?"

I was deliberate in taking the initiative because I wanted to protect George from any direct criticism from others, which would be easy to do, because he was expressing an "unfashionable" opinion. Secondly, some members of the group might be threatened by what George had said because it was a feeling that they themselves were struggling to control and [they might be] prompted to attack him in an effort to protect their own equilibrium. Thirdly, I wanted to give official sanction to George's comments—not as a correct point of view but one which was acceptable for open discussion. Fourthly, I suspected that many in the group had hostile feelings toward abusive parents (you would have to be either pretty callous or pretty saintly not to, after some of the things we had all seen) and might welcome a chance to discuss it now that it was brought out in the open. Consequently, I was more directive than usual in taking the initiative here but did it consciously and deliberately for the reasons cited.

In saying what I said, to focus the discussion on the point of view raised, I tried to depersonalize it and universalize the comment. Not "What do you think about what George has said?" but "Social Workers might feel this way. What do you think?" Having said what I said I sat back, physically withdrawing, my intent being to give the initiative back to the group and suggest that they were once again in control and responsible for the proceedings.

It didn't work. George's comment was too threatening or too tempting. Perhaps some felt that once they started expressing hostility to the abusive parents, they might not be able to control themselves. I really don't know what was operating internally in members of the group. I do know that nobody responded to what I had said and the continuing silence was growing more oppressive. Something needed to be done and I, as the one officially in charge of the group (the leader?), had the responsibility for doing it.

After a silence which seemed eternal (but was really only about seven to ten seconds) I intervened again. I was also pressured by the fact that I was conscious that George, for all the vehemence with which he had said what he had said, was now growing more and more uncomfortable about being responsible for getting us into this impasse—so I felt an obligation to protect him again. My intervention this time was designed to deliberately sanction negative feelings toward abusive parents and consequently to make acceptable the open expression of such feelings in the group.

Very briefly I told the group about a call I had made in response to a report about a baby crying continuously, apparently uncared for. The apartment was in a run-down rooming house, and the baby, in a crib, had apparently not been fed for some time. It was covered with sores and the diaper had not been changed for days. Feces and urine had dribbled down the child's legs and covered the bottom of the crib. In addition, the child's face was bruised as a result of a beating. The mother was lying on a bed in a drugged or drunken stupor. As I stood there taking in the situation I kept saying to myself openly but in a low voice, "You shit. You lousy bastard"—because that's the way I felt at the moment.

Having finished, I sat back again. I shared this with the group in giving further sanction to expression of negative feelings. Assuming that some in the group identified with me, openly sharing my own reactions might prompt a response.

I had, during the seven-to-ten-second silence, briefly considered, and then rejected, an alternative intervention. I knew from our individual conference meetings that Sandra had strong negative feelings about abusive parents. I was tempted to use this knowledge and call on Sandra to share her feelings with the group. However, I felt that would be a breach of confidentiality which Sandra might resent. It might also make the others anxious about my use of any information they had confided in the individual conference.

An uneasy silence followed what I said and then Paul (bless him) said that as he thought about it this reminded him of his reaction with the "R" family. (Paul, twenty-seven, who did a two-year stint with the Peace Corps in Guatemala, is the indigenous leader of the group.) Paul's comment started a general discussion which lasted for about thirty-five minutes during which I said nothing. The initiative and control remained with the group throughout. All I did was nod and "mmm-mmm" on occasion and in general indicated I was an active, interested, accepting listener.

Paul's comment, focused on his hostile feelings toward some parents, was followed by similar expressions of feeling by Ann, Cathy, Bill, and George again. As each one took the ball in turn, there was less hesitancy and stronger feelings expressed. The sense of group contagion was almost palpable. There was, particularly at first, a good deal of embarrassment, tension-relieving laughter—the kind one hears in middle-aged, middle-class groups when sex is discussed. Neither Lillian nor Ruth said anything, but they listened avidly and reacted, nonverbally, with approval to what was said. They really enjoyed hearing the group tear into abusive parents. It was clear (at least to me) that the effect was cathartic (and needed) by the group—and was not as likely to have happened in the individual conference where each member of the group reacted in isolation.

After a time, however this expression of such previously suppressed feelings kind of ran its course. Once again, Paul initiated a change in direction of the group discussion. He said something to the effect that that's all well and good but how does that help the kids. Perhaps it was satisfying to feel punitive toward the parents, but we all knew that in most instances the courts would not terminate parental rights even if we petitioned for it and furthermore, in most instances, we would be abusing the child if we opted for removal and placement. He used the "R" case, once again, to discuss that fact that even though, sure, he felt hostile toward the parents, his job was to do what was best for the kid and even here he felt that preserving the home for the kid by helping the parents change was the best thing he could do to protect the child.

This changed the direction of the discussion. It returned to the earlier focus—how does one help the abusive parent to change, but with a difference. There was a conviction that this was a necessary and correct approach in helping the child and that, while hostility toward the parents was an understandable and acceptable reaction, it got us nowhere. We needed to control our feelings because if we all responded punitively toward the parents, this would get in our way in trying to establish a therapeutic relationship with them. If we were going to keep the child in the home by changing the parents, we would kill our chances by communicating hostility toward them.

Once again the discussion with regard to this question was pretty general and for the most part I stayed out of it completely. Members of the group used their own caseload (as did Paul with the "R" case) and their own experience to illustrate the futility of hostility toward parents if your aim was to help the child.

The meeting went about ten minutes beyond scheduled time. At the official end-time the discussion was still pretty active so I let it run for a while. When it began to slow down and get somewhat repetitious I intervened to sum up and recapitulate. I rapidly reviewed the course the meeting had taken from general discussion on approaches in helping abusive parents to change, to a cathartic expression of hostility, to a discussion of the pragmatic need to control negative feelings if we were going to do our job effectively.

I was conscious of the need to do this rapidly (three to five minutes), because once the scheduled time is past some people stop listening and get restive ("overtime," is an imposition), others get anxious because they may have interviews scheduled. But I was also conscious of the need for closure and for a transition to the next meeting. Consequently I kept the group a moment longer and said that, while we had established a pragmatic reason for self-discipline of feelings, perhaps we could discuss what makes abusive parents act this way. Perhaps we could come to the desirability of self-discipline of hostile feelings through understanding. I threw in the old "to understand is to forgive," first in French (pandering a bit to my narcissism—a venal sin). I proposed that we think about this as the focus for our next group meeting, and if the group thought that this would be helpful to discuss, to let me know before next Tuesday (meetings are on Thursday afternoon).

The supervisor in this example has acted consciously and deliberately to help the group move productively toward the achievement of some significant learning related to their work. Each intervention he makes is the result of a disciplined assessment of the needs of the group at that moment. The exercise of direction is not restrictive but tends to enhance group participation. The supervisor tries to limit interventions to those necessary to expedite the work of the group, giving direction and control back to the group as soon as possible. He shows a sensitivity to verbal and nonverbal reactions of individual members of the group as well as perceptiveness to the general climate of the group as a whole.

At every point the supervisor is faced with a series of possibilities. For instance, when the group was silent, the supervisor might have chosen to focus on group dynamics or steer the discussion in a direction that developed greater group awareness of group dynamics interaction: "I wonder what prompts the silence; perhaps it might be productive to discuss how each of us is feeling now." This would have encouraged a transition away from the question of dealing with abusive parents, and it would have led to teaching regarding group process. By focusing group attention, by interventions on one or another aspect of the situation, the supervisor can narrow, widen, or change the focus of discussion.

Summary

Group supervision is the use of the group setting to implement the administrative, educational, and supportive functions of supervision. It is most frequently used as a supplement (rather than a substitute) for individual supervision.

Among the advantages of the use of the group setting for supervision are:

- it ensures economical use of administrative time and effort;
- it ensures efficient utilization of a wider variety of teaching-learning experiences;
- it provides a forum for discussion of problems and experiences common to group members that not only aids in the formulation of possible solutions but also provides a wider variety of experiences to each worker;
- it provides emotional support;
- it provides an opportunity for the supervisees to share their own knowledge and give support to others;
- it aids in the maintenance of morale;
- it provides a comfortable learning environment, one that is potentially less threatening than the individual supervisory conference;
- it provides an opportunity for the supervisees to confront the supervisor with some degree of safety;
- it provides each worker with an opportunity to compare his or her work with that of the other supervisees;
- it gives the supervisees a chance to feel more involved with and a part of the agency as a whole;
- it provides the supervisor with the chance to see the supervisees in a different light;

- it allows the sharing of supervisory functions between the supervisor and the group;
- it facilitates modification of the supervisees' behavior through giving them a chance to learn from peers;
- it allows the supervisees to see the supervisor in a different light; and
- it permits the development of greater supervisee autonomy; it offers the possibility of multicultural education.

Among the disadvantages of the use of the group setting for supervision are:

- group learning needs take precedence over individual learning needs;
- it fosters peer competition; the supervisee can abdicate responsibility for developing his own work-problem solutions;
- it threatens the loss of the supervisor's group control; group pressures to conform may stifle individual creativity; and
- it demands considerable group-work skills from supervisors.

The basic principles of group process and dynamics and the general principles of learning are applicable to group supervision. As group leader, the supervisor shares with the group the responsibility for stimulating and focusing group interaction.

10 | Problems and Innovations

At different points in earlier chapters, we have alluded to persistent problems that confront supervisors in social work. Some problems are methodological, related to how supervisors observe and teach social work practice. Others, addressing supervisory goals and environments, are more basic. The first series of problems is primarily technical in nature. The second series deals with professional policy issues. The intent in this chapter is to pull together and make explicit the different sets of problems and to review the innovative methods and procedures that have been proposed to deal with them.

Observation of Performance: The Nature of the Problem

The supervisor faces a technical problem related to access to the supervisee's performance. If the supervisor is to be administratively accountable for the worker's performance and if he or she is to help the worker learn to perform the work more effectively, the supervisor needs to have clear knowledge of what the worker is doing. However, the supervisor most often cannot directly observe the worker's performance. This is particularly true in casework. The caseworker-client contact is a private performance, deliberately screened from public viewing. Concealment of what takes place in the physically isolated encounter is reinforced and justified by dictates of "good" practice and professional ethics. Protecting the privacy of the encounter guarantees the client his or her right to confidentiality and guards against the disturbances to the worker-client relationship that, it is thought, would result from intrusion of an observer. What Freud said of analysis is applied to the social work interview: "The dialogue which constitutes the analysis will permit of no audience; the process cannot be demonstrated."

The group worker's performance is more open to observation. Miller points out that "what goes on between the worker and the group is directly visible to many people" (1960:72)—to group members, to other workers, and to supervisors. However, "observations of a worker's activity take place . . . on an informal, not a deliberately planned, basis" (Miller 1960:75).

Though the community worker's activities also seem to be open to observation, this openness is more apparent than real. As Brager and Specht note,

> Community organization practice is at once more visible and more private than casework. Although it takes place in the open forums of the community, where higher authorities may be present, this is usually only on ceremonial occasions. Surveillance of the workers' *informal* activities is another matter. The real business of community workers is less likely to occur within the physical domain of higher ranking participants than the activities of other workers. Thus the community worker has ample opportunity, if he wishes, to withhold or distort information. (1973:240)

Many of the community organizer's activities are highly informal and unstructured. "Whereas casework interviews can be scheduled and group workers conduct meetings on some scheduled basis, the activities of community workers defy regulation and schedule. Much time is absorbed with informal telephone conversations, attending meetings in which they may have no formal role, talking to other professionals and other difficult-to-specify activities" (Brager and Specht 1973:242).

By far the most common source of information used by supervisors in learning about a worker's performance is the written case-record material supplemented by a verbal report prepared and presented by the supervisee (Kadushin 1992a; McCarthy, Kulakowski, and Kenfeld 1994; Rogers and McDonald 1995). Thus, in most instances, the supervisor "observes" the work of the supervisee secondhand, mediated through the supervisee's perception and recording of it. A medical social worker supervisee writes, "The only information my supervisor receives about my clients is through my filter, what I tell her at patient staffing and what she reads when I do all my charting. Her thoughts and recommendations are manipulated by what information I chart and choose to share."

A worker in an adolescent treatment facility writes,

> It's pretty scary. In reality my supervisor has no clear idea of what I am doing. She knows only what I choose to tell her. Sometimes I feel pleased that she trusts my judgments. But sometimes I feel we might be placing my supervisor, as well as my clients, at risk and she could end up on the hot seat on the "Oprah Show."

Discussing the supervision of psychiatric residents, Wolberg says,

> A professional coach who sends his players out to complete a number of practice games with instructions on what to do and who asks them to provide him at intervals with a verbal description of how they had played and what they intend to do next would probably last no more than one season. Yet this is the way much of the teaching in psychotherapy is done. What is lacking is a systematic critique of actual performances as observed by peers or supervisors. (1977:37)

The problem of access to worker performance is compounded by the fact that not only is the performance itself "invisible" but the outcomes of the performance are vague and ambiguous. The fact that automobiles come off an automobile assembly line is assurance of the competence of the worker's performance without actually having to see the performance. Social work supervisors never see a clear visible product of performance.

The traditional and current heavy dependence on record material and verbal reports for information regarding workers' performance necessitates some evaluation of these sources. Studies by social workers (Armstrong, Huffman, and Spain 1959) as well as other professionals (Covner 1943; Froehlich 1958; Ladany et al. 1996; Muslin et al. 1967; Wilkie 1963; Yerushalmi 1992; Yourman and Farber 1996) indicate that case records and self-reports present a selective and often distorted view of worker performance.

To examine the nature, extent, and importance of what supervisees withhold from their supervisors, Ladany et al. (1996) surveyed 20 counseling and clinical psychology training programs and received 108 usable responses from graduate students. Therapists-in-training acknowledged withholding negative aspects of their performance, such as clinical mistakes, evaluation concerns, impressions of their clients, negative reactions to clients, countertransference reactions, and client-counselor attraction. The reasons provided for withholding information were that supervisees perceived the information as unimportant or too negative or personal to reveal to the supervisor, that information was withheld to manage the supervisor's impression of the supervisee, and that revealing information was a form of political suicide. In most cases, nondisclosures remained secret because neither the supervisee nor the supervisor brought them up. Some findings from the study suggested that withholding information from the supervisor was related to perceptions of supervisory styles and relationships; supervisees often revealed the same information withheld from their supervisors to their peers or friends in the field, particularly if the information was perceived as important. A replication by Yourman and Farber (1996) reported a similar pattern of findings.

Distorted reports and withheld information are self-protective measures against the possibility of criticism and rejection by the supervisor (Yerushalmi 1992). They are also an effort to obtain approval and approbation for work seemingly well done, perhaps even an integral part of the social worker's professional development (Lazar and Itzhaky 2000). It needs to be remembered that approval and criticism are intensified by inevitable transference elements in the relationship with the supervisor and that autonomous decision making is a cornerstone of professional practice.

Studying the use of records by agency workers, Pithouse noted that, among other things, they were sometimes constructed as a gloss, a protective device vindicating the worker's practice. He noted that supervisors, having themselves once been workers, recognized records as presenting the appearance of expected practice, not necessarily a record of actual practice (Pithouse 1987:36–37).

Case records are used not only to collect and store information for use but also to justify a worker's decisions, reconcile conflicting impressions, document events for worker protection, and present an understandable picture of a confusing situation to communicate an impression of success (Bush 1984).

Comparisons of process recordings with tape recordings of the same contacts indicated that workers failed to hear and remember significant, recurrent patterns of interaction. Workers do not perceive and report important failings in their approach to the client. This omission is not necessarily intentional falsification of the record to make the worker look good, although that does happen. It is rather the result of selective perception in the service of the ego's attempt to maintain self-esteem (Yerushalmi 1992). Fifty years ago, Elon Moore (1934) wrote an article entitled "How Accurate Are Case Records?" He indicated that case records are not particularly accurate; this issue is still pertinent today. Supervision based on written records supplemented by verbal reports is supervision based on "retrospective reconstructions which are subject to serious distortions" on the part of the supervisee (Ward 1962:1128). A supervisee writes candidly,

> The tendency in writing process notes is to sort of gloss over things that you found embarrassing or that you found difficult. I think there are times when I've made super boo-boos that I've left out purposely. And my reason for leaving out super mistakes is that I don't feel like being embarrassed. And if I know it's a mistake, why I have to present it to the supervisor? (Nash 1975:67)

Seeking approval through selective reporting, another supervisee says, "If I'm concerned about my supervisor writing down in his evaluation that I tend to ignore transference phenomena, then, even if I don't believe it, I'll make sure to include material that shows transference phenomena, because he happens to be interested in that" (Nash 1975:68). There is some inevitable distortion of the realities of the encounter in the intellectualized reconstruction for the purpose of verbal and/or written communication. Imposing order, sequence, and structure on the interview in reporting the typically discontinuous, redundant, haphazard interactions presents it differently from the way it actually happened.

Stein et al. (1975) compared the psychiatric evaluations of patients made under two conditions. In one condition, the psychiatric resident described the patient in a supervisory conference and the supervisor completed an evaluation statement. In the second condition, supervisors directly observed the interview between the psychiatric resident and the same patient and completed an evaluation on the basis of this observation. "The results of the study supported the hypothesis that a supervisor who does not see the patient is handicapped in his evaluation of the patient's psychopathology. . . . Indirect supervision results in decreased accuracy" (Stein et al. 1975:267, 268). Differences between reports provided supervisors and independent assessments by observers of the same interaction were again confirmed in a study of intake interviews (Spitzer et al. 1982).

Even if worker reports formed a valid basis for educational supervision, using only those reports for evaluating worker performance would be a hazardous procedure. Valid evaluation requires that we know what the workers actually did, not what they think they did or what they say they did. If we apply what we know about human behavior to the supervisees reporting on their own performance, we recognize the inadequacies of such a procedure as a basis for either good teaching or valid evaluation. As a consequence of anxiety, self-defense, inattention, and ignorance of what they should look for, the workers are not aware of much that takes place in the encounter in which they are active participants; some of what they are aware of they may fail to recall; if they are aware of it and do recall it, they may not report it. The comment by two supervisors of child-psychotherapy trainees is applicable to social workers:

> In supervision of child psychotherapists over the year the authors have become impressed with . . . the unexpected degree to which direct observation of the trainee's psychotherapeutic hours reveals important and often flagrant errors in the trainee's functioning—errors which are somehow missed during supervision which is not supplemented by direct observation. This seems to be the case despite the trainee's attempt to be as honest as possible in talking with his supervisors, his use of the most detailed and complete process notes or his attempt to associate freely about the case without looking at his notes. (Ables and Aug 1972:340)

This clinical observation is confirmed in an empirical study by Muslin, Turnblad, and Meschel (1981). They systematically compared the actual interview material as recorded on videotape with an audiotape of the reports of these interviews to supervisors. The interviews were conducted by medical students during their psychiatric rotation. They found that less than half of the material was actually reported to the supervisor, and some degree of distortion was present in 54 percent of the interview reports. The four clinicians who independently studied the actual videotaped interviews and the reports to supervisors also made a judgment on the significance of the interview material that was not reported to supervisors. Forty-four percent of the material that the judges felt would totally alter the evaluation of the patient was omitted, and 9 percent of such material was distorted. "These results indicate that to proceed in supervision *as if* an adequate data base were present is misleading" (Muslin, Turnblad, and Meschel 1981:824, emphasis in original; see also Wolfson and Sampson 1976). Some additional studies on the problem of assessment of performance on the basis of supervisee self-reports were cited in the chapter on evaluation.

In response to these difficulties, various innovations have been proposed to give the supervisor more direct access to the worker's performance. A review of the literature by Goodyear and Nelson (1997) enumerates twenty-two strategies that supervisors have used to observe worker performance. Of these, direct observation and the indirect observation of audio- and video-taped interviews have been rated highly by clinical supervisors and their trainees (Wetchler, Piercy, and Sprenkle 1989), although few social work supervisors use either method (Kadushin 1992a). For both supervisors and workers, the postsession observation of videotaped practice is perhaps the most highly rated supervisory method (Wetchler, Piercy, and Sprenkle 1989; Bernard and Goodyear 1998; Gould and Bradley 2001).

Direct Observation of Performance

The simplest procedure is direct observation of the interview, either by un-obtrusively sitting in on the interview or by observing the interview through a one-way screen. Such methods are used by more than 40 percent of the marriage and family therapy supervisors (Wetchler, Piercy, and Sprenkle 1989) and almost never by social workers (Kadushin 1992a). Of course, the client's permission is needed for this and any other procedure that opens the client-worker contact to outside observation. (Whether social work's invol-untary clients can give valid informed consent for direct observation is a controversial issue.)

Sitting In

Kadushin (1956a, 1956b, 1957) tested the feasibility of sitting in on an in-terview in both a family service agency and a public assistance agency. Very few clients objected to the introduction of an observer. Postinterview dis-cussion with both the worker and the client, supplemented by some objective measures of interview contamination attributable to observation, indicated that an unobtrusive observer had little effect on the interview.

Schuster and colleagues utilized this procedure in the supervision of psy-chiatric residents. "We decided on a simple direct approach to the matter. We decided to have the supervisor sit with each new patient and the resident, as a third party, relatively inactive and inconspicuous but present. . . . In very few instances did our presence seem to interfere significantly with either the resident or the patient" (Schuster, Sandt, and Thaler 1972:155). Duncan (1963), Kohn (1971), Leader (1968), and Liddle (1991) have also reported on the successful use of direct observation of worker performance in super-vision and training.

One-Way Mirrors

The one-way vision screen permits observation without the risk or necessity of participation and minimizes observer intrusion on the interview or group session (Fleischmann 1955). The supervisor can see and hear the interview without being seen or heard. Peer group observation of the interview or group session is also possible. One-way viewing requires a special room, and it has its own hazards. Gruenberg, Liston, and Wayne noted that "the physical setting of the one-way mirror arrangement has been less than conducive to continuous alertness in the supervisor. The darkened room is more often conducive to languor than attentiveness" (1969:96; see also Adler and Levy 1981).

In a study of ten social work graduate students on the other side of the one-way mirror, Wong (1997) found that social work students expected and experienced anxiety before and during supervision. In time, however, the trainees begin to relax, and by the end of their training they generally perceived this form of supervision as a valuable experience.

Co-therapy Supervision

The supervisor-observer, sitting in on an interview, can easily move to a new role, that of co-worker or co-therapist (Tuckman and Finkelstein 1999). Co-therapy has also been termed multiple therapy and, in group work, co-leadership. If supervision through co-therapy is offered, it is generally provided as a supplement to rather than a substitute for individual supervision.

Supervision conducted by sitting in with the worker and client has been championed for safeguarding client welfare, immersing the supervisor in the direct-practice experience, and allowing clients to observe supervision in action (Bernard and Goodyear 1998). One of the principal advantages of co-therapy is that the supervisor, as an active participant in the supervisee's performance, is in a position to witness firsthand the behavior of the supervisee (Finkelstein and Tuckman 1997). Having initiated co-therapy, one supervisor noted that he became immediately aware of a supervisee's problematic approach to the client—a problem that "had not been clear to me during the few months of traditional supervision we had had" (Rosenberg, Rubin, and Finzi 1968:284). In analyzing the experience over a six-month period of co-therapy between a supervising psychotherapist and students, Rosenberg, Rubin, and Finzi note that "the direct observation of the student did away with retrospective falsification in the student's traditional role in reporting his work to the supervisor" (1968:293).

Manifestations of countertransference are more open to the supervisor as he or she experiences this firsthand. Co-therapy then makes more information and more valid information available to the supervisor. Consequently, it is an innovation that helps resolve the problem regarding the information needed by the supervisor for effective supervision.

Munson (1993) ranks the live co-therapy interview as the most effective method of social work supervision, but the use of co-therapy for educational supervision presents problems. If the supervisor becomes active in the worker-client meeting, then the dynamics may resemble those of co-therapy conducted by a novice paired with an experienced practitioner (Smith, Mead, and Kinsella 1998), in which "the junior therapist" tends to defer to the senior therapist, who tends "to take over" (Altfeld and Bernard 1997:381).

During the co-therapy session, it is advisable for the supervisor to allow the supervisee to take primary responsibility for the interaction. The supervisor intervenes only when the supervisee is experiencing some difficulty, when the supervisee signals a request for intervention, or when the supervisor sees a clear opportunity of modeling behavior that he or she is anxious to teach.

Productive use of co-therapy for purposes of supervision "requires a conscious effort by the supervisor to modify what tendency he might have to take over and be the expert and for the [supervisee] to resist a tendency to sit back and be an observer" (Sidall and Bosma 1976:210).

The helping professions employ and evaluate co-therapy supervision differentially (Carlozzi et al. 1997). McKenzie et al. (1986) found that 64.9 percent of marriage and family therapy supervisors engaged in co-therapy supervision, but social workers use this form of direct observation infrequently (Kadushin 1992a). Those reporting on the use of the co-therapy procedure in supervision cite the dangers of inhibiting the worker's autonomous learning or promoting dependency on the supervisor (Rosen and Bartemeier 1967; Smith, Mead, and Kinsella 1998).

Co-therapy provides the supervisee not only with an opportunity for direct observation of the work of a skilled practitioner, but also with a stimulating basis for joint discussions. "The supervisory conference takes on new meaning as the [supervisor] evaluates for the [supervisee's] benefit not only the [supervisee's] performance, but also his own" (Ryan 1964:473). The co-therapy experience is most productive if prepared for carefully and if followed, as soon as possible, by a joint discussion of the experience they have jointly shared.

Observation Via Tapes: Indirect Observation of Performance

Dependence on retrospective written and verbal reports of the worker-client interaction means that the experience as it actually occurred is lost forever. Similarly, direct interview observation and observation through a one-way screen or co-therapy leave no record for retrieval, study, or discussion. To correct this deficiency, some social workers record their interviews on audio- or videotape. The use of such procedures has become widespread in human service professions generally (Carlozzi et al. 1997; Goodyear and Nelson 1997; Robiner et al. 1997; Whisenhunt et al. 1997), although less so in social work (Kadushin 1992a). The importance of such technical aids for supervision is that their use enables us to observe performance indirectly and reenact the performance for examination.

Videotaping is done through an unobtrusive port from an adjoining control room containing the equipment. Alternatively, the lens sees through a one-way mirror. The simplest procedure is to turn the equipment on at the beginning of the interaction and off at the end. However, in agencies with more elaborate equipment, additional cameras are used, and wide-angle shots, zoom close-ups, superimpositions, and split-screen images are recorded and edited. Group meetings and conferences require special wide-angle cameras and omnidirectional or multiple microphones.

The National Association of Social Workers (NASW) Code of Ethics (1999) requires social workers to obtain informed consent from their clients before audiotaping or videotaping interviews and before permitting supervisors and other third parties to observe the recordings. Informed consent requires clear and understandable language that informs clients of the purpose of the recording, the risks and benefits involved, the clients' right to refuse or withdraw consent, and the time frame covered by the consent. Social workers should give clients the option of specifying that the tape be erased after use in supervision and invite clarifying questions. Videotaping through camera ports in the wall rather than inside the interview or conference room is designed primarily to reduce distraction, not to hide the fact of taping from the clients.

Video- and audiotaping provide considerable advantages for teaching and evaluation in addition to making available complete, reliable, and vivid information regarding the worker's performance. The availability of recordings retrieves the client for the supervisory conference. The supervisor who knows the client only from the supervisee's written record and verbal reports may have difficulty in holding the client as the focus of attention of the conference. The client is a disembodied, dehumanized abstraction. Audio- or videotape makes the client's presence immediate and vivid. This increases the certainty that the client is not "forgotten" during the supervisory conference, that clinical supervision remains truly triadic, including the supervisor, supervisee, and client.

Audio- and videotapes allow the supervisor to discuss the client in a way that makes more vivid what he or she says to the supervisee. To be told is not as effective as to be shown. Seeing for ourselves (made possible by tapes) is perhaps the most insightful method of learning. Supervisees, through tape replay, face themselves in their own performances rather than the supervisor's definition of them. One rather cocksure resident denied feeling much anxiety in the interview situation. On a replay of his videotape, however, he saw himself chewing gum rapidly during several tense moments during the hour. In the discussion of his behavior, he was able to recall his tension and consider the possibilities of its origin (Hirsh and Freed 1970:45).

The disjunction between a supervisee's mental image of his or her behavior and the actuality becomes undeniably clear on tape replay. One student said, "You get an idea of what you really look like and project to the [client] but often this is not what you intended" (Suess 1970:275). The experience of self-discovery that follows video playback has been aptly described as "self-awkwardness." One worker said, "I discovered by watching the tape that I was too halting in my speech and that there was not enough continuity in what I was saying. Without videotape it might have taken months for a [supervisor] to convince me of this" (Benschoter, Eaton, and Smith 1965:1160).

Tape playback involves confrontation with self and by self—not, as so often is the case, confrontation by reflection from others. "A therapist was shocked when she saw and heard herself making cumbersome and convoluted interpretations of such semantic complexity that *she* could barely understand them while later viewing the tape. However, months of reporting had given her supervisor the impression that her interventions were precise and articulate." Another "recognized while watching a tape that he gratuitously mumbled 'uh huh' throughout the session regardless of the patient's words" (Rubenstein and Hammond 1982:149–50).

Audiovisual playback permits considerable self-learning. It thus encourages the development of self-supervision and independence from supervision. The supervisee has the "opportunity of distinguishing between the model he has of his own behavior and the reality of his behavior" (Gruenberg, Liston, and Wayne 1969:49). He or she has a chance for a second look at what he or she did, an opportunity to "integrate multilevel messages" perhaps missed in the heat of the interaction. Playback provides a less pressured, more neutral opportunity to detect missed interventions or formulate what might have been more appropriate ones. As a supervisor said in pointing to the advantages for self-instruction in videotape, "Sometimes there is no need to point out a mistake. The tape speaks for itself" (Benschoter, Eaton, and Smith 1965:1160).

As participants-observers in the interview, group meeting, or conference, the supervisees can devote only part of their time and energy to self-observation and introspective self-analysis. They must devote most of their time and energy to focusing on client needs and reactions. Furthermore, much of their behavior is beyond self-observation. They cannot see themselves smile, grimace, arch their eyebrows, or frown. Retrieving the interaction on tape, supervisees can give their undivided attention to the role of self-observer. Videotape comes close to implementing Robert Burns's wish "to see ourselves as others see us."

Supervisees can play the tape when they are more relaxed and less emotionally involved; they can therefore examine their behavior somewhat more objectively. At the same time, repeating their contact with the full imagery of the event as it took place tends to evoke some of the same feelings they felt at the time. The tape allows the supervisees-observers to relive the experience with some of the associated affect.

Viewing themselves on videotape or listening to themselves on audiotape may be ego-supportive for supervisees. For many, their self-image is reinforced positively by what they see and hear. In response to the playback experience, supervisees said, "I look better, sound better than I thought"; "I did better than I realized." Adjectives used to describe themselves, elicited after playback, were similar to and as positive as those elicited before playback (Walz and Johnston 1963:233). The direction of the limited change that had taken place was toward a more objective view of their performance. It was a humbling rather than a humiliating experience. Without supervisory intervention, but as a consequence of the playback alone, supervisees' perceptions of their work tended to become more congruent with the supervisor's perceptions (Walz and Johnston 1963:235). Seeing oneself engaged in behaving competently, intervening in ways that are helpful, tend to reinforce such behavior. Replay not only helps correct errors but also helps reinforce learning.

The nature of tape technology permits considerable flexibility in how it might be used in supervision. Through the use of audio- and videotapes the supervisor and supervisee can review the work repeatedly at their own time and at their own pace (Farmer 1987).

The opportunity for repeated replaying of the interactional events permits supervisor and supervisee to focus exclusively on a single aspect each time. At one time they can focus on the client; another time they can focus on the worker. The same one or two minutes of interaction can be played repeatedly to focus on worker-client interchange. Shutting off the sound on videotape permits exclusive concentration on nonverbal behavior; shutting off the visual image permits exclusive attention to verbal content.

Tapes do not diminish the desirability of supervision even though they do provide the supervisee with a rich opportunity for critical, retrospective self-examination of his or her work. Seeing and hearing this material in the presence of a supervisor who asks the right provocative questions and calls attention to what otherwise might be missed provides the supervisee with greater opportunities for learning. The procedure has been institutionalized in counselor training by Norman Kagan and his associates (Kagan, Krath-wohl, and Miller 1963; Kagan and Kagan 1997) in what they term Interpersonal Process Recall (IPR). The supervisee watches a playback of the video-taped interview in the presence of a trained counselor. Through sensitive questioning, the counselor encourages the supervisee to describe the feelings he or she experienced during the interview and to translate body movements and to reconstruct the thinking that led him or her to do and say the particular things he or she did and said at specific points in the interview.

Self-defensive activity by the supervisee is just as probable in playback observation as during the interview itself. The use of tapes is optimally productive only when there is a supervisor available who can gently (but insistently) call attention to what the supervisee would rather not hear or see. Mark Twain once said that "you can't depend on your eyes when your imagination is out of focus." The supervisor, watching or listening to the tape alongside the supervisee, helps keep imagination in focus.

Videotapes are employed in group supervision as a stimulus for discussion. Chodoff (1972) played tapes of interviews in group supervisory meetings, stopping the tape at various points in an interview to elicit comments from supervisees as to how they would have handled the situation at that point if they were the interviewer and to speculate on what would happen next in the interview.

Supervisor evaluation feedback is likely to have greater effect under conditions of high visibility of worker performance. Any assessment is likely to be easily dismissed by the worker if he or she has little confidence in the supervisor's evaluation because of limited opportunity to observe performance. Taped material can be used in evaluation to demonstrate or validate patterns of changing performance over a period of time. An interview, or group session, taped at one point in time can be compared with a similar interview or group session taped several months or a year later.

Tapes can also be used, as records are currently, to induct new staff. A library of audio- and videotapes can be developed that give the new worker a clear and vivid idea of the work the agency does.

There are some disadvantages, however, in the use of audio- and video-tapes. Conscious of the fact that their entire performance is being recorded, with no possibility of change or revision, the supervisees may be somewhat more guarded and less spontaneous in their behavior. They may tend to take more seriously La Rochefoucauld's maxim, "It is better to remain silent and be thought a fool, than to speak and remove all doubt."

The worker is more likely than the client to feel anxious, "since the therapist can feel himself being examined while the [client] sees himself as being helped" (Kornfeld and Kolb 1964:457). For most supervisees, the gains from taping their performance appear to offset the risks. Itzin (1960) found that supervisees who taped their interviews for supervision were very much in favor of the procedure. They felt it introduced a desirable objectivity into supervision and helped them overcome evasions, distortions, and other defenses manifested in written reports of their work. One supervisee said, "I feel certain that the supervisor was able to pin down my problems quite early—and understood me much better than he could have had I been able to hide behind process recording" (Itzin 1960:198). Another commented, "It gave [the supervisor] a much more accurate account of what went on during the interview. When reporting happenings we tend to flavor them with our own thoughts, feelings and needs. I fail to see how it could be otherwise. He knew what we were doing rather than what we said we were doing" (Itzin 1960:198). One student said, "I can read a thousand books on theory but when I actually saw what was happening it was a great awakening" (Ryan 1969:128). Social work students who videotaped their interviews gained self-awareness and sensitivity in a study by Hanley, Cooper, and Dick (1994); social work students who received feedback on their audiotaped or video-taped client interviews reported significantly more satisfaction with their field practicum than those who did not (Fortune and Abramson 1993); and both supervisors and supervisees awarded their highest rating to reviewing videotaped interviews when Wetchler et al. (1989) asked marriage and family therapists to evaluate supervisory formats in use.

One of the principal advantages of the use of tapes for supervision is also one of its principal disadvantages. Audio- and videotapes are complete and indiscriminate. The supervisor faces an embarrassment of riches and may be overwhelmed by the detail available. It is possible to avoid the danger of being overwhelmed, however, by selecting limited sections for viewing, judiciously sampling the interaction, and taking an "audiovisual biopsy."

The time involved in using the videotape for supervision can be reduced by asking the supervisee to select the points on the tape that he or she wants to discuss and identify the counter numbers where this interaction appears on the tape, giving this information to the supervisor in advance. Rather than reviewing an entire hour-long tape, the supervisor can simply spot-check and then focus on those interactions that the supervisee would like to discuss.

Taping procedures presents a possibly hazardous challenge to the supervisor. If the supervisor can observe the supervisee's performance through use of these procedures, the supervisee can likewise have access to the supervisor's performance. There is an implied invitation to have the supervisor conduct an interview or lead a group so that the supervisee can observe how it should be done. The supervisee who is dependent solely on hearing the supervisor talk about social work has to extrapolate from the supervisor's behavior in the conference how he or she might actually behave with clients. The role model available to the supervisee is largely imaginary. Direct observation of the supervisor in action would make available a more vivid, authentic, and realistic role model for emulation.

Videotaping of interviews by the supervisor with clients allows the worker to "see their teachers at work removed from the unrealistic vacuum of didactic pontification. In seeing their supervisor's sessions firsthand, warts and all, the [supervisees] not only see their supervisor's skills and learn from them but may also be given the chance to renounce the previous idealization of the supervisor" (Rubenstein and Hammond 1982:159).

Supervisors as well as supervisees can profit from taping and reviewing their work. There is no reported use of such procedures in social work, but supervisors in education and psychology (Robiner et al. 1997) have tape-recorded their conferences for self-study.

There is a persistent question of the distortion of the worker-client interaction resulting from the use of all observational procedures and the threat to confidentiality. Reports by psychologists, psychiatrists, and social workers who have used audio- and videotape in recording individual or group interviews are almost unanimous in testifying that no serious distortions of interaction had taken place. With considerable consistency, professionals state that very few clients object to the use of these devices; that whatever inhibiting effects these devices have on client communication are transient; that clients are less disturbed than the workers, who are anxious about exposing their performance so openly to the evaluation of others; and that workers take longer to adapt comfortably to this situation than do clients.

The subjective reports of those who have used audio- or videotape for service, research, and supervision are consistently supported by systematic research on the effects of such procedures. Some years ago Kogan (1950) found that the use of an audiotape recorder had no significant intrusive effect on social casework interview. Subsequent studies (Harper and Hudson 1952; Lamb and Mahl 1956; Poling 1968; Roberts and Renzaglia 1965) confirm this conclusion.

That is not to say that such procedures have no effects. Any change makes for some change. The important question is whether the effects are significant, whether the intrusive consequences are sufficiently deleterious to offset the clear advantages in the use of tapes. The answer clearly seems to be that there are no serious deleterious effects when used with good judgment.

The use of tapes cannot be careless or indiscriminate. Some clients are affected more than others (Gelso 1972; Gelso and Tanney 1972; Van Atta 1969), and particularly with paranoid clients these procedures would be contraindicated. Niland et al. (1971) have observed some of the inhibitory consequences of the use of tape recordings; they emphasize the need for sensitivity to the supervisee's "index of readiness" to utilize audio and video recording.

Balancing the advantages and disadvantages and comparing audio- and videotaping with alternative supervisory procedures, these observational approaches might be seriously considered as desirable innovations. This was the conclusion of family therapist supervisors. In a questionnaire study of 318 approved family therapist supervisors and 299 of their supervisees, both groups agreed that "reviewing videotapes of therapy sessions with supervisors" was the most effective supervisory technique (Wetchler et al. 1989:39, table 1, and 42, table 2). "Review written verbatim transcripts with supervisor" was given the lowest effectiveness rating by both supervisor and supervisee among eighteen different procedures listed.

Use of these measures, which provide direct and indirect access to the worker's performance, helps mitigate the problem associated with the supervisors secondhand, perhaps distorted knowledge of what the worker is actually doing. Some additional innovations include not only direct observation but also live supervision during the time the interview is actually conducted.

Live Supervision During the Interview

Even if the supervisor can observe the work of the supervisee more fully and directly, he or she is still denied the possibility of teaching at the moment when such intervention is likely to be most effective. Whether the supervisor sits in on the interview, observes through a one-way mirror, or listens to and sees the work of the supervisee on audio- and videotape, the discussion of the worker's performance is retrospective. For the worker, supervision comes after the interview, at a point in time removed from his or her most intense affective involvement in the problem situation, when he or she might be most amenable to learning. The advantages of immediacy and heightened receptivity to suggestion while under stress are diluted. Assuming that the record of practice shows room for improvement, any retrospective benefits of supervision may be lost on the client. Consequently, there have been a number of attempts to use modern technology to permit the supervisor to supervise while the worker is actually engaged in an interview. However, if the supervisor's direct observation of the worker-client interaction is intrusive, live supervision intrudes more.

The main thrust of live supervision is to move supervisory interaction closer to where the action is taking place and to increase the immediacy and spontaneity of the supervisor's teaching. Live supervision also permits the supervisee to immediately test his or her ability to implement the supervisor's suggestions and to ascertain immediately the client's response to suggested interventions. This supposedly has a potent impact on learning (Munson 1993).

Having decided to supervise during the actual course of the interview, the supervisor has to decide on the method of intervention. The choice involves use of the bug-in-the-ear and related methods of contact with the supervisee, calling the supervisee out of the session for a conference (Gold 1996) or walking into the session to engage in supervision.

Bug-in-the-Ear and Bug-in-the-Eye Supervision

A miniaturized transmitter used by the supervisor and a receiving apparatus worn as a small, unobtrusive, lightweight, behind-the-ear hearing aid allow the supervisor to communicate with the supervisee during the course of the interview or group meeting. Watching and listening behind a one-way mirror or through a video camera pickup, the supervisor can make suggestions that only the supervisee can hear. The communication is in the nature of a space-limited broadcast, and no wires impede the movements of the supervisee.

Korner and Brown (1952) first reported the use of such a procedure more than thirty years ago, calling it the mechanical third ear. Ward (1960, 1962) and Boylsten and Tuma (1972) reported on the use of this device in psychiatric training in medical schools; Montalvo (1973) detailed use of a similar procedure in a child guidance clinic; and Levine and Tilker (1974) described the use of the device in supervision of behavior modification clinicians.

Gallant and Thyer (1989), Goodyear and Nelson (1997), Bernard and Goodyear (1998), and Bradley and Ladany (2001) have reviewed the literature on the use of the bug-in-the-ear in a variety of disciplines, citing the advantages and disadvantages of the procedure. An empirical study of the effects of the use of bug-in-the-ear supervisory feedback with four marriage and family therapy trainees found that the procedure produced significant improvement in trainees' clinical skills (Gallant, Thyer, and Bailey 1991).

For a beginning worker, such a device may help lower "his initial encounter anxiety, thus allowing him more freedom to focus on the patient's anxieties. The fact that a supervisor is immediately available provides significant support so that the therapist is able to be more relaxed, spontaneous, and communicative" (Boylsten and Tuma 1972:93).

In defense of directive intrusions by the supervisor during the therapy, Lowenstein and Reder (1982) state that for the beginning therapist "there is a feeling of gratitude for a 'powerful voice' which offers generous help in moments of stagnation, perplexity, and chaos" (1982:121). They note further that the supervisor does or should know better than the supervisee, and directivity is not antithetical to development of creativity, as "it is only reasonable to expect that creativity will be developed *after* fundamental techniques are mastered" (Lowenstein and Reder 1982:121, emphasis in original).

The supervisor can call attention to nonverbal communication (which is often missed) to the latent meaning of communication (to which the worker fails to respond) or to significant areas for exploration that have been ignored. As Montalvo (1973:345) notes, "This arrangement assumes that you do not have to wait until the damage is done to attempt to repair events." Becoming aware of these considerations on the spot promotes immediate learning and helps offer the client more effective service, as illustrated in the following vignette. A nine-year-old was very late for his interview, and the therapist was annoyed and upset. When the boy came in,

> he was obviously anxious. He looked at the therapist and stated that the therapist looked different—his hair was "all messed up." Misunderstanding the communication, the therapist commented on his hair. When it was pointed out to the therapist (via the bug) that the boy recognized his more curt voice, the therapist was able to comment on the boy's fear that perhaps the therapist was angry at him for being late. The interpretation of the boy's fears of the therapist's anger led to the patient's being able to relax and promoted further psychotherapeutic intervention. (Boylsten and Tuma 1972:94)

Such a procedure enables the supervisor to evaluate directly the supervisee's effectiveness in using supervision. It has an additional advantage for the supervisor, in that he or she is in a better position to deter possible legal action against him- or herself by stopping the supervisee if there is any danger of harm to the client. The procedure combines client protection with enhancing the professional growth of the supervisees.

Direct supervisory interventions can differ in degree of concreteness and specificity. It can be a general statement or a very specific prescription for action. The intervention can differ in the degree of directiveness. The supervisee can be directed to do something, or the intervention can be in the nature of a suggestion. The intervention can differ in terms of the degree of annotation. The supervisor can be very brief in explaining the reasons for what is being communicated or can elaborate on the justifications for the communication. The interventions can differ in the level of their intensity and can be communicated with considerable emphasis or in a mild tone. Interventions can be more specific, more directive with beginning workers and more general with experienced ones.

Comments might be peremptory instructions, telling the supervisee to do this or that. "Explore the parent's conflicts on discipline"; "confront father with his failure to respond to son"; "get mother to negotiate with daughter on homework"; or "include grandmother in the discussion." More often their supervisory comments tend to be suggestive: "Think about—; if you have a chance, —; see if you can—; it might help to try—." Or their comments may be supportive: "That was good; keep it up; fine intervention." Or they can be suggestive: "Perhaps a short role-play might help at this point."

Although informed consent is required for the ethical use of bug-in-the-ear and related procedures (NASW 1999), family cooperation is sometimes solicited by being told that services to them would be more effective if monitored by a more experienced supervisor (Kaplan 1987). Clients rarely ask about the hearing aid, but they should be informed in advance about methods of supervision in use.

A questionnaire study of the use of the bug-in-the-ear in psychiatric residency training found that it had been utilized by 36 percent of the seventy-four programs responding. Patients were not adversely affected by its use. Problems for the supervisee, including possible loss of control of the interaction, creation of dependency, and disturbance and distraction, depended to a considerable extent on the supervisee-supervisor relationship. Where the supervisor was sensitive to the needs of the supervisee and was not dominant or intrusive, the procedure presented little difficulty (Salvendy 1984).

Certain dangers associated with the use of the device are clearly recognized. These include the possibility of confusing and disconcerting the worker by too frequent interventions , the possibility of addictive dependence on outside help, the possibility of interference with the worker's autonomy and opportunity for developing his or her own individual style (Barker 1998). The danger lies in "robotizing" the worker or having him or her operate by "remote control" as a "parrot." "A trainee pointed out that in my enthusiasm to be helpful via the ear—that 'comments came so thick and fast it was hard to do any thinking of my own!' I think it is important for the bug to be a word in the ear rather than a cartridge in the brain!" (Hildebrand 1995: 175).

To manage these risks, the approach suggested by those who have used the device is for the supervisor to broadcast only during silences or when the worker is making notes; to limit such interventions to clearly important points in the interaction, such as when the worker is seriously in error or in difficulty; and to make suggestions that are phrased in general terms, leaving the actual dialogue and action pattern to the students. "Most trainees point to the fact that the real value for them lies in interpretations of general themes in the psychotherapy process rather than in specific interpretive remarks" (Boylsten and Tuma 1972:95).

Furthermore, supervisor and supervisee might agree in advance that if the supervisor's interventions are at any point confusing or not helpful, the supervisee can take the bug out of the ear using some agreed-in signal. In general, although the bug-in-the-ear is among the least intrusive of the live supervisory approaches, the recent innovation of bug-in-the-eye supervision (Klitzke and Lombardo 1991; Smith, Mead, and Kinsella 1998) is even less so. In this method, the supervisor employs a computer or video screen to communicate with the supervisee. Visible to the worker but not to the client, a bug-in-the-eye provides visual supervisory feedback. Available when the supervisee wants it—unlike bug-in-the-ear feedback that may come when the supervisor deems it prudent—this form of feedback is less demanding of the worker's immediate attention. Sometimes, for that very reason, messages from the supervisor can be ignored.

These procedures, involving supervisory guidance of the supervisee while he or she works, are discussed, explained, and evaluated by Whiffen and Byng-Hall (1982), Munson (1993), Goodyear and Nelson (1997), Bernard and Goodyear (1998), and Bradley and Ladany (2001).

In offering criteria for determining when personal contact with the supervisor is necessary and when a phone call via bug-in-the-ear will suffice, Berger and Dammann say:

> We find it helpful to call the therapist out of the room to talk with the supervisor when changes in strategy are proposed . . . It is difficult for the therapist to comprehend a change in strategy while in the presence of the family. Once a joint strategy is developed, however, phone calls from the supervisor to the therapist suggesting changes in tactics (e.g., "Have the therapist persuade his wife to go along with" or "tell the family you must explain the tasks further") are very useful. (1982:340–41)

With some empirical support, Bernard and Goodyear (1998) propose that live supervision has a number of putative advantages over less intrusive forms of supervised practice: (1) there is an increased probability that practice directed by a more experienced clinician will be effective; (2) live supervision protects client welfare; (3) the supervisor is more directly accountable for the outcomes of practice in live supervision; (4) live supervision prevents the clinician from becoming enmeshed in client family systems; and (5) supervisees may learn more efficiently in live supervision. Other reviews of the empirical literature, however, suggest that live supervision has counterbalancing disadvantages (McCollum and Wetchler 1995): (1) live supervision takes time, is expensive, and is difficult to schedule; (2) skills learned in live supervision may not generalize to other practice situations; (3) live supervision may produce passive practitioners who take little initiative; and (4) live supervision is unduly disruptive. Although a study of clients' views of live supervision and satisfaction with therapy found that clients were generally satisfied with live-supervised therapy as long as the perceived helpfulness of live supervision outweighed its perceived intrusiveness (Locke and McCollum 2001), the impact and efficacy of live supervision have been the subject of more speculation than research (Wark 1995a, 1995b; Goodyear and Nelson 1997; Bernard and Goodyear 1998; Smith, Mead, and Kinsella 1998; Bradley and Ladany 2001).

Social workers may feel some hesitancy about the use of such direct measures of observing and directing the supervisee's performance. Where a social work supervisor strives for a collaborative relationship with her supervisee, the relationship in live supervision is more overtly hierarchical and directive. Wong (1997) is one of the few social workers reporting the use of live supervision. Family therapy supervisors have been less hesitant and less apologetic about being openly directive and acknowledge that such procedures clearly reflect the hierarchical nature and structure of their supervisor-supervisee relationships, although Bernard and Goodyear (1998) and Bradley and Ladany (2001) believe that this attitude in family therapy supervision has softened somewhat.

Observing Worker Performance: A Recapitulation

A principal problem for supervision concerns the supervisor's access to the supervisee's performance. Administrative supervision for evaluation and accountability, educational supervision for professional development, and (to a lesser extent) supportive supervision all require the supervisor's firsthand knowledge of what the supervisee is actually doing. The nature of the social work interview is said to require privacy and protection from any intrusion. Consequently, the supervisor learns what the supervisee has done after some delay and from the supervisee's verbal and/or written self-report.

Case-record material supplemented by the supervisee's verbal report has served a long and useful purpose in social work supervision, despite its deficiencies. There is nothing to suggest that it should be discarded. There is much to indicate that it does require selective supplementation through more frequent use of the other procedures discussed in this chapter. Despite the availability and clear utility of such procedures in meeting some of the problems of supervision, social workers by and large have made very limited use of them (Kadushin 1992a).

Admittedly, the use of videotape does require large initial expense for an agency, consultation in the selection of equipment from the bewildering array available, and some technical knowledge in the use of the equipment. These considerations may act as deterrents. However, audio- and videotape equipment of high quality requires little expense, needs minimal knowledge for use, and is unobtrusive; in addition, its use is familiar and acceptable to most clients. Observation through one-way mirrors and through sitting in on an occasional interview requires even less imposition. There seems little justification for the neglect of these various methods for direct supervisory access to worker performance.

The Problem of Interminable Supervision

The innovative procedures we have been discussing are all intended to provide the supervisor with more open, more complete access to the worker's performance. Another series of innovations has been proposed in response to the historical controversy regarding the continued need for supervision of professionally competent workers. In 1950 the U.S. Census Bureau questioned the advisability of listing social work as a profession, "since its members apparently never arrived at a place where they were responsible and accountable for their own acts" (Stevens and Hutchinson 1956:51). Kennedy and Keitner (1970:51) noted that "there is no other profession where self-determination applies to the client and not the worker."

Arguments about autonomy derive more often from considerations regarding the professional status of social work than from the demands of direct service workers. The limitations on autonomy implied in a system of supervision is perceived as an insult to the professional status of social work. A worker once said: "Supervision creates a poor image of social work in relation to other professions. As a mature, experienced, professional social worker, I am embarrassed to refer to someone as 'my supervisor.'"

The literature reverberates with charges that supervision perpetuates dependency, inhibits self-development, violates the worker's right to autonomy, and detracts from professional status. In the 1930s, Reynolds complained of supervision as cultivating "perpetual childhood" in workers: "Much of the time, one must admit, supervision is a necessary evil and it becomes more evil as it becomes less necessary" (1936:103). During the 1970s, continued supervision not only became professionally inappropriate but also appeared to violate the tenets of egalitarian participatory democracy.

More recently, Veeder (1990) expressed a more general concern with continued supervision as related to the problem of the professional status of social work. Continued supervision, it was asserted, denied the worker of full autonomy in practice, one of the principal attributes of a profession.

Most of the assertions with regard to "interminable" supervision are perhaps merely that—assertions based on limited evidence. There are, however, few factual data available that would permit us to know how many social workers are supervised for how long and whether supervision is, in fact, "interminable" for any sizable number of professionally trained workers.

Fieldwork manuals of graduate schools of social work in the United States define the minimum requirements for appointment as supervisors (field instructors) to the school's graduate students and field placement. A review of the manuals of fifty U.S. graduate schools of social work indicates that in 95 percent of cases workers were eligible for appointment as supervisors after only two years of direct service experience as MSWs. State civil service announcements for supervisor generally require only two years of full-time supervised experience or appropriate licensure as direct service workers for eligibility for the position.

The fact that most entry-level positions in supervision require only one or two years of post–master's degree experience would imply that few professionally qualified practitioners are themselves supervised routinely by the time they reach their sixth year of practice.

It is no longer true that graduate social workers with practice experience are the only professionals who are supervised. Professionally accredited teachers, engineers, and nurses continue to be responsible to supervisory personnel after years of practice. A study of professionals in industry shows that "industrial laboratories tend not to grant autonomy to scientists regardless of their academic training until after they have proved themselves over a period of time" (Abrahamson 1967:107). Furthermore, the highly independent professions of medicine and law are facing increasing supervision as many of their members now find employment in organizational settings (for example, see Hoff 1999). In some respects, this trend will likely continue for all helping professions governed by the privatization of health and social services (Jarman-Rhode and McFall 1997), case law (Reamer 1994; Schamess and Lightburn 1998), and the burgeoning managed care practice environment (Donner 1996; Kalous 1996; Munson 1998a, 1998b; Coffey et al. 2000).

Interminable Supervision and Worker Autonomy

There is an additional point of controversy regarding the question of interminable supervision. At the same time that the contention was made that social workers were supervised too much and too long, there was the argument that social workers were unsupervised and had too much autonomy and discretion. While social workers, regarding themselves as professionals, pressed for more autonomy, more discretion, and fewer administrative controls over their actions, client advocates and civil libertarians, acting in defense of clients' rights, pressed for greater restrictions on worker discretion (Handler 1973, 1979; Gummer 1979; Shnit 1978).

It is clear that occupational dissatisfaction and an increased likelihood of burnout is associated with infringements on professional autonomy (Arches 1991). The question is the extent to which employment in the social agency bureaucracy actually restricts professional autonomy.

Studies of worker autonomy and discretion in a variety of settings, such as public welfare (Kettner 1973), child welfare (Gambrill and Wiltse 1974; Shapiro 1976; Satyamurti 1981), rural social work (Kim, Boo, and Wheeler 1979), and in studies by McCulloch and O'Brien (1986), Prottas (1979), and Butler (1990) supplemented by relevant studies in England (Parsloe and Stevenson 1978; Barclay Report 1985; Pithouse 1987; Davies 1990) and Israel (Eiskovitz et al. 1985) tend to confirm the fact that in reality workers do exercise a considerable amount of autonomy and discretion in the performance of their work.

The detailed studies by Prottas (1979) and Lipsky (1980) of the actual decision-making procedures of street-level bureaucrats—their term for the direct service worker—confirms a picture of considerable discretionary behavior on the part of such workers. Lipsky concluded that two characteristic interrelated aspects of the direct service position in the human service profession were the "relatively high degree of discretion and relative autonomy from organizational authority" (1980:13). Prottas (1979:388) observed, "There is a surprisingly large degree of autonomy and self-direction displayed in the behavior" of the direct service worker and workers are successful in capturing the autonomy they need to "respond to a complex and unpredictable" situation (Prottas 1979:7). Though the amount of discretion formally allocated to the direct service public welfare worker is modest, the study indicated "that considerable discretion is in fact exercised" (Prottas 1979:18). This had been noted previously by Handler (1973, 1979), who pointed to the considerable autonomy exercised by social workers in making daily decisions.

A questionnaire study of social work professionalization asked a nationwide sample of 1,020 NASW members about the level of autonomy they experienced in their practice (Reeser and Epstein 1990). Of the respondents, 68 percent indicated they had considerable autonomy in their work. Only 16 percent indicated that "any decision I make has to have the supervisor's approval" (Reeser and Epstein 1990:91, table 3.7). "The profile that emerges from their responses—suggests that social workers in the eighties experience[d] relatively high autonomy in their work—social workers have more discretionary power in dealing with clients than is generally assumed" (Reeser and Epstein 1990:92), reflecting the general conclusions of the studies cited above.

Attitudes Toward Interminable Supervision

The research raises questions about the reality of the negative aspects of continued supervision. The continuation of supervision gets support from advocates who point to the positive aspects of continued supervision.

There have been cogent defenses of support provided by extended supervision (Eisenberg 1956a, 1956b; Levy 1960). Eisenberg points to the continuing supportive needs of the supervisee: "It would be an extraordinary worker who did not, at times, experience some burden and some guilt, some anger and some despair—even a mature and experienced practitioner [does]. . . . In all of this the supervisor stands as helper of the caseworker for the agency; the worker is not alone" (1956a:49). The argument is also made that supervision of even the most experienced worker is necessary because help is always needed in objectifying the complex interpersonal relationships in which the worker is involved. The nature of the work may require continuation of the availability of supportive supervision.

Reflecting on her years of experience in supervision, Norman (1987:379) says, "During my early years of supervising I would have said that one's emotional dependency on supervision lessens with experience. However, experience has taught me that this is not true. Although at some point a therapist may no longer need the educational aspects of supervision, he or she continues to need the emotional support of supervision or consultation because of the nature of clinical work."

The principal dissatisfaction with continued supervision seems to lie with prolonging educational supervision. Continuing obligatory educational supervision suggests that the worker does not know enough, is not fully competent, and is incapable of autonomous practice. As Toren (1972:79) says, "Trained social workers are willing to concede administrative authority to their supervisors as part of the limitations imposed by the organizational framework; however, they resent and resist the teaching function of the supervisor which they perceive as encroaching upon their professional judgment, responsibility, and competence."

However, one might see continuing supervision not as a reflection on the worker's professional competence but as a procedure to help the worker continue to improve and upgrade his or her practice. This is a professional obligation that has no termination. Even the skill of the most advanced practitioners can stand improvement. Such a perspective justifies continuation of clinical supervision. We are all in the process of becoming; none of us has ever fully arrived. The need for continuing professional education receives support in the requirement in most states that maintenance of a professional license requires annual continuing education. Trained, experienced workers who do not have supervision available express a need for this in furtherance of professional development (Garrett and Barretta-Herman 1995)

In contrast to the opposition to prolonged educational supervision, there is a readier acceptance of the necessity for continued administrative supervision. One of the earliest advocates of freedom from supervision believed that because social workers "work in agencies that are accountable for the performance of each staff member," autonomous practice would still require "that agencies continue to maintain structural channels for enabling staff to be most effectively accountable to administration" (Henry 1955:40). As Leyendecker notes, freedom from authority of others in autonomous practice does "not seem to be truly applicable to the operation of a social agency requiring, as it does, an organizational structure in which responsibility and accountability are clearly defined and allocated" (1959:56). The recognition that someone in the hierarchical agency structure must continue to perform the functions of administrative supervision has been echoed and reechoed by those who have advocated greater independence from supervision (Aptekar 1959:9; Austin 1961:189; Leader 1957:407; Lindenberg 1957:43).

Even if all the workers were well trained, were objectively self-critical, and had developed a level of self-awareness that eliminated the need for educational supervision, even if all workers were so highly motivated, self-assured, rich in inner resources that they felt no need for supervisory support, administrative supervision would continue to be necessary as long as the workers were employees of an agency.

Administrative supervision functions to protect the client from possible abuse of worker autonomy. The possibility that the worker's real power may be used in oppressive, arbitrary, or inequitable ways argues for the need for some continuing procedural controls (Wilding 1982).

Handler notes that good supervision serves the same function as a fair hearings appeal on the part of the client. Both serve to check discriminatory practices and failure to comply with rules and regulations—matters that can have an adverse effect on client rights and interests (1979:101–102).

The advent and growth of social work credentialing has renewed professional interest in supervision for licensure (Gray 1986, 1990). Although some academic interest in alternative models of supervision for licensed social workers was visible in the 1990s (Hardcastle 1991; Barretta-Herman 1993; Garrett and Barretta-Herman 1995; Powell 1996; Kuechler and Barretta-Herman 1998), few experienced social workers endorsed unsupervised practice. In a national survey of 885 members of NASW, although "a high percentage of both supervisors (48 percent) and supervisees (52 percent) agreed that as the worker developed professional competence, the relationship should be 'changed to consultation to be used when, and as, the supervisee decides' . . . [but] A sizeable percentage of both supervisors and supervisees (38 percent supervisors; 41 percent supervisees) indicated a preference for continued moderated supervision" (Kadushin 1992a:25). Apparently, as social workers develop practice wisdom on a par with their supervisors, experienced social workers yearn for more "highly skilled . . . more senior level supervision" (Greenspan et al. 1992:41) with a clinical focus (Rich 1992; Schroffel 1998), not practice without supervision. In this light, social workers are revisiting their attitudes toward prolonged supervision (Attoma-Matthews 2001; Rothstein 2001).

Despite the fact that the negative aspects of continued supervision seem to be less serious than had been presumed, and despite the fact that there are positive aspects of continuing supervision and an expressed desire for ongoing instruction, there is continuing controversy about the need for modification if not termination of "interminable" supervision. In response to this concern, proposals have been offered to deal with this problem.

The charge of interminable supervision may be factually dubious and yet psychologically correct. This paradox results from the lack of any formalized procedure for termination of supervision. The physician is supervised for a prolonged period after graduation, but there is a clearly understood and accepted date of termination for the period of internship. The social work profession might well consider adopting a formal, institutionalized procedure for termination of educational supervision after a given period.

There is some disagreement about the time needed to achieve freedom from supervision and what aspects of supervision might need to continue to operate. Sixty years ago, the Jewish Children's Bureau in Chicago had a classification of workers independent of supervision, achieved after workers had been under supervision for "three or four years" (Richman 1939:261). Despite efforts to clarify the criteria of readiness for worker emancipation from supervision (Henry 1955; Lindenberg 1957), they are still very ambiguous. Time in practice is often given as a criterion, but the recommendations vary from one year in practice following graduation from a school of social work (Stevens and Hutchinson 1956:52) to three years (Leader 1957:464) to four to six years (Hollis 1964:272).

Wax (1963) reports on one agency's use of time-limited supervision for MSW social workers, permitting them to move toward independent practice within a period of two years in the agency. Supervision is followed by formal and informal peer consultation, and "social pressure from the colleague group replaces the pressure of the parent surrogate supervisor" (Wax 1963:41).

In one highly professionalized agency, the procedure in 1982 was to have regularly scheduled supervision with new staff members "until the worker and supervisor agree that it was no longer needed. Generally this is six months to one year after hiring. Supervision in group continues beyond this" (Dublin 1982:234).

The NASW statement on *Standards for the Classification of Social Work Practice* (NASW 1981:9) requires "at least two years of post–master's experience under appropriate professional supervision" before achieving the level of independent professional practice.

Others regard time in practice as an artificial criterion that denies differences in the tempo at which workers move toward readiness for independent practice. In addition to professional competence, Hardcastle (1991:74) argues that the state of the art and environment of social work practice should govern emancipation from supervision. Supervision becomes less important, for example, to the extent that the process and outcomes of social work practice "technologies" become more reliable, but supervision becomes more important if the fiscal or political agency environments become turbulent.

Innovations for Increasing Worker Autonomy

The need for a structured approach to granting the experienced professional worker progressively increasing freedom from supervision is generally recognized. What innovations have been reported in social work that seek to achieve this goal?

Peer Group Supervision

We noted in chapter 9 that group supervision can offer the worker a greater measure of autonomy than that permitted through individual supervision. Peer group supervision is an extension of this procedure in the direction of still greater independence. Bernard and Goodyear (1998) describe peer group supervision as a popular forum for the examination of practice experiences, peer review, transmitting new knowledge, and preventing burnout. As distinguished from group supervision, peer group supervision invests the peer group with control of group meetings; the supervisor, if he or she sits in at all, is just another member of the group. It has been defined as a process by which "a group of professionals in the same agency meet regularly to review cases and treatment approaches without a leader, share expertise and take responsibility for their own and each other's professional development and for maintaining standards of [agency] service" (Hare and Frankena 1972:527). In such peer supervision, each member of the group feels a responsibility for the practice of the others and for helping them improve their practice (Marks and Hixon 1986). What a worker does with the suggestions and advice offered by peers is his or her own responsibility. Peer supervision is suggested as a substitute for or supplement to educational supervision (Weinbach and Kuehner 1987; Remley et al. 1987; Hardcastle 1991; Benshoff 1993; Shamai 1998; Gillig and Barr 1999).

Peer group supervision symbolizes the capacity for greater independence of the worker; it also allows greater spontaneity and freedom in the absence of an authority figure. Nonetheless, it presents its own difficulties. Rivalry for leadership and control is often present, and unless the group is composed of workers with somewhat equal education and experience, some staff members may be reluctant to participate, feeling that they cannot learn much from peers who know less than they do.

In describing a productive peer group supervision experience, Schreiber and Frank attribute the success to the fact that the group was composed of social workers of "comparable experience, length of training and background" (1983:31). Difficulties related to exposure of practice to peers with whom they felt competitive and to the fact that members felt hesitant about being vigorously critical (see also Borders 1991b).

Although peer supervision "has received only modest coverage in the professional literature" (Bernard and Goodyear 1998:127), there is some empirical support for a conclusion that it offers enhanced learning opportunities in feedback from peers under conditions of greater independence and lower anxiety (Christensen and Kline 2001).

Peer Consultation

A less authority-bound version of peer group supervision is peer consultation. Peer consultation can be organized in the context of the individual conference. For example, Fizdale discusses a worker in her agency who had

> done considerable interviewing of both partners together in marital counseling cases. She had, therefore, developed a special skill in handling these "joint" interviews and had special knowledge about when they can be productive. It is quite usual for any staff member to consult with her about the value of a joint interview in a particular case or to get her help in preparing for such an interview or in reviewing the results. (1958:446)

Asking for consultation with peers is not without its consequences. The consultee admits to a limited measure of competence. He or she must accept some measure of dependence as well as lower status, however temporary, in the dyad. Frequent requests from the consultee accentuates these negatives.

Peer supervision works best among peers with approximately equal levels of competence, so that the consultee today may be a consultant tomorrow to the consultant of yesterday. This possibility of reciprocation equalizes status.

As reflected in the material presented above, the term "peer group supervision" as used in the literature is very loosely defined. In one sense, it is an extension of the informal kind of consultation that goes on in bull sessions between workers in any agency as they talk with each other about their clinical experiences. In another sense, it applies to a program of continuing education organized by peers employing their own case material as the basis for group discussion (Schreiber and Frank 1983; Richard and Rodway 1992; Garrett and Barretta-Herman 1995; Powell 1996; Bernard and Goodyear 1998; Kuechler and Barretta-Herman 1998).

These procedures do encourage greater autonomy and independence in the examination of clinical practice, but peer group supervision and peer consultation as reported do not attempt to take responsibility for the necessary administrative functions of supervision. At best, peer supervision is an adjunct to and supplement to traditional supervision, not a substitute for it.

Interminable Supervision and Debureaucratization

Other proposals for dealing with the negative reactions to continuing supervision concern alterations in administrative structure or relationships.

Suggestions for changes in the administrative structure involve a redistribution of power and responsibility so that a greater measure of both is given to worker peer groups (Weber and Polm 1974). Instead of an agency whose administrative structure is sharply pyramidal—large numbers of workers at the base, supervised by a more limited number of middle managers, topped by an administrator—the suggested shape is somewhere between pyramidal and rectangular. Instead of an agency with a hierarchical orientation, the suggested orientation is more egalitarian.

Intensified implementation of participatory management procedure tends to enhance the autonomy of the worker. Deliberate efforts have been made in some agencies to involve direct-service workers actively in the determination of significant policy decisions and in formulation of operating procedures (Weber and Polm 1974; Pine, Warsh, and Malluccio 1998).

Similar efforts have involved application of the principles of management by objectives to supervision (Raider 1977; Kwok 1995). Management by objectives (or, more appropriately, supervision by objectives) is an effort to establish a procedure of control that is acceptable and measurable. With the participation and cooperation of the supervisee, definite objectives are formulated for achievement in each case. These objectives are stated in precise and explicit terms that lend themselves to observation and measurement. Once objectives have been formulated in conferences between worker and supervisor and measurable outcome criteria have been defined, a time limit is established for achievement of objectives and the different objectives are ranked in priority. The process is monitored by the supervisor with active worker participation (Fox 1983). Work efforts are evaluated by establishing the extent to which such objectives are achieved in each case.

Another innovation involves team service delivery (Brieland, Briggs, and Leuenberger 1973; Gillig and Barr 1999). A team of workers, working together as a unit, is given responsibility for supervision. The supervisor is merely one of the team members, although on somewhat more higher ground than the others. He or she acts as a consultant, coordinator, and resource person to team members and, when necessary, as team leader. However, the responsibility for work assignments, monitoring quantity and quality of team members' work, and meeting educational needs of team members is invested in the group.

Supervisory functions still need to be performed in team service delivery. They can be differently allocated and distributed, but such functions cannot be eliminated or ignored. Team service delivery takes group supervision one step further as a procedure for augmenting worker autonomy. It gives administrative mandate to the peer group to perform the main functions previously performed by the supervisor. The team can, as a team, engage in much significant decision making, but the imperatives of organizational life still have to be implemented. Final decisions have to be validated by the supervisor, who has ultimate administrative responsibility for team performance.

The problems of organizational coordination and communication may even be intensified with team service delivery, making the functions of supervision especially important. Because different members of the team may be involved with the same family at different times, this approach requires having up-to-date records and reporting material available. It also requires constant coordination to see that team members are not tripping over each other in offering service to the family. See Shamai (1998) for a case study of the salutatory benefits of team supervision during periods of traumatic political upheaval.

Interdisciplinary teams, as contrasted with intradisciplinary teams, face the additional problems of differences in status between members and the understanding and acceptance of the claims of expertise of team members from different disciplines. A counterbalancing factor, however, is the benefit of transdisciplinary teaching and learning (Gillig and Barr 1999). Wood and Middleman (1989) see the team approach to supervision as a growing and desirable alternative to more traditional supervision.

Quality circles are voluntary problem-solving groups of employees from the same work group formed to identify, analyze, and solve work-related problems (McNeely, Schultz, and Naatz 1997). Springer and Newman (1983) report on the use of a quality circle system in social work. The quality circle system, as used by the Texas Department of Human Resources, "consists of a small group of staff members who usually work in related areas, meeting regularly to identify, analyze and propose solutions to problems of productivity, quality of operations service and work life" (Springer and Newman 1983:417). The quality circle program supposedly emphasizes a more humanistic, democratic, and collaborative relationship between labor and management. It encourages greater managerial receptivity to worker grassroots input in organizational problem solving. Although this and related forms of worker participation in management (e.g., Gowdy and Freeman 1993) may improve worker morale (Baird 1981) and ameliorate or prevent worker burnout (Cherniss 1985), Smith and Doeing (1985) raise questions about the problems in applying the approach to social work administration, and any benefits may be short-lived (Lawler and Mohrman 1985). Work groups manage service by monitoring customer satisfaction in total quality management (Martin 1993), for example, but this alternative to supervision is rarely implemented in settings that offer human services (Boettcher 1998). Although new forms of management periodically become fashionable in social work, following private sector trends, Abrahamson and Fairchild (1999) view many of their putative benefits as management superstition.

Workers may be given greater control over the supervisory process by instituting a contract system (Fox 1974). The supervisee negotiates a contract with the supervisor, specifying the kinds of things he or she feels is necessary to learn within a specific period of time. Osborn and Davis (1996) recommend a structured contract to define: (1) the purpose, goals, and objectives of supervision; (2) the context of supervision; (3) the duties and responsibilities of supervisor and supervisee; (4) supervision procedures; (5) performance evaluation; and (6) the scope of supervisory competence. Others encourage contracts that define the supervisor's and worker's legal and ethical duties to agency clients (Saltzman and Proch 1990; Reamer 1994; Bullis 1995; Swenson 1997; Knapp 1997; Knapp and VandeCreek 1997; NASW 1999). Munson (1993) believes that supervision agreements should be negotiated for renewable six-month periods, specifying what procedures will be followed if either party fails to fulfill the contract conditions.

If the purpose of supervision contracts is to bring key practice issues into the conscious awareness of both parties, contracts will have modest value unless both parties participate psychologically in the process of their development (Shulman 1999). Nevertheless, Holloway contends that a supervision contract "increases the probability that both participants will behave congruently with established expectations," by inviting the supervisee "to participate in the construction of the [supervisory' relationship" (1995:255).

Not everyone is sanguine about the benefits of supervisory contracts, however. Designed to empower workers by articulating the reciprocal obligations and duties of supervisor and supervisee, supervision contracts may not be legally binding (Holloway 1995; Bernard and Goodyear 1998), and their advocates rarely take into account the power differences in the supervisory dyad (Munson 1993). Thus, although the American Association of State Social Work Board encourages social workers seeking licensure to file written supervision plans with state licensing boards (AASWB 1997), and although NASW receives and adjudicates grievances over poor supervision (Strom-Gottfried 1999), contracts with heavy-handed supervisors may be difficult to negotiate or enforce from the subordinate position.

Supervision in the Managed Care Context

Recent trends in health-care financing and delivery have affected all human services (Rehr and Rosenberg 2000). With national health-care expenditures reaching $1 trillion in 1996 (U.S. House of Representatives Committee on Ways and Means 2000), the nation has turned to privatization and managed care to regulate the pace of this burgeoning growth (Coffey et al. 2000; Rehr and Rosenberg 2000). This has had a profound effect on social work in health care (Cornelius 1997; Bell 1999; Gilstrap 1999), the largest field of social work practice (Gibelman and Schervish 1997b).

Managed care has rapidly affected other areas of practice, such as child welfare, as well. An ever-increasing number of social workers are affiliated directly or indirectly with managed care programs (Edinburg and Cottler 1995; Schamess and Lightburn 1998; Emenhiser, Barker, and DeWoody 1995; Child Welfare League of America 1999). Corcoran and Vandiver define *managed care* as "any health care delivery system in which various strategies are employed to optimize the value of provided services by controlling their cost and utilization, promoting their quality, and measuring performance to ensure cost-effectiveness [by actively managing] both the medical and financial aspects of a patient's care" (1996:309). Now the dominant form of health care delivery in the United States (Almgren 1998), managed care is changing social work practice (Riffe 1995). Through its refusal to reimburse agency assignment of supervisors as field instructors for social work students in fieldwork placements, managed care negatively affects the future of the profession. Schools are currently finding it more difficult to find adequate placement providing professional supervision of students in placement. (Jarman-Rhode and McFall 1997; Raskin and Bloom 1998).

What are the consequences of these changes for social work supervision? One general effect has been a decline in the number of social work supervisors and a reduction in the significance of supervisory functions. Gibelman and Schervish (1997a) examined changes in the status of social work supervision between 1991 and 1997 based on NASW membership data. The overall conclusion was that "resources of staff time and allocation of personnel costs associated with supervision are shrinking" (Gibelman and Schervish 1997a:4). There has been a decrease in the number of members listing supervision as their primary function. Most of the supervisors indicated that the time they allocated to purely supervisory functions has been reduced.

Schroffel quotes the American Board of Examiners in the *Clinical Supervisor* to the effect that "there is currently less agency support for consistent individual sessions between supervisee and supervisor" (1999:92–93). A questionnaire study of more than 300 hospitals affiliated with the American Hospital Association found that one-on-one supervision by social workers decreased between 1992 and 1996. "Traditional models of supervision are beginning to erode while non-social work supervision experienced a significant increase over all three years of the study" (Berger 2002:15).

In one practice pattern, based on an analysis of the membership of NASW, Gibelman and Schervish (1996) observed that not long ago new social workers began supervised practice in social service agencies, earned licenses to practice clinical social work independently, and then developed unsupervised private practices in solo or group or settings within several years (Cornelius 1997). But as managed care is loath to pay for unlicensed social work practice (Brooks and Riley 1996; Jarman-Rhode and McFall 1997; Munson 1998a, 1998b) or social work supervision (Jarman-Rhode and McFall 1997; Munson 1998a, 1998b), more current reports indicate that social work supervision is becoming harder to find for students and beginning social workers in agency settings (Gibelman and Schervish 1997a; Austrian 1998; Urdang 1999; Berger and Ai 2000), even more so for experienced workers (Schroffel 1999). Thus, in one care-managed pattern, 69.9 percent of surveyed workers received group supervision, 50 percent received brief episodes of individual supervision, and 32.9 percent received no supervision at all (Schroffel 1999:98). In a second, more anecdotal pattern, social workers now begin their practice in host settings with administrative supervision by other disciplines (Gibelman and Schervish 1997a;

Almgren 1998; Berger and Ai 2000; Long and Heydt 2000) and purchase social work supervision toward and after licensure in the marketplace (Attoma-Matthews 2001; Rothstein 2001).

Managed care may not be totally responsible for such changes, but the ideology and orientation of managed care practice is pushing and pulling the profession inexorably in this direction. Cost containment, maximization of productivity, increased efficiency, and rigorous fiscal management exert financial pressure to flatten organizational structures, implement horizontal integration of related functions, eliminate positions of lesser priority, and reduce time allotted to unprofitable functions.

Gibelman and Schervish note that although retrenchment stimulated by managed care pressures affects all organizational levels, down-sizing tends to target middle-management positions, and that supervisory positions are classified within the middle management categories (1996:14).

It is instructive to note that a nationwide survey in 1998 by the Child Welfare League of America about the management of child welfare services consistent with managed care models (McCullough and Schmitt 1999) found nothing to say about supervision. This signal of the reduction in significance of social work supervision may herald a trend in response to the pervasive bottom-line ideology of managed care. The managed care insistence on measurable outcome results in this management model makes the supervisory cadre vulnerable unless it can demonstrate clearly that supervisory functions and activities make a significant contribution to positive client improvement.

Managed care has had a different impact on each of the three principal supervisory functions.

Administrative Supervision and Managed Care

There has been a reduction in the supervisory role in staff recruiting and hiring. Managed care organizations, not supervisors, determine which workers will become providers of reimbursable services.

Managed care organizations evaluate worker performance by requiring documentation of the practice outcomes achieved by contracted social work employees. The parallel performance reviews conducted by supervisors have little bearing on quality assurance in the managed care context.

Supervisory decisions regarding choice of clients to be assigned, the nature of services to be provided, and the duration of treatment are often preempted by managed care organizational decisions.

Because managed care systems are driven by data, supervisors have to make certain that details are clearly, accurately, and completely documented in the record of service. Monitoring of worker activity becomes detailed and precise. The supervisor's increased concern with precise documentation, details of activities, and results is an inevitable consequence of reimbursement by external sources.

Clinical-Educational Supervision and Managed Care

Generally educated before the advent of managed care, many supervisors and social workers need to learn the language of the corporate market culture of managed care. The client is a consumer; the worker is a service provider; case management is benefits management; service planning is benefit design. Capitation, co-payment, and utilization reviews are not only terms to be mastered but concepts that need to be accepted (Sabin 1999). The origin and development of managed care is another important supervisory lesson for teaching and learning.

The frequent requirement by managed care organizations for specific Axis I diagnosis of clients in accordance with the *Diagnostic and Statistical Manual* of the American Psychiatric Association (APA 2000) requires that both supervisors and supervisees have considerable familiarity with the current nosological system.

For educational purposes, many supervisors have to reorient their traditional biopsychosocial perspective to include a significant new element. The reorientation is toward a biopsychosocial-fiscal perspective, and cost-consciousness concerns have to become part of the supervisee's perspective as well.

Managed care systems demand rapid assessments of presenting problems, the ability to conclude client contacts within a limited time frame, and the ability to competently employ the interventions for which managed care agencies are most likely to earn reimbursement. Corcoran and Vandiver (1996) argue that supervisors should be prepared to help their supervisees master the art of demonstrating the medical necessity of treatment and formulating behavioral treatment goals informed by the signs and symptoms of mental disorders codified in the *Diagnostic and Statistical Manual* of the APA (2000).

The professional social work curriculum has generally not included a strong emphasis on solution- and symptom-focused brief interventions utilizing behavior modification or cognitive-behavioral therapy approaches. These may have to become part of the supervisor's educational agenda in the managed care context.

The necessity for such training and retraining is confirmed by studies that examine what social workers need to know to operate effectively in the managed care context (Brooks and Riley 1996; Vandivort 1996; Corcoran and Vandiver 1996; Kane, Hamlin, and Hawkins 2000; Kolar et al. 2000).

Supportive Supervision and Managed Care

The managed care context presents the social worker with situations that are likely to generate considerable professional and ethical stress.

Managed care practice is stressful because its policies and procedures erode the worker's professional autonomy and prerogatives. As a competent professional, the worker might expect to determine, along with the client, the nature and content of the service that the presenting problem requires, the appropriate duration of service, and the desirable outcomes of social work practice. These decisions, however, are made by the managed care organization through prospective, concurrent, and retroactive utilization reviews. The managed care organization authorizes the necessity, appropriateness, applicability, and duration of the reimbursable service, providing practice guidelines and protocols that detail how approved treatment modalities should be implemented. An altogether different approach might be selected by a worker with professional freedom.

The result of such constraints is the standardization and routinization of performance—the antithesis of autonomous professional practice. If autonomy and decisional prerogatives are a source of job satisfaction, as research suggests they are (Poulin 1994), then curtailing professional autonomy leads to a loss or reduction of job satisfaction (Riffe 1999).

Operating in the managed care context exposes the social worker to a host of ethical problems. Restricting access to services for unprofitable consumers—the disabled, those with chronic illnesses, the aged, those requiring heroic treatment—is in conflict with the ethical mandate of providing unfettered access to social work treatment for vulnerable persons and groups.

Restricting the number of reimbursable service contacts that a client may have implies that his or her worker may have to terminate services unethically before the presenting problem is resolved. When client health-care requirements exceed managed care limits, the social worker may feel torn between practicing pro bono and the malpractice specter of client abandonment. The worker is under pressure to assign a not altogether appropriate "diagnosis" to a client who he or she is convinced needs continuing treatment, unethically increasing the designated severity of the client's presentation. For some workers, who may feel that assigning a "diagnosis" violates a client's individuality through labeling, managed care requirements may pose an ethical problem for supervisory discussion.

Following the time-limited treatment protocols dictated by managed care utilization review, managers may compromise the social worker's ethical duty to champion every client's right to self-determine the course and nature of treatment.

Having to share details about clients and practice interventions with managed care organizations for monitoring and review purposes results in some loss of control of how and by whom the information will ultimately be used. For many social workers, this is tantamount to an unethical violation of the client's right to privacy (Cooper and Gottlieb 2000).

Constraints on professional autonomy reduce job satisfaction and worker morale. Ethical conflicts engender anxiety and guilt in the worker. These consequences of practicing in a managed care environment call for increased time and effort devoted to supportive supervision to help workers manage their feelings. Because supervisors may also find it difficult to balance the financial, humanitarian, ethical, and legal dilemmas of managed care practice (Lemieu-Charles and Hall 1997), these conditions and constraints have a negative impact on them as well.

Despite the fact that managed care appears to increase the need for clinical and supportive supervision, both aspects of supervision are likely to receive less attention in the managed care environment because time and energy devoted to clinical and supportive supervision does not directly generate revenue. Time devoted to these functions is not financially reimbursable. Professional education and development and sustaining worker morale are not perceived to be responsibilities of the managed care system. The result is a relative increase in the administrative supervisory function and a likely reduction in the total time devoted to supervision.

Despite the creeping spread of managed care throughout social work a word of perspective may be in order. Tracking the location of where people identifying themselves as social workers are employed, we find that 57 percent are employed in the public sector by federal, state, or local governmental agencies, organizations that are relatively impervious to the encroachment of managed care and operate with less concern for bottom-line profits. Only 18 percent of social workers are employed in private, for-profit organizations. Workers in such agencies may be most vulnerable to in-roads by managed care organizations (Barth 2001:37). The balance may shift somewhat with privatization of social services.

In addition, it needs to be noted that there is a growing public backlash against some of the limitations and restrictions associated with managed care. Pressure for legislative and judicial redress has increasing public support.

Agency Debureaucratization Experiences

Against the backdrop of managed care and the privatization of health and human services, no systematic information is available that would enable us to know how many agencies have flattened their organizations by adopting quality circles, team supervision, total quality management, or related innovations in participatory management. By the same token, little is known about the adoption of management by objective procedures, supervision contracts, or other related techniques used to sharpen the focus of supervised social work services.

Generally the reports of peer supervision and consultation describe workers who were professionally trained, had considerable practice experience, and also often had advanced training (Barretta-Herman 1993; Garrett and Barretta-Herman 1995; Powell 1996; Getz and Agnew 1999). Agency administration had confidence that the workers were sufficiently competent, committed, and self-disciplined to operate autonomously without harm to clients. Such experienced workers, as a rule, have been emancipated from supervision as a consequence of having social work licenses (Munson 1996a, 1996b; Getz and Agnew 1999). Nevertheless, there is reason to believe that many still yearn for supervision from colleagues with advanced practice wisdom and skill (Rich 1992; Kenfield 1993; Schroffel 1998).

Agencies reporting successful efforts to reduce or eliminate supervision recognize that these innovative efforts were made possible by virtue of special staff and structural qualities. Reporting on debureaucratization of a professional voluntary child welfare agency, Taylor noted the agency's success in eliminating some supervisory positions and in assigning cases on a peer level. Success of the innovation was explained in part by the fact that peers were comparable in experience and skill at a high level. The agency, however, was still struggling with the problem of "how evaluations of caseworker performance will be done" (Taylor 1980:587).

The success of increasing autonomy through agency debureaucratization, increased participation in decision making on the part of the workers, and increased responsibility of supervisory task performance by workers is largely predicated on conditions that obtain in only a minority of agencies. A collegial model requires a highly trained and experienced staff with a consensual commitment to clearly understood objectives and a mutual sense of trust and regard—conditions that are not easy to achieve.

The innovations outlined above are expressions of a series of fundamental and related problems. These concern the place of the professional in organizations and the larger society, the distribution of power in the organization, and the prerogatives of worker autonomy. Such questions are of particular relevance to the focus of this text because they get played out in the organization most explicitly at the supervisory level.

Problem: The Professional and the Bureaucracy

The problem of professional worker autonomy in a bureaucratic context raises again the central question encountered earlier in the chapter on administrative supervision. It speaks to the strain between the requirements for worker discretion dictated by the nature of social work practice and the need to accommodate to the requirements that have to do with working in an organization (Glastonbury, Cooper, and Hawkins 1980). This tension is mediated by the supervisor, who represents both the worker and the organization.

Social workers have always conceded (however grudgingly) the need for some sort of control structure to accomplish the work of the agency. But the clearly preferred control structure was that of the profession rather than that of the bureaucracy. The orientation of a profession and that of a bureaucracy are supposedly inherently in conflict. The needs of the bureaucracy for standardization, uniformity, role specificity, efficiency, impersonality, and rule adherence are antithetical to the needs of the professional for flexibility, maximum discretion and autonomy, sensitivity to the uniqueness of individual situations, and a primary concern with client needs. What is professionally correct is more important than what is organizationally desirable. There is recognition that a complex organization requires the performance of certain tasks, but the basis for obtaining conformity to organizational needs, ensuring coordination, and limiting individual, idiosyncratic behavior lies not in hierarchically delegated authority but in professional self-discipline—voluntary adherence to professional norms and peer governance. The essential difference between these control structures is outlined by Toren:

> The distinctive control structure of the professions . . . is fundamentally different from bureaucratic control exercised in administrative organizations. Professional control is characterized as being exercised from "within" by an internalized code of ethics and special knowledge acquired during a long period of training and by a group of peers which is alone qualified to make professional judgments. This type of authority differs greatly from bureaucratic authority which emanates from a hierarchical position. (1972:51)

The difference lies in the basis of the legitimate authority that supports the differing control systems, one based on expertise that prompts voluntary compliance, the other based on power vested in a position that obligates compliance. The professional control structure recognizes colleagues as having equal authority and power rather than supervisor and supervisee with differing amounts.

The strain between the professionals' preference for self- and peer government and the bureaucratic-hierarchical control structure encountered in working in complex organizations (such as social agencies) is the subject of considerable discussion (Abrahamson 1967; Billingsley 1964a, 1964b; Guy

1985; Raelin 1986; Benveniste 1987; Von Glinow 1988; Shapero 1989; Hodson et al. 1994; Getz and Agnew 1999). However, with the bureaucratization of the professions and the "professionalization of bureaucracies," there has been increasing accommodation between the two control systems. "Organizations are increasingly governed by professional standards and professionals are increasingly subject to bureaucratic controls" (Kornhauser 1962:7). The basis for accommodation efforts lies in the fact that the professional needs the organization almost as much as the organization needs the professional.

There has been some rethinking generally about the inevitability of conflict between professionals and the bureaucracy (Blouke 1997). There is greater current acceptance of the idea, first proposed by Harris-Jenkins (1970), that "the contemporary professional who works in an organizational setting is quite likely to feel at home and at ease there because professions and organizations are fused into a new social form" (Blankenship 1977:38). A questionnaire study of 267 professional social workers in health and welfare agencies found that bureaucratic and professional value orientations were not necessarily in conflict. The two sets of values were perceived as separate, rather than polar opposites on one continuum (Wilson, Voth, and Hudson 1980). "The findings clearly indicate that while social workers may value autonomy, flexibility, and innovation in their work situations they may at the same time value bureaucratic organizational arrangements. Assertions that bureaucratic values, which guide the policies and procedures of organizations, are antithetical to the professional values of workers are highly questionable" (Wilson, Voth, and Hudson 1980:29). (See also Eagerton 1994). Heraud notes that

> the relationship between bureaucracy and the profession is not, as is frequently depicted, in all cases one of conflict and in social work in particular there is considerable congruence between bureaucratic and professional criteria. Concepts such as organizational professionalism or bureau-professionalism have been developed to express this relationship. Bureaucracy and professionalism have, for example, both been seen as subtypes of a wider category, that of rational administration. (1981:135)

Thus, it might be concluded that although there is a dynamic tension between the needs of the professional and the needs of the organization, these differences are reconcilable, that bureaucratization does not necessarily result in deprofessionalization, and that identification with the organization does not necessarily occur at the expense of identification with the profession. Supervision and professionalism are not necessarily antithetical concepts.

The difference (however subtle) between professional autonomy and accountability needs clarification. Professional autonomy suggests that professionals are responsible to themselves for the services they offer. Accountability requires something beyond professional autonomy and personal responsibility for service offered. Accountability requires that, beyond responsibility to oneself as a professional, the worker is also responsible to agency administration and, beyond agency administration, to the community for the service offered. Accountability is based on the fact that the social worker's licensed actions not only are sanctioned by professional expertise, which justifies professional autonomy, but also based on "delegated discretion," the authority to provide service deriving from the agency's administration and third-party payers. "Professional autonomy" suggests that social workers are free agents. "Accountability" points to the fact that as agency employees social workers are not free agents but are acting as representatives of the agency and through the agency as representatives of the community. The worker is not carrying a personal caseload but an agency caseload.

Related to this is the distinction that needs to be made between autonomy over ends and autonomy over means (Raelin 1986). Determining the mission of the organization is the proper responsibility of agency administration. Generally, the professional cedes autonomy of such ends to administration. Professionals are more likely to advocate for autonomy over means. What they should do in treating the client and how they should do it is their prerogative—an autonomy earned by specialized knowledge and skills—but is constrained by public and private demands for efficiency in the face of limited resources. The justification for managerial control in the face of agreeing to grant the professional autonomy regarding means is that there needs to be some certainty that the professional is employing appropriate means to achieve the goals of the agency and its external stakeholders (Lewis 1988).

There might be less conflict than supposed between the professional and the bureaucracy, but there are also significant advantages for the professional in operating in an organizational context. Although worker and supervisor autonomy has been associated with job satisfaction (Poulin 1994, 1995), the counterbalancing variables of adequate organizational resources, supervisory support, and co-worker trust have also been identified as correlates of job satisfaction (Poulin and Walter 1992). Through the agency the professional is provided with community and legal sanction and support for the work he or she is doing. The organization provides the professional with clients so that he or she does not need to expend energy in developing a clientele. The agency provides resources that assist the professional in task performance—clerical and financial help, technical materials, paraprofessional assistance, insurance coverage, specialized consultation, and so on. The organization provides the stimulation that derives from immediate, close contact with other professionals, the emotional support that comes from an immediately accessible peer group, and the technical advisement that comes from good supervision. Within the context of a complex organization, the professional has available a rich network of related specialists with whom to coordinate his or her own activities.

If bureaucratic controls limit the worker's discretion and autonomy, they make for reliable, predictable, nondiscriminating decision making. The statement that may come closest to reality is that professionalism and bureaucracy, being multidimensional, may be in conflict with regard to some considerations but congruent and mutually supportive with regard to others (Anderson and Martin 1982).

Ethical Dilemmas in Supervision

In discussing ethics in relation to supervision, there is no problem regarding the obligations of a supervisor to act in an ethical, humane manner toward supervisees. There is an ethical obligation to meet the legitimate needs of the supervisee, evaluate objectively and fairly, refrain from taking advantage of differences in power, and implement the functions of supervision conscientiously and responsibly. It is unethical for supervisors to assign a case to a supervisee who is without the necessary skills and knowledge to offer effective service. Reamer (1989) notes that supervisors are ethically liable if they fail to meet regularly with supervisees to review their work and provide timely evaluations, if they fail to provide adequate coverage in a supervisee's absence, or if they fail to detect or stop a negligent treatment plan.

It is unethical for either supervisors or supervisees to present themselves as competent to deliver professional services beyond their training level of experience and competence.

The supervisor is obligated to respect the confidentiality of material shared with him or her in the process of supervision. If information obtained in supervision needs to be communicated to others, the supervisor should inform the supervisee about the person(s) to whom it will be communicated and for what purpose. The supervisor has a gatekeeper function in protection of clients. If it is clear that a supervisee is not competent and is not likely to become competent, the supervisor is responsible for advising a change of career or terminating employment. There is an ethical responsibility on the part of supervisors to avoid dual relationships with supervisees, particularly roles related to sexual exploitation. Supervisors have an ethical responsibility to make explicit their expectations of the supervisee and the arrangements for working together. Supervisors have an ethical responsibility for continued self-development, upgrading skills, and monitoring their own effectiveness.

The supervisor has to make him- or herself available in case of emergencies or at any time when crisis decisions need to be made. Throughout, the supervisor's responsibility is initially and primarily to the needs of the client and only secondarily to the needs of the supervisee.

These statements make up the consensually accepted, standard, noncontroversial ethical obligations that a supervisor must observe vis-à-vis the supervisee. Beyond this, however, a supervisor might be asked to address a number of ethical questions that are more controversial and about which there may be little consensus. Such problems relate to the kinds of ethical dilemmas that might be posed for the supervisee, who then turns to the supervisor for help in resolving them. A dilemma for the supervisee becomes a dilemma for the supervisor. A dilemma poses a question to which any answer has some negative consequences and/or violates an alternative significant value.

The narrowing conception of rights and entitlements to health and social services, managed care, and the growing diversity of the nation now frequently pose ethical questions for supervisors for which ready answers are easier in principle than in practice.

In addition to providing opportunities for discussion and for clarification and catharsis, workers might legitimately feel that their supervisor should provide some direction, some suggestions for resolving ethical questions. But neither the profession nor the community has formulated clear-cut answers to many of the ethical questions that have confronted workers with growing frequency recently. Supervisors consequently often find that they have only themselves to look to in offering guidance to supervisees faced with such problems.

A pervasive, ubiquitous ethical problem is how to resolve the disjunction between what we are ethically obligated to do for the client and the reality of what we can do, a dilemma exacerbated by practice in a managed care and increasingly litigious environment. This is a conundrum with two forms.

> The first involves difficult choices when social workers believe that complying with managed care guidelines compromises the quality of care that clients receive. The second involves potential violations of ethical standards in social work and, possibly, lawsuits alleging malpractice or some other form of negligence. (Reamer 1997b:98)

The NASW Code of Ethics requires that the social worker act to "ensure that all people have equal access to the resources, employment, services, and opportunities they require to meet their basic human needs and develop fully" (1999:6.04). What adjustments does the supervisor advise the worker to make when "**needed**" resources or services are denied? Should the supervisor authorize services to clients in need, even if managed care companies refuse to authorize payments?

Strom-Gottfried and Corcoran identify the root of such problems as conflicts of interest that requires supervisors to act as triple agents, "with concurrent responsibilities to clients, [to supervisees,] and to employers or other entities that have a stake in the helping process" (1998:110). For an ethical solution, they recommend making clients aware of potential conflicts of interest and giving priority to providing quality of care. Appelbaum (1999) calls this the duty to disclose. Making clients aware of conflicts of interest is an element of obtaining informed consent for social work services, an ethical social work mandate. In this light, Reamer (1997b) believes that clients should be informed of how the delivery of services may be affected by third-party policies and restriction, made aware of procedures for service authorization, advised of their right to appeal, and forewarned that appeals compromise their privacy. Moreover, as client advocates social work supervisors have an ethical duty to protest third-party decisions contrary to professional judgment. Appelbaum (1999) calls this the duty to appeal adverse decisions. Illuminating the conflict of interest is the subsequent risk of providing services pro bono, counterbalanced by the ethical prohibition against abandoning clients and the corollary risk of a malpractice lawsuit, which Appelbaum describes as the duty to continue treatment. To avoid ethics violations and malpractice lawsuits, supervisors should direct workers to obtain informed consent for social work services, protest any premature service cessation, assess clients for risks of suicide and other behaviors injurious to the client or others, seek consultation when clients need services beyond the scope of supervisory expertise, and monitor supervisees closely, conscientiously, and carefully (Reamer 1997b). Along broader lines, Knapp (1997) asserts the importance of managing helping relationships, anticipating problems, documenting services carefully, and consulting with knowledgeable peers. Even with such guidelines, however, the available evidence suggests that supervisors find it difficult to balance the financial, humanitarian, and ethical issues of managed care practice (Lemieu-Charles and Hall 1997).

A classic illustration of an ethical dilemma is posed by the limits of confidentiality. In an interview, a client vehemently threatens violence to his wife. In warning his wife, we violate confidentiality. In not warning his wife, we are an accessory to her injury if she is subsequently hurt. How absolute are the limits of confidentiality that the supervisor asks the supervisee to observe? Increasingly, the answer is found in malpractice case law (Reamer 1995; Knapp 1997; Strom-Gottfried and Corcoran 1998).

What position does the supervisor take in resolving the dilemma of a supervisee whose client has disclosed that he has AIDS, has not told his wife, and does not intend to tell her? What if a parent has been told that a newborn has a number of serious congenital abnormalities, needs an operation to survive, and is faced with the question of consenting to the operation or allowing the child to die. What if a pregnant thirteen-year-old seeks the help of the social worker in obtaining an abortion and does not want either her parents or the father of the child notified of her decision?

What is the ethical balance involved in forcing mentally impaired adults off the streets and into shelters during the winter because of concern for their safety? This example points to the conflict between the client's right to self-determination and the worker's responsibility for a client's safety, between doing right and doing good. Is there a duty to warn siblings of a client who was found to have breast cancer mutation on genetic testing?

Given an increasingly multicultural society, how does the supervisor assess behavior that appears to be harmful to children but is in accordance with the client's culture, as in the case of immigrant families that practice traditional clitoridectomy on minor females to enhance their marriageability? How far does respect for cultural differences extend?

What are the limits of self-determination in the case of a Temporary Assistance for Needy Families (TANF) mother who wants help in finding day care for a three-year-old child so that she can be free to accept a well-paying offer to act in a legal but pornographic film? Is the worker obligated to give the client a kind of Miranda warning to the effect that if, in the course of casework counseling, she shares information about sexual or physical abuse of her children, the worker will report this?

A virginal thirty-two-year-old man seeks the help of the worker for referral to a sexual surrogate to overcome his inhibitions and for agency financial support for the service. A terminally ill cancer patient requests the help of the worker as an advocate in persuading the medical staff to withhold life support so that she might die. A head-injured client has refused medication, exercising his right to refuse treatment; during two brief interludes that might have been managed by medication, he abused a six-year-old boy and frightened women by exposing himself in a crowded department store. In response to each of these situations, the general orientation is that the clients have the right and the obligation to make the decision for themselves, the worker's responsibility being to help the clients come to a decision. But with regard to these example situations, and other equally difficult questions, the worker is involved in helping the client implement the decision. Community funds and agency resources often need to be allocated in support of the decision. Conflicts can arise between client rights and public interest.

Consequently, the worker—and through the worker, the supervisor—find it difficult to be entirely neutral in response to the decision the client selects. Which way do they lean, or should they lean, in response to these situations? The problem for supervision is that many of these situations pose ethical dilemmas that are as yet unresolved (Yelaja 1971; Levy 1982; Edelwich and Brodsky 1982; Rhodes 1986; Reamer 1989; Harrar, VandeCreek, and Knapp 1990; Congress 1992; Reamer 1994, 1995; Knapp 1997; Reamer 1997a, 1997b, 1998; Strom-Gottfried and Corcoran 1998; Appelbaum 1999).

Many questions faced by the worker do not yield to technical solutions because they are primarily ethical rather than technical questions. No amount of technical skill can help a worker answer a question regarding situations in which confidentiality might need to be set aside to protect threatened people, in which agency rules and regulations might need to be "bent" to accommodate highly individualized client needs, or in which a white lie might be considered to mitigate a client's pain or suffering. In instances of difficult ethical decisions between one good and another conflicting good, the worker might find that the opportunity to talk things over with a supervisor provides relief and a sense of direction—provided that the supervisor has formulated a sense of direction.

Sexism and Social Work Administration

Sexism is defined as discrimination based on gender. There is a problem in social work relating to equitable access of women to administrative positions. The term "social work administration" covers a variety of levels from the lowest supervisory position to agency executive director. For both men and women, supervisor is the entry-level position to the administrative hierarchy.

Though the majority of social workers are women, the administrative enclave in many social work agencies has been disproportionately male (Szakacs 1977; Chernesky 1980). However, in a national study of NASW members, Gibelman and Schervish (1997b) have found that the majority of social work administrators are now female. Although women are still underrepresented as administrators, they are closing the gap, particularly as entry-level administrators, where women now account for 72.5 percent of the supervisors in the NASW membership (Gibelman and Schervish 1997b:table 5.14).

When male social workers still held the majority of administrative roles in a female profession (Fortune and Hanks 1988; Zunz 1991; Hipp and Munson 1995), this paradox demonstrated that women were at a disadvantage both for recruitment and selection to managerial positions and, as staff members, for promotion to such positions (Knapman 1977; Ezell and Odewahn 1980). Beyond entry-level managerial positions, women complained of a glass ceiling that impeded further upward mobility in the organizational hierarchy, a gender-biased view of female administrators by the so-called boys' club, and a dearth of mentors to provide guidance, information, support, and legitimacy in their efforts to become administrators (Hanes 1989). Some attributed the underrepresentation of women in upper agency administration to a more limited interest in career advancement in conflict with family interests, a limited preference for administrative activities, and discontinuous work history (Brager and Michael 1969; Valentich and Gripton 1978; Sutton 1982; Shann 1983; Kravetz and Jones 1982). Stereotypes that reflected negatively on females' capacity for managerial performance were seen to impact adversely on selection, evaluation, and promotion decisions.

Women who occupy administrative social work positions earn significantly less income than their male counterparts (Gibelman and Schervish 1995), suggesting that sexism still holds sway in the agency settings where most social workers practice. But as women have gained access to the power of the supervisory role, examinations of gendered supervision have shifted in focus from analyses of access, wage, and power differentials to analyses of the gendered nuances of interpersonal supervisory behavior, producing four literature reviews, examining more than 100 studies, by three women and three men.

In a review of the literature examining gender and power, for example, Granello concluded that

> current research drawn from counseling and other supervisory relationships suggests that gender can have consequences for the supervisory dyad. There is, however, no consistent research to measure the type or extent of the influence. As the individual with the inherent power and often more experience, the counseling supervisor must assume responsibility for minimizing the effect of gender on the dyad. (1996:64)

A second reviewer, Osterberg, contends that

> despite years of inconclusive and contradictory research, conclusions regarding gender differences in leadership and supervisory styles regarding continue to exaggerate whatever difference there may be between the genders, while minimizing the differences among women and among men. Such research frequently focuses solely on gender, reflecting and reinforcing popular cultural assumptions that gender is primary and that men and women are opposites, thus inadvertently contributing to perceptions of gender difference. (1996:69)

In a review of the research examining gender combinations and matching in the supervisory dyad, Ellis and Ladany (1997:469) are succinct: "With the abundance of nonsignificant findings compared to the infrequent significant findings, inferences pertaining to gender effects in supervision seem inappropriate." Finally, Bernard and Goodyear speak to both research and practice: "Empirical support for gender differences related specifically to supervision is modest, the most examined gender-related issue being the execution of power within supervision" (1998:48–50).

The Problem of Education for Supervision

We have noted above that lack of training is one of the problems encountered by direct service workers making the transition to supervision. Education for supervision is a problem for the profession as well.

In the 1970s, Olmstead and Christensen, in concluding a national study of social work personnel problems, called attention to the need for formal and explicit training for supervision. "There appears to be a pressing need for supervisory training. The function of supervision is too critical to leave to trial-and-error learning. Systematic instruction in the fundamentals of supervision warrants a high place on any list of training requirements" (1973:6, report no. 2).

Educating supervisors to supervise remains a problem today. Relatively few supervisors have had any extended systematic education in supervision. Aiken and Weil (1981) note that role adoption (learning to do the job after being assigned the title) and emulation or modeling (imitating supervisors previously encountered) are the principal ways of learning to supervise. A program of didactic education in supervision is rarely required for promotion to a supervisory position, reducing the new supervisor's motivation for specialized supervisory training.

Researching social work graduate school offerings in the area of social work supervision, Munson (1983:13) found that only 13 percent of the schools required a course in supervision; 28 percent of the schools did not have a course in supervision; and 58 percent offered such a course as an elective (1983:15). Perhaps because the 1994 curriculum policy statement of the Council on Social Work Education did not require schools to offer a course in supervision, our more recent survey (Harkness and Kadushin 2001) of 154 accredited graduate programs and programs in candidacy found modest evidence of significant change in the number of schools offering course content, seminars, workshops, and courses on social work supervision. Of the sixty-nine programs responding to the questions we posed about their supervisory offerings over the previous two years, 71 percent reported offering content on social work supervision in courses or seminars on social work administration and/or social welfare policy (N = 49); 48 percent reported offering a workshop on social work supervision (N = 33); and 65 percent reported offering a course or seminar on social work supervision (N = 45). Merely 3 percent of program respondents reported no supervisory offerings at all (N = 2). Despite the somewhat low (45 percent) survey return rate, we are cautiously optimistic that schools of social work are offering somewhat more training for social work supervision.

Unlike social work (Blankman, Dobrof, and Wade 1993; Erera and Lazar 1993; Munson 1993), counselor education has taken action in response to the problem. A national survey of counselor education programs determined that training in supervision was rarely offered, even at advanced levels of training. In response to a recognition of the importance of such training, the Council for Accreditation of Counseling and Related Educational Programs in 1988 mandated instruction in supervision in post–master's degree counseling programs (Borders and Leddick 1988:272); in 1993 the Association for Counseling Education and Supervision adopted ethical guidelines for clinical supervisors (Bernard and Goodyear 1998). The American Association for Marriage and Family Therapy has developed a certified Approved Supervisor status for those who meet the clinical and training requirements.

A Perspective: The Positive Values of Professional Supervision

Focusing on the problems of supervision tends to obscure the very real contribution made by supervision to the effective operation of social work agencies and the general satisfaction with current supervisory procedures. At the outset in discussing the positive values of supervision, we should like to call the reader's attention to the chapter 6 review of the significance and value to the supervisee of supportive supervision.

Despite some dissatisfaction, agency supervision is, for the most part, doing the job with which it is charged. A nationwide sample of approximately 400 professionally trained supervisees anonymously answered the following question: "In general, how satisfied do you feel with the relationship you now have with your supervisor?" Responses were in terms of a five-point scale ranging from "I am extremely satisfied" to "I am extremely dissatisfied." Some 28 percent of the respondents indicated extreme satisfaction, and an additional 32 percent indicated that they were "extremely" or "fairly satisfied"—a total of 60 percent of respondents expressing a reasonable degree of satisfaction in the supervisory experience. Only 15 percent were "fairly dissatisfied" or "extremely dissatisfied" (Kadushin 1974).

A more recent replication of the study involving 377 MSW supervisees obtained similar responses to the same question. Of the respondents, 30 percent indicated that they were "extremely satisfied" and 36 percent were "fairly satisfied" with their relationship with their supervisor. Only 5 percent indicated they were "fairly" or "extremely" dissatisfied (Kadushin 1992a).

Olmstead and Christensen's study of 1,660 workers throughout the country showed that, overall, 77 percent were satisfied with the supervision they were receiving. The fact that 78 percent of the respondents answered "no" to the question "Would you prefer a different type of supervision than you get?" further confirms the generally positive attitude of these workers toward supervision (Olmstead and Christensen 1973:205). Other studies available also tend to indicate considerable satisfaction with social work supervision (Greenleigh Associates 1960:132; Scott 1969:95; Galambos and Wiggens 1970:18).

The level of satisfaction with supervision reported by social workers responding to standardized job satisfaction questionnaires is close to the level reported for a normative sample of workers (Harrison 1980:38; see also Cherniss and Egnatios 1978). Parsloe and Stevenson, in a detailed interview study of more than 300 British social workers, found that rather than being antagonistic or resistive to supervision, "most social workers expected and wanted supervision" (1978:205).

Munson's study of sixty-five supervisees from a variety of agencies indicated that satisfaction scores with supervision are "fairly high, indicating that there is overall satisfaction with supervision" (1980:7). A survey of the job satisfactions of some 370 workers in mental health settings found that "respondents tended to be most satisfied with their supervision, followed closely by satisfaction with co-workers and with their work" (Webb et al. 1980).

A study of job satisfaction of school social workers in Iowa found that satisfaction with supervision was significantly associated with job satisfaction. "If respondents were satisfied with supervision they were more likely to be satisfied with their job" (Staudt 1997:481).

Studying job satisfaction in a department of human resources, Newsome and Pillari (1991) found that overall job satisfaction and the overall quality of supervision were positively correlated.

Evans and Hohenshil (1997), in a study of substance abuse counselors, found a relationship between job satisfaction and the quantity of supervision received.

In a study of the experience with supervision of 222 workers in child welfare agencies, Shapiro (1976:137) says "respondents' evaluation of the quality of their supervision was more likely to be positive than negative." Sixty-three percent thought their supervisors were always or usually helpful, 26 percent found their supervisors only occasionally or rarely helpful, and the remainder indicated that helpfulness varied with the case discussed. The most commonly named areas of helpfulness were "implementing casework skills and adding to the worker's general knowledge of the field" (Shapiro 1976:137–38).

At a state human services agency, 636 supervisees rated their supervisors on seven dimensions reflecting their attitudes toward supervisees. The dimensions included such aspects as communication, unit management, personnel policies, and personnel evaluations. Overall the supervisors rated a mean of 3.27 on a 5-point scale from 1 (not at all) to 5 (very well), indicating a reasonable level of satisfaction with supervisors on the part of the 636 supervisees (Russell, Lankford, and Grinnell 1984: 4, table 1).

Forty caseworkers employed by a department of human resources were asked to assess the factors that they perceived as hindering their efficiency and effectiveness. Of the variety of factors rated, supervision was marked as being least significant as a hindrance (Grinnell and Hill 1979:121).

Olmstead and Christensen's nationwide study concluded that good supervision is an important determinant of agency effectiveness. "The data are conclusive. High agency scores on the supervision variable were accompanied by greater employee satisfaction, better individual performance, less absenteeism, better agency performance, and higher agency competence" (1973:304).

In a study of 102 child-care workers, Shinn (1979) found that the quality of supervision was positively correlated with job satisfaction and negatively correlated with anticipated turnover at levels of high statistical significance. In a contemporary study of eighty-four clinicians serving clients with mental illness in a managed care environment, Schroffel (1999:101) found that individual supervision was "always" or "very helpful" for 64 percent of the surveyed practitioners, and that satisfaction with group supervision was significantly correlated with job satisfaction.

A study of eighty social work supervisor-supervisee dyads found that a close, quality supervisory relationship as perceived by the worker was related to high job satisfaction and low burnout (Cotter Mena 2000). A meeting of the California Assembly Human Service Committee reported in *NASW News* (October 2001, 49, no. 9, p. 4) indicated testimony to the effect "that good supervision is key to retaining social workers."

The value of supervision for more effective agency administration is noted in several studies. Community mental health centers are among the agencies that depend heavily on third-party payments for support and consequently face legislative mandates for rigorous accountability. A questionnaire study of community mental health center supervisors' perceptions of effective accountability mechanisms found that all 117 respondents saw "a well-coordinated and explicit system of supervision as the most preferred approach to facilitating a community mental health center based quality assurance program" (Smith 1986:9).

Sosin (1986) studied the effects of supervisor inputs in implementing administration of child welfare permanency planning programs in all seventy-two Wisconsin counties. There were wide variations in the extent to which supervisors in different counties reminded workers to conduct case reviews of children in placements, monitored reviews, conducted discussions of case reviews, and reviewed workers' records regarding permanency planning. In analyzing the effects of supervisor actions on permanent planning outcomes, Sosin concluded that supervisors' actions in reminding workers to conduct reviews was significantly related to reducing time in care. Other administrative actions of the supervisor ("discuss routine review results" and "perform review from records") were modestly related to time in care (Sosin 1986:372, table 4).

Program review teams surveying child welfare programs in Illinois repeatedly mention the relationship between supervision and performance. A 1988 program review of an area office notes that

> positive indicators such as case documentation and case closing were found within those teams whose supervisors were more structured and formal in their management. Within those teams where supervision was vacant, sporadic and inconsistent, we found a lower rate of case closing and documentation.

Another area reviewed by the Office of Program Review noted that "those teams where the supervisor had developed systems for periodic review of case records had noticeably better quality records than those who had not."

We have earlier noted the value of good supervision as a prophylactic for burnout.

The importance of supervision in preventing child maltreatment in institutions for children is cited by Rindfleisch (1984). In asking for suggestions as to what is likely to reduce the incidence of maltreatment, different respondents to a questionnaire returned by some 1,000 institutional personnel suggested better supervision, experienced supervision, thorough supervision, strong supervision, effective supervision, regular supervision, accessible supervision, consistent supervision, and quality supervision.

It might be noted that the research cited indicates the positive effects of supervision on supervisee job satisfaction and administrative procedures. A question might be raised about the consequences of effective supervision for client change.

Harkness and Poertner (1989) reviewed the social work supervision research literature between 1955 and 1985 and noted that such research neglected the effects of supervision on clients and clients' outcomes (see also Galassi and Trent 1987). Some evidence suggests that client-focused supervision may improve client satisfaction with the helping relationship, worker helpfulness, and goal attainment (Harkness and Hensley 1991; Harkness 1995; Harkness 1997). But see Ellis and Ladany (1997:485) for a critical review of this and related research.

Some research supports the contention that workers supervised by more professionally competent supervisors were less critical of supervision than those workers who experienced less adequate supervision (Scott 1965:81). Supervisors who hold an MSW degree appear to be more effective than non-MSW supervisors in enabling their supervisees to use their knowledge and skills. In testing students entering a graduate school of social work after having worked in the field, Torre (1974) found that professional background of the supervisors was one of only two factors related to how well the students performed. Students who, as workers, had been supervised by professionally trained supervisors did statistically better than those who had been supervised by non-MSW supervisors.

Further data "contain at least the suggestion that professionally oriented supervisors were the more effective group in motivating workers to perform as measured by agency criteria" (Torre 1974:101). Consequently, to improve agency effectiveness, greater time and attention need to be devoted to improving current supervisory practice. Many of the complaints about supervision are not the result of problems in supervision as such, but rather of the improper application of supervisory procedures.

The profession might seriously consider, as a partial solution to the problems posed by supervision, a more active program of explicit, formal training for social work supervision to increase the number of better supervisors doing good supervision. In a companion initiative, we encourage our colleagues to advance social work's portfolio of supervision research. It is comforting to know that supervision makes a significant contribution to worker's job satisfaction and that agency administration operates more effectively as a result of the availability of supervision. A very important question that needs to be far more adequately addressed by research is the extent to which good supervision is significantly related to the certainty of client improvement—a problem alluded to a number of different times in different ways in various contexts throughout the text.

Summary

The lack of direct access to supervisees' performance is a problem for supervisors. Workers' reports of their activities often suffer from significant omissions and distortions. Procedures such as direct observation, audio- and videotapes, and co-therapy supervision are being used in response to this problem. Tapes provide the supervisor with a complete, reliable view of the worker's performance and provide the worker with the opportunity for self-supervision.

Peer supervision and time-limited supervision have been proposed in response to the problem of prolonged supervision. There is agreement that the supervisory relationship should yield to consultation, although some administrative supervision will continue to be required.

A variety of procedures have been tried to debureaucratize the agency and redistribute managerial decision-making power. These include team service delivery, participatory management, and a supervisory contract system. Many such initiatives are difficult to advance in a managed care environment.

The problem of the professional in a bureaucracy was discussed, suggesting the possible sources of reconciliation between these two sources of control. Sexism and managerial opportunities for women were reviewed.

Studies show that most supervisees express satisfaction with the supervision they are receiving and that supervisors do a more effective job as a result of formal training.

» Bibliography

Abbott, A. and S. C. Lyter. 1998. "The Use of Constructive Criticism in Field Supervision." *Clinical Supervisor* 17 (2):43–57.

Abels, Paul A. 1977. *The New Practice of Supervision and Staff Development.* New York: Association Press.

Aber, J. Lawrence. 1983. "Social Policy Issues in Prevention of Burn-Out: A Case Study." In Barry A. Farber, ed., *Stress and Burn-out in the Helping Professions*, pp. 213–26. New York: Pergamon.

Ables, Billie S. and Robert G. Aug. 1972. "Pitfalls Encountered by Beginning and Child Psychotherapists." *Psychotherapy: Theory, Research, and Practice* 9 (August):340–45.

Abrahamson, Arthur C. 1959. *Group Methods in Supervision and Staff Development.* New York: Harper.

Abrahamson, Eric and Gregory Fairchild. 1999. "Management Fashion: Lifecycles, Triggers, and Collective Learning Processes." *Administrative Science Quarterly* 44 (4):706–40.

Abrahamson, Mark. 1967. *The Professional in the Organization.* Chicago: Rand McNally.

Abramczyk, Lois W. 1980. "The New M. S. W. Supervisor: Problems of Role Transition." *Social Casework* 61:83–89.

Acker, G. 1999. "The Impact of Clients' Mental Illness on Social Workers' Job Satisfaction and Burnout." *Health and Social Work* 24 (2):112–19.

Adelson, M. J. 1995. "Clinical Supervision of Therapists with Difficult-to-Treat Patients." *Bulletin of the Menninger Clinic* 59 (1):32–52.

Adler, Jacqueline and Carmela Levy. 1981. "The Impact of the One Way Screen: Its Uses as a Teaching Aid." *Contemporary Social Work Education* 4 (1):66–74.

Aikin, Gib and Marie Weil. 1981. "The Prior Question: How Do Supervisors Learn to Supervise?" *Social Casework* 62:472–79.

Alexander, Leslie B. 1972. "Social Work's Freudian Deluge: Myth or Reality?" *Social Service Review* 46:517–38.

Allen, G. J., S. J. Szollos, and B. E. Williams. 1986. "Doctoral Students' Comparative Evaluation of Best and Worst Psychotherapy Supervision." *Professional Psychology: Research and Practice* 17 (2):91–99.

Almgren, Gunnar. 1998. "Mental Health Practice in Primary Care: Some Perspectives Concerning the Future of Social Work in Organized Delivery Systems." *Smith College Studies in Social Work* 68 (2):233–53.

Alonson, Anne and Scott J. Rutan. 1978. "Cross-Sex Supervision for Cross-Sex Therapy." *American Journal of Psychiatry* 135 (8):928–31.

Alpher, Victor S. 1991. "Interdependence and Parallel Processes: A Case Study of Structured Analysis of Social Behavior in Supervision and Short-Term Dynamic Psychotherapy." *Psychotherapy* 28 (2):218–31.

Altfeld, David A. and Harold S. Bernard. 1997. "An Experiential Group Model for Group Psychotherapy Supervision." In C. Watkins, ed., *Handbook of Psychotherapy Supervision*, pp. 381–99. New York: Wiley.

Amacher, Kloh-Ann. 1971. "Explorations Into the Dynamics of Learning in Field Work." DSW diss., Smith College School of Social Work.

American Association of State Social Work Boards Model Law Task Force. 1997. *Model State Social Work Practice Act.* Culpeper, Va.: American Association of State Social Work Boards.

American Psychiatric Association. 2000. *Diagnostic and Statistical Manual of the American Psychiatric Association,* 4th ed. Washington, D.C.: American Psychiatric Association.

American Psychological Association. 1992. *American Psychological Association Ethical Principles of Pyschologists and Code of Conduct.* Washington, D.C.: APA. (Online document retrieved December 3, 2001, from http://www.apa.org/ethics/code.html#1.11.)

American Public Human Services Association. 1998. "Local Welfare Reform: Organizational Structure, Services, and Devolution of Authority." *Survey Notes* 1 (6/7):1–16.

——. 1999. "Local-Welfare Reform Implementation: Baseline Data, Work and Employment, Child Care, Transportation, Data and Program Evaluation." *Survey Notes* 1 (8/9):1–16.

American Public Welfare Association. 1990. *Factbook of Public Child Welfare Services and Staff.* Washington, D.C.: American Public Welfare Association.

Anderson, D. 2000. "Coping Strategies and Burnout Among Veteran Child Protection Workers." *Child Abuse and Neglect* 24 (6):839–48.

Anderson, J. and M. Adams. 1992. "Acknowledging the Learning Styles of Diverse Student Populations: Implications for Instructional Design." In L. Border and N. Van Note Chism, eds., *Teaching for Diversity*, pp. 19–34. San Francisco: Jossey-Bass.

Anderson, S., M. Schlossberg, and S. Rigazio-DiGilio. 2000. "Family Therapy Trainees' Evaluations of Their Best and Worst Supervision Experiences." *Journal of Marital and Family Therapy* 26 (1):79–91.

Anderson, William A. and Patricia Y. Martin. 1982. "Bureaucracy and Professionalism in the Social Services—A Multi-Dimensional Approach to the Analysis of Conflict and Congruity." *Journal of Social Service Research* 5 (3/4):33–51.

Apaka, Tusencko K., Sidney Hirsch, and Sylvia Kleidman. 1967. "Establishing Group Supervision in a Hospital Social Work Department." *Social Work* 12:54–60.

Appelbaum, Paul S. 1999. "Legal Liability and Managed Care." In Donald N. Bersoff, ed., *Ethical Conflicts in Psychology*, 2d ed., pp. 561–65. Washington, D.C.: American Psychological Association.

Aptekar, Herbert H. 1959. "The Continued Education of Experienced Workers." *Child Welfare* 38:7–12.

Arches, J. 1991. "Social Structure Burnout and Job Satisfaction." *Social Work* 36 (3):202–6.

——. 1997. "Burnout and Social Action." *Journal of Progressive Human Services* 8 (2):51–62.

Arkin, N. 1999. "Culturally Sensitive Student Supervision: Difficulties and Challenges." *Clinical Supervisor* 18 (2):1–16.

Armstrong, Katherine. 1979. "How to Avoid Burn-Out: A Study of the Relationship Between Burn-Out and Worker, Organizational and Management Characteristics in Eleven Child Abuse and Neglect Projects." *Child Abuse and Neglect* 3:145–49.

Armstrong, Margaret, Margaret Huffman, and Marianne Spain. 1959. "The Use of Process and Tape Recordings as Tools in Learning Casework." MA thesis, State University of Iowa.

Arvey, R. D. and K. R. Murphy. 1998. "Performance Evaluation in Work Settings." *Annual Review of Psychology* 49:141–68.

Attoma-Matthews, C. 2001. "On My Own: My Experiences Finding Supervision." *Reflections: Narratives of Professional Helping* 7 (1):73–79.

Austin, D. 1961. "The Changing Role of Supervisor." *Smith College Studies in Social Work* 31:179–95.

———. 1998. *A Report on Progress in the Development of Research Resources in Social Work*. Austin: School of Social Work, University of Texas at Austin.

Austin, M. S. 1981. *Supervisory Management for the Human Services*. Englewood Cliffs, N.J.: Prentice-Hall.

———. 1988. "Managing Up: Relationship Building Between Middle Management and Top Management." *Administration in Social Work* 19 (4): 29–45.

Austrian, Sonia G. 1998. "Clinical Social Work in the 21st Century: Behavioral Managed Care Is Here to Stay!" In Rachelle A. Dorfman, ed., *Paradigms of Clinical Social Work*, vol. 2, pp. 315–36. Philadelphia: Taylor and Francis.

Babcock, Charlotte G. 1953. "Social Work as Work." *Social Casework* 36: 415–22.

Baird, J. 1981. "Quality Circles May Substantially Improve Hospital Employees' Morale." *Modern Healthcare* 11 (9):70–74.

Bannerjee, M. 1995. "Desired Service Outcomes: Toward Attaining an Elusive Goal." *Administration in Social Work* 19 (1):33–53.

Barber, C. and M. Iwai. 1996. "Role Conflict and Role Ambiguity as Predictors of Burnout Among Staff Caring for Elderly Dementia Patients." *Journal of Gerontological Social Work* 26 (1/2):101–16.

Barclay Report. 1982. *Social Workers: Their Roles and Tasks*. London: Bedford Square Press for the National Institute for Social Work.

Baril, G. L. 1989. "Are Androgynous Managers Really More Effective?" *Group and Organizational Studies* 14 (2):234–49.

Barker, P. 1998. *Basic Family Therapy*, 4th ed. London: Blackwell Science.

Barnard, Chester. 1938. *The Functions of the Executive*. Cambridge, Mass.: Harvard University Press.

Barretta-Herman, A. 1993. "On the Development of a Model Supervision for Licensed Social Work Practitioners." *Clinical Supervisor* 11 (2):55–64.

Barth, Michael. 2001. *The Labor Market for Social Workers: A First Look*. New York: John A. Harford Foundation.

Baudry, F. D. 1993. "The Personal Dimension and Management of the Supervisory Situation with a Special Note on the Parallel Process." *Psychoanalytic Quarterly* 62:588–613.

Bauman, William F. 1972. "Games Counselor Trainees Play: Dealing with Trainee Resistance." *Counselor Education and Supervision* 12:251–57.

Bazelon Center for Mental Health Law. 1997. *Protecting Consumer Rights in Public Systems' Managed Mental Health Care Policy*. Washington, D.C.: Bazelon Center for Mental Health Law.

Becker, Dorothy G. 1961. "The Visitor to the New York City Poor, 1843–1920." *Social Service Review* 35 (4):382–97.

——. 1963. "Early Adventures in Social Casework: The Charity Agent 1800–1910." *Social Casework* 44:253–61.

Beckett, J. O. and D. Dungee-Anderson. 1997. "A Framework for Agency-Based Multicultural Training and Supervision." *Journal of Multicultural Social Work* 4 (4):27–48.

Behling, John, Carolefta Curtis, and Sara A. Foster. 1982. "Impact of Sex Role Combination on Student Performance in Field Instruction." *Clinical Supervisor* 6 (3):161–68.

Beiser, Helen. 1966. "Self-Listening During Supervision of Psychotherapy." *Archives of General Psychiatry* 15:135–39.

Bell, Joanne I. n.d. *Staff Development and Practice Supervision: Criteria and Guidelines for Determining Their Appropriate Function.* Washington, D.C.: U.S. Department of Health, Education and Welfare, Social and Rehabilitation Service, Assistance Payments Administration.

Bell, Peggy L. 1999. "Changes in Therapeutic Process Integrity." In Karen Weisgerber, ed., *The Traumatic Bond Between the Psychotherapist and Managed Care,* pp. 87–101. Northvale, N.J.: Jason Aronson.

Bennett, C. and S. Blumenfield. 1989. "Enhancing Social Work Practice in Health Care: A Deeper Look at Behavior in the Work Place." *Clinical Supervisor* 7 (2/3):71–88.

Benschoter, R. A., M. T. Eaton, and D. Smith. 1965. "Use of Videotape to Provide Individual Instruction in Techniques of Psychotherapy." *Journal of Medical Education* 40:1159–61.

Benshoff, J. M. 1993. "Peer Supervision in Counselor Training." *Clinical Supervisor* 11 (2):89–102.

Benveniste, G. 1987. *Professionalizing the Organization.* San Francisco: Jossey-Bass.

Berger, Candyce S. In Press. "An Evolving Paradigm of Supervision Within a Changing Health Care Environment." *Health and Social Work* in press.

Berger, Candyce S. and Amy Ai. 2000. "Managed Care and Its Implications for Social Work Curricula Reform: Clinical Practice and Field Instruction." *Social Work in Health Care* 31 (3):83–106.

Berger, Michael and Cassell Dammann. 1982. "Live Supervision as Context in Treatment and Training." *Family Process* 21 (3):337–44.

Berkeley Planning Associates. 1977. *Project Management and Worker Burnout Report.* Berkeley, Calif.: Berkeley Planning Associates.

Berkman, B., E. Bonander, B. Kemler, M. J. Isaacson Rubinger, I. Rutchick, and P. Silverman. 1996. "Social Work in the Academic Medical Center: Advanced Training—A Necessity." *Social Work in Health Care* 24: 115–35.

Bernard, H. S. 1999. "Introduction to Special Issue on Group Supervision of Group Psychotherapy." *International Journal of Group Psychotherapy* 49 (2):153–57.

Bernard, J. M. and R. K. Goodyear. 1998. *Fundamentals of Clinical Supervision,* 2d ed. Needham Heights, Mass.: Allyn and Bacon.

Bernardin, J. H. 1986. "Subordinate Appraisal: A Valuable Source of Information About Managers." *Human Resource Management* 25 (3):421–40.

Bernardin, J. H. and C. S. Walters. 1977. "The Effects of Rater Training and Diary Keeping on Psychometric Error in Ratings." *Journal of Applied Psychology* 62:64–69.

Billingsley, Andrew. 1964a. "Bureaucratic and Professional Orientation Patterns in Social Casework." *Social Service Review* 38:400–407.

——. 1964b. *The Role of the Social Worker in a Child Protection Agency: A Comparative Analysis.* Boston: Society for the Prevention of Cruelty to Children.

Birk, J. M. and J. R. Mahalik. 1996. "The Influence of Trainee Conceptual Level, Trainee, Anxiety, and Supervision Evaluation on Counselor Developmental Level." *Clinical Supervisor* 14 (1):123–38.

Bishop, J. B. 1971. "Another Look at Counselor, Client and Supervisor Ratings of Counselor Effectiveness." *Counselor Education and Supervision* 10:310–23.

Bishop, Maxine H. 1969. *Dynamic Supervision: Problems and Opportunities.* New York: American Management Association.

Black, Janet E., M. Maki, and J. Nunn. 1997. "Does Race Affect the Social Work Student-Field Instructor Relationship?" *Clinical Supervisor* 16 (1):39–54.

Blackey, Eileen. 1957. *Group Leadership in Staff Training.* Bureau of Public Assistance, H.E.W. Report no. 29. Washington, D.C.: U.S. Government Printing Office.

Blake, R. R. and S. S. Mouton. 1961. *The Managerial Grid.* Houston: Gulf.

Blane, Stephen M. 1968. "Immediate Effect of Supervisory Experiences on Counselor Candidates." *Counselor Education and Supervision* 8:39–44.

Blankenship, Ralph L. 1977. *Colleagues in Organization—The Social Construction of Professional Work.* New York: Wiley.

Blankman, J., J. Dobrof, and K. Wade. 1993. "Moving Up Without Falling Down: Forming Groups to Aid New Supervisors. *Clinical Supervisor* 11 (2):135–44.

Blau, Peter M. 1960. "Orientation Toward Clients in a Public Welfare Agency." *Administrative Science Quarterly* 5:341–61.

Blau, Peter M. and W. Richard Scott. 1962. *Formal Organizations.* San Francisco: Chandler.

Bloom, Leonard and Cherie Herman. 1958. "A Problem of Relationship in Supervision." *Journal of Social Casework* 39:402–6.

Blouke, Peter S. 1997. "Musings of a Bureaucratic Psychologist." *Professional Psychology: Research and Practice* 28 (4):326–28.

Blum, D. and S. Euster-Fisher. 1983. "Clinical Supervisory Practice in Oncology Settings." *Clinical Supervisor* 1 (1):17–27.

Blumberg, Arthur. 1980. *Supervisors and Teachers: A Private Cold War,* 2d ed. Berkeley, Calif: McCuthan.

Boettcher, R. 1998. "A Study of Quality-Managed Human Service Organizations." *Administration in Social Work* 22 (2):41–56.

Bogo, M. 1993. "The Student/Field Instructor Relationship: The Critical Factor in Field Education." *Clinical Supervisor* 11 (2):23–36.

Bogo, M. and E. Vayda. 1988. *The Practice of Field Instruction in Social Work.* Toronto: University of Toronto Press.

Bonosky, N. 1995. "Boundary Violations in Social Work Supervision: Clinical, Educational, and Legal Implications." *Clinical Supervisor* 13 (2):79–95.

Borders, L. D. 1991a. "Supervisors' In-Session Behaviors and Cognitions." *Counselor Education and Supervision* 31:32–47.

——. 1991b. "A Systematic Approach to Peer Group Supervision." *Journal of Counseling and Development* 69:245–51.

——. 1992. "Learning to Think Like a Supervisor." *Clinical Supervisor* 10 (2):135–48.

——. 1996. "Review of Clinical Supervision: A Systems Approach." *Counselor Education and Supervision* 36 (1):85–90.

Borders, L. D., J. M. Bernard, H. A. Dye, M. L. Fong, P. Henderson, and D. W. Nance. 1991. "Curriculum Guide for Training Counseling Supervisors: Rationale, Development, and Implementation." *Counselor Education and Supervision* 31:58–79.

Borders, L. Dianne and George R. Leddick. 1988. "A Nation-Wide Survey of Supervision Training." *Counselor Education and Supervision* 7 (3): 271–83.

Bowers, B., S. Esmond, and M. Canales. 1999. "Approaches to Case Management Supervision." *Administration in Social Work* 23 (1):29–49.

Boylsten, William H. and June M. Tuma. 1972. "Training of Mental Health Professionals through the Use of the 'Bug in the Ear.'" *American Journal of Psychiatry* 129:92–95.

Brackett, Jeffrey. 1904. *Education and Supervision in Social Work.* New York: Macmillan.

Bradley, Loretta and Nicholas Ladany, eds. 2001. *Counselor Supervision: Principles, Process, and Practice,* 3d ed. Philadelphia: Brunner-Routledge.

Bradshaw, Walter H. 1982. "Supervision in Black and White: Race as a Factor in Supervision." In Michael Blumenfield, ed., *Applied Supervision in Psychotherapy,* pp. 199–220. New York: Grune and Stratton.

Brager, George and Harry Specht. 1973. *Community Organizing.* New York: Columbia University Press.

Brager, George and John A. Michael. 1969. "The Sex Distribution in Social Work: Causes and Consequences." *Social Casework* 50:595–601.

Bramford, Terry. 1978. "The Gulf Between Managers and Practitioners." *Social Work Today* 10:11–12.

Brandon, Joan and Martin Davies. 1979. "The Limits of Competence in Social Work: The Assessment of Marginal Students in Social Work Education." *British Journal of Social Work* 9:297–347.

Brandt, D. E. 1996. "Similarities Between Psychoanalytic Supervision and Other Forms of Analytic Consultation." *Clinical Supervisor* 14 (2):99–107.

Brashears, F. 1995. "Supervision as Social Work Practice: A Reconceptualization." *Social Work* 40 (5):692–99.

Braver, M., N. Graffin, and W. Holahan. 1990. "Supervising the Advanced Trainee: A Multiple Therapy Training Model." *Psychotherapy* 27 (4): 561–67.

Brearley, Paul C. 1982. *Risk and Social Work.* Boston: Routledge and Kegan Paul.

Brennan, E. Clifford. 1982. "Evaluation of Field Teaching and Learning." In Bradford W. Sheafer and Louise E. Jenkins, eds., *Quality Field Instruction in Social Work,* pp. 76–97. New York: Longman.

Brennan, E. Clifford, Morton L. Arkava, David E. Cummins, and Leona K. Wicks. 1976. "Expectations for Baccalaureate Social Workers." *Public Welfare* 34:19–23.

Bretz, Robert, G. Milkovich, and W. Read, W. 1992. "The Current State of Performance Appraisal Research and Practice: Concerns, Directions, and Implications." *Journal of Management* 182:321–52.

Brieland, Donald, Thomas L. Briggs, and Paul Leuenberger. 1973. *The Team Model of Social Work Practice.* Syracuse, N.Y.: Syracuse University School of Social Work.

Brintnall, Michael. 1981. "Caseloads, Performance and Street-Level Bureaucracy." *Urban Affairs Quarterly* 16:281–98.

Briscoe, Catherine and David Thomas. 1977. *Community Work: Learning and Supervision.* London: Allen and Unwin.

Brodsky, Annette M. 1980. "Sex Role Issues in the Supervision of Therapy." In Allen K. Hess, ed., *Psychotherapy Supervision: Theory, Research, and Practice,* pp. 509–22. New York: Wiley.

Brodsky, A. and J. Edelwich. 1980. *Burn-Out: Stages of Disillusionment in the Helping Professions.* New York: Human Sciences Press.

Bromberg, Phillip. 1982. "The Supervisory Process and the Parallel Psychoanalysis." *Contemporary Psychoanalysis* 18 (1):92–111.

Brooks, Deanna, and Priscilla Riley. 1996. "The Impact of Managed Health Care Policy on Student Field Training." *Smith College Studies in Social Work* 66 (3):307–16.

Brown, A., and I. Bourne. 1995. *The Social Work Supervisor.* Philadelphia: Open University Press.

Bruck, Max. 1963. "The Relationship Between Student Anxiety, Self-Awareness and Self-Concept, and Competence in Casework." *Social Casework* 44:125–31.

Bruner, Jerome S. 1963. *The Process of Education.* New York: Vintage.

Bruss, K., C. Brack, G. Brack, H. Glickhauf-Hughes, and M. O'Leary. 1997. "A Developmental Model for Supervising Therapists Treating Gay, Lesbian, and Bisexual Clients." *Clinical Supervisor* 15 (1):61–73.

Bullis, R. K. 1995. *Clinical Social Worker Misconduct.* Chicago: Nelson-Hall.

Bunker, D. R. and M. H. Wijnberg. 1988. *Supervision and Performance—Managing Professional Work in Human Services Organizations.* San Francisco: Jossey-Bass.

Burack-Weiss, A. and F. Brennan. 1991. *Gerontological Social Work Supervision.* New York: Haworth.

Burke, Donald and Douglas S. Wilcox. 1971. "Basis of Supervisory Power and Subordinate Job Satisfactions." *Canadian Journal of Behavioral Science* 3:184–93.

Burke, P. 1997. "Risk and Supervision: Social Work Responses to Referred User Problems." *British Journal of Social Work* 27:115–39.

Burns, Mary E. 1958. "The Historical Development of the Process of Casework Supervision as Seen in the Professional Literature of Social Work." Ph.D. diss., School of Social Service Administration, University of Chicago.

Bush, James. 1977. "The Minority Administrator: Implications for Social Work Education." *Journal of Education for Social Work* 13 (1):15–22.

Bush, Malcolm. 1984. "The Public and Private Purpose of Case Records." *Children and Youth Services Review* 6:1–18.

Busso, R. J. 1987. "Teacher and Student Problem-Solving Activities in Educational Supervisory Sessions." *Journal of Social Work Education* 3:67–73.

Butler, B. B. 1990. "Job Satisfaction: Management's Continuing Challenge." *Social Work* 35:112–17.

Calligor, Leopold. 1981. "Parallel and Reciprocal Process in Psychoanalytic Supervision." *Contemporary Psychoanalysis* 17 (1):1–27.

Caplow, Theodore. 1954. *The Sociology of Work.* Minneapolis: University of Minnesota Press.

Caragonne, Penelope A. 1979. "Implementation Structures in Community Support Programs: Manpower Implications of Case Management Systems." Reprinted in *Selected Readings on the Enhancement of Social Service*

Management Systems. DHHS Publication no. (OHDS) 80-30273. Washington, D.C.: U.S. Government Printing Office.

Cardy, Robert L. 1998. "Performance Appraisal in a Quality Context: A New Look at Old Problems." In James W. Smither, ed., *Performance Appraisal: State of the Art in Practice,* pp. 132–62. San Francisco: Jossey-Bass.

Cardy, R. L. and G. H. Dobbins. 1986. "Affect and Appraisal Accuracy: Liking as an Integral Dimension in Evaluating Performance." *Journal of Applied Psychology* 71:672–78.

——. 1994. "Performance Appraisal: Alternative Perspectives." Cincinnati, Ohio: Southwest.

Carifio, M., and Hess, A. 1987. "Who Is the Ideal Supervisor?" *Psychology: Research and Practice* 18 (3):244–50.

Carless, Sally A., L. Mann, and A. Wearing. 1998. "Leadership, Managerial Performance, and 360-Degree Feedback." *Applied Psychology: An International Review* 474:481–96.

Carlozzi, A. F., J. S. C. Romans, D. L. Boswell, D. B. Ferguson, and B. J. Whisenhunt. 1997. "Training and Supervision Practices in Counseling and Marriage and Family Therapy Programs." *Clinical Supervisor* 15 (1): 51–60.

Cashwell, C. S., E. J. Looby, and W. F. Housley. 1997. "Appreciating Cultural Diversity through Clinical Supervision." *Clinical Supervisor* 15 (2):75–85.

Charles, G., P. Gabor, and J. Matheson. 1992. "An Analysis of Factors in the Supervision of Beginning Child and Youth Care Workers." *Clinical Supervisor* 10 (1):21–33.

Chernesky, Roslyn H. 1980. "Women Administrators in Social Work." In Elaine Norman and Arlene Mancuso, eds., *Women's Issues and Social Work Practice,* pp. 241–61. Itasca, Ill.: Peacock.

Cherniss, C. 1985. "Stress, Burnout, and the Special Services Provider." *Special Services in the Schools* 2 (1):45–61.

Cherniss, Cary. 1980. *Professional Burn-Out in Human Service Organizations.* New York: Praeger.

Cherniss, Cary and E. Egnatios. 1978. "Clinical Supervision in Community Mental Health." *Social Work* 23 (3):219–23.

Chevron, Eve and Bruce J. Rounsaville. 1983. "Evaluating the Clinical Skills of Psychotherapists—A Comparison of Techniques." *Archives of General Psychiatry* 40:1129–32.

Child Welfare League of America. 1999. *1998 State and County Survey Results.* Washington, D.C.: Child Welfare League of America.

Children's Bureau. 1976. *Child Welfare in 25 States—An Overview.* U.S. Department of Health, Education and Welfare Publication no. OHD 76-30090. Washington, D.C.: U.S. Government Printing Office.

Ching, S. 1993. "Structure in Counseling Supervision." *Asia Pacific Journal of Social Work* 5 (2):88–102.

Chodoff, Paul. 1972. "Supervision of Psychotherapy with Videotape: Pros and Cons." *American Journal of Psychiatry* 128:819–23.

Christensen, T. M. and W. B. Kline. 2001. "The Qualitative Exploration of Process-Sensitive Peer Group Supervision." *Journal for Specialists in Group Work* 26 (1):81–89.

Cloud, J. 1998. "Sex and the Law." *Time* (March 23):48–54.

Coffey, R. M., T. Mark, H. Harwood, D. McKusick, J. Genuardi, J. Dilonardo, and J. A. Buck. 2000. *National Estimates of Expenditures for Mental Health and Substance Abuse Treatment, 1997.* SAMHSA Publication no. SMA-00-3499. Rockville, Md.: Center for Substance Abuse Treatment and Center for Mental Health Services, Substance Abuse and Mental Health Services Administration.

Cohen, Neil and Gary B. Rhodes. 1977. "A View Toward Leadership Style and Job Orientation in Education and Practice." *Administration in Social Work* 1 (3):281–91.

Cohen, Ruth. 1972. "Student Training in Geriatric Center." In Florence W. Kaslow and Associates, eds., *Issues in Human Services,* pp. 168–84. San Francisco: Jossey-Bass.

Coleman, H. K. 1999. "Training for Multicultural Supervision." In E. Holloway and M. Carroll, eds., *Training Counselor Supervisors: Strategies, Methods, and Techniques,* pp. 120–61. Thousand Oaks, Calif.: Sage.

Compton, Beulah and Burt Galaway. 1975. *Social Work Processes.* Homewood, Ill.: Dorsey.

Congress, E. P. 1992. "Ethical Decision Making of Social Work Supervisors." *Clinical Supervisor* 10 (1):157–70.

Consalvo, C. 1989. "Humor in Management: No Laughing Matter." *Humor* 2 (3):285–97.

Constantine, M. G. 1997. "Facilitating Multicultural Competency in Counseling Supervision: Operationalizing a Practical Framework." In D. B. Pope-Davis and H. L. K. Coleman, eds., *Multicultural Counseling Competencies: Assessment, Education and Training, and Supervision,* vol. 7, pp. 310–24. Thousand Oaks, Calif.: Sage.

Conte, Jon R. et al. 1981. *A Qualitative Evaluation of Citizen's Review of Boards in Four States.* Chicago: University of Illinois Center for Policy and Research.

Conway, P. and M. S. Ellison. 1995. "The Development of a Behaviorally Anchored Rating Scale for Master's Student Evaluation of Field Instructors." *Clinical Supervisor* 13 (1):101–20.

Conyngton, Mary. 1909. *How to Help: A Manual of Practical Charity Designed for the Use of Nonprofessional Workers Among the Poor.* New York: Macmillan.

Cook, D. A. 1994. "Racial Identity in Supervision." *Counselor Education and Supervision* 34:132–41.

Cook, D. A. and J. E. Helms. 1988. "Visible Racial/Ethnic Group Supervisees' Satisfaction with Cross-Cultural Supervision as Predicted by Relationship Characteristics." *Journal of Counseling Psychology* 35:268–74.

Cooper, Caren C. and M. C. Gottlieb. 2000. "Ethical Issues with Managed Care: Challenges Facing Counseling Psychology." *Counseling Psychologist* 282:179–236.

Cope, Ronald. 1982. "Concurrent Validity of a Written Test for Entry Level Social Workers." *Educational and Psychological Measurement* 42 (4):1181–188.

Corcoran, K. 1997. "Managed Care: Implications for Social Work Practice." In *1997 Supplement to the Encyclopedia of Social Work,* 19th ed., pp. 191–200. Washington, D.C.: NASW Press.

Corcoran, Kevin and Vikki Vandiver. 1996. *Maneuvering the Maze of Managed Care.* New York: Free Press.

Cormier, L. Sherilyn and Janine M. Bernard. 1982. "Ethical and Legal Responsibilities of Clinical Supervisors." *Personnel and Guidance Journal* 60:486–91.

Cornelius, Donald S. 1997. "Social Work Practice and Industrialized Managed Care: A Case Study." Ph.D. diss., City University of New York. University Microfilms International no. 9720080.

Costa, L. 1994. "Reducing Anxiety in Live Supervision." *Counselor Education and Supervision* 34:30–40.

Cotter Mena, Kristin Marguerite. 2000. "The Impact of the Supervisory Relationship on Worker Job Satisfaction and Burnout." Ph.D. diss., University of Houston.

Covner, B. S. 1943. "Studies in the Phonographic Recorders of Verbal Material: III. The Completeness and Accuracy of Counselor Interview Reports." *Journal of General Psychology* 30:181–203.

Crespi, Tony D. 1995. "Gender Sensitive Supervision: Exploring Feminist Perspectives for Male and Female Supervisors." *Clinical Supervisor* 13 (2):19–30.

Crisp, B. R. and L. Cooper. 1998. "The Content of Supervision Scale: An Instrument to Screen the Suitability of Prospective Supervisors of Social Work Student Practicums." *Journal of Teaching in Social Work* 17 (1/2):201–11.

Cross, Darryl and David Brown. 1983. "Counselor Supervision as a Function of Trainee Experience: An Analysis of Specific Behaviors." *Counselor Education and Supervision* 22:333–40.

Cruser, Robert W. 1958. "Opinions on Supervision: A Chapter Study." *Social Work* 3:18–25.

Csikszentmihalyi, M. and I. Csikszentmihalyi. 1988. *Optimal Experience: Psychological Studies of Flow in Consciousness.* New York: Cambridge University Press.

Culatta, Richard and Herbert Seltzer. 1976. "Content and Sequence Analysis of the Supervisory Session." *ASHA* 18:8–12.

——. 1977. "Content and Sequence of the Supervisory Session: A Report of the Clinical Use." *ASHA* 19:523–26.

Curtis, P. and J. Boyd. 1997. *1995 Salary Study.* Washington, D.C.: Child Welfare League of America.

Dailey, Dennis M. 1983. "Androgyny, Sex Role Stereotypes, and Clinical Judgement." *Social Work Research and Abstracts* 19 (1):20–24.

Daley, Dennis M. 1992. *Performance Appraisal in the Public Sector: Techniques and Applications.* Westport, Conn.: Quorum.

D'Andrea, M. and J. Daniels. 1997. "Multicultural Counseling Supervision: Central Issues, Theoretical Considerations, and Practical Strategies." In D. Pope-Davis and H. Coleman, eds., *Multicultural Counseling Competencies,* pp. 290–309. Thousand Oaks, Calif.: Sage.

Daniels, J., M. D'Andrea, and B. Soo Kyung Kim. 1999. "Assessing the Barriers and Changes of Cross-Cultural Supervision: A Case Study." *Counselor Education and Supervision* 38:190–203.

Davidson, Terrence N. and Edmund T. Emmer. 1966. "Immediate Effect of Supportive and Nonsupportive Supervisor Behavior on Counselor Candidates' Focus of Concern." *Counselor Education and Supervision* 6:27–31.

Davies, M. 1990. "Work Satisfaction in Probation and Social Work." *British Journal of Social Work* 20:433–43.

Davis, Edward W. and Marjie C. Barrett. 1981. "Supervision for Management of Worker Stress." *Administration in Social Work* 5:55–64.

Dawson, John B. 1926. "The Case Supervisor in a Family Agency." *Family* 6:293–95.

Decker, W. H. 1987. "Job Satisfaction: Effect of Supervisors' Sense of Humor." *Social Behavior and Personality* 15 (2):225–32.

Decker, W. H. and D. M. Rotondo. 1999. "Use of Humor at Work: Predictors and Implications." *Psychological Reports* 84:961–68.

DeMartini, J. and L. B. Whitbeck. 1987. "Sources of Knowledge for Practice." *Journal of Applied Behavioral Science* 23 (2):219–31.

Demos, George. 1964. "Suggested Uses of Tape Recordings in Counseling Supervision." *Personnel and Guidance Journal* 42 (7):704–5.

Dendinger, C. and E. Kohn. 1989. "Assessing Supervisory Skills." *Clinical Supervisor* 7 (1):41–55.

DeNisi, A. H. and L. H. Peters. 1996. "Organization of Information in Memory and the Performance Appraisal Process: Evidence from the Field." *Journal of Applied Psychology* 816:717–37.

Deutsch, C. J. 1984. "Self-Reported Sources of Stress Among Psychotherapists." *Professional Psychology: Research and Practice* 15 (6):833–45.

Devine, Edward. 1901. *The Practice of Charity.* New York: Handbook for Practical Workers.

Dhooper, S. S., M. B. Huff, and C. M. Shultz. 1989. "Social Work and Sexual Harassment." *Journal of Sociology and Social Welfare* 16 (3):125–35.

Dimock, Hedley S. and Harleigh B. Trecker. 1949. *The Supervisor of Group Work and Recreation.* New York: Association Press.

DiNitto, D., A. McNeece, and D. Harkness. 1997. "Educating and Credentialing Social Workers." In D. DiNitto and A. McNeece, eds., *Social Work: Issues and Opportunities in a Challenging Profession,* 2d ed., pp. 17–44. Boston: Allyn and Bacon.

Doehrman, Margery. 1976. "Parallel Processes in Supervision and Psychotherapy." *Bulletin of the Menninger Clinic* 40:3–104.

Donner, S. 1996. "Field Work Crisis: Dilemmas, Dangers, and Opportunities." *Smith College Studies in Social Work* 66 (3):317–31.

Dooley, Dickey, K., W. F. Housley, and C. Guest Jr. 1993. "Ethics in Supervision of Rehabilitation Counselor Trainees: A Survey." *Rehabilitation Education* 7:195–201.

Dornbusch, Sanford M. and W. Richard Scott. 1975. *Evaluation and the Exercise of Authority.* San Francisco: Jossey-Bass.

Drake, B. and J. Washeck. 1998. "A Competency-Based Method for Providing Worker Feedback to CPS Supervisors." *Administration in Social Work* 22 (3):55–74.

Drake, B. and G. Yadoma. 1996. "A Structural Equation Model of Burnout and Job Exit Among Child Protective Services Workers." *Social Work Research* 20:179–87.

Duan, Chang-Ming and Helen Roehlke. 2001. "A Descriptive 'Snap-Shot' of Cross-Racial Supervision in University Counseling Center Internships." *Journal of Multicultural Counseling and Development* 29:131–45.

Dublin, Richard A. 1982. "Supervision as an Orienting and Integrating Process." *Social Casework* 63:233–36.

Duncan, Mina G. 1963. "An Experiment in Applying New Methods in Field Work." *Social Casework* 44:179–84.

Duncan, W. J. 1984. "Perceived Human and Social Network Patterns in a Sample of Task-Oriented Groups." *Human Relations* 37 (11):895–907.

Eagerton, John C. 1994. "Mental Health Professionals' Attitudes Toward Judicial Intervention: Bureaucracy, Organizational Loyalty, and Professionalism as Determinants." *Dissertation Abstracts International Section A: Humanities and Social Sciences* 54 (10-A):3871.

Edelwich, Jerry and Archie Brodsky. 1982. *Sexual Dilemmas for the Helping Professional.* New York: Bruner-Mazel.

Edinburg, Golda M. and Joan M. Cottler. 1995. "Managed Care." In Richard L. Edwards, ed., *Encyclopedia of Social Work,* 19th ed., pp. 1635–41. Washington, D.C.: NASW Press.

Edwards, Mark R. and A. J. Ewan. 1996. *360° Feedback: The Powerful New Model for Employee Assessment and Performance Improvement.* New York: American Management Association.

Efstation, J. F., J. M. Patton, and C. M. Kardash. 1990. "Measuring the Working Alliance in Counselor Supervision." *Journal of Counseling Psychology* 37:322–29.

Eiskovitz, Z. et al. 1985. "Supervision in Ecological Context: The Relationship Between the Quality of Supervision and the Work and Treatment Environment." *Journal of Social Service Research* 8 (4):37–58.

Eisenberg, Sidney. 1956a. "Supervision as an Agency Need." *Social Casework* 37:233–37.

——. 1956b. *Supervision in the Changing Field of Social Work.* Philadelphia: Jewish Family Service of Philadelphia.

Ekstein, Rudolf and Robert S. Wallerstein. 1972. *The Teaching and Learning of Psychotherapy,* 2d ed. New York: International Universities Press.

Ellis, M. V. 1991. "Critical Incidents in Clinical Supervision and in Supervisor Supervision: Assessing Supervisory Issues." *Journal of Counseling Psychology* 38 (3):342–49.

Ellis, M. V. and N. Ladany. 1997. "Inferences Concerning Supervisees and Clients in Clinical Supervision: An Integrative Review." In C. Watkins, ed., *Handbook of Psychotherapy Supervision,* pp. 447–507. New York: Wiley.

Ellis, M. V. and E. S. Robbins. 1993. "Voices of Care and Justice in Clinical Supervision: Issues and Interventions." *Counselor Education and Supervision* 32 (3):203–13.

Emenhiser, David, R. Barker, and M. DeWoody. 1995. *Managed Care: An Agency Guide to Surviving and Thriving.* Washington, D.C.: Child Welfare League of America.

Epstein, Irwin. 1970. "Professionalization, Professionalism, and Social Worker Radicalism." *Journal of Health and Social Behavior* 11:67–77.

Erera, I. P. 1991a. "Role Conflict Among Public Welfare Supervisors." *Administration in Social Work* 15 (4):35–51.

——. 1991b. "Supervisors Can Burn-Out Too." *Clinical Supervisor* 9 (2):131–48.

Erera, I. P. and A. Lazar. 1993. "Training Needs of Social Work Supervisors." *Clinical Supervisor* 11 (1):83–94.

——. 1994a. "Operationalizing Kadushin's Model of Social Work Supervision." *Journal of Social Service Research* 18 (3/4):109–22.

——. 1994b. "The Administrative and Educational Functions in Supervision: Indications of Incompatibility." *Clinical Supervisor* 12 (2):39–56.

Etgar, T. 1996. "Parallel Processes in a Training and Supervision Group for Counselors Working with Adolescent Sex Offenders." *Social Work with Groups* 19 (3/4):57–69.

Etzioni, Amitai. 1961. *A Comparative Analysis of Complex Organizations.* New York: Free Press.

Evans, W. N. and T. H. Hohenshil. 1997. "Job Satisfaction of Substance Abuse Counselors." *Alcoholism Treatment Quarterly* 15 (2):1–13.

Ewalt, Patricia L. 1980. "From Clinician to Manager." In Stephan White, ed., *New Directions for Mental Health Services—Middle Management in Mental Health,* pp. 1–10. San Francisco: Jossey-Bass.

Ezell, Hazel F. and Charles A. Odewahn. 1980. "An Empirical Inquiry of Variables Impacting on Women in Management in Public Social Service Organizations." *Administration in Social Work* 4 (4):53–70.

Family Service Association of America. 1957. *A Guide to Classification of Professional Positions and Evaluation Outlines in a Family Service Agency.* New York: Family Service Association of America.

Farber, Barry A. and Louis J. Heifetz. 1981. "The Satisfactions and Stresses of Psychotherapeutic Work: A Factor Analytic Study." *Professional Psychology* 12 (5):621–29.

——. 1982. "The Process and Dimensions of Burn-out in Psychotherapists." *Professional Psychology* 13(2):293–301.

Farmer, S. S. "Visual Literacy and the Clinical Supervisor." *Clinical Supervisor* 5 (1):45–72.

Favaro, J. L. and D. R. Ilgen. 1989. "The Effects of Ratee Prototypicality on Rater Observation and Accuracy." *Journal of Applied Social Psychology* 19:932–46.

Feldman, S. 1999. "The Middle Management Muddle." *Administration and Policy in Mental Health* 26 (4):281–90.

Feldman, Yonata, Hyman Sponitz, and Leo Nagelberg. 1953. "One Aspect of Casework Training through Supervision." *Social Casework* 34:150–56.

Ferris, G. R., T. A. Judge, K. M. Rowland, and D. E. Fitzgibbons. 1994. "Subordinate Influence and the Performance Evaluation Process: Test of a Model." *Organizational Behavior and Human Decision Processes* 58: 101–35.

Fiedler, Fred E. 1967. *A Theory of Leadership Effectiveness.* New York: McGraw.

Field, M. 1980. "Social Casework Practice During the 'Psychiatric Deluge'." *Social Service Review* 54 (4):482–507.

Fields, Mrs. James T. 1885. *How to Help the Poor.* Boston: Houghton.

Fineman, S. 1985. *Social Work Stress and Intervention.* London: Gower.

Finkelstein, H. and A. Tuckman. 1997. "Supervision of Psychological Assessment: A Developmental Model." *Professional Psychology: Research and Practice* 28 (1):92–95.

Fisher, B. L. 1989. "Differences Between Supervision of Beginning and Advanced Therapists: Hogan's Hypothesis Empirically Revisited." *Clinical Supervisor* 7 (1):57–74.

Fizdale, Ruth. 1958. "Peer Group Supervision." *Social Casework* 39:443–50.

Fleischmann, O. 1955. "A Method of Teaching Psychotherapy. One-Way-Vision Room Technique." *Bulletin of the Menninger Clinic* 19:160–72.

Fleming, Joan and Therese Benedek. 1966. *Psychoanalytic Supervision.* New York: Grune.

Fong, M. and S. Lease. 1997. "Crosscultural Supervision: Issues for the White Supervisor." In D. Pope-Davis and H. Coleman, eds., *Multicultural Counseling Competencies,* pp. 387–405. Thousand Oaks, Calif.: Sage.

Ford, Julian D. 1979. "Research on Training Counselors and Clinicians." *Review of Educational Research* 49:87–130.

Ford, K. and A. Jones. 1987. *Student Supervision.* Hampshire, Eng.: Macmillan.

Fortune, A. E. and J. S. Abramson. 1993. " Predictors of Satisfaction with Field Practicum Among Social Work Students." *Clinical Supervisor* 11 (1):95–110.

Fortune, A. and L. Hanks. 1988. "Gender Inequities in Early Social Work Careers." *Social Work* 33:221–25.

Fox, Raymond. 1974. "Supervision by Contract." *Social Casework* 55:247–51.

——. 1983. "Contracting in Supervision: A Goal Oriented Process." *Clinical Supervisor* 1 (1):65–76.

——. 1998. "An Essay on Mutuality and Parallel Process in Field Instruction." *Clinical Supervisor* 17 (2):59–73.

Fox, Raymond and M. Cooper. 1998. "The Effects of Suicide on the Private Practitioner: A Professional and Personal Perspective." *Clinical Social Work Journal* 26 (2):143–57.

Frantz, T. G. 1992. "Learning from Anxiety: A Transtheoretical Dimension of Supervision and its Administration." *Clinical Supervisor* 10 (2):29–56.

Frawley-O-Dea, M. G., and J. E. Sarnat. 2001. *The Supervisory Relationship—A Contemprorary Psychodynamic Approach.* New York: Guilford.

Freeman, S. C. 1993. "Structure in Counseling Supervision." *Clinical Supervisor* 11 (1):245–52.

French, John R. P. Jr. and Bertram Raven. 1960. "The Bases of Social Power." In D. Cartwright and A. Zander, eds., *Group Dynamics,* pp. 607–23. Evanston, Ill.: Row, Peterson.

Freudenberger, Herbert. 1980. *Burn-Out.* New York: Anchor.

Friedlander, G. 1983. "Trainees' Expectations for the Supervision Proseminar." *Counselor Education and Supervision* 22:342–48.

Friedlander, M. L. and L. G. Ward, 1984. "Development and Validation of the Supervisory Styles Inventory." *Journal of Counseling Psychology* 31 (4):541–57.

Friedlander, M. L., S. M. Siegel, and K. Brenock. 1989. "Parallel Processes in Counseling and Supervision: A Case Study." *Journal of Counseling Psychology* 36 (23):149–57.

Friedman, D. and N. J. Kaslow. 1986. "The Development of Professional Identity in Psychotherapists: Six Stages in the Supervision Process." *Clinical Supervisor* 4:29–49.

Friedson, Eliot and Buford Rhea. 1965. "Knowledge and Judgment in Professional Evaluations." *Administrative Science Quarterly* 10:107–24.

Friesen, Deloss D. and G. B. Dunning. 1973. "Peer Evaluation and Practicum Supervision." *Counselor Education and Supervision* 13:229–35.

Froehlich, Clifford P. 1958. "The Completeness and Accuracy of Counseling Interview Reports." *Journal of General Psychology* 58:81–96.

Fukuyama, M. A. 1994. "Critical Incidents in Multicultural Counseling Supervision: A Phenomenological Approach to Supervision Research." *Counselor Education and Supervision* 34:144–51.

Furlong, M. 1990. "On Being Able to Say What We Mean: The Language of Hierarchy in Social Work Practice." *British Journal of Social Work* 20: 570–90.

Gadsby-Waters, J. 1992. *The Supervision of Child Protection Work.* Brookfield, Vt.: Avebury.

Galambos, Eva C. and Xenia R. Wiggens. 1970. *After Graduation: Experiences of College Graduates in Locating and Working in Social Welfare Positions.* Atlanta: Southern Regional Education Board.

Galassi, J. P. and P. J. Trent. 1987. "A Conceptual Framework for Evaluating Supervision Effectiveness." *Counselor Education and Supervision* 15: 260–69.

Gallant, J. Paul and Bruce A. Thyer. 1989. "The 'Bug in the Ear' in Clinical Supervision: A Review." *Clinical Supervisor* 7 (2/3):43–58.

Gallant, J. Paul, Bruce A. Thyer, and Jon S. Bailey. 1991. "Using 'Bug-in-the-Ear' Feedback in Clinical Supervision." *Research on Social Work Practice* 1 (2):175–87.

Galm, Sharon. 1972. *Issues in Welfare Administration: Welfare—An Administrative Nightmare.* Subcommittee on Fiscal Policy of the Joint Economic Committee, U.S. Congress. Washington, D.C.: U.S. Government Printing Office.

Gambrill, Eileen and Kermit Wiltse. 1974. "Foster Care Plans and Activities." *Public Welfare* 32:12–21.

Gardiner, D. 1895. "The Training of Volunteers." *Charity Organization Review* 11:2–4.

Gardiner, D. 1989. *The Anatomy of Supervision: Developing Learning and Professional Competence for Social Work Students.* Philadelphia: Open University Press.

Garrett, C. 1999. "Stress, Coping, Empathy, Secondary Traumatic Stress, and Burnout in Healthcare Providers Working with HIV Infected Individuals." Ph.D. diss., New York University.

Garrett, K. J. and A. Barretta-Herman. 1995. "Moving from Supervision to Professional Development." *Clinical Supervisor* 13 (2):97–110.

Gasiorowicz, Nina. 1982. "The Parallel Process Supervision and Psychotherapy—An Empirical Study." *Smith College Studies in Social Work* 53:67.

Gatmon, Dafna, Daniel Jackson, Lisa Koshkarian, Nora Martos-Perry, Adriana Molina, Neesha Patel, and Emil Rodolfa. 2001. "Exploring Ethnic, Gender, and Sexual Orientation Variables in Supervision: Do They Really Matter?" *Journal of Multicultural Counseling and Development* 29:102–13.

Geideman, H. and P. Wolkenfield. 1980. "The Parallelism Phenomenon in Psychoanalysis and Supervision." *Psychoanalytic Quarterly* 49 (2):234–55.

Geller, C. 1994. "Group Supervision as a Vehicle for Teaching Group Work to Students: Field Instruction in a Senior Center." *Clinical Supervisor* 12 (1):199–214.

Gelso, Charles. 1972. "Inhibition Due to Recording and Clients' Evaluation of Counseling." *Psychological Reports* 31:675–77.

Gelso, Charles and Mary F. Tanney. 1972. "Client Personality as a Mediator of the Effects of Recording." *Counselor Education and Supervision* 22:109–14.

Getz, H. and D. Agnew. 1999. "A Supervision Model for Public Agency Clinicians." *Clinical Supervisor* 18 (2):51–62.

Getzel, G. S. and R. Salmon. 1985. "Group Supervision: An Organizational Approach." *Clinical Supervisor* 3 (1):27–43.

Gibelman, M. 1999. "The Search for Identity: Defining Social Work—Past, Present, Future." *Social Work* 44 (4):298–310.

——. 2000. "Say It Ain't So Norm! Reflections on Who We Are." *Social Work* 45 (5):463–66.

Gibelman, M. and P. Schervish. 1995. "Pay Equity in Social Work: Not!" *Social Work* 40 (5):622–30.

——. 1996. "The Private Practice of Social Work: Current Trends and Projected Scenarios in a Managed Care Environment." *Clinical Social Work Journal* 24 (3):323–38.

——. 1997a. "Supervision in Social Work: Characteristics and Trends in a Changing Environment." *Clinical Supervisor* 16 (2):1–15.

——. 1997b. *Who We Are: A Second Look.* Washington, D.C.: NASW Press.

Gibson, F., A. McGrath, and R. Ried. 1989. "Occupational Stress in Social Work." *British Journal of Social Work* 29:1–16.

Gillespie, David F. and Susan Cohen. 1984. "Causes of Worker Burn-Out." *Children and Youth Services Review* 6:115–24.

Gillig, Paulette M. and Andrew Barr. 1999. "A Model for Multidisciplinary Peer Review and Supervision of Behavioral Health Clinicians." *Community Mental Health Journal* 35 (4):361–65.

Gilstrap, Roger L. 1999. "The Health of Mental Health Organizations and Their Employees: A Phenomenological Study." Ph.D. diss., Gonzaga University. University Microfilms International no. 9931543.

Ginsberg, M. R., R. P. Weisberg, and E. L. Cowan. 1985. "The Relationship Between Supervisors' Satisfaction with Supervision and Client Change." *Journal of Community Psychology* 13 (October):387–92.

Gizynski, M. 1978. "Self Awareness of the Supervisee in Supervision." *Clinical Social Work Journal* 6 (3):202–10.

Gladstone, Bernard. 1967. *Supervisory Practice and Social Service in the Neighborhood Center.* New York: United Neighborhood Homes.

Glastonbury, Bryan, David M. Cooper, and Pearl Hawkins. 1980. *Social Work in Conflict—The Practitioner and the Bureaucrat.* London: Croom Helm.

Gleeson, J. 1992. "How Do Child Welfare Caseworkers Learn?" *Adult Education Quarterly* 43 (1):15–29.

Glendenning, John M. 1923. "Supervision through Conferences on Specific Cases." *Family* 4:7–10.

Glidden, C. and T. Tracey. 1992. "A Multidimensional Scaling Analysis of Supervisory Dimensions and their Perceived Relevance Across Trainee Experience Levels." *Professional Psychology: Research and Practice* 23 (2):151–57.

Glisson, C. 1989. "The Effect of Leadership on Workers in Human Service Organizations." *Administration in Social Work* 13 (3/4):99–116.

Glisson, C. and M. Durick. 1988. "Predictors of Job Satisfaction and Organizational Commitment in Human Service Organizations." *Administrative Science Quarterly* 33:61–81.

Goffman, Erving. 1952. "On Cooling the Mark Out: Some Aspects of Adaptation to Failure." *Psychiatry* 15:451–63.

——. 1959. *The Presentation of Self in Everyday Life*. Garden City, N.Y.: Anchor.

Goin, Marcia K. and Frank M. Kline. 1976. "Countertransference: A Neglected Subject in Clinical Supervision." *American Journal of Psychiatry* 133 (1):41–44.

Gold, J. M. 1996. "Call-Out Supervision." *Clinical Supervisor* 14 (2):157–63.

Goldhammer, Robert. 1969. *Clinical Supervision: Special Methods for the Supervision of Teachers*. New York: Holt.

Goldstein, Arnold P., Kenneth Heller, and Lee B. Sechrest. 1966. *Psychotherapy and the Psychology of Behavior Change*. New York: Wiley.

Goodridge, M., P. Johnston, and M. Thomson. 1996. "Conflict and Aggression as Stressors in the Work Environment of Nursing Assistants: Implications for Institutional Elder Abuse." *Journal of Elder Abuse and Neglect* 8 (1):49–67.

Goodyear, R. K. 1990. "Gender Configurations in Supervisory Dyads: Their Relation to Supervisee Influence Strategies and to Skill Evaluations of the Supervisee." *Clinical Supervisor* 8 (2):67–80.

Goodyear, R. and J. M. Bernard. 1998. "Clinical Supervision: Lessons from the Literature." *Counselor Education and Supervision* 38:6–22.

Goodyear, R. and Nelson, M. 1997. "The Major Formats of Psychotherapy Supervision." In C. Watkins, ed., *Handbook of Psychotherapy Supervision*, pp. 328–44. New York: Wiley.

Goodyear, R., P. Abadie, and F. Efros. 1984. "Supervisory Theory into Practice: Differential Perceptions of Supervision by Ekstein, Ellis, Polster and Rogers." *Journal of Counseling Psychology* 31 (2):228–37.

Gould, K. 2000. "Beyond *Jones v. Clinton*: Sexual Harrassment Law and Social Work." *Social Work* 14 (2):237–48.

Gould, L. J. and Loretta J. Bradley. 2001. "Evaluation in Supervision." In Loretta J. Bradley and Nicholas Ladany, eds., *Counselor Supervision: Principles, Process, and Practice*, 3d ed.,, pp. 271–303. Philadelphia: Brunner-Routledge.

Gouldner, Alvin. 1954. *Patterns of Industrial Democracy*. New York: Free Press.

Gowdy, E. A. and E. M. Freeman. 1993. "Program Supervision: Facilitating Staff Participation in Program Analysis, Planning, and Change." *Administration in Social Work* 17 (3):59–79.

Granello, Darcy Haag. 1996. "Gender and Power in the Supervisory Dyad." *Clinical Supervisor* 14 (2):54–68.

Granvold, Donald K. 1978. "Training Social Work Supervisors to Meet Organizational and Worker Objectives." *Journal of Education for Social Work* 14 (2):38–46.

Grater, H. A. 1985. "Stages in Psychotherapy Supervision: From Therapy Skills to Skilled Therapist." *Professional Psychology: Research and Practice* 16 (5):605–10.

Gray, Deering C. 1994. "Parallel Process in the Supervision of Child Psychotherapy." *American Journal of Psychotherapy* 48 (1):102–10.

Gray, Laurie A., Nicholas Ladany, Jessica A. Walker, and Julie A. Ancis. 2001. "Psychotherapy Trainees' Experience of Counter-Productive Events in Supervision." *Journal of Counseling Psychology* 48 (4):371–85.

Gray, S. 1986. "The Impact of State Licensure on the Structure, Content, and Context of Supervision in Social Work Practice." Ph.D. diss., Barry University.

Gray, S. W. 1990. "The Interplay of Social Work and Supervision: An Exploratory Study." *Clinical Supervisor* 8 (1):53–65.

Gray, S. W., D. E. Alperin, and R. Wik. 1989. "Multidimensional Expectations of Student Supervision in Social Work." *Clinical Supervisor* 7 (1): 89–102.

Green, A. D. 1966. "The Professional Social Worker in the Bureaucracy." *Social Service Review* 40:71–83.

Green, Solomon H. 1972. "Educational Assessments of Student Learning through Practice in Field Instruction." *Social Work Education Reporter* 20:48–54.

Greenleigh Associates. 1960. *Addenda to Facts, Fallacies, and Future: A Study of the AFDC Program, Cook County, Ill.* New York: Greenleigh Associates.

Greenspan, R., S. Hanfling, E. Parker, S. Primm, and D. Waldfogel. 1992. "Supervision of Experienced Agency Workers: A Descriptive Study." *Clinical Supervisor* 9 (2):31–42.

Grinnell, Richard M. and Linda Sue Hill. 1979. "The Perceived Effectiveness and Efficiency of DHR Employees." *Social Service Review* 53:116–22.

Grossbard, Hyman. 1954. "Methodology for Developing Self-Awareness." *Social Casework* 35:380–85.

Grotjohn, M. 1945. "The Role of Identification in Psychiatric and Psychoanalytic Training." *Psychiatry* 12:141–45.

Grube, M. N. and S. W. Painton. 1990. "Effective and Ineffective Clinical Supervisors: Looking Back." *Health Care Supervisor* 8 (4):45–53.

Gruenberg, Peter B., Edward H. Liston Jr., and George J. Wayne. 1969. "Intensive Supervision of Psychotherapy with Videotape Recording." *American Journal of Psychotherapy* 23:95–105.

Guest, C. L. Jr. and K. Dooley. 1999. "Supervisor Malpractice: Liability to the Supervisee in Clinical Supervision." *Counselor Education and Supervision* 38:269–79.

Gummer, Burton. 1979. "On Helping and Helplessness: The Structure of Discretion in the American Welfare System." *Social Service Review* 53: 215–28.

——. 1990. *The Politics of Social Administration: Managing Organizational Politics in Social Agencies.* Englewood Cliffs, N.J.: Prentice-Hall.

Gurka, M. D. and E. D. Wicas. 1979. "Generic Models of Counseling, Supervision, Counseling Instruction, Dichotomy, and Consultation Meta-Model." *Personnel and Guidance Journal* 57:407–9.

Gurteen, Humphrey S. 1882. *A Handbook of Charity Organizations.* Buffalo, N.Y.: privately published.

Guy, M. E. 1985. *Professionals in Organizations: Debunking a Myth.* New York: Praeger.

H. C. D. 1949. "Through Supervision with Gun and Camera: The Personal Account of a Beginning Supervisor." *Social Work Journal* 30:161–63.

Hage, Jerald and Michael Aiken. 1967. "Relationship of Centralization to Other Structural Properties." *Administrative Science Quarterly* 12:72–91.

Hagler, P. and P. L. Casey. 1990. "Games Supervisors Play in Clinical Supervision." *ASHA* 32 (2):53–56.

Haj-Yahia, M. M. 1997. "Culturally Sensitive Supervision of Arab Social Work Students in Western Universities." *Social Work* 42 (2):166–74.

Halberg, I. R., A. Berg, and L. T. Arlehman. 1994. "The Parallel Process in Clinical Supervision with a Schizophrenic Client." *Perspectives in Psychiatric Care* 30 (2):26–32.

Hale, K. K. and C. D. Stoltenberg. 1988. "The Effects of Self-Awareness and Evaluation Apprehension of Counselor Trainee Anxiety." *Clinical Supervisor* 6 (1):49–70.

Haley, J. 1977. *Problem Solving Therapy.* San Francisco: Jossey-Bass.

Hall, Richard H. 1968. "Professionalization and Bureaucratization." *American Sociological Review* 33:92–104.

Handler, Joel F. 1973. *The Coercive Social Worker.* Chicago: Rand McNally.

——. 1979. *Protecting the Social Service Client—Legal and Structural Controls on Official Discretion.* New York: Academic Press.

Hanes, K. S. 1989. *Women Managers in Human Services.* New York: Springer.

Hanlan, Archie. 1972. "Changing Functions and Structures." In Florence W. Kaslow and Associates, eds., *Issues in Human Services,* pp. 39–50. San Francisco: Jossey-Bass.

Hanley, B., S. Cooper, and G. L. Dick. 1994. "Videotaping as a Teaching Tool in Social Work Education." *Journal of Continuing Social Work Education* 6:10–14.

Hansen, James and Richard W. Warner. 1971. "Review of Research on Practicum Supervision." *Counselor Education and Supervision* 11:261–72.

Hansen, James, Ronald Pound, and C. Petro. 1976. "Review of Research on Practicum Supervision." *Counselor Education and Supervision* 16:107–16.

Hansen, James, Terri H. Robins, and John Grimes. 1982. "Review of Research on Practicum Supervision." *Counselor Education and Supervision* 15:15–24.

Hardcastle, D. A. 1991. "Toward a Model for Supervision: A Peer Supervision Pilot Project." *Clinical Supervisor* 9 (2):63–78.

Hare, Rachel T. and Susan T. Frankena. 1972. "Peer Group Supervision." *American Journal of Orthopsychiatry* 42:527–29.

Haring, Barbara. 1974. *Workload Measurement in Child Welfare: A Report of CWLA Member Agencies, Activities, and Interests.* New York: Child Welfare League of America.

Harkness, D. 1995. "The Art of Helping in Supervised Practice: Skills, Relationships, and Outcomes." *Clinical Supervisor* 13 (1):63–76.

——. 1997. "Testing Interactional Social Work Theory: A Panel Analysis of Supervised Practice and Outcomes." *Clinical Supervisor* 15 (1):33–50.

Harkness, D. and H. Hensley. 1991. "Changing the Focus of Social Work Supervision: Effects on Client Satisfaction and Generalized Contentment." *Social Work* 36 (6):506–12.

Harkness, D. and Kadushin, A. 2001. "Social Work Supervision in the Graduate Curriculum: A Survey of Accredited Graduate Social Work Programs." Unpublished data.

Harkness, D. and J. Poertner. 1989. "Research and Social Work Supervision: A Conceptual Review." *Social Work* 34 (2):115–19.

Harkness, D., M. Swenson, K. Madsen-Hampton, and R. Hale. 2001. "The Development, Reliability, and Validity of a Clinical Rating Scale for Codependency." *Journal of Psychoactive Drugs* 33 (2):159–71.

Harkness, L. and P. Mulinski. 1988. "Performance Standards for Social Workers." *Social Work* 33:339–44.

Harper, Robert A. and John W. Hudson. 1952. "The Use of Recordings in Marriage Counseling: A Preliminary Empirical Investigation." *Marriage and Family Living* 14:332–34.

Harrar, W. R., L. VandeCreek, and S. Knapp. 1990. "Ethical and Legal Aspects of Clinical Supervision." *Professional Psychology: Research and Practice* 21 (1):37–41.

Harris, Patrick. 1977. "Staff Supervision in Community Work." In Catherine Briscoe and David N. Thomas, eds., *Community Work: Learning and Supervision,* pp. 33–42. London: Allen and Unwin.

Harris-Jenkins, G. 1970. "Professionals in Organizations." In J. A. Jackson, ed., *Professions and Professionalization,* pp. 55–108. New York: Cambridge University Press.

Harrison, W. David. 1980. "Role Strain and Burn-Out in Child-Protective Service Workers." *Social Service Review* 54:31–44.

Harshbarger, Dwight. 1973. "The Individual and the Social Order: Notes on the Management of Heresy and Deviance in Complex Organizations." *Human Relations* 26:251–70.

Hart, Gordon M. 1982. *The Process of Clinical Supervision.* Baltimore, Md.: University Park Press.

Hartman, C. and K. Brieger. 1992. "Cross-Gender Supervision and Sexuality." *Clinical Supervisor* 10 (1):71–81.

Hasenfeld, Yeshkel. 1983. *Human Service Organizations.* Englewood Cliffs, N.J.: Prentice-Hall.

Hathway, Marion. 1943. "Utilizing Available and New Personnel." *Compas* 24:41–42.

Hawkins, P. and R. Shohet. 1989. *Supervision in the Helping Professions.* Milton Keynes, UK: Open University Press.

Hawthorne, Lillian. 1975. "Games Supervisors Play." *Social Work* 20:179–83.

Hayes, R. 1986. "Men's Decision to Enter or Avoid Nontraditional Occupations." *Career Development Quarterly* 35:89–101.

Hayes, Richard L., Lorie S. Blackman, and Carolyn Brennan. 2001. "Group Supervision." In Loretta J. Bradley and Nicholas Ladany, eds., *Counselor Supervision: Principles, Process, and Practice,* 3d ed., pp. 183–206. Philadelphia: Brunner-Routledge.

Haywood, Christine. 1979. *A Fair Assessment—Issues in Evaluating Counselors.* London: Central Council for Education and Training in Social Work.

Hegarty, W. H. 1974. "Using Subordinate Ratings to Elicit Behavioral Changes in Supervisors." *Journal of Applied Psychology* 59:764–66.

Henderson, C., C. Cawyer, and C. E. Watkins. 1999. "A Comparison of Student and Supervisor Perceptions of Effective Practicum Supervision." *Clinical Supervisor* 18 (1):47–74.

Henry, Charlotte S. 1955. "Criteria for Determining Readiness of Staff to Function without Supervision." In *Administration, Supervision, and Consultation,* pp. 34–45. New York: Family Service Association of America.

Heppner, Paul P. and Patrick G. Handley. 1981. "A Study of Interpersonal Influence Process in Supervision." *Journal of Counseling Psychology* 28 (5):437–44.

Heppner, Paul P., Dennis M. Kivlighan, Jeffery W. Burnett, Thomas R. Berry, et al. 1994. "Dimensions that Characterize Supervisory Interventions Delivered in the Context of Live Supervision of Practicum Counselors." *Journal of Counseling Psychology* 41 (2):227–35.

Heraud, Brian. 1981. *Training for Uncertainty—A Sociological Approach to Social Work Education.* Boston: Routledge and Kegan Paul.

Herrick, Christine D. 1977. "A Phenomenological Study of Supervisees' Positive and Negative Experiences in Supervision." Ph.D. diss., University of Pittsburgh.

Herzberg, Frederick. 1968. "One More Time—How Do You Motivate Employees?" *Harvard Business Review* 46:220–38.

Herzberg, Frederick, B. Mausner, and B. B. Snyderman. 1959. *The Motivation to Work,* 2d ed. New York: Wiley.

Herzlinger, Regina E. 1981. "Management Control Systems in Human Service Organizations." In Herman D. Stein, ed., *Organization and the Human Services Cross Disciplinary Reflections,* pp. 205–32. Philadelphia: Temple University Press.

Hildebrand, J. 1995. "Learning through Supervision: A Systemic Approach." In M. Yelloly and M. Henkel, eds., *Learning and Teaching in Social Work: Towards Reflective Practice,* pp. 182–88. London: Jessica Kingsley.

Himle, D. P., S. Jayaratne, and P. Thyness. 1989. "The Effects of Emotional Support on Burnout Work Stress and Mental Health Among Norwegian and American Social Workers." *Journal of Social Service Review* 13 (1): 27–45.

Hipp, J. L. and C. E. Munson. 1995. "The Partnership Model: A Feminist Supervision/Consultation Perspective." *Clinical Supervisor* 13 (1):23–38.

Hirsh, Herman and Herbert Freed. 1970. "Pattern Sensitization in Psychotherapy Supervision by Means of Video Tape Recording." In Milton M. Berger, ed., *Videotape Technique in Psychiatric Training and Treatment.* New York: Bruner-Mazel.

Hodson, Randy, S. Creighton, C. Jamison, S. Rieble, and S. Welsh. 1994. "Loyalty to Whom? Workplace Participation and the Development of Consent." *Human Relations* 47 (8):895–909.

Hoese, J. A. 1987. "An Exploratory Investigation of Group Supervision: Trainees, Supervisors, and Structure." Ph.D. diss., University of Wisconsin, Madison.

Hoff, Timothy F. 1999. "The Social Organization of Physician-Managers in a Changing HMO." *Work and Occupations* 26 (3):324–51.

Hogan, R. A. 1964. "Issues and Approaches to Supervision." *Psychotherapy—Theory, Research, and Practice* 2:139–41.

Hollis, Florence. 1964. *Casework: A Psycho-Social Therapy.* New York: Random House.

Holloway, E. 1995. *Clinical Supervision: A Systems Approach.* Thousand Oaks, Calif.: Sage.

Holloway, E. et al. 1989. "Relation of Power and Involvement to Theoretical Orientation in Supervision: An Analysis of Discourse." *Journal of Counseling Psychology* 36 (1):88–102.

Holloway, E. L. 1987. "Developmental Models of Supervision: Is It Development?" *Professional Psychology: Research and Practice* 18:209–16.

Holloway, E. L. and R. Johnson. 1985. "Group Supervision: Widely Practiced but Poorly Understood." *Counselor Education and Supervision* 24:332–40.

Holloway, S. and G. Brager. 1989. *Supervising in the Human Services: The Politics of Practice.* New York: Free Press.

Horwitz, M. 1998. "Social Worker Trauma: Building Resilience in Child Protection Social Workers." *Smith College Studies in Social Work* 68 (3): 363–77.

Howard, M. and J. Jensen. 1999. "Clinical Practice Guidelines: Should Social Work Develop Them?" *Research on Social Work Practice* 9 (3):283–301.

Howe, E. 1980. "Public Professions and the Private Model of Professionalism." *Social Work* 25:179–91.

Hughes, L. and P. Pengelly. 1997. *Staff Supervision in a Turbulent Environment: Managing Process and Task in Front-Line Services.* London: J. Kingsley.

Hunt, Winslow. 1981. "The Use of Countertransference in Psychotherapy Supervision." *Journal of the American Academy of Psychoanalysis* 9 (3):361–73.

Hurlbert, D. F. 1992. "Changing the Views of Social Work Supervision: An Administrative Challenge." *Clinical Supervisor* 10 (2):57–69.

Iberg, J. R. 1991. "Applying Statistical Control Theory to Bring Together Clinical Supervision and Psychotherapy Research." *Journal of Consulting and Clinical Psychology* 59 (4):575–86.

Ilgen, Daniel R., J. L. Barnes-Farrell, and D. B. McKellin. 1993. "Performance Appraisal Process Research in the 1980s: What Has It Contributed to Appraisals in Use?" *Organizational Behavior and Human Decision Processes* 54:321–68.

Iliffe, G. and L. Steed. 2000. "Exploring the Counselor's Experience of Working with Perpetrators and Survivors of Domestic Violence." *Journal of Interpersonal Violence* 15 (4):393–412.

Itzhaky, H. and R. Aloni. 1996. "The Use of Deductive Techniques for Developing Mechanisms of Coping with Resistance in Supervision." *Clinical Supervisor* 14 (1):65–76.

Itzhaky, H. and R. Atzman. 1999. "The Role of the Supervisor in Training Social Workers Treating HIV Infected Persons in a Hospital." *Social Work in Health Care* 29 (1):57–74.

Itzhaky, H. and A. Aviad-Hiebloom. 1998. "How Supervision and Role Stress in Social Work Affect Burnout." *Arete* 22 (2):29–43.

Itzhaky, H. and A. Eliahu. 1999. "Do Students Reflect Their Field Instructors? The Relationship Between Supervisory and Learning Styles in Social Work Field Instruction." *Clinical Supervisor* 18 (1):75–84.

Itzhaky, H. and D. S. Ribner. 1998. "Resistance as a Phenomenon in Clinical and Student Social Work Supervision." *Australian Social Work* 51 (3): 25–29.

Itzin, Frank. 1960. "The Use of Tape Recording in Field Work." *Social Casework* 41:197–202.

Jacobs, C. 1991. "Violations of the Supervisory Relationship: An Ethical and Educational Blind Spot." *Social Work* 36 (2):130–35.

Jacobs, Jerry. 1969. "Symbolic Bureaucracy: A Case Study of a Social Welfare Agency." *Social Forces* 47:513–22.

Janeway, Elizabeth. 1980. *Power of the Weak.* New York: Knopf.

Jarman-Rhode, Lilly and JoAnn McFall. 1997. "The Changing Context of Social Work Practice: Implications and Recommendations for Social Work Educators." *Journal of Social Work Education* 33 (1):29–46.

Jay, Anthony. 1967. *Management and Machiavelli.* New York: Bantam.

Jayaratne, S., H. V. Brabson, L. M. Gant, B. A. Nagda, A. K. Singh, and W. A. Chess. 1992. "African-American Practitioners' Perceptions of their Supervisors: Emotional Support, Social Undermining, and Criticism." *Administration in Social Work* 16 (2):27–43.

Jayaratne, Srinika and Wayne A. Chess. 1982. "Some Correlates of Job Satisfaction Among Social Workers." *Journal of Applied Social Sciences* 7 (1):1–17.

——. 1984a. "Job Satisfaction, Burnout, and Turnover: A National Study." *Social Work* 29:448–53.

——. 1984b. "The Effects of Emotional Support on Perceived Job Stress and Strain." *Journal of Applied Behavioral Science* 20 (2):141–53.

Jayaratne, Srinika, Tony Tripodi, and Wayne A. Chess. 1983. "Perceptions of Emotional Support, Stress and Strain by Male and Female Social Workers." *Social Work Research and Abstracts* 19 (2):19–29.

Jaynes, S. et al. 1979. "Clinical Supervision of the Initial Interview: Effects on Patient Care." *American Journal of Psychology* 136 (11):1454–457.

Jeanquart-Barone, S. 1993. "Trust Differences Between Supervisors and Subordinates: Examining the Role of Race and Gender." *Sex Roles* 29 (1/2):1–10.

Joelson, J. 1982. "Friday Afternoon at the Board—Group Supervision in School Practice." *Social Work in Education* 4 (4):26–34.

Johnson, B. A. and T. Meline. 1997. "A Survey of Supervisor-Workload Practices: Communication Disorders Programs in Colleges." *Clinical Supervisor* 16 (1):79–96.

Judd, Jawiga, Regina E. Kohn, and Gerda L. Shulman. 1962. "Group Supervision: A Vehicle for Professional Development." *Social Work* 7 (1):96–102.

Judd, P., S. R. Block, and C. L. Calkin. 1985. "Sexual Harassment Among Social Workers in Human Service Agencies." *Arete* 10 (1):12–21.

Judge, Timothy A. and G. Ferris. 1993. "Social Context of Performance Evaluation Decisions." *Academy of Management Journal* 361:80–105.

Kadushin, Alfred. 1956a. "The Effects of Interview Observation on the Interviewer." *Journal of Counseling Psychology* 3:130–35.

——. 1956b. "Interview Observation as a Teaching Device." *Social Casework* 37:334–41.

——. 1957. "The Effect on the Client of Interview Observation at Intake." *Social Service Review* 31:22–38.

——. 1968. "Games People Play in Supervision." *Social Work* 13:32.

——. 1973. *Supervisor-Supervisee: A Questionnaire Study.* Madison: School of Social Work, University of Wisconsin.

——. 1974. "Supervisor-Supervisee: A Survey." *Social Work* 19:288–98.

——. 1976. *Supervision in Social Work.* New York: Columbia University Press.

——. 1981. "Professional Development: Supervision, Training, and Education." In Neil Gilbert and Harry Specht, eds., *Handbook of the Social Services,* pp. 638–65. Englewood Cliffs, N.J.: Prentice-Hall.

——. 1990. *Final Report of Updated Survey: Supervisors-Supervisees.* Madison: School of Social Work, University of Wisconsin.

——. 1992a. "Social Work Supervision: An Updated Survey." *Clinical Supervisor* 10 (2):9–27.

——. 1992b. "What's Wrong, What's Right with Social Work Supervision." *Clinical Supervisor* 10 (1):3–19.

——. 1999. "The Past, the Present, and the Future of Professional Social Work." *Arete* 23 (3):76–91.

Kagan, H. K. and N. I. Kagan. 1997. "Interpersonal Process Recall: Influencing Human Interaction." In C. E. Watkins Jr., ed., *Handbook of Psychotherapy Supervision,* pp. 296–309. New York: Wiley.

Kagan, Morris. 1963. "The Field Instructor's Evaluation of Student Performance: Between Fact and Fiction." *Social Worker* 3:15–26.

Kagan, Norman, David R. Krathwohl, and Ralph Miller. 1963. "Stimulated Recall in Therapy Using Video-Tape: A Case Study." *Journal of Counseling Psychology* 10:237–43.

Kagle, Jill D. 1979. "Evaluating Social Work Practice." *Social Work* 24:292–96.

Kahill, S. 1988. "Symptoms of Professional Burnout: A Review of the Empirical Evidence." *Canadian Psychology* 29 (3):284–97.

Kahn, Eva. 1979. "The Parallel Process in Social Work Treatment and Supervision." *Social Casework* 60:520–28.

Kahn, Robert L. 1964. *Organizational Stress.* New York: Wiley.

Kaiser, T. L. 1992a. "The Supervisory Relationship: A Study of the Relationship Between Supervisor and Supervisee in the Clinical Supervision of Marriage and Family Therapists." Ph.D. diss., University of Minnesota.

——. 1992b. "The Supervisory Relationship: An Identification of the Primary Elements in the Relationship and an Application of Two Theories of Ethical Relationships." *Journal of Marital and Family Therapy* 18 (3):283–96.

——. 1997. *Supervisory Relationships.* Pacific Grove, Calif.: Brooks/Cole.

Kalous, T. 1996. "Conducting Psychotherapy Supervision in the Managed Care Era". In N. Cummings, M. Pallak, and J. Cummings, eds., *Surviving the Demise of Solo Practice: Mental Health Practitioners Prospering in the Era of Managed Care,* pp. 93–116. Madison Conn.: Psychosocial Press.

Kane, Michael N., E. R. Hamlin, and W. Hawkins. 2000. "Perceptions of Field Instructors: What Skills Are Critically Important in Managed Care and Privatized Environments?" *Advances in Social Work* 12:187–202.

Kaplan, David M. 1983. "Current Trends in Practicum Supervision Research." *Counselor Education and Supervision* 22:215–26.

Kaplan, R. E. 1986. "Is Openness Passé?" *Human Relations* 39 (3):229–43.

——. 1987. "The Current Use of Live Supervision Within Marriage and Family Therapy Training Programs." *Clinical Supervisor* 5 (3):43–52.

Kaplan, S. J. 1991. "Consequences of Sexual Harassment in the Workplace." *Affilia* 6 (3):50–65.

Kaplan, T. 1991. "Reducing Student Anxiety in Field Work: Exploratory Research and Implications." *Clinical Supervisor* 9 (2):105–17.

Kaslow, F. W. 1972. "Group Supervision." In Florence W. Kaslow and Associates, eds., *Issues in Human Services,* pp. 115–41. San Francisco: Jossey-Bass.

Kaslow, F. W. et al., eds. 1977. *Supervision, Consultation, and Staff Training in the Helping Professions.* San Francisco: Jossey-Bass.

Kaufman, Herbert. 1960. *The Forest Ranger.* Baltimore, Md.: Johns Hopkins University Press.

——. 1973. *Administrative Feedback: Monitoring Subordinate Behavior.* Washington, D.C.: Brookings Institution.

Keller, J. F., H. O. Protinsky, M. Lichtman, and K. Allen. 1996. "The Process of Clinical Supervision: Direct Observation Research." *Clinical Supervisor* 14 (1):51–63.

Kenfield, J. 1993. "Clinical Supervision of Licensed Psychologists: Nature of and Satisfaction with the Supervisory Relationship." Ph.D. diss., University of Minnesota.

Kennard, B. D., S. M. Stewart, and M. R. Gluck. 1987. "The Supervision Relationship: Variables Contributing to Positive Versus Negative Experiences." *Professional Psychology: Research and Practice* 18 (2):172–75.

Kennedy, A. J. and K. Ferra. 1935. *Social Settlements in New York City.* New York: Columbia University Press.

Kennedy, Miriam and Lydia Keitner. 1970. "What Is Supervision? The Need for a Redefinition." *Social Worker* 38:51–52.

Kettner, Peter M. 1973. "Some Factors Affecting Use of Professional Knowledge and Skill by the Social Worker in Public Welfare Agencies." DSW diss., School of Social Work, University of Southern California.

Kim, Dong I., L. Sung Boo, and Allan Wheeler. 1979. "Professional Competency, Autonomy, and Job Satisfaction Among Social Workers in an Appalachian Rural Area." *Social Thought* 5:47–59.

Kivlighan, D., E. Angelone, and K. Swafford. 1991. "Live Supervision in Individual Psychotherapy: Effects on Therapist's Intention Use and Client's Evaluation of Session Effect and Working Alliance." *Professional Psychology: Research and Practice* 22:489–95.

Kleinman, L. S. and J. W. Lounsbury. 1978. "Validating Procedures for Selecting Social Work Personnel." *Social Work* 23:481–88.

Klitzke, M. J. and T. W. Lombardo. 1991. "A 'Bug-in-the-Eye' Can Be Better than a 'Bug-in-the-Ear': A Teleprompter Technique for On-Line Therapy Skills Training." *Behavior Modification* 15:113–17.

Knapman, N. S. 1977. "Sex Discrimination in Family Agencies." *Social Work* 22:461–65.

Knapp, Samuel. 1997. "Professional Liability and Risk Management in an Era of Managed Care." In Diane Marsh and Richard Magee, eds., *Ethical and Legal Issues in Professional Practice with Families,* pp. 271–88. New York: Wiley.

Knapp, S. and L. VandeCreek. 1997. *Treating Patients with Memories of Abuse: Legal Risk Management.* Washington, D.C.: American Psychological Association.

Knight, C. 1996. "A Study of MSW and BSW Students' Perceptions of Their Field Instructors." *Journal of Social Work Education* 32 (3):399–415.

Koeske, G. and S. Kirk. 1995a. "Direct and Buffering Effects of Internal Locus of Control Among Mental Health Professionals." *Journal of Social Service Research* 20 (3/4):1–28.

——. 1995b. "The Effect of Characteristics of Human Service Workers on Subsequent Morale and Turnover." *Administration in Social Work* 19 (1):15–31.

Koeske, G. and R. Koeske. 1989. "Structural and Theoretical Validity of the Maslach Burnout Inventory: A Critical Review and Reconceptualization." *Journal of Applied and Behavioral Science* 25:131–32.

Kogan, Leonard S. 1950. "The Electrical Recording of Social Casework Interviews." *Social Casework* 31:371–78.

Kohn, Regina. 1971. "Differential Use of Observed Interview in Student Training." *Social Work Education Reporter* 19:45–46.

Kolar, Patricia, M. A. Patchner, W. V. Schutz, and L. S. Patchner. 2000. "Assessing the Impact of Managed Care of Field Instruction in Schools of Social Work." *Arete* 242:39–52.

Kolb, David A. 1981. "Learning Styles and Disciplinary Differences." In Arthur A. Chickering and Associates, eds., *The Modern American College*, pp. 232–55. San Francisco: Jossey-Bass.

Kolevson, Michael. 1979. "Evaluating the Supervisory Relationship in Field Placements." *Social Work* 24 (3):241–44.

Korner, Ija N. and William H. Brown. 1952. "The Mechanical Third Ear." *Journal of Consulting Psychology* 16:81–84.

Kornfeld, D. S. and L. C. Kolb. 1964. "The Use of Closed Circuit Television in the Teaching of Psychiatry." *Journal of Nervous and Mental Diseases* 138:452–59.

Kornhauser, William. 1962. *Scientists in Industry: Conflict and Accommodation.* Berkeley, Calif.: University of California Press.

Krause, A. A. and G. J. Allen. 1988. "Perceptions of Counselor Supervision: An Examination of Stoltenberg's Model from the Perspectives of Supervisor and Supervisee." *Journal of Counseling Psychology* 35:77–80.

Kravetz, Diane and Linda E. Jones. 1982. "Career Orientation of Female Social Work Students: An Examination of Sex Differences." *Journal of Education for Social Work* 18 (3):77–84.

Kruger, Louis J. et al. 1988. "Group Supervision of Paraprofessional Counselors." *Professional Psychology: Research and Practice* 19 (6):609–16.

Kruzich, J. M. et al. 1986. "Assessment of Student and Faculty Learning Styles: Research and Application." *Journal of Social Work Education* 3 (Fall):22–29.

Kuechler, C. F. and A. Barretta-Herman. 1998. "The Consultation Circle: A Technique for Facilitating Peer Consultation." *Clinical Supervisor* 17 (1):83–94.

Kutzik, Alfred. 1977. "The Social Work Field." In Florence W. Kaslow and Associates, eds., *Supervision Consultation and Staff Training in the Helping Professions,* pp. 25–60. San Francisco: Jossey-Bass.

Kwok Lai Yuk Ching, S. 1995. "The Use of Supervision by Objectives in Fieldwork Teaching." *Asia Pacific Journal of Social Work* 5 (2):88–102.

Ladany, N., C. S. Brittan-Powell, and R. K. Pannu. 1997. "The Influence of Supervisory Racial Identity Interaction and Racial Matching on the Supervisory Working Alliance and Supervisee Multicultural Competence." *Counselor Education and Supervision* 36:284–303.

Ladany, N., A. G. Inman, M. G. Constantine, and E. W. Hofheinz. 1997. "Supervisee Multicultural Case Conceptualization Ability and Self-Reported Multicultural Competence as Functions of Supervisee Racial Identity and Supervisor Focus." *Journal of Counseling Psychology* 44 (3):284–93.

Ladany, N., C. E. Hill, M. M. Corbett, and E. A. Nutt. 1996. "Nature, Extent, and Importance of What Psychotherapy Trainees Do Not Disclose to Their Supervisors." *Journal of Counseling Psychology* 43 (1):10–24.

Ladany, N., D. Lehrman-Waterman, M. Molinaro, and B. Wolgast. 1999. "Psychotherapy Supervisor Ethical Practices: Adherence to Guidelines, the Supervisory Working Alliance, and Supervisee Satisfaction." *Counseling Psychologist* 27 (3):443–75.

Lamb, Richard and George Mahl. 1956. "Manifest Reactions of Patients and Interviewers to the Use of Sound Recording in the Psychiatric Interview." *American Journal of Psychiatry* 112:733–35.

Lambert, M. J. 1980. "Research and the Supervisory Process." In A. K. Hess, ed., *Psychotherapy Supervision: Theory, Research, and Practice,* pp. 423–50. New York: Wiley.

Lambert, M. J. and B. M. Ogles. 1997. "The Effectiveness of Psychotherapy Supervision." In C. Watkins, ed., *Handbook of Psychotherapy Supervision,* pp. 421–46. New York: Wiley.

Lambert, M. S. and E. G. Beier. 1974. "Supervisory and Counseling Process: A Comparative Study." *Counselor Education and Supervision* 14:54–60.

Landau, R. and P. Baerwald. 1999. "Ethical Judgement, Code of Ethics, and Supervision in Ethical Decision Making in Social Work: Findings from an Israeli Sample." *Journal of Applied Social Sciences* 23 (2):21–29.

Langs, Robert. 1979. *The Supervisory Experience.* New York: Jason Aronson.

Lanning, Wayne L. 1971. "A Study of the Relation Between Group and Individual Counseling Supervision and Three Relationship Measures." *Journal of Counseling Psychology* 18:401–6.

Larrabee, M. J. and G. M. Miller. 1993. "An Examination of Sexual Intimacy in Supervision." *Clinical Supervisor* 11 (2):103–26.

Latting, J. K. 1991. "Eight Myths on Motivating Social Services Workers: Theory-Based Perspectives." *Administration in Social Work* 15 (3): 49–66.

Lawler, E., and S. Mohrman. 1985. "Quality Circles After the Fad." *Public Welfare* 43 (2):37–44.

Lazar, A. and Z. Eisikovits. 1997. "Social Work Students' Preferences Regarding Supervisory Styles and Supervisor's Behavior." *Clinical Supervisor* 16 (1):25–37.

Lazar, A. and H. Itzhaky. 2000. "Field Instructors' Organizational Position and Their Instructional Relationships with Students." *Arete* 24 (2):80–90.

Lazar, A. and A. Mosek. 1993. "The Influence of the Field Instructor-Student Relationship on Evaluation of Students' Practice." *Clinical Supervisor* 11 (1):111–20.

Leader, Arthur L. 1957. "New Directions in Supervision." *Social Casework* 38:462–68.

——. 1968. "Supervision and Consultations through Observed Interviewing." *Social Casework* 49:288–93.

Lee, Porter. 1923. "A Study of Social Treatment." *Family* 4:191–99.

Lee, R. E. 1997. "Seeing and Hearing in Therapy and Supervision: A Clinical Example of Isomorphism." *Journal of Family Psychotherapy* 8 (3):51–57.

Lemieu-Charles, L. and M. Hall. 1997. "When Resources Are Scarce: The Impact of Three Organizational Practices on Clinician-Managers." *Health Care Management Review* 22 (1):58–69.

Lemkau, J. P. 1984. "Men in Female Dominated Professions: Distinguishing Personality and Background Factors." *Journal of Vocational Behavior* 24:110–22.

Leon, A., J. Altholz, and S. Dziegielewski. 1999. "Compassion Fatigue: Considerations for Working with the Elderly." *Journal of Gerontological Social Work* 32 (1):43–62.

Leong, F. T. L. and N. S. Wagner. 1994. "Cross-Cultural Counseling Supervision: What Do We Know? What Do We Need to Know?" *Counselor Education and Supervision* 34:117–31.

Leung, P. and K. Cheung. 1998. "The Impact of Child Protective Service Training: A Longitudinal Study of Workers' Job Performance, Knowledge, and Attitudes." *Research on Social Work Practice* 8 (6):668–84.

Levine, F. M. and H. A. Tilker. 1974. "A Behavior Modification Approach to Supervision of Psychotherapy." *Psychotherapy: Theory, Research, and Practice* 11 (2):182–88.

Levinson, Daniel and Gerald Klerman. 1967. "The Clinician-Executive." *Psychiatry* 30:13–15.

——. 1972. "The Clinician-Executive Revisited." *Administration in Mental Health* 6:53–67.

Levy, Charles S. 1960. "In Defense of Supervision." *Journal of Jewish Communal Service* 37:194–201.

——. 1982. *Guide to Ethical Decisions and Action for Social Science Administrators—A Handbook for Managerial Personnel.* New York: Haworth.

Levy, Gerald. 1970. "Acute Workers in a Welfare Bureaucracy." In Deborah Offenbacher and Constance Poster, eds., *Social Problems and Social Policy,* pp. 168–75. New York: Appleton.

Lewis, W. 1988. "A Supervision Model for Public Agencies." *Clinical Supervisor* 6 (2):85–92.

Leyendecker, Gertrude. 1959. "A Critique of Current Trends in Supervision." In *Casework Papers, National Conference on Social Welfare.* 48–63 New York: Family Service Association of America.

Liddle, H. A. 1991. "Training and Supervision in Family Therapy: A Comprehensive and Critical Analysis." In A. S. Gurman and D. P. Kniskern, eds., *Handbook of Family Therapy,* vol. 2, pp. 638–97. New York: Brunner/Mazel.

Lieberman, S. 1956. "The Effects of Change in Roles on the Attitudes of Role Occupants." *Human Relations* 9:385–402.

Likert, Rensis. 1967. *The Human Organization: Its Management and Value.* New York: McGraw.

Lindenberg, R. 1957. "Changing Traditional Patterns of Supervision." *Social Work* 2:42–46.

Lindenberg, Sidney. 1939. *Supervision in Social Group Work.* New York: Association Press.

Lipsky, Michael. 1980. *Street Level Bureaucracy—Dilemmas of the Individual in Public Services.* New York: Russell Sage Foundation.

Liston, Edward, Joel Yager, and Gordon D. Strauss. 1981. "Assessment of Psychotherapy Skills: The Problem of Interrater Agreement." *American Journal of Psychiatry* 138 (8):1069–74.

Littrell, J. M. et al. 1979. "A Developmental Framework for Counseling Supervision." *Counselor Education and Supervision* 19:129–36.

Litwak, Eugene. 1964. "Models of Bureaucracy Which Permit Conflict." *American Journal of Sociology* 67:177–84.

Lochner, B. T. and T. P. Melchert. 1997. "Relationship of Cognitive Style and Theoretical Orientation to Psychology Interns' Preferences for Supervision." *Journal of Counseling Psychology* 44 (2):256–60.

Locke, L. and E.McCollum. 2001. "Client's Views of Live Supervision and Satisfaction with Therapy." *Journal of Marital and Family Therapy* 27 (1):129–33.

Lohmann, R. 1997. "Managed Care: A Review of Recent Research." In *1997*

Supplement to the Encyclopedia of Social Work, 19th ed., pp. 200–213. Washington, D.C.: NASW Press.

Long, Dennis D. and Margo J. Heydt. 2000. "Qualitative Analysis of a BSW Field Placement with a Hospital-Owned Physician Practice in a Skilled Nursing Facility." *Health and Social Work* 25 (3):210–18.

Lopez, S. 1997. "Cultural Competence in Psychotherapy: A Guide for Clinicians and Their Supervisors." In C. Watkins, ed., *Handbook of Psychotherapy Supervision,* pp. 570–88. New York: Wiley.

Lowenstein, Sophie and Peter Reder. 1982. "The Consumer Response: Trainees' Discussion of the Experience of Live Supervision." In Rosemary Whiffen and John Byng-Hall, eds., *Family Therapy Supervision—Recent Developments in Practice,* pp. 115–30. New York: Grune and Stratton.

Lutz, Werner A. 1956. *Student Evaluation: Workshop Report, 1956. Annual Program Meeting of the CSWE.* Buffalo, N.Y.: New York Council on Social Work Education.

Maccoby, M. 1976. *The Gamesman.* New York: Simon and Schuster.

MacEachron, A. E. 1994. "Supervision in Tribal and State Child Welfare Agencies: Professionalization, Responsibilities, Training Needs, and Satisfaction." *Child Welfare* 73 (2):117–28.

Magnuson, S., S. A. Wilcoxon, and K. Norem. 2000. "A Profile of Lousy Supervision: Experienced Counselors' Perspectives." *Counselor Education and Supervision* 30 (3):189–202.

Mahrer, A. R. 1998. "A New Departure in Experiential Supervision: Discovering the Trainee's Deeper Personal Approach to Psychotherapy." *Clinical Supervisor* 17 (1):125–34.

Malos, Stanley B. 1998. "Current Legal Issues in Performance Appraisal." In James W. Smither, ed., *Performance Appraisal: State of the Art in Practice,* pp. 49–94. San Francisco: Jossey- Bass.

Mandell, Betty. 1973. "The 'Equality' Revolution and Supervision." *Journal of Education for Social Work* 9:43–54.

Marcus, Grace. 1927. "How Casework Training May Be Adapted to Meet Workers' Personal Problems." In *Proceedings of the National Conference of Social Work, 1927.* Chicago: University of Chicago Press.

Marks, J. L. and D. F. Hixon. 1986. "Training Agency Staff through Peer Group Supervision." *Social Casework* 67:418–23.

Marohn, Richard C. 1969. "The Similarity of Therapy and Supervisory Themes." *International Journal of Group Psychotherapy* 19:176–84.

Martin, L. 1993. "Total Quality Management: The New Managerial Wave." *Administration in Social Work* 17 (2):1–16.

Martin, L. and P. Kettner. 1997. "Performance Measurement: The New Accountability." *Administration in Social Work* 21 (1):17–29.

Maslach, Christina. 1982. *Burn-Out—The Cost of Caring.* Englewood Cliffs, N.J.: Prentice-Hall.

Maslow, Abraham. 1968. *Toward a psychology of being* (2nd. ed.). Princeton, N.J.: Van Nostrand.

Maslow, Abraham. 1979. *Malpractice: A Guide for Mental Health Professionals.* New York: Free Press.

Matheson, W., C. Van Dyk, and K. Millar. 1995. *Performance Evaluation in the Human Services.* New York: Haworth.

Mathews, G. 1983. *Supervision in Human Services in Kent and Muskegon Counties, Michigan.* Kalamazoo: Western Michigan University.

Matorin, Susan. 1979. "Dimensions of Student Supervision—A Point of View." *Social Casework* 60:150–56.

Mattinson, Janet. 1975. *The Reflection Process in Casework Supervision.* Washington, D.C.: NASW Press.

Mayer, John E. and Aaron Rosenblatt. 1973a. "Sources of Stress Among Student Practitioners in Social Work: A Sociological Review." Paper read at the annual meeting Council on Social Work Education, San Francisco, January 1973.

——. 1973b. "Strains Between Social Work Students and Their Supervisors: A Preliminary Report." Paper read at the National Conference on Social Welfare, Atlantic City, N.J., May 1973.

——. 1975a. "Encounters with Danger—Social Workers in the Ghetto." *Sociology of Work and Occupations* 2:227–45.

——. 1975b. "Objectionable Supervisory Styles: Students' Views." *Social Work* 20:184–89.

Maypole, Donald E. 1986. "Sexual Harassment of Social Workers at Work: Injustice Within." *Social Work* 31:29–34.

Maypole, Donald and Rosemarie Skaine. 1982. "Sexual Harassment of Blue Collar Workers." *Journal of Sociology and Social Welfare* 9:682–95.

McCarthy, P., D. Kulakowski, and J. A. Kenfeld. 1994. "Clinical Supervision Practices of Licensed Psychologists." *Professional Psychology: Research and Practice* 25:177–81.

McCarthy, P., S. Sugden, M. Koker, F. Lamendola, S. Maurer, and S. Renninger. 1995. "A Practical Guide to Informed Consent in Clinical Supervision." *Counselor Education and Supervision* 35:130–38.

McClelland, D. C. and D. H. Burnham. 1976. "Power: The Great Motivator." *Harvard Business Review* 54:100–110.

McColley, S. H. and E. L. Baker, 1982. "Training Activities and Styles of Beginning Supervisors: A Survey." *Professional Psychology: Theory and Practice* 13 (2):283–92.

McCollum, E. E. and J. L. Wetchler. 1995. "In Defense of Case Consultation:

Maybe 'Dead' Supervision Isn't Dead After All." *Journal of Marital and Family Therapy* 21 (2):155–66.

McCroy, R., E. Freeman, S. Logan, and B. Blackmon. 1986. "Cross-Cultural Field Supervision: Implications for Social Work Education." *Journal of Social Work Education* 22:50–56.

McCue, R. B. II and R. C. Lane. 1995. "Parallel Process and Perspective: Understanding, Detecting, and Intervening." *Psychotherapy in Private Practice* 14 (3):13–33.

McCulloch, A. and L. O'Brien. 1986. "The Organizational Determinants of Worker Burnout." *Children and Youth Services Review* 8:175–90.

McCullough, Charlotte and Barbara Schmitt. 1999. *Managed Care and Privatization Child Welfare Tracking Project:1998 State and County Survey Results.* Washington, D.C.: Child Welfare League of America Press.

McDaniel, S. H., T. Weber, and S. McKeever. 1983. "Multiple Theoretical Approaches to Supervision: Choices in Family Therapy Training." *Family Process* 22:491–500.

McKenzie, P. N., B. J. Atkinson, W. H. Quinn, and A. W. Heath. 1986. "Training and Supervision in Marriage and Family Therapy: A National Survey." *American Journal of Marriage and Family Therapy* 14:293–303.

McNeely, R. L. 1987. "Predictions of Job Satisfaction Among Three Racial Ethnic Groups of Professional Female Human Service Workers." *Journal of Sociology and Social Welfare* 14 (4):115–36.

McNeely, R. L., Beth Schultz, and Frederick Naatz. 1997. "Quality Circles, Human Service Organizations, and the Law." *Administration in Social Work* 21 (1):65–71.

McNeill, B. W. and V. Worthen. 1989. "The Parallel Process in Psychotherapy Supervision." *Professional Psychology: Research and Practice* 20 (5):329–33.

McNeill, B. W., K. L. Hom, and J. A. Perez. 1995. "The Training and Supervisory Needs of Racial and Ethnic Minority Students." *Journal of Multicultural Counseling and Development* 23:246–58.

Mechanic, David. 1964. "Sources of Power of Lower Participants in Complex Organizations." In W. W. Cooper, M. W. Shelly, and H. J. Leavitt, eds., *New Perspectives in Organizational Research,* pp. 136–49. New York: Wiley.

Megargee, Edwin I. 1969. "Influence of Sex Roles on the Manifestation of Leadership." *Journal of Applied Psychology* 53 (2):27–34.

Memmott, J. and E. Brennan. 1998. "Learner-Learning Environment Fit: An Adult Learning Model for Social Work Education." *Journal of Teaching in Social Work* 16 (1/2):75–95.

Menefee, D. and J. Thompson. 1994. "Identifying and Comparing Competencies for Social Work Management: A Practice Driven Approach." *Administration in Social Work* 18 (3):1–25

Merton, Robert. 1957. *Social Theory and Social Structure,* rev. ed. New York: Free Press.

Meyer, Carol H. 1966. *Staff Development in Public Welfare Agencies.* New York: Columbia University Press.

Meyer, Herbert A., Emanual Kay, and John R. P. French. 1965. "Split Roles in Performance Appraisal." *Harvard Business Review* 43:123–29.

Miars, Russel D. 1983. "Variations in Supervision Process Across Trainee Experience Levels." *Journal of Counseling Psychology* 30:403–12.

Middleman, R. R. and G. B. Rhodes. 1985. *Competent Supervision: Making Imaginative Judgements.* Englewood Cliffs, N.J.: Prentice-Hall.

Milford Conference Report. 1929. *Social Work: Generic and Specific.* New York: American Association of Social Workers.

Millar, K. L. 1990. "Performance Appraisal of Professional Social Workers." *Administration in Social Work* 14 (1):65–75.

Miller, Harry L., Sidney Mailick, and Marilyn Miller. 1973. *Cases in Administration of Mental Health and Human Service Agencies.* New York: Institute for Child Mental Health.

Miller, Irving. 1960. "Distinctive Characteristics of Supervision in Group Work." *Social Work* 5 (1):69–76.

——. 1977. "Supervision in Social Work." In *Encyclopedia of Social Work,* 17th ed., pp. 1544–1551. Washington, DC: NASW Press.

Miller, L. and J. G. Twomey. 1999. "A Parallel Without a Process: A Relational View of Supervisory Experience." *Contemporary Psychoanalysis* 35 (4):557–80.

Miller, Ronald and Lawrence Podell. 1970. *Role Conflict in Public Social Services.* New York: State of New York Office of Community Affairs, Division of Research and Innovation.

Montalvo, Braulio. 1973. "Aspects of Live Supervision." *Family Process* 12:343–59.

Moore, Elon H. 1934. "How Accurate Are Base Records?" *Social Forces* 12:501.

Moore, Stewart. 1970. "Group Supervision: Forerunner or Trend Reflector: Part I—Trends and Duties in Group Supervision." *Social Worker* 38:16–20.

Moore, Stewart. 1971. "Group Supervision: Forerunner or Trend Reflector: Part II—Advantages and Disadvantages." *Social Worker* 39:3–7.

Moore, Wilbert E. 1970. *The Professions: Rules and Roles.* New York: Russell Sage.

Mothersole, G. 1999. "Parallel Process: A Review." *Clinical Supervisor* 18 (2):107–21.

Mueller, K. 1995. "The Relationship Between Social Support and Burnout Among Social Work Caregivers and HIV/AIDS Clients." Ph.D. diss., New York University.

Mueller, William S. and Bill L. Kell. 1972. *Coping with Conflict: Supervisory Counselors and Psychotherapists.* New York: Appleton.

Munson, Carlton E., ed. 1979. *Social Work Supervision—Classic Statements and Critical Issues.* New York: Free Press.

Munson, Carlton. 1979a. "An Empirical Study of Structure and Authority in Social Work Supervision." In Carlton E. Munson, ed., *Social Work Supervision—Classic Statements and Critical Issues,* pp. 286–96. New York: Free Press.

——. 1979b. "Evaluation of Male and Female Supervisors." Social Work 24:104–110.

——. 1980. "Differential Impact of Structure and Authority in Supervision." *Arete* 6:3–15.

——. 1981. "Style and Structure in Supervision." *Journal of Education for Social Work* 17 (1):66–72.

——. 1983. *An Introduction to Clinical Social Work Supervision.* New York: Haworth.

——. 1993. *Clinical Social Work Supervision,* 2d. ed. New York: Haworth.

——. 1996a. "Autonomy and Managed Care in Clinical Social Work Practice." *Smith College Studies in Social Work* 66 (3):241–60.

——. 1996b. "Credentialing and Managed Care." *Clinical Supervisor* 14 (2): 1–4.

——. 1996c. "Risk Management in Mental Health Practice." *Clinical Supervisor* 14 (1):1–18.

——. 1997. "Gender and Psychotherapy Supervision." In C. Watkins, ed., *Handbook of Psychotherapy Supervision,* pp. 549–69. New York: Wiley.

——. 1998a. Societal Change, Managed Cost Organizations, and Clinical Social Work Practice." *Clinical Supervisor* 17 (2):1–41.

——. 1998b. "Evolution and Trends in the Relationship Between Clinical Social Work Practice and Managed Cost Organizations." In Gerald Schamess and Anita Lightburn, eds., *Humane Managed Care?,* pp. 308–24. Washington, D.C.: NASW Press.

——. 2001. *Clinical Social Work Supervision,* 3d ed. New York: Haworth.

Murphy, K. R. and W. K. Balzar.1989. "Rating Errors and Rating Accuracy." *Journal of Applied Psychology* 74:619–24.

Murphy, Kevin R. and J. N. Cleveland.1995. *Understanding Performance Appraisal: Social, Organizational, and Goal-Based Perspectives.* Thousand Oaks, Calif.: Sage.

Mushlin, M., H. Levitt, and L. Anderson. 1986. "Court Ordered Foster Family Care Reform: A Case Study." *Child Welfare* 62 (2):141–54.

Muslin, Hyman, Alvin G. Burstein, John E. Gedo, and Leo Sadow. 1967.

"Research on the Supervisory Process. I. Supervisor's Appraisal of the Interview Data." *Archives of General Psychiatry* 16:427–31.

Muslin, Hyman, Robert J. Turnblad, and George Meschel. 1981. "The Fate of the Clinical Interview: An Observational Study." *American Journal of Psychiatry* 138 (6):822–25.

Mutschler, Elizabeth and S. Jayaratne. 1993. "Integration of Information Technology and Single System Designs: Issues and Promises." *Journal of Social Service Research* 18 (1/2):121–45.

Nadelson, Carol and Notman Maikan. 1977. "Psychotherapy Supervision: The Problem of Conflicting Values." *American Journal of Psychotherapy* 31:275–83.

Nader, Ralph, Peter J. Petkas, and Kate Blackwell, eds. 1974. *Whistle Blowing: Report of the Conference on Professional Responsibility.* New York: Grossman.

Napier, N. and Latham, G. 1986. "Outcome Expectancies of People Who Conduct Performance Appraisals." *Personnel Psychology* 39 (4):827–37.

Nash, V. C. 1975. "The Clinical Supervisor of Psychotherapy." Ph.D. diss., Yale University.

Nathanson, Theresa. 1962. "Self-Awareness in the Educative Process." *Social Casework* 43:31–38.

National Association of Social Workers. 1971. *NASW Standards for Social Work Personnel Practices: Professional Standards.* Washington, D.C.: NASW Press.

——. 1981. *NASW Standards for Social Work Practice in Child Protection.* Washington, D.C.: Author. (Online document retrieved December 2, 2001, from http://www.naswdc.org/pubs/standards/child.htm.)

——. 1990. *NASW Standards for Social Work Personnel Practices (Revised).* Washington, D.C.: NASW Press.

——. 1999. *NASW Code of Ethics (Revised).* Washington, D.C.: NASW Press.

——. 1999. *Guidelines for Clinical Social Work Supervision.* Washington, D.C.: NASW Press.

——. n.d. *Reference for Candidates for Admission to the Academy of Certified Social Workers.* Washington, D.C.: Academy of Certified Social Workers, NASW.

National Social Welfare Assembly, 1961. *Salaries and Working Conditions of Social Welfare Manpower, 1960.* New York: National Social Welfare Assembly.

Nelsen, Judith C. 1973. "Early Communication Between Field Instructors and Casework Student." DSW diss., School of Social Work, Columbia University.

——. 1974. "Relationship Communication in Early Fieldwork Conferences, Part I–II." *Social Casework* 55:237–43.

Nelson, Mary Lee and Myrna L. Friedlander. 2001. "A Close Look at Conflictual Supervisory Relationships: A Trainee's Perspective." *Journal of Counseling Psychology* 48 (4):384–95.

Nelson, M. L. and E. L. Holloway. 1990. "Relation of Gender to Power and Involvement in Supervision." *Journal of Counseling Psychology* 37:473–81.

Neufeldt, S. and M. Nelson. 1999. "When Is Counseling an Appropriate and Ethical Supervision Function?" *Clinical Supervisor* 18 (1):125–35.

Neufeldt, S., L. Beutler, and R. Banchero. 1997. "Research on Supervisor Variables in Psychotherapy Supervision." In C. Watkins, ed., *Handbook of Psychotherapy Supervision*, pp. 508–24. New York: Wiley.

Newsome, M. Jr., and V. Pillari. 1991. "Job-Satisfaction and the Worker-Supervisor Relationship." *Clinical Supervisor* 9(2):119–30.

Nichols, Margo and Judy Cheers. 1980. "The Evaluation of the Praticum." *Contemporary Social Work Education* 3 (1):54–71.

Niland, Thomas M., John Duling, Jada Allen, and Edward Panther. 1971. "Student Counselors' Perception of Videotaping." *Counselor Education and Supervision* 11:97–101.

Niolon, R. 1997. "Experiences of Gays and Lesbians as Students in Psychology Training Programs." Ph.D. diss., St. Louis University.

Norman, S. S. 1987. "Supervision: The Effective Process." *Social Casework* 68:374–79.

Norris, Dan. 1990. *Violence Against Social Workers—The Implications for Practice.* London: Jessica Kingley.

O'Bryne, K., and J. I. Rosenberg. 1998. "The Practice of Supervision: A Sociocultural Perspective." *Counselor Education and Supervision* 38:34–42.

O'Connor, Brian P. 2000. "Reasons for Less than Ideal Psychotherapy Supervision." *Clinical Supervisor* 19 (2):173–83.

O'Connor, Robert and Larry Spence. 1976. "Communication Disturbances in a Welfare Bureaucracy: A Case for Self Management." *Journal of Sociology and Social Welfare* 4 (2):178–204.

Olmstead, Joseph A. 1973. "Organizational Structure and Climate: Implications for Agencies." National Study of Social Welfare and Rehabilitation Workers, Work and Organizational Contexts, Working Paper no. 2. Washington D.C.: U.S. Government Printing Office.

Olmstead, Joseph A. and Harold E. Christensen. 1973. "Effects of Agency Work Contexts: An Intensive Field Study." Research Report no. 2. Washington, D.C.: Department of Health, Education, and Welfare, Social and Rehabilitation Service.

Olyan, Sidney D. 1972. "An Explanatory Study of Supervision in Jewish Community Centers as Compared to Other Welfare Settings." Ph.D. diss., University of Pittsburgh.

Osborn, C. J. and T. E. Davis. 1996. "The Supervision Contract: Making It Perfectly Clear." *Clinical Supervisor* 14 (2):121–34.

Osterberg, M. J. 1996. "Gender in Supervision: Exaggerating the Differences Between Men and Women." *Clinical Supervisor* 14 (2):69–84.

Overholser, James C. 1991. "The Socratic Method as a Technique in Psychotherapy Supervision." *Professional Psychology: Research and Practice* 22 (1):68–74.

Owens-Patterson, M. 2000. "The Black Supervisor: Racial Transference and Countertransference in Interracial Psychotherapy Supervision." In Beverly Green and Leslie C. Jackson, eds., *Psychotherapy with Black Women: Innovations in Psychodynamic Perspective and Practice,* pp. 145–65. New York: Guilford.

Paige, Clara P. 1927. "Supervising Casework in a District Office." *Family* 8:307–9.

Paine, Whiton S. 1982. *Job Stress and Burn-Out—Research Theory and Intervention Perspectives.* Beverly Hills, Calif.: Sage.

Parihar, E. 1983. "Group Supervision: A Naturalistic Field Study in a Speciality Unit." *Clinical Supervisor* 1 (4):3–14.

Parsloe, Phyllida and Olive Stevenson. 1978. *Social Service Teams: The Practitioner's View.* London: Her Majesty's Stationery Office.

Parsons, T. 1951. *The Social System.* Glencoe, Ill.: Free Press.

Patti, Rino J. 1977. "Patterns of Management's Activity in Social Welfare Agencies." *Administration in Social Work* 1 (1):5–18.

——. 1983. *Social Welfare Administration: Managing Social Programs in a Developmental Context.* Englewood Cliffs, N.J.: Prentice-Hall.

——. 1984. "Who Leads the Human Services—The Prospects for Social Work Leadership in the Age of Political Conservatism." *Administration in Social Work* 8 (1):17–29.

——. 1987. "Managing for Service Effectiveness in Social Welfare Organizations." *Social Work* 32:377–81.

Patti, Rino J. et al. 1979. "From Direct Service to Administration: A Study of Social Workers' Transitions to Clinical to Management Roles." *Administration in Social Work* 3:131–51.

Patton, M. J. and D. M. Kivlighan Jr. 1997. "Relevance of the Supervisory Alliance to the Counseling Alliance and to Treatment Adherence in Counselor Training." *Journal of Counseling Psychology* 44 (1):108–15.

Pawlak, Edward J. 1976. "Organizational Tinkering." *Social Work* 21:376–80.

Peabody, Robert L. 1964. *Organizational Authority: Superior-Subordinate Relationships in Three Public Service Organizations.* New York: Atherton.

Pearson, Geoffrey. 1975. "Making Social Workers." In Roy Bailey and Mike Brake, eds., *Radical Social Work,* pp. 18–45. New York: Pantheon.

Pecora, P. J. 1984. "Improving the Quality of Child Welfare Services: Needs Assessment of Training Staff." *Child Welfare* 68 (4):403–19.

Pecora, Peter and J. Hunter. 1988. "Performance Appraisal in Child Welfare: Comparing the MBO and BARS Methods." *Administration in Social Work* 2 (11):55–72.

Pecora, Peter J. et al., eds. 1996. *Quality Improvement and Evaluation in Child and Family Services: Managing into the Next Century.* Washington, D.C.: Child Welfare League of America Press.

Pegeron, J. 1996. "Supervision as an Analytic Experience." *Psychoanalytic Quarterly* 65:693–710.

Pelz, O. C. and F. M. Andrews. 1976. *Scientists in Organizations: Productive Climates for Research and Development.* Ann Arbor: University of Michigan Press.

Pepper, N. G. 1996. "Supervision: A Positive Learning Experience or an Anxiety Provoking Exercise?" *Australian Social Work* 49 (3):55–64.

Perlman, Helen H. 1947. "Content in Basic Social Casework." *Social Service Review* 21:76–84.

——. 1950. "Teaching Casework by the Discussion Method." *Social Service Review* 24:334–46.

Perlmutter, F. D. 1990. *Changing Hats: From Social Work Practice to Administration.* Silver Spring, Md.: NASW Press.

Peters, Charles and Taylor Branch. 1972. *Blowing the Whistle: Dissent in the Public Interest.* New York: Praeger.

Pettes, Dorothy E. 1979. *Staff and Student Supervision—A Task Centered Approach.* London: Allen and Unwin.

Petty, M. M. and R. H. Miles. 1976. "Leader Sex Role Stereotyping in a Female-Dominated Work Culture." *Personnel Psychology* 29:393–404.

Petty, M. M. and C. A. Odewahn. 1983. "Supervisory Behavior and Sex Role Stereotypes in Human Service Organizations." *Clinical Supervisor* 1 (2):13–20.

Pickvance, D. 1997. "Becoming a Supervisor." In G. Shipton, ed., *Supervision in Psychotherapy and Counseling—Making a Place to Think,* pp. 131–42. Philadelphia: Open University Press.

Pine, B., R. Warsh, and A. Malluccio. 1998. "Participatory Management in a Public Child Welfare Agency: A Key to Effective Change." *Administration in Social Work* 22 (1):19–32.

Pines, Ayala. 1982. "On Burn-Out and the Buffering Effects of Social Support." In Barry A. Farber, ed., *Stress and Burn-Out in Human Service Professions*, pp. 155–69. New York: Pergamon.

Pines, Ayala and C. Maslach. 1978. "Characteristics of Staff Burn-Out in Mental Health Settings." *Hospital and Community Psychiatry* 29:233–37.

Pines, Ayala, Elliot Aronson, and Ditsa Kafry. 1981. *Burn-Out—From Tedium to Personal Growth*. New York: Free Press.

Pithouse, A. 1985. "Poor Visibility—Case Talk and Collegial Assessment in a Social Work Office." *Work and Occupations* 12 (1):77–89.

——. 1987. *Social Work: The Social Organization of an Invisible Trade*. Brookfield, Eng.: Avebury.

Piven, Herman and Donald Pappenfort. 1960. "Strain Between Administrator and Worker: A View from the Field of Corrections." *Social Work* 5: 37–45.

Poertner, John and Charles A. Rapp. 1983. "What Is Social Work Supervision?" *Clinical Supervisor* 1:53–67.

Pointer, Avis Y. and Jacob R. Fishman. 1968. *New Careers: Entry Level Training for the Human Service Aide*. Washington, D.C.: New Careers Development Program, University Research Corp.

Poling, E. G. 1968. "Video Tape Recordings in Counseling Practicum. I. Environmental Considerations." *Counselor Education and Supervision* 8:348–56.

Porter, N. 1994. "Empowering Supervisees to Empower Others: A Culturally Responsive Supervision Model." *Hispanic Journal of Behavioral Sciences* 16 (1):43–56.

Poulin, J. 1994. "Job Task and Organizational Predictors of Social Work Job Satisfaction Change: A Panel Study." *Administration in Social Work* 18 (1):21–38.

Poulin, J. 1995. "Job Satisfaction of Social Work Supervisors and Administrators." *Administration in Social Work* 19 (4):35–49.

Poulin, J. and C. Walter. 1992. "Retention Plans and Job Satisfaction of Gerontological Social Workers." *Journal of Gerontological Social Work* 19:99–114.

Powell, David J. 1980. *Clinical Supervision: Skills for Substance Abuse Counselors*. New York: Human Sciences Press.

——. 1993a. *Clinical Supervision in Alcohol and Drug Abuse Counseling: Principles, Models, Methods*. New York: Lexington.

——. 1993b. " 'She Said . . . He Said' Gender Differences in Supervision." *Alcoholism Treatment Quarterly* 10 (1/2):187–93.

——. 1996. "A Peer Consultation Model for Clinical Supervision." *Clinical Supervisor* 14 (2):163–78.

Presthus, Robert. 1962. *The Organizational Society.* New York: Knopf.

Pretzer, Clarence A. 1929. "Significant Facts Regarding the Turnover of Case Workers in Family Welfare Agencies During 1927 and 1928." *Family* 10:163–73.

Prieto, L. R. 1996. "Group Supervision: Still Widely Practiced but Poorly Understood." *Counselor Education and Supervision* 35:295–307.

Prottas, Jeffrey. 1979. *People Processing—The Street Level Bureaucrat in Public Service Bureaucracies.* Lexington, Mass.: Lexington.

Pruger, R. and L. Miller. 1991. "Efficiency and the Social Services: Part B." *Administration in Social Work* 15 (1/2):25–44.

Putney, M. W., E. L. Worthington, and M. E. McCullough. 1992. "Effects of Supervisor and Supervisee Theoretical Orientation and Supervisor-Supervisee Matching on Interns' Perceptions of Supervision." *Journal of Counseling Psychology* 39:258–65.

Rabinowitz, F. E., P. P. Heppner, and H. J. Roehlke. 1986. "Descriptive Study of Process and Outcome Variables of Supervision Over Time." *Journal of Counseling Psychology* 33:292–300.

Raelin, J. A. 1986. *The Clash of Cultures: Managers and Professionals.* Boston: Harvard Business School Press.

Raichelson, S. H., W. G. Herron, L. H. Primavera, and S. M. Ramirez. 1997. "Incidence and Effects of Parallel Process in Psychotherapy Supervision." *Clinical Supervisor* 15 (2):37–48.

Raider, Melvyn C. 1977. "Installing Management by Objectives in Social Agencies." *Administration in Social Work* 1 (3):235–44.

Ralph, Norbert. 1980. "Learning Psychotherapy: A Developmental Perspective." *Psychiatry* 43:243–50.

Rapoport, Lydia. 1954. "The Use of Supervision as a Tool in Professional Development." *British Journal of Psychiatric Social Work* 2:66–74.

Rapp, Charles A. and Poertner, John. 1987. "Moving Clients Center Stage through the Use of Client Outcomes." *Administration in Social Work* 11 (3/4):23–38.

——. 1992. *Social Administration: A Client-Centered Approach.* New York: Longman.

Rasheed, M. 1997. "The Experiences of African American Male Clinical Social Work Supervisors in Cross-Racial Supervision: A Hermeneutic Phenomenological Analysis." Ph.D. diss., Loyola University of Chicago.

Raskin, M. and W. Bloom. 1998. "The Impact of Managed Care on Field Instruction." *Journal of Social Work Education* 343:365–74.

Ratliff, D. A., K. S. Wampler, and G. H. Morris. 2000. "Lack of Consensus in Supervision." *Journal of Marital and Family Therapy* 26 (3):373–84.

Rauktis, M. E. and G. F. Koeske. 1994. "Maintaining Social Worker Morale: When Supportive Supervision Is Not Enough." *Administration in Social Work* 18 (1):39–60.

Reamer, Frederic G. 1989. "Liability Issues in Social Work Supervision." *Social Work* 34:445–48.

——. 1994. *Social Work Malpractice and Liability: Strategies for Prevention.* New York: Columbia University Press.

——. 1995. "Malpractice Claims Against Social Workers: First Facts." *Social Work* 40 (5):595–601.

——. 1997a. "Ethical Standards in Social Work: The NASW Code of Ethics." In *1997 Supplement to the Encyclopedia of Social Work,* 19th ed., pp. 113–23. Washington, D.C.: NASW Press.

——. 1997b. "Managing Ethics Under Managed Care." *Families in Society* 78 (1):96–101.

——. 1998. *Ethical Standards in Social Work: A Critical Review of the NASW Code of Ethics.* Washington, D.C.: NASW Press.

Reeser, Linda C. and Irwin Epstein. 1990. *Professionalization and Activism in Social Work: The Sixties, the Eighties, and the Future.* New York: Columbia University Press.

Rehr, Helen, and Gary Rosenberg. 2000. "Social Work and Health Care Yesterday, Today, and Tomorrow." In June Gary Hopps and Robert Morris, eds., *Social Work at the Millennium: Critical Reflections on the Future of the Profession,* pp. 86–122. New York: Free Press.

Reich, Charles A. 1970. *The Greening of America.* New York: Random House.

Reising, Gregory and M. Harry Daniels. 1983. "A Study of Hogan's Model of Counselor Development and Supervision." *Journal of Counseling Psychology* 30:235–44.

Remley, T. P. et al. 1987. "Postgraduate Peer Supervision: A Proposed Model for Peer Supervision." *Counselor Education and Supervision* 15:53–60.

Resnick, Herman and Rino J. Patti. 1980. *Change from Within: Humanizing Social Welfare Organizations.* Philadelphia: Temple University Press.

Reynolds, Bertha C. 1936. "Art of Supervision." *Family* 17:103–7.

——. 1942. *Learning and Teaching in the Practice of Social Work.* New York: Farrar.

Rhodes, M. L. 1986. *Ethical Dilemmas in Social Work Practice.* Boston: Routledge and Kegan Paul.

Rich, P. 1992. "Barriers to the Clinical Supervision of Direct Care Staff in a Human Service Organization: A Case Study." Ph.D. diss., University of Massachusetts.

Richard, R. and M. R. Rodway. 1992. "The Peer Consultation Group: A Problem-Solving Perspective." *Clinical Supervisor* 10 (1):83–100.

Richman, Leon. 1939. "Continued Stimulation of Growth and Staff Experience." In *Proceedings of the National Conference on Social Work, June 26–July 2, 1938*, pp. 251–65. Chicago: University of Chicago Press.

Richmond, Mary. 1897. "The Need for a Training School in Applied Philanthropy." In *Proceedings of the National Conference of Social Welfare, 1897.*

——. 1899. *Friendly Visiting Among the Poor: A Handbook for Charity Workers.* New York: Macmillan.

Riffe, Holly A. 1995. "The Changing Nature of Clinical Social Work: Managed Care and Job Satisfaction." Ph.D. diss., Ohio State University. University Microfilms International no. 9544669.

——. 1999. "Managed Health Care and Job Satisfaction: Impact of Third-Party Payers." *Journal of Applied Social Sciences* 232:43–49.

Rindfleisch, N. 1984. *Identification, Management, and Prevention of Child Abuse and Neglect in Residential Institutions*, vol. 3. Columbus: Ohio State University Research Foundation.

Risely-Curtiss, C. and Hudson, W. 1998. "Sexual Harassment of Social Work Students." *Affilia* 13 (2):190–210.

Rivas, F. 1984. "Perspectives on Dismissal as a Management Prerogative in Social Service Organizations." *Administration in Social Work* 8 (4): 787–91.

Robbins, T. L. and A. S. DeNisi. 1994. "A Closer Look at Interpersonal Affect as a Distinct Influence on Cognitive Processing in Performance Appraisal." *Journal of Applied Psychology* 793:341–53.

Roberts, Ralph R. and G. A. Renzaglia. 1965. "The Influence of Tape Recording on Counseling." *Journal of Counseling Psychology* 12:10–15.

Robiner, W., S. Saltzman, H. Hoberman, and J. Schirvar. 1997. "Psychology Supervisors' Training, Experiences, Supervisory Evaluation and Self-Rated Competence." *Clinical Supervisor* 16 (1):117–44.

Robinson, Virginia. 1936. *Supervision in Social Casework.* Chapel Hill, N.C.: University of North Carolina Press.

——. 1949. *The Dynamics of Supervision Under Functional Controls.* Philadelphia: University of Philadelphia Press.

Rodenhauser, P. 1995. "Experiences and Issues in the Professional Development of Psychiatrists for Supervising Psychotherapy." *Clinical Supervisor* 13 (1):7–22.

Rogers, G. and P. L. McDonald. 1995. "Expedience Over Education: Teaching Models Used by Field Instructors." *Clinical Supervisor* 13 (2):41–66.

Romans, J. S. C. 1996. "Gender Differences in Counselor/Therapist Trainees." *Clinical Supervisor* 14 (1):77–86.

Rosen, A. 1994. "Knowledge Use in Direct Practice." *Social Service Review* 68:561–77.

Rosen, A., E. Proctor, N. Morrow-Howell, and M. Staudt. 1995. "Rationales for Practice Decisions: Variations in Knowledge Use by Decision Task and Social Work Service." *Research on Social Work Practice* 5:501–23.

Rosen, Harold and Leo H. Bartemeier. 1967. "The Psychiatric Resident as Participant Therapist." *American Journal of Psychiatry* 123:1371–78.

Rosenberg, Louis M., Sam S. Rubin, and Hilda Finzi. 1968. "Participation Supervision—The Teaching of Psychotherapy." *American Journal of Psychotherapy* 22:280–95.

Rosenthal, L. 1999. "Group Supervision of Groups: A Modern Analytic Perspective." *International Journal of Group Psychotherapy* 49 (2):197–213.

Ross, R. R., E. M. Altmaier, and D. W. Russell. 1989. "Job Stress Social Support and Burnout Among Counseling Center Staff." *Journal of Counseling Psychology* 36 (4):464–70.

Rothman, Beulah. 1973. "Perspectives on Learning and Teaching in Continuing Education." *Journal of Education for Social Work* 9:39–52.

Rothman, Jack. 1974. *Planning and Organizing for Social Change: Action Principles from Social Science Research.* New York: Columbia University Press.

Rothstein, J. 2001. "Clinical Supervision—Then and Now: The Professional Development of Social Workers." *Reflections: Narratives of Professional Helping* 7 (1):61–71.

Rowbottom, Ralph, Anthea Hay, and David Billis. 1976. *Social Service Departments—Developing Patterns of Work and Organization.* London: Heinemann.

Rowley, Carl M. and Eugene Faux. 1966. "The Team Approach to Supervision." *Mental Hygiene* 50:60–65.

Royster, Eugene C. 1972. "Black Supervisors: Problems of Race and Role." In Forence W. Kaslow and Associates, eds., *Issues in Human Services,* pp. 72–84. San Francisco: Jossey-Bass.

Rubenstein, Mark and David Hammond. 1982. "The Use of Video Tape in Psychotherapy Supervision." In Michael Blumenfield, ed., *Applied Supervision in Psychotherapy,* pp. 143–63. New York: Grune and Stratton.

Rubin, S. S. 1997. "Balancing Duty to Client and Therapist in Supervision: Clinical, Ethical, and Training Issues." *Clinical Supervisor* 16 (1):1–23.

Rushton, A. and J. Nathan. 1996. "The Supervision of Child Protection Work." *British Journal of Social Work* 26:357–74.

Russell, G. M. and E. M. Greenhouse. 1997. "Homophobia in the Supervisory Relationship: An Invisible Intruder." *Psychoanalytic Review* 84 (1):27–42.

Russell, Pamela A., Michael W. Lankford, and Richard M. Grinnell. 1984. "Administrative Styles of Social Work Supervision in a Human Service Agency." *Administration in Social Work* 8 (1):1–16.

Ryan, A. S. and C. O. Hendricks. 1989. "Culture Communication: Supervising the Asian and Hispanic Social Worker." *Clinical Supervisor* 7 (1):27–40.

Ryan, C. 1969. "Video Aids in Practicum Supervision." *Counselor Education and Supervision* 8:125–29.

Ryan, Francis. 1964. "Joint Interviewing by Field Instructor and Student." *Social Casework* 45:471–74.

Ryan, G. 1999. "Treatment of Sexually Abusive Youth: The Evolving Consensus." *Journal of Interpersonal Violence* 14 (4):422–36.

Sabin, James E. 1999. "How to Teach Residents About Ethical Managed Care—Even if the Mention of 'Managed Care' Makes Your Blood Boil." *Harvard Review of Psychiatry* 7 (1):64–67.

Sachs, D. M. and S. H. Shapiro. 1976. "On Parallel Process in Therapy and Teaching." *Psychoanalytic Quarterly* 45:394–415.

Sales, Esther and Elizabeth Navarre. 1970. *Individual and Group Supervision in Field Instruction: A Research Report.* Ann Arbor: School of Social Work, University of Michigan.

Saltzman, A. and K. Proch. 1990. *Law in Social Work Practice.* Chicago: Nelson-Hall.

Salvendy, J. T. 1984. "Improving Interviewing Techniques through the Bug-in-the-Ear." *Canadian Journal of Psychiatry* 29:302–5.

Sarnat, J. E. 1992. "Supervision in Relationship: Resolving the Teach-Treat Controversy in Psychoanalytic Supervision." *Psychoanalytic Psychology* 9 (3):387–403.

Satyamurti, Carole. 1981. *Occupational Survival.* Oxford: Basil Blackwell.

Savaya, R. and S. E. Spiro. 1997. " Reactions of Practitioners to the Introduction of a Standard Instrument to Monitor Clinical Outcomes." *Journal of Social Service Research* 22 (4):39–55.

Savickas, M. L., C. D. Marquart, and C. R. Supinski. 1986. "Effective Supervision in Groups." *Counselor Education and Supervision* 14:17–25.

Schacht, J., H. E. Howe, and J. J. Berman. 1989. "Supervisor Facilitative Conditions and Effectiveness as Perceived by Thinking- and Feeling-Type Supervisees." *Psychotherapy: Theory, Research and Practice* 26 (4):475–83.

Schamess, G. and D. Lightburn, eds. 1998. *Humane Managed Care?* Washington, D.C.: NASW Press.

Schein, Edgar H. 1970. *Organizational Psychology,* 2d ed. Englewood Cliffs, N.J.: Prentice-Hall.

Scher, Maryonda. 1981. "Gender Issues in Psychiatric Supervision." *Comprehensive Psychiatry* 22 (2):179–83.

Schiavone, D. D. and J. C. Jessell. 1988. "Influence of Attribute Expertness and Gender in Counselor Supervision." *Counselor Education and Supervision* 28:28–42.

Schilit, Warran K. and Edwin Locke. 1982. "A Study of Upward Influence in Organizations." *Administrative Science Quarterly* 27:304–15.

Schmidt, Frances and Martha Perry. 1940. "Values and Limitations of the Evaluation Process. I: As Seen by the Supervisor. II: As Seen by the Worker." In *Proceedings of the National Conference of Social Work,* pp. 629–47. New York: Columbia University Press.

Schneck, D., B. Grossman, and U. Glassman. 1990. *Field Education in Social Work.* Dubuque, Iowa: Kendall Hunt.

Schreiber, Pamela and Elaine Frank. 1983. "The Use of a Peer Supervision Group by Social Work Clinicians." *Clinical Supervisor* 1 (1):29–36.

Schroffel, A. 1998. "To What Extent Does the Availability, Quality, and Style of Supervision Correlate with the Degree of Clinician Job Satisfaction?" Ph.D. diss., Smith College School for Social Work, Northampton, Mass.

Schroffel, Alan. 1999. "How Does Clinical Supervision Affect Job Satisfaction?" *Clinical Supervisor* 182:91–105.

Schubert, G. and J. Nelson. 1976. "An Analysis of Verbal Behaviors Occurring in Speech Pathology Supervisory Sessions." *Journal of the National Student Speech and Hearing Association* 4:17–26.

Schuster, Daniel B., John J. Sandt, and Otto F. Thaler. 1972. *Clinical Supervision of the Psychiatric Resident.* New York: Brunner/Mazel.

Schutz, Benjamin M. 1982. *Legal Liability in Psychotherapy.* San Francisco: Jossey-Bass.

Schwartz, H. 1990. "Transition to Administration: A Comparative Study of Social Workers and Psychologists." Ph.D. diss., University of Tennessee, Knoxville.

Scott, D. and J. Farrow. 1993. "Evaluating Standards of Social Work Supervision in Child Welfare and Hospital Social Work." *Australian Social Work* 46 (2):33–41.

Scott, W. Richard. 1965. "Reactions to Supervision in a Heteronomous Professional Organization." *Administrative Science Quarterly* 10:65–81.

——. 1969. "Professional Employees in a Bureaucratic Structure." In Amitai Etzioni, ed., *The Semiprofessions and Their Organization,* pp. 82–140. New York: Free Press.

Scurfield, Raymond, M. 1981. "Clinician to Administrator: Difficult Role Transition?" *Social Work* 26:495–501.

Searles, Harold F. 1955. "The Informational Value of the Supervisor's Emotional Experiences." *Psychiatry* 18:135–46.

Sennett, Richard. 1981. *Authority*. New York: Vintage Books.

Shaefor, Bradford and Lowell Jenkins. 1982. *Quality Field Instruction in Social Work*. New York: Longman.

Shamai, M. 1998. "Therapist in Distress: Team-Supervision of Social Workers and Family Therapists Who Work and Live Under Political Uncertainty." *Family Process* 37 (2):245–59.

Shanfield, S. B., K. L. Matthews, and V. Hetherley. 1993. "What Do Excellent Psychotherapy Supervisors Do?" *American Journal of Psychiatry* 150:1081–84.

Shanfield, S. B., P. C. Mohl, K. L. Matthews, and V. Hetherly. 1992. "Quantitative Assessment of the Behavior of Psychotherapy Supervisors." *American Journal of Psychiatry* 149 (3):352–57.

Shann, M. H. 1983. "Career Plans of Men and Women in Gender-Dominant Professions." *Journal of Vocational Behavior* 22:343–56.

Shapero, A. 1989. *Managing Professional People: Understanding Creative Performance*. New York: Free Press.

Shapiro, Constance H. 1982. "Creative Supervision—An Underutilized Antidote." In Whiton S. Paine, ed., *Job Stress and Burn-Out: Research, Theory, and Intervention Perspectives*. Beverly Hills, Calif.: Sage.

Shapiro, Deborah. 1976. *Agencies and Foster Children*. New York: Columbia University Press.

Shinn, M. B. 1979. "Burnout in Human Service Agencies." In Kenneth Reid and Rebecca Quinlan, eds., *Burnout in the Helping Professions*, pp. 1–22. Kalamazoo: Western Michigan University.

Shinn, Marybeth and Hanne Morch. 1982. "A Tripartite Model of Coping with Burn-Out." In Barry A. Farber, ed., *Stress and Burn-Out in the Human Service Professions*, pp. 227–38. New York: Pergamon.

Shnit, Dan. 1978. "Professional Discretion in Social Welfare Administration." *Administration in Social Work* 2 (4):439–50.

Shriberg, L. et al. 1975. "The Wisconsin Procedures for Appraisal of Clinical Competence." *ASHA* 17:158–65.

Shulman, Lawrence. 1982. Skills of Supervision and Staff Management. Itasca, Ill.: Peacock Publishers.

——. 1991. Interactional Social Work Practice: Toward an Empirical Theory. Itasca, Ill: Peacock.

——. 1993. Interactional supervision. Washington, DC: NASW Press.

——. 1995. "Supervision and Consultation." In R. Edwards, ed. in chief, *Encyclopedia of Social Work*, 19th ed., pp. 2373–379. Washington, D.C.: NASW Press.

——. 1999. *The Skills of Helping Individuals, Families, Groups, and Communities*, 4th ed. Itasca, Ill.: Peacock.

Shyne, Ann W. 1980. "Who Are the Children? A National Overview of Services." *Social Work and Abstracts* 16:28–33.

Sidall, Lawrence B. and Barbara J. Bosma. 1976. "Co-Therapy as a Training Process." *Psychotherapy: Theory, Research, and Practice* 13 (3):209–13.

Sigman, M. 1989. "Parallel Process at Case Conferences." *Bulletin of the Menninger Clinic* 53 (4):340–49.

Silver, P. T., J. E. Poulin, and R. C. Manning. 1997. "Surviving the Bureaucracy: The Predictors of Job Satisfaction for the Public Agency Supervisor." *Clinical Supervisor* 15 (1):1–20.

Simon, Herbert A. 1976. *Administrative Behavior. A Study of Decision-Making Processes in Administrative Organization,* 2d ed. New York: Free Press.

Simpson, Richard L. and Ida H. Simpson. 1969. "Women and Bureaucracy in the Semiprofessions." In Amitai Etzioni, ed., *The Semiprofessions and Their Organization,* pp. 96–265. New York: Free Press.

——. 1985. "Confidence and Anxiety in Student Clinicians." *Clinical Supervisor* 3 (3):25–48.

——. 1990. "Off-campus Supervisor Self-evaluation." *Clinical Supervisor* 8 (1):163–74.

Singer, M. I., L. Song, and B. Ochberg. 1994. "Sexual Victimization and Substance Abuse in Psychiatrically Hospitalized Adolescents." *Social Work Research* 18:97–103.

Stites, E. W., J. A. Brengarth, and M. S. Warefella. 1983. "Yes, Virginia, There Is Sexual Harassment in Social Work." Paper presented at the Annual Program Meeting, Council on Social Work Education, Fort Worth, TX.

Slovenko, Ralph. 1980. "Legal Issues in Psychotherapy Supervision." In Allen K. Hess, ed., *Psychotherapy Supervision—Theory, Research, and Practice,* pp. 453–73. New York: Wiley.

Smergut, P. 1998. "Total Quality Management and the Not-for-Profit." *Administration in Social Work* 22 (3):75–86.

Smith, Donald M. 1972. "Group Supervision: An Experience." *Social Work Today (London)* 3:13–15.

Smith, H. L. and C. P. Doeing. 1985. "Japanese Management: A Model for Social Work Administration?" *Administration in Social Work* 9 (1):1–11.

Smith, Harrison. 1986. "Use of Supervision to Facilitate Quality Assurance in Community Mental Health Centers." *Social Work Research and Abstracts* 22 (1):3–9.

Smith, R. C., D. E. Mead, and J. A. Kinsella. 1998. "Direct Supervision: Adding Computer-Assisted Feedback and Data Capture to Live Supervision." *Journal of Marital and Family Therapy* 24 (1):113–25.

Smith, Zilpha D. 1884. "Volunteer Visiting, The Organization Necessary to

Make it Effective." In *Proceedings of the National Conference of Charities and Corrections.* Boston: George H. Ellis.

——. 1887. "How to Get and Keep Visitors." In *Proceedings of the National Conference of Charities and Corrections,* pp. 156–62. Boston: George H. Ellis.

——. 1892. "The Education of the Friendly Visitor." *Charities Review* 2 (1):48–58.

——. 1901a. "Friendly Visitors." *Charities* 7:159–60.

——. 1901b. "How to Win and How to Train Charity Visitors." *Charities* 7:46–47.

Soderfeldt, M. B. and L. Warg. 1995. "Burnout in Social Work." *Social Work* 40 (5):638–43.

Sosin, M. R. 1986. "Administrative Issues in Substitute Care." *Social Service Review* 60:360–76.

Spain, D. 1999. "The Debate in the United States Over Immigration." *U.S. Society and Values: The Electronic Journal of the U.S. Information Agency* 4 (2).

Spellman, Dorothea. 1946. "Improving the Quality of Social Group Work Practice through Individual Supervisory Conferences." 122–131 In *Toward Professional Standards.* New York: Association Press.

Spitzer, Robert et al. 1982. "Supervising Intake Diagnosis." *Archives of General Psychiatry* 39:1297–305.

Springer, M. and M. A. Newman. 1983. "Improving Productivity in Child Welfare Programs." *Child Welfare* 57 (5):409–20.

Starling, B., S. Baker, and L. Campbell. 1996. "The Impact of Structured Peer Supervision on Practicum Supervisees." Paper presented at the American Psychological Association, Toronto, Canada.

Staudt, M. 1997. "Correlates of Job Satisfaction in School Social Work." *Social Work in Education* 1 (43):43–52.

Steggert, Frank X. 1970. "Organization Theory: Bureaucratic Influences and the Social Welfare Task." In Harry A. Schatz, ed., *Social Work Administration: A Resource Book,* pp. 43–56. New York: Council on Social Work Education.

Stein, Herman. 1961. "Administrative Implications of Bureaucratic Theory." *Social Work* 6 (3):14–21.

——. 1965. "Administration." In Robert Morris, ed., *Encyclopedia of Social Work,* New York: NASW.

Stein, Stafan P. et al. 1975. "Supervision or the Initial Interview—A Study of Two Methods." *Archives of General Psychiatry* 32:265–68.

Steiner, Richard. 1977. *Managing the Human Service Organization—From Survival to Achievement.* Beverly Hills, Calif.: Sage.

Steinhelber, J. et al. 1984. "An Investigation of Some Relationships Between Psychotherapy Supervision and Patient Change." *Journal of Clinical Psychology* 40 (6):1346–53.

Stelling, Joan and Rue Bucher. 1973. "Vocabularies of Realism in Professional Socialization." *Social Science and Medicine* 7:661–75.

Stenack, R. J. and H. A. Dye. 1982. "Behavioral Descriptions of Counseling Supervision Roles." *Counselor Education and Supervision* 22:295–304.

Stevens, Ruth N. and Fred A. Hutchinson. 1956. "A New Concept of Supervision Is Tested." *Social Work* 1 (3):50–55.

Stiles, Evelyn. 1963. "Supervision in Perspective." *Social Casework* 44:19–25.

Stiles, E. W., J. A. Brengarth, and M. S. Warefella. 1983. "Yes, Virginia, There Is Sexual Harrassment in Social Work." Paper presented at the Annual Program Meeting, Council on Social Work Education, Fort Worth, TX.

Stodgill, R. M. and A. E. Coons. 1957. *Leader Behavior: Its Description and Measurement.* Columbus: Bureau of Business Research, Ohio State University.

Stoesz, D. and H. Karger. 1990. "Welfare Reform: From Illusion to Reality." *Social Work* 35 (2):141–47.

Stoltenberg, C. D. 1981. "Approaching Supervision from a Developmental Perspective: The Counselor Complexity-Model." *Journal of Counseling Psychology* 28 (1):59–65.

Stoltenberg, C. D. and U. Delworth. 1987. *Supervising Counselors and Therapists: A Developmental Approach.* San Francisco: Jossey Bass.

Stoltenberg, C. D., B. W. McNeill, and H. C. Crethar. 1994. "Changes in Supervision as Counselors and Therapists Gain Experience: A Review." *Professional Psychology: Research and Practice* 25 (4):416–49.

Stoltenberg, C. D. and B. W. McNeill. 1997. "Clinical Supervision from a Developmental Perspective: Research and Practice." In C. Watkins, ed., *Handbook of Psychotherapy Supervision*, pp. 184–202. New York: John Wiley & Sons.

Stoltenberg, C. D., R. A. Pierce, and B. W. McNeill. 1987. "Effects of Experience on Counselor Trainees' Needs." *Clinical Supervisor* 5 (1):23–32.

Stone, G. 1997. "Multiculturalism as a Context for Supervision: Perspectives, Limitations, and Implications." In D. Pope-Davis and H. Coleman, eds., *Multicultural Counseling Competencies*, pp. 263–89. Thousand Oaks, Calif.: Sage.

Streepy, Joan. 1981. "Direct Service Providers and Burn-Out." *Social Casework* 62:352–61.

Strom-Gottfried, Kimberly. 1997. "The Implications of Managed Care for Social Work Education." *Journal of Social Work Education* 33 (1):7–18.

Strom-Gottfried, Kimberly. 1999. "When Colleague Accuses Colleague: Adjudicating Personnel Matters through the Filing of Ethics Complaints." *Administration in Social Work* 23 (2):1–16.

Strom-Gottfried, Kimberly, and Kevin Corcoran. 1998. "Confronting Ethical Dilemmas in Managed Care: Guidelines for Students and Faculty." *Journal of Social Work Education* 34 (1):109–19.

Studt, Elliot. 1959. "Worker Client Authority Relationships in Social Work." *Social Work* 4:18–28.

Suess, James F. 1970. "Self-Confrontation of Videotaped Psychotherapy as a Teaching Device for Psychiatric Students." *Journal of Medical Education* 45:271–82.

Sullivan, I. G. 1989. "Burnout—A Study of A Psychiatric Center." *Loss, Grief, and Care* 3 (1/2):83–93.

Sumerel, M. B. and L. D. Borders. 1996. "Addressing Personal Issues in Supervision: Impact of Counselors' Experience Level on Various Aspects of the Supervisory Relationship." *Counselor Education and Supervision* 35:268–86.

Sutton, Jacquelyn A. 1982. "Sex Discrimination Among Social Workers." *Social Work* 27:211–17.

Swanson, Al and John A. Brown. 1982. "Racism, Supervision, and Organizational Environment." *Administration in Social Work* 5 (2):59–67.

Swenson, L. C. 1997. *Psychology and Law for the Helping Professions.* Pacific Grove, Calif.: Brooks/Cole.

Switzer, Elaine. 1973. "Chicago Settlement, 1972: An Overview." *Social Service Review* 47:581–92.

Szakacs, J. 1977. "Survey Indicates Women Losing Ground in Leadership." *NASW News* 22:12.

Taibbi, R. 1995. *Clinical Supervision: A Four-Stage Process of Growth and Recovery.* Milwaukee: Families International.

Talen, M. R. and N. Schindler. 1993. "Goal-Directed Supervision Plans: A Model for Trainee Supervision and Evaluation." *Clinical Supervisor* 11 (2):77–88.

Taylor, James B. 1968. "Rating Scales as Measures of Clinical Judgment: A Method for Increasing Scale Reliability and Sensitivity." *Educational and Psychological Measurement* 28:747–66.

Taylor, James B., E. Haefele, P. Thompson, and C. O'Donoghue. 1970. "Rating Scales as Measures of Clinical Judgement II: The Reliability of Example-Anchored Scales Under Conditions of Rater Heterogeneity and Divergent Behavior Sampling." *Educational and Psychological Measurement* 36:301–10.

Taylor, Joseph L. 1980. "A Practice Note on Staff Reorganization." *Child Welfare* 59 (9):583–87.

Tebb, S., D. W. Manning, and T. K. Klaumann. 1996. "A Renaissance of Group Supervision in Practicum." *Clinical Supervisor* 14 (2):39–51.

Tenny, Mrs. 1895–1896. "Aid to Friendly Visitors." *Charity Review* 5:202–11.

Thing, Pen. 1979. "Perceptual Differences in the Supervision of Paraprofessional Mental Health Workers." *Community Mental Health Journal* 15:139–48.

Thomas, David N. and William Warburton. 1978. "Staff Development in Community Workers in Social Service Departments." In C. Briscoe and D. Thomas, eds., *Community Work: Learning Supervision*, pp. 22–32. London: Allen and Unwin.

Thomas, George and Anthony LaCavera. 1979. "Evaluation of the South Carolina Department of Social Services Child Protective Services Certification Training Program." Research paper, Georgia Regional Institute of Social Welfare Research.

Thwing, A. W. 1893. "The 'Friendly Visitor' at Boston, U.S.A." *Charity Organization Review* 19:234–236.

Toren, Nina. 1969. "Semiprofessionalism and Social Work: A Theoretical Perspective." In Amitai Etzioni, ed., *The Semiprofessions and Their Organization*, pp. 141–95. New York: Free Press.

——. 1972. *Social Work: The Case of a Semiprofession.* Beverly Hills, Calif.: Sage.

Torre, Elizabeth. 1974. "Student Performance in Solving Social Work Problems and Work Experience Prior to Entering the MSW Program." *Journal of Education for Social Work* 10:114–17.

Towle, Charlotte. 1945. *Common Human Needs.* Washington, D.C.: U.S. Government Printing Office.

——. 1954. *The Learner in Education for the Professions: As Seen in Education for Social Work.* Chicago: University of Chicago Press.

——. 1962. "Role of Supervision in the Union of Cause and Function in Social Work." *Social Service Review* 36:396–411

Tracey, T. J., et al. 1989. "Reactance in Relation to Different Supervisory Environments and Counselor Development." *Journal of Counseling Psychology* 36:336–44.

Tsui, M. 1997. "Empirical Research on Social Work Supervision: The State of the Art (1970–1995)." *Journal of Social Service Research* 23 (2):39–51.

Tsui, M. and W. Ho. 1997. "In Search of a Comprehensive Model of Social Work Supervision." *Clinical Supervisor* 16 (2):181–205.

Tsui, M. 2001. *Towards a Culturally Sensitive Model of Social Work Supervision in Hong Kong.* Doctoral Thesis, The University of Toronto.

Tuckman, A. and H. Finkelstein. 1999. "Simultaneous Roles: When Group Co-Therapists Also Share a Supervisory Relationship." *Clinical Supervisor* 18:185–201.

Turner, J. and M. Fine. 1997. "Gender and Supervision: Evolving Debates." In T. C. Todd and C. L. Storm, eds., *The Complete Systemic Supervisor: Context, Philosophy, and Pragmatics*, pp. 72–82. Boston: Allyn and Bacon.

Tyler, Ralph W. 1971. *Basic Principles of Curriculum and Instruction.* Chicago: University of Chicago Press.

Um, M. H. and D. Harrison. 1998. "Role Stressors, Burnout, Mediators, and Job Satisfaction: A Stress-Strain-Outcome Model and an Empirical Test." *Social Work Research* 22 (2):100–115.

U.S. Bureau of the Census. 1998. *Statistical Abstract of the United States:1998* (118th ed.). Washington, D.C.: Bureau of the Census.

U.S. Bureau of Labor Statistics. 2000a. *Employment and Earnings* 47 (1):179–214.

——. 2000b. *Occupational Employment Statistics.* Available online at *stats.bls.gov.OEShome.htm.*

——. 2000c. *2000–2001 Occupational Outlook Handbook.* Washington, D.C.: Bureau of Labor Statistics.

——. 2001. "Table 11—Employed Persons by Detailed Occupation, Sex, Race, and Hispanic Origin." In *Employment and Earnings* 48 (11), p. 179. Washington, D.C.: U.S. Government Printing Office.

U.S. Civil Service Commission. 1955. *Leadership and Supervision: A Survey of Research Findings.* U.S. Civil Service Commission, Personnel Management Series no. 9. Washington, D.C.

U.S. Department of Health, Education and Welfare. 1978. *Systems of Social Services for Children and Families: Detailed Design.* DHEW Publication no. (OHDS) 73-30131. Washington, D.C.: U.S. Government Printing Office.

U.S. House of Representatives Committee on Ways and Means. 2000. *2000 Green Book* (WMCP:106-14). Washington, D.C.: U.S. Government Printing Office.

Urbanowski, M. and M. M. Dwyer. 1988. *Learning through Field Instruction: A Guide for Teachers and Students.* Milwaukee, Wis.: Family Service America.

Urdang, Esther. 1999. "The Influence of Managed Care on the M.S.W. Social Work Student's Development of the Professional Self." *Smith College Studies in Social Work* 70 (1):3–25.

Valentich, M. and J. Gripton. 1978. "Sexism and Sex Differences in Career Management of Social Workers." *Social Science Journal* 15 (2):101–11.

Van Atta, R. E. 1969. "Co-Therapy as a Supervisory Process." *Psychotherapy: Theory, Research, and Practice* 6:137–39.

Vandivort, Warren R. 1996. "Focus Group Exploration of Social Work Skills Needed for the Managed Care Environment." In S. Wilson, E. Francis, and W. Vandivort, eds., *Preparing Social Workers for a Managed Care Environment.* Washington, D.C.: CSWE/NASW.

Van Soest, D. and J. Kruzich. 1994. "The Influence of Learning Styles on Student Field Instructor Perceptions of Field Placement Success." *Journal of Teaching in Social Work* 9 (1/2):49–69.

VanderKolk, C. 1974. "The Relationship of Personality, Values, and Race to Anticipation of the Supervisory Relationship." *Rehabilitation Counseling Bulletin* 18:41–46.

Vargus, Ione D. 1980. "The Minority Administrator." In Simon Slavin and Felice D. Perlmutter, eds., *Leadership in Social Administration*, pp. 216–29. Philadelphia: Temple University Press.

Varma, A., A. S. DeNisi, and L. H. Peters.1996. "Interpersonal Affect and Performance Appraisal: a Field Study." *Personnel Psychology* 492:341–60.

Veeder, N. W. 1990. "Autonomy, Accountability, and Professionalism: The Case Against Close Supervision in Social Work." *Clinical Supervisor* 8 (2):33–47.

Vinokur, Diane K. 1983. *The View from the Agency: Supervisors and Workers Look at In-Service Training for Child Welfare.* Ann Arbor: National Child Welfare Training Center, University of Michigan School of Social Work.

Vinokur-Kaplan, D. and A. Hartman. 1986. "A National Profile of Child Welfare Workers and Supervisors." *Child Welfare* 65 (4):323–35.

Vinter, Robert D. 1959. "The Social Structure of Service." In Alfred J. Kahn, ed., *Issues in American Social Work*, pp. 242–69. New York: Columbia University Press.

Vinton, K. L. 1989. "Humor in the Workplace: It's More than Telling Jokes." *Small Group Behavior* 20 (2):151–66.

Von Glinow, M. A. 1988. *The New Professional—Managing Today's High-Tech Employees.* Cambridge, Mass.: Ballinger.

Vonk, M. E. and B. A. Thyer. 1997. "Evaluating the Quality of Supervision: A Review of Instruments for Use in Field Instruction." *Clinical Supervisor* 15 (1):103–13.

Vonk, M. E. and E. Zucrow. 1996. "Female MSW Students' Satisfaction with Practicum Supervision: The Effect of Supervisor Gender." *Journal of Social Work Education* 32 (3):415–20.

Wade, D. C., E. Cooley, and V. Savicki. 1986. "A Longitudinal Study of Burnout." *Children and Youth Services Review* 8:161–73.

Wade, K., N. Beckerman, and E. J. Stein. 1996. "Risk of Posttraumatic Stress Disorder Among AIDS Social Workers: Implications for Organizational Response." *Clinical Supervisor* 14 (2):85–98.

Walker, Sydnor H. 1928. *Social Work and the Training of Social Workers.* Chapel Hill, N.C.: University of North Carolina Press.

Wallace, J. and M. Brinkeroff. 1991. "The Measurement of Burnout Revisited." *Journal of Social Service Research* 14 (1–2):85–111.

Walter, C. and T. Young. 1999. "Combining Individual and Group Supervision in Educating for the Social Work Profession." *Clinical Supervisor* 18 (2):73–89.

Walton, Mary. 1967. "Rats in the Crib, Roaches in the Food." *Village Voice* (May 11):5–12.

Walz, G. R. and J. A. Johnston. 1963. "Counselors Look at Themselves on Video Tape." *Journal of Counseling Psychology* 10:232–36.

Ward, C. H. 1960. "An Electronic Aide for Teaching Interviewing Techniques." *Archives of General Psychiatry* 3:357–58.

Ward, C. H. 1962. "Electronic Preceptoring in Teaching Beginning Psychotherapy." *Journal of Medical Education* 37:1128–29.

Wark, L. 1995a. "Defining the Territory of Live Supervision in Family Therapy Training: A Qualitative Study and Theoretical Discussion." *Clinical Supervisor* 13 (1):145–62.

——. 1995b. "Live Supervision in Family Therapy: Qualitative Interviews of Supervision Events as Perceived by Supervisors and Supervisees." *American Journal of Family Therapy* 23 (1):25–37.

Warren, D. I. 1968. "Power, Visibility and Conformity in Formal Organizations." *American Sociological Review* 6:951–70.

Watkins, C. E. Jr. 1990. "The Separation-Individuation Process in Psychotherapy Supervision." *Psychotherapy: Theory, Research, and Practice* 27 (2):202–9.

——. 1992a. "Psychotherapy Supervision and the Separation-Individuation Process: Autonomy Versus Dependency Issues." *Clinical Supervisor* 10 (1):111–22.

——. 1992b. "Reflections on the Preparation of Psychotherapy Supervisors." *Journal of Clinical Psychotherapy* 48 (1):145–47.

——. 1994. "The Supervision of Psychotherapy Supervisor Trainees." *American Journal of Psychotherapy* 48 (3):417–31.

——. 1995a. "Psychotherapy Supervision in the 1990s: Some Observations and Reflections." *American Journal of Psychotherapy* 49 (4):568–82.

——. 1995b. "Researching Psychotherapy Supervisor Development: Four Key Considerations." *Clinical Supervisor* 13 (2):111–18.

——. 1996. "On Demoralization and Awe in Psychotherapy Supervision." *Clinical Supervisor* 14 (1):139–48.

——. 1997. "The Ineffective Psychotherapy Supervisor: Some Reflections About Bad Behaviors, and Offensive Outcomes." *Clinical Supervisor* 16 (1):163–70.

——. 1999. "The Beginning Psychotherapy Supervisor: How Can We Help?" *Clinical Supervisor* 18 (2):63–72.

Watkins, C. E. Jr., ed. 1997. *Handbook of Psychotherapy Supervision.* New York: Wiley.

Watkins, C. E. Jr., L. J. Schneider, J. Haynes, and R. Nieberding. 1995. "Measuring Psychotherapy Supervisor Development: An Initial Effort at Scale Development and Validation." *Clinical Supervisor* 13 (1):77–90.

Watson, C. 1988. "When a Woman Is the Boss: Dilemmas in Taking Charge." *Group and Organization Studies* 13 (2):163–81.

Wax, John. 1963. "Time-Limited Supervision." *Social Work* 8 (3):37–43.

Wayne, J. 1988. "A Comparison of Beliefs About Student Supervision Between Micro and Macro Practitioners." *Clinical Supervisor* 6 (3/4): 271–98.

Weatherly, Richard et al. 1980. "Accountability of Social Service Workers at the Front Line." *Social Service Review* 54:556–71.

Webb, Linda et al. 1980. "Employees' Satisfaction Among Workers in Mental Health Settings." *Psychological Reports* 47:30.

Weber, Max. 1946. *Essays in Sociology.* Translated and edited by H. H. Gerth and C. Wright Mills. New York: Oxford University Press.

Weber, Shirley and Donald Polm. 1974. "Participatory Management in Public Welfare." *Social Casework* 55:297–306.

Weinbach, Robert W. 1990. *The Social Worker as Manager: Theory and Practice.* New York: Longman.

——. 1992. "Meeting a Supervisory Responsibility: Shared Evaluation of Supervisory Potential." *Clinical Supervisor* 10 (2):195–210.

Weinbach, R. W. and K. M. Kuehner. 1987. "Improving the Use of Agency Resources through Peer Training." *Social Work* 32:221–24.

Weiner, Myron E. 1990. *Human Services Management: Analysis and Applications,* 2d ed. Belmont, Calif.: Wadsworth.

Weinger, Susan. 2000. *Security Risk: Preventing Client Violence Against Social Workers.* Washington, D.C.: NASW Press.

Werstlein, P. and A. D. Borders. 1997. "Group Process Variables in Group Supervision." *Journal for Specialists in Group Work* 22 (2):120–36.

Westheimer, Ilse J. 1977. *The Practice of Supervision in Social Work: A Guide for Staff Supervisors.* London: Ward Lock Educational.

Wetchler, J. L., F. P. Piercy, and D. H. Sprenkle. 1989. "Supervisors' and Supervisees' Perceptions of the Effectiveness of Family Therapy Supervisory Techniques." *American Journal of Family Therapy* 17 (1):35–47.

Wetchler, J. L. and K. A. Vaughn. 1991. "Perceptions of Primary Supervisor Interpersonal Skills: A Critical Incident Analysis." *Contemporary Family Therapy* 13 (1):61–69.

——. 1992. "Perceptions of Primary Family Therapy Supervisory Techniques: A Critical Incident Analysis." *Contemporary Family Therapy* 14 (2):127–36.

Wexler, S. and R. Engel. 1999. "Historical Trends in State-Level ADC/AFDC Benefits: Living on Less and Less." *Journal of Sociology and Social Welfare* 26 (2):37–61.

Whiffen, Rosemary and John Byng-Hall. 1982. *Family Therapy Supervision— Recruit Developments in Practice.* New York: Grune and Stratten.

Whisenhunt, B., J. Romans, D. Boswell, and A. Carlozzi. 1997. "Counseling Students' Perceptions of Supervisory Modalities." *Clinical Supervisor* 15 (2):79–90.

White, Mark B. and Candyce S. Russell. 1995. "The Essential Elements of Supervisory Systems: A Modified Delphi Study." *Journal of Marital and Family Therapy* 21 (1):33–53.

——. 1997. "Examining the Multifaceted Notion of Isomorphism in Marriage and Family Therapy Supervision." *Journal of Marital and Family Therapy* 23 (3):315–33.

White, William A. 1978. *A Systems Response to Staff Burn-Out.* Rockville, Md.: ITCS.

Wilbur, M., J. Roberts-Wilbur, G. Hart, J. Morris, and R. Betz. 1994. "Structured Group Supervision (SGS): A Pilot Study." *Counselor Education and Supervision* 33:262–69.

Wilbur, Michael P., et al. 1991. "Structured Group Supervision: Theory into Practice." *Journal of Specialists in Group Work* 16 (2):91–100.

Wilding, Paul. 1982. *Professional Power and Social Welfare.* Boston: Routledge and Kegan Paul.

Wiley, M. O. and P. B. Ray. 1986. "Counseling Supervision by Developmental Level." *Journal of Counseling Psychology* 33 (4):439–45.

Wilkie, Charlotte H. 1963. "A Study of Distortions in Recording Interviews." *Social Work* 8:31–36.

Wilkinson, A. D. and R. M. Wagner. 1993. "Supervisory Leadership Styles and State Vocational Rehabilitation Counselor Job Satisfaction and Productivity." *Rehabilitation Counseling Bulletin* 37 (1):15–24.

Williams, A. B. 1997. "On Parallel Process in Social Work Supervision." *Clinical Social Work Journal* 25 (4):425–35.

Williams, S. and R. P. Halgin. 1995. "Issues in Psychotherapy Supervision Between the White Supervisor and the Black Supervisee." *Clinical Supervisor* 13 (1):39–61.

Williamson, Margaretta. 1961. *Supervision: New Patterns and Processes.* New York: Association Press.

Wilmot, C. 1998. "Public Pressure and Private Stress." In Richard Davies, ed., *Stress in Social Work,* pp. 21–32. London: Jessica Kinsley.

Wilson, Gertrude and Gladys Ryland. 1949. *Social Group Work Practice.* Boston: Houghton.

Wilson, Paul A., Victor Voth, and Walter A. Hudson. 1980. "Professionals and the Bureaucracy: Measuring the Orientations of Social Workers." *Journal of Social Service Research* 4 (1):15–30.

Wilson, Suanna J. 1981. *Field Instruction: Techniques for Supervisors.* New York: Free Press.

Wimpfheimer, S., Marge Klein, and Marge Kramer. 1993. "The Impact of Liability Concerns on Intraorganizational Relationships." *Administration in Social Work* 17 (4):41–55.

Wisconsin Department of Health and Social Services. 1977. *A Study in the Job Tasks and Associated Knowledge Areas of the Supervisor I Position in Wisconsin.* Milwaukee: School of Social Welfare—Center for Advanced Studies in the Human Services, University of Wisconsin.

Wolberg, Lewis R. 1977. *The Techniques of Psychotherapy,* 3d ed., part 2. New York: Grune and Stratton.

Wolfson, Abby and Harold Sampson. 1976. "A Comparison of Process Notes and Tape Recordings." *Archives of General Psychiatry* 33:558–63.

Wong, Y. S. 1997. "Live Supervision in Family Therapy: Trainee Perspectives." *Clinical Supervisor* 15 (1):145–58.

Wood, G. and R. R. Middleman. 1989. *The Structured Approach to Direct Practice in Social Work.* New York: Columbia University Press.

Woodcock, G. D. C. 1967. "A Study of Beginning Supervision." *British Journal of Psychiatric Social Work* 9:66–74.

Worthen, V. and B. W. McNeill. 1996. "A Phenomenological Investigation of 'Good' Supervision Events." *Journal of Counseling Psychology* 43 (1):25–34.

Worthington, E. L. 1987. "Changes in Supervision: Supervision vs. Counselor and Supervisors Gain Experience—A Review." *Professional Psychology: Research and Practice* 18 (3):189–208.

Worthington, E. L. Jr. and A. Stern. 1985. Effects of Supervisor and Supervisee Degree Level and Gender on the Supervisory Relationship." *Journal of Counseling Psychology* 32:252–62.

Wulf, Jonathan and Mary Lee Nelson. 2000. "Experienced Psychologists' Recollections of Internship Supervision." *Clinical Supervisor* 19 (2):123–45.

Yelaja, Shankar A., ed. 1971. *Authority and Social Work: Concept and Use.* Toronto. University of Toronto Press.

——, ed. 1982. *Ethical Issues in Social Work.* Springfield, Ill.: C. C. Thomas.

Yerushalmi, H. 1992. "On the Concealment of the Interpersonal Therapeutic Reality in the Course of Supervision." *Psychotherapy* 29 (3):438–96.

——. 1993. "Stagnation in Supervision as a Result of Developmental Problems in the Middle-Aged Supervisor." *Clinical Supervisor* 11 (1):63–82.

York, Reginald O. 1988. "Sex Role Stereotypes and the Socialization of Managers." *Administration in Social Work* 12 (1):25–40.

York, R. O. and R. T. Denton. 1990. "Leadership Behavior and Supervisory Performance: The View from Below." *Clinical Supervisor* 8 (1):93–108.

York, R. O. and T. Hastings. 1985–1986. "Worker Maturity and Supervisory Leadership Behavior." *Administration in Social Work* 9 (4):37–46.

Yourman, D. B. and B. A. Farber. 1996. "Nondisclosure and Distortion in Psychotherapy Supervision." *Psychotherapy* 33 (4):567–75.

Zetzel, E. 1953. "The Dynamic Basis of Supervision." *Social Casework* 34: 143–49.

Zucker, P. J. and E. L. Worthington. 1986. "Supervision of Interns and Post-doctoral Applicants for Licensure in University Counseling Centers." *Journal of Counseling Psychology* 33:87–89.

Zunz, S. 1991. "Gender-Related Issues in the Career Development of Social Work Managers." *Affilia* 6 (4):39–52.

——. 1998. "Resiliency and Burnout: Protective Factors for Human Services Managers." *Administration in Social Work* 22 (3):39–53.

Index